PUBLIC
SPEAKING

PUBLIC SPEAKING

BUILDING COMPETENCY IN STAGES

SHERRY DEVEREAUX FERGUSON
University of Ottawa

New York   Oxford
OXFORD UNIVERSITY PRESS
2008

Oxford University Press, Inc., publishes works that further Oxford University's
objective of excellence in research, scholarship, and education.

Oxford New York
Auckland Cape Town Dar es Salaam Hong Kong Karachi
Kuala Lumpur Madrid Melbourne Mexico City Nairobi
New Delhi Shanghai Taipei Toronto

With offices in
Argentina Austria Brazil Chile Czech Republic France Greece
Guatemala Hungary Italy Japan Poland Portugal Singapore
South Korea Switzerland Thailand Turkey Ukraine Vietnam

Published by Oxford University Press, Inc.
198 Madison Avenue, New York, New York, 10016
http://www.oup.com

Oxford is a registered trademark of Oxford University Press

Library of Congress Cataloging-in-Publication Data

Ferguson, Sherry Devereaux.
   Public speaking : building competency in stages / by Sherry Devereaux Ferguson.
      p. cm.
   Includes index.
   ISBN 978-0-19-518777-9
    1. Public speaking. I. Title.

 PN4129.15.F47 2007
 808.5'1--dc22

                                                              2006049479

Printing number: 9 8 7 6 5 4 3 2 1

Printed in the United States of America
on acid-free paper

This book is dedicated to the men in my life,
especially my husband Stewart

I dedicated an earlier book to the women in my life— my grandmother, mother, sisters, daughters, and granddaughters. I dedicate this book to the men who play a continuing and important role—Stewart, Eric, Bruno, George, Dick, Patrick, and grandchildren Morgan, Solan, and William. I also dedicate this book to those no longer with me except in poignant memory: my grandfathers John Solon Gunn and Reason Lemuel Devereaux, my father Aden Nelson Devereaux, and my dear friend Henry Murphy. And since three little girls (Ella, Sasha, and Gabrielle) were not fast enough at being born to make it into my earlier dedication, I add your names to this one. Your importance in my life cannot be overstated, and I offer this dedication to all of you as a small token of my caring. Thank you, Stewart, for being an extraordinary partner on my journey.

CONTENTS

3   Listening with a Purpose
Exercises in Perception and Listening

4   Acquiring the Basic Skills
The Speech of Introduction

5   Researching, Analyzing, and Adapting to Your Audience
The Speech of Welcome

8   Researching and Supporting Your Ideas
The Informative Speech

9 The Building Blocks of Persuasive Discourse
A Debate Involving Minority Voices

10 Arguing Eloquently and Convincingly
Speech to Convince, Stimulate, or Actuate

11 The Language of Propaganda
A Coffee-Shop Discussion on Ethics

12 Speaking in Social Contexts
A Speech for Special Occasions

13 Speaking in Classroom Contexts
A Team Presentation

Appendix:
Memorable Speeches, Historical Moments

PREFACE

I have been involved in the study or teaching of speech for almost a half century. So in career terms, this book is long overdue. Obviously, there are disadvantages to coming so late into a fairly saturated market, populated by so many credible academics. There are, however, also advantages. The first is lack of commitment to the past—the opportunity to begin with a fresh perspective, rather than making incremental changes over a number of years. As some well-publicized cases have demonstrated, problems can arise if people undergo too many cosmetic surgeries. The same is true for books!

A second advantage is the opportunity to synthesize knowledge gained over the course of a career—to bring a lifetime of experiences to bear on the project. This book will be very different from the one that I would have written in the early 1970s. And even as I have worked on the project, I have continued to question prior assumptions about what works best in an undergraduate speech class.

When I engaged in early talks with Oxford representatives about this project, they told me that—given the enormous resources that go into producing an introductory book and the number of well-established books on the market—they did not want to add another book to the market unless I could offer a novel approach. Since the teaching of public speaking relies on classical principles, that request would seem to be a difficult one. But over the years, I have struggled with certain dilemmas in teaching the introductory speech course—dilemmas that I know others also confront. In this book, I have tried to overcome some of these problems. The following discussion describes characteristics of the book that make it appealing to instructors of the undergraduate speech course. The approach is assignment-based, additive, flexible, comprehensive, innovative, realistic, friendly, substantial, and current in its perspectives.

Assignment-Based

First, the approach is assignment-based. The large majority of instructors adopt assignment-based approaches to teaching the undergraduate speech course. This book responds, as others do not respond, to the important need to recognize the way in which most instructors *actually teach* the undergraduate speech course. Let me explain.

With existing books on the market, instructors confront the difficult decision as to which materials to cover first. The dilemma arises because the authors have adopted a *topic-focused* rather than *assignment-focused* approach to the organization of their books. For some 50 years or more, the typical introductory speech book has been organized around discrete subject areas such as knowing your audience, conducting research, developing your outline, supporting your ideas, and presenting the speech. In other words, each chapter addresses a *different step* in the public speaking process. To cover all of the steps, you must read the entire book. To make matters more confused, the discussions of different types of speeches (informative, persuasive, social occasion, and other), which form the basis for the speaking assignments, appear in yet another chapter—often positioned at the end of the textbook.

Since every step in the speech process is relevant to the preparation of any speech, theoretically students should have completed all of the readings before they present the first speech. Of course, that is an impossible expectation. So how does one time the order chapters of often equal importance such as communication apprehension, audience adaptation, research techniques, organizational formats, attention-getting devices, language, delivery, ethics, and listening styles? Everyone has a different idea of what should go first, including the authors of introductory textbooks.

Whatever the final ordering of chapters, the same question eventually comes into play for the instructor of speech. Where to begin when so much is relevant to the first speaking assignments? Instructors respond to this dilemma in a variety of ways. Some paste together their reading assignments, asking the students to read bits and pieces of different chapters. Others delay assignments such as informative speaking until late in the term, leaving little time for other major speaking assignments. Many experienced instructors have generated their own materials handouts or manuals, which they distribute or place on the web. Frustrated by the shortcomings of books that fail to get their students quickly into the material, a number avoid the use of textbooks altogether.

A large number of instructors spend more time than they would like to spend on lectures, in order to give sufficient orientation to their students in their early assignments. Since they cannot expect their students to have read all of the chapters until later in the term, they are confronted with the need to respond to ongoing queries about assignments. The process of putting together an outline for courses is time-consuming and frustrating for the beginning teacher of speech, and the adoption of a new book requires that experienced instructors engage in yet another patchwork exercise.

An assignment-based approach eliminates these kinds of problems. Each chapter presents the information and orientation required to fulfill the assignment for that chapter (contained in the *Instructor's Manual*, available to adopting professors). The student does not need to read the entire book to prepare the speaking assignments. In short, an assignment-based approach makes the work of instructors much easier. You are able to use class time to discuss ideas from the readings, conduct exercises that illustrate points, view films and videos, and get students quickly into presentations. You can lecture less often and listen and react more often. Graduate assistants and new instructors of speech need only prepare one chapter at a time. Ensuring uniformity across multiple sections of a course becomes much easier. Finally, the structure of this book is more appropriate for on-line courses than any other speech text presently on the market. The assignment-based modular nature of the approach works well with WebCT and blackboard applications.

Additive

This book assumes that an additive approach works best. Each new assignment allows the student to apply principles learned earlier in the course, but also to acquire new knowledge and skills. The chapter overview, which follows, demonstrates the way in which this book encourages the student to build competency in stages.

Chapters One through Three suggest introductory exercises that allow students to consider their ethical obligations as speakers, confront their public speaking fears, and come to a better understanding of how listeners process information and share responsibility for the success of a speech event. The Critical Communication Model (CCM), introduced in Chapter One, provides a framework for looking at speech events. This model includes a strong focus on both the audience-centered nature of public speaking and its ethical dimensions. Likewise, Chapter Three focuses on the way in which audiences perceive and process information.

By Chapter Four, the students have the opportunity to become involved in their first speaking assignment—the speech of introduction. This chapter suggests steps to follow in creating a speech of introduction. The assignment introduces students to the basics—writing an introduction, thesis and preview statements, transitions, and conclusions. The chapter also discusses common organizational schemes that apply to a speech of introduction. The focus in terms of theory is on strategies for gaining and holding audience attention.

Chapter Five provides the opportunity for students to apply principles of audience research, analysis, and adaptation in a speech of welcome. After conducting research on their classmates, the students prepare welcoming comments for a fictitious event. While every chapter in the book recognizes the importance of an audience-centered approach to speaking, this chapter details the most common strategies for meeting the basic needs of audiences, recognizing their belief and value orientations, and adapting to speaking situations. The chapter includes a stress on immediacy strategies.

Chapter Six enables the students to put aside content issues long enough to focus on principles of delivery. The chapter discusses both delivery options (extemporaneous, impromptu, memorized, manuscript speaking, and speaking from a teleprompter) and ways to build credibility through delivery of a one-point speech.

Chapter Seven looks at purposes and types of visual aids, as well as principles governing the delivery of speeches with visual supports. Extensive coverage is given to the preparation and delivery of PowerPoint and other computer-generated presentations. While the content of this chapter is relevant to a number of speaking assignments covered in this book, this chapter suggests the possibility for a speech that debriefs an organization on the results of a project or undertaking. Students of business will find this assignment particularly relevant to their career paths.

An informative speaking assignment, discussed in Chapter Eight, asks the students to engage in research, choose appropriate organizational schemes, make effective use of visual aids, and speak extemporaneously from note cards. One option for the informative speaking assignment is a speech of demonstration.

Chapter Nine examines the building blocks of persuasive discourse: *ethos*, *pathos*, and *logos*. The chapter exposes the reader to strategies for achieving and maintaining credibility, using emotional appeals, and employing logic and reasoning in arguing points of view. Fallacies in logic and reasoning are also described.

Chapter Ten introduces the student to purposes of persuasive speaking and organizational schemes that apply to this genre of speaking. The chapter leads the student through the process of writing and delivering a persuasive speech. Like earlier assignments, the persuasive speech assignment requires the students to engage in research, adapt ideas to their audiences, select the best organizational formats, and use sound logic and reasoning. However, the assignment also asks the students to employ various linguistic devices in appealing to the emotions of their audiences. The students are expected to use repetition, metaphors, analogies, antithesis, and other linguistic devices. The nature of the assignment requires that the students memorize large segments of their speeches, even if they use note cards in delivering them.

Although every chapter of the book asks the students to look at ethical questions related to speechmaking, Chapter Eleven suggests the importance of engaging in an in-depth "coffee-shop" discussion of such questions. More specifically, the chapter looks at the boundaries of ethical communication, along with instances where speakers have crossed these boundaries. Individual and modern concepts of propaganda provide a framework for understanding these transgressions. Issues raised in ethics boxes, which appear throughout the book, can be revisited in this chapter. The students can also refer to speeches included in the Appendix.

Chapter Twelve describes the special occasion speech (wedding toast, roast, tribute, or other social occasion speech). As noted in this chapter, a number of these genres present the opportunity for speakers to incorporate humor. The discussion of the use of humor emphasizes the importance of following ethical guidelines.

Large increases in college and university enrollments have created the necessity for instructors to require team (rather than individual) presentations. Chapter Thirteen prepares students for those assignments by discussing the creation and delivery of a team presentation using PowerPoint. This kind of presentation engages the audience in a variety of learning activities, reflecting educational theories addressed in the chapter. Various topics addressed in the chapter include setting teaching and learning objectives, applying learning theories in developing content, managing group dynamics, and making the presentation.

Chapter Fourteen discusses ghostwriting, that is preparing a speech for delivery by a second party (local politician, bureaucrat, or businessperson). This chapter examines the history of ghostwriting; its established place in the functioning of modern organizations; and the preparation of ghostwritten manuscript. Also discussed are the necessity for professional ghostwriters to relinquish ownership of the speech at some point, the importance of providing feedback to speechwriting organizers and speakers, strategies for getting work as a professional speechwriter, and the ethics of ghostwriting.

Chapter Fifteen looks at the major components in a rhetorical analysis. Many of the theories discussed in the book are pulled together in this chapter. The chapter also returns the students to the critical communication model featured in Chapter One.

In conclusion, an additive approach ensures that students will not feel intimidated by having to acquire all of the information at one time. Instructors, for their part, can place a focus on different elements as the course progresses. A marginal glossary introduces the reader to new terms in each chapter. In line with the additive approach, the glossary also recalls and reviews terms appearing in earlier chapters.

Flexible

The approach is flexible. Chapters One through Eleven introduce the student to the basic principles of speechmaking, with each new chapter adding layers of information. Chapters Twelve through Fifteen offer information that will be of interest to specific audiences. A standard approach will include assignments such as one-point and informative speeches, persuasive speeches, and social occasion speeches. An instructor in a speechwriting course, on the other hand, might decide to omit the chapters on delivery and team presentations but require the chapters on ghostwriting and rhetorical analysis. The instructor of a speech course populated by business or engineering students might place more emphasis on team presentations and related subject matter. A continuing education instructor might want to focus on the kinds of speech situations that are commonly encountered by the particular mix of adult students in the class. The book has sufficient content for special audiences that the instructor can pick and choose from a range of concepts, including some assignments and omitting others.

The approach also assumes that some instructors will want to substitute favorite assignments for those suggested for this text. So long as the assignment demonstrates principles discussed in the chapter, no problem should arise from the substitution. An instructor of speech in a fashion design program, for example, may want to require a process demonstration for the informative speaking assignment but substitute a sales talk for the more conventional persuasive speech assignment. The structure of the book lends itself to easy substitutions or adaptations of assignments.

Comprehensive

The coverage is comprehensive. Many concepts discussed in the book are standard to every public speaking text. People have studied the psychology of audiences and the canons of speech since the days of Aristotle. Speech is the oldest of arts and a fast developing science. Any book that omitted the important learnings, acquired over centuries, would be seriously deficient. So I have included lengthy discussions of informative, persuasive, and social occasion genres. This book addresses standard subject areas such as communication apprehension and stresses the importance of audience adaptation. Speech instructors have indicated, in surveys, that speech textbooks should include an emphasis on both topics. This book also responds to a demand for in-depth discussions of support materials (source credibility, emotional, and logical supports). Throughout the book, I talk about the importance of taking cultural considerations into account in adapting to audiences. In essence, all of the basics appear in this book. The coverage is comprehensive including discussion questions at the end of each chapter, references within the chapters to online and other resources, and an appendix with memorable speeches by historical and contemporary.

   The book has a number of supplementary materials:

- An Instructor's Manual and Test Bank, prepared by myself, Stefne Broz of Wittenberg University, and Alexandra Hendricks (Ph.D., University of Arizona, and a consultant for the Government of Canada). Beyond containing the **Suggested Assignment** for each chapter, the Instructor's Manual and Test Bank is full of extra assignments, exercises, and teaching tips that will help bring this innovative book to life in the classroom.
- An Instructor's CD with PowerPoint presentations, featuring a powerful computerized test-maker
- A companion website, with resources for both instructor and learner

Innovative

In addition, the approach incorporates a number of features not included in other speech textbooks. The assignment-based and additive approach of the book is certainly novel. However, other features are equally innovative. The critical communication model, appearing in the first chapter, includes an ethical component, not captured in other speech models. While every speech text openly recognizes the importance of ethical considerations, I do not know of any that incorporate this component into their models. The model also includes a number of environmental variables, unique to this book. The book uses a large number of contemporary examples to illustrate the dilemmas faced by speakers in today's environment.

The book also includes such novel assignments as a coffee shop discussion on ethics and a speech of welcome. The speech of welcome enables students to focus, early in the course, on the audience-centered nature of public speaking. The assignment also allows them to put audience adaptation theories into practice. A number of the points raised in the discussion on PowerPoint presentations are also not offered in other books.

A chapter on ghostwriting draws on the experiences of the author, involved for ten years in writing speeches for politicians and high-level government bureaucrats. Other books do not include this topic, even though the majority of professional communicators must engage in ghostwriting at some point in their careers. In fact, the large majority of professional communicators do far more writing of speeches for others and coaching than delivering speeches.

Another novel feature of the book is the inclusion of a chapter on rhetorical analysis. Many instructors ask their students to attend and analyze a live public speaking event as one of their speaking assignments; others request that the students analyze a videotaped performance or the script of a speech. Yet no other introductory textbook discusses the basics of how to put together a rhetorical analysis. Usually, this material appears in a second or third year (or even a graduate) course that is specific to rhetorical analysis. While not as sophisticated as these upper-level discussions, the basic approach for preparing a rhetorical analysis, described in this chapter, will help the student to understand the most critical components of public speaking. The various categories of analysis also provide a summary of concepts covered in earlier chapters.

Realistic

The book is realistic in its expectations. The fifteen-chapter format enables the instructor to assign one chapter per week. Admittedly, teachers of the introductory speech class will need to make some choices on assignments. However, the coffee shop discussion on ethics, the classroom debate on minority policy issues, and the one-point impromptu speaking assignment can be completed within the time frame of a single class meeting. So can exercises related to communication apprehension, public speaking anxiety, and listening. The speeches of introduction, as well as the welcoming addresses, take approximately one hour of presentation time for a group of 20 students (plus time for feedback). Social occasion speeches are also typically short in duration. Other oral assignments (typically two or three in a term, depending upon the number of students) require more time for preparation, presentation, and feedback. Here the instructors must make choices on which assignments to require for delivery. The assignments on ghostwriting and rhetorical analysis do not require oral presentation time, which is at a premium in speech classes.

Friendly

I have aimed for a book that is highly readable, with an abundance of examples, tips from professionals, sample student speeches, and visuals. Lecture time is limited in speech courses, and instructors like to use the class time to focus on skills acquisition. So students must acquire most of the theory through readings, undertaken outside of class. For that reason, I have tried to achieve a "student-friendly" style of writing. I have tried, in the book, to anticipate a number of the questions that I find myself answering year after year for students. When their textbook answers these questions, the students do not need to go to the instructors for so much explanation. Thus, the life of the instructor becomes much easier. The book also includes a large number of photos, original cartoons, and other visuals that increase the look and appeal of the book for undergraduate students.

Substantial and Current

At the same time that I have aimed for a student-friendly book, *I have tried to offer content that is substantial and current.* I tried to incorporate some of the latest theories (as referenced in journals such as *Communication Education*) in this book. Some public speaking texts are so elementary (compared to their peer texts in psychology, sociology, engineering, and other disciplines) that the discrepancy becomes painfully apparent, and our students complain (in their words) that we are "dumbing down" the content. This book seeks to achieve readability without sacrificing substance.

In conclusion, I have sought to create a book that meets the needs of both students and instructors—using an approach that is assignment-based, additive, flexible, comprehensive, innovative, realistic, friendly, substantial, and current in its offerings. I hope that the readers will concur on this point.

ACKNOWLEDGMENTS

Peter, Peter, Peter (Labella, of course). Thank you for your support at the beginning, middle, and conclusion of this project. You have been a delightful correspondent and wonderful enthusiast. I have appreciated your wit, commitment to excellence, *and* your willingness to invest in yet another speech book. I have never worked with a company that I like better than Oxford. You have re-energized my sometimes flagging faith in the publishing industry. I recommend your company to any author who would like to have a positive experience. And not least important, Oxford has not merged or sold out to another company in the last three years. There are advantages to going with a publishing house that can trace its history to 1478!

I would also like to give special thanks to Chelsea Gilmore, a critical newcomer to the Oxford team and my project. Your quick turnaround time on questions, cheerful manner of dealing with authors, and obvious experience and competence have impressed me. I am privileged to have such a dedicated person working on my behalf. I am also grateful to Karen Shapiro for shepherding the book through the production process—no easy task given the large number of visuals and supplementary materials. Art director Liz Cosgrove did an amazing job with the design of the book. Thank you!

Thanks also to Kim Rimmer and Jill Crosson for their efforts in marketing and selling my book. I would also like to acknowledge other less visible members of the Oxford team! I know that many of you have had a part in the project, even if I have not had the opportunity to meet or correspond with all of you.

I am profoundly grateful to the many reviewers who recommended and/or helped to guide the development of the book. Thank you for your time and thoughtful comments. I have incorporated a very large number of your recommendations into this final product and given serious consideration to all of them.

I also appreciate the generosity of authors, public figures, and personalities who have allowed me to use their work without fee—James McCroskey and Earl Charles Spencer, as well as others whose work appears in the book. (These names appear in the credits section.) I thank Brian Robinson, Juline Ranger, Laura Peck, and Brian Creamer for contributing professional advice. I am especially pleased to include motivational speaker Brian Robinson, the son of my best friend in high school and university. I also thank Garrett Patterson for sharing a speech schedule.

Other contributors (identified throughout the book and in the end notes) include former students, who did excellent work in my classes, and members of Toastmaster clubs, who took the time to share their experiences. Thanks to Erika Adams for taking time to help with the final look of the PowerPoint presentation that appears with Chapter 7. I am pleased to incorporate photographs taken by a long-time work colleague, Lois Siegel.

On a personal *and* professional level, I would like to thank some members of my family. Gill Ferguson produced a large number of the photographs that appear in the book. Since Gill lives in London, England, we have corresponded at all hours of the day and night. An extremely talented photographer, she has generated a number of interesting and creative images for the book. Alexandra Hendriks, my oldest daughter, produced the test bank for the book. She also helped with creating some of the line and bar graphs in the book. My youngest daughter Cameron Ferguson, who worked part-time as a graphic artist for the CBC in earlier years, has contributed the cartoons, models, and other illustrations that appear in the book. I thank Bruno Lepage, son in spirit, for rescuing me when I became absolutely befuddled, unable to figure out how to complete some action on the computer. Without his intervention, the book would be missing some necessary diagrams. Bruno also helped with inputting some of the images that appear in the PowerPoint presentation. Thanks to Maristela Carrera for contributing photos of Brazil, Joe Ferguson for taking the time to draw a map of Brazil, Desirée Devereaux for sharing some professional experiences, and Claire and George Smith for contributing a photograph.

On a strictly personal level, I would like to acknowledge the love and support of my husband Stewart Ferguson and mother Maureen Devereaux. On a daily basis, I draw strength from their presence in my life. And finally, even though my son Eric has not participated in this project, he is often in my thoughts; and he has been a valuable contributor for earlier book projects.

Sherry Devereaux Ferguson

PUBLIC
SPEAKING

Outline

PUBLIC SPEAKING IN THE AGE OF ACCOUNTABILITY

A Critical Model

Learning Objectives

- To learn more about the birth of critical society
- To understand influential trends in the environment
- To become acquainted with the critical communication model (CCM)

The rhetoric of protest in the United States has increased in presence and volume in recent years, with representation by both liberal and conservative forces. Native, feminist, labor, religious, ethnic, and environmental groups vigorously promote their causes in a variety of media. Antiglobalization demonstrations pockmark every world summit. An expanding number of political and social activists use civil disobedience, teach-ins, and marches to make their voices heard. Participants in a "Reclaim the Streets" campaign stop cars and hold parties on blocked roads to protest the loss of public space in urban centers. "Culture jammers" replace the faces of Gap models with hollow skulls and redraw an Obsession ad to show a Calvin Klein model leaning over a toilet bowl.[1] In May 2005, more than 2,500 activists, educators, policymakers, journalists, and concerned citizens met in St. Louis, Missouri, to plan strategies for repairing a "broken media system."[2]

These protests evoke memories of the civil rights and antiwar rhetoric of the 1960s. Unlike the 1960s, however, the protests address a crazy quilt of political, social, and economic issues stretched out along the full length of the political spectrum. Alliances shift from issue to issue, with often puzzling results. Environmentalists join hands with flat earth advocates, gay and lesbian activists, union workers, and members of the John Birch Society to demonstrate against free trade.[3] Backlash against the *Patriot Act* legislation has brought together the Gun Owners of America, the American Library Association, the Green Party, and the American Civil Liberties Union.[4] A United for Peace network pulls in members of the National Organization for Women, Greenpeace, the National Council of Churches, the American Friends Service Committee, the War Resisters League, Black Voices for Peace, Not In Our Name, September 11 Families for Peaceful Tomorrows, Veterans

for Peace, pro-Palestinian groups, and many others. People with highly disparate views on one issue come together on other issues. As one editorialist commented, the result is "strange marchfellows."[5] Even more interesting, they dust off their protest signs from one rally and carry them to the next, without acknowledging that the theme of the rally has changed.

E-activists press their causes on the worldwide web, and growing numbers of online petitions engage people of all ages, including seniors, previously on the sidelines of politics. In short, these patterns herald a new critical era for the United States. And they have relevance for public speakers, who enter an existing climate, larger than the auditorium in which they speak. This climate has *political, social, cultural, economic, legal,* and *technological* dimensions, as well as *rhetorical conventions,* which shape how people respond to public discourse. We are living in an age of accountability, and not even our most prominent politicians and community leaders are exempt from the demands for transparency and forthrightness in their public communications. Thus, this chapter takes a *macro* perspective, looking at the "big picture" within which contemporary speech events occur. Other chapters examine public speaking from the *micro* perspective—concentrating on specific characteristics of the speaker, message, channel, and audience.

This chapter will consider the birth of critical society in the United States, as well as trends in the environments within which contemporary speakers operate. I will also propose a critical model for evaluation of public speaking efforts.

Rhetorical conventions
The rules that govern styles of public speaking

Macro
A "big picture" perspective

Micro
A tightly focused perspective

The Roots of Critical Society

Public reaction to a number of recent events reveals reduced levels of tolerance for lying and deception by public figures. This trend makes its way back in time to former President Richard Nixon, who resigned from the U.S. presidency in 1974 after investigation revealed his role in the Watergate cover-up. Prior to that date, Americans had a relatively high tolerance for claims of executive privilege and secrecy on the part of government. The public assumed that government leaders acted on its behalf when they withheld information. Nixon was surprised to find that the rules of the game had changed so drastically from a time when "cloak and dagger" operations still wore the mantle of respectability. Even during the presidency of John F. Kennedy, no one looked closely at the personal habits of the president or complained about lack of access to information. In a period characterized as the "Cold War," government critics were often labeled as supporters of communism.

The groundwork for these shifts in public attitudes occurred in the late 1960s, when prominent journalists condemned the government for lying and withholding information about the Vietnam war. Revelations of deceit led to large-scale demonstrations, acts of civil disobedience, and sometimes violent protests. The civil rights protesters joined with the antiwar protesters to create a large "critical" mass. Although the United States had been born of the parents of revolution, the country had avoided large-scale revolts since the Civil War. But now again, a century later, a new generation of critics had been birthed.

In the decades to follow, many would accuse the media—which had played such a prominent role in the decision of Lyndon Johnson not to seek a third term in the presidency and the resignation of Richard Nixon—of growing placid and conservative in the 1980s. But even without the same political agendas, the media have played a definitive role in transforming audiences from passive observers to trained cynics. In 1972, I wrote about the occasion when U.S. Senator Edward ("Ted") Kennedy went on national television to explain the events of July 18, 1969, that led to the drowning death of Mary Jo Kopechne. Kopechne was a secretary to Robert F. Kennedy. On the return home from an office party, the car in which Kopechne was a passenger (driven by Edward Kennedy) plunged into a pond in Chappaquiddick, Massachusetts. Kennedy escaped from the submerged vehicle, but his young passenger died. Kennedy did not report the accident or alert police to the whereabouts of Kopechne until the following morning. Newspaper accounts heavily criticized Kennedy for his lack of action, and journalists speculated that he was intoxicated when the accident occurred. Few believed or accepted the televised account that Kennedy gave on July 25, 1969, and he was never able to regain the full confidence of the Democratic Party or the American public—at least not sufficiently to pursue presidential office. I ascribed the failure of Kennedy's speech, in significant part, to changes that had taken place in American audiences since the 1950s—changes that had transformed audiences from willing participants in staged dramas to cynics and critics.[6] As media critic John Leonard noted, "The Sixties, as Ted Kennedy found out after he tried to explain Chappaquiddick on television to an unbelieving public, required more than squeezing your sincerity like a lemon."[7]

This cynicism has edged its way into the present. Few believed the disclaimers of President Bill Clinton when he said that he had not had an affair with Monica Lewinsky. And when President George W. Bush posed for a photo opportunity with two girls of African-American descent in Gulfport, Mississippi, following hurricane Katrina, critics quickly identified his action as a public relations ploy to appease critics. In a letter submitted to the *New York Times*, writer George Cameron Grant said: "[When he visits the Gulf coast region], will he appear in hip boots and Air Force One windbreaker? A National Guard outfit? A Red Cross jacket and matching hat? What will the fancy slogan be on the inevitable banner that will hang behind him?"[8] In the months following Katrina, some questioned whether the nomination of John Roberts to the Supreme Court was timed to divert media attention from the government response to hurricane Katrina. In short, the trusting Americans of the 1950s have become sophisticated media consumers, who recognize and decry attempts to manipulate their emotions or divert their attention. This predisposition to question crosses political lines.

Trends in the Environment

The following discussion looks at trends in the political, economic, cultural, technological, social, legal, and rhetorical environments in which contemporary speakers operate. An understanding of these trends is important in the framing of discourse. We do not speak in a vacuum, and we do not talk to ourselves. We speak within a context, and audience adaptation requires that we comprehend the dynamics of that environment. We need to understand audience expectations of speakers in today's environment, the limits of the possible in terms of what we can achieve, and trends that are influencing and transforming our speaking contexts. Speaking is an audience-centered activity with purposes of informing, persuading, entertaining, and inspiring. The old adage says, "If a tree falls and no one sees it fall, has it really fallen?" The same applies to speaking. If someone speaks but the audience is not listening, has a speaking event really occurred?

Audience adaptation
Taking into account the diverse makeup of the group to whom one speaks

INCREASING ACTIVISM IN THE POLITICAL SPHERE

Since the early 1970s, many public figures have fallen casualty to the reconfigured political climate, defined most recently by the yin and yang of a moral right and a liberal left. More than one serious contender for president, including Democrat Gary Hart, resigned from consideration after the media subjected his personal life to intense scrutiny. Republican Robert Livingston withdrew from consideration as Speaker of the House of Representatives in 1998 after revealing details of an extramarital affair. On June 25, 2004, Republican candidate Jack Riley dropped out of the running for U.S. Senate amid allegations of sex club forays with his wife. In August 2004, New Jersey (Democratic) Governor James McGreevey publicly admitted that an extramarital homosexual affair was the reason for his intended resignation from office. Former President Bill Clinton faced Senate impeachment proceedings for perjury and obstruction of justice in a grand jury investigation of his affair with Monica Lewinsky. Both Hillary and Bill Clinton came under fire through a special prosecution investigation of failed real estate dealings of the late 1970s. Like the impeachment proceedings that would follow in later years, the probe ultimately came to focus as much on the reliability of words as on activities.[9]

The 9/11 Commission, established to assess malfunctioning in the U.S. intelligence and administrative systems prior to the September 11, 2001, terrorist attacks in the United States, released its report in the fall of 2004. The authors of the report pointed to shortcomings in the performance of the Democratic government of Bill Clinton and the Republican administration of George W. Bush. Most relevant to this discussion, the investigators looked for evidence of whether the heads of government had been honest and open with the American people about how they had performed in the period leading up to September 11, 2001. The Abu Ghraib prison scandal also raised questions about whether the administration had lied about its complicity in the abuses there. Revelations that 380 tons of explosives had disappeared in Iraq led to further questioning of the Bush administration. Some asked whether the administration had deliberately hidden this blunder from the American public in the months leading to the official announcement. In a startling first, a number of retired U.S. generals (including retired commanders of key forces in Iraq) called for the resignation of Defense Secretary Donald Rumsfeld.

A large number of interest groups have taken the stage to argue their causes in a very public fashion. Issues related to funding of stem cell research, the right of gays and lesbians to marry and have full legal rights, immigration, euthanasia, abortion, the war in Iraq, the management of homeland security and the Patriot Act, the health care system, the role of religion in state politics, and the transfer of jobs to other countries have mobilized the population. This activism is not limited to one political party or one ideology. Groups on both ends of the political spectrum have organized to question the policies and practices of government, and their issues invade the rhetoric of communities around the country. People are asking serious questions of their leaders and those who would aim to be leaders. Approximately 60 percent of the American population voted in the November 2004 election, a larger percentage than any election year since 1968, the period of civil disobedience and the Vietnam war.[10]

Speakers must be aware of the issues that perforate the political landscape, as well as the beliefs, opinions, and values of their listeners with regard to these issues. They should also recognize that they do not face a public that is easily manipulated or prone to accept unsupported assertions. With access to a preponderance of information on the Internet, audiences are more likely to question authority. As many protest marches demonstrate, people of vastly different political orientations may come together to promote shared issues. While speakers must honor their own beliefs, they must also recognize the limitations of what they can accomplish with particular audiences and realize that their listeners expect sound evidence to support assertions. The current wisdom is that public figures, forced to defend their actions, will do well to take responsibility and admit their mistakes because ultimately their words (not their actions) may be the nails in their coffins.

INCREASING ACTIVISM IN THE ECONOMIC SPHERE

With the publication of *The Manufacturing of Consent* in 1988, Noam Chomsky and Edward S. Herman became the apostles of the new critical era. Arguing that elitist interests had replaced public interests, Chomsky and Herman decried the size, profit orientation, wealth, and concentrated ownership of a handful of media giants. They pointed to the dependency of mass media on advertising as their primary source of income and on government, business, and "experts" as the dominant sources of information.[11] These dependencies, they claimed, create a bias that supports financial interests. The next major influence in the construction of critical society came in the person of Naomi Klein, the daughter of activist filmmaker Bonnie Klein. Bonnie Klein made her mark in the 1970s with the highly controversial antipornography film *Not a Love Story*. Following in the footsteps of her mother, Naomi Klein became somewhat of a cult figure in the 1990s with the publication of *No Logo*, a powerful discourse against the branding of North America by large corporations.[12] She has been a major force in the international antiglobalization movement. While not everyone agrees with Klein's anarchist stance on some issues, few would dispute that her book has helped to shape a more cynical and critical society—a society that trusts less and asks more questions.

At home, the collapse of Enron Corporation spelled the loss of life savings for thousands of employees who owned shares in the energy company. Employees, investors, and retirees lost billions when Enron closed its doors. This largest bankruptcy in U.S. history opened the books of the financial world to intense scrutiny, not only in New York but also in markets around the world. As the investigation unfolded, the focus centered increasingly on a complex network of lies and deception by top executives at Enron. In a nervous financial market transfigured by the fall of Enron, international homemaker Martha Stewart became the next prominent casualty:

> The Stewart case is one of a number of criminal indictments that prosecutors have brought against corporate executives in recent years. While comparatively small in terms of the dollars at stake and the gravity of the crime, Stewart's obstruction of justice case has been a powerful public relations vehicle for government officials to send the broad message that corporate malfeasance will not be tolerated.[13]

In July 2004, Stewart received a sentence of five months in prison and two years' probation for lying to investigators about her 2001 sale of ImClone Systems stock. The original claim was that she acted on insider information, but no one tried her for that offense. Her words, not her actions, ultimately took her into the courtroom.

A skeptical public now looks with suspicion on most large corporate executives, and watchdogs such as the Corporate Library track the annual salary increases of Fortune 500 CEOs.[14] The outcry against malfeasance on the part of public figures comes from all political spheres and finds its way into the public discourse. Corporate leaders and politicians face the necessity to respond to these criticisms and to recognize the concerns of their shareholders and constituents. Many of the topics explored by student speakers concern these same issues.

INCREASING ACTIVISM IN THE LEGAL SPHERE

We live in an age of class action suits and legal accountability. *Class action* suits are brought to the court by one or more individuals who represent a larger group of people with a grievance against a company. A growing number of legal firms specialize in class action lawsuits. Prominent employers sued in recent years include such a diverse range of businesses as Coca Cola, Detroit Edison, Winn-Dixie, Wal-Mart, Bank of America, Home Depot, and Boeing. Plaintiffs have even named the U.S. Justice Department and the D.C. Department of Corrections as defendants in other class action lawsuits. Charges filed against these employers range from racial and gender discrimination to sexual harassment to failure of employers to pay overtime to workers. Other lawsuits concern alleged misrepresentation of policies and services or illegal seizure of funds.[15]

In a much publicized case, McDonalds was sued for serving coffee so hot that it burned a customer who spilled the coffee in her lap. After withdrawing Vioxx from the medical market in the fall of 2000, Merck Pharmaceuticals waited for the inevitable lawsuits to follow. (Some studies had revealed that prolonged use of Vioxx doubles the risk of heart attacks, strokes, and blood clots in users.) By October 2004, users in Illinois and Vermont had already filed lawsuits against Merck Frosst, the manufacturer of Vioxx. The tobacco industry continues to be a prime target for class action suits, and class action suits in the environmental area also continue to dominate the legal landscape. Automobile insurance premiums have skyrocketed as a consequence of large settlements and payments to victims of accidents, to the point that many people can no longer afford to drive their own automobiles. Many medical physicians, especially surgeons, have moved to states with a better history

of ruling in favor of doctors charged with malpractice suits. Others have jacked up their fees to pay the rising insurance costs.

These legal issues inspire much of our most contentious public discourse, whether on television or in college classrooms. Speakers have always had to consider the legal implications of their words. In the current environment, they must be especially careful. Meticulous research and adequate documentation are critical in preparing to speak in public.

INCREASING DIVERSITY IN THE CULTURAL ENVIRONMENT

A number of changes have occurred in the social demographics of the United States since 1990. Approximately half of the country's foreign-born population entered the country in 1990 or later. The 2003 American Community Survey (reported by the U.S. Census Bureau) reveals that approximately one out every eight respondents is foreign-born. Survey participants listed twenty-seven different countries as their ancestral origins.[16] Regions of origin include (in order of numbers) Latin America, Asia, Europe, Africa, North America, and Oceania. Fourteen percent claim Hispanic or Latino origins (Mexican, Puerto Rican, Cuban, or other). About one out of five participants in the census speaks a language other than English at home; one out of ten speaks English "less than very well."[17]

The changing nature of our cultural mosaic has implications for the makeup of audiences. Audiences are increasingly multicultural. Their values and experiences, especially in their first years of residency, sometimes differ from those who are born and raised in the country. The account of a young student illustrates this point:

> My parents Ruth and Kurt Chuop met in the midst of a Cambodian genocide, a time when all sense of humanity seemed to have vanished. Yet in this sea of despair and destruction, they were each other's anchors. They were hopeful that, when the war ended, they could start a new life together. Although the prospect of moving to a foreign land was intimidating, they instinctively knew that if they worked hard enough, nothing would be impossible. As you can probably guess, that was before they had four children. My poor naïve parents! They had no idea that raising children in this country would be a little different from raising children in the Cambodian countryside. I can remember the first time that I approached my mother about dating. She looked at me in shock and stated that good Cambodian girls never date. They marry good Cambodian men chosen by their parents. Ahh, arranged marriages. Yeah, this wasn't going to work. Needless to say, my parents abandoned the idea pretty quickly amidst our forceful protests.[18]

A number of studies have sought to identify the American value system. The following list indicates the most often-referenced values—those qualities that we esteem most highly in a person: achievement-oriented, active, hard-working, competent, caring, humanitarian, competitive, conformist, cultured, democratic, dominant, efficient, egalitarian (believing in equality), free, imaginative, independent, individualistic, intelligent, logical, materialistic, hedonistic, moral, optimistic, patriotic, peaceful, progressive, idealistic, responsible, social, and family-oriented.[19] When speakers address mainstream audiences, they may assume that the majority

Audience analysis
Research into the makeup of the group to whom one will speak

will hold these values in high regard. In reality, a number of subcultures place certain values significantly higher than others (e.g., Asians may value collectivism over individualism). Audience analysis helps the speaker to understand the needs of audiences with unique cultural profiles. As speakers, we must show respect for the cultural differences in audiences and their varying perspectives on dating, marriage, and other social and political issues. After all, the act of speaking is *not about the speaker*. It is *about the audience*.

Other changes have also occurred in the cultural portrait of the United States. The education level of Americans has increased dramatically since 1940. The 1940 census reported, for example, that 5.4 percent of men and 3.7 percent of women (twenty-five years or older) were college graduates. By way of contrast, the 2003 population survey showed that 29 percent of men and 25 percent of women (twenty-five years or older) had completed at least a B.A. degree.[20] By 2003, 85 percent of the population in the same age category had finished high school. Literacy levels are correspondingly on the incline. The increasing education and literacy levels of Americans means that speakers must assume that most listeners have at least a high school education; almost one out of three has a university degree.

CHANGES IN TECHNOLOGICAL ENVIRONMENTS

In today's wired world, speakers have many different audiences, often scattered through the community or dispersed around the state, country, or globe. Some are present in the immediate speaking environment, but many are not visible to the

speaker. The auditorium may have a seating capacity of three hundred persons; but television, radio, and the web do not respect such limitations. In the case of a political speech, many advocacy groups, politicians, bureaucrats, and members of the general public listen to the speech on the radio, observe the speech on television, or read excerpts from the speech on the Internet or in a newspaper. A speaker may have no idea of the range of his audience or the numbers for any given speech:

> The speakers of today's online community sit in wired caves, sometimes clothed in only their underwear, using Adobe Photoshop (a popular graphics editing program) and cryptic computer language codes to convey their character to the receivers of the message: the web surfing public. Not only is the speaker him or herself now invisible to the audience, but we, as the audience, cannot even be certain that the speaker is limited to a single person. Such constructs of character have led, in extremes, to the "big brother" feelings of paranoia towards "faceless corporate America." After all, how can we trust that which we not only cannot see, but also that for which we cannot determine a number of speakers?[21]

As new technologies proliferate, more extensive collections of speeches become available in audio and video formats. The ready availability of these archived speeches promotes the necessity for authenticity. Speakers can no longer craft one message for Ohio audiences and another for California audiences. As speeches become accessible on the Internet, anyone can verify the stances of speakers on various issues. This potential for authentication means that speakers have little incentive to lie or deceive their publics. Recognizing this new environment, organizations (especially governments) have placed an increasing stress on consistency in messaging.

CHANGES IN SOCIAL ENVIRONMENTS

We are living in less formal days than did the speakers we study in history books, films, and videos. That lack of formality intrudes into all aspects of our social interactions. When I was growing up, everyone wore formal black attire to funerals, just as women wore hats to Easter church service, and no one ever wore white shoes with a black or navy dress. Specific conventions governed the dress of both men and women, and different occasions called for different kinds of dress. But times and expectations of what is appropriate and acceptable have changed, at least for the average person. Recently, I was surprised to see that some people arrived at a funeral service in jeans. On a second occasion, I watched the news coverage of the memorial service for Terri Schiavo, the Florida woman who died after the courts ordered the removal of her feeding tube. The father of Terri Shiavo sat on the front row of the televised memorial service in shorts and a casual shirt.

Even so, expectations vary across cultures, and we hold people in high positions of influence to different standards. In January 2005, French President Jacques Chirac, Russian President Vladmir Putin, and other global figures gathered in southern Poland to recognize the 60th anniversary of the liberation of Auschwitz. With the exception of Vice President Dick Cheney, who represented the United States at this solemn occasion, the world leaders were attired in dark, formal clothing and footwear. Because the ceremony took place outside on a cold windy day, the men also wore "gentlemen's" hats. Cheney, on the other hand, was clad in a military green parka with a fur-trimmed hood, embroidered with his name. His footwear was brown lace-up hiking boots, and his knit ski cap bore the words "Staff 2001." Washington Post staff writer Robin Givhan described the hat as the kind "a conventioneer might find in a goodie bag" and the embroidered name as "reminiscent of the way in which children's clothes are inscribed with their names before they are sent away to camp."[22] He offered the following commentary on Cheney's choice of clothing: "Some might argue that Cheney was the only attendee with the smarts to dress for the cold and snowy weather. But sometimes, out of respect for the occasion, one must endure a little discomfort."[23] The fact that Cheney would have appeared at all in such informal garb, however, says something significant about social conventions in North America in the 21st century.

Rules of social interaction have also changed in other ways. An increasing number of people are choosing interactive media, watching reality shows that encourage their participation, and listening to radio and television talk shows that solicit their feedback. If hockey and soccer fans want to get on the ice or field with the players, it should not be surprising in today's environment. On a visit to New Orleans (in the year preceding hurricane Katrina), I noticed that many of the establishments on Bourbon Street no longer featured paid entertainment.

They relied, instead, on tourists and students to climb on the stage, join the musicians, and become part of the act. In the same way, speakers are finding that their audiences do not want to be passive observers, witnessing events in which they have no role to play. They want to be involved and engaged.[24]

While some would argue that television has created a culture of passive observers who expect only to be entertained,[25] I would say that this trend has reversed itself in this decade. If you look at the success of shows such as *The Apprentice, Survivor*, and *The Amazing Race*, you can see that viewing audiences seek shows that engage them. By the hundreds of thousands, they apply to compete on the shows; and they watch them, in large part, to figure out who will emerge as victor or survivor. The same is true of Court TV and forensic crime shows such as *American Justice* and *48 Hours Mystery*, where audiences follow the trail of evidence to see where it leads. Shows such as *American Idol* and *The Bachelor(ette)* require that audience select the final winners of the competition or figure out who will remain at the end of the show. Almost every kind of contemporary programming, from *Larry King Live* to *Fear Factor*, allows for feedback and the acquisition of additional information on subjects of interest.

CHANGES IN RHETORICAL CONVENTIONS

Like the social traditions that govern dress, the rules that govern speaking have undergone a transformation. A short journey to nineteenth-century Britain, eighteenth-century France, and nineteenth-century America—periods in which emotion played a strong role in delivery—allows a glimpse of how speaking styles have changed over the years. In Britain, orators such as Richard Sheridan sometimes fainted in mid-delivery of their speeches—a calculated action that conveyed their emotional attachment to the subject of their speeches. In France, the chaotic days of the French Revolution produced a master orator, Maximilien Robespierre. In highly emotional and ritualized speeches, Robespierre declared his personal sufferings and his anticipated place in martyrdom. He used elaborate gestures and dressed in a flamboyant style. Female members of his audience, in anticipation of the climactic moments of the speech, would hold their handkerchiefs in waiting, poised to weep upon cue from the speaker.[26]

Elocution
Formal study of public speaking that dates back to the 1770s, associated with highly contrived gestures and movements

In nineteenth-century America, students studied the art of elocution in classrooms, and the more affluent also received private tutoring. Textbooks gave explicit instructions on how to express various emotions through voice, movement, and gestures. Speakers sought to mimic the mannerisms of great and noble men.[27] Works such as John Walker's *The Elements of Gesture* and Gilbert Austin's *Chironomia* set the standard for instruction.[28] (See Reflections box.) The line sketches demonstrate the most common postures and gestures. A hand to the brow, an extended arm, a broad sweeping movement—each gesture carried an explicit meaning to the audience. The speakers learned how to apply the stylized gestures to memorized passages, not unlike the rote exercises practiced by schoolboys in the Roman Empire or the declamations of the Hellenistic period in Greece.[29] The line sketches in the illustration on page 19 demonstrate the most common postures and gestures taught to students in formal learning environments in the 1800s.

Reflections

Excerpt from a Nineteenth-Century Book on Elocution

When the pupil has got the habit of holding his hand and arm properly, he may be taught to move it. In this motion he must be careful to keep the arm from the body. He must neither draw the elbow backwards, nor suffer it to approach to the side, but while the hand and lower joint of the arm are curving towards the shoulder, the whole arm, with the elbow, forming nearly an angle of a square, should move upwards from the shoulder, in the same position as when gracefully taking off the hat; that is, with the elbow extended from the side, and the upper joint of the arm nearly on a line with the shoulder; and forming an angle of a square with the body; . . . this motion of the arm will naturally bring the hand, with the palm, downwards, into a horizontal position, and when it approaches to the head, the arm should, with a jerk, be suddenly straightened into its first position, at the very moment the emphatical word is pronounced. This coincidence of the hand and voice, will greatly enforce the pronunciation; and, if they keep time, they will be in tune, as it were, to each other; and to force and energy, add harmony and variety.

Source: John Walker, "The Elements of Gesture," in William Scott, *Scott's New Lessons in Reading and Writing* (Philadelphia: A. Walker, 1816), p. 16.

Audiences of the day rewarded this highly theatrical style of delivery with rapt attention and accolades.

In the late 1800s, a movement called Chautauqua developed. Initially, the movement involved the development of community programs, first on Lake Chautauqua in New York and later in other locations (especially the Midwest). The community events featured a series of speakers who lectured on a wide diversity of religious, cultural, scientific, and political topics. As the movement matured in the early 1900s, speakers began to move from location to location on the "Chautauqua circuit." Programs typically lasted from three to seven days. At the peak of the movement in the mid-1920s, lecturers on the circuit were speaking to more than 45 million people in more than 10,000 communities in forty-five states.[30] Over time, a variety of entertainers (magicians, actors and actresses, and opera singers) joined the group of tent performers; however, the core event continued to be the public speakers:

> Lecturers were the backbone of Chautauqua. Every topic from current events to travel to human interest to comic storytelling could be heard on the Circuits. Chautauqua would swell by the thousands to see William Jennings Bryan, the most popular of all Chautauqua attractions. Until his death in 1925 his populist, temperance, evangelical, and crusading message could be heard on Circuits across the country. Another popular reformer, Maud Ballington Booth, the "Little Mother of the Prisons," could bring her audiences to tears with her description of prison life and her call to reform. In a more humorous vein, author Opie Read's homespun philosophy and stories made him an enduring presence on the platform.[31]

The lectures could last for hours, and families saw the events as a form of entertainment.

At the same time that the Chautauqua movement was flourishing, students studied the art of elocution in the classroom and delivered memorized speeches as a form of entertainment at school events. In legislatures and other political settings, it was not unusual for politicians to speak for four or more hours to packed rooms. British Parliamentarian Richard Sheridan spoke for four days at the impeachment trial of Warren Hastings.[32] If a politician in Congress or the Senate were to speak for several hours in today's environment, we would consider that he was filibustering, seeking to delay a vote on some bill or policy. In short, prior to the advent of movies and television, audiences had a high tolerance for listening to speakers for extended periods of time—a situation that has changed dramatically.

Over the last five decades, the media have created a generation of audiences that expect short and provocative speeches, as opposed to long and entertaining speeches. When I write speeches for politicians and bureaucrats, I find that the average time requirement for speeches is ten to fifteen minutes. About ten years ago, I was asked to write speeches that were twenty minutes in length. When I was growing up in the 1950s, political figures often spoke for thirty to forty-five minutes, considerably shorter than the famed Chautauqua speakers such as William Jennings Bryan but notably longer than their peers in this century. The speeches get shorter and shorter as attention spans collapse and audiences turn to alternative media for information.

Other changes have also marked the rhetorical landscape. Most notably, we have moved from an eloquent and emotional past to an informal and conversational present. As early as 1915, John Winans (a pioneer in establishing the field of speech communication) urged speakers to adopt a more natural and conversational mode of delivery.[33] Even some elocutionists advocated more informal styles of language and presentation. But until the second half of the twentieth century, their advice fell mostly on deaf ears.[34] Unlike the audiences of Sheridan and Robespierre, modern audiences view histrionic and contrived modes of delivery as inappropriate. For the majority of occasions, people expect a warm, conversational, and spontaneous delivery—not a grand oratorical happening. Reflecting this trend, which took strong hold in the 1960s, literary critic Northrop Frye observed that high style can exist in ordinary speech.[35]

This move from the formal to the conversational can be attributed in large part to the onset of television:

> Because of the size of a television receiver screen, subjects being televised generally are portrayed by shots of sufficiently close range to show significant detail. . . . The television director uses panoramic shots to establish a setting and a series of close shots to record the event. The communicator in a television event . . . usually can assume that he is being observed at close range. Thus, his safest approach may be to assume that he is acting within personal or intimate distance of his audience and to rely on the nonverbal style of delivery most appropriate to such proxemic zones. Gestures or body movement that characterizes the actor in a theatre or the public speaker will seem exaggerated, affected, or even ludicrous on television. In the vernacular of the theatre, such techniques give the appearance of a "ham" performance.[36]

In addition, speakers must take "audio distance" into account. Unlike the ancient orator, who did not have the benefit of voice amplification, today's speakers will almost always operate in the close audio zone. Also, regardless of the immediate setting in which the communicator is operating, television audiences will receive the communication in the intimate territory of their homes. Such a setting for the transaction favors an informal style of delivery. For most occasions, the communicator should strive for verbal and nonverbal styles suitable for intimate personal space: "Not only will the physical elements of the communication be bound by the demands of intimate address, but also the *content* and *language* of the communication must conform to such criteria."[37]

Others have also described the influence of television on public address. In the late 1960s, media guru Marshall McLuhan observed that television would require the emergence of a more flexible and casual politician,[38] and in the 1970s, critic John Leonard proclaimed that "television creates style as much as it records it."[39] By the 1980s, the media effects literature had captured this theme, and politicians struggled to learn the new grammar—so different from that of the stump speech. Dubbed "the Great Communicator," Ronald Reagan became known for his mastery of this style. This new definition of eloquence has resulted in an increased emphasis on narrative (storytelling), self-disclosure, and visual modes of persuasion; and a number of speech scholars urge that we give more recognition to what actually works in speeches.[40]

Narrative
Story-telling

At the same time that audiences like to see the "real" person, they do not always want to see excessive emotion. Listeners feel uncomfortable when speakers become too personal in their display of emotions. Sally Field learned that lesson in 1984 when she accepted the Academy Award for her role as leading actress in *Places in the Heart*. In a moment of uncontained happiness, she gushed: "I haven't had an orthodox career, and I've wanted more than anything to have your respect. The first time I didn't feel it, but this time I feel it, and I can't deny the fact that you like me, right now, you like me!" Field's acceptance speech became the object of mockery and cynical commentary. Critics believed that she had gone "over the top" with this outpouring of emotion. Like other shifts in public speaking demands, the rejection of excessive emotion dates back to the establishment of television as a dominant medium.[41]

Occasionally, however, audiences react differently. When Cuba Gooding, Jr., received the award for best supporting actor in *Jerry Maguire* in 1997, he shouted, "I love you! Tom Cruise! I love you, brother! I love you, man! . . . Everybody, I love you. I love you all. Cameron Crowe! James L. Brooks! James L. Brooks, I love you. Everybody who's involved with this, I love you. I love you. Everybody involved." Perhaps the difference in the audience reactions to the two displays of emotion derived from the fact that Sally Field focused on herself in a very personal way, revealing her insecurities, whereas Cuba Gooding, Jr., focused on the audience.[42] When speakers are unable to maintain their composure in speaking about a highly personal topic, they create a situation that is uncomfortable for the audience. On more than a few occasions, students have begun to cry while talking about the death of a parent or sibling. The audience does not know how to react in these situations.

Despite the tendency of many contemporary audiences to feel uncomfortable with strong displays of emotion, such displays are allowed—and even expected—when someone experiences a serious loss. On these occasions, audiences anticipate that speakers will display emotion. As Scott Peterson (tried for the murder of his wife Laci Peterson) and other defendants have discovered, audiences judge them badly if they do not show sufficient emotion in the courtroom and in front of the television cameras. The Russian public criticized Premier Vladimir Putin for his stoic response to the deaths of Beslan hostages in September 2004. They wanted him to show more emotion.[43]

Finally, changes have also occurred (within certain settings) in the topics deemed appropriate for public consumption. When Ellen DeGeneres "came out" on *Ellen* in 1997, she soon lost her place on primetime television. Now she has a popular talk show, and all of the major networks have added programs such as *Queer Eye for the Straight Guy* and *The L Word*. *The Vagina Monologues* could not have been performed on university and college campuses in the early 1990s.

A Critical Model for Public Speaking

In this transformed society, words are sometimes more important than actions. Martha Stewart was indicted not for insider trading, but because she lied about her actions. Bill Clinton faced the possibility of impeachment not because he had an

Critical Communication Model (CCM)
A model used to help illustrate how communication occurs, and its possible impact

affair with Monica Lewinsky, but because he lied about the affair. People have high expectations of public personalities. They expect transparency and honesty, and they hold public figures to high standards of accountability. These expectations are part of the environment within which speakers function. Thus, any communication model should include an ethical dimension.

The critical communication model CCM below includes the traditional elements (speaker, message, channel or medium, audience, noise, feedback, and

Critical Communication Model (CCM)

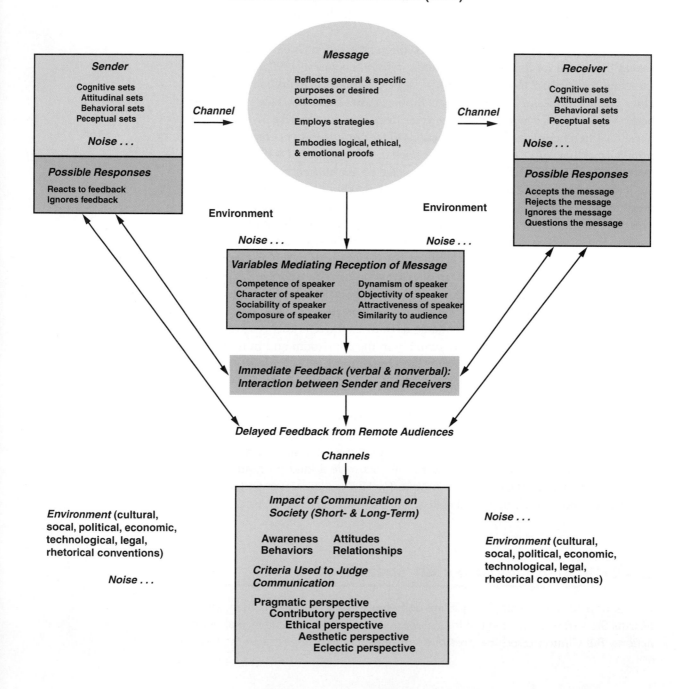

environment). However, this model goes further to incorporate the concepts of intent, purpose, and outcomes of a speech—all part of ethical considerations. The model also adds political, technological, social, legal, and economic influences, as well as rhetorical conventions, to the more usual cultural variables that constitute environment or speech context. Like other communication models, this one seeks to explain the communication process, visually depict relationships, and assist in identifying points of communication breakdown.

SENDER

The sender, or source of the message, provides the starting point in any model of public speaking. In the case of public speaking, the sender translates ideas into symbols or language codes. Speakers come in all varieties, from politicians to activists to comedians; and they represent public, private, and voluntary spheres. They have specific purposes in giving speeches. In the most general terms, their purposes may be to *inform, persuade, entertain,* or *inspire.* They may seek, for example, to inform about a new border security policy, persuade the audience to accept new security screening procedures, entertain the audience with stories about humorous episodes at border crossings, or inspire the audience to join the fight against terrorism. Sometimes speakers have motives or purposes in delivering a speech that they do not share with the audience: to repair a damaged image, to encourage the audience to vote for their party in the next election, or to explain their many absences from congressional sessions.

The credibility of any speaker influences our acceptance of the person's message. When speakers arrive at the podium, they come with baggage. We call this baggage *source credibility.* The term *source credibility* refers to the perceived intelligence, knowledge, and tangible attainments; sociability; appearance; character and reputation; personality; sincerity; dynamism; and composure of a speaker. Numerous studies demonstrate that the greater the credibility of a source, the greater the chance that the audience will accept the message of the speaker. In other words, credibility mediates reception of the message. Roman orator Cicero stated that audiences take the actions of a person's life into account when they judge a message: "It contributes much to success in speaking that the morals, principles, conduct, and lives of those who plead causes, and of those for whom they plead, should be such as to merit esteem, and that those of their adversaries should be such as to deserve censure."[44]

Speakers have intent when they speak—some purpose or set goal—that we must consider when evaluating their speech efforts. Most people would argue that we are most responsible when we commit an intentional act. In the court system, we hold people more accountable if they act with purpose and understand the possible consequences of their actions. In the same way, audiences judge messages, at least in part, on the intent of the speaker.

MESSAGE

A speech is the message delivered by a speaker to an audience—an oral form of communication, at least at some point in time. (I say "at some point in time"

Sender
The source of the message

Inform
To impart information

Persuade
To attempt to convince through the making of an argument

Entertain
To amuse

Inspire
To motivate, instill with feeling

Source credibility
The perceived attributes of a speaker (e.g., intelligence, honesty, etc.), which affect receptivity to a message

Message
Information conveyed from sender to receiver

because archived speeches may appear in written formats.) Usually speakers have a strategy for achieving their purposes. The strategy may not be obvious to the audience, but a scholar of rhetoric should be able to uncover speech strategies. A politician may choose, for example, to focus a speech on international rather than domestic concerns if her performance in office has been stronger in the international arena. This is a strategic choice that she makes. In another situation, a speaker may use extensive appeals to the American value system as a means of achieving his purposes. In seeking to reverse the court decision to remove the feeding tube of their daughter, the parents of Terri Schiavo appealed to one of our most cherished values, the sanctity of life.

Speakers use *logical*, *emotional*, and *ethical* proofs to develop their speeches. *Logical* proofs include evidence, reasoning, and argumentation. *Emotional* proofs involve psychological appeals to the emotions of the audience. By *ethical* proofs, we mean the building of source credibility—demonstrating intelligence, character, and good will. (See the Question of Ethics box.)

Logical proofs
Proofs involving reason, argument, and evidence

Emotional proofs
Proofs that appeal to the feelings of an audience

Ethical proofs
Proofs aimed at building source credibility

A Question of Ethics

An antigay website features a picture of Matthew Shepard "burning in hell." (Matthew Shepard was the victim of a hate crime against homosexuals. His death by beating received extensive media coverage.) The click of a button allows the web visitor to hear Matthew "scream in hell." Another website gives detailed instruction on how to build explosive devices. You learn that two website visitors were later involved in a massacre of high school students. A group of protesters carries placards with the words "Down with the government." A speaker argues that prochoice advocates are murderers; the next day, two people die in the bombing of an abortion clinic. A student writes an essay that advocates violence against adherents to the Muslim faith. A website carries pornographic images of children, while another hosts images of women who appear to be victims of violent rape. A personal ad, which requests the services of a hit man, appears in a magazine for mercenaries. An organization called "Victims for Justice" (VFJ) distributes information on former convicts to potential employers and landlords. The materials contain statements of an inflammatory nature, intended to create fear and hate in the readers. When ex-convicts move into a neighborhood, VFJ members demonstrate outside of their homes, delivering speeches over loudspeakers. They call for neighborhood dwellers to use whatever means necessary to drive the offenders from their neighborhood.

What are the limits of free speech? What constitutes hate speech? Images that degrade or words that defile? The perpetration of false information that unfairly depicts some racial, religious, or minority group? Language that inflames or encourages people to take violent action against others? Language that results in deaths or injuries? Should we protect all groups in society, even those who break the law? Should we consider the outcomes of the speech event? What happens when we put limits on the rights of people to speak freely in a democratic society? Do significant differences exist in how we should treat the cases described here? What are the implications of censorship? Try to define "hate speech."

CHANNEL

Channel refers to the medium by which a message is transmitted. At the most basic level, the air that carries our messages is a medium. We may also use radio or television signals to convey our messages to larger numbers of people. Speakers can reach audiences via audio and video conferences. An increasing number of communicators are choosing the Internet as a means of reaching audiences. Like other communicators, speakers have an increasingly diverse number of channels, or media, for transmitting their messages. In the case of new technologies, however, they also have less control than in live situations over what happens to the message. Once the words leave the mouths of speakers, they have little control over how far or where they travel. Their messages may appear in whole or in part in a variety of media. A magazine may reprint the entire text of a speech, but chat groups on the Internet or newspapers may select passages out of context for inclusion in their discussions. Television coverage often includes extremely brief "sound bites" of speeches.

Channel
The medium through which the message is transmitted

ENVIRONMENT

The environments in which we seek to inform, persuade, motivate, and entertain are too diverse to justify mention. However, in the broadest terms, speechmaking occurs in political, social, economic, cultural, legal, and technological contexts. For the public speaker, rhetorical conventions are part of this context. When critics engage in rhetorical analysis of the type discussed in Chapter Fifteen, they consider all of these variables. Communication models, however, often fail to elaborate on the contexts in which speakers operate. Yet these contexts frame the speech acts and help us to understand possible reasons that speakers (ourselves and others) succeed or fail.

Environment
The many contexts in which public speaking takes place

RECEIVER

Language symbols become ideas in the minds of listeners, who decode the messages received from speakers. The resulting ideas may or may not be the same as those in the speaker's head. Understanding and acceptance of messages rely upon the successful negotiation of a number of internal variables in audiences, including cognitive, attitudinal, behavioral, and perceptual sets. Listening is hard work, requiring that we hear what someone says; selectively perceive, assimilate, and categorize the information; and, finally, develop a mental response to the message. We filter out a large part of what we hear every day, especially information that jars with what we already know and accept to be the truth. We perceive selectively, ignoring information that does not conform to our expectations. In today's environment, the challenge faced by many speakers is even greater than in the past. When speakers attempt to reach their audiences by means of radio, television, or the Internet, they compete with a variety of stimuli. The members of a target audience may be preparing a meal, reading a newspaper, or watching a video at the same time that they are listening to the speaker. Multiple media may be operating in the listening space.

Receiver
The recipient of a message

NOISE

Noise
Anything that interferes with the communication act

Noise often occurs in the attempt to communicate our ideas and opinions. By *noise* we mean any form of interference in the communication process. This noise can manifest itself in the speaker, the environment, the channel, or the listener. A speaker may be tired, confused, or unsure of how to communicate her ideas. She may be insecure with a particular audience, and the lack of confidence may cause her to lose her composure or to forget her speech. Listeners may be biased or prejudiced on the topic addressed in the speech. They may also feel tired, overworked, or stressed by some event in their personal lives. These factors may prompt audience members to allow their thoughts to drift in other directions. If someone is hungry, the person will think about food instead of the content of the speech. Cultural misunderstandings can short-circuit the reception process. Audience expectations related to social norms in dress or codes of behavior can create communication problems. Factors in the external environment—a loud air conditioning unit, an overheated room, a ringing cell phone or pager, coughing, or whispering among audience members—can also cause an audience to lose focus. A malfunctioning microphone or computer can interrupt the ability of the speaker to convey information. Thus, noise in the environment can be internal or external impediments to communication, psychological or physiological in nature.

FEEDBACK

Feedback
Response to a message

The process of public speaking is interactive and iterative in nature. In the immediate situation, a dynamic exchange occurs between speaker and listener, in which the two trade roles, offering feedback and asking and responding to questions. When the listener becomes speaker, a feedback loop occurs. In a live situation, audiences provide nonverbal (and sometimes verbal) feedback to the speaker. The term *feedback* refers to the discernible response of a listener to a message. Nonverbal feedback may take the form of a shake of the head, smile, yawn, or nod. The listener may turn away from the speaker or look at his watch. There may be a delay in the processing of verbal information because many listeners provide their feedback via the web, e-mails, letters, telephone calls, and personal contact following a speech event. Ultimately, the listener decides whether to accept, reject, ignore, or question the intent, means, and outcomes of the speech.

Outside of a classroom situation, listeners do not feel bound to remain in a speaking environment that does not meet their expectations. Today's audiences do not adhere to the same social conventions as their parents—conventions that required people to stay in their seats and to look interested even when they were bored or tired of listening to the speaker. So the ultimate form of feedback in a speaking situation is to leave. If listeners do not get what they want from a speaker, they have other options, over which they have a much higher measure of control. That is, the vanishing audience members can decide when to acquire the information (morning, afternoon, or evening), how much to acquire (skimming of material versus in-depth research), and from what sources (television, radio, the Internet, magazines, books, or live speech event). Attending a live speech event requires a relatively high investment—negotiating traffic, fitting the event into a hectic work and personal schedule, and sacrificing some other activity. Since the costs are high, the benefits must be high.

Speakers, for their part, may choose to respond to—or disregard—listener feedback. If they respond, the loop begins again: speaker-listener-speaker. Speakers may acknowledge the validity of a comment, respond to a question, or ask a question of the audience member who shows nonverbal signs of confusion or upset. Remote audiences also provide feedback to the speaker. As discussed earlier in the chapter, these audiences may be remote in time or space. Although delayed, this feedback can have a dramatic effect on how the speech is perceived and judged. Opinion leaders in the media and the larger society react to speeches that reach them through various media—newspapers, radio, television, the Internet—and interpersonal channels such as family, friends, and work colleagues. Other audiences do not receive the communcations within the lifetime of the speakers. In those cases, the speaker never receives the feedback; but he or she may have defenders and detractors who study, analyze, and judge the worthiness of the speech.

IMPACT AND CRITERIA FOR JUDGING SPEECH

From an audience perspective, positive outcomes of a speech could be increased understanding, positive attitudes, higher levels of commitment to take action, pleasurable feelings, or improved relationships. Negative outcomes are also possible, such as confused understanding of a topic, a stronger commitment to a preexisting point of view (contrary to the position espoused by the speaker), a feeling of apathy or powerlessness, or worsened relationship. Speaking is a *results-oriented, audience-centered* activity. When the speaker does not recognize and take audience needs and expectations into account, the speech will fail to achieve its desired results.

We can judge a speech on whether the speaker achieved his or her purposes, made a contribution, produced an aesthetically pleasing product (in terms of words and delivery), and conformed to ethical standards of conduct. Audience members usually judge speeches on a mix of these criteria, and they are often willing to tolerate a less than perfect delivery if a speaker has something of value to offer to them. In other words, audiences value the speaker who makes a contribution. Novice speakers, on the other hand, often place an unjustified high emphasis on factors of delivery.

Without ignoring aesthetics and delivery, this book places a fair amount of stress on making a contribution and adhering to ethical standards in speechmaking. In an age of accountability, we must look at the *costs of achieving outcomes*. That is, we must go beyond results to judge speakers on such criteria as motives and truthfulness (*intent*), the extent to which the message has been framed and delivered in an ethical manner (*means*), and the consequences of the speech act (*end*). An ethical perspective requires that we judge the costs of our rhetorical efforts to ourselves and others. Did we have honorable motives (*intent*)? Did we intend for our words to bring harm to others (*intent*)? Did we tell the truth (*means*)? Did we avoid the use of inflated or vague language (*means*)? Did we incur damage to our reputation or standing in the community (*end*)? Did our words result in physiological or psychological harm to others (*end*)? If we attempt to sell a faulty product to someone, have we breached the ethical model? If we reveal a confidence that harms a third party, have we broken an ethical contract with the person who shared the information with us? (See the Question of Ethics box.)

For scholars of rhetoric, a focus on ethics makes complete sense. From the time of Aristotle, Isocrates, Cicero, and Quintilian, rhetoricians have stressed the importance of character and honesty in speaking. A survey of seventy-nine communication programs in 1996 found that almost 40 percent were teaching stand-alone courses in ethics.[45] The numbers are doubtless much greater now. The growth of critical society gives new energy to the argument of classical and modern scholars that speakers should truly be "good men [or good women] with good speech skills."[46]

A Question of Ethics

Is lying ever justified? Should truth be a relative commodity? Consider the following examples.

Example #1. You are a political figure. Someone asks, "Have you had an affair with Susie Smith?" You consider the impact of the affair on your family and the likelihood that your marriage will be destroyed. Moreover, you have never put Susie Smith on payroll or done anything to favor her with regard to your official duties as a politician. You answer, "No, I don't know Susie Smith." Later you go on national television and deny having had an affair.

Example #2. Your friend asks if you like her new hairstyle. You think that it is extremely unattractive, but you respond, "Yes, it's really nice."

Example #3. You live in a military state. A soldier arrives at your home in the middle of the night. He demands, "Is anyone else in the house?" You know that your brother is sleeping in the other room and he will be at risk if you say "yes." You respond, "No, no one is here."

What is the difference, if any, in these three situations? Can you suggest criteria for determining when (if ever) lying is acceptable? Should the criteria vary from situation to situation—public versus private, number of people affected, level of harm, or other?

Is omission the same thing as lying? If an audience member questions a speaker on some point and she avoids responding or answers a different question, has she behaved in an unethical way? If a persuasive speaker gives only the positive attributes of a facial cream and ignores the negative, has the person committed an unethical act?

Imagine that someone is trying to sell exercise equipment to you. The person selectively includes some facts and omits others. Is it reasonable to expect that salespersons should talk about the weaknesses of their products? What if the product is prescription medication? Advertising rules now require that drug companies list all of the potential side effects of medications, in addition to telling about the benefits. Do you think that speakers have the same obligation to give complete information, even if it harms their cases? In answering this question, should we consider the potential costs of using the products in determining ethical criteria for speechmaking? Alternately, should we apply the same criteria to promotion of all products?

Conclusion

Recent events have demonstrated changes in levels of societal tolerance for lying, deception, and irresponsible behavior by public figures. Public speakers face this same cynical public when they go to the podium. Gone are the days when audience members bowed to authority figures or accepted words on faith. They expect politicians and other public figures to be able to back up their opinions, to speak with transparency, and to stand behind their words. And if television or radio commentators expose inconsistencies—shifts in position or language—audiences react. While not all of us will become public figures, we confront the same expectations when we speak in public. We must be prepared to speak directly and honestly, to respond to questions, and to translate our words into actions. We are living in an age of accountability.

This chapter has introduced the reader to the CCM model. The chapters that follow address, in detail, the components of this model—speaker, message, channel, specific environments, and listener. Vignettes, intended to provoke discussion of ethical considerations in public speaking, appear throughout the book.

Questions for Discussion

1. Describe examples of "noise" in your classroom environment. Consider internal and external distractions with which speakers may have to contend.

2. How many live speech events (outside of the classroom) have you attended in the last year? What prompted you to attend the live events, as opposed to acquiring the information from some other source (media, secondhand accounts, etc.)? Did the speakers meet your expectations? Why or why not?

3. Identify some speech topics that would have been unacceptable until recent years? Identify some speech topics that would still be unacceptable within a classroom setting.

4. Do you agree that we are living in an age of accountability? Give examples to support your reasoning.

Outline

COMMUNICATION APPREHENSIVENESS

Learning to Cope with Anxiety

Learning Objectives

· To learn about the causes of communication anxiety
· To understand the nature of speech anxiety
· To learn how to cope with speech anxiety

Social phobia
A fear of being judged in social situations

Leslie was a quiet retiring man, gentle in manner and soft-spoken. Superficially, he looked like any other person. But appearances were deceptive. Leslie suffered from a condition called *social phobia*, a fear of evaluation that creates a state of confusion and anxiety in individuals placed in a social situation. Literally any interpersonal encounter—whether ordering a meal at a restaurant, interacting with a grocery clerk, or responding to a request for directions—created mental havoc in Leslie, causing him to stammer, turn red, and become generally incoherent. In order to cope with these extreme levels of social anxiety, Leslie planned every communication event. At home with family members, he would sit alone in a corner, practicing for possible interpersonal encounters, planning even the laughs that he could insert into the conversation. In a restaurant, he would follow the lead of the first person to order, "I'll have the same." Any successful social interaction was a major life accomplishment for Leslie, cause to celebrate by repeating the conversation over and over again once he returned home. His brother once remarked that Leslie's tension was so palpable that it could be felt by everyone in a crowded room.

I suspect that Leslie's case (a true one) is more extreme than most. However, the National Institute of Mental Health says that anxiety disorders affect 13 percent of Americans between the ages of eighteen and fifty-four. Moreover, a professor at the Anxiety Disorders Clinic (Centre for Addiction and Mental Health, University of Toronto Medical School) believes that social phobia is *the* most common anxiety disorder:

> The illness is associated with an intense fear of evaluation in social or performance situations. . . . Among individuals with social phobia, the problem is not only shyness, but also the negative thoughts and feelings that get triggered by their feared situations, which cause them to avoid the situation altogether. Even signing a cheque in front of someone else can be potentially humiliating, because there is the possibility of a nervous shake of the hand. Social phobia is intensely painful and disruptive for those who crack under pressure. Physical symptoms include rapid heart rate, shortness of breath, trembling, and urgency—or failure—to urinate. Other situations commonly feared are public speaking, eating and drinking in a restaurant, and meeting new people. In some cases, the fear escalates to a point where individuals experience panic attacks. . . . For many sufferers of social phobia, what fuels their fears is the desire to be perfect. An array of hypothetical questions floods their minds: What if I say something silly? What if I start sweating? What if I pass out? . . . There are artists who never show their work purely because they are afraid of being evaluated. One question they constantly ask themselves is, "What if it's not good enough?"[1]

Communication apprehension
Fear of speaking in public

As suggested by this discussion, communication apprehensiveness is a large part of the problem experienced by social phobics. Most feared are situations such as public speaking and meeting new people because they carry the highest threat of evaluation.[2] This chapter focuses on the causes of communication apprehensiveness, situational anxiety of the type experienced by public speakers, and coping strategies.

Causes of Communication Apprehension

In 2003, Paul A. Broughton presented a paper at the National Communication Association convention in Miami that summarized twenty years of research into the causes of communication apprehension. Broughton based his review on research

Keep in Mind

We feel more anxious when communicating . . .

- In unfamiliar and novel situations
- With strangers or people who seem unlike us
- In situations involving evaluation
- With larger audiences
- In more formal situations
- In a nonnative language
- In situations where others have high expectations of our performance

- In situations where we set high personal standards for ourselves
- In situations where we are conspicuous
- In situations where we are ignored
- With people who are of a higher status than ourselves
- After we experience failure

published in *Communication Education*.[3] Those and other findings help us to understand the kind of anxiety experienced by public speakers. (See the Keep in Mind box.)

Unfamiliar and novel situations create anxiety.[4] The situations that cause the highest levels of anxiety are those in which we face the unfamiliar. Actor Antonio Banderas confessed to being terrified to make his Broadway debut in the musical *Nine*. Although a seasoned stage performer in his native Spain, he felt completely intimidated by the idea of performing on the historic stages of New York City. He said, "You don't even know how you're gonna respond on the stage. You can sing at home, but it's a different deal. You have to go on stage with an orchestra, having to project for two-and-a-half hours in a play."[5] Banderas worried unnecessarily; the Outer Critics Circle Broadway/Off-Broadway nominated his production for twelve awards. To overcome his fear of the unfamiliar, French actor Jean-Louis Barrault hid on the set of the stage play *Volpone* until the director, actors, and stage crew had departed for the night. Then he spent the night sleeping in Volpone's bed before an imaginary audience to prepare for the next day's performance.[6]

We experience greater states of anxiety when communicating with strangers than with people whom we know well.[7] Some people stutter and stammer when they communicate with strangers; and children sometimes develop a condition called *selective mutism*, in which they stop speaking entirely to avoid situations where they must speak to strangers. The term *xenophobia* refers to an irrational fear and dislike of

Selective mutism
Ceasing speaking entirely to avoid speaking to strangers

Xenophobia
Irrational fear of strangers

people who are different from us. Some people use the term to refer exclusively to racial discrimination; however, the meaning is sufficiently broad to encompass differences of race, gender, culture, sexual orientation, ethnicity, or other distinguishing feature. In general, we tend to gravitate toward people who are similar to us in "values, religion, group affiliation, skills, physical attributes, age, language, occupation, social class, nationality, ethnicity, [and] residential location."[8] Such situations have fewer novel elements and unknown features. We know what to anticipate in interactions with these groups.

Evaluation
Judgment

We feel heightened states of anxiety in situations involving evaluation.[9] When surveyed in 1993–1994 about major sources of stress, competitive gymnasts with the Tops National Team in the U.S. revealed that fear of negative evaluation, fear of making a mistake, and high expectations of self or others were three major sources of stress. One gymnast said that she felt stress "when all of these people are watching you, other people who are better than you, judges watching your every move." Another said, "I'm afraid I'll mess up and embarrass myself."[10] Some studies have found that the strongest indicator of speech anxiety is our personal judgment of the kind of impression that we will make.[11] With a touch of humor, Virgin Records

founder Richard Branson recounted his reaction to a situation requiring formal evaluation by the audience:

> [Microsoft CEO] Bill Gates invited me to talk to thirty or forty chief executives from around the world. Just before I got up on stage, forms were handed out to everybody, and Gates said, "It's very important that all of us are tested in our lives. Richard's about to speak and I'd like you all to mark him out of 10." Now, that intimidated me. . . . I thought I'd gotten out of school thirty five years ago. I turned to the guy on my right—I think he was the head of Amazon—and said, "I'll give you a 10 if you give me a 10."[12]

The fear of evaluation, in some cases, derives from feelings of vulnerability in situations where our fate moves out of our control, into the hands of someone other than ourselves. The more serious the potential consequences of that loss of control, the more likely we are to feel apprehensive, as in a job interview or custody hearing. The importance of making a positive impression affects our level of anxiety.[13]

We feel more anxious in larger and more formal situations.[14] For the majority of people, this principle holds true. The larger the audience, the greater will be the number of evaluations of the performance. The more formal the situation, the more restrictions and rules apply. However, for some speakers, the reverse is the case. The intimacy of small classroom settings throws off speakers who are used to performing in large formal settings. I have noted, over many years, that some of my most experienced student speakers (e.g., former debaters) are surprised to find that they feel a much higher level of anxiousness in the intimacy of a classroom environment where you can notice every micro-expression that crosses the faces of your audience.

We feel more nervous when we are communicating in a nonnative language.[15] We fear the negative evaluations of those who speak the language more fluently. For anyone who has tried to practice a second language, this principle seems so obvious as not to require extensive authentication.

We feel greater anxiety when others have high expectations of our performance or when we set high personal standards for ourselves.[16] In the competitive figure skating world, people know that the greatest pressure is always upon those who hold last year's medal. The expectations of a repeat award-winning performance can create excruciatingly high levels of anxiety, even among seasoned performers. The daughters and sons of well-known actors and actresses often experience the same feelings. Actress Bridget Fonda suffered from stage fright for the first two years of her career. She attributes her fears to the fact that people associated her name with Peter Fonda (her grandfather) and Jane Fonda (her aunt). The association carried the probability that she would be judged by different and possibly higher standards than those applied to other fledgling actresses.[17] (See the Question of Ethics box.)

We experience greater apprehension if we anticipate or experience failure.[18] After forgetting the words to several songs in a 1967 concert in Central Park, New York City, Barbra Streisand refused to sing in public for twenty-seven years. At the height of his career, while directing and acting at the National Theatre in London, Sir Lawrence Olivier began to worry that fatigue would cause him to forget his lines; the phobia persisted for five years. One of my own experiences also illustrates the way in which our fears can become self-fulfilling prophesies. I was acting in a

A Question of Ethics

Lisa had a deep fear of speaking in any position other than number three. At the end of the first class meeting, she privately informed her speech instructor that she *had* to speak in third position in every assignment. According to Lisa, she had never made a presentation in any other position to that point in her life. The instructor believed that the speech class was an opportunity for the young woman to confront an irrational fear that appeared to cause her great emotional distress. Since the class policy was to allow the students to volunteer for speaker positions, she told Lisa that she would have to open the question of speaking order to the entire group.

When another student requested the third speaking position, Lisa panicked. She firmly informed her classmate that she could not take that position. Believing the request to be unreasonable and reacting with some surprise to the authoritarian tone of the demand, her classmate took a staunch position and refused to change. Lisa was dismayed. Panic-stricken, she continued her efforts to persuade the other student to change speaker position until it was clear that the student would not yield. If you were the instructor in this class, how would you deal with this kind of situation—one where the student has extreme communication apprehensiveness or a panic disorder?

college play when the thought struck me that I had never felt stage fright or forgotten a line in a play. As the time approached for that evening's performance, I could not get the thought out of my head. Then I began thinking that I *could* forget a line; and that night, for the first time in four years of acting, I blanked on one of my lines. After that night, I never felt the same sense of sureness as before the incident. In the same way, if we forget a speech, we are likely to feel more anxious in our next presentation.

We feel greater anxiety in situations where we are conspicuous or in situations where we are totally ignored.[19] One contributor to an Internet forum explained that he is fine sitting at a table with a group of twelve or more people. But if he begins to feel that he is on display, he panics. He said that he has dropped classes to avoid oral presentations, and he avoids social situations where he could become the center of attention. At the other extreme, we become uncomfortable in situations where we are ignored. We wonder why no one will look at us, and we search our minds for reasons to explain the lack of responsiveness. We become more anxious when we think that the audience is disinterested or unresponsive.[20] Audiences do not realize to what extent speakers are aware of small movements, fleeting expressions, yawns, and exits from auditoriums.

We experience greater apprehension when speaking to individuals or groups of higher status than ourselves.[21] These feelings of apprehension often translate into more rigid and tense postures, which typify low-status individuals.[22] Once we have transmitted signals of insecurity and lack of confidence to audience members, we have a harder time gaining their respect and attention.

Situational Anxiety and Public Speaking

Psychologists differentiate between anxiety associated with particular personality traits (*trait* anxiety) and tension generated by specific situations (*situational* anxiety). While someone with trait anxiety will experience high levels of anxiety in *many different* communication environments, a person with situational anxiety will feel tense *only in certain situations*—public speaking, for example, or job interviews.

Situational anxiety afflicts virtually everyone at some point, including celebrities. When sitcom star Jennifer Aniston won the October 2002 Hollywood Film Award for her starring role in *Friends*, her acceptance speech was less than memorable. Afterwards Aniston explained, "I understand the whole crying thing now. I forgot the cast! I'm just terrified. I have stage fright unless I have something written for me to say. I couldn't speak. I'm a blithering idiot."[23] One of the most humorous accounts of stage fright comes from the experience of British actor Alfred Edward Matthews, who performed in a West End London production. A pivotal scene required that he answer a telephone on stage. When the telephone rang on cue, Matthews crossed the stage, picked up the receiver, and froze. Realizing that he had forgotten his line, he turned to another actor and said, "It's for you."[24]

Lacking the option of such a creative exit from the situation, speakers with stage fright seek other ways to deal with their anxieties. Following the advice of professionals, they may begin by assessing their level of comfort in speaking situations. James C. McCroskey designed the Personal Report of Communication Apprehension (PRCA) to measure more generalized communication anxiety (trait anxiety)[25] and the Personal Report of Public Speaking Anxiety (PRPSA) to measure anxiety

Trait anxiety
Fears that stem from particular personality features

Situational anxiety
Fears that stem from the specific circumstance one is in

that is specific to public speaking (situational anxiety).[26] McCroskey and his colleagues at West Virginia University have largely defined the study of communication apprehension since 1970. See the Measuring Up boxes on pages 39 and 41.

Public speaking ranks very close to the top of high anxiety–producing situations. A 1997 study found that 20 percent of public speaking students experience anxiety of a severe nature,[27] and a 2001 Gallup poll found that fear of public speaking ranked second only to fear of snakes among the general population.[28] Earlier polls have generated similar findings, with fear of death occupying a significantly lower ranking than public speaking.[29] Referring to these results, comedian and television actor Jerry Seinfeld once joked, "Now this means, to the average person, if you have to go to a funeral, you're better off in the casket than doing the eulogy!"[30]

Some speakers experience the kind of panic described by Katzman, where they have difficulty breathing or continuing. When delivering a speech, one student would bring her child to the front of the classroom with her so that, if she succumbed to panic, the child could lead her from the room. Research suggests that panic disorders of this variety tend to occur more than twice as often in women as men (4.9 percent of women as opposed to 1.2 percent of men).[31] Studies also show that women experience higher levels of communication anxiety, in general, than men.[32] The problem of succumbing to irrational fears is not restricted to inexperienced speakers. Surveys suggest that 76 percent of experienced speakers feel anxious prior to reaching the podium.[33] (See the Reflections box.)

We can look at signs of speech anxiety in terms of what we would feel, what others would see and hear, and what mechanical devices (connected to the body) would register.

- *As a speaker, we would feel* tightness in the throat and a dry mouth, frequent swallowing, weak knees, shortness of breath, cold hands, faintness, sinking feeling in stomach, inability to focus, a sense of confusion and disorganization, and blankness of mind or blockages of memory. We might have difficulty sleeping during the period leading to the presentation.
- *Others would see* the avoidance of eye contact, licking of lips, flushed face, awkward posture and unnatural movements, restless pacing, aimless gesturing, fidgeting with objects, and shaking hands.
- *Others would hear* an abnormally fast or slow rate of speech, weaker voice, higher pitched voice, breaking or quivering voice, blurred or unclear speech, more slips of the tongue, nonfluencies such "um" and "uh," and lack of vocal variety.
- *Mechanical devices, attached to the body, would detect* increased perspiration, dilation of pupils, faster pulse rate, higher blood pressure, increase in blood sugar, increased glandular secretions, reduced digestive processes due to diversion of blood from the stomach and intestines to the brain and muscles, and irregular breathing.

Measuring Up

Personal Report of Communication Apprehension (PRCA-24)

The PRCA-24 is the instrument which is most widely used to measure communication apprehension. It is preferable above all earlier versions of the instrument (PRCA, PRCA10, PRCA-24B, etc.). It is highly reliable (alpha regularly >.90) and has very high predictive validity. It permits one to obtain subscores on the contexts of public speaking, dyadic interaction, small groups, and large groups. However, these scores are substantially less reliable than the total PRCA-24 scores because of the reduced number of items. People interested only in public speaking anxiety should consider using the PRPSA rather than the public speaking subscore drawn from the PRCA-24. It is much more reliable for this purpose.

This instrument is composed of twenty-four statements concerning feelings about communicating with others. Please indicate the degree to which each statement applies to you by marking whether you: **Strongly Disagree = 1; Disagree = 2; Are Neutral = 3; Agree = 4; Strongly Agree = 5**

_____ 1. I dislike participating in group discussions.

_____ 2. Generally, I am comfortable while participating in group discussions.

_____ 3. I am tense and nervous while participating in group discussions.

_____ 4. I like to get involved in group discussions.

_____ 5. Engaging in a group discussion with new people makes me tense and nervous.

_____ 6. I am calm and relaxed while participating in group discussions.

_____ 7. Generally, I am nervous when I have to participate in a meeting.

_____ 8. Usually, I am comfortable when I have to participate in a meeting.

_____ 9. I am very calm and relaxed when I am called upon to express an opinion at a meeting.

_____ 10. I am afraid to express myself at meetings.

_____ 11. Communicating at meetings usually makes me uncomfortable.

_____ 12. I am very relaxed when answering questions at a meeting.

_____ 13. While participating in a conversation with a new acquaintance, I feel very nervous.

_____ 14. I have no fear of speaking up in conversations.

_____ 15. Ordinarily I am very tense and nervous in conversations.

_____ 16. Ordinarily I am very calm and relaxed in conversations.

_____ 17. While conversing with a new acquaintance, I feel very relaxed.

_____ 18. I'm afraid to speak up in conversations.

_____ 19. I have no fear of giving a speech.

(Continued)

Measuring Up

Personal Report of Communication Apprehension (PRCA-24)—cont'd

_____ 20. Certain parts of my body feel very tense and rigid while giving a speech.

_____ 21. I feel relaxed while giving a speech.

_____ 22. My thoughts become confused and jumbled when I am giving a speech.

_____ 23. I face the prospect of giving a speech with confidence.

_____ 24. While giving a speech, I get so nervous I forget facts I really know.

Scoring

Group Discussion: 18 − (scores for items 2, 4, & 6) + (scores for items 1, 3, & 5)

Meetings: 18 − (scores for items 8, 9, & 12) + (scores for items 7, 10, & 11)

Interpersonal: 18 − (scores for items 14, 16, & 17) + (scores for items 13, 15, & 18)

Public Speaking: 18 − (scores for items 19, 21, & 23) + (scores for items 20, 22, & 24)

Group Discussion Score: _____

Meetings Score: _____

Interpersonal Score: _____

Public Speaking Score: _____

To obtain your total score for the PRCA, simply add your sub-scores together. _____ Scores can range from 24–120. Scores below 51 represent people who have very low CA. Scores between 51–80 represent people with average CA. Scores above 80 represent people who have high levels of trait CA.

Norms for the PRCA-24

Based on over 40,000 college students; data from over 3,000 nonstudent adults in a national sample provided virtually identical norms, within 0.20 for all scores.

	Mean	Standard Deviation	High	Low
Total Score	65.6	15.3	> 80	< 51
Group	15.4	4.8	> 20	< 11
Meeting	16.4	4.2	> 20	< 13
Dyad (Interpersonal)	14.2	3.9	> 18	< 11
Public	19.3	5.1	> 24	< 14

Source: J. C. McCroskey, *An Introduction to Rhetorical Communication*, 4th ed. (Englewood Cliffs, NJ: Prentice-Hall, 1982). Also available in more recent editions of this book, now published by Allyn & Bacon.

Measuring Up

Personal Report of Public Speaking Anxiety (PRPSA)

This was the first scale we developed in our work on communication apprehension. It is highly reliable (alpha estimates >.90) but it focuses strictly on public speaking anxiety. Hence, we moved on to develop the PRCA and ultimately the PRCA-24.

This is an excellent measure for research which centers on public speaking anxiety, but is an inadequate measure of the broader communication apprehension construct.

Directions: Below are thirty-four statements that people sometimes make about themselves. Please indicate whether or not you believe each statement applies to you by marking whether you:
Strongly Disagree = 1; Disagree = 2; Are Neutral = 3; Agree = 4; Strongly Agree = 5.

_____ 1. While preparing for giving a speech, I feel tense and nervous.

_____ 2. I feel tense when I see the words "speech" and "public speech" on a course outline when studying.

_____ 3. My thoughts become confused and jumbled when I am giving a speech.

_____ 4. Right after giving a speech I feel that I have had a pleasant experience.

_____ 5. I get anxious when I think about a speech coming up.

_____ 6. I have no fear of giving a speech.

_____ 7. Although I am nervous just before starting a speech, I soon settle down after starting and feel calm and comfortable.

_____ 8. I look forward to giving a speech.

_____ 9. When the instructor announces a speaking assignment in class, I can feel myself getting tense.

_____ 10. My hands tremble when I am giving a speech.

_____ 11. I feel relaxed while giving a speech.

_____ 12. I enjoy preparing for a speech.

_____ 13. I am in constant fear of forgetting what I prepared to say.

_____ 14. I get anxious if someone asks me something about my topic that I don't know.

_____ 15. I face the prospect of giving a speech with confidence.

_____ 16. I feel that I am in complete possession of myself while giving a speech.

_____ 17. My mind is clear when giving a speech.

_____ 18. I do not dread giving a speech.

_____ 19. I perspire just before starting a speech.

(Continued)

Measuring Up

Personal Report of Public Speaking Anxiety (PRPSA)—cont'd

_____ 20. My heart beats very fast just as I start a speech.

_____ 21. I experience considerable anxiety while sitting in the room just before my speech starts.

_____ 22. Certain parts of my body feel very tense and rigid while giving a speech.

_____ 23. Realizing that only a little time remains in a speech makes me very tense and anxious.

_____ 24. While giving a speech, I know I can control my feelings of tension and stress.

_____ 25. I breathe faster just before starting a speech.

_____ 26. I feel comfortable and relaxed in the hour or so just before giving a speech.

_____ 27. I do poorer on speeches because I am anxious.

_____ 28. I feel anxious when the teacher announces the date of a speaking assignment.

_____ 29. When I make a mistake while giving a speech, I find it hard to concentrate on the parts that follow.

_____ 30. During an important speech I experience a feeling of helplessness building up inside me.

_____ 31. I have trouble falling asleep the night before a speech.

_____ 32. My heart beats very fast while I present a speech.

_____ 33. I feel anxious while waiting to give my speech.

_____ 34. While giving a speech, I get so nervous I forget facts I really know.

Scoring

To determine your score on the PRPSA, complete the following steps:

Step 1. Add scores for items 1, 2, 3, 5, 9, 10, 13, 14, 19, 20, 21, 22, 23, 25, 27, 28, 29, 30, 31, 32, 33, & 34.

Step 2. Add the scores for items 4, 6, 7, 8, 11, 12, 15, 16, 17, 18, 24, & 26.

Step 3. Complete the following formula: PRPSA = 72 − Total from Step 2 + Total from Step 1

Your score should be between 34 and 170. If your score is below 34 or above 170, you have made a mistake in computing the score.

High = > 131

Low = < 98

Moderate = 98–131

Mean = 114.6; SD = 17.2

Source: J. C. McCroskey, "Measures of Communication-Bound Anxiety," _Speech Monographs_ 37 (1970): 269–277.

Reflections

At the age of fifty-five, I had been speaking and performing in public situations for forty years. While in school, I had participated actively in competitive debate, interpretive reading, extemporaneous and impromptu speaking, oratory events, and theater productions. My professional career had involved teaching speech, theater, and a broad range of communication courses; and I had been involved in community theatre, as well. I assumed that I would never again experience speech anxiety. I thought that the shaky hands, the weak knees, and the trembling voice were vestiges of a long abandoned youth. But I was wrong! I learned that, at any point in our lives, we can become a casualty of speech anxiety.

On the occasion in question, I had been asked to speak to a group of program evaluation experts on approaches to evaluating communication programs, a little researched topic at that time. The audience was large, and I believed that they knew a great deal more about the topic of program evaluation than I knew. Although I was one of a slate of speakers, I was the sole representative from the communication community. So I was already a bit nervous about my competency to speak to this particular group (*first cause of anxiety—fearing that others know more than you know*). The group was also unfamiliar to me, since they came from another discipline; and the auditorium was filled to capacity (*second cause of anxiety—large and unfamiliar audience*). Moreover, I was in a hectic work period and I had had little time to prepare for the speaking occasion. The lack of preparation time made me still more nervous (*third cause of anxiety—lack of preparedness*). That nervousness escalated to panic when I arrived at the auditorium, fifteen minutes before the opening speaker,

to find that the overhead projector had been positioned at least ten feet from the speaker's podium (*fourth cause of anxiety—last-minute arrival and lack of time to adjust to physical environment*).

To make matters worse, the podium and equipment were on two different levels! Because I had planned to use both a manuscript and visuals, I did not know what to do. Too late to ask for changes in the physical setting and too flustered to ask someone else to assist with the visuals, I assumed the role of roadrunner. I dashed from one level to the next as I delivered my speech to a room filled with hundreds of people. I was breathless and exhausted from the tension and unexpected high level of physical exertion. My knees and hands shook uncontrollably, and even while I was speaking, I worried that the negative experience would permanently undermine my self-confidence in speaking situations.

In fact, it did take a few months and several speaking events to recover the sense of security that I had felt prior to this calamitous presentation. On a subsequent speaking occasion, for example, I was in a small conference room with a group of six academics, and I experienced the same high level of anxiety that I had felt with the audience of hundreds. Had I stopped speaking at that point in time, I might have been an anxious presenter for the rest of my career. I chose, however, a different route. And for many people, that decision as to whether to withdraw from public speaking or to face another audience is key to overcoming speech anxiety. If you stop speaking at a point when you have had a bad experience, you will never have a good experience.

Sherry Ferguson

Coping Strategies

Like other successful performers, speakers have to learn to channel nervousness to their benefit. Anxiety generates energy, which seasoned performers harness and use to their advantage. News anchor Walter Cronkite once joked that the difference between a professional and a novice is that the professional has taught his butterflies to fly in formation.[34] Studies demonstrate that students typically report much lower levels of speech anxiety by the end of a public speaking course. As competency increases, levels of anxiety decrease.[35] Even by the end of the fourth speech, students experience significantly reduced levels of anxiety.[36] Suggestions for coping with speech anxiety include the following.

BEFORE THE SPEECH

Select a subject with which you are comfortable. One student chose to give his demonstration speech on how to polish shoes. Afterward he confessed that his own lack of interest in the topic and the fear of boring his audience caused him to feel extremely nervous. Another student delivered a speech on how to do an Axel, a standard jump in figure skating. Since only a few students had been involved in competitive figure skating, the technical details were tedious and hard for most to understand. At the other end of the spectrum, the figure skaters in the group already knew the material, and the speech rehashed old ideas. A recognition of the situation generated anxiety in the speaker, which could have been avoided by choosing a different topic.

Prepare thoroughly in advance of the speech occasion. Speakers do not always realize the critical role of preparation in feeling comfortable before an audience.[37] If you are concerned about filling the time, forgetting your speech, or not knowing the answer to questions, you are more likely to be nervous. If you are worried that the audience may know more than you about the subject, you need to exert still more effort to feel comfortable with your topic. On the other hand, if you have

Keep in Mind

Coping: Before the Speech

· Choose a topic with which you are comfortable.
· Prepare thoroughly.
· Concentrate on your introduction and conclusion.
· Find out who will be present at the speech.
· Practice delivering and timing your speech.
· When practicing, don't stop until you've reached the end of the speech.

· Familiarize yourself with equipment and the physical setting for the speech.
· Use visualization techniques to imagine an ideal presentation.
· Get enough sleep the night before the speech event.

invested time in your topic, your audience should be able to recognize and respect the effort.

Concentrate in particular on your introduction and conclusion, which you may choose to memorize. Research demonstrates that speaker anxiety diminishes considerably after the first thirty seconds of a presentation.[38] Moreover, first impressions do count.

Do not try to memorize the entire speech. Prepare notes from which you can speak. You are less likely to lose your place, and you will sound more spontaneous.

Find out who will be present at the speech. The unfamiliar is unnerving. If you have researched and adapted your speech to your audience, you will feel less nervous delivering the speech. If you face a hostile audience, you need to devise strategies for reaching the group. If you know that you are speaking to experts, you should gear your language and presentation style to that level.

Practice delivering and timing your speech so that you do not exceed time limits. Realizing that you are significantly over your time limit can cause you to become anxious and flustered. You may rush to complete the speech and, in the process, leave out important sections that cause the speech to seem disorganized and disjointed. You also risk losing focus and forgetting parts of the speech.

When practicing, do not stop until you have reached the end of the speech—even if you forget part of the speech. Learning how to overcome moments of failed memory or to cope with mistakes is part of the process of becoming an accomplished speaker. Do not expect every session to be the same. With extemporaneous speaking, your words will vary somewhat with each practice. (See Tips from a Professional.)

Familiarize yourself with the equipment and physical arrangements of the setting in which you will speak. If you have planned to deliver your speech to a small intimate

Extemporaneous
Speaking without having memorized the entire speech, often from note cards

---

TIPS FROM A PROFESSIONAL

Regardless of natural talent and ability, anyone can become a great speaker by following five key rules.

Tell a story, make a point. Everyone loves a good story. Think about it. At church, school, or when hanging out with friends, a good storyteller would always catch your attention. The same holds true when giving speeches.

Recently I gave a speech titled "Uncomfortable." The speech was about how personal growth requires us to become uncomfortable. In support of my thesis, I told a story about my fear of flying—white knuckles, sweating, praying on the flight, and taking medication to cope with my fears. In other words, to get from one point to another, we sometimes have to do things that make us uncomfortable.

My second story was about the discomfort that I felt selling encyclopedias door to door one summer in between college semesters. Selling door to door was very uncomfortable; however, it helped me become a great salesperson and taught me about persistence. Your listeners need *visuals*—words that paint images—something to "hold on to" when they are listening. Tell a story . . . visuals, humor, drama . . . and make a point.

(Continued)

TIPS FROM A PROFESSIONAL—CONT'D

Provide a road map. Tell 'em what you are going to tell 'em, tell 'em, and tell 'em what you told them. That's it. That's a road map. In the role of guide, you have to provide directions for where you will be taking your listeners so they don't get lost. Always present the central theme of your speech in the first thirty seconds so they don't begin thinking, "Where is he going with this?" Then tell them the two, three, or four points you are going to discuss (*tell 'em what you going to tell 'em*) and then discuss the points (*tell 'em*). In your conclusion, repeat the points and the theme of your speech (*tell 'em what you told 'em*). It's easy for listeners to get distracted with thousands of things on their minds. Constantly remind them where they are, where you are taking them, and where they have been. A good speaker provides a great road map.

Be enthusiastic. Ever hear a speaker who put you to sleep? No excitement, no energy, no enthusiasm? One of my best mentors was Arlo Pierson, my boss the summer I sold encyclopedias door to door. He was a captivating speaker. Why? He smiled, used wild gestures, and made great eye contact. He always talked as if he was sharing the most important news in the world. People loved him because he was so enthusiastic. Audiences love speakers with passion and enthusiasm.

What's in it for me? Another mentor taught me that, when I'm speaking, I should always remember that my audience is thinking these words: So what? What's in it for me? You have to address the *needs of your audience*. What are the benefits of your message? Will they make more money, have better sex, become wiser and richer, or lead a more meaningful life? How will they *benefit* from your message? Tell them how you will *help* them. Spell out what's in it for them.

Get enough stage time. Darren Lacroix, the 2001 Toastmasters International World Champion of Public Speaking, began his speaking career as a stand-up comic in 1994. He was awful. Darren said that he would frequently "bomb" and get booed off the stage. However, year after year, he got back on stage, presented new material, and spoke as often as possible. Eventually he joined Toastmasters International in the late 1990s. His local memberships extended to five different Toastmasters clubs so he could speak frequently. Darren videotaped almost every speech and enlisted the help of other veteran Toastmasters to critique his work. The result of all his years of "stage time"? He beat more than 50,000 contestants to win the Toastmasters International 2001 World Championship of Public Speaking. He says he went from "chump to champ" because of all his stage time. Great speakers jump at every speaking opportunity.

Third place winner in the 2005 International Toastmaster Speech Contest (District 46, Metropolitan New York and New Jersey), Brian Robinson has spoken to more than 30,000 people in his capacity as a trainer and motivational speaker for Skillpath Seminars, the Doe Fund, and his own keynote workshops. See more at www.brianrobinson.name.

group and you find yourself in an auditorium setting, you may lose your confidence. Similarly, some speakers lose their confidence when lecterns are removed.[39] Be sure that you have tested the equipment and identified problems in advance of the speaking event. Also be certain that the room will hold the same equipment and the same seating arrangement on the day that you are to present. If you suspect that you will have to rearrange furniture, plan to come early or to request necessary changes.

Visualization
Creating or recreating an event in one's mind

Use visualization techniques to imagine an ideal presentation. Speakers who train and practice visualization techniques report decreased levels of communication

anxiety and improved performance.[40] The most convincing evidence of the benefits of visualization comes, however, from the athletic world. Some Olympians say that it accounts for 90 percent of their success because the time that separates winners from losers is often seconds.[41] According to Olympic competitor Curt Clausen, "The difference between you and the guy next to you is almost completely mental. At the highest level, that's what makes the difference." In the period preceding the 2000 Olympic trials, diver Laura Wilkinson broke three bones in her right foot, an injury that kept her from practicing some required dives for seven weeks. During her period of recuperation, she used mental imagery to sustain her skills; in Sydney, Australia, she broke China's sixteen-year dominance to capture the gold medal in women's platform diving.[42]

With visualization, you create or re-create an event in your mind, using all of your senses to imagine the experience. Visualization helps to make unfamiliar situations more familiar. You anticipate the details of the moment when you will stand before the audience, so that the actual event appears like a rerun of what you imagined as a perfect performance. The perspective from which you visualize the event can be either internal or external.

With the *internal* perspective, you are completely "in the body"—seeing, feeling, and experiencing the event from the perspective of the participant. Being "in the body" limits your vision to what you would see as a participant in the event. If you

Internal perspective
Visualizing an event from your perspective as speaker

are up to bat on the baseball field, for example, you would see the pitcher and the people on the field, but you would not see the back of their heads, the umpire, the catcher, or the players sitting on the bench. Laurie Graham, winner of five World Cup races in alpine skiing, describes how she takes an internal perspective in her imaging:

> All of us use visualization a lot in our sport. You have to know the course one hundred percent; all the bumps, which way the turns go, what the terrain is like, what the snow is like, the optimum line you want to be on, and the optimum position. All that goes in and we watch ourselves in our minds run the course and run it well. If we make a mistake in our mind we rewind, go back and just see ourselves doing it right, from start to finish. Actually I don't watch myself, I visualize it as if I'm running the race; the course is coming at me. There are different ways to visualize. You can go through the course just skiing the gates, so you know where the gates are. But then you have to ski through the course fast, feeling the way you want to ski.[43]

In the case of public speaking, internal imaging involves seeing, hearing, and feeling the sensations from the perspective of the speaker. With an *external* perspective, on the other hand, you are "out of the body." You have become a spectator at the event, a member of the audience. In the case of public speaking, external imaging involves witnessing the event from the perspective of an audience member. The position of observer enables you to see things that you might not perceive from inside the body, and you have less of an emotional connection to the event. You might see yourself standing before the audience—confident and erect in posture, smiling, making eye contact with different audience members, using natural easy gestures, and receiving applause as you finish your speech. Whereas the internal perspective emphasizes the kinesthetic, the external perspective stresses the visual. The following visualization by Olympic diver Sylvie Bernier illustrates the process of visualization from an external perspective:

> At night, before going to sleep, I always did my dives. Ten dives. I started with a front dive, the first one I had to do at the Olympics, and I did everything as if I was actually there. I saw myself on the board with the same bathing suit. Everything was the same. . . . If the dive was wrong, I went back and started all over again. It takes a good hour to do perfect imagery of all my dives, but for me it was better than a workout. Sometimes I would take the weekend off and do imagery five times a day.[44]

Both perspectives are important. Gaetan Boucher, double gold medalist in speed skating at the 1984 Olympics, described how he moved between internal and external perspectives in imaging:

> I always do the same thing. When I go from the warm-up bench to the starting line, I go to the same spot, flex a couple of times, make the hole for my blades where I start, get in position and picture the way I will skate. I try to get inside myself, instead of having a video view. The video view is more visual. You see yourself. If I am inside myself, it is really me that is skating and I do not see myself going around the corner like a video. I am trying to picture from the inside but sometimes I cannot. I usually see myself start the race from the back and then it is like I get closer and follow right behind. Then I see the turn from the side. But then I move back inside myself and I come around the turn, seeing the turn coming. Then I see the same corner from the front.[45]

External perspective
Visualizing an event from the perspective of your audience

Suggestions for how to practice visualization vary among different sports psychologists. The following, however, embodies the principles included in most instructions. To prepare for visualization, write a description of what you want to imagine—that is, your "perfect performance," including as many details as possible. Visualization should involve all of the senses. Imagine the sound of the fan, the brightness of the lighting, the smell of lilacs outside the window, the sound of papers rustling while you wait for students to put away their notebooks, the smiles on faces of friends, and other details about the speaking environment. Sometimes speakers or others record this description on an audiotape that they can replay. A gifted NCAA basketball player, for example, recorded his visualization of scoring a basket. In his description, he included hearing the "swoosh" of the ball as it enters the net. He played the audiotape each evening before he went to sleep and when he awoke in the mornings.[46] Others watch videotapes of performers they would like to emulate.

Before beginning the first visualization exercise, read through the written script or listen to the audiotape. Then prepare for the mental imagery by doing a relaxation exercise. After relaxing, imagine a simple experience, such as going to the front of the classroom to speak. *Assume an internal perspective in the beginning*, relying on all of your senses to experience the moment from a physiological and emotional perspective. If you experience the sensation of fear or you feel your body tensing in anticipation of speaking, engage in self-talk and use trigger words to quiet your negative emotions. Practice shutting out distracting or negative thoughts and focusing on the speech and the audience. *After you have attempted this exercise a few times, include an external perspective.* Imagine your perfect performance from the perspective of the audience. Visualize the moment when you rise from your seat to go to the front of the classroom. Place an emphasis on the visual and auditory elements of the speaking environment. What will observers see and hear? If you see yourself experiencing some problem, visualize yourself recovering from the situation with grace and confidence. Ten minutes of practice each day can make a significant difference to performance.

    Finally, get enough sleep the night before the speech event. A late night can compromise your ability to think clearly on the day of your speech event.

DURING THE SPEECH

Dress appropriately and comfortably. Avoid question marks when you choose outfits for a speaking event. You want to be able to concentrate on your speech, not to worry about whether you are dressed appropriately. If you think that a skirt might be too short or a tie too loud, return them to the closet. If you think that you will feel shaky in a pair of high heels, make a different choice. If you are worried that an outfit could emphasize an attribute that you would rather not share with your

Keep in Mind

Coping: During the Speech

- Dress comfortably—but appropriately.
- Be on time to deliver the speech.
- While waiting, tense and relax your hand, leg, and other muscles.
- Before beginning, take a couple of deep breaths.
- Concentrate on what you are saying instead of how you are saying it.
- Concentrate on the audience instead of yourself.
- Deliver the speech with outward signs of confidence.
- Do not verbalize your anxiety.
- If your mouth becomes dry, pause and take a swallow of water.

- Recognize that even the best speakers make mistakes.
- Use visual aids, which shift attention from speaker to speech and give meaningful actions to your hands.
- Substitute larger controlled movements for fidgety uncontrolled ones.
- Shift into positive self-talk if you feel lack of confidence.
- Recognize that seemingly negative responses from the audience may have nothing to do with you.
- If you panic, get past the moment.

audience, select another item. Choose clothing that allows freedom of movement. You want to feel comfortable when you speak. If you are unsure about the expectations of the audience or the occasion, err on the conservative side. Prescriptions are difficult, but you should always try to look your personal best. Much communication anxiety derives from factors related to physical appearance.[47]

Be on time to deliver the speech. If you are racing to get to the event, you will be emotionally fatigued, flustered, and breathless before you begin your speech. In an April 2005 episode of *The Apprentice*, Donald Trump eliminated candidate Angie from the competition after she choked on a presentation. Angie attributed her poor presentation to the tension that she felt after being stuck in New York traffic, unable to arrive at her destination until the last minute, and to an unexpected glitch in her presentation (loss of a jacket to be worn by a fashion model).

While waiting to speak, take measures to relax your body and voice. First, tense and relax your hand, leg, and other muscles. Such actions help to rid your body of excess tension created by the rush of adrenaline. Then take a couple of deep breaths. The most visible signs of nervousness are a fast-paced delivery, accompanied by breathlessness; a higher pitched voice that is thin rather than full in tone; a failure to pause for emphasis; and garbled and inarticulate speech. Anxiety restricts the chest and throat muscles. A deep breath, on the other hand, will open the airway and send oxygen to your lungs and brain. Sitting straight against the back of your chair, hold your breath for four to five seconds before slowly exhaling. If you can find a private corner, you might also want to do some facial exercises designed to loosen facial and jaw muscles. One such exercise requires you to open your mouth wide and then close tightly. Just as athletes use visualization to prepare for events, they also use visualization to relax prior to an event. Race-walker Andrew Hermann says that he imagines a smooth blue liquid running through his body. If that does not work, he proceeds to a second image: "I picture brown sugar and pouring water over it. I see it dissolve and it makes the tensions dissolve wherever they are."[48] Speakers can use these same strategies.

When delivering the speech, concentrate on what you are saying instead of how you are saying it; eliminate distractions. If you focus on the ideas in your speech, you will have less time to worry about your shortcomings. Sports psychologists use the term *peak performance* to describe times when athletes are at their personal best. Sports psychologist Peter Jensen says that athletes who have experienced a peak performance describe it in the following way:

> You're focused and relaxed—athletes always say it's as if things are happening in slow motion. They see everything, they anticipate, and yet the time went by very quickly. And that kind of duality . . . where at the end, it changes to, "Gee, I just got out here, I would have liked to stay out here longer—and yet while I was out there, everything was so slow. I could see everything, I had time for everything, I didn't feel rushed."[49]

Some athletes describe their peak performances as "out-of-body" experiences. Others describe the experience as "being in a cocoon," totally detached from distractions in the environment. Many describe peak performances as being "in the flow," where the person has a feeling of absolute control, confidence, and absorption in the happening.[50] Golfers talk about being "in the zone." U.S. Olympic Training Center sports psychologist James Bauman said that numerous studies have confirmed that successful athletes have a higher-than-average capacity to deal with distractions:

> Olympic athletes in particular find ways to remain focused on an event to the exclusion of negative influences such as unruly crowds, inclement weather, even family problems. While the vast majority of us spend lots of time worrying about things we can't control, successful athletes attend primarily to those cues or stimuli that are relevant, or within their control.[51]

Experts say that the focus must always be on the activity being performed. Focusing on someone else's performance just serves to distract.

While speaking, concentrate on the audience instead of yourself. (See the Reflections box.) Look for signals of understanding. If you see your audience drifting or looking uncertain, insert an attention-getting device, ask a question, or find an alternate way to explain an idea that may have generated confusion. Try not to respond to signs of disinterest by drawing into yourself. Maintain direct eye contact with your audience and focus on friendly faces if you feel that your confidence is waning. Once you have received positive reinforcement from those audience members, you can try again with those who appear bored or negative.

Deliver the speech with outward signs of confidence and do not verbalize your anxiety. Studies in nonverbal communication have demonstrated that psychologists can experience the feelings of patients by assuming the postures of the patients. If you assume more confident postures, your audience also will feel more comfortable. If you perceive your status to be lower or your assets less than that of your audience, remember that you may be superior in some other domain. The theory of multiple intelligences, discussed in Chapter Thirteen, focuses on our multidimensionality as human beings. So while I may be better at writing or speaking, you may better at art or music. Judge yourself as a whole person in moments when you feel insecure—a person with as much value and as many abilities as anyone sitting in the audience.

If you feel your mouth becoming dry during your presentation, take the time to pause and take a swallow of water. Bring a bottle of water with you to the speaker's stand.

Recognize that even the best speakers make mistakes; regain your focus and continue if you make a mistake. No one is perfect. Much of the time, your audience will not

Reflections

Rae Tattenbaum, a certified instructor in biofeedback, told the story of a talented mezzo-soprano, who came to her for help with concentrating during performances. The young woman explained that she always noticed the tightness of her pantyhose when she was singing, and when that happened, she lost focus: "My pantyhose," she told me. "That's what I think about when I'm performing."

Source: R. Tattenbaum, "Want to Beef up Your Performance? Forget the Pantyhose!" *Inner Act Peak Performance and Training* website, http://www.inner-act.com/Media/Article, p. 1. Accessed November 10, 2003.

notice a mistake unless you point it out, and they will accept small mistakes.[52] Famed golf champion Tiger Woods talked about the importance of regaining focus after you make a mistake: "My father and I call it *zoning*. If you mis-hit a shot, hit it out of bounds, put it in the water, you have to get your focus back. You've got to start thinking ahead, don't look behind."[53] In your practice sessions, plan how to improvise if you get off track. Prepare note cards even if you think that you will not need them. You can put them in a pocket or on a nearby table— just in case.

Use visual aids, which shift attention from speaker to speech and give meaningful actions to your hands.[54] Beginning speakers often feel as if they have gained three or four extra appendages. Visual aids offer an activity for your hands and give you a purpose for moving around as you point to, explain, and change your visuals.

If you become aware that you are making uncontrolled and fidgety movements, substitute larger controlled movements that add instead of detract from your speech. Fidgeting sometimes reflects a need to express oneself more naturally and openly. You should always use a presentation mode that seems comfortable to you.[55]

If you begin to doubt the effectiveness of your presentation, shift into positive self-talk (before and during the presentation).[56] Just as listeners have time to think about other topics while they are listening, you have time to take mental side trips while delivering a speech. With this excess time, you may begin to worry that your audience looks bored, inattentive, lethargic, or hostile. When confronted with self-doubts, engage in positive conversation with yourself. Say, for example, "OK, I'm doing pretty well. Most people look interested." Or, "This next section should be easy to explain." Or, "I think this next example will get the audience's attention."

Many Olympic competitors carry on conversations with themselves throughout their competitive events. U.S. runner Curt Clausen used cue words such as "relax, smile, low arms."[57] The internal dialogue of U.S. kayaking champion Kathy Ann Colin was somewhat different: "Come on. Just do it. . . . Ten strokes for power. Ten for rhythm. Ten for legs." Sometimes in competitions, she blurted out, "Legs, legs, legs"![58] Others might use trigger words such as "smooth and easy," "let it happen," or "focus." A 1992 study of Olympic gymnasts confirmed that the more positive the self-talk, the higher the chances that an athlete will excel, whereas negative self-talk has the opposite effect on an athlete's success.[59] A 1994 study found that junior tennis players who used self-talk won more points than players who did not.[60]

Recognize that audience members have many different issues and preoccupations and that their reactions to your speech may have absolutely nothing to do with you. When I first began teaching, I interpreted lack of student attention or knitted brows as a personal criticism. I thought that I must be doing something wrong when students looked preoccupied or angry or frustrated—that my lecture was boring, that I had made some statement that offended, or that the students disliked me as an individual. But then I began teaching the first-year course in interpersonal communication, where I asked students to keep journals of their communication experiences. I learned a great deal from those journals, which were often emotional reading. At any given moment, the students were undergoing a vast range of experiences, which had to have an impact on their ability to listen and

Zoning
Getting back into focus quickly after being thrown off

Visual aids
Props or illustrations, which can serve to shift attention from speaker to speech

Self-talk
Internal conversations with one's self, used to build confidence

to perform in the university classroom. I never went through a semester that some students did not lose close family members or friends to disease and accidents. A significant number underwent loss of relationships with boyfriends and girlfriends. Almost all expressed self-doubt and concern about being evaluated unfavorably by peers. One young woman had just learned that her partner had HIV, and she had to take a series of tests over six months to determine whether she had contracted the disease.

In short, I came to realize that nine times out of ten the student lost in her thoughts or frowning into her books was probably not thinking about my class. More often, she was thinking about a broken relationship, a hospitalized grandparent, or whether she had forgotten to put money in the parking meter. I came to realize that the sleepy-looking young man in the back row might be working double shifts to pay for next semester's tuition. You should not ignore nonverbal signals from listeners. You should always try to capture and maintain the attention of all listeners. *But* you should not necessarily assume responsibility for failure. Many internal and external factors influence audience behaviors. What you see as a bored countenance may be the face of a student who studied or worked all night. What you interpret as negativity may be deep sadness or frustration, whose source has nothing to do with your speech. If your presentation is at 7:00 P.M., after your classmates have been in classes since 8:30 A.M., your efforts to hold their attention will not always be successful. Moreover, you should remember that, when people leave the classroom at the end of the period, they are more likely to be thinking about their problems than about your speech. So put matters into perspective—both as you speak and when you engage in self-evaluation after the fact.

Recognize that different cultures react in different ways to speakers. In a situation where approximately 150 million people live outside the countries of their birth, and two or three million more join them each year, audiences will be diverse.[61] As speakers, we need to understand and appreciate the cultural differences in our audiences. If you are using eye contact as a measure of attentiveness, you might reach conclusions that are the opposite of the truth.[62] Patterns of eye contact vary greatly between mainstream and some minority cultures. Americans of European heritage tend to look at a person while listening and away from the person while speaking. African Americans do the opposite, maintaining eye contact while speaking but not while listening. Studies of listening patterns in German and American students have identified other cultural differences, leading to the conclusion that we need to be careful when interpreting nonverbal responses of listeners.[63]

If you freeze or panic, get past the moment. If a student says that he is unable to finish a speech, talk (as a group) about the situation. Class members can share their perceptions with the speaker, as well as the feelings that they have experienced at the podium. On occasion, I offer to alter the speaking environment in some way to help the person to overcome his fears. I usually allow the speaker to select an alternative arrangement, perhaps delivering the speech from a sitting position or even cross-legged on the floor with other students positioned in a circle. On one occasion, the speaker requested that the audience sit on the floor while he spoke from a standing position! Strange perhaps, but he was able to finish his speech; and the next time he spoke, he did not request any special seating arrangement. He had conquered his fear.

AFTER THE SPEECH

If you have not performed at your personal best, put the occasion into perspective by applying the "ten-year rule." Ask yourself, "In ten years' time, will this event be important?" In all likelihood, no one but you will remember the occasion after a year or two. More importantly, no one but you will really care. In fact, some studies suggest that audiences prefer speakers who are less than perfect.[64] The following story offers a philosophical perspective from which to consider events of less than earth-shattering importance.

> Charles never worried a great deal about what others thought about him—a source of some frustration to his family, since that lack of concern often translated into idiosyncratic dress and a disregard for conformity in general. When questioned on one occasion about why he placed so little importance on the views of other people, he said that his attitude had come from his days as a bomber pilot in World War II. At 17, he had joined Britain's Royal Air Force (RAF), and subsequently he had flown many missions over Hitler's Germany. War statistics reveal that no more than half of RAF pilots returned from their missions. While British commanders did not share these grim statistics with the pilots and moved the men frequently

Ten-year rule
A device used to put a speaking experience in perspective

among locations to mask the high mortality rate, the pilots knew that, at the end of the day, many of their comrades did not rejoin them at Saracen's Head—the Lincoln pub that was a gathering place for not only British, but also Canadian, American, and other Allied military. Faced with the need to come to terms with the fragility and uncertainty of life, Charles and many of his fellow officers had little time for the trivial and inconsequential. They had learned to differentiate between matters of life-altering importance and those of lesser import. For Charles, this experience had translated into a philosophy that governed how he chose to lead the rest of his life.

Doing well in a speech is important, but unless we are in the defendant's box at a murder trial, few speeches are life-and-death matters. We should never allow this fear to dominate our professional and personal lives or discourage us from participating fully in life.[65] Strive to do your best, but recognize that a less than perfect performance will not usually result in long-term damage to more than your ego or occasionally your wallet (in the case of a failed sale or business transaction). As sports psychologist Peter Jensen noted, "On a bad day, you might say, "I'll just try this and then I'll reevaluate myself and see where I'm at."

Conclusion

Although communicators with trait anxiety may make some progress in a supportive speech environment and should not dismiss the potential value of the experience, introductory speech classes are not the best place to learn coping techniques for severe problems. Social phobics such as Leslie, for example, require the help of counselors who specialize in treating severe social anxiety. The use of techniques such as desensitization, cognitive restructuring, hypnosis, biofeedback, group therapy, and skills training help the person to learn how to cope in social environments. Some psychologists believe in combining medications with these techniques. Obviously, introductory speech classes do not allow for these kinds of intensive therapeutic approaches to dealing with serious social phobias.[66] Speech classes, on the other hand, are the perfect environment for giving people the skills to cope with situational anxiety; and they offer a more limited avenue to dealing with generalized anxieties.

Questions for Discussion

1. Describe any physical or emotional symptoms that you experience when speaking before an audience. Have you ever panicked in these circumstances?

2. Review some of the causes of communication anxiety. Using this list of causes, analyze a situation in which you felt nervous.

3. How do you cope when you experience apprehensiveness associated with public speaking? Before the speech? During the speech? During the question period? Can you offer any advice to others?

4. When delivering a speech, what makes you most nervous? Fear of forgetting the speech? Lack of confidence in your knowledge or expertise? Audience reactions to your speech? Discomfort or issues with your dress? The physical environment? Equipment or technology problems? Difficulty in relating to different linguistic or cultural groups? Other?

5. Have you ever tried visualization as a means of controlling your apprehension? In what context? Preparing for a sports competition? A speaking competition? Other? Did you adopt an in-body or out-of-body approach to the visualization?

6. Describe your most successful and least successful speaking experiences. What were the characteristics of each situation?

Outline

LISTENING WITH A PURPOSE

Exercises in Perception and Listening

Learning Objectives

- To identify common listening purposes
- To understand how listeners process information
- To appreciate the reciprocal responsibilities of speakers and listeners

As a society, we suffer from attention deficit disorder (ADD). When tested immediately after a ten-minute presentation, the average listener hears, comprehends, and remembers only about 50 percent of the information. After forty-eight hours, the amount retained has diminished to 25 percent.[1] In classroom situations, 10 percent is a common retention rate.[2]

Experts tell us that these poor listening skills carry a price tag in the business world.[3] The Sperry Corporation in New York concluded that, if each one of its 87,000 employees made a $10 mistake each year due to not listening (e.g., taking a wrong number or wrong order), the financial consequences to the company would be close to $1 billion a year.[4] Others tell us that poor listening skills are equally expensive in our personal relationships. As reported in the book *Women and Love*, the number one complaint of women is that men do not listen; but author Sharon Hite says that women are not much better than men at listening.[5] Admittedly, these statistics on retention and recall suggest a serious problem, but we can gain a more sophisticated understanding if we take perception studies into account. The experience of one man, who regained his sight after thirty years of blindness, illustrates that knowing *what to retain* and *what to discard* is far more important than grasping every detail in our environments. He explained, "When I could see again, objects literally hurled themselves at me. One of the things a normal person knows from long habit is what not to look at. Things that don't matter, or that confuse, are simply shut out of their seeing minds. I had forgotten this, and tried to see everything at once; consequently I saw almost nothing."[6] The term *selective perception* refers to the process by which we selectively perceive and retain certain kinds of information, while we ignore or discard other information. Because we are bombarded by approximately 1,600 bits of information a minute, we must disregard a great deal of what we receive. As listeners, the challenge is to retain the significant.

This chapter explores common listening purposes, the influence of perception on message reception, and the reciprocal responsibilities of listeners and speakers in a public speaking situation. This discussion aims to expand our understanding of the receiver portion of the communication model introduced in Chapter One.

Retention
That part of the message we hold in our memory

Perception
The process by which we acquire, organize, and assign meaning to sensory information

Selective perception
The unconscious process by which we attend to and retain some details while we ignore or discard others

Purposeful listening
The reasons why we choose to listen

Purposeful Listening

Our purposes for attending speech events govern how we perceive much of the information that we receive from speakers. People attend speech events for many different reasons. Some of the most common relate to acquiring information, connecting with an important person, being inspired personally or professionally, offering support to a speaker or cause through our presence as an audience member, or recognizing the accomplishment of someone who is receiving an award, graduating, or retiring. Sometimes we attend a speech event in order to occupy the same physical space as an admired political figure or entertainer. We may go, for example, to hear a speaker who is a noted humanitarian, the winner of a Pulitzer Prize, or an intellectual of great note. We enjoy telling our family and friends that we attended a lecture by former South African president Nelson Mandela, a reading by author J. K. Rowling of *Harry Potter* fame, or a speech by the Dalai Lama.

At other times, we may want to feel a vicarious connection with someone or something bigger than ourselves or to participate in a historical event. Many Americans traveled to Rome to say a final farewell to Pope John Paul II. We may attend some events out of a sense of obligation or to show respect and friendship for a colleague. Through our presence, we express our support for a person, a cause, or a policy. During World War II, the British often risked their lives to attend sell-out performances of public events in support of the war cause. We may look for inspiration or emotional support from a lecturer. For twenty-two days and 2,286 miles in 1999, Lance Armstrong made the gruelling journey across some of the most intimidating terrain in Europe to capture the first of seven straight Tour de France victories. This remarkable accomplishment did not compare to Armstrong's personal victory two years earlier against the most aggressive form of testicular cancer. After crossing the finish line on the Champs Elysée in Paris, Armstrong offered inspiration to all who face life-threatening illnesses: "If there's one thing I say to those who use me as their example, it's that if you ever get a second chance in life, you've got to go all the way."[7] In subsequent years, many cancer patients and their families filled the auditoriums where Lance Armstrong spoke about the importance of personal strength and resolution. The audiences knew the story, but they went to experience the man and to draw emotional support from his words.

Like the audiences of the Chautauqua Circuit, we sometimes attend a speech event to be entertained. We may not plan to spend time in Tibet, but we may enjoy listening to someone else talk about their adventures in the Himalayas. We may look for speakers like Jim Carey or Chris Rock, who will make us laugh. Comedians often double as speakers at public events. We attend graduation speeches, award ceremonies, and other speaking occasions for a host of other reasons. Part of preparing for a public speaking event involves recognizing the purposes of audiences in attending the event. The speaker then accepts responsibility for trying to meet those audience goals.

The assumption that we listen predominantly to obtain information is highly flawed. While this purpose may dominate classroom and professional situations, it is less salient as a reason for listening in many other contexts. For that reason, it is useful to distinguish between deliberative and empathic listening. *Deliberative listening* involves hearing, understanding, and storing information for later recall, as well as analyzing and drawing conclusions from the information.[8] Anticipating the possibility that we may use the information at a later date, we attempt to receive the message without distortion. Also we evaluate the quality, relevance, and usefulness of the information. The motives for deliberative listening are logical, rational, and critical in nature. The process stresses comprehension and evaluation. Deliberative listening plays an important role in societies that value free speech. The viability of democracies depends on the ability of citizens to judge the quality of the messages that they receive. In an environment where information moves freely, with few restrictions, we must be able to differentiate between fact and opinion, truth and exaggeration.

In other situations, however, deliberative listening may be less useful. In many social and classroom situations, we want to do more than judge the other person. We want to offer encouragement and support to the speaker. We want to build a relationship. We want to convey our respect for the person. In those cases, some blend between deliberative and empathic listening may be most appropriate. *Empathic listening* means listening to understand the person as well as the message.[9]

This kind of listening has an emotional, as well as intellectual, component; and we pay attention to the verbal and nonverbal. Mutual respect, support, and trust characterize the process. Some Asian cultures place a higher value than Americans do on the emotional aspects of listening.[10]

Deliberative listening
Listening with the intent of judging the information

Empathic listening
Assuming the perspective of the speaker when we listen

How Listeners Process Information

The following discussion looks at the nature of perception, the influence of listening frames on message reception, and the way in which our information processing abilities have an impact on listening.

NATURE OF PERCEPTION

Perception is learned and culture-bound, backward-looking, selective, value-laden, and relative.

Perception Is Learned and Culture-Bound

As infants, we learn to organize information received through senses such as sight, touch, smell, sound, and taste. Consider the everyday learning that occurs with a sense such as sight, which we take so much for granted. The retina of the eye registers an image such as a child looking at coconut ice candies. The optic nerve cluster collects the image of the child and transmits it to the brain for processing. Although the retina of the eye acts like a camera lens in capturing the image, the optic nerve does not retain any form of organization in transmitting the image. Rather the bits and pieces of information, which constitute the image, arrive in the brain in a random, chaotic, and completely disorganized fashion. That is, the nerves that carry the thousands of bits of information may not terminate in places adjacent or even close to each other. The individual must learn that a specific nerve terminal in the brain represents a particular point in space. No replication of the image exists until the brain processes and organizes all the bits of information. Visual systems are designed to recognize learned patterns among the vast overload of available information.[11]

In a well-known experiment, a researcher constructed special glasses that not only distorted his vision but also turned the world upside down. He wore the glasses day and night for an extended period of time. By the end of the orientation period, his vision was so good that he was able to fly an airplane and ride a motorcycle while wearing the goggles. At the completion of the experiment, the researcher removed the glasses, to find that his world without the glasses had turned upside down. The person had to retrain his brain to organize the incoming information in a way that allowed him to function normally.[12]

Just as we learn sight by experience, we also learn touch by experience. To illustrate the point, ask another person to close his eyes. After he closes his eyes, touch his arm *lightly* with varying combinations of fingers (e.g., three fingers from one hand and two fingers from the second hand), placed simultaneously on the skin. On the first couple of tries, he will not be able to differentiate a total of one from four, five, or even ten fingers on the skin. After several tries, however, he will learn to discriminate. A person who has learned Braille can discriminate between various combinations of six raised dots, representing the letters of the alphabet, placed about an eighth of an inch apart. In the same way as with sight and touch, people can learn to distinguish between sounds that are initially indistinguishable.[13]

Culture-Bound
The ways in which our geography, ethnicity, and other personal factors affect our perceptions

How we perceive taste is also learned. When grocery shopping with a friend from Greece, I was amused to see that she made a sour face when she came to the beef liver. She commented, "I can't understand how anyone can eat liver." Being from the South, I included liver and onions on my menu of appealing dishes. I did not say anything, however, and soon after we arrived at the seafood counter.

With much animation in her voice, my friend announced, "Octopus! I love baby octopus!" It was my turn to pause and take a second look at the "baby octopus" curled under the plastic wrap. I tried to visualize how the legs would appear on my plate, and I became a bit queasy. I was keenly aware, in that moment, of the acquired nature of our reaction to different foods. People in some Middle Eastern countries regard the eyes of sheep as a delicacy. Favorites of my Scottish husband are steak and kidney pie and tripe (the stomach lining of cows). Natives of Louisiana list alligator on their menus, and some cultures eat grub worms found under rotting logs. Unappealing, you say? Well, it is all in the mouth (and nose) of the beholder. Perception is both learned and culture-bound.

Perception Is Backward-Looking

The learned nature of perception means that it is backward-looking in its interpretation of the present. We constantly anticipate the past. Films such as *The Others* are able to succeed in building plot lines based on deception because audiences have learned perceptual sets about horror films. These sets are based on prior encounters with the conventions of the genre. In *The Others*, Nicole Kidman plays the role of a single mother with two children. Her children's life-threatening allergies to sunlight enable the movie producers to establish a dark, foreboding, and suspenseful setting. The mother and children grow increasingly fearful that they are living in a haunted house with servants whom they suspect to be the living dead. We follow the movie, convinced that we know the familiar plot line. We ignore many signs, such as the failure of the children to respond to sunlight, the ability of the wife to communicate with her obviously dead husband, the historical dress, the archaic speech, the strange mannerisms of those who live in the house, and the

Backward-looking
Our reliance on past history to interpret the present

interactions between the children and a young boy, whom we suspect to be a spirit presence. In short, we ignore many signs that could have led us to a different conclusion about what was going on. In the end, however, we realize that our perceptions have led us to the wrong assumptions. We have been duped. Yes, the house is haunted; but no, the haunted are not the ones we believe them to be.

These same kinds of deception occur in *Sixth Sense*, when audiences ignore sign after sign that things are not as they perceive them to be. If you watch the film a second time, you see many signs that you did not see on the first viewing. Listeners within speech settings fall prey to the same perceptual traps. We interpret new information in the light of past experiences and predispositions. *We hear what we expect to hear.*

Because much of our perceptual learning occurs when we are young, we face a difficult task when we have only fifteen or twenty minutes to influence the knowledge and belief sets of audiences. Even when listeners are positively disposed to learn something new, they must use old frameworks and schemes of classification to interpret and file the information. In *The Act of Creation*, Arthur Koestler argues that creative leaps often come from people in dream states or outside of a particular field of study because they are not constrained by the old conceptual frameworks.[14] The more we know about a subject, the more expertise we acquire, the more difficult it becomes to think "outside of the box." As audience reactions to the films *The Others* and *Sixth Sense* demonstrate, we pick

out what we regard to be significant detail in any event and interpret the information in the light of what we expect to see. A wire photograph of an Olympic event offers an interesting example of how we have to revise our first response to accept a different interpretation of reality.

Perception Is Selective

Numerous studies of eyewitness accounts demonstrate the selective nature of perception.[15] Judges and lawyers know that two people may see the same robbery from virtually the same angle and distance, yet disagree on almost every detail of the event. These discrepancies in perception include such basics as the height, weight, eye color, hair color, and manner of dress of the robbery suspect. The learned nature of perception leads us to focus on some details and to ignore others. An athlete, for example, might notice the degree of muscularity in the robbery suspect. A fashion designer might notice the dress. A plastic surgeon might make mental notes about the bone structure of the person. *In other words, we see what we know.*

Numerous eyewitnesses to the 2001 sniping murders in Washington, D.C., described the presence of a white truck or van at the locations of the sniping incidents. For weeks police searched for a white van before apprehending the suspects in a very different kind of automobile. In the end, the "white van" turned out to be an older model blue four-door Chevrolet sedan. And even the guilty sometimes

Selective
The focusing on some details while ignoring others

get upset with the unreliability of eyewitness accounts. On June 25, 2004, Mark Allen Patterson walked into the offices of the *Gadsden Times* in Alabama to complain that the eyewitness to his robbery (a robbery he had committed) had given incorrect information. He wanted the newspaper to correct their inaccurate reporting of his truck as green (rather than burgundy).[16]

A litany of perception slides demonstrates the selective nature of perception. The collection of photographs on pages 68-73 allows us to understand the criteria by which we select detail from the vast overload of information in our environments.

Perception Is Value-Laden

Perception is also value-laden. A study by Leo Postman, Jerome Bruner, and Elliott McGinnies demonstrated that audience members are quicker to perceive information that fits with their existing value orientations.[18] After testing people to identify their values, the researchers flashed the words representing those values on a screen for a brief millisecond. Then they gradually increased the time that words appeared on the screen until all participants in the experiment could recognize the words. The findings follow:

> Those persons with a strong religious value orientation were able to see the word *religion* when it was on the screen for a very brief instant. Others, less religiously oriented, required that the word be on the screen for a longer period before they recognized it. Things that are important to us, those which we value, are the ones we perceive.[19]

In shorthand language, *we are most likely to see what we already believe to be the truth.*

Values
Personal principles or standards that color perceptions

We notice objects that are intense—loud or colorful.[17]

We notice ideas and objects that violate our expectations—objects that are larger or smaller than we expect.

Novelty draws our attention.

We pay attention to contrasts.

Relative
Comparative

Perception Is Relative

A six-foot-tall individual might perceive a 5'5" suspect as short, whereas someone five feet tall might perceive the suspect as tall. Serious consequences can result from such perceptual discrepancies. Kirk Bloodsworth spent eight years in jail (two on death row) before being exonerated for the rape and murder of a nine-year-old girl. Part of his problem stemmed from an inaccurate description of the guilty party. The authorities were looking for a 6'5" man. In the end, the confessed murderer proved to be only 5'7" tall. In the movie *Annie Hall*, the viewer sees Alvin Singer (Woody Allen) talking to his psychiatrist on one side of a split screen. The psychiatrist asks about Alvin's relationship with Annie Hall (Diane Keaton): "How often do you sleep together?" Alvin replies, "Hardly ever, maybe three times a week." On the other side of the split screen, Annie speaks with her counsellor. Asked the same question, Annie responds, "Constantly, I'd say three times a week."[20]

Sign
Something that stands for an object or idea

We also read signs within a context. The signs acquire meaning, depending upon the context that surrounds them. If someone is smoking a cigarette in front

When objects or ideas repeat themselves, we notice them.

of an office building, we assume the person is smoking tobacco. If the same person is holding what appears to be a cigarette in an alleyway, surrounded by homeless people, we assume the person could be smoking an illicit drug. As discussed in Chapter One, public speakers communicate within a larger context that includes social, political, economic, legal, technological, and cultural factors, as well as personal experiences that affect the perceptions of listeners. Before September 11, 2001, the term *9-1-1* had only one meaning: the number that you call to ask for help in an emergency. And before 2001, we would not have flinched at the sight of white powder on envelopes or imagined the necessity to remove our shoes for security checks at airports. Our perspectives change from day to day and year to year.

INFLUENCE OF LISTENING FRAMES ON MESSAGE RECEPTION

Media analysts talk a lot about framing theory—a reference to how journalists structure and tell their stories. Framing theory says that journalists put a "spin" on their reporting of issues. Choices made in the telling of the story influence our interpretations of what we read and hear.[21] But we also have frames within which we receive the information. In the case of public speaking, our "listening" frames dictate whether and how we will perceive, understand, accept, and/or act on information. In the context of this discussion, we could define *listening frames* as "perceptual and attitudinal sets that allow the entry of certain kinds of information and block other kinds of information." Communication can fail when we devalue the

Framing
How journalists choose to structure and tell a story

Listening Frames
What we bring to a listening situation that determines what we absorb, understand, and accept, and what we do not

We notice incongruity and objects that seem out of place.

source, set our listening frames to block information with which we disagree, ignore or discard information that appears to be of little interest or value, or lack the background to process the information. All of these tendencies are grounded in perception theory.

Devaluing of the Source

We may reject information from sources that we do not value. Perception theory tells us that we do not seek out, hear, or remember information that jars with our value frameworks.[22] A smoker will not recall the specifics of an antitobacco advertisement. A believer in conspiracy theories will not note or remember the details of a documentary that negates his theory. People maintain their equilibrium by filtering out dissonant or uncomfortable information.[23] Sometimes our dismissal of a speaker's words may come from such superficial markers as physical appearance or other status cues.

We pay attention to objects that are near at hand.

Disagreement with Information

Sometimes we set our listening frames to reject information with which we disagree. We silently criticize the speaker, preparing arguments in our heads instead of listening to what the person has to say. We rely on stereotypes or react to uncomfortable information by cutting the lines of communication. If a journalist or speaker tells a story using an unacceptable frame, we may simply ignore or distort the information to fit our expectations or needs. In line with the backward-looking nature of perception, we rely on past experiences or stereotypes to interpret new information. We also perceive selectively, in a way that is congruent with our values and beliefs. The My Lai massacre of Vietnamese citizens by American troops in 1968 illustrates the kinds of omissions and distortions that can occur when listeners selectively perceive and filter information:

> A war correspondent was present when a hamlet was burned down by the United States Army's First Air Cavalry Division. Inquiry showed that the order from division headquarters to the brigade was "On no occasion must hamlets be burned down." The brigade radioed the battalion: "Do not burn down any hamlets unless you are absolutely convinced that the Vietcong are in them." The battalion radioed the infantry company at the scene: "If you think there are any Vietcong in the hamlet, burn it down." The company commander radioed his troops: "Burn down that hamlet."[24]

Our attitudes toward certain kinds of information also influence how we configure our listening frames. We set the frames to filter certain kinds of information, much like we set levels of security for filtering spam from our computers. If we set the level of security too high, we may miss some of the messages because the program does not recognize the information as worthwhile or significant. Figuratively speaking, the computer program diverts the messages to the spam folder; and we may never know that the messages arrived in the system unless something happens (as in the My Lai incident) to draw our attention to the inappropriate setting.

Lack of Interest in Topic

Communication can fail if we have no interest in the topic. We may be apathetic about the speaker, the subject matter, or the occasion. The speech may contain no novel information. We may tune out discussions that require too much mental exertion. Seeing no purpose to a speech, we may set our listening frames to discard the information before it can be processed. In these situations, we often fake attention. Most of us share this tendency from time to time, and we may become quite good at concealing our "out-of-body" trips. In line with perception theory, we must necessarily ignore a large amount of the information that comes to us each day. So these actions are understandable, even if they do not always serve our best interests.

Lack of Background to Interpret Information

Sometimes we simply lack the knowledge or experience to recognize patterns. In those situations, the holistic nature of perception leads us to fill in the gaps. I used to show excerpts from a film titled *The Good Times Are Killing Me* to a class of Canadian students. This film depicts the rural Mardi Gras celebrated in southwestern Louisiana.[25] I did nothing to prepare the students for the subject matter of the film because I wanted to demonstrate the ways in which we add, drop, and distort information that is incomprehensible within our listening frames. I wanted to illustrate processes such as *levelling* (the elimination of details from a story), *sharpening* (the exaggeration and accentuation of striking features of stories), and *assimilation* (fitting stories to our preconceptions and cultural frameworks).

Levelling
Eliminating details from a story

The film about the Acadian Mardi Gras was an ideal vehicle for illustrating these points. Rural Acadians celebrate a Mardi Gras quite unlike the world-famous carnival of New Orleans. In the traditional celebration, masked men in clown outfits, pointed hats, and colorful pajamas decorated with fringe ride on horseback through the countryside, begging for chickens, sausages, rice, vegetables, and other donations. Dressed in black capes and cowboy hats, their *capitaines* carry

Count the number of "Fs" in this statement:

Full flavourful cuisine is made of everything that we value in fantastic foods—fine herbs, lots of fresh ingredients, and a touch of genius!

Compare your answers.

white flags. A lone individual, accompanied by a band of musicians, sings the haunting Mardi Gras song. The rules of conduct are as follow:

> The authority of *le capitaine* is absolute. He leads the procession and distributes any liquor that is consumed. No member of the colorful band of beggars may enter private property without his permission. He approaches each farmhouse with raised white flag to ask permission from the homeowners for *les Mardi Gras* to enter. If he receives an invitation, he drops or waves the flag to signal the others. They are expected to sing and dance and beg with great energy at homes that are donating to the gumbo.[26]

Before departing, the masked beggars and their *capitaines* chase down live chickens to take back to the villages, where the women prepare chicken and sausage gumbos for the evening celebration. The dancing and festivities continue at the local dance hall until midnight, the beginning of the Lenten season.

Apart from the costumes and the drinking, no familiar cues exist in this film about the Acadian Mardi Gras. No floats, grand balls, or krewes (groups that stage the parades and costumed balls) characterized the cinematic depiction of this rural Mardi Gras. No throwing of beads or crowning of royalty in $100,000 costumes took place in the locations where this film was made—places like Churchpoint, Basile, and Mamou. When I asked my students (following the viewing of the film) to describe the seemingly bizarre events in the film, they had no context within which to interpret the events. They did not understand why masked men would be riding through the countryside begging for chickens. They found the wringing of a chicken's neck to be unsettling. Unable to speak French, most students had no idea of what the Mardi Gras song meant or represented. They did not understand the context or meaning of the celebration. In short, they had no relevant frames within which to position the information, and their accounts gave great insight into how listeners try to make sense of culturally alien information. The next section describes some of their responses.

HOW LISTENERS RESPOND

When confronted with information that conflicts with existing values and beliefs, holds no obviously useful or interesting characteristics, or contains alien concepts that they do not understand, how do listeners respond? What do they retain of the information? What do they ignore when they do not agree with the information or find it so alien that they cannot process it? What do they add in an effort to make sense of the concepts? How do they distort the information to fit their perceptual frames? The following discussion will use the class exercise with the Mardi Gras film as a means of illustrating these points. As in the telephone game, one student (who had seen the film) was asked to relay her interpretation of the film to a second individual who was not present for the viewing. That individual then relayed his understanding of the film to a third person, absent from the classroom for the viewing and the earlier descriptions. The entire class heard the descriptions.

Retention in Perceptual Frames

Sharpening
Exaggerating or accentuating details in a story

In the class experiment, what was retained? First, the recounting of the events demonstrated the *sharpening* effect in perception—how receivers of communication tend to retain the most outrageous and sensational details, such as the wringing of the chicken's neck. Students also remembered the colorful beggars and caped men riding on horseback through the countryside. Some remembered the highly sensory images of boiled crawfish and corn cobs being poured from vats onto picnic tables. Typically students remembered that the Cajuns like to drink, party, go horseback riding, and chase chickens.

Losses from Perceptual Frames

What was dropped? Overall, the accounts were simplistic and underdeveloped (*levelling* effect), with much lost from the original account. As the information passes from one student to the next, the transmission time grows shorter. A classic article argued that people can usually recall no more than seven points, "plus or minus two";[27] and some argue that the number may be closer to five than seven. In this situation, the students tended to omit major contextual details such as the costumes and the music, pervasive forces in the film. Yet context is so important to our sensing of the world, as well as to communicating our perceptions to others. When questioned about the omissions, one student said, "I heard the music in my head all of the time that I was recounting the story. I just didn't think to mention it."

Additions to Perceptual Frames

What was added? Students often embellished the story, adding details not present in the film. They might make up a conversation where the women on farms beg the costumed men to sing a song for them; or they might say that the men were on their way to a masquerade ball. The added details made the person appear better informed and the story more interesting. The new information often added "spice" to the story. The students might say, for example, that the women were frightened when the masked men arrived or that the masked men were drinking heavily. At other times, the additions seemed to be attempts to make sense of what they had seen and heard—to find some logical and reasonable explanation for the events that they had witnessed (*assimilation* to their cultural expectations).

Assimilation
Filtering stories through our own experiences

Distortions of Perceptual Frames

What was distorted? The students often changed the story to fit their understanding of the world. When some aspect of the film did not make sense, the person invented an explanation or changed the story line (also illustrating *assimilation*). They might say, for example, that *les capitaines* were modern-day pirates who rode in bands through the countryside, forcing people to give chickens to them. They might say the film was a music video featuring John Fogarty. (Fogarty appeared in the film, singing "Don't Mess with My Toot-Toot.")

An exercise such as this one allows one to go inside the head of the listener to see how people deal with culturally alien or unfamiliar information. The film's usefulness as a vehicle for teaching derived in part from its weaknesses. The Cajun population of Louisiana loudly protested this depiction of their culture and decried the way in which the filmmakers provided no context for the happenings in the film. One source, for example, noted:

> The final version . . . portrayed the Cajuns as a strange tribe of vulgar, hard-partying, drunks, the front-line in a losing battle for cultural and ethnic survival in America. . . . Louis Landreneau is presented dressing as a woman, complete with brassiere and pantyhose, wig and makeup, under the careful supervision of his mother, without explaining that he is preparing for his community's Mardi Gras celebration. The Mardi Gras is eventually presented with no explanation other than the definitions gathered by the fascinated but unenlightened crew from drunken participants.

When working with different kinds of materials (e.g., Eskimo folklore), students react in the same way. They try to explain folk stories and myths in rational, scientific terms. Dreams become reality in the telling of the stories. The students winnow down the details so that they reach a very low level. And they distort and exaggerate the most outrageous moments—the moment, for instance, when an Eskimo hunter turns into a bearskin. They lose the cultural context for the stories. What the students hear depends greatly on what they already know. And when the students pass the information from one to another, the accounts get shorter and shorter as more and more details disappear. (See the Keep in Mind box.)

In addition to perceptual and attitudinal issues, the gap between speaking and listening rates explains some of the difficulties experienced by listeners. Numerous studies have found that listeners can process information significantly faster than speakers can speak. Some studies set average listening rates at 300 words per minute[28] and speaking rates at 125 words per minute.[29] Other studies identify an even wider gap between the rates at which people listen and speak. They have shown that people can listen effectively at speeds four or five times greater than normal speech.[30] A number of years ago, researchers found that blind and partially

Keep in Mind

When processing culturally alien information . . .
We tend to retain
     . . . the most outrageous and sensational details.
We tend to add
     . . . embellishments and "spice" to secure interest.
     . . . logical causes and explanations for events.
     . . . details that make us look more informed.
We tend to drop
     . . . story lines that do not fit our culture experience.

blind students effectively developed the ability to "speed listen" to recorded play-backs of their professors' lectures. By increasing the playback speed, they could listen to a sixty-minute lecture in forty minutes. Despite the "chatterbox" effect, they were able to comprehend the content at this significantly faster rate.[31] Our brains are able to handle information at jet speed, but speakers deliver the information at a locomotive pace. In such a situation, listeners tend to succumb to distractions in their heads and physical environments.

INFLUENCE OF SETTING ON MESSAGE RECEPTION

Furnishings, acoustics, lighting, and general ambience of a setting influence the receptiveness of audiences to messages. Classic studies by Abraham Maslow and Robert Mintz found that more positive exchanges occur in "beautiful" rooms, surroundings that are visually and aesthetically pleasing to the eye.[32] Through choices of colors and furniture, some rooms convey a sense of warmth, while others are cold and uninviting.[33] To create a sense of immediacy with the audience, speakers often remove physical obstacles such as podiums that separate them physically and psychologically from their listeners.

The comfort and arrangement of chairs or auditorium seating also have an impact on reception of a message. Some studies have found that people make harsher judgments of others in uncomfortable settings.[34] The design of some chairs encourages people to remain in the environment for long periods of time (e.g., seating in lounges), whereas other chairs are designed to become uncomfortable after a few minutes.[35] The unfriendly and uncomfortable seating arrangements in airports encourage people to move into the restaurants and bars. The same principles apply to auditorium and other settings where speech events occur. Audiences, especially older people, may be prone to avoid the discomfort of some physical settings; or they may find it difficult to pay attention in certain settings. Seating that relaxes people too much, of course, can have the equally undesirable effect of putting people to sleep.

The presence of perfumes creates an impossible environment for those with allergies or asthma. In unpleasant environments, windows offer a route of escape; and speakers lose listeners to the fall foliage, squirrels scampering in the park, and the muted conversations of passing pedestrians. Other detractors include background noise, overheated or cold rooms, musty or unpleasant smells, sounds of traffic, or music that jars with the personal tastes of listeners. Conversations between audience members also offer competition to speakers. One researcher contends that the average room contains forty-three decibels of sound.[36]

Researchers in one study observed instruction by sixteen teachers in thirty-two classrooms of first-, sixth-, and eleventh-grade students.[37] The principal finding was the following:

> The main determinant of whether a student was actively and directly engaged in the process of classroom communication was his or her *location*, or place in the setting. In a typical straight-row seating arrangement, the researchers identified an "action zone" or center of activity where most interaction takes place. This area . . . extends from the front of the room directly up the center line, diminishing in intensity

as it moves farther away from the teacher. In this zone are the students to whom the teacher talks. The process is reciprocal, for it is these same students who talk to the teacher.[38]

Their findings were consistent across all teachers, subjects, and grade levels. Subsequent studies have confirmed that those in the front row and the center of other rows tend to participate the most actively. Other studies have found that overall participation diminishes as you go from the front to the back of the room. In seminar rooms, the most active participants sit across from the instructor.[39] Studies tie these participation patterns to the tendency of speakers to communicate in a kite-shaped or diamond-shaped pattern. When listeners fall outside of these communication zones, the level of their engagement diminishes. Since a tombstonelike (row-by-row) seating arrangement still characterizes 90 percent of university classrooms,[40] these studies have relevance for listeners who are sitting in the "dead zone." The studies are also relevant to public speakers, who must take care not to restrict eye contact and body orientation to the "action zone."

Reciprocal Responsibilities of Listeners and Speakers

Speakers are not the only ones with a responsibility for communicating ideas. Audiences bear as much responsibility for a successful speaking event as speakers do. Speakers respond with less anxiety and greater confidence when they perceive the audiences to be congenial.[41] An early study by Ivey and Hinkle demonstrated the importance of supportive feedback.[42] In this experiment, six participating students began a psychology class in a nonattentive mode. They slouched in their seats, showed no interest in taking notes, and avoided eye contact with the instructor. The instructor, for his part, lectured in a monotone, used no gestures, and paid little or no attention to the students. At a prearranged signal, the students switched from passive to active listening behaviors. They sat up straight in their chairs or leaned forward to show interest in the lecture, engaged in direct eye contact, and took notes. Once the students showed interest in the lecture, the instructor began to gesture; he spoke more rapidly; and the class session became animated. At a second prearranged signal, the students reverted to their passive listening behaviors; and after a painful attempt to regain the interest of the group, the instructor returned to his lackluster performance.

GIVING NONVERBAL FEEDBACK

Through positive and supportive feedback, audiences can encourage speakers to perform optimally. A good audience gives nonverbal feedback by paying close attention to the speech—nodding on occasion, smiling, looking for eye contact with the speaker, leaning slightly forward or otherwise orienting the body toward the speaker. Courteous and attentive audiences put away notes and avoid conversations (spoken or written) while speeches are underway. As speakers, we are most drawn to those audience members who give us highly positive feedback, or at the

Nonverbal feedback
Audience behaviors such as nodding, smiling, fidgeting, leaning forward, etc., that let speakers know how effective they are

other extreme, highly negative feedback. We look at the people who are smiling and nodding to gain strength. We make eye contact with those who are giving negative feedback to try to figure out what is wrong and to effect a change in their attitudes. Sometimes, the negative feedback causes us to become nervous and to lose our concentration. If we fail repeatedly to get any response to our efforts, we may tune out that part of the audience in order to avoid the negative contact. (See the Keep in Mind boxes.)

Keep in Mind

Tips on Good Listening Attitudes

- Be a selfish listener; think about what you can get from the speech.
- Try to understand what the speaker is saying; focus on main ideas.
- Avoid anticipating what the person is going to say; you may be surprised.
- Be open-minded; don't listen with the purpose of finding fault.
- Withhold judgment until the end of the speech; don't stop listening or plan your arguments while the person is still speaking.
- Put yourself in the position of the speaker; ask why the person has this perspective.

- Be compassionate when the person makes mistakes in delivery; no one is perfect.
- Pay more attention to content than to delivery.
- Pay more attention to ideas than to the way in which they are expressed.
- Avoid stereotyping speakers; don't make assumptions on the basis of ethnicity, sex, age, or other factors.
- Block distracting thoughts and noises, which impede listening effectively.

Keep in Mind

Tips on Good Listening Behaviors

- Use nonverbal language to encourage the speaker to do his or her best—smiling when appropriate, nodding occasionally, and orienting your body toward the speaker.
- Avoid talking to friends or making distracting noises during the speech.
- Don't read or engage in other work assignments while the person is speaking.
- Don't mumble or leave your seat if you disagree with the speaker; give the person a chance to finish the speech before challenging the ideas.

- Ask questions *after* the speech; don't use frowns and shakes of the head to question while the speech is still in progress.
- Control "micro-expressions," those fleeting looks that last a second but have a long-term impact on speakers.
- If the speaker hesitates, use nonverbal signals to encourage him or her to continue.
- Combine praise with criticism when you comment on the speech.

GIVING VERBAL FEEDBACK

Verbally, audiences give feedback when they respond to questions by the speaker, ask questions at the end of the speeches, or provide oral or written comments. Some regulations govern the giving of feedback. First, feedback should convey, in a timely fashion, what worked well and what requires improvement. Immediate feedback makes a stronger impression than delayed feedback. Second, the feedback should be specific. Ryan Seacrest, host of *American Idol*, often criticizes Simon Cowell (one of the judges of the competition) for his failure to be specific in criticizing the efforts of contestants. He says that the contestants cannot improve if they do not know what they are doing wrong. If the feedback is sufficiently specific and descriptive, speakers can also learn a great deal from constructive feedback. In other words, as an audience member, you should never say, "Great speech!" or "I hated the speech." Such comments not only offend (in the latter case), but they also offer no constructive direction for change. Speakers learn nothing from such vague comments. In addition, generalities demonstrate lack of awareness and knowledge on the part of the person providing the feedback. With experience in speaking and listening, feedback should become increasingly concrete and sophisticated.

Feedback should employ descriptive rather than judgmental language. You could say, for example, "You have a tendency to shift from foot to foot while you speak," or, in shorthand language, "too much shifting from foot to foot." That would be descriptive. The same statement, framed in evaluative language, would be, "It's annoying when you shift from foot to foot." Useful feedback offers specific directions for change, such as, "Try to eliminate some of the lower body movement in your next speech."

Feedback should focus on the modifiable. Pointing to a lisp or stutter, an unpleasantly nasal voice, or a thick accent serves no purpose. These kinds of problems are best noted by the instructor in a private session with the student, at which time the instructor can direct the student to appropriate resources such as speech therapists or language departments. Repeated critiques by peers just serve to demoralize, since these kinds of deficiencies require time and expert help to correct.

Limiting individual feedback to the identification of two strengths and two areas for improvement allows listeners to focus on major points. Asking for feedback in the form of numbers is less useful, since standards among novice speakers vary so greatly. Also, people use numbers as crutches, allowing them to avoid identifying strengths and diagnosing problems. The importance of requesting strengths as well as challenges cannot be overstated. A supportive atmosphere is essential to learning. As discussed in Chapter Two, many enroll in speech classes to gain confidence, overcome communication anxiety, and better their chances of doing well in careers that require competency in speaking to groups. They look for skills for coping in their everyday lives. They have no intention of signing up to be motivational speakers. In a negatively charged atmosphere, little improvement will take place. In a positive atmosphere, the students establish close friendships, offer support to each other through responsive attitudes and constructive feedback, and learn to better their own speaking and critical listening skills.

At the same time that speakers bear a responsibility to audiences, audiences bear a responsibility to speakers—to pay attention and model supportive behaviors, listen to the whole message before passing judgment, and realize that some

Verbal feedback
Oral responses from audiences that could involve asking or answering questions or providing comments

A Question of Ethics

The auditorium was filled to capacity, both with people and the noise of many small conversations. The audience of new immigrants was heterogeneous in composition. The purpose of the gathering was to prepare the group for the challenges they would confront in adjusting to a new country. Attendance was compulsory.

Samantha, the event organizer, moved to the speaker's podium, where she called for order. Several guest speakers filed onto the stage, seating themselves behind her. She introduced the first speaker. There was a ripple of applause at the conclusion of the speech. At the conclusion of the second speech, the audience again applauded, less enthusiastically this time. Finally, an attractive, young, and well-dressed woman rose to talk about the challenges of raising children in Canada—the need to understand and tolerate differences in cultural approaches to such matters as child rearing and socializing.

By this time, many members of the audience were tired. They yawned and talked quietly among themselves. Many held jobs that required them to rise at 5:00 in the morning or earlier; so they had been awake for many hours and they resented having to attend an evening event. To make matters worse, a large number spoke English as a second language. So they had to pay close attention to understand the speeches. As the evening continued, many did not bother. Some showed signs of upset at the advice offered by the speaker. They interpreted her comments as saying that they should tolerate behaviours in youth that violated their cultural and religious values. Part of their reaction derived from their judgment of the speaker's age and dress. They thought that she was too young to be speaking on child-rearing, and they thought that she was from an environment of privilege, unable to understand their situation.

The speaker reacted to their inattentiveness and unrest by growing more nervous. She stammered and repeated portions of her speech. She referred more often to her notes; her complexion turned a bright red. To those sitting closest to the stage, it was obvious that her hands were shaking uncontrollably. She spoke faster and slurred her words, making it still more difficult for her audience to understand the speech. The audience read these signs as a lack of self-confidence and inadequacy. How does this example reflect some of the principles discussed in this chapter? Who was responsible for the failed speech?

speakers have important messages even if their delivery is weak. The audience must judge the truthfulness of the speaker, the accuracy and value of the message, and the ethics of the presentation. (See the Question of Ethics box.)

Conclusion

Listening is hard work, requiring that we hear what someone says; selectively perceive, assimilate, and categorize the information; and, finally, develop a mental response to the message. We frequently hear what we expect to hear. We tend to switch off when we do not understand or disagree with an idea. Nervousness and frustration also interfere with comprehension of messages. Our listening frames are set to filter out a large amount of the information that we receive each day. If the filter levels are set too high, we will not hear, comprehend, or retain important information. If they are set too low, however, we will suffer the effects of information overload. If our interest flags at times when listening to a speech, we should remind ourselves that we had a purpose in coming to the event. We should ask ourselves, "What can I get out of the situation?" Even if the quality of the speech is less than we had anticipated, we may still be able to fulfill our initial purposes in attending the event.

This chapter has expanded upon the characteristics and needs of the listener, as introduced in the CCM model. In later chapters, I will explore some of the ways in which speakers can overcome these internal and external obstacles to effective listening. We will discuss, for example, how speakers can tie their discussion to existing perceptual frames to facilitate assimilation by the audience, add novel ideas that sharpen the information, use concrete and memorable details to avoid leveling effects, and rely on multiple sensory channels to reach the audience.

Questions for Discussion

1. Close your eyes for a moment. Think about what you recall of your immediate surroundings. Keeping one hand over your lowered eyes, make a few notes about the features in the physical environment that come to the top of your mind. Then look up and compare your notes with those of other members of the class. Note the differences in what you have noticed from what other people have noticed.

2. How do your purposes for listening shift from one situation to another? Give examples.

3. Describe a situation in which you have had little interest in listening. What were the characteristics of that situation? What could have increased your interest in listening?

4. Do you listen more often in a deliberative or empathic fashion? Recount some incident in which you reacted negatively to deliberative listening on the part of your parents, friends, or partner and/or positively to empathic listening.

5. The following adjectives have been used to describe characteristics of perception: culture-bound and value-laden, holistic, backward-looking, relative, and selective. Give examples from your experience to illustrate these characteristics of perception.

6. Do you think that your classroom setting has a positive or negative impact on the listening patterns of your fellow students? Explain.

7. Evaluate the impact of audience behaviors on your speech experiences to this point in time. What kinds of listening and feedback behaviors have made your speaking experiences more pleasant? What kinds of behaviors have made your experiences more difficult or unpleasant? Identify class members who have demonstrated supportive listening behaviors. Evaluate your own listening behaviors. Based on the readings and class discussion, what could you do to become a better listener and to make your classmates feel more comfortable when they are speaking?

8. Describe some dominant stereotypes (e.g., used car salesmen, morticians, professors, hockey players, scientists, accountants, artists, engineers, etc.). How do the stereotypes impede our ability to send and receive messages?

Outline

ACQUIRING THE BASIC SKILLS

The Speech of Introduction

Learning Objectives

- To learn how to select a topic and write clear thesis and purpose statements for a speech of introduction
- To learn how to get organized, including making an outline and writing a preview statement
- To learn how to get audience attention in an introduction
- To discover how to develop the body of the speech
- To learn to connect ideas and parts of the speech
- To learn to close the speech with a memorable thought
- To understand the importance of practicing the speech, using an extemporaneous style of delivery

Speeches of introduction are common in workplace, social, and classroom contexts. Within some African cultures, they rank alongside speeches of welcome and appreciation as *the* most common speech given by the average person.[1] In this chapter, we will consider seven steps in preparing and practicing a speech of introduction. Those steps include (1) getting started by choosing a theme, deciding upon the purpose of the speech, and writing a thesis statement; (2) getting organized by identifying and ordering the main ideas and writing a preview statement; (3) writing an introduction; (4) developing the main body of the speech; (5) using connectives to link ideas and internal summaries to orient listeners; (6) concluding with a memorable thought; and (7) practicing the speech, using an extemporaneous mode of delivery.

Step 1: Getting Started

Theme
The unifying idea of a speech

The first step in the speech process involves choosing a theme, deciding on the purpose of the speech, and writing a thesis statement.

CHOOSING A THEME

The process of deciding upon a speech topic generally entails library research. With a speech of introduction, however, *you* are the subject of the speech. Therefore, you can skip the research step and begin by identifying a theme or central organizing principle for your speech. You can use some physical object (ring, ticket, figure skates, old running shoes, T-shirt, mug, or other physical representation) as a catalyst for talking about your personality, relationships, interests, or experiences. The selected object allows you to pursue a theme in the speech, rather than just telling us that you have two sisters, a brother, and a cat; you like Italian food; and you are in first year of college. Although these latter points may define you, audiences are bored by such listings.

To introduce herself to the class, one student brought a teacup to the front of the class to talk about how her shaking disorder had influenced her life. Another brought a pair of boots and described all of the places that her boots had traveled. She allowed the boots to tell the story. Another student brought a piece of bent medal to explain how the twisted medal reflected characteristics of his personality. Others brought a blue bunny or a collection of uniforms. Objects such as T-shirts carry messages about our personality or travels. An agenda book can launch a discussion of organizational abilities or interest in attending certain kinds of events.

In looking through your music collection, you may find that your likes in music (hip hop, rap, classic rock, or other) or artists (Black Eyed Peas, Gwen Stefani, JayZ, Radiohead, and Kelly Clarkson) reflect stages in your life or relationships that mattered to you. Other objects will represent passions or causes to which you have contributed. Sometimes passions become obsessions, which, if not too serious, can present an opportunity to add humor to a speech. Audiences enjoy speakers who can laugh about their own shortcomings and foibles. To the extent that you can

Sample Speech

I've Got a Lot of Things to Hang

I've got a lot of things to hang. My cowboy hat, ball cap, and fedora hang on my bedposts. My Pink Floyd, Hank Williams, and Mötley Crüe posters plaster my walls. (You didn't hear this from me, but one of them is covering the aftermath of a less-than-intelligent frosh week event.) My guitars, and I've got a few, are hung neatly in my dorm room to keep them off the war zone that I call a floor. I'm desperately trying to keep my grades up and hang on to my scholarships. I'm Brock, your run-of-the-mill country bumpkin from Napanee, who doesn't know Avril Lavigne, and I've got a lot of things to hang.

My roommate says I am harder to read than an Arabic book, and I am. Some say I wear my mood, interests, and attitudes on my sleeve. I suppose I do, but it's more complicated than that. Music is a gigantic part of my life. If you see me walking down the halls, you can bet the farm that I'm humming a song. Any song. I like them all. On my iTunes, my Nelly's next to my Nirvana, which is next to my Nitty Gritty Dirt Band. I've also got enough jackets for an army. When I watch too much *That '70s Show*, and I feel like dressing like Hyde—I throw on my corduroy jacket and aviators. I rock to Pink Floyd and walk around like I don't have a care in the world. When all you hear is punk rock blaring from my room, it's likely that I'll be donning the same leather jacket and spiked hair that used to embarrass my parents to no end. Sometimes, I throw on the plaid shirt and cowboy hat. My greeting changes from "Hey, how's it goin?'" to "G'dayhowareyaduday." This week I've watched *Walk the Line* several times, and it doesn't take a rocket scientist to figure out the inspiration behind today's outfit.

My mom says I'm whimsical. Maybe she's right. My aunt thinks I'm eclectic. Maybe that's it. I'm pretty sure my dad thinks I've got a few screws loose. Maybe. You can never be sure what to expect from me. In fact, the only sure-fire thing about this run-of-the-mill country bumpkin from Napanee, who doesn't know Avril Lavigne, is that I got a lot of things to hang.

Brock Young

---

choose an original theme, you should do so, passing up themes that are likely to be overused. The most creative themes usually produce the most interesting speeches. Perhaps you can think in terms of experiences that could have been frightening, embarrassing, or life-defining. (See the Sample Speech by Young.)

DECIDING UPON A PURPOSE

Speeches may be serious and informative or light and entertaining in tone and purpose. The most often cited speech purposes are to inform, persuade (convince, stimulate, or move to action), or entertain. Some persuasion speeches seek to inspire or motivate listeners to achieve higher purposes or goals in their lives. Some informative speeches pay tribute to the lives of people who have made some contribution to society. So many more specific purposes reside under the broad purposes of informing, persuading, and entertaining. Moreover, purposes are not always easy to label. A speaker may prepare a talk, for example, on how to get ready for hurricanes. Ostensibly, the speech is informative, offering instruction on steps

Purpose
What one intends to accomplish through the speech act

to follow in preparations. However, the speaker may also be trying to persuade—to convince people not to be laissez-faire in their attitudes toward hurricanes.

In a second case, the most important purpose of the speaker may be unstated. Politicians regularly deliver talks at Rotary Clubs, women's business luncheons, and meetings of educators. In these speeches, they explain their positions on issues and update constituents on what is happening in Congress or municipal government. They may talk about their commitment to reducing crime or plans related to a new transit system. Ostensibly, these purposes are informative in nature. The primary intent of the politician, however, may be to establish good will, demonstrate accessibility, and obtain votes in the next election. At other times, speakers simply seek to transmit the messages of their organizations. So the distinctions among speech purposes may be less clear in practice than on paper.

In-class speech assignments usually designate a general purpose (inform, convince, actuate, entertain, or inspire), but the student decides upon the specific purpose of the speech. Examples of specific purposes in speeches *to inform* could be "to explain how to get involved in student government" or "to describe how to conduct a meeting." If the general purpose is *to persuade*, the specific purpose could be "to convince people to stop smoking," "to reinforce the importance of eating a healthy diet," or "to encourage people to give more money to charities." If the general purpose is *to entertain*, the specific purpose could be "to give a mock graduation speech designed to entertain." The statement of specific purpose should appear in the introduction of the speech, and outlines should include statements of general and specific purpose.

FRAMING A THESIS STATEMENT

Thesis statement
A single declarative sentence that expresses the main point of your speech

Every speech should be unified, governed by one central idea that all other points support. This single declarative sentence, or *thesis statement*, should encapsulate everything that you want to say. The more carefully you have framed the purpose statement, the easier it will be to articulate the thesis. Examples of thesis statements include:

- This old sweatshirt and these running shoes have seen some remarkable sights.
- This photograph of Mount Everest tells you where I want to be in five years' time.
- My experience with bungee jumping is one that I would not want to repeat.
- This journal reveals how my life changed after I came to university.

Note that each statement refers to a single idea, which becomes the organizing principle for the speech. Every other statement in the speech must support and develop the thesis statement. If you cannot relate some part of your speech to this thesis statement, the point does not belong in the speech. Sometimes, you will discover that your thesis statement cannot contain the points that you wish to make. When that happens, you must rewrite the thesis statement to cover what you intend to say. *The main point of the speech should be clear—to you and to your audience.* The thesis statement gives unity and coherency to the speech.

Step 2: Getting Organized

The organizational process involves three major tasks: identifying and ordering major points, developing an outline of the points, and writing a preview statement for your introduction.

IDENTIFYING AND ORDERING MAJOR POINTS

After writing purpose and thesis statements, you must decide upon the major points to be covered in your speech and the organizational scheme. In two- to three-minute speeches, you will not have time to develop more than two or three major points. The following discussion compares how you could organize a speech on hotel fires, using the various organizational schemes. All of the rules apply, however, to speeches of introduction. The most common patterns in speeches of introduction are *chronological*, *spatial*, *topical*, *narrative*, and *comparative*.

Chronological patterns are time-based: first to last, last to first, past to present, present to past, past to future, or future to past. A speech about the worst hotel fires, for example, might employ a time-based form of organization. A chronologically ordered speech on major hotel fires could begin with the Winecoff Hotel in Atlanta, Georgia (1946), before proceeding to the Taeyokale Hotel in Seoul, Korea (1971); the MGM Grand Hotel and Casino fire in Las Vegas (1980); the Dupont Plaza Hotel in San Juan, Puerto Rico (1986); and the Manor Hotel in Manila, the Philippines (2001). (See the Sample Speech by St-Cyr on pg. 90 for an example of a chronological pattern.)

The *spatial* pattern organizes content according to location or relationship of the parts in space. Often we are talking about some kind of geographical ordering. In the case of a speech on the worst hotel fires, for example, the speaker could talk about catastrophic hotel fires in Korea, Puerto Rico, the Philippines, and the United States. Alternatively, the speaker could organize the discussion of hotel fires according to where they began in the buildings. Perhaps some fires began in hotel rooms situated on different levels, others in kitchens or common areas. Like the ordering by regions of the country, this latter form of organization qualifies as spatial ordering. (See the Sample Speech by Montgomery on pg. 91 for an example of a spatial pattern.)

A *topical* form of organization groups ideas according to subject matter. The organization follows some logical ordering of the ideas. On the subject of major hotel fires, for example, the speaker could have four major headings: (1) *origins* or *causes* of the hotel fires (cigarettes, explosions, faulty wiring), (2) *motivations* behind the fires (accidental or deliberate), (3) *effects* of the fires (numbers of people killed and injured), and (4) *follow-up actions* taken by governments (e.g., new building and fire codes). Note that *causes* and *effects* constitute two (out of many) possibilities for topical ordering of material. If you seek, however, to establish a *relationship* between causes and effects, you have chosen the *cause-effect* pattern of organization, which will be covered in Chapter Ten. (See the Sample Speech by Mennie on pg. 92 for an example of a speech that uses topical organization.)

The increasingly popular *narrative* pattern of organization involves telling a story.[2] The experience can be your own or someone else's. If you choose to recount a personal experience with surviving a hotel fire, you will probably use this

Chronological patterns
Time-based methods of organizing content in a speech

Spatial
Organizing content based on location or relationship of the parts in space (usually geographical)

Topical
Organizing content by subject matter

Narrative
Organizing content through story-telling

Sample Speech

My Life in Uniform

How many of you can identify with this scenario? You wake in the morning and put on your school uniform. After school, you put on a second uniform to go to work. After work, you put on yet another uniform to go to an extracurricular activity. Sound familiar? At one point, this was my life—uniform, after uniform, after uniform. I did not buy any new clothes for almost three years! In many ways, these uniforms have come to represent me as a person. And in this speech, I will introduce you to some of the uniforms that reflect my school, work, and extracurricular experiences. My name is Sabrina St-Cyr, and this is my life.

At age eight, I joined Brownies and Girl Guides. [*Show uniforms.*] When I turned thirteen, I joined the Air Cadets. [*Display uniform.*] This period in my life was difficult. In junior high, all of my friends chose different social groups. So my parents suggested that I join Air Cadets, partly because my dad is in the Air Force. The result: six years of hard work and dedication and many precious friendships.

These badges represent those six years. This first badge shows the different camps that I attended; the second represents my status in cadets. I aged out as a warrant officer second class. This next badge means I was a drum major. After starting the brass and reeds band, I took charge of the group. I was also on the drill team, an instructor, and a participant in all fundraisers. The Legion Medal was my most important accomplishment as a cadet. I earned this medal, at the end of my fourth year, for outstanding citizenship. This cadet uniform reflects a very important part of my life. In this uniform, I learned leadership and discipline. I will never forget my time in Air Cadets.

This next uniform represents my entrance into the workforce. [*show uniform.*] I wore this uniform for two and a half years in my first job at Wendy's Family Restaurant. During my time at Wendy's, I was trained in every area except the grill. On the basis of my performance, I got a number of pins. I really enjoyed my time at Wendy's, even if it was a fast-food restaurant. This experience also represents my passing from child to adult: earning money, having more responsibility. It would prepare me for future jobs.

This is my high school uniform. [*Show uniform.*] It reflects my academic side, the years when I prepared for university. During high school, I was part of band, badminton, and track and field.

After high school and Air Cadets, I followed the military tradition and joined the reserves. [*Show uniform.*] In the reserves, I am a supply technician, meaning that I support members and other units. This past summer, I completed my trade course and participated in a training exercise. My experiences in supply work have been rewarding, and I work with a wonderful group of people.

So as you can see, my life is full of uniforms, each one representing different aspects of my life: my childhood, my school, my jobs, Air Cadets, and the military. What about the future? What kind of uniform still awaits me? Only time will tell. I can only hope that the uniform will fit what I hope to accomplish in my life.

Sabrina St-Cyr

Sample Speech

Boots

Last fall I took a three-month journey to a number of different countries. I wanted to learn more about myself—and about other people. I did just that while walking in these boots, and I would like to share those experiences with you.

Just imagine my excitement and anticipation of crossing the Pacific Ocean for the first time to discover a whole new world, crossing fifteen time zones and flying 32,000 miles round trip. And on one part of my trip, I spent time in a place where time doesn't really exist. The trek that I took to Nepal was the most emotional of my journey. To this day I can still smell the fresh air of the Mount Everest region. Seeing the mountain for the first time from the base camp stunned me. It was so beautiful. It is a scene of so much triumph and tragedy that I couldn't wait to get closer. I walked 194 kilometers in these boots to 17,500 feet above sea level, only to be defeated hours from my goal because I was too ill to continue.

One of the ways I was able to get over that defeat was by reflecting on how far I had come and what I had seen along the way, from the children who knew nothing of the Western world to one night where the air was so clear that I saw more stars than I ever knew existed. I was proud of my accomplishment.

From Nepal, my boots walked me into a hospital in Thailand. My first hospital experience consisted of a one-week stay in Bangkok—alone and afraid. After getting out, I recovered the only way I knew how. I spent five days in Phuket by the pool sipping strawberry daiquiris!

From there, my boots and I flew to Kuala Lumpur, Malaysia, where I spent a lot of time quietly observing. I made it to the observation deck of the Petronas Towers, where Sean Connery and Catherine Zeta-Jones recently stole billions in their movie *Entrapment*. In Singapore, I reflected on the beauty of the women. I have never seen so many faces of porcelain and grace.

Before I returned home, I had one last adventure. I spent six weeks in Australia, where I ate crocodile and discovered freedom when I jumped out of an airplane at 14,000 feet! I met people who will be my friends for life, as well as the man of my dreams. I also spent Christmas with my best friend of sixteen years who had married an Aussie the year before.

Upon my return home, I realized that—out of everything I had experienced—what mattered most was that I had learned something important about myself. I had learned that I had courage I never knew I had—courage to pursue a dream that mattered to me. My boots still have mud caked to their soles and I'm not going to remove it. The mud has been with me since the start of my journey, and I only collected more as I went. As I continue through life and gain more experience, I think I should gain more mud along the way too.

Heather Montgomery

organizational format. (See the Sample Speech by Kalata on pg. 93 for an example of narrative organization.)

Using the *comparative* form of organization, you could compare the *actions taken by people who survived major hotel fires* with *actions taken by those who lost their lives in the fires*. The thesis of your speech, in that case, could be: "People who survive major hotel fires behave differently from those who perish in the smoke and flames." (See the Sample Speech by Dillman on pg. 94 for an example of comparative organization.)

Comparative
Organizing content by contrasting one thing with another

Sample Speech

My Secret Addiction

My name is Joanna, and I am an addict. When I was fifteen, my mother (of all people) introduced me to a toxin that has forever changed my life. I grew up a home where my ultimate role model exposed me to her problem and convinced me that living life her way was okay. I can still see it now. There we would sit, mother and daughter, indulging in our family cycle of addiction, drinking cappuccinos and latte. And now, without coffee, I don't know if I could get through a day.

Some of you may be wondering how a generic Tim Horton's double-double could really be seen as an artifact that says a lot about me. You should realize, however, that this cup of coffee—as well as many others like it—not only reflects who and what I am, but also gives me the kick that I need to keep being me. In this speech, I will tell you a little about how coffee reflects my personality, the disastrous consequences of not having my daily fix of coffee, and how coffee contributes to my successes.

The erratic energy that we associate with a strong cup of coffee reflects my active, social, and somewhat scattered nature. In kindergarten, Mrs. Fortin named me the tiny little chatterbox, and since then, I've been known to shamefully assume the role of the "overly drunk girl making a fool out of herself" from time to time.

In a constant state of caffeination, I buzz through life. But when I don't have sufficient levels of caffeine coursing through my veins, the real disasters unfold. Without caffeine, I am often late, sleep-deprived, overly spontaneous, and oblivious to my physical surroundings. On the first day of school, my third year here, I had to call a friend in the morning to ask whether the library was in Morrisett or Montpetit. I also had to ask where these buildings are located on campus.

Another revealing incident occurred at the beginning of my first year in university. Having awakened a little late, I decided to forego my morning coffee and got ready as usual. I gathered my books, got dressed, and strolled out to the bus stop, proud of myself for having made good time. As I entered the bus shelter, two businessmen, who had been chatting pleasantly, stopped mid-sentence and stared right at me. I assumed that they were creepy and faced the other way. It was only when people, passing by in cars, pointed and laughed that I realized what was going on. There I stood with flawless makeup and straightened hair, my toothbrush hanging out of my mouth, complete with a chin full of toothpaste. And really, how does one recover from such a thing gracefully? I just swallowed, gagged, wiped the toothpaste off my face, and placed my toothbrush in my purse. Now Joanna does not skip her morning coffee!

Beyond kick-starting my day, a little caffeine gives me a boost when it's time to perform. I have always been extremely creative, and I write constantly. Whether it's time to act, deliver a speech, compete at improvisation in front of a screaming crowd, or sing opera for a panel of musical elite, coffee is part of my preparatory ritual.

Though I may not be as dark, mysterious, or Italian as coffee, I'd say that we certainly have more than a few things in common. I like it, need it, and am often wearing it to some degree. I guess my dependence could be seen as an addiction, but I choose to call my relationship with the beverage a life choice—and one of which my mom is proud.

Joanna Mennie

Sample Speech

Blue Bunny—a Piece of Home

I want you to imagine a market, like the one here in Ottawa—but bigger, with thousands of people shouting, bargaining. Shawls, scarves, and scraps of material are draped on top of large metal poles—an attempt to create a canopy to protect people from the exhausting heat of the sun. Merchants flank both sides of the cobbled, winding road. The air is so thick with the smells of sweat and spices that the only thing keeping you from passing out is your excitement and wonder. Then suddenly sirens go off. A loud booming voice comes over the intercom and says something, but you don't understand the words. Your heart starts to pound. A sinking feeling hits the bottom of your stomach, and you begin to run. Then BANG—an explosion. You hit the ground. When you get back to where you're staying, you grab your stuffed animal or GI Joe or your diary or picture of your family and you hold it tight and you begin to feel better.

"Home is where the heart is," or at least that's what someone famous once said. But what happens if you're away from home? For me, I like to take a piece of home with me wherever I might go. I call him "Blue Bunny."

When I was five, my mom remarried—this great big bear of a man whom I now call *dad*. To anyone else, his 6'3", 275-pound stature is slightly intimidating; but when you get to know him, he's as gentle and soft-spirited as a bunny rabbit. And when he won a blue bunny, this stuffed animal, on our first father-daughter adventure, Blue Bunny and I became almost as close as my dad and I. From that point on, Blue Bunny and I became inseparable.

Vegas, Mexico, Israel, Denmark, England, Barbados, Virginia, New York, Muskoka, and Ottawa—Blue Bunny has been there. Blue Bunny has seen the Dead Sea. He has climbed to the top of Mount Masada and watched the sun rise. He has been awakened by gunfire, but he has also heard the soft soothing call of a loon. He has sat in the grid-locked traffic of New York City and ridden through the valleys of Virginia and the mountains of Barbados. He has wandered the streets of Copenhagen and swum among the coral reefs of Cuba.

There is something to be said about things that make you feel at home, no matter your geographic location. Poets have written about the strong appeal of home, and musicians have sung songs about its relentless pull. Home is very important to me. When I feel scared, nervous, excited, or angry, home is the place I go to feel okay; and when I'm with my blue bunny, I'm home.

Natalie Kalata

Sometimes the major headings in a speech follow one organizational scheme (e.g., chronological), whereas the subheadings adhere to a different pattern (e.g., topical). Figure 4.1 illustrates this point.

DEVELOPING AN OUTLINE

The next step is to develop an outline. Figure 4.2 shows standard outline form taken to the fourth level of detail: first-level headings (I, II, III, etc.), second-level headings (A, B, C, D, etc.), third-level headings (1, 2, 3, etc.), and fourth-level headings (a, b, c, d, etc.). Six rules apply in developing your outline.

Outline
An organizational device that lays out only the essential parts, in order

Sample Speech

The Shape of My Personality

In case you are wondering why I would have brought such a strange prop to the podium, I would like to tell you a little about its history and relevance to this speech of introduction.

First its history. My initial contact with this piece of bent metal occurred shortly after I began working at in a bicycle repair shop in the summer of 2002. One day, a customer brought a used bicycle to the store. The rear wheel needed to be replaced. And so I ordered and fitted the new wheel onto the bike. When I returned the bike to its owner, I kept the bent wheel.

Having little to do for parts of every day, I found that the metal offered some source of entertainment. I experimented with twisting and bending it into various shapes. Over the course of the summer, I began to reflect on its qualities and value. In doing so, I saw parallels with some of my own personality, some findings that I would like to share with you today.

Metaphorically, the bent rim has many of the qualities that I like to see in myself: seemingly opaque, yet sometimes you can see right through

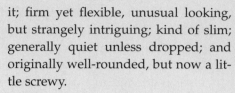

it; firm yet flexible, unusual looking, but strangely intriguing; kind of slim; generally quiet unless dropped; and originally well-rounded, but now a little screwy.

My experimentation with the rim also symbolizes my more creative instincts. The ability to shape what some might see as a piece of junk into a unique piece of art. The ability to see art in what others might see as a twisted piece of metal. I am a wannabe artist myself.

The rim also demonstrates my enjoyment of simple pleasures. When it comes to having summer jobs, there are few rules that I value. However, I do believe in working hard until you master a task and then gradually relaxing into an easier posture.

I value having a good time. Life is more than just work. And so I have transformed the bent wheel from a tool used only to perform work into a source of amusement and pleasure.

I hope that this strange-looking object has helped you to learn a little bit about me—my interests, quirks, and values.

Jeff Dillman

First, limit the number of subheadings in speeches. Three reasons explain this limitation. Every level carries additional details, which require time to develop. Since you do not have time to develop a large number of points in a short speech, you should limit the number of levels. Also, too many levels of detail confuse the listener. If a speech proceeds into great detail on one point, the listener can lose her place in the larger structure of the speech. Finally, if you use more than three levels in a five-minute speech, you are probably pursuing a tangent and giving undue time to one idea at the expense of a more balanced presentation. If you use more than four levels of detail in a ten- to fifteen-minute speech, you are probably developing some points more fully than others. In a balanced presentation, you give equal time to all major points. With three or four levels, you should use internal summaries to keep the structure and progress of the speech before the listeners. For a short speech, such as

Mixed Pattern of Organization: Chronological Headings/ Topical Subheadings

I.   Fire at Winecoff Hotel, 1946
   A.   Origins
   B.   Causes
   C.   Effects

II. Fire at Taeyokale Hotel, 1971
   A.   Origins
   B.   Causes
   C.   Effects

III. Fire at MGM Grand Hotel and Casino, 1980
   A.   Origins
   B.   Causes
   C.   Effects

IV. Fire at Dupont Plaza Hotel, 1986
   A.   Origins
   B.   Causes
   C.   Effects

V.   Fire at Manor Hotel, 2001
   A.   Origins
   B.   Causes
   C.   Effects

Figure 4.1

a two- to three-minute speech of introduction, you will probably use no more than two or three levels of detail. Otherwise, your speech will appear incoherent and unfocused to listeners who cannot go back to refresh their memories.

Second, do not mix sentences and phrases in an outline. You should not, for example, use a phrase such as "types of fighter planes" as a heading in your outline and a sentence such as "One type of fighter plane is the F-16." for the first subpoint. The first cluster of words "types of fighter planes" is not a sentence; it is a phrase. To correct the inconsistency, you can change the phrase into a sentence such as "Several types of fighter planes are common in the U.S. Air Force." Alternatively, you can change the sentence into a phrase such as "the F-16 fighter plane." Either format is acceptable (phrase or sentence), but you must be consistent. Choose one or the other.

Sub-points
Points made after main points have been laid out

Standard Outline Format

I.

    A.

    B.

        1.

        2.

        3.

            a.

            b.

            c.

        4.

    C.

II.

    A.

    B.

    C.

Figure 4.2

Third, standard outline format requires that each level have at least two subpoints. In the event that you have only one subpoint, you should combine that point with the heading that it supports. So if you have only "A," you should combine "A" with the Roman numeral that it supports (I, II, III, etc.). If you have only "1," you should combine "1" with the letter that it supports (A, B, C, etc.) If you have only "a," you should combine "a" with the number that it supports (1, 2, 3, etc.).

The fourth rule in outlining is to use parallel construction. The ideas that appear at each level (i.e., under the same heading) should reflect the same organizing principle. If your speech is about rollover risks for various classes of vehicles, the major headings in your discussion could be frontal risk, side risk, and rollover resistance. The next level of headings could identify vehicle types such as sport utility vehicles (SUVs), vans, passenger cars, and trucks. The third level could identify specific kinds of sport utility vehicles, vans, passenger cars, and trucks. To include specific vehicles such as the RAV-4 or Chevrolet Tracker in a list of vehicle types would violate the organizational principle for that level. Figure 4.3 illustrates this point.

The fifth rule requires that you indent each new point and capitalize the first word in every statement or phrase. See the sample outlines throughout this chapter.

The sixth and final rule obliges you to assign only one idea to each point. The following illustrates an *inappropriate* inclusion of multiple ideas in one statement: "Accidents result when boaters do not have any kind of operating license; also they should not drink when they are operating a boat." This statement contains two different ideas. The first idea concerns rules of licensing; the second concerns issues related to

Parallel construction

In an outline, when the ideas that appear at each level operate under the same organizing principle

Standards for Judging Rollover Risks in Vehicles

I. Frontal risk
    A. SUVs
        1. RAV-4
        2. Chevrolet Tracker
    B. Automobiles
        1. Audi A4
        2. Mazda RX 8
    C. Trucks
        1. Chevrolet Silverado
        2. Dodge Ram
II. Side risk
    A. SUVs
        1. RAV-4
        2. Chevrolet Tracker
    B. Automobiles
        1. Audi A4
        2. Mazda RX-8
    C. Trucks
        1. Chevrolet Silverado
        2. Dodge Ram
III. Rollover resistance
    A. SUVs
        1. RAV-4
        2. Chevrolet Tracker
    B. Automobiles
        1. Audi A4
        2. Mazda RX-8
    C. Trucks
        1. Chevrolet Silverado
        2. Dodge Ram

Figure 4.3 Consistency Within Levels

drinking and operating a boat. The two statements should appear as separate points.

Figures 4.4 and 4.5 illustrate the six principles of outlining, applied to the sample speech by Sabrina St-Cyr. The first outline employs phrases; the second uses sentences.

Phrase Outline

General Purpose: To inform

Specific Purpose: To introduce myself by talking about the role of uniforms in my life

Thesis: My name is Sabrina St-Cyr, and this is my life in uniform.

Preview statement: In this speech, I will introduce you to some of the uniforms that reflect my school, work, and extracurricular experiences.

I. A multitude of uniforms in our lives—school, work, and recreational activities
    A. The meaning of uniforms in our lives
    B. Uniforms as a way of introducing myself
II. Uniforms as a reflection of activities and periods in my life
    A. Joining Brownies and Girl Guides at age eight
    B. Entering Air Cadets at age thirteen
        1. A way to bridge a gap in my social life
        2. A tie to my father's life in the military
        3. Badges earned in Air Cadets
        4. Acquisition of discipline and leadership skills
    C. Entering the workforce at Wendy's Family Restaurant
        1. Training received
        2. Pins awarded for performance
        3. Benefits of experience in terms of maturity and income
    D. Participating in high school activities
        1. Academic achievements
        2. Experiences in band
        3. Sports activities
    E. Following the military tradition by joining the reserves
        1. Acting as a supply technician
        2. Completing my trade course and participating in a training exercise
        3. Satisfaction gained from a life in the reserves
III. A future of yet unknown uniforms

Figure 4.4

Sentence Outline

General Purpose: To inform

Specific Purpose: To introduce myself to the class by talking about the role that uniforms have played in my life

Thesis: My name is Sabrina St-Cyr, and this is my life in uniform.

Preview statement: In this speech, I will introduce you to some of the uniforms that reflect my school, work, and extracurricular experiences.

I. Like many of you, I wear a multitude of uniforms—for school, work, and recreational activities.

    A. In many ways, these uniforms have come to represent me as a person.

    B. My name is Sabrina St-Cyr, and this is my life in uniform.

II. My uniforms reflect activities and periods in my life.

    A. At age eight, I joined Brownies and Girl Guides.

    B. When I turned thirteen, I joined the Air Cadets.

        1. Air Cadets helped to fill a gap in my social life.

        2. Since my father is in the military, my parents thought this was a good idea.

        3. During my six years in Air Cadets, I earned a number of badges.

        4. In the uniform of the Air Cadet, I learned leadership and discipline.

    C. This next uniform, worn for two and a half years at Wendy's Family Restaurant, represents my entrance into the workforce.

        1. During my time at Wendy's, I was trained in every area except the grill.

        2. On the basis of performance, I got a number of pins.

        3. This experience helped me to mature and to earn money.

    D. My high school uniform reflects my academic side, as well as my experiences in band and sports.

    E. After high school and Air Cadets, I joined the reserves.

        1. I am a supply technician.

        2. I completed my trade course and participated in a training exercise.

        3. These experiences have been rewarding.

III. The uniforms that I will wear in the future are still unknown.

Figure 4.5

WRITING A PREVIEW STATEMENT

Preview statement
A statement that tells the audience what you are about to discuss

Preview statements, also called *statements of structural progression* or *orientation*, announce what you will cover in the speech. The following example illustrates this point: "First, I want to tell you who Bill Matthews is. Then I want to tell you why he is important to this organization. Finally, I want to tell you how you can all become a little more like the Bill Matthewses of this world." As in the following example, statements of structural progression can be extremely brief—sometimes only one sentence—in short speeches: "In this speech, I will address three major points: the dramatic increases in cases of AIDS in some African countries, the lack of resources to combat the spread of AIDS, and the role that the United States can play in halting the march of AIDS across the African continent."

Unlike readers, listeners cannot refer back to the previous page or flip ahead to see where the speaker is going. For this reason, you must advertise where you are going with a speech. The old adage says: You should tell an audience what you are going to tell them. Then you should tell them. Then you should tell them what you told them. The statement of orientation should appear in the introduction to the speech.

Step 3: Writing the Introduction

Although this chapter places writing of the introduction as the third step in the speechmaking process, many speakers prepare their introductions and conclusions before organizing and writing the main text. While the body of the speech should be logical and clear in its development, the introduction and conclusion should be creative, interesting, and memorable. For this reason, speeches should begin with an attention-getting device (followed by purpose and thesis statements and a preview of the organization of the speech).

Early studies in the psychology of attention identified the average attention span of audiences as ranging between two seconds and one minute—not a long time.[3] Reflecting the conclusions of these early scholars, Walter Dill Scott observed:

> In public address it is seldom that we are able to hold the full and undivided attention for more than a few seconds or a few minutes at best. The hearer's attention is constantly wandering or decreasing in force. He may renew it by personal effort, or else something we say or do may bring back the wandering or waning attention.[4]

If we accept the often made assertion that television has decreased attention spans of audiences,[5] we might conclude that the situation has further deteriorated over the last century. In the public speaking realm, part of the problem derives from the fact that typical speaking rates vary between 100 and 140 words per minute,[6] and audiences comprehend at a rate of 300 words per minute.[7] Therefore, audiences have time to engage in daydreaming about a multitude of subjects—relationships, agendas, food, assignments, and responsibilities at work, to mention but a few.

Although listeners have a responsibility to pay attention, this chapter focuses on techniques employed by speakers to maintain that attention. In speeches of introduction, the most common include immediacy strategies; references to the novel; suspense and shock techniques; linguistic strategies such as the use of sensory-laden language and quotations; activity, drama, and conflict; and humor. Gimmicks come with a price tag.

The attention-getting step should not be too lengthy. It takes about two minutes (sometimes less, depending on rate of speech) for the average speaker to get through one page of typed material (double spaced, twelve-point Times Roman font). Beginning speakers often overestimate what they can cover in the time allotted, causing them to run seriously overtime in speeches. In a speech of introduction, one short paragraph (about a third of a page) with attention-getting device, thesis statement, and preview statement should be sufficient. In longer speeches (five to fifteen minutes), the introduction could vary between half and three-quarters of a page in length, and the conclusion could be as much as half of a page.

Attention-getting statement
A statement, appearing early in the speech, that draws the audience in

IMMEDIACY STRATEGIES

Immediacy strategies act to close the psychological distance between speaker and audience. Speaking is an audience-centered activity, and when we use immediacy strategies, we engage in audience adaptation. While Chapter Six discusses immediacy techniques from the perspective of delivery, this chapter introduces the topic from the perspective of content. In a speech of introduction, the speaker may make a *reference to someone in the audience*, extend a *personal greeting or compliment*, mention *the occasion or surroundings*, mention a *recent event*, share *personal* details (i.e., self-disclose), adopt a *conversational style*, and/or ask a *question*. In the following example, a student speaker greets his audience, refers to some members by name, compliments the audience, and talks about recent events.

Immediacy strategies
Techniques employed to bring the speaker closer to the audience, figuratively and/or literally

> Good afternoon everyone, or should I say "Nuqneh!" I'm very happy to see you all. We've got a great turnout this year, and I see lots of people have dressed for the occasion, which is great! I see a number of new faces among you, as well as some familiar ones. Bob, I see you managed to make it again. This must be your tenth convention. Welcome everybody to the thirty-second annual Star Trek convention. We have a wonderful program lined up for you, so let's get to it![8]

Conversational language conveys the impression that a speaker is "in the moment," speaking on a one-to-one basis to audience members, as in the following excerpt from a student speech:

Conversational language
Speaking as if you are talking one on one, but to entire audience

> On January 1, 2004, my parents will celebrate their twenty-fifth anniversary—a quarter of a century of marriage. To this day, I don't know how they did it. I asked, on one occasion, what their secret was. My dad replied, "When you've had all you can take, and you can't take it any more, mark an X on the calendar. If things haven't improved by exactly six months from that day, pack your bags and leave. It's over." My mom smiled. She said that, for her, the answer to their staying together was simple. They had agreed that whoever left first had to take the kids.[9]

References to the familiar also bring a sense of immediacy to speeches. In the following example, Kristen Pidduck begins her speech of introduction by talking about a situation with which many students can identify, especially students in a

References to the familiar
Using an example that is easily related to by the audience

public speaking course. She also engages in self-disclosure, another immediacy technique:

> I would make a bet that at some point or another almost every person in this class has suffered from a case of the shakes. Maybe it happened in a situation such as this one, where you had to stand up and give a talk. Or maybe it was because your blood sugar level was low, or you had not eaten in a while. Maybe you were very tired. I would also bet that, at that time, you became very aware of yourself, your actions, and your fine motor skills. Think of how you felt in those moments. Were you upset because you couldn't pour milk properly? Or you couldn't focus on the words in a book because your hand was shaking? Maybe you had trouble signing your name or writing an essay. Now imagine going through your whole life in this way. You would be surprised by the number of people who do. I do. My name is Kristen Pidduck, and the cup of tea that I am holding represents all of the things that I cannot drink or eat because of my shaking disorder.[10]

By beginning with a reference to shared experiences, Kristen encourages the audience to fit the information into an existing perceptual framework.

A final example of an immediacy strategy entails *asking questions of the audience*. In this way, you bring the audience into your speech. Sometimes speakers ask for an actual show of hands or a verbal response from their audience. At other times, the questions are rhetorical in nature. By *rhetorical*, I mean that the speaker does not expect the audience to respond in any visible or audible way to the question. Well-phrased rhetorical questions, such as the following, stimulate the audience to think about—but not to verbalize—the response: "Did you have problems finding affordable housing this semester? Are you eating Kraft dinner and tuna delight because your rent is too high? Has a landlord ever refused to return a $100 damage deposit that he wasn't supposed to collect from you in the first place?" When listeners respond to the questions, they become active participants in the speech event.

Several criteria apply to the use of rhetorical questions. Rhetorical questions should be acceptable to the audience. They should also be realistic. Audience members tune out the speaker who asks an unrealistic question such as, "How many of you would like to earn a million dollars on your spring break?" Finally, the questions should be sufficiently simple that the audience members can respond without conducting complex mathematical exercises in their heads. They could probably respond fairly easily, for example, to the question "How much did you spend last year on DVDs?" But if you asked how much they spent last year on recreation, you would lose them. First, they would have to figure out what you meant by *recreation*. Then they would have to think about the cost of each item. Finally, they would have to multiply the figures. When speakers ask questions, they should pause long enough for the audience to consider the answer. In the latter case, for all practical purposes, the speaker might as well sit down after asking the question because the calculations would consume the class period. Of course, that does not happen. What does happen is that audience members lose interest when they are asked complicated questions.

Additional criteria apply when you expect a show of hands or other visible response to your questions. Ask questions that do not call for embarrassing or incriminating responses. Do not ask, for example, how many students have failed to report their summer income, cheated on an examination, used ecstasy, or engaged in sex without using a condom.

Rhetorical question
Question to which a speaker does not expect an answer, posed to provoke interest in the audience

Sometimes speakers overrely on rhetorical questions as an attention-getting strategy in the introduction to speeches. They ask questions when they have not devoted sufficient time to preparation or cannot think of a more interesting or creative way to begin their speeches. One study found that one-third of amateur writers begin their essays with rhetorical questions, whereas *no* professional writers open an essay in this way. If they employ them, they use them later in their essays.[11] Questions should be combined with vivid and concrete description or some other attention-getting strategy. Evaluation of speeches should consider the extent to which the speaker has integrated questions into the fabric of the speech and used them in combination with other strategies. I have heard many boring speeches that included all of the technical elements but lacked luster and interest.

REFERENCES TO THE NOVEL

Whereas reference to the familiar *gains* our attention, reference to the unfamiliar *holds* our attention. When speakers fail to make the transition from known to unknown, they lose their audiences. The following example illustrates the offering of novel information to an audience:

> Many of you have heard the term *obsessive compulsive disorder*. In shorthand, the term is *OCD*. I would like to introduce you to some little known facts about this potentially crippling psychological disorder. People with OCD may spend hours fighting the need to clean everything around them. They cringe at the thought that they might touch a doorknob or sink that is inhabited by unseen microbes. They don't check doors once each night. They check them three or four times. Other people with OCD collect useless items—old clothing, magazines, newspapers, and pots and pans. They spend hours going through garbage cans, and they find it almost impossible to sort and give away anything. Some people with OCD are excessively slow in completing tasks because they want to ensure that everything is perfect. I am a "cleaner" and a "repeater"; and I struggle daily to overcome these compulsions. They do not define me, but they have a huge impact on my life.

Perception studies tell us that intensity and contrast, in particular, draw our attention. We tend to notice extremely large and extremely small objects, as well as those that are different or unusual.

SUSPENSE AND SHOCK TECHNIQUES

The producers of reality shows have mastered the art of building and maintaining suspense. They continually add new twists or change the rules and dynamics of the game. To add conflict and uncertainty to *Survivor* and *The Apprentice*, the producers switch people to different teams. They bring unexpected guests to the house of *The Bachelor*, and they ask unsuspecting contestants to take lie detector tests on *Who Will Marry My Dad?* On *For Love or Money*, they change the value of the checks held by contestants. *Big Brother 5* added what they call a "DNA factor" to the show. Hostess Julie Chen explains the meaning of *DNA* in this way: "This year's theme is *Do Not Assume. Project DNA* for short. Nothing is as it seems. Everything is open to interpretation." (See the Question of Ethics box.)

References to the novel
Using an example that is unexpected, to gain or hold attention

Suspense and shock techniques
Using examples that are deliberately mysterious or even disturbing, to gain or hold the interest of the audience

A Question of Ethics

Many of the reality shows use shock techniques to capture audience attention. On *Survivor*, the producers replayed an event in which a woman claimed that she was sexually harassed by one of the participants, who was naked at the time. A participant on *Who Will Marry My Dad?* was shown abandoned at a church in full wedding garb. Subsequently, she learned that the daughters of the prospective groom had chosen her for elimination from the show. After dividing the contestants from *American Idol* into two groups, the producers asked the popular Taylor Hicks to stand with the group that he considered to be the winning team. The programs that feature wife and husband swapping often include highly derogatory comments about participants, retained for their entertainment value. The producers of *My Big Fat Obnoxious Boss* (a spoof on "The Apprentice") deceived the participants into thinking that they were participating in a real competition. In fact, their "boss" was an actor who asked them to panhandle on the streets of Chicago, lie to people, sleep on pillows stuffed with dollar bills, and eat Spam. (They were told the Spam was an expensive cuisine.) In short, many reality shows are characterized by their focus on sensational and shocking moments, as well as deceit.

Sometimes speakers also use shock techniques. They write a shocking word on a blackboard, show a disturbing photograph, or select a topic for its shock value. A speaker may show photographs of animals abused in cosmetic testing or graphic images of accident victims. Sometimes they use language that is politically incorrect in an effort to demonstrate the problem of racism or sexism. Some speakers also use the same kind of attention-getting devices for humorous effect. They argue that, if they are members of the disadvantaged group, they have the right to call themselves whatever they please.

Should motive be taken into account in judging the ethics of the technique? If the speaker uses one of these shock strategies to shake listeners from an apathetic posture, is he or she justified in using the strategy? How do you feel about the use of shock techniques of this nature? What criteria determine whether a shock technique is ethical? Does the end purpose (awareness versus humorous effect) make a difference in judging the ethics? Should members of the same racial or gender group be able to poke fun at themselves?

The public speaker works within a much more constrained time bracket than producers of reality shows do. When speakers use suspense techniques, they engage audience members by arousing their curiosity or provoking them to question the meaning of a statement. Sometimes the speaker mentions some point to be addressed later in the speech, information to be provided, or questions to be answered. If the information or questions hold interest for audience members, they will listen to get answers to the questions. Speakers also use shock techniques to grab our attention, as in the following example:

> In 1850, you could purchase a slave in the United States for approximately $1000. In 2005, you can purchase a young girl in Amsterdam and Bangkok for $600. You can purchase an adult slave on the Ivory Coast of Africa for $40. There are more slaves in the early years of this century than in any other period in the history of civilization.[12]

LINGUISTIC STRATEGIES

In the next instance, the speaker relies on highly *evocative and sensory laden language* to gain the attention of her audience. By accessing multiple channels of perception (sight, sound, touch, feel, taste, and smell), she increases the chances that audiences will note and absorb the information.

> Imagine! It's June. You're on vacation with family and friends. After living off Ramen noodles for months, you have saved enough money to reach your destination. Clear blue skies above. You face great iron gates that welcome you to an enchanted castle. You smell cotton candy and hot dogs. Every color in the rainbow surrounds you in the form of brilliant costumes. You see adventurous rides that go faster than the speed of light. You hear captivating music and children squealing with excitement. You can almost taste and feel the sticky sweetness of a candied apple. Life can't get better. As you take everything in, you notice something out of the corner of your eye. Suddenly you are overcome with nervousness. All those years of anticipation have finally led to this moment. You try to catch your breath, but you have lost the ability to speak. Your palms are sweating, your knees are shaking, and you are face to face with your dream. You are finally meeting Mickey Mouse.[13]

Linguistic strategies
using highly descriptive and sensual language or quotations to gain the attention of the audience

Quotations are commonly used to get attention in the introductions and conclusions of speeches. Lines from poets such as Maya Angelou and songwriters such as Paul McCartney and John Lennon have appeared in many inspirational speeches over the years. A popular quotation by Mark Twain has been making the rounds of the Internet in recent years: "Dance like nobody's watching; love like you've never been hurt. Sing like nobody's listening; live like it's heaven on earth." In using quotations, you should always cite the source: Seemingly ageless baseball player Satchel Paige once wryly observed, "Age is a case of mind over matter. If you don't mind, it don't matter." Motivational speakers rely heavily on quotations to inspire audiences.

The pithy quotation usually works best, but you should explain the quotation in an interesting way or tie it to other attention-getting strategies. The audience needs time to orient to the speaker. A longer introduction gives this opportunity. In conclusions, however, quotations can more readily stand on their own as attention-getting strategies. Other linguistic strategies are described in Chapter 10.

ACTIVITY, DRAMA, AND CONFLICT

Americans love competitive sports such as football, baseball, and wrestling. Millions buy lottery tickets every week. References to activity, drama, and conflict capture audience attention. In political races, the media quickly narrow the race to a manageable number of contenders (two or three) that they can follow and depict as winners or losers. They talk about the frontrunners and the laggards. They build drama as the race progresses.[14] Audiences like plots that develop quickly. The reality shows must eliminate someone each week in order for the audience to maintain

its interest. In the same way, speakers hold the interest of audiences by adding conflict and drama to their speeches and maintaining a relatively fast pace in developing story lines. The following example illustrates this point:

> What is it like to be poor in America? On a recent bus trip from Chicago to Houston, I got at least a partial answer to that question from a nineteen-year-old named Dolores Rodriguez. Over the course of the twenty-four-hour ride, Dolores told me about her life—a story that introduced me to the realities of being poor in one of the nation's largest cities. She explained that she was traveling to Houston to explore the possibilities of getting work in that city. Her husband Alonso remained at home with their two children. In south side Chicago, she lived in a neighborhood where the average income was under $20,000 a year. Worse, the neighborhood was controlled by two warring gangs, the Latin Kings and the Vice Lords. Because Dolores and Alonso had refused to join either of the gangs, they were under constant threat by both. Whenever they left their apartment, they exited by the back door to avoid contact with gang members who hung around the front of their building. When they traveled in a car, her husband wore a large sombrero to hide his age. Dolores never took her little girl to the park near her apartment, and she feared every step of her two-block walk to the grocery store. She spent most of her days at home watching TV, unable to go out of the apartment. She told me that she was looking forward to the building of a new Wal-Mart in Englewood because the store would have a number of security guards. Sadly, the situation of Dolores and Alonso is not unusual. Between January and May 2004, the Chicago Police Department recorded almost 15,000 incidences of violent crime in their city. Multiply Chicago by all of the other urban environments in the United States, and you will obtain some sense of the scope of the problem. Also realize that these are the *reported* crimes. Large numbers of crimes go unreported, especially where victims fear retribution from their attackers.

A study by the National Council of the Teachers of English found that 60 percent of professional writers begin their essays with narratives. By way of contrast, only 10 percent of student amateurs use this strategy to begin their essays.[15]

HUMOR

Many speakers employ humor as a means of warming up the audience, in the same way that comedians warm up studio audiences prior to the taping of television shows. The use of humor in speeches can, however, be risky. Not everyone shares the same sense of what is funny; and used inappropriately, humor can be highly offensive. Some standard rules apply to its use. First, always avoid racist or sexist humor. Even self-deprecating humor carries limits. Second, the joke should be fresh enough to capture the interest of the audience. Third, the joke or humorous experience should be relevant to the topic of the speech and to the audience.

Not everyone is comfortable using humor that employs a punch line. Many people stumble on the punch line or fail to time its delivery properly. Sometimes they confuse the telling of the joke. Traditionally, women have been less comfortable than men with stock jokes, especially in mixed gender situations.[16] Women often prefer to recount an experience with humorous content rather than tell a joke with a punch line.

To resonate with audiences, humor must be based on real experience. Many older audiences could identify with the humor of comedian George Burns because they had experienced situations similar to the ones that became the brunt of his jokes. On one occasion, for example, Burns quipped: "You know you're getting old when you bend over to tie your shoe and think, 'What else can I do while I'm down here?'" For more information on the use of humor in speeches, see Chapters Twelve and Fourteen.

GIMMICKS

Sometimes speakers use gimmicks such as tearing up dollar bills or bringing live animals to class to capture the attention of their audiences. Gimmicks, however, are always extremely risky; and live animals draw attention away from the speaker.

Step 4: Developing the Body of the Speech

You have decided upon a topic and purpose for the speech, developed an outline of major points that you want to cover, and written an introduction with attention-getting, thesis, and preview statements. The next step is to develop each of the points in your outline, using concrete and interesting language. A speech of introduction or personal experience will not employ supporting materials such as statistics and expert testimony. The speech will, however, depend on such supports as *personal experiences*, *examples*, *stories*, *quotations*, and *humor*. Later chapters will go into depth on the use of these support materials.

Step 5: Connecting Your Thoughts

Transitions, *signposts*, and *internal summaries* ensure that the speech moves easily from one idea to the next. They tie the speech together into a coherent whole.

TRANSITIONS

Transitions
Verbal cues that alert an audience to a shift in the speech

Transitions act as connectors of thoughts, establishing the relationship between different paragraphs or major points in a speech. Examples of transitions are *in addition to*, *also*, *moreover*, *however*, *next*, *so much for*, and *now*. Transitions also can include longer phrases such as: "The next point that we will discuss . . ."; "So much for . . . now we will turn to . . ."; "Now that we have explored the nature of the problem, we will look at solutions."; "This is one part of the problem, the second part is . . ."; and "We have spent a lot of time talking about the problem, it's time to discuss the solution." Sometimes transitions serve the secondary function of placing emphasis on certain points: "Above all else, you need to understand . . ." (See the Keep in Mind box for additional examples of common transitions.)

Keep in Mind

Common Transitions

Comparison likewise, in the same way, in relationship to, in comparison with, similarly, in a similar fashion, once more, like, analogous to, just as, in a like manner, comparable to, mimicking, typical of, duplicating, akin to, not unlike

Contrast nevertheless, on the contrary, on the one hand . . . on the other hand, but, rather, instead, still, yet, however, despite, by way of contrast, nonetheless, although, even so, notwithstanding, regardless, in spite of, even though

Time before, after, in the meantime, during, as soon as, next, at last, first, then, immediately, subsequently, currently, at the same time, usually, to begin with, eventually, meanwhile, recently, once, simultaneously, finally

Emphasis most important, above all, in fact, surely, the most striking, indeed, truly, certainly, furthermore, most assuredly, without doubt, most critical, most substantial, in truth, beyond doubt, unquestionably, notably, of course

Location near, above, beyond, adjacent to, beneath, in front of, behind, to the left, to the right, opposite, between, below, alongside, away from, bringing up the rear, elsewhere, further from, the far side of, beyond, atop, parallel to

Addition moreover, in addition to, once again, also, not only . . . but also, as well as, besides, another, equally important, along with, additionally, together with, also, so too, another significant, also under consideration, aggravating

Clarification for example, for instance, specifically, to illustrate, namely, in particular, such as, stated differently, simply stated, in other words, to demonstrate, the following example, put another way, exemplifying, to clarify, because

Conclusion as a result, thus, consequently, hence, accordingly, as noted, in my view, in conclusion, in short, briefly, as mentioned earlier, in closing, in summary, in the final analysis, to conclude, therefore, on the whole, all things considered

Concession although, granted that, I admit that, naturally, admittedly, certainly, even though, while it may be true, failing that, the worst case scenario, at any rate, at least, it may appear that, all kidding aside, given that, without doubt

SIGNPOSTS

Like bookmarks, *signposts* position the listener in the speech. Typically, they relate back to the statement of structural progression (preview or orientation statement that appears in the introduction to the speech). As in the following example, they alert the listener to major divisions or headings in the speech: "The first life-altering event in my life was . . . The second life-altering event was . . . The third life-altering circumstance happened when . . ." An alternative way of signposting is to ask questions as you enter each new area of discussion. For example, a speaker may introduce the problem section of a persuasive speech by asking, "What is the problem?" Once he reaches the solution part of the speech, he asks, "What can the company do about the problem?" He concludes by asking, "What can *you* do about the problem?" Like transitions, signposts also act as connectors.

> **Signposts**
> Devices that remind the audience of the structure of the speech

INTERNAL SUMMARIES

Internal summaries
Brief recaps within the body of the speech, keeping the audience focused

Internal summaries also help to ensure the continuity of a speech. Especially important to longer speeches, they remind the audience of the logical progression of the speech. The following example illustrates this point: "In short, understanding figure skating entails learning a whole new vocabulary. Once you understand that vocabulary, you can gain entry to the world of figure skate judging. As I have explained, however, that experience can be a disillusioning one for many novice skaters and their parents." Notice that the internal summary, in this instance, is brief. A two- to three-minute speech of introduction may not require an internal summary. The brevity and simplicity of the speech eliminate the need.

Step 6: Closing with a Memorable Thought

Conclusions should leave audiences with a memorable thought. In a speech of introduction, the speaker can use a quotation, poem, or anecdote that relates closely to the main point of the speech. Alternatively, the speaker can incorporate a moment of humor in a light-hearted speech. In the following example from a student speech, the young woman talked about her addiction to coffee. She concluded her speech with the following statement:

> Although I may not be as dark, mysterious, or Italian as my favourite coffee, I'd say that we have more than a few characteristics in common. I like it, need it, and am

often wearing it some degree or another. I guess that some would say I am addicted, but I like to say I've made a life choice. Cappuccino, latte, et moi! Partners for life![17]

Just take the plunge!

Sometimes speakers tie the speech into a neat package by linking their conclusion to the opening thought of the speech. In the introduction to a student speech titled "Bungee Jumping," Mary Kathryn Roberts talked about the importance of facing your fears:

> Everyone has his or her own ideas about the meaning of fear. For some of you, fear may be coming in front of a group and speaking, as I am doing now. For me, fear presented itself in September 2003 in the form of Velcro, awkward harnesses, and a really big rubber band! Last summer I faced my fear. After much trembling, sweating, and giggling, I finally leapt, screamed, and then glowed in the realization that I had done it. I had bungee jumped!

In the conclusion of the speech, the speaker returned to this initial idea:

> And I believe that is what life is about: facing your fears, crossing the boundaries that you place upon yourselves. Sure, I may never go bungee jumping again, and I still get shaky atop a ladder. But I can say that I did it. And I will always have this tape of my sloppy, awkward leap to remind me to *just jump*. There is never any regret in taking a safe risk. Just jump.[18]

The conclusions to longer speeches often include summaries of major points, as in the following example:

> In the introduction to this speech, I told you that I had made three influential decisions during the course of skating career. My first decision was to move to Lake Placid to skate when I was only fifteen years old. That decision led to my studying under a coach of Olympic fame. The second major decision was to change from singles to pairs skating. I met my partner for life when I made that decision. My third decision, which still causes me grief, was to give up my Olympic dreams and turn professional at the age of twenty. American businessman and author Joe Karbo once said, "The only things I regret . . . are the things I didn't do." Never give up your dreams!

Like introductions, conclusions conform to set rules. They should not be too lengthy. They should not introduce new material. They *should* provide closure. In an eight- to ten-minute speech, the latter conclusion is an appropriate length. The conclusion to a five-minute speech should be half that length. The conclusion to a two- to three-minute speech of introduction should be no more than several sentences. When you put together the introduction and conclusion to a speech, they rarely will consume more than 20 percent of your speaking time. A final point about conclusions concerns the tendency of novice speakers to apologize or thank their audiences for listening. They may make statements such as "I hope that I haven't taken up too much of your time," "I will stop boring you now," or "That's it!" As a speaker, you offer something to the audience. Listeners should thank you rather than the reverse.

The Sample Speech on pg. 112 illustrates the most common elements in a speech of introduction: an effective attention-getting step, thesis statement, preview statement, signposts, and conclusion. In this speech, the signposts also serve as transitions between different parts of the speech.

Sample Speech

Passages

Attention-Getting Step

I squeezed my mother's hand as tight as I could. The cool metal from the gun pressed against my ear. A woman wearing all white was holding the gun. In a calm and soothing voice, she said to me, "I am going to count to three and then shoot. Ready? 1 . . . 2 . . . 3 . . . BANG!" I let out a loud shriek. Then I glanced at the mirror in front of me. That was when I saw the piercing through my right ear. These are the earrings from that day. [*Show earrings*.]

Thesis Statement (underlined)

My name is Alyssa Jacobs. I am twenty one years old, and I have eighteen unnecessary holes in my body. <u>My parents would never have fathomed that, after this first encounter with the piercing gun, I would go through a series of stages of piercing various parts of my body, each with symbolic significance.</u>

Preview Statement (to orient audience to organization of speech)

Three acts of piercing, in particular, stand out as marking transition stages in my maturation and in my relationship with my parents: my first earrings, the piercing of my belly button, and my tongue piercing.

Signpost to First Major Point (underlined)

<u>When I had my first piercing</u>, I was only eight years old. But after having my ears pierced, I felt really grown up. My parents' supportive attitudes helped me to feel that I had entered a new and more mature stage in my life. In my mind, I had moved from childhood into preadolescence.

Signpost to Second Major Point (underlined)

<u>The next piercing</u>, which marked my transition to adolescence, occurred when I was thirteen. This was my belly button period. The man who did the piercing took me into a small room, which was probably a converted closet. If the two of us had wanted to stand up at the same time, it would not have been possible. Afraid of sharing my decision with my parents, I hid the piercing for months. This is the ring from my belly button piercing. [*Show ring*.]

By the time I went to the doctor for my yearly checkup, months later, the piercing was severely infected. As the doctor was examining it, my mother walked into the room and saw it for the first time. She flipped out and ran out of the office. She wouldn't talk to me for weeks.

That night, when my father came home, my mother was still crying and screaming. My father thought that the whole family had died in a common tragedy. My parents eventually got over their upset, but to this day they can't look at that ring without cringing. My parents' reaction underscored the fact that I had entered my teenage years, and we were negotiating a new relationship.

Signpost to Third Major Point (underlined)

<u>The third piercing came</u> when I was eighteen. The piercing of my tongue marked my transition from adolescence to adulthood. [*Show piercing*.] I had just graduated from high school and was about to start CEGEP. My parent's reaction was calm, considering that I had just put a hole in my tongue. All they said was, "You've lost your mind." They had finally accepted that I was grown up and they couldn't stop me from doing what I wished.

I have since taken out my tongue ring, an action that pleases my parents greatly, even though they won't admit it. I have grown out of my "tongue piercing phase," but I am not quite yet finished with putting holes in my body. My last piercing occurred when I was twenty.

Conclusion

Body piercing has been practiced for centuries in many different cultures. Some believe that the practice originated as much as five thousand years ago. Body piercing is one of the oldest forms of body modification; yet the reasons for piercing the body are as diverse as the cultures from which they come.

In my case, the piercing of each new part of my body came at a time when I was undergoing a transition—from childhood to preadolescence, from preadolescence to adolescence, from adolescence to adulthood. And each piercing drew a unique reaction from my parents that reinforced the transition that I was undergoing. Eventually I will take out all of the piercing; however, the impressions created in my memories will never disappear.

Alyssa Jacobs

Step 7: Practicing and Delivering the Speech

The term *extemporaneous speaking* refers to a situation where a speaker prepares and practices a speech but limits memorization to the introduction and conclusion of the speech.

Extemporaneous speaking
Speaking without having memorized the entire speech

USING NOTE CARDS

Typically, the person speaks from 3″ × 5″ or 4″ × 6″ index cards that contain key words. Sometimes, however, these note cards also include quotations and key passages that the speaker wants to say word for word. Since only the speaker sees the

note cards, he can put anything that he wants on the cards. When a speaker chooses to place the entire speech on the cards, however, he runs the risk of being tempted to read the speech. Many students have told me that, no matter how hard they try, they cannot get away from reading speeches that appear in their entirety on note cards. Also, it is hard to see the major points on a card if the format is full text. If you lose your place, it is harder to locate it. For that reason, the best advice is to limit the information on note cards to a few quoted phrases and key points. When you speak from key points, you can add ideas to your note cards at the last minute. You may decide, for example, to add a reference to someone in the audience, another person's speech, or some unexpected news. These references add a sense of immediacy to your speech and encourage the audience to feel that you are speaking spontaneously and sincerely.

Depending on the length of the speech, two to five cards usually are sufficient. Follow your outline format. Do not include too many words on a single note card and put the key words in a sufficiently large font or handwriting. Some people use color codes or highlight points that they want to emphasize or have trouble remembering. You should be able to grasp the ideas quickly when you look at the note cards. Printing in all capital letters is harder to read than a mix of lower- and upper-case letters. Numbering the cards ensures that you can find your place if you drop them, as sometimes happens. (See Figures 4.6 and 4.7)

PRACTICING AND TIMING THE SPEECH

Practice the speech in front of a mirror or do a trial run with your roommate, but do not try to repeat the same words each time that you deliver it. Slight variations

---

Sample Note Card

Julie Huot   1/2

Do you know someone with an invisible disability? I do. We all do. According to statistics, at least three of us in this class have an invisible disability. What do I mean? Let's start with a few facts.

U.S. Department of Health and Human Services—over 2.9 million school-age children or 15% of the population

Total numbers of students attending our university—30,000

Total number of students in Faculty of Arts—3,000

How many cope with the challenges of an invisible disability? Close to 1 in 6 Americans

Potentially 5,000 students affected on our campus

Translates into 450 students in Faculty of Arts

35% of students identified with a learning disability drop out of high school—2× the rate of nondisabled peers

Figure 4.6

in wording give the impression that you are "in the moment." Typically, speakers memorize only the introduction and conclusion to speeches. Do not read from note cards; instead glance at the cards from time to time as a reminder of the next thought sequence. Maintaining consistent eye contact is critical to a good delivery. Hold the cards in one hand and do not play with them while delivering your speech. When you move from one card to the next, look at your audience so that their attention is on you, not the note cards. Never substitute pieces of paper for note cards. The rustling of large pieces of paper distracts the listener, and small scraps of paper look unprofessional.

Studies have found a positive relationship between the quality of a presentation and the amount of time spent preparing, processing, and practicing the speech (silently and aloud).[19] For this reason, extemporaneous speaking is the preferred form of delivery in most situations. An extemporaneous delivery ensures a well-rehearsed speech, but you retain the impression of spontaneity when you do not memorize it. When practicing your speech, time it. You show little respect for your classmates when you go over the time limit, since the extra time can only come from their allotment. The speeches of novice speakers *almost always* extend longer than they plan. The reverse is rarely the case.

USING VISUAL AIDS

Some studies suggest a correspondence between time spent in preparing a visual aid and the overall quality of the speech, including content and delivery.[20] Several cautions apply, however, to the use of visual aids. When showing a three-dimensional object, be sure that audience members can see the object from their

---

Sample Note Card

Huot   2/2

Three Key Points:

(1) Learning disabilities are often unrecognized and invisible to people not directly affected by it.

(2) Students with learning disabilities attending university can succeed with minimum accommodations.

(3) To ensure equal access to higher education, society must assign resources to provide for people with learning disabilities.

Definitions:

Learning disabilities—"unusual difficulties with spelling, writing, math, concentration, and memory"

Accommodations—what people with learning disabilities need from the outside world in order to be successful

For example: extra time on an exam, quiet room, access to a computer.

Figure 4.7

seats. When objects are too small, too large, too awkward, or inappropriate to bring to class, you should construct a model or display a photograph of the object. You can enlarge the photograph at a print shop, for example, and mount it on a poster board. Alternatively, you can use an overhead projector, slide projector, or the computer to display the photograph. (See the Reflections box.)

Do not circulate objects or photographs among the audience when you are speaking. When you are ready to talk about the object, place it between yourself and the audience. Sometimes speakers place objects at selected points in the room, sufficiently close for the audience to see without straining. At other times, they wait until the conclusion of the speech to display the object at close range or to pass it around the room. Sometimes they place photocopies, face down, at individual seats and ask that the audience not look at the material until requested. When you have finished using a visual aid, cover or remove it from the view of the audience. Additional material on the use of visual aids appears in Chapter Seven.

Reflections

Speakers Beware!

Be careful when you use live visual aids! I can remember one speaker who brought a young, two-foot alligator as a prop. Although it was muzzled, all attention was on the alligator for the five minutes she was speaking; and as a result, nobody really heard her speech. That's visual overkill.

John Busby

Conclusion

In this chapter, I have considered seven steps to be taken in preparing and practicing a speech of introduction. Those steps include *getting started* by choosing a theme, articulating the purpose of the speech, and writing a thesis statement; *getting organized* by identifying and ordering the main ideas and writing a preview statement; *writing an introduction*; *developing the main body of the speech*; *using connectives* to link ideas and *internal summaries* to orient listeners; *concluding with a memorable thought*; and *practicing the speech*, using an extemporaneous mode of delivery.

Questions for Discussion

1. Identify three objects that represent some aspect of your experiences, personality, or values. Explain why you selected these objects. What do they say about you? Why are they important? How could you use them to communicate your personality in a speech of introduction?

2. Think about some of your classes at the university. Without identifying specific professors, talk about what gets your attention in lectures. What about in other public speaking situations?

3. Identify some celebrity or politician who is good at making audiences feel a sense of immediacy or psychological closeness. Which characteristics of the person's speaking style encourage this reaction?

4. What kind of humor appeals to you? What kind of humor do you find offensive?

Outline

RESEARCHING, ANALYZING, AND ADAPTING TO YOUR AUDIENCE

The Speech of Welcome

Learning Objectives

- · To learn about researching and analyzing your audience
- · To learn about researching and analyzing the speaking environment
- · To learn strategies for adapting your speech to your audience and the occasion
- · To understand the importance of taking ethical considerations into account

Oprah Winfrey is, without doubt, the diva of television talk shows. Her success as a daytime talk show host has brought her enormous wealth and popularity. In October 2002, *Fortune* ranked Oprah number ten among the world's most powerful women in business. In 2004, she occupied the number three spot on Forbes' top celebrity list. While Oprah's down-to-earth personality, sense of humor, optimistic approach to life, and altruism play a critical role in her appeal to audiences, her success is based on more than just personality. Oprah is a virtuoso in the art of *audience adaptation*—a term that refers to the practice of taking the values and beliefs, interests, needs, and knowledge levels of an audience into account in the process of communicating with a group.

Public speaking is an *audience-centered*—not a speaker-centered—activity. Therefore, definitions of success depend to a significant degree on answering questions such as the following: Did I meet audience member expectations and fulfill their needs? Did I make a contribution to their levels of awareness, offering additional knowledge and information? Did I influence their attitudes or behaviors? In other words, did I have an impact? Did my speech make a difference? Too often, novice speakers think almost exclusively in terms of performance: Was my delivery without glitches? Did I maintain my composure? Did I use the right number of hand movements? Did I fidget? The fact is, however, that audience members are willing to overlook presentation flaws if they think that the speaker has recognized and attempted to meet their needs. Understanding the composition and values of your audience is the key to meeting their needs. Thus, this chapter considers how to research, analyze, and adapt to your audience, taking ethical considerations into account. The chapter also considers the need to take situational variables into account.

Audience adaptation

Using what one knows about one's audience to communicate more effectively with them

Audience-centered

Focused on the audience and their needs

Researching and Analyzing Your Audience

In an early communication model, Wilbur Schramm said that our success as communicators depends, to a great extent, on the degree to which our fields of experience overlap with those of our audience.[1] By *field of experience*, Schramm refers to the totality of what we are at the moment of communication. Since we constantly learn from new experiences, we are never the same at any two moments in time. In accordance with Schramm's model, the most effective communication occurs

Fields of experience

What we are—our values, interests, life experiences—at the moment we are communicating

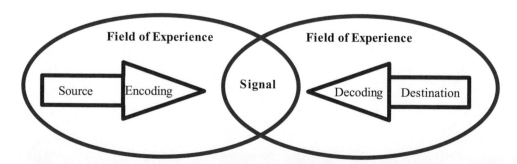

Figure 5.1 Wilbur Schramm's Field of Experience Model

among people who share the same background, language and culture, beliefs, attitudes, and values. That is, we can communicate with others to the extent that we have overlapping fields of experience.

Audience research requires the collection of the following four kinds of information: *demographic*, *psychographic*, *personality*, and *situational*. This information can come from many different sources. You can contact representatives of host organizations. You can conduct research on the Internet (web pages and references to the organization), request the annual report or publications that describe the operations of the organization, or schedule interviews with members of the group. Some organizations maintain profiles of employees, which they will share with speakers or training directors. Speakers often engage in conversation with audience members at the speaking event in order to learn more about their interests and priorities. Even last-minute information can often be worked into a speech. For more information on researching the audience and occasion, see Chapter Eight.

Audience research
Various methods of learning about one's audience

CREATING A DEMOGRAPHIC PROFILE

As a speaker, the first stage in researching your audience is to construct a *demographic profile* of the audience, taking factors such as age, sex, gender, marital and parental status, race, ethnicity, culture, income, education, and occupation into account. If you are speaking on education reform, for example, you should ask whether you will have school board members, teachers, or students—or a combination of the three groups—in your audience (*occupation*). If you choose to speak against the violent content of some popular song lyrics, you should learn whether your audience will be over forty or under twenty (*age*) and predominantly men or

Demographic profile
A picture of an audience that takes age, gender, ethnicity, income, education, etc., into account

women (*gender*). A successful speech to inform the audience about black holes in space requires knowing whether the majority of your audience members are astrophysicists, students in an undergraduate astronomy class, or science fiction writers (*education* and *expertise*). Deciding to speak on the rising costs of college tuition to a group of university students requires that you understand their economic situation, such as level of access to bursaries and employment (*income*). A speech on police brutality or ethnic profiling requires that the speaker be sensitive to demographic variables such as *race* and *ethnicity*. *Cultural* considerations are always important, as the United States is an increasingly diverse and multicultural society.

The *Oprah* show offers a model for studying the fundamental principles of audience adaptation. Like any good speaker, the producers of *Oprah* understand the demographics of their audience. As a result, they are able to identify topics and guests of interest to this audience. Based on the subject matter of *Oprah*, we should not be surprised that most viewers are women between the ages of eighteen and fifty-four.[2] Oprah explicitly acknowledges the "stay-at-home" status of many viewers when she makes comments such as, "Now put down your laundry and pay attention" or "Give your children some crayons and listen to what Dr. Phil has to say." Many of the themes for the talk show appeal to women in their early and middle adulthood, trying to identify what they want from life or seeking to revitalize their marriages. A common theme is the importance of taking time away from the children to reflect on one's priorities and engage in activities that result in self-actualization. Other popular themes include weight loss, fitness, and makeovers.

A smaller number of the discussion topics are aimed at older women who confront the "empty nest" syndrome or face a crisis in their marriage or lives—serious illness, loss of a family member or valued friend, employment difficulties, or other catalytic events that cause the person to reevaluate priorities and make lifestyle adjustments. Although men frequently appear on the show, almost invariably they accompany women, offering support for their wives or partners and explaining

their relationship problems from the male perspective. One often suspects that the motivation for appearing on the show has originated with the female partner. Oprah also demonstrates an awareness of the female demographics of her television audience when she selects guests to appear on the show. Women appear more often than men as guests on her show.

The level of language and the topics discussed on the show suggest that most viewers would have at least a high school education. A large number would be college or university graduates. The *Oprah* producers recognize this demographic when they invite psychologists, educators, social workers, and other professionals to appear on the show. Many of the celebrity guests reflect the cultural diversity of North American society. Not infrequently, Oprah's guests include individuals with mixed ethnic or cultural heritages, reflecting the melting pot nature of American society. When Oprah acknowledges acts of altruism by her viewing audience, she honors representatives of many different demographic groups, taking factors such as gender, ethnicity, occupation, education, and income into account.

In short, it is obvious that both Oprah and the producers of her show appear to be keenly aware of demographics when they plan the content of their programs. For that reason, her show offers an excellent example of audience research, analysis, and adaptation to these groups. Any successful speaker takes similar measures in preparing for the public speaking occasion.

CREATING A PSYCHOGRAPHIC PROFILE

The term *psychographic* refers to psychological factors such as beliefs, attitudes, and values. Audience adaptation requires knowledge of these psychological variables, as well as an awareness of the strength with which audience members hold their convictions.

Psychographic profile
A picture of the audience that takes their beliefs, attitudes and values into account

Beliefs

A *belief* is faith in the credibility of some concept or idea. We may believe, for example, that taxes are too high, drinking is a problem on college campuses, and crime is on the rise. The average person has hundreds of thousands of beliefs about people, politics, health, relationships, and countless other topics. We may believe that private schools are better than public schools, immigration policies are unfair, or California is the best state in which to live. We may believe that purple is the most aristocratic color, brunettes are more attractive than blondes, or cats carry more diseases than dogs. Our beliefs may be valid or invalid, supported or unsupported by evidence. A belief does not have to be true for us to accept it. (See the Reflections box on page 124.)

Beliefs
Faith in an idea or set of ideas.

Attitudes

Clustered together, beliefs constitute attitude sets. An *attitude* is a predisposition to respond in a given way to objects, situations, or people—in other words, to display our likes and dislikes. If we believe, for example, that crime is on the rise, that our children are vulnerable to being kidnapped or molested, and that the government

Attitudes
Settled ways of thinking about people, ideas, objects, or situations

Reflections

I Believe . . .

"I believe that computers are the most incredible tool we can use to feed our curiosity and inventiveness."

Bill Gates, chairman of Microsoft,
September 19, 2005

"I believe in a broad definition of what art is and who artists are: Barbers, cooks, auto detailers, janitors and gardeners have as much right to claims of artistry as designers, architects, painters and sculptors."

Frank X. Walker, poet, March 27, 2006

"I believe in the connection between strangers when they reach out to one another."

Miles Goodwin, real estate agent
and Vietnam veteran, Milwaukee,
May 1, 2006

"I believe it is possible for ordinary people to achieve extraordinary things."

Jody Williams, founding
coordinator of the International
Campaign to Ban Landmines,
January 9, 2006

is not spending enough on crime prevention, we may hold negative attitudes toward the government in power. If we believe that marijuana alleviates pain and that terminal cancer patients should be able to select their drugs of choice, we may have a positive attitude toward legalization of marijuana for palliative purposes. In other words, a set of related beliefs leads to attitudes (our likes and dislikes), which in turn influence our actions.

Beliefs and attitudes vary greatly across audiences. If a speaker suspects that some beliefs held by an audience are erroneous or ill-founded, she may need to address those misperceptions to accomplish her speech purposes. Also, she may need to consider audience attitudes toward her topic and likely reactions to her approach to the subject matter. She may need to assess her level of credibility with the audience. Audiences may be interested or disinterested in any given topic, receptive or unreceptive to the position advocated, and friendly or unfriendly toward the speaker. Sometimes speakers have captive audiences, required by their employers or professors to attend the speaking occasion. At other times, audience members may go to considerable trouble to attend a speech event. The speaker should take these motivations and perceptions, which often exist prior to the speech event, into account. (See the Reflections box on page 125.)

Values

Values
Personal principles or standards that color perceptions

Whereas people have thousands of attitudes, they have only dozens of values. The term *value* refers to an ideal or moral principle that is at the foundation of our belief structures. In benchmark studies, Milton Rokeach identified thirty-six values common to most cultures.[3] Eighteen are *instrumental*, pertaining to ideal ways to behave. Examples include the importance of being caring, ambitious, patriotic, competent, competitive, efficient, progressive, individualistic, egalitarian, dominant, logical, independent, social, optimistic, family-oriented, and active. Another

Reflections

My attitudes.

I Like . . . books . . . skiing . . . racing . . . relaxing at home . . . *CSI Miami* . . . monkeys . . . cats . . . dogs . . . drawing . . . dancing . . . Chinese lyrics . . . old cafes . . . rock concerts . . . Jessica Simpson . . . collecting stamps . . . traveling abroad.

I Dislike . . . honking in traffic . . . airline food . . . knitting . . . words like *policy* . . . anti-intellectualism . . . girls that talk to my boyfriend . . . fraternities . . . the opera . . . fast food . . . C++ for large projects . . . politicians who lie . . . getting up early.

eighteen values are *terminal*, relating to ideal states of existence. Examples include a world at peace, family security, freedom, a comfortable life, happiness, self-respect, a sense of accomplishment, wisdom, equality, national security, true friendship, salvation, inner harmony, mature love, a world of beauty, social recognition, pleasure, and an exciting life.

While most researchers believe that the same values appear in all cultures, they acknowledge that differences exist in the *priority level* of the value, the *number of people who hold the value*, and the *strength of their convictions*. Western countries place a higher importance than most Middle Eastern countries do on change and progress. The importance of the individual versus the collective varies from country to country. In periods of war, patriotism assumes a higher level of importance than in periods of peace. In the same way, values related to personal and national security may eclipse values such as right to privacy and self-determination when countries or people feel threatened. So while all countries may report the same repertoire of values, the level of importance assigned to the value, the number of people who hold the value, and the strength of individual conviction may wane or grow stronger in some historical periods and cultural settings. (See the Reflections box on page 126.)

How do values relate to beliefs and attitudes? If the CEO of a company accepts the *values* of efficiency, innovation, and competitiveness, he may hold the *belief* that organizations should periodically restructure their processes in order to operate more efficiently, creatively, and competitively. These beliefs, in turn, may lead to an *attitude* that supports organizational layoffs in poor economic times and in situations where new expertise could upgrade the company's operations and increase profit margins. If the same CEO had placed a greater priority on values such as generosity and caring, he might have made different choices. A strong adherence to the *value* of caring, for example, could lead to the *belief* that loyalty to the company produces greater long term advantages for the company. This conviction could lead to the *attitude* that the company should not institute a policy of layoffs.

Returning to our earlier example, the producers of the *Oprah* show demonstrate a sound knowledge of the values of those who watch their program, as well as the reference groups with which they identify. *Oprah* clearly appeals to a specific kind of audience. It is obvious, for example, that viewers of *Oprah* are (or aspire to be) optimists in their approach to life, adherents to the value that "the best is yet to be," upwardly mobile, and believers in the values of achievement, self-fulfillment, and

Reflections

I Value . . .

"Service is important to me because I feel that I must do my best to make this world beautiful."

Jessica Lauren Friedman,
Washington University,
St. Louis, 2006

"My faith is important to me."

Uwem Akpan, author, 2005

"Education and the continuing quest for knowledge is important to me. Honesty, truthfulness, respect, kindness, looking after one's environment . . . also rank among my most important things."

Chantel, blogger, Australia, 2006

"Loyalty is important to me."

Bart Scott, Baltimore Ravens, 2006

"Time is important to me because I want to sing long enough to leave a message."

Mahalia Jackson, gospel singer, deceased

"Work is important to me!"

Kathleen Ryan, Inclusion
International, Ireland, 2005

"Winning is important to me, but what brings me real joy is the experience of being fully engaged in whatever I'm doing."

Phil Jackson, NBA coach and former player

---

independence. Many members of this audience are likely to place a strong emphasis on spiritualism and altruism and to be reasonably liberal in their approach to issues of politics, religion, and race and ethnicity. Family values are close to the top of their list of priorities. They are patriotic, proud of their American heritage, but they also value multicultural traditions and ethnic associations. Many are on a common quest for improved relationships, spiritual growth, physical fitness, and better management of their health and financial affairs. Whether decorating small spaces in their homes or allocating time to various household responsibilities, they aim to make the maximum use of available resources in the most efficient and effective way. Most members of *Oprah's* audiences have reached a point in their lives where they have the time and resources to ponder more than survival issues, and they value quality of life. They believe in taking action and assuming personal responsibility for their choices. They care about the environment and the kind of world their children will inherit.

When creating psychographic profiles, speakers must be careful not to stereotype audiences. Not all Southerners are Republicans, not all women are feminists, and some used car dealers are honest. (See the Reflections box on page 127.)

Needs

Needs
Things we identify as essential to our being

The basic needs of people remain constant across all groups and periods in time. Work by Abraham Maslow presents a staircase of human needs, beginning with *physiological and safety* needs and progressing to *love, esteem,* and ultimately *self-actualization* needs.[4] According to Maslow, we are only able to concentrate on satisfying self-esteem and self-actualization needs after we have satisfied the three

Reflections

"As much as being Indian is my identity, that is not all I am. I am not just an 'Indian'; I am a woman, a business student, an artist, a writer, an adventurer, and a sensitive yet bold person who cannot be summarized in one word."

Aarti Shaw

Source: www.isp.msu.edu/oiss/essay/essays05/AartiShah.pdf.

lower-level needs (physiological, security, and love). A starving man may be obsessed by the thought of food; but once fed, he can think about satisfying other needs such as security (finding a safe place to stay), love (finding a companion), and esteem (status within the community).

In many regards, the higher-level needs represent luxuries to people in many developing countries, who face the daily threat of starvation and inadequate resources to deal with earthquakes or other natural disasters. Those people will be too occupied with providing food and shelter for their families, tending to ill children, and making a much-needed contribution to the community to think about self-esteem or self-fulfillment. Even in the most affluent countries, relatively few people achieve self-actualization, a state characterized by independent lifestyles, freedom from restraint, and the ability to pursue personal goals. Creativity and curiosity are markers of self-actualizing behaviors. Most often, people satisfy these interests and goals outside of the workforce, through pursuit of hobbies and other personal interests.

The advertising industry appeals to the full range of human needs. Vitamin and food advertisements cater to the physiological needs of audiences. Insurance companies typically appeal, in their advertisements, to our drive for security and love. Advertisements for hair products and makeup appeal to love and esteem needs. Such appeals suggest that the products will improve your looks, job opportunities, and ability to hold or attract a mate. Prestige appeals to self-esteem often appear in advertisements for automobiles and designer clothes. Recruitment advertisements for universities and military institutions often play to the self-actualization needs of individuals. In the same way as advertisers, speakers may stress the way in which their information or proposed solutions to problems will help audience members to meet their physiological, security, love, esteem, or self-actualization needs. The section on adaptation strategies gives examples to illustrate this point.

CREATING A PERSONALITY PROFILE

Personality factors also mediate the possibility that a speaker can influence audience opinion.[5] Some audience members embrace change relatively fast. Others are rigid on every issue, steadfast in maintaining their initial position. Two personality variables in particular have an influence on how people respond to persuasive

messages: the extent to which individuals are open- or close-minded and their level of self-esteem.

Although the creation of an audience profile based on personality attributes is probably unrealistic most of the time, recognition of the existence of these personality types within the audience is important. Occasionally, you face a fairly homogeneous audience that fits one of these profiles. An audience of CEOs, for example, is not likely to have esteem issues. People of low self-esteem do not tend to achieve these positions. In the same way, some audience members are more open-minded in their approach to issues than others. The organizational affiliations of individuals may give clues as to their levels of open-mindedness and their willingness to contemplate new ideas.

Dogmatism

Dogmatism
Rigidity and closed-mindedness

The term *dogmatic* refers to people who are closed-minded.[6] Compared to more open-minded individuals, dogmatics place a high value on trusted sources and have a hard time accepting messages that conflict with their existing beliefs. They tend to be more pessimistic than open-minded individuals are, to see problems in a narrow way, and to reject the ideas of those who do not agree with trusted authorities. An open-minded individual, on the other hand, does not believe that authorities absolutely determine policies, and they are willing to consider and accommodate new and more controversial ideas.[7]

Eric Hoffer published a classic work in 1951 called *The True Believer*.[8] He indicated that the fanatical personality types that one finds at the far left side of the political spectrum match those that appear on the far right side of the spectrum. Both share a frustration and alienation from mainstream society; and, according to Hoffer, their engagement with mass political movements comes not from political conviction, but from a lack of belief in self. Most people fall between the extremes identified by Hoffer.

Self-Esteem

Like dogmatic individuals, listeners with high self-esteem are more difficult to persuade than are individuals with low self-esteem. The former tend to resent highly directive messages and to resist outside pressures. They are more likely to respond to optimistic than pessimistic messages. Low-esteem individuals, on the other hand, are more likely seek the approval of others, pay more attention to pessimistic messages, and feel little ability to influence their situation.[9] People with high levels of anxiety regarding decisions also tend to resist persuasive messages.[10]

Self-esteem
Sense of self-worth

Researching and Analyzing Your Speaking Environment

Understanding the particulars of the speaking environment (occasion and place) is also important to a speaker. What is the occasion? Will other speakers precede or follow the speaker? Will the situation be formal or informal? Will a podium be available to the speaker? The speaker needs to know what to expect in terms of the physical environment—for example, the arrangement of the room (auditorium seating or chairs arranged in a circle) and the furniture (movable or bolted to the floor). Will the audience expect to participate in an interactive session, with a lengthy question-and-answer period following the more formal comments by the speaker? Chapter Six considers how speakers can use the physical environment to create a sense of psychological closeness to their audiences.

Adapting to Your Audience

Speakers adapt to their audiences in many different ways. Some of the most common strategies include choosing an appropriate topic, framing a realistic purpose, and recognizing the audience through a variety of means. The following discussion will consider these adaptation strategies in more depth.

CHOOSING A TOPIC AND APPROACH

Knowledge of demographic variables (age, occupation, gender, education, income, race, and ethnicity) and psychographic variables (values, beliefs, and attitudes) can guide the speaker's choice of subject matter and approach. The immediate situation and historical context also influence the acceptability of certain topics.

Some topics are inappropriate with certain audiences and in certain circumstances. One student, who worked for a funeral home, gave a demonstration speech on how to apply makeup to corpses. For his informative speech, another student chose to explain various positions that could be assumed in lovemaking. It became obvious, as soon as the young man began his speech, that he was painfully uncomfortable with the topic. As he progressed with his speech, his complexion turned a bright red, and he began to stutter and stammer. His classmates felt his embarrassment, and they became equally uncomfortable. As a professor, I was not sure how to respond to the situation. I did not want to further embarrass the young man, who had already realized his mistake. On the other hand, I felt uneasy leaving the topic of subject matter untouched. Eventually, I chose to note that we should always feel comfortable with our subject matter and take the audience and speaking environment into account. (See the Question of Ethics box.)

Other topics, such as basic dental hygiene, are so ordinary or familiar that no one cares about the subject matter. One student, who worked part-time at McDonald's,

A Question of Ethics

Michael knew that a number of his classmates were smokers. They often stood outside the school doors, smoking between classes. They also smoked in bars and restaurants. Even though he knew that he might upset the smokers in the class, he believed strongly that no one should smoke on school premises or in other public places. But his speech teacher had cautioned that students must adapt their speeches to the class. Michael was not sure what this warning implied. To what extent should he try to adapt his speech purpose to his audience? Should he temper his point of view or offer some excuses for the smokers in the audience? Ethically, what was his obligation? Michael thought that, if he decided to argue against smoking, he could say that he had been a smoker at one time himself. That way, the audience would think that he could identify with their feelings. Also, they would assign more credibility to him as a speaker. In actual fact, Michael had never smoked.

Maria planned to deliver a speech with a feminist perspective, focused on ways for women to protect themselves against sexually transmitted diseases (STDs). She had delivered a similar talk on several occasions to a women's group. Two student members of the Silver Ring Thing, dedicated to virginity outside of marriage, objected to the topic on moral grounds. Some others said that if Maria were giving the speech in another kind of environment (for example, a sex education class), the content might be appropriate. Several male students indicated that they had little interest in the topic. They also felt excluded from the speech purpose. Was it appropriate to exclude some members of her audience in selecting and developing her talk? Are all topics appropriate for all occasions? Do you agree that another occasion would be more appropriate for delivery of such a talk?

Linda wanted to speak on her phobia, her intense dislike of using public bathroom facilities. She planned to deliver the talk in fulfillment of her after-dinner speaking assignment, which required humorous content.

How do you feel about these speech topics? Do you think that the audience has the right to define point of view and subject matter for a speaker? Should speakers change their topics just because an audience disagrees with the subject matter? To what extent should speakers adapt their speeches to meet audience expectations or biases? Should they ever exaggerate or fabricate expertise and experience in order to win the audience to their point of view?

delivered a demonstration speech on how to make a Big Mac. The class could have cared less, as everyone knew what went into a Big Mac. Since the speaker could not divulge the ingredients of the sauce, she had no new information to convey. Another student instructed the class on how to make Kraft macaroni and cheese, which entails boiling water and opening a package. The choice of topic was an insult to college students. The speaker could have made the speech more interesting to the group, however, by talking about variations on the basic recipe—different kinds of ingredients (vegetables, sauces, etc.) that could add flavor and nutrition to the meal. Many college students do eat macaroni and cheese dinners as part of their staple diet. So talking about ways to add variety to the meal, to combine the dish with other complementary courses, or to make macaroni and cheese as the featured course in an inexpensive candlelight dinner for friends could have been appropriate. But the speech would have needed to have a creative or innovative twist to capture attention and some novel information to maintain that attention.

Issues that are immediate and vital to the individual have more meaning than those that are remote in time, place, or likelihood of occurrence. Although we may be concerned about famine in Ethiopia and earthquakes in Japan, we call for drastic action when mudslides threaten homes in California or hurricanes bear down on the Gulf coast. Our concern deepens and penetrates the veneer that we build around ourselves.

Some topics, however, are too current and too sensitive to discuss in certain time periods and situations. As a general rule, we should avoid topics related to religion. We should recognize that the classroom is a captive situation for students, who do not have the option of staying or leaving. In the days immediately following September 11, 2001, many Americans (including members of the country's Muslim community) were shocked and disturbed by an event that they could not begin to understand. In the early days following the attack, before all of the facts were known, many Muslim students would have been very uncomfortable listening to a speech that decried the terrorist acts—not because they identified with the terrorists but because they felt vulnerable to attacks themselves. Some racist acts were taking place in isolated parts of the country, where Muslims were targeted because of their ethnic and religious affiliations.

Sometimes speakers have difficulty in handling highly sensitive issues such as racism, or they may find themselves unable to finish speeches with highly painful or emotional content. With topics such as the death of a parent or sibling, for example, the risk that the speaker may lose control is high. So speakers need to think carefully about whether they can manage a topic of this nature. Audiences become uncomfortable when speakers lose control. At the same time, however, speakers should care about their topics. The best speeches come from situations where the speakers feel passionately about their subject matter. So a balance must be achieved. Ultimately, the choice of topics is a highly personal one, for which no one set of criteria exists.

FRAMING A REALISTIC PURPOSE

Similar cautions apply when discussing speech purposes. Some purposes are simply not achievable. If you are speaking to an audience of pig farmers, you are not likely to persuade them to endorse vegetarianism. You may be able, however, to

convince them to take more care in the management of manure and to avoid water and crop contamination—serious problems that pose a threat to water and food supplies.

A speech to persuade members of a conservative church group to support same-sex marriages will probably have little impact—or certainly not a positive impact. The large majority of church members will have a stable attitude set, formed over many years and tied to traditional concepts of family and community. Their beliefs will have been reinforced by authority figures with whom they identify. Confronted with an audience opposed to liberalization of church policies, the speaker should either choose a different topic or adjust the purpose to a more realistic one. In this instance, the speaker might aim to persuade audience members to condemn acts of intolerance and violence that violate church principles. If you are speaking to a more liberal organization, on the other hand, an achievable purpose could be arguing for the legitimacy of same-sex marriages. The following excerpt from a student speech illustrates the way in which one student recognized the limits of what she could accomplish in her speech:

> I am sure that all of you have heard about the recent controversy surrounding the legalization of same-sex marriages. I have to admit that it surprises me to learn that there are still people who say that homosexuality is wrong, that it is sinful or immoral. It surprises me, but I am not here to convince anyone to reconsider his or her views. And I am not here to tell you that your views are wrong or outdated. I

am here to persuade you to look for common ground, where we can all find a place to stand and agree. I believe that common ground is tolerance. We must learn to be tolerant of other people's beliefs and orientations. And even if we do not share the beliefs, we should respect each other for our life choices. Mr. Garrison, a character in one of my favorite cartoons, *South Park*, said it best: "Look, just because you have to tolerate something doesn't mean you have to approve of it! *Tolerate* means that you're putting up with it!" We need to get better at putting up with each other.[11]

Social judgment theory tells us that the initial attitudes of an audience have a significant effect on the speaker's potential to achieve attitudinal or behavioral changes. Listeners have latitudes of acceptance, noncommitment, and rejection. Persuaders are most likely to effect change if they stay within a person's "latitude of acceptance." By *latitude of acceptance*, we mean that the position of the persuader is consistent with—and highly favorable to—audience views on the topic. If the arguments of the persuader fall within the audience's latitude of acceptance, the speaker has a good chance of achieving attitudinal or behavioral change.

If the arguments fall into the *latitude of noncommitment* (meaning that audience members neither accept nor reject the ideas), more limited change is possible. Prior to hearing the speech, listeners may lack sufficient information to form an opinion, or they may not care very much about the topic. If the speaker provides the missing information and motivates the audience to think seriously about the subject, listeners may experience attitudinal or (occasionally) behavioral change. But if the position and arguments of the persuader fall into a *latitude of rejection* (meaning that they are highly objectionable to listeners), no change is likely.[12] In fact, a boomerang effect may occur. One European experiment, for example, demonstrated that highway postings of 100 km/hour speed limits on a six-lane highway did more to decrease the speed of travelers than highway postings of 80 km/hour. In other words, someone accustomed to driving 110 km/hour would be inclined to comply with a speed limit of 100 km/hour. However, the same person would reject a specified limit of 80 km/hour and continue to drive at an unreduced speed of 110 km/hour. Social scientists explained their findings by saying that 80 km/hour fell outside the drivers' latitudes of acceptance.[13]

Large latitudes of rejection characterize individuals who feel passionately opposed to a topic. Subjects such as religion, politics, and sex polarize people, leading to situations where the noncommittal zone holds few members. Such polarizing topics also are tied to our most central beliefs; according to Milton Rokeach, little change occurs over time in beliefs that are at the center of our value systems.[14]

Latitude of acceptance
When the listener's views are likely to be aligned with the speaker

Latitude of noncommitment
When the listener's views neither agree nor disagree with the speaker

Latitude of rejection
When the listener's views are likely to be opposed to those of the speaker

RECOGNIZING YOUR AUDIENCE

Strategies for recognizing the audience include establishing personal connections, making reference to a shared perspective or common struggle or fate, connecting through reference groups, complimenting the audience on achievements and recognizing their sacrifices, acknowledging audience beliefs and attitudes, recognizing commitment to shared principles and values, talking in terms that are meaningful, using appropriate language, relating to the knowledge levels of the audience, and recognizing multiple audiences. (See the Keep in Mind box.)

Keep in Mind

Strategies for recognizing your audience

- Establishing personal connections
- Making reference to a shared perspective or common struggle or fate
- Connecting through reference groups
- Complimenting audience members on achievements and recognizing their sacrifices
- Acknowledging audience beliefs and attitudes
- Recognizing commitment to shared principles and values
- Talking in terms that are meaningful
- Using appropriate language
- Relating to the knowledge levels of the audience
- Recognizing multiple audiences

Establishing Personal Connections

Sometimes speakers thank the people who introduced them or the audience that issued the invitation to speak:

> Thank you for your kind introduction, James. Good to see you again, this time in your home state. Not more than six months ago, in Delaware, James and I shared the same platform. And here we are again, on the other side of the country, in Seattle, swapping stories and experiences with another great audience. I am also happy to see other committed colleagues—Lisa Berry, Joan Conner, and Larry Mills. Thank you for inviting me to participate in your event. I hope that this will become an annual exchange.

Sample Speech

Speech of Welcome

Welcome to the information session on the Students Abroad Program. I would like to extend a big thanks to the university administration for allowing us to talk with you about our program. We are here today because we understand that traveling on a student budget can be problematic. The Students Abroad Program (SAP) is your chance to take that extended vacation while covering costs of living and adding international work experience to your CV.

With offices around the world, our goal is to help you to have a rewarding experience in a country of your choice. You may want to snorkel on the Great Barrier Reef of Australia or visit the amazing sets of *Lord of the Rings* in New Zealand. As communication students, you may want to learn about the inner workings of the British Broadcast Corporation in England or help advertise the Cannes Film Festival in France. Whatever you are seeking, SAP can help you to find it. Fifteen percent of our participants come from your region.

Traveling can be scary, especially for young adults. Going to a new place with a new language and culture can be confusing. But SAP will assist you with travel and accommodation arrangements. You will be able to travel in a group, where you have the comfort of friends, or you can travel solo, giving you an opportunity to extend your group of acquaintances. No matter your preference, a SAP team will be there to greet you and to assist you in settling into your new community.

At this time, I would like to introduce you to Jerome Newman, our president, who will walk you through the details of the program and answer your questions. Jerome began this program more than ten years ago, but he is as enthusiastic about its benefits as the day that he registered the first participants. Jerome, you're on.

Dana Troster

Sometimes speakers refer specifically to the comments of speakers who preceded them. For example, a sales presentation aimed at convincing an audience to purchase a home security system could begin with the following kind of statement:

> I was really interested in John's comment on the high cost of maintaining home security systems. You may be surprised to learn that I absolutely agree with what he had to say. However, he didn't mention one interesting point. He didn't mention the high cost of *not having* home security systems. I would like to share some statistics on break-ins that have occurred in your neighborhood in recent months.

Use of second person language—"you"—also helps to establish a personal connection with audiences. (See the Reflections box.)

Sharing a Common Perspective, Struggle, or Fate

Often speakers talk about sharing a common perspective or fate with the audience—the concept of *oneness*. At the 2004 Democratic national convention in

Reflections

What Did Y'all Say?

British slang words, which often aren't slang at all, are a mystery to Americans. These words, which appear commonly in Great Britain, have entirely different meanings (or no meaning at all) to most of us. Imagine that you heard the word *gob*, dropped in conversation. Like me, you'd probably think of a droplet of something, or maybe the music group. But to a Brit, the word *gob* is simply slang for mouth.

Imagine that you are at a pub and you want something to put in your gob. You could ask for bangers and mash, or sausage and mashed potatoes. Others of you might request a chip buddy. Chip buddies take those calorie-soaked potatoes to a whole new level. By slapping some chips between two pieces of bread, you can enjoy a French fry sandwich!

Looking around the pub, you find yourself staring at a very fine-looking boy or girl. To be a true Brit, you could say something like, "That bloke is quite fit" in lieu of "That guy is hot." And if the pub is located in London, you can say "I fancy that Cockney; he is so tick, man."

OK, so now you've left the pub and you're walking down the street. Suddenly, a man begins to yell at you, "Find a bobby! They're copping it up. There's claret all over the place!" At this moment, you might be tempted to give the man a dirty look and walk the other way. But if you know that bobby means policeman, copping it up means getting in trouble, and claret is another word for blood, you might actually try to help. The distraught man is just trying to say, "Find a policeman! They're getting in trouble. There's blood all over the place!" If you want to calm the man, you can say, "Hold it down an ickle, mate."

Your next stop is a local sports venue, which carries supplies for football (of course, I mean soccer), rugby, and cricket. You see that kits and trackies are for sale; and after wandering around the shop, you realize that they must be referring to uniforms and sweat shirts. But why didn't they just say so? You overhear a nearby conversation that refers to one side being "skinned on the pitch" during the last match. You flinch but then realize that the two speakers are simply saying that one side was badly beaten during the last game.

After leaving the sports store, you wander onto a soccer field to watch the team practice. You hear your friend exclaim that the coach is *awesome*. Well, now, this is one you can figure out on your own—until you realize that the word has a much more negative connotation in Britain and no one wants to be labeled as awesome.

On your tour of Britain, you have noticed that many of the slang words apply to females and those who have consumed too much alcohol. If you want to refer to a girl, she's a bird. If she's plain, she's a Doris; unattractive, a minger; or extremely unattractive, a moose. If she's young, she's a skirt; if she's loose, she's a salt. Should we see an inebriated man leaving the pub, we could say that he is tooled, ramped, off-your-face, or mullered. With so much attention on the fairer sex and alcoholic beverages, one can only assume that men must have had a significant influence on the creation of slang on the island!

You're finally back at your apartment building, where your friend gets a phone call. When she hangs up, you learn that it was her boss. You ask how her new job is going, and she replies, "I'm well made up with it. It's brilliant! But my boss is a bloody twit. I caught him snogging his secretary the other day!" Seeing your confused face, she explains that she's really happy with her new job but her boss is an idiot. She adds that she saw him kissing his secretary the previous day.

Returning to your room, you pass some neighbors in the hall. They smile and nod, but behind your back, they whisper, "She must be gutted since her fella left her. She was mad about him. What a git he turned out to be! Always in a strop!" Having been in Great Britain long enough to decipher the gossip, you know that strop means bad mood and git refers to a jerk. You're well aware that your neighbors are exchanging stories about you and your ex.

Finally, after a long day, and just when you think that you've lost the plot—that you are out of the trees—you crawl into your bed and fall asleep.

Believe it or not, I've exposed you to thirty British slang words and expressions. And although an American-British dictionary may seem like a good idea, you should realize that slang changes from region to region. As soon as you leave one area for another, you're up against a whole new vocabulary. No matter where you go, you will confront some novel and incomprehensible words and expressions—not to mention the accents that go with them. So enjoy—and good luck! And the next time that you entertain someone from Great Britain, remember that *y'all* also have some very strange expressions.

Kristen Pidduck

Sources: *Bend It Like Beckham*, Twentieth Century Fox Film Corporation (2002); T. Byrne, "The Cockney" (1996). www.thecockney .btinternet.co.uk, accessed February 5, 2004; T. Duckworth, *A Dictionary of Slang*, www.peevish.co.uk.slang, accessed February 4, 2004.

Atlanta, Georgia, U.S. Senate candidate Barack Obama from Illinois affirmed that he was one with his audience in the gripping words that he delivered to delegates:

> If there's a child on the south side of Chicago who can't read, that matters to me, even if it's not my child. If there's a senior citizen somewhere who can't pay for her prescription and has to choose between medicine and the rent, that makes my life poorer, even if it's not my grandmother. If there's an Arab American family being rounded up without benefit of an attorney or due process, that threatens my civil liberties. It's that fundamental belief—I am my brother's keeper, I am my sister's keeper—that makes this country work. . . . *E pluribus unum.* Out of many, one.[15]

At other times, politicians talk about the fact that they would not introduce a policy that would harm some member of their family—their mother, grandmother, or other symbolic individual. In other words, they argue that they stand to profit or gain by the same policies that their audience does.

In an eloquent speech delivered on November 1, 2001, Assembly of First Nations Chief Matthew Coon Come focused on the psychic ties that bind First Nations peoples of Canada to Americans.

> First, I want to convey to you the sense of seriousness that First Nations peoples hold the September 11, 2001 events. This is our homeland. Our Elders refer to it as mother earth, and when anyone harms our mother in whatever form, be it through the destruction of the environment or by the taking of human life that was put here, it hurts us. We feel for the families who senselessly lost their loved ones, for we too have known loss. We have been here for many, many generations and too have known terror in our homelands, but never on the scale recently experienced. Skilled Mohawk Ironworkers helped build those buildings which were destroyed, and, in fact, were the first on the scene to help with rescue attempts. First Nations citizens feel the same fear as other Canadians. Our people travel on both sides of the border

because our homelands and our relatives are on both sides. Our ancestors are buried on both sides of the border and we have many friends in the United States. With this unspeakable act the world has changed; our world has changed, and we are prepared to do our part to return to the sense of security that we formerly had.[16]

This concept of identification reflects a well-known communication theory called *dramatism*, associated with theorist Kenneth Burke.[17]

Connecting Through Reference Groups

Reference group
A group to which we belong or aspire to belong

At other times, speakers adapt by pointing to audience members with whom others can identify. The term *reference group* refers to those groups in which we hold or aspire to membership. Former President Bill Clinton often invited members of various demographic groups to be present in his audience for major state addresses. At some point during the evening, he directed the spotlight to these individuals, carefully selected to represent the diversity of the American population. On one occasion, the honored group included people with disabilities, the military, and minority populations. Clinton was certainly not the first political figure—or the last—to apply this strategy. After the catastrophic events of September 11, 2001, President George W. Bush invited Lisa Beamer (the wife of Todd Beamer, who died on Flight 93) to attend a major speaking occasion. As a result of his apocalyptic call to action, "Let's roll," Beamer is probably the best-known of the Flight 93 passengers. The presence of Lisa Beamer in the audience allowed the president to connect with the audience through this reference group.

George W. Bush may have taken his cue from his father, former President George H. W. Bush, who relied on a similar strategy when he delivered his declaration of war against Iraq in 1991. The senior George Bush stated:

> Listen to Hollywood Huddleston, Marine lance corporal. He says, "Let's free these people so that we can go home and be free again." . . . Listen to one of our great officers out there—Marine Lieutenant General Walter Blumer. He said, "There are things worth fighting for; a world in which brutality and lawlessness are allowed to go unchecked isn't the kind of world we're going to want to live in." Listen to Master Sergeant J. P. Kendall of the 82nd Airborne: "We're here for more than the price of a gallon of gas; what we're doing is going to chart the future of the world for the next hundred years. It's better to deal with this guy now than five years from now." And finally, we should all sit up and listen to Jackie Jones, an army lieutenant, when she says, "If we let him get away with this, who knows what's going to be next." I've called upon Hollywood and Walter, J. P. and Jackie, and all their courageous comrades in arms to do what must be done. Tonight, America and the world are very proud of them and their families, and let me say that everyone listening or watching tonight, when the troops we've sent in are finished their work, I'm determined to bring them home as soon as possible.[18]

Hollywood Huddleston, Walter Blumer, J. P. Kendall, and Jackie Jones stood for all of the military—from the lowly level of lance corporal to the prestigious level of lieutenant general. In other situations, the reference groups may be regional, occupational, ethnic, or other.

Sample Speech

Welcoming Comments

Good afternoon. Welcome to the fourth annual Writers Coalition conference and congratulations to each of you for being selected to participate in this four-day event! This auditorium is filled with talented young writers who worked hard to qualify for a place in our workshops. It is an honor to welcome such an impressive pool of talent to our city—participants, workshop facilitators, and guest speakers.

If you will take a moment to look around the room, you will recognize some familiar faces. Margaret Walker has helped to organize the Writers Coalition for the past two years, and we are proud to have her back again. Joining us, as well, are acclaimed novelist Steven Styles and playwright Kenneth Adams. They are here to share their experience and offer their advice to you. Thank you so much for accepting our invitation, Steven and Kenneth.

The next four days will give all competition winners the opportunity to polish your writing skills in areas of your choice. You will be able to choose from categories such as poetry, novels, short stories, and nonfiction. You will also have a chance to network with our workshop facilitators, seasoned writers who can open doors for you in the professional world of writing.

So over the next few minutes, I will give you a short overview of the workshops, as well as discuss our expectations of you. Today you will be assigned to groups where you will become acquainted with other aspiring young writers. Tomorrow's workshops will proceed as follows. . . .

Mary Kathryn Roberts

Complimenting the Audience

Where appropriate, a speaker may offer a compliment, as in the following example:

> I am so pleased to be in New York for the opening ceremonies of Little Italy week. Thank you, Angelo and Mary, Dr. Antonelli and Mayor Con Di Nino, for inviting me to share this special occasion with you. One of the things that I always enjoy about New York is the opportunity to reexperience the true spirit of America—our multiculturalism and history as a country that welcomes all who come to our shores. Standing in this lobby today—with its fountain, its cobblestone floors, and its wonderful murals—we can all appreciate the part of America that is Italy. How much less would this country be if you had not chosen to make it your home!

On other occasions, speakers have connected with their audiences by recognizing their suffering or sacrifices. On September 11, 2002, at the crash site in Shanksville, Pennsylvania, first lady Laura Bush delivered a beautifully crafted tribute to the victims of Flight 93. In the following passage, she recognized the suffering of her audience: "America is learning the names, but you know the people. And you are the ones they thought of in the last moments of life. You are the ones they called and prayed to see again. You are the ones they loved."[19]

Engaging in Self-Disclosure

Self-disclosure
Sharing personal information to break down barriers

Speakers can also establish a relationship with the audience by engaging in appropriate amounts of self-disclosure.[20] On August 19, 1992, Mary Fisher stepped before the Republican National Convention in Houston, Texas, to deliver an address now recognized as one of the top 100 speeches ever delivered by an American. In this speech, Fisher spoke openly of her own HIV status and asked the Republican Party to "lift the shroud of silence which has been draped over the issue of HIV and AIDS":

> I have come tonight to bring our silence to an end. . . . I would never have asked to be HIV positive, but I believe that in all things there is a purpose; and I stand before you and before the nation gladly. Tonight, I represent an AIDS community whose members have been reluctantly drafted from every segment of American society. Though I am white and a mother, I am one with a black infant struggling with tubes in a Philadelphia hospital. Though I am female and contracted this disease in marriage and enjoy the warm support of my family, I am one with the lonely gay man sheltering a flickering candle from the cold wind of his family's rejection.

Through the act of self-disclosure, speakers such as Mary Fisher establish a close psychological connection with their audiences, a phenomenon known as *immediacy*. (See Chapters Six, Eight, and Ten for more detailed discussions of the concept of *immediacy*.)

Acknowledging Audience Beliefs and Attitudes

In declaring war against Iraq in 1991, former President George H. W. Bush recognized that many middle-age Americans still remembered the long, drawn-out engagement in Vietnam. Moreover, many had fought in the war, participated in antiwar protests, or fled the country to avoid the draft. Hundreds of thousands had lost friends and family members in a conflict that few were willing to defend in subsequent years. In 1991, the sons and daughters of these former soldiers and activists were of fighting age. How would they view a president who was ready to lead the country into another conflict? Recognizing the potential resistance of his audience to his basic speech purpose—to declare war to drive Iraqi forces out of Kuwait—Bush attempted to reassure his audience that the conflict with Iraq would not be long, costly in lives, or ill-supported in logistical terms: "This will not be another Vietnam. . . . Our troops will have the best possible support in the entire world, and they will not be asked to fight with one hand tied behind their backs. I'm hopeful that this fighting will not go on for long and that casualties will be held to an absolute minimum."[21]

Understanding that many audience members were opposed to the military draft policies of the Vietnam war, Bush also stated, "Ours is an all volunteer force." Anticipating that some might recall the poorly trained youths who had barely graduated from high school when they were conscripted to fight in Vietnam, he said that the soldiers who fight in Iraq will be "magnificently trained." In response to the argument that many Americans never really understood why the country had entered the civil war in Vietnam, Bush proclaimed that the troops are "highly motivated" and that they "know why they are there." Anticipating that some would accuse him of economic motives in entering the war, Bush declared that "we're here for more than the price of a gallon of gas."

In conclusion, the speech illustrates how speakers take audience beliefs and attitudes into account when they structure their discourse. Sometimes they acknowledge the gap that separates speaker from audience; at other times, they look for common ground that will facilitate communication.

Recognizing Audience Commitment to Shared Principles and Values

When former first lady (currently U.S. Senator) Hillary Clinton rose to speak before women gathered in Beijing, China, on September 5, 1995, she faced a formidable rhetorical task. While she had a sympathetic audience, she also had a highly diverse one. The women in attendance at the Fourth UN Conference on Women came from around the globe. They had vastly different backgrounds and experiences and widely diverse social, political, and religious beliefs. Hillary Clinton had to move to the level of the most basic human experiences to find a common meeting place. She adapted to this rhetorical challenge by beginning her speech in the following way:

> This is truly a celebration a celebration of the contributions women make in every aspect of life: in the home, on the job, in their communities, as mothers, wives, sisters, daughters, learners, workers, citizens and leaders. It is also a coming together, much the way women come together every day in every country. We come together in fields and in factories. In village markets and supermarkets. In living rooms and board rooms. Whether it is while playing with our children in the park, or washing clothes in a river, or taking a break at the office water cooler, we come together and talk about our aspirations and concerns. And time and again, our talk turns to our children and our families. However different we may be, there is far more that unites us than divides us. We share a common future. And we are here to find common ground so that we may help bring new dignity and respect to women and girls all over the world—and in so doing, bring new strength and stability to families as well. By gathering in Beijing, we are focusing world attention on issues that matter most in the lives of women and their families: access to education, health care, jobs, and credit, the chance to enjoy basic legal and human rights and participate fully in the political life of their countries.[22]

Hillary Clinton's examples draw upon the values shared by all members of her audience—values such as love of family, freedom, independence, and human dignity.

Where diversity is present, speakers must be sensitive to the needs of the various groups. If you have a mix of the groups in your audience, you should acknowledge the diversity but, at the same time, identify underlying values and principles that unite the group. In the following example, Sarah Johnson recognized—after arriving at the occasion—that the subject of her speech was ill-suited to the values of her audience. She had to make an immediate adjustment to the situation:

> I was a member of a progressive speech club with a dynamic membership. A club member asked if I would speak at the meeting of another group who wanted to start a similar club. The location was a church, not unusual because churches often

give up their basements for free. As it turned out, however, my audience was the church congregation. (I figured this out when I walked through the door.) The topic of my planned speech was the story behind the large (very large) tattoo on my back. Not exactly the best topic for a conservative church group. As you can well imagine, I was pretty nervous. I did not have another speech in my back pocket, and I could not back out because I was the only speaker. Since I knew my material, I was able to improvise, which is what I did for most of my presentation. I still told the story behind the image, but I never mentioned the word *tattoo*. The tattoo image of an infant appealed strongly to the mothers and grandmothers in the audience, and I changed my speech from educational (yet shocking) to a warm and earthy celebration of motherhood. The audience never knew that I had planned a very different speech![23]

Recognizing Audience Needs

In the speech cited earlier, Hillary Clinton appealed to the most basic needs of audiences—*physiological and safety* (references to health), *security* (references to jobs and credit), *love* (references to family and children), *esteem* (references to dignity and respect), and *self-actualization* (references to education and personal aspirations).

Speakers recognize audience needs when they use examples to which audience members can relate. Translating information into terms that are immediate and meaningful to the audience also helps, as in the following example:

> How would you feel if I told you that one out of three of you will be dead in five years time? Scared? Shocked? Incredulous? If I were speaking this morning to a group of adults in Botswana, Africa, my audience would not be shocked or incredulous. Why? Because they live every day with the tragic reality that 36 per cent of their friends and family members will die with the HIV virus. Most will never receive treatment. Their prognosis is terminal.

The Institute of Medicine found that almost 100,000 Americans die each year as a result of medical errors. To make this statistic as meaningful as possible to a class of medical students, you could say:

> According to a 1999 report by the Institute of Medicine, as many as 98,000 Americans die each year as a result of medical mistakes by well-meaning health care workers. Statistically speaking, a large number of these deaths will occur in our state—perhaps as many as 5,000 over the next ten years. That means that, at some point in your life, you have probably met—or will meet—at least one of the people who have made such a mistake. Perhaps your professor, your family physician, or your local pharmacist. It could be that you will work with this person at some point in the future. Unless you maintain the most dedicated vigil, that offending person could be you. We are all human, but our mistakes cost more when we are doctors.

When the examples and statistics reflect situations that are close at hand and important to the audience, they mean more than examples and statistics that concern remote places and situations. The closer the proximity of the example, the illustration, or the statistic in terms of time, place, and potential impact, the more meaningful the material will be to your audience. Thus, for college students, the most meaningful examples will relate to your chosen area of study, your university, your town, your state, and your country. The examples are also more meaningful when

Sample Speech

Speech of Welcome

Take a minute. Sit back in your chairs and imagine this situation. You're one-on-one with someone—someone whom you find very attractive, someone who seems to be stimulating you in all the right ways, someone whose eyes say it all up to that climactic moment. Then suddenly, after only three minutes, it's all over and they get up and walk away. Would you be upset? You shouldn't be. "Why?" you ask. Because this is the only time when three minutes is enough! Welcome everyone to the wonderful world of speed dating.

It's good to see such an enthusiastic group, eager to meet the many singles who have joined you in tonight's quest for the right partner. For many of you, this is your first acquaintance with this new and unconventional form of dating. So for our newcomers, let me explain the process. Speed dating is a quick form of dating in which the men circulate about the room, spending three to five minutes with each of the women, who will sit at tables of two. On these mini-dates, you will get the chance to become somewhat acquainted with the other person. You will have some basis for deciding if you want to pursue the acquaintance further.

After five minutes is up, a buzzer will signal the end of the date. On the cards provided to each individual, you will check the "yes" or "no" box, indicating whether you want to see the person again. The men will proceed to the next table. At the end of the night, we will collect the cards, calculate the matches, and e-mail the contact information of the people with whom you had a positive connection.

I am happy to report that I have looked at the profiles of several audience members, and I am quite certain that we already have some matches in the making. A striking number of you are football and soccer fans; so already we're seeing similar interests. Good news for the young women seeking older men, as we have one in the group waiting to talk to you! Another common area of interest was people who enjoy reality TV shows. Look around, singles. The person sitting across the room could be your future significant other, and he or she is only a mini-date away.

We've all been through the hardships of dates from hell. Perhaps someone drank too much, they said too much, or they were just too much themselves. These are the dates that drag on and on, when you would give anything for them to have ended after five minutes. Worry no longer, friends. Speed dating has arrived, and Cupid is ready to strike you with his arrow.

I know that you are anxious to try your hand at the "lance-romance" talk, but before we begin, I would like to invite Elizabeth Snowden to say a few words. Lizbeth met her husband at these very tables last year—proof positive that speed dating works. Here to offer words of optimism, please join me in welcoming Lizbeth.

Jenn Thomlinson

---

they relate to our basic psychological and physiological needs. No medical student would want to imagine, for example, that they could actually contribute to the harm of an individual in their care.

Choosing Appropriate Language

The use of gender-neutral language is important with audiences that include members of both genders. Terms such as *policeman, fisherman, manhandled, chairman, tradesman*, and *manpower* are offensive to some female members. The more politically correct terms are *police officers*, *fishers*, *handled roughly*, *chairperson* or the *chair*, *skilled worker*, and *human resources*. Rather than saying *mankind*, say *human beings* or *humanity*. Substitute *member of Congress* for *congressman*, *firefighter* for *fireman*, and *letter carrier* for *mailman*. The use of politically correct language is important in addressing audiences. You should use terms such as *young woman* instead of *girl*, *woman* instead of *lady*, and *young man* instead of *boy*.

Terms such *older adults* or *seniors* are preferred to *old people*. Since many people (including a number of older Americans) live in relationships outside of marriage, the reference to *partner* is safer than marital-specific terms such as *husband* or *wife* or *spouse*. Avoid unnecessary descriptors such as *lady* lawyer or *gay* athlete.

When referring to people with disabilities, public speakers should avoid the use of terms such as the *handicapped*, the *disabled*, or the *blind*. Instead speakers should say *people with disabilities* or *people who are blind*. Like all of us, people who are blind or deaf prefer to see themselves as people first, with assets and liabilities. Their disabilities or illnesses do not define their potential. Also speakers should avoid terms like *wheelchair-bound*, *people suffering from HIV*, or *cancer victims*. People with disabilities usually see themselves as coping with their challenges, not bound or handicapped by them. Many overcome remarkable obstacles in their quest to lead independent lives; they are fighters, not victims. People who are deaf, for example, have their own language; and many consider their communication system to be equal or superior to that of people who communicate with verbal language. They even have their own unique system for expressing humor. They resent being stigmatized by words that imply an inferior status.

The language used to refer to members of minorities must also be politically correct. The term *Asian* is preferable to *Oriental*, and a reference to a specific national origin such as *Japanese*, *Chinese*, or *Thai* is preferable to *Asian*. Since many families of Asian, African, and other national origins have been in America for generations, however, not all want to be labeled by the countries of their long-dead ancestors.

Over time and among different groups, variations occur in what is deemed desirable or acceptable. Terms such as *Aboriginals* and *natives* refer to the Inuit and First Nations people of Canada. However, some natives prefer to maintain the designation of *Indian*. In the same way, Americans of African descent have shifted their preferred names over time from *colored* to *Negro* to *Afro-American* to *black* to *African American* to *people of color* (a developing trend, which clusters more than one ethnic population). Some Americans of Spanish descent ask to be called *Latino*; others prefer *Hispanic*, *Hispano*, *Mexican-American*, or even *Chicano* (a term used by some political activists).[24] Some Latino residents of Texas have coined the term *Tejano*. The term AHANA stands for African-Americans, Hispanics, Asians, and Native Americans.

As exemplified by the show *Queer Eye for the Straight Guy*, gays and lesbians have added positive content in recent years to words such as *queer*, a politically incorrect term in the 1950s. In 2005, the *Passionate Eye* aired a documentary on *fag hags*, a term that refers to women who like gay men. One woman discussed how two negative words (*fag* and *hag*) have acquired positive connotations for women with strong ties to gay men.[25] Residents of some South and Central American countries have begun to argue that the designation *Americans* should not be applied only to residents of the United States. In brief, speaker beware! Political correctness has a short life, and not everyone agrees on the appropriate terminology. (See the Reflections box.)

Level of language is also important when you attempt to reach audiences of varying backgrounds and education levels. Despite the popular conception that speakers should always avoid jargon and technical language, jargon can be very useful in communicating with others within a professional culture (legal, medical, or other). In the same way, despite its negative connotations, "bureaucratese" can be effective in communicating within government environments,

Reflections

Are Chicanos the Same as Mexicans?

"Spanish People"

This term is used frequently in the United States to refer indiscriminately to any person that speaks Spanish. As such, it is imprecise and often inappropriate in that it includes people from more than two dozen countries, spanning all of the American continent, the Caribbean and Spain. The term does apply specifically, however, as the proper name for the native people of Spain, and for this reason it is as incorrect to use it to refer to any and all Spanish-speakers as the term "English" would be to refer to citizens of New Zealand, Australia or the United States.

Hispanics

This term is often used to refer collectively to all Spanish-speakers. However, it specifically connotes a lineage or cultural heritage related to Spain. As many millions of people who speak Spanish are not of true Spanish descent (e.g., na-

tive Americans), and millions more live in Latin America (cf., "Latino" below) yet do not speak Spanish or claim Spanish heritage (e.g., Brazilians) this term is incorrect as a collective name for all Spanish-speakers, and may actually be cause for offense.

Latino

This term is used to refer to people originating from, or having a heritage related to, Latin America, in recognition of the fact that this set of people is actually a superset of many nationalities. Since the term "Latin" comes into use as the least common denominator for all peoples of Latin America in recognition of the fact that some romance language (Spanish, Portuguese, French) is the native tongue of the majority of Latin Americans, this term is widely accepted by most. However, the term is not appropriate for the millions of native Americans who inhabit the region.

(Continued)

Reflections

Are Chicanos the Same as Mexicans?—cont'd

Mexican

Specifically, the nationality of the inhabitants of Mexico. Therefore, the term is used appropriately for Mexican citizens who visit or work in the United States, but it is insufficient to designate those people who are citizens of the United States (they were born in the US or are naturalized citizens of the US) who are of Mexican ancestry. The various terms used to properly designate such people are described below, however, it is important to explain why these people feel it is important to make such a distinction. US citizens who are troubled by this often point out that most immigrants do not distinguish themselves by point of origin first (i.e., German-American), but simply as "Americans" (another troublesome term, but we won't get detoured by that here). Here are some reasons why many US citizens of Mexican extraction feel that it is important to make the distinction:

Mexican-American

This term is commonly used to recognize US citizens who are descendants of Mexicans, following the pattern sometimes used to identify the extraction of other ethnic Americans (e.g., "African-American"). This term is acceptable to many Mexican descendants, but for those who do not identify with a Mexican heritage, but rather with a Spanish heritage, it is unacceptable (cf., "Hispano," below). Also, for those who do not view themselves as "Americans" by choice, this term is problematic, and for others the implication that the identity of the bearer is unresolved, or in limbo, between two antipodal influences, belies their self-concept as a blend that supersedes its origins and is stronger, richer and more dynamic than either of its cultural roots.

Hispano

This term is preferred by that subpopulation, located primarily in the US southwest, who identify with the Spanish settlers of the area and not with the Mexican settlers (specifically, the Creole Spanish-native American race). There is in fact an important number of these people located along the Rio Grande Valley of New Mexico and in the northern Sangre de Cristo mountain range of the same state. This group has been traditionally a very closed and conservative one, and recent evidence provides important explanations for this: they seem to be descendants of persecuted Jews who fled Spain during the 16th and 17th centuries and sought refuge in what were then the farthest reaches of the known world. They survived by minimizing their contact with outsiders and by hiding or disguising their religious and cultural identities as much as possible. Historical researchers call them "cryptic Jews."

Chicano

A relatively recent term that has been appropriated by many Mexican descendants as unique and therefore reflective of their unique culture, though its first usage seems to have been discriminatory. The most likely source of the word is traced to the 1930 and 40s period, when poor, rural Mexicans, often native Americans, were imported to the US to provide cheap field labor, under an agreement of the governments of both countries. The term seems to have come into first use in the fields of California in derision of the inability of native Nahuatl speakers from Morelos state to refer to themselves as "Mexicanos," and instead spoke of themselves as "Mesheecanos," in accordance with the pronunciation rules of their language. . . . An equivocal factor is that in vulgar Spanish it is common for Mexicans to use the "CH" conjunction in place of certain consonants in order to create a term of endearment. Whatever its origin, it was at first insulting to be identified by this name. The term was appropriated by Mexican-American activists who took part in the Brown Power movement of the 60s and 70s in the US southwest, and has now come into widespread usage. Among more "assimilated" Mexican-Americans, the term still retains an unsavory connotation, particularly because it is preferred by political activists and by those who seek to create a new and fresh identity for their culture rather than to subsume it blandly under the guise of any mainstream culture.

Source: Movimiento Estudiantil Chicano/o de Aztlan (MECHA de Tejaztlan), student organization at the University of Texas at Austin, "Are Chicanos the Same as Mexicans?" (April 30, 1998), http://studentorgs.utexas.edu/mecha/archive/chicano.html, accessed April 18, 2006, page maintained by Jorge Tapia.

where diplomacy of wording protects relationships and ambiguity provides a safety net for its users. But when you attempt to communicate with members of the larger public, who do not understand the language, you risk being misunderstood. Speakers who communicate with a lay audience should use direct and conversational language—never jargon that could confuse or alienate. You should avoid terms such as *stakeholders*, *target groups*, *strategies*, and *portfolios* when speaking to lay audiences. You should also avoid overly ornate and pretentious language. (See the Reflections box.)

A common technique for adapting to an audience in linguistic terms is to speak in the first person plural ("we") and the second person ("you"). In the first instance, the speaker pulls the audience into her frame of reference. In the second case, the speaker communicates with the audience in a direct and personal fashion.

Adaptation also requires that the speech be "sayable." That is, you should be able to breathe at regular intervals in the speech. If the words do not sound right,

Sayable
A passage that is easy and comfortable to speak aloud

Reflections

Always use clear terminology. I remember an occasion when a wannabe nurse peppered her speech with a great number of medical terms and acronyms (e.g. TLC, ECG, SMAC, ICU, and the like), none of which the audience understood. While the speaker gained a position of power within the group, she did not follow good speaking practice. It's always better to tell the audience what the terms mean; then everyone is on an even playing field. I can fill your ears with railway engineering terms, which my compatriots would understand, but others would wander away from the conversation with glazed eyes.

John Busby

cluster properly, or convey a thought in memorable language, reword the thought. If the cadence and rhythm of the speech are not right, begin again. *Speech is for the ear, not the eye.* Tune yourself to the aural dimensions of language when you write a speech. Pretentious language is usually "unsayable." Eloquence resides in simplicity—the nice turn of phrase, the lyrical thought, the compelling analogy.

Relating to the Knowledge Level of the Audience

Correctly diagnosing the level of knowledge held by your audience is critical to audience adaptation. The following example illustrates the experience of Milton Himsl:

> I was to present a two hour Unix System Administrator's course at the annual user's conference. The course was fully booked, and about 30 people showed up. I was very nervous; so I just introduced myself and then launched right into my talk. I didn't really make eye contact with anyone until I relaxed about five minutes later. When I finally looked away from my notes, I found one shining-eyed person, hanging onto my every word, and another 29 people staring like deer caught in the headlights. I stopped and asked what was wrong. It turned out that 29 of the 30 people didn't know anything about Unix and thought that a System Administrator was the person responsible for the General Ledger activities of the store. I had a class full of accountants![26]

Once the speaker had regained his composure, he asked what the group expected from the seminar and whether they had any specific questions. He knew nothing about accounting or the general ledger function of the company software, but he offered to note their questions and to post the answers in the computer lab. As the questions were posed, class members began to share answers and experiences; and the instructor assumed the role of facilitator. He asked the class to move into the computer lab and break into groups so that they could better share their expertise. When he announced that the session was over, only half of the participants looked up from their computers to wave *OK*. The others were too engrossed in what they were doing to notice. To the instructor's surprise, the feedback at the end of the session was extremely positive. The instructor had managed to adapt to the knowledge level of his audience and to the situation by maintaining a flexible attitude.

Recognizing Multiple Audiences

Multiple audiences
The idea that some speeches are not only heard by the people in the room, but are also transmitted or recorded so that others will hear them in other places or at other times

In today's wired world, speakers have many different audiences, often scattered throughout the community or dispersed around the state, country, or globe. Some are present in the immediate speaking environment, but many are not visible to the speaker. The auditorium may have a seating capacity of three-hundred persons; but television, radio, and the web do not respect such limitations. In the case of a political speech, many advocacy groups, politicians, bureaucrats, and members of the general public may be listening to the speech on the radio, observing the

speech on television, or reading excerpts from the speech on the Internet or in a newspaper.

Sometimes the audiences are contemporaries of a speaker; at other times, the speaker writes for future generations and remote constituencies. An example would be the June 1964 speech of Nelson Mandela, delivered in a courtroom in Pretoria, South Africa, immediately prior to his sentencing to a lifetime in jail. Facing a possible death sentence, Nelson Mandela delivered a four-hour speech, judged to be the most emotionally gripping of his political career. He concluded with the words:

> During my lifetime I have dedicated myself to the struggle of the African people. I have fought against white domination, and I have fought against black domination. I have cherished the ideal of a democratic and free society in which all persons live together in harmony and with equal opportunities. It is an ideal which I hope to live for and to achieve. But, if need be, it is an ideal for which I am prepared to die.[27]

Mandela knew that the future generations of South Africans and influential leaders in other countries would read his speech and pay attention to the words. At the same time, he knew that the people present in the courtroom that day would probably pay no heed to what he had to say. Nor would they circulate his words to other South African blacks for fear of revolt. The real impact of the speech would be felt over an extended period of time. So Mandela had more than one audience. In many regards, his least important audience was his immediate one, composed of jurors, judge, and spectators who had been privileged with entry to the courtroom setting. He did not have his true audience—present and future generations of South African blacks or sympathetic leaders and constituencies from other countries—in the courtroom.

Sometimes speakers explicitly acknowledge these more remote audiences—those not present in the auditorium or the bleachers or even in the same historical period. For example, President John F. Kennedy addressed a number of international, as well as domestic, audiences in his 1961 inaugural address delivered in Washington, DC:

> To those old allies whose cultural and spiritual origins we share, we pledge the loyalty of faithful friends. . . . To those new states whom we welcome to the ranks of the free, we pledge our word that one form of colonial control shall not have passed away merely to be replaced by a far more iron tyranny. . . . To those peoples in the huts and villages of half the globe struggling to break the bonds of mass misery, we pledge our best efforts to help them help themselves. . . . To our sister republics south of our border, we offer a special pledge: To convert our good words into good deeds. . . . Let all our neighbors know that we shall join with them to oppose aggression or subversion anywhere in the Americas. And let every other power know that this hemisphere intends to remain the master of its own house. To that world assembly of sovereign states, the United Nations, our last best hope in an age where the instruments of war have far out-paced the instruments of peace, we renew our pledge of support. . . . Finally, to those nations who would make themselves our adversary, we offer not a pledge but a request: That both sides begin anew the quest for peace, before the dark powers of destruction unleashed by science engulf all humanity in planned or accidental self-destruction.[28]

Speakers face unique challenges when their speaking environment includes two audiences—the audience that is present in the auditorium and the television viewing audience. Yet public speakers often face this dilemma, and many politicians and members of Congress tailor their speeches to appeal to their remote viewers. By adopting a more conversational and personal style of delivery, sprinkled with occasional witticisms, the speakers are able to encourage a feeling of physical and psychological proximity. President Ronald Reagan was said to have been a master at using the intimate eye of the television camera to reach Americans. But this kind of delivery, as we will discuss in the next chapter, may be less suited to members of the immediate audience, who would prefer a more animated style of delivery with greater variations in movement and voice.

ADAPTING TO THE SITUATION

Strategies for adapting to the situation include making references to the location of the speech and the occasion (including historical context).

Reference to location
Connecting to your audience by talking about the place where the speech is being presented

Reference to Location

Reference to location is a common instrument for audience adaptation. By creating awareness of shared physical and psychological space, speakers bridge the gap that separates them from their audience. The following example illustrates reference to place as a means of audience identification:

> It is always a special pleasure for me when my itinerary takes me to Savannah. The city of gardens and tea rooms. A city that seems, like few others of its size, to enjoy an inner peace, a tranquillity that comes with age and knowing who you are. It is a city without an identity crisis. Savannah is a wonderful blending of the old and the new. Is there any other city in America with trees as old and grand as Savannah? Gas lanterns and carriages left over from another era. And, as close as the nearby waterfront, structures of iron and steel to remind us that the future is never far away.

Reference to Historical Occasion

On the fortieth anniversary of D-Day, former President Ronald Reagan spoke to veterans gathered at the U.S. Ranger Monument at Pointe du Hoc, France. He referenced the historical events that created the need for the speech:

> We stand on a lonely, windswept point on the northern shore of France. The air is soft, but forty years ago at this moment, the air was dense with smoke and the cries of men, and the air was filled with the crack of rifle fire and the roar of cannon. At dawn, on the morning of the 6th of June, 1944, 225 Rangers jumped off the British landing craft and ran to the bottom of these cliffs. Their mission was one of the most difficult and daring of the invasion: to climb these sheer and desolate cliffs and take out the enemy guns. . . . Behind me is a memorial that symbolizes the Ranger daggers that were thrust into the top of these cliffs. And before me are the men who put them there. These are the boys of Pointe du Hoc. These are the men who took the cliffs. These are the champions who helped free a continent. These are the heroes who helped end a war. Gentlemen, I look at you and I think of the words of Stephen Spender's poem. You are men who in your "lives fought for life . . . and left the vivid air signed with your honor."[29]

Reference to historical occasion
Connecting to your audience by talking about the events that occurred at that location

Words of Caution

In advance of presentations, news commentators often predict the words and positions of political and celebrity speakers, analyze and interpret their strategies, and offer critiques of their speech content. When audience adaptation or other rhetorical strategies become transparent, they lose their effectiveness. So if television commentators on CBS or *Larry King Live* predict that the president will make appeals to the international community in his next address—and he makes those appeals—the audience becomes acutely aware of the rhetorical strategies. If this enhanced awareness leads to the perception that the speaker is attempting to manipulate us, we react accordingly, rejecting the arguments and appeals and resisting movement in the direction urged by the speaker. We become cynical and skeptical.

As discussed in Chapter One, the environment in which we deliver our speeches is a vastly changed one from the last century, when "stump" speakers could present different messages to different audiences as they traveled across the country. Often they took audience adaptation to the extreme, changing their stance on issues from one location to another. In this century, however, television and radio stations can—and do—replay the words of public communicators at will, allowing audiences to witness and hear the previous positions and commitments of the speaker. In such a situation, honesty and consistency are not only desirable characteristics for public communicators; they are compulsory. More than ever, audiences need to know that speakers are sincere in their motivations and that they have some personal stake in what they advocate. Audiences expect, in current lingo, a "connect" between what speakers say and do. In the eyes of the audience, the insincere speaker is the companion of the glib salesperson who talks for money and the slick politician who talks for power and position. So while audience adaptation means recognizing, respecting, and trying to reach your audience, the term does not mean lying to your audience, attempting to influence them by unethical means, or pretending to be someone other than yourself. Critical to long-term credibility is consistency in the messages conveyed to audiences.

Conclusion

This chapter has expanded upon the audience component in the critical communication model (CCM). Audience adaptation is more than just recognizing individuals in your audience. Adaptation also involves telling your audience members why a topic should matter to them and how your solution can help to satisfy their physiological, safety, love, esteem, and self-actualization requirements. Audience adaptation is explicitly acknowledging the beliefs, opinions, and values of your audience. Television reality shows such as *Survivor* and *Big Brother* illustrate well the importance of understanding how to adapt your message to different audience members. To stay alive in the game—to avoid eviction—survivors must constantly monitor their personal communications and create messages that resonate with the other players. What works with one individual will not necessarily achieve the same results with a second. So the framing of messages changes as the players seek to persuade the other competitors to keep them in the game. The final vote, which determines the ultimate survivor, comes from the players themselves. So the participants must be constantly aware of individual peer reactions, as well as group alliances that may have formed.

In the same way as the competitors on *Survivor* and the other reality shows, speakers must become familiar with their audience, plan their communications carefully, monitor reactions to their communications, and adjust their strategies. In short, they must engage in ongoing audience adaptation. Unlike the TV reality shows, however, audience adaptation does not imply presenting an erroneous picture of your position, compromising your values, or catering to your audience by shifting positions to accommodate the person or the occasion. The chapters on persuasion will look, in more depth, at the different kinds of audiences faced by persuasive speakers and the strategies adopted to meet the challenges posed by apathetic, unreceptive, or hostile audiences.

Questions for Discussion

1. Identify demographic characteristics that you share in common with your class mates. In which areas do you differ?

2. Can you think of some topics that might be of more interest to men? Women? Seniors? Lawyers? Musicians? A particular cultural or ethnic group? People in your hometown or region of the country?

3. Identify some reference groups to which you belong or aspire. What can someone learn about your values by knowing the reference groups to which you belong? How do these groups help to define you as a member of an audience?

4. Explain how speaking strategies on a topic such as date rape would need to take demographic variables such as gender, age, culture, and marital status into account. How could you make the speech relevant to a group with diverse demographic characteristics?

5. Discuss some of the ethical considerations related to audience adaptation strategies.

Outline

PUTTING PRINCIPLES OF DELIVERY INTO PRACTICE

The One-Point Speech

Learning Objectives

- To learn how to prepare a one-point speech
- To discover how to build credibility through delivery
- To understand and learn how to cope with technical challenges
- To set realistic goals for progress in public speaking

An early study by Alan H. Monroe found that most people see effective public speaking as synonymous with effective delivery.[1] In my experience, the same holds true today. If you ask your students to analyze a speech without specifying criteria, they will almost invariably focus on the delivery (rather than the words) of the speaker. In this chapter, we will examine the nature of one-point speeches (a useful vehicle for focusing on delivery), delivery options, strategies for building credibility through delivery, technical challenges, and realistic goals for progress in presenting your ideas.

Preparing One-Point Speeches

One-point speech
A speech designed to develop only one main idea

As the name suggests, one-point speeches develop one main idea, such as "Co-op programs help students to get jobs when they graduate" or "Video lottery terminals (VLTs) are responsible for many suicides." Some one-point speeches address values, such as "By helping our neighbor, we help ourselves" (value of *generosity*) or "Count your life not by the breaths you take, but by the moments that take your breath away" (value of *beauty*). Quotations are good launches for one-point speeches.

One-point speeches have an introduction with standard elements, a main point, and a clear conclusion. The speaker uses several examples to support a one-point speech. The structure of the speech is circular, like a wheel with spokes. At the center of the wheel is the single point of the speech. The supporting examples and stories are the spokes to the wheel. So the speaker moves between giving or reminding the audience of the point of the speech and illustrating that point with supporting evidence. This kind of organizational pattern is common in many traditional societies. Kenyans, for example, use mostly anecdotes and personal testimonials to support a single point in their speechmaking; they use few statistics.[2] The Navajo also rely strongly on personal experience with the subject matter; they use a form of testimony called *enactment*. With *enactment*, speakers use themselves as proof of what is said: "The speaker actually becomes a method of verification or validation of the point being made."[3] This focus on self-disclosure through personal stories and anecdotes also typifies the trend in American rhetoric, which presently favors a narrative style.[4]

Preparation for a one-point speech follows the same path as preparation for other speaking engagements: (1) development of an introduction (attention-getting strategies, statement of purpose, thesis, and preview or orientation statement), (2) development of one point (supported by examples, anecdotes, parables, and personal testimonials), and (3) a concluding statement with a brief summary and link back to the opening thought. Sometimes speakers define one or more terms in order to establish a frame of reference for the audience. The personal testimonials allow an opportunity for self-disclosure. For an example of a one-point student speech, see the Sample Speech on page 157. This speech uses several supporting examples to illustrate a single personality trait.

Speakers should avoid thesis statements that identify several (as opposed to one) point, such as "Co-op programs have three major benefits"; "Rising costs in university education have involved increases in tuition, books, and health fees"; or

Sample Speech

Accident Prone

Picture a 1978 Chevrolet Malibu driving in circles in a parking lot. The couple inside has become increasingly frustrated because they can't find a space. A two-year-old in the back seat is crying and a four-year-old is whining. Suddenly, just as the couple is about to lose it, a parking space appears, as if Moses himself had parted the cars. The driver is poised to take it, but just as the car is about to move, a loud horn blares. When the couple looks back, they notice two things: (1) The driver in the car behind them is frantically waving his arms, his eyes bulging out of his head; (2) the baby is missing.

Switch the scene to beneath the rear tire of the car, and you find me, at two years old. I'd evidently given up on finding a space and decided to exit the car prematurely. My name is Sebastian Samur, and from my earliest years, I have always been prone to accidents. From cracking my head open while jumping on the bed to breaking my arm trying to ride a tricycle in the baby pool, I have never been one to make the most intelligent decisions.

A second perfect example occurred in my grade eight shop class. It was my fourth time taking the class; so I felt confident as I shaped the wheels of the toy car I had designed. So confident that, when the band saw jammed, I figured I could easily shove my way through. And shove I did. My finger went straight into the blade. Now you would think that—upon seeing my finger drenched in blood, the rusty band saw blade stained red, and a digit dangling far from where it should have been—I might have decided to panic. But no, not me! I wasn't that smart. After turning off the machine and calmly putting my work away, I proceeded to stand in the five-person line-up. When my turn finally came, the only thing I said was, "Uh," as I indicated my finger. My teacher muttered an equally enthusiastic, "Oh dear," after which he wrapped it up rather shabbily, and soon I was off to the hospital to have it fixed. Here is the result of that surgery (photo).

Thankfully, despite my lack of reaction, my finger healed quite well, and the large scars are all that remain of the accident. I have many such scars all over my body, and yet despite all these reminders, I continue to make stupid decisions. So please: If you happen to glance over and find me unconscious, bleeding profusely, or my limbs somewhat askew, offer some help, because chances are I'll need it.

Sebastian Samur

"Video lottery terminals (VLTs) yield high profits for business but pose a high risk to individual users." In each of these examples, the speaker would be obligated to develop two or more main points.

Choosing Mode of Delivery

When speaking, you have a choice of several modes of delivery. Those options include extemporaneous, impromptu, memorized, and manuscript speaking. Other options include speaking from a teleprompter or PowerPoint deck. The one-point speech offers a good opportunity to gain practice in extemporaneous or impromptu speaking. Other chapters provide an opportunity to practice the other modes of delivery.

EXTEMPORANEOUS SPEAKING

Extemporaneous speaking
Speaking without having memorized the entire speech, often from note cards

As noted in Chapter Four, the term *extemporaneous speaking* refers to a situation where you prepare and practice a speech without memorizing more than the introduction and conclusion. Typically, you speak from 3″ × 5″ or 4″ × 6″ index cards that contain key words and phrases or quotations. Speaking from key points enables you to add ideas to your note cards at the last minute—a reference to someone in the audience, another person's speech, or a happening in today's news. These references add a sense of being "in the moment." Depending on the length of the speech, two to five cards usually are sufficient. Limit the number of words on a card, put them in large print or font, and number them. A mix of lower- and upper-case letters is more readable than "all caps." See the Keep in Mind box for a more comprehensive review of points to remember in using note cards.

Practice the speech before a mirror or in front of your roommate, but do not try to remember the exact words. Glance at the cards from time to time to remind yourself of the thought sequence. Avoid shuffling or playing with the cards when speaking. Direct eye contact with audience members is important. Typically, extemporaneous speakers memorize only the introduction and conclusion to speeches. Properly delivered, an extemporaneous speech sounds spontaneous even if you have practiced a number of times. This perception of spontaneity comes from the fact that the wording changes slightly from one practice to the next. For that reason, whenever possible, the extemporaneous speaking situation is preferred to impromptu speaking, the next type of delivery discussed here. See the Keep in Mind box on how to sound extemporaneous with a well-practiced speech. Studies show that better speeches result from time invested in the preparation and practice of a speech.[5]

Impromptu speaking
Speaking without benefit of preparation, usually in an unexpected situation

IMPROMPTU SPEAKING

Impromptu speaking refers to an unexpected speaking occasion—a time when you are forced to think on your feet, without benefit of more than a few minutes of preparation time. Some believe, however, that no speech is truly impromptu

Keep in Mind

Tips for Using Note Cards

· Use 3″ × 5″ or 4″ × 6″ index cards—never regular paper!
· Write clearly and legibly, large enough to see easily.
· Use mostly key words.
· Write out quotations and statistics; note sources.
· Limit the number of points on cards to five or six.

· Highlight or underline hard-to-remember points.
· Avoid using more than five cards.
· Number the cards.
· When you deliver, hold the cards with one hand.
· Maintain eye contact; do not read from cards.

Keep in Mind

Tips to Practice by Listening

I have a technique for practicing my speeches that allows them to sound extemporaneous even though I have practiced them. I write out my speech well in advance. Then I record myself reading the speech on one of the little hand recorders. For the week leading to the speech, I never look at notes but simply listen to the speech over and over—sometimes in the car, sometimes in other situations. I do not memorize the speech, but I do become extremely familiar with the material, details, and order of points. The technique works well because it is like listening to yourself deliver a speech flawlessly over and over again. The lack of memorization allows for a natural delivery and a little improvisation upon delivery. Clients marvel at my never using notes—not even to deliver factual content with dates and dollars interspersed. This is not a technique I was ever taught or read about. I got the idea from techniques used in sport where you visualize over and over the perfect performance.

Mary Charleson

because people collect stories in their heads that they use on occasions when they must speak unexpectedly. They also draw on experiences from their past. As F. E. Smith (Lord Birkenhead) once said of former British Prime Minister Winston Churchill, "Winston has devoted the best years of his life to preparing his impromptu speeches." (See the Keep in Mind box.)

To the extent possible, people tend to avoid impromptu speaking. Faced with the need to perform spontaneously, speakers often use parts of speeches that have worked for them in the past. Some have favorite passages that they insert in numerous speeches. (Classical rhetoricians applied the term *commonplaces* to these recycled passages). Government leaders rarely have only one version of any speech. Their speechwriters typically prepare multiple versions of the same speech, adapted to various circumstances and audiences. At other times, speechwriters in large organizations such as government prepare *speech modules* (policy statements and examples that anyone in the organization can use). Faced with the need to produce speeches on short notice, speakers paste together relevant points from the speech modules.

Keep in Mind

Tips for Impromptu Speaking

- Think in advance about stories with morals that could apply to many different topics.
- Do not reveal your topic prior to speaking.
- Begin with an attention-getting device.
- Proceed to a thesis statement.

- If the speech has more than one point, offer a preview of major points to be covered.
- Develop major point or points of speech.
- Have a clear, interesting conclusion that ties together the speech.

These modules serve much the same function as the form letters that organizations use to respond to public requests for information.

Communicators also prepare what are called "Qs and As" (questions and answers) to ensure that bureaucrats and politicians make as few impromptu remarks as possible. In fact, communicators often quake if their government leaders depart from a set script because consistency in messaging is extremely important. We live in a period of time when the media can press a button to replay the words of a politician, government leader, or CEO. Organizations are legally and socially responsible for public statements. So they must take particular care when they speak "off the cuff." Tips from a Professional talks about the importance of being prepared for these "ambushes."

When I was in high school, students prepared for impromptu speaking competitions by doing two things: (1) reading the most recent issues of *Time* magazine and *Newsweek* (quick and easy to digest) and (2) memorizing stories and quotations that they could apply to almost any topic. I recall that one competitor had a

---

TIPS FROM A PROFESSIONAL
Avoiding the "Deer in the Headlights"

You have just emerged from a televised committee appearance on a critical issue of public importance, and, feeling good about how it went, you see a crush of reporters, cameras, and technicians in front of you. A "fight-or-flight" feeling in the pit of your stomach triggers a glistening sweat on your forehead and your palms start to sweat.

If you feel this way, you certainly wouldn't be alone in your feelings toward the "ambush." Thinking in these terms, however, may not do justice to the opportunities that a media encounter can offer.

First, the speaker must reduce the downside risk of the "sound bite from hell," which most people fear. How to prevent such a career-limiting opportunity? First, you should realize that the reporters are looking for a usable sound bite to use in "clip city," not a detailed explanation. So give them what they came for—a seven-second sound bite that cuts to the heart of your point. Secondly, use the "ambush" to drive your messages, rather than merely a "Q & A" session, in which you react to all the questions without any attempt to steer the interview to what you want to say. Finally, avoid the "deer in the headlights" look by fixing your gaze on some chosen spot during the questions—either down or at a place just slightly to one side or beyond the reporters, who are immediately in front of you. By focusing on that spot, you can gain a few seconds to think before beginning your response. That will reduce the pressure—and temptation—to blurt out a response without the time to think. When you are ready to speak, you can look more directly toward the reporter or the camera.

So, even if you never to grow to love the "ambush," you can at least learn to survive the experience—and in media interviews, that is absolutely essential.

Laura Peck, vice president and cofounder of McLoughlin Media in 1984, has conducted thousands of communication skills programs for senior executives globally. Laura is a graduate of Dalhousie University with a B.A. and B.Ed. Laura also completed the Executive Leadership Program at the John F. Kennedy School of Government at Harvard University. Her consulting firm has offices in Washington, DC, and Ottawa, Ontario.

favorite story that he adapted to almost every occasion. He told a parable of the person who is allowed to visit both "hell" and "heaven." When he visits "hell," he sees people sitting at a grand banquet hall. Chained together, the people are unable to eat the wonderful dishes that lie before them. When the visitor goes to a second room, he is surprised to see a similar situation. As in the first room, the people sit chained to a long banquet table, unable to feed themselves. But this time the people are eating! By cooperating, they can feed each other.

At this point, my friend launched into whatever happened to be the main topic of the impromptu speaking assignment. In today's terms, that could be the war in Iraq, the plight of hurricane victims, or immigration issues. The parable could lead into a discussion of unemployment, homelessness, or the high debt load incurred by university graduates who obtain school loans. Cooperation is a generic concept applicable to the solution of almost any crisis experienced by individuals, institutions, or governments. Experienced speakers often rely on these kinds of planned passages to carry them through moments when they must speak "without preparation." Another story that could be adapted to many different speech topics is the following:

> When poachers want to capture monkeys, they go about it in a surprisingly simple way: They place fruit or nuts in an open jar. The mouth of the jar is sufficiently large for the monkey to insert his paw in an open fashion, but not large enough for the monkey to remove the fruit with a clenched fist. The jar is also too heavy to be carried away by the monkey. Because the monkey refuses to give up the fruit, the poachers are able to walk up to the jar and capture the exhausted monkey without any real resistance. Obviously, the fruit is not worth the price that the monkey has to pay with his life. But he steadfastly refuses to relinquish the valued prize. Such are many of the sacrifices that we make in our own lives. We refuse to recognize when we have invested too much in a worthless enterprise, surrendered too much for too little return, or paid the ultimate price for victory. Like the monkey, we become entrapped, overcommitted.

A web search allowed me to identify a number of different contexts in which people have applied this story. Interestingly, the applications ranged from discussions of the Indo-Pakistani conflict to matters pertaining to global financial economies to the importance of persevering in troubled relationships. The possibilities for the application of this tale are limitless.

MEMORIZING THE SPEECH

Even though the practice of memorizing a speech is largely a relic of the past, exceptions exist. Some contests in oratory still demand that competitors learn their speeches by heart. Ceremonial speakers tend to memorize their speeches or to speak from a manuscript. Also, many motivational and political speakers become so familiar with their material that the delivery is virtually memorized. Some of the most eloquent speakers, such as Martin Luther King, Jr., delivered speeches that included finely honed passages, which could not have been the product of extemporaneous or impromptu delivery. The language was too precise. So while memorizing a speech may not be the most common or the preferred form of delivery, the practice still exists.

Memorizing
Committing an entire speech to memory

Most speaking occasions allow speakers to bring whatever memory devices they choose to the podium. So even if you plan to deliver a memorized speech, you may feel more comfortable bringing a few notes to the stand with you—just in case you forget. If you do not want your audience to see the cards, you can place them on a shelf under the speaker's podium or on a nearby table. The major difference between memorized and extemporaneous delivery is the extent to which you aim for spontaneity in wording. With extemporaneous delivery, you aim to vary the wording from one practice to the next. With a memorized speech, you strive to reproduce the exact wording of the speech as you have written it. You want the audience to savor the words and appreciate the carefully turned phrase.

In practicing the speech, think about the sequence of ideas. Memorize the sequence and then memorize the wording. When delivering the speech, focus your attention on your purpose in speaking and on your audience so that you do not sound robotic. If you forget a part of the speech, stop and find your place. If necessary, improvise until you are back on track.

MANUSCRIPT SPEAKING

Manuscript speaking
Speaking from the entire manuscript of a speech, but not reading it word for word

In formal situations, executive speakers often work from manuscripts or Power-Point decks prepared by speechwriters. Many speeches of the good will variety will be manuscript speeches, especially those prepared by communication staff members or professional speechwriters. When delivering a manuscript speech, the speaker may bring a full sheath of pages to the speaker's podium. (See the Keep in Mind box.) When delivering from a manuscript, place the open folder containing the papers on the podium. The podium should be high enough to allow you to maintain an erect head as you scan the manuscript, but low enough to allow the audience to see your face. Slide the papers from one side of the folder to the other as you progress through the speech. If you choose not to use a podium, hold the folder (containing the manuscript) with one hand, somewhat above waist level.

Whichever approach you select (podium or free-standing delivery), assume a posture that enables you to maintain eye contact with the audience. Lower your eyes, not your head, as you scan the manuscript for meaning. Decide, in advance, the points at which you will refer to the manuscript. (No ghostwriter can identify those points for a speaker.) Adequate practice enables you to refer less often to the manuscript. A general rule of thumb is that you should be able to look at your audience at least eighty percent of the time. In other words, you should have eye contact with the audience for eight out of ten minutes.

In reading the manuscript speech, look for thought clusters and focus on meaning and ideas rather than individual words. Some pauses will be shorter and others longer. Prior marking of the manuscript (see Chapter Fourteen) will tell you *where* to pause; but—in my experience—will rarely you *how long* to pause. So adhere to the following advice when delivering the manuscript: Pause briefly when ideas in different word clusters are linked to each other; take a longer pause after an introduction, the conclusion of a major thought sequence, and when you want to achieve dramatic effect.

The goal of most manuscript speaking is to sound as if you are engaged in direct conversation. You should be keenly aware of what you are saying and very

Keep in Mind

Tips for Delivering from Manuscript

- Prepare the manuscript copy in advance, indicating places for pauses, passages to be emphasized, and so on.
- Be sure that any last-minute additions (e.g., references to members of audience) do not clutter the manuscript so that it becomes unreadable.
- Practice in advance so that you know the speech well.
- If using a microphone, arrive early to be sure that the system is working.
- If you are using a podium, adjust it to appropriate height before the speech begins.
- In absence of a podium, place the manuscript in a folder and hold at waist level.
- As you read, slide papers from right to left side of the folder.

- Lower your eyes, not your head, to the paper.
- Look ahead to grasp clusters of words.
- Concentrate on ideas, not individual words.
- Maintain a conversational, personal delivery.
- Project energy and dynamism through voice and body.
- Vary your inflection, pitch, rate, and volume.
- Maintain eye contact at least 80 percent of the time.
- Smile when appropriate.
- Use pauses effectively.
- Do not exaggerate movements and expressions unless for humorous effect.
- Do not be afraid to move away from the podium.

much "in the moment," cognizant of the audience and their reactions to the speech. Adding spontaneous introductory comments that give the impression of immediate engagement is often appropriate. You should build the feeling that your comments are specific to *this* audience at *this* time. Using pauses effectively helps to transmit the impression of spontaneity. Moving too rapidly through material gives the impression of reading the speech. By speaking too fast, less skillful readers almost always give their audience little time to react to thoughts. The only real formula for delivering an excellent manuscript speech, however, involves practicing the speech multiple times and visualizing yourself in the situation of actual delivery.

Speakers often make last-minute changes to manuscripts written by others. In the situation of speaker, you should review the manuscript sufficiently in advance to ask for typewritten changes. Last-minute changes entered between the lines or in the margins can clutter the manuscript to the point that the text becomes unreadable. You should also avoid crossing out words. The exception to this rule involves the addition of impromptu references to the audience, occasion, or context that may be unknown at the time of writing the speech.

SPEAKING FROM A TELEPROMPTER

For televised speeches, speakers use teleprompters. Even when speakers rely on teleprompters, however, they often choose to present the appearance of delivering a manuscript speech. See the Keep in Mind box for rules to observe in speaking from a teleprompter.

Teleprompter
An electronic device that scrolls the text of a speech so that the speaker can read from it

Keep in Mind

Tips for Reading from a Teleprompter

- Practice at least one time (more if possible) with the teleprompter.
- Identify any words that could pose pronunciation problems.
- Make changes in the script, as necessary, for readability.
- Speak in a conversational and energetic manner.
- Imagine that you are speaking to a live person, not the camera.
- Avoid looking at the monitor; it looks unnatural.
- Read the text from the upper third, not the bottom, of the screen.

- Avoid giving the appearance of being a rotating fan.
- When reading ahead, look for idea clusters.
- Use controlled gestures when speaking from a teleprompter.
- Use appropriate facial expressions.
- Employ pauses for attention and emphasis.
- Avoid rushing delivery; the operator will follow your speed.
- Keep your head and chin elevated; don't slouch or slump.
- Keep a glass of water close at hand.
- When you finish, look at the camera until the director yells "cut."

Building Credibility Through Delivery

Studies have found that audiences judge speakers on the basis of the following factors: perceived *composure, dynamism, trustworthiness, sociability, status, competence,* and *objectivity*. Most of these factors include elements on which delivery has an impact. (See the Keep in Mind box on page 165.)

COMPOSURE

Composure

Exercising control over posture and movements, a poised and fluent delivery, which increases your credibility in the eyes of audiences

American audiences are more likely to accept the messages of speakers who appear to be *composed*.[6] A recent study uncovered the reason that audiences may feel uncomfortable when speakers make too many mistakes:

> Why is it so annoying to watch someone else make a mistake? Maybe because it affects the same areas of the brain as when a person makes his or her own mistake, Dutch researchers say. Experiments in which volunteers tried a computer task and then watched each other do the same thing showed the brain reacted in a similar way whether the observer made the mistake, or watched someone else make it. . . . For their experiment Hein van Schie and colleagues hooked up 16 men and women to electrodes to measure brain activity and then sat them in front of a display screen with a joystick. The task was simple—to move the joystick in the same direction as certain arrows appearing on the screen. . . . After each trial, the volunteers were told whether they were correct. When people realised they had made an error, a distinctive electrical signal arose from a brain region called the anterior cingulate cortex. The same thing happened when the volunteers watched other volunteers try the experiment and make the occasional mistake.[7]

Keep in Mind

Improve Your Credibility Through Delivery

- Dress appropriately.
- Practice in advance if you will be using equipment.
- Be energetic when speaking.
- Maintain eye contact with your audience.
- Engage your audience in some activity, if time permits.
- Be natural and conversational.
- Smile when appropriate; avoid smirks and inappropriate smiles.
- If you make a mistake, collect your thoughts and continue.
- Stand straight; do not slump or hang your head.
- Be purposeful in your movements.
- Do not fidget with your hands or shift from foot to foot.
- Pause if you are tempted to use fillers such as *uh*, *um*, *like*, and so on.
- Use silence to your benefit—for emphasis or effect.
- Avoid strong emotional displays such as crying.
- Vary your rate, volume, pitch, and inflection.
- Avoid rushing your speech.
- Practice your speech so that it is smooth; avoid a choppy delivery.
- Use high quality, professional-looking visual aids.

The Dutch researchers concluded that the same mechanisms apply when we monitor our own actions and the actions of others. Outward signs of composure include a relaxed and confident posture and controlled body movements, a fluent delivery, a controlled use of silence, and the exercise of control over emotional displays. Audiences also judge speakers on the basis of how well they recover from mistakes. See the Reflections box for an example of how one speaker turned an embarrassing moment to her advantage by joking about the situation.

Reflections

As I was speaking, the buttons of my blouse began to set themselves free, opening my chest for all to see. As my situation worsened, people started to notice. I could hear some audience members begin to "snicker" and giggle. What could I do? I made a joke and said: "Umm . . . is it getting colder in here? Or is it just me?" People laughed, after which I was able button my blouse and refocus the audience's attention—on my message rather than my breasts! Lessons learned: No problem is without a solution. Think on your feet. Learning to laugh about yourself is important, and doing it in a positive way keeps your credibility as a speaker. People may remember your embarrassing moment, but they will also remember how skillfully you got out of the situation.

Christine Vallières

Controlling Posture and Body Movements

Audiences often connect external behaviors with inner states of mind. They may interpret tension in hands, arms, and facial muscles, for example, as signs of anxiety. They may attach similar meaning to lack of gestures, a soft or monotone voice, and emotionless facial expression. So if a speaker manifests these behaviors, the audience might see the person as wanting in confidence, intimidated by the speaking event.[8] Sometimes we extrapolate personality characteristics from behaviors. We might conclude, for example, that a person is inflexible or boring—or perhaps too meek to be interesting. We associate deadpan facial expressions with lack of warmth.

In the same way, audiences see uncontrolled movements as indicators of nervousness and lack of confidence. The nervous and uncertain speaker has a large repertoire of awkward postures and uncontrolled movements upon which to call. Some of the most common postures include slouching against the speaker's stand, leaning against a table or chair, crossing legs, and standing with one hip out of place or feet spaced too widely apart to be natural. The most common uncontrolled movements include rocking back and forth (sometimes back to front, sometimes side to side), kicking a leg, and bobbing the body. Uncontrolled hand and arm movements include tightly clutched hands (in front or behind the body), hands on the hip, a tight grip on the two sides of the speaker's podium, swinging arms, holding or rubbing one arm, touching the hair, flipping the hair, and playing with an object such as a rubber band or pen. Not surprisingly, audiences see increased reliance on these kinds of movements and *manipulators* (the term applied to the massaging, rubbing, or holding of our own bodies) as signs of discomfort.[9]

The importance of gaining control over extraneous body movements and gestures cannot be overemphasized. The inexperienced speaker will be most comfortable with feet spaced slightly apart, a stance that carries an impression of balance. As the speaker grows more comfortable with the audience and the act of speaking, she may practice taking the occasional step toward one side of the audience or the other. These movements should be purposeful, and the speaker should assume positions that are fixed for a period of time. Pacing is a sign of nervousness, lack of confidence, and indecision or weakness. Any kind of movement should appear motivated, not random or aimless.

In my experience, women face a particular challenge in public speaking. A major problem occurs when women adopt mannerisms that are "little girl" in nature—twisting a strand of hair, tugging on clothing, hunching their shoulders, or giving little kicks of their feet as they speak. I make this observation on the basis of many years of teaching public speaking, as well as attending professional workshops, where members of the audience have discounted the views of otherwise competent speakers who model these characteristics. Consciously or unconsciously, we associate these kinds of gestures with children. While all speakers (male and female) risk loss of credibility, in my experience, the risk is especially high for women and for speakers with a naturally youthful appearance.

Achieving Fluency

Fluency
Not stumbling over words

Fluency (not stammering, stuttering, or relying on *mmhs* and *uhs*) and appropriate use of pauses are also important. Most speakers have crutches upon which to rely when they face an uncertain moment in a speech. The speaker might say *uh, OK, um, ah, you know, well, whatever, ur, anyway,* and *like.* The smacking of lips and other noises also serve as filler in those moments when the alternative is silence. In reality, moments of silence can build suspense or allow an audience to think about a point that the speaker has made. As with other aspects of delivery, the mantra should be, "Eliminate anything that detracts from the message." Filler sounds intrude, like white noise, into the consciousness of the audience and take the focus away from the speech. The noises also detract from the impression that the speaker is confident and composed. We associate fluency and calm during silence with composure.[10]

Taking Control of Silence

Experienced speakers use silence to gain and maintain control over their speaking environments. When they reach the front of the room or the podium, they pause before beginning the speech. They wait for audience members to stop talking, to put down their pens and paper, and to turn their attention to the front. When they ask a rhetorical question of the audience, they pause long enough to allow the audience members to respond to the question in their minds. After making a statement with strong emotional impact, experienced speakers wait long enough for the comment to have maximum effect. Sometimes speakers pause before stating a startling fact, waiting for the undivided attention of the group. Just as seasoned speakers pause before beginning their speeches, they also pause after concluding their speeches. They allow the audience time to process the final thought before they vacate the stage or speaker's platform. Inexperienced speakers, on the other hand, rush from one sentence to the next and often complete their last sentence on the way to their seats. In summary, pauses allow speakers to demonstrate control over their subject matter and the situation.

Public speakers, however, are often afraid of silence; and if they forget a point or lose their place, they feel great embarrassment. In English literature, we speak of "pregnant pauses" as if they have great weight and significance. They are "heavy" moments, often emotional, to be avoided whenever possible. But the speaker who has lost his place or breath should not hesitate to pause, collect his thoughts, and then continue. Sometimes a drink of water will give a speaker the required time to remember the next point and alleviate the dryness of throat that comes with tension. Pauses also serve other functions, as the later discussion on dynamism will consider.

The easiest way to separate experienced from inexperienced actors and actresses is to examine their use of silence. (See the Reflections box.) Actors such as Robert Redford, Richard Gere, and Jodie Foster have mastered the art of silence; and we read strength and power into their dialogues. American speakers also can learn from the Asians or Apaches, who are comfortable with lapses in speaking: "The Taoist view is that one who speaks doesn't know, one who knows doesn't speak."[11] Similarly, in the Apache culture, strangers gathering for work may not break their silence for days.

Controlling Emotional Displays

As discussed in Chapter One, North American audiences are usually uncomfortable with high levels of emotionalism in presentations; and speakers typically

Reflections

Silence in Singapore

Sitting on the plane, I ran through the routines that I would be teaching in a two-week "hip hop" workshop, scheduled to begin upon my arrival in Singapore. While I had been teaching "hip hop" for a long time, I had never ventured so far from home; nor had I ever taught in a cultural environment other than my own. I had no idea what it would be like to instruct students in the tiny country of Singapore. But I soon found out.

Amidst nerves and uncertainty, I took the stage to teach my first class. And there they were—a room full of students—so poised, prepared, and expressionless that I felt like a drill sergeant in my own hip hop army! At home, I usually have to spend the first five minutes settling down a rowdy room before giving choreography; but in my class in Singapore, you could have heard a pin drop. Everyone was attentive and focused. The silence was deafening. I didn't know how to interpret it. I was used to separating people who were making a disturbance and calling for quiet. I immediately felt that no one was enjoying himself or herself, and I decided to lighten the mood. My voice got louder, my tone got shriller, and I did not let anyone escape from my most direct eye contact. No change at first. Then slowly I heard a quiet mumble begin to make its way around the room. It sounded like friendly banter. Relieved and happy that the room was finally alive with noise and movement,

I increased my level of activity still further. I waved my arms. I jumped about the stage. I used the most animated facial expressions at my disposal. This had to be my best performance ever. Meanwhile, the mumbling grew into a loud rumble, and I could hear nearly every student saying *aiyah*.

The class ended on this note, after which a student approached me to ask if I knew the meaning of what everyone was saying. Cheerfully, I said that I wasn't sure but I thought that it might be some sort of laughter or acknowledgment. Politely but firmly, she said that I was wrong; and she explained the meaning of the exclamation. *Aiyah* meant "a universal feeling of surprise and disappointment"! To say the least, I was horribly embarrassed and more than a little anxious for my next class. But a fellow staff member talked me through some "less North American" techniques, which served me well through the remainder of the two-week workshop. I learned that it is very important to have background knowledge of the culture. While I thought that I was being funny, other people found me offensive. Had I simply taken the time to learn more about the Singapore culture, my first teaching experience in Asia would have gone a lot more smoothly.

Jamie Hodgins

attempt to control such displays. A few years ago, I led a discussion of media coverage of the Oka, Quebec, crisis—a situation where the Mohawk of Kanesatake mounted an armed protest against the building of a municipal golf course on sacred burial grounds. One of the politicians speaking publicly on the topic was Ethel Blondin (now Blondin-Andrew), who represents the western Arctic region of the Northwest Territories. The consensus in the discussion (especially among the men) was that Blondin, a Dene, had destroyed her credibility by displaying excessive emotion before the television cameras. In the eyes of many television viewers, she had appeared close to tears as she delivered her speech. And, in fact, in the days following her speech, some television commentators criticized her for an overly emotional presentation. One of the factors that contributed to the impression of extreme emotionalism was the rising inflection that characterized the ends of her sentences. Combined with a relatively high-pitched voice that often seemed to be breaking, the inflection pattern suggested to listeners that Blondin was close to tears. Although some women believed that the emotional delivery increased the credibility of Blondin on the sincerity dimension, others reacted negatively to the display.

Sometime later I was watching *North of 60*, a television drama about Lynx River, a small town in the Northwest Territories. To my surprise, I realized that the inflection of the female Native speakers on *North of 60* sounded remarkably close to that of Ethel Blondin. The pattern of rising inflection at the ends of sentences did not, however, connote excessive emotion at all. Rather, the pattern characterized the normal discourse of Native speakers living in the region. The perception that Blondin was close to tears in her earlier speech was probably erroneous. Nonetheless, the lesson to be learned from Blondin's experience remains intact. Mainstream audiences in North America do not like speakers to lose their composure and become overly emotional in a public situation. Sally Field's experience, recounted in an earlier chapter, offers a second support for this conclusion. For that reason, when speakers are unsure that they can speak on a topic without breaking down, they should select another topic.

DYNAMISM

American audiences appreciate speakers who are *dynamic*.[12] External signs of dynamism in a speech include movement and gestures, animated facial expressions, and sufficient volume, emphasis, and variety in the voice. Dynamic speakers also engage the audience. In a public speaking context, presenters who lean on the podium, lower their heads to speak, talk in low voices, and mumble will not convey the required degree of dynamism. Charisma appears in some discussions as a source credibility factor that is associated with dynamism and attractiveness.[13]

Dynamism
Displays of physical energy, such as gestures or raised voice, which can increase a sense of connection to audiences

Making Appropriate Use of Movement, Gestures, and Facial Expressions

Within some cultural settings, absence of gestures can convey boredom, blandness of personality, and lack of energy.[14] If you are speaking to an audience of Greeks, Italians, Arabs, South Americans, or Africans, they may expect you to use broad and animated gestures. The Japanese, on the other hand, expect a minimum of hand gestures in public speaking. A sudden and unanticipated movement of the hand can completely distract a Japanese listener.[15] If animated hand and body movements are part of the culture of your audience, try to use a more dynamic mode of delivery. If you are speaking to an audience of Asian businesspeople, on the other hand, you may want to employ fewer gestures and more controlled facial expressions.

These suggestions come with a caution, however. If you use gestures that do not match your personality or comfort level, they may appear awkward or flamboyant. Rather than contribute to the sense that you are a dynamic speaker, the gestures

may convey the impression that you are insincere. Many beginning speakers are overwhelmed by the number of points to be considered when they deliver a speech—voice, posture, volume and enunciation, pronunciation, proper breathing, and control of the speech content. They find it difficult to employ new and unfamiliar gestures in their first speeches. Since no prescription exists for appropriate use of gestures, the goal should be to strive for a natural and sincere style of delivery and to take audience expectations into account. For some speakers or occasions, that implies using more gestures; for others, it means fewer. The main criterion is that gestures should complement your speech but not draw attention to themselves. In the same way, Americans appreciate animated but controlled facial expressions. They associate deadpan expressions with lack of energy and uninteresting personalities.

Pitch
The highness or lowness of one's voice

Inflection
Changes in pitch

Conveying Dynamism Through Pitch, Inflection, and Rhythm

Every culture uses pitch, inflection, and rhythm to give meaning to speech. The term *pitch* refers to the highness or lowness of the voice, and the term *inflection* refers to changes in pitch. Through pitch and inflection, speakers convey both emotion and energy. When people lack variation in pitch and inflection, we say that they speak in a *monotone* (one level). An early study identified a monotonous voice as the most serious barrier to an effective presentation.[16] Clear strong vocal presentations convey a sense of dynamism and energy, whereas voices that are weak and thin transmit the opposite impression. Most Americans follow an inflection pattern that ends with a lowering of inflection at the end of sentences. Some other cultures end their sentences with a rising inflection.

The term *rhythm* refers to a "harmonious flow of vocal sounds"[17] or patterns. Speakers often vary their rhythm according to the seriousness of the occasion. To convey seriousness of purpose, for instance, East Indians adopt a "slow ponderous . . . rhythm and a low pitch."[18] In general, however, speakers should avoid excessive predictability in speech rhythm. Like the lapping of the tide against the seashore, predictable patterns of rising and falling speech can lull an audience to sleep. Predictable patterns can also give the impression that the person is reading the speech. (We tend to fall into patterns when we read out loud.) The speaker who is criticized for falling into a pattern can insert pauses to eliminate the impression of reading or delivering a memorized speech. Pauses interrupt patterns and help speakers to sound more spontaneous.

Even though an animated delivery is preferable for most occasions, you should avoid a choppy delivery. Choppiness in delivery—or the breaking of speech into bits and pieces—is one of the most common problems among beginning speakers. To avoid choppiness, you should practice the speech aloud, identifying the places to take a break and to breathe. In that way, the speech does not become fragmented in delivery. Too many breaks, too often, destroy the aesthetic quality of speeches. The strategic placement of pauses, as discussed in another section, allows the speaker to maintain fluency of presentation and to breathe at the right places. The following example illustrates how a speaker can break a passage into readable, but flowing, segments:

> We face a crisis in health care./ We stand at the edge of a precipice/ and if we do not take care/we will be in freefall/ unable to control where or how we land./ We know that we must find a way to bridge the gap between what we have and what we need./ However/ we also know that/ at present/ we lack the resources to make a credible effort./ So we continue tottering at the edge of disaster./

Conveying Dynamism Through Rate and Volume

Audiences attach a higher level of dynamism to individuals who speak in a relatively rapid and animated fashion with sufficient volume. However, the nature of the content; the language skills, cultural expectations, and knowledge of the audience; the occasion; the personality and linguistic skills of the speaker; and the speaking environment (physical and technical) influence choices regarding both rate and volume of speech.

The nature of the content should have an impact on rate of speech. When talking about a concept that is complex and difficult to understand, using technical language, or defining terms, you should speak more slowly. The audience needs time to process more complex information. When you are giving statistics or asking the audience to relate an idea to their own experiences, allow more time for thought. A faster rate of speech, on the other hand, works well with lighter topics. In recounting

Rhythm
Measured flow of words in speaking

Rate
Rapidity

Volume
Loudness

a story, giving an example, or talking about an idea that can be easily grasped, you can speak more quickly. Public speakers tend to speak more rapidly when they are excited or interested in a topic. Sometimes they speak more rapidly when they build toward a climactic moment in a speech, as happened in the speech "I Have a Dream" by Martin Luther King, Jr. King's pace quickened from an average rate of 92 words a minute in the early part of his speech to a rate of approximately 145 words per minute at the climax.[19]

If a speaker addresses a topic about which he feels strongly (e.g., imposing a draft or laws governing sex offenders), he may raise his voice from time to time to show emotional engagement with the topic. People associate loud and rapid speech with strong emotions and high levels of involvement with a topic.[20] But many audiences react negatively to an angry speaker, viewing the person as out of control. Establishing a contrast between softness and loudness in delivery is often the best approach. The most commanding moments in a speech may be the times when the speaker lowers her voice and speaks in soft tones for dramatic effect—to build suspense or to add a more tempered emotional energy to the speech.

The language skills and knowledge level of the audience also influence choices regarding rate of speech and volume. A presenter may speak at a faster rate with audiences who share his linguistic profile; or he may speak louder with some audiences (e.g., Latinos and Arabs) than with others (Japanese and Chinese).[21]

The nature of the occasion also influences choices regarding rate of speech. The greater the sense of occasion, the slower the rate of speech is likely to be. Racing through a eulogy, a state speech, or a declaration of war would be inappropriate. In summary, while a faster-paced speech conveys dynamism and energy, speakers may need to slow their rates to connect with some more somber occasions.

The average rate at which people speak varies between 120 and 180 words per minute,[22] but rates of delivery often reflect the *personality of the speaker* or the *level of confidence with the language.* When I wrote speeches for ministers whose first language was French, I wrote shorter speeches because they typically spoke at a slower rate in English than in French. In short, no one rate of speech may be best for every speaker.

Environmental factors (physical and technical) also deserve consideration. The acoustics of the room or auditorium, the lighting, and equipment have an impact on delivery options. Microphones pose special challenges in speaking. When using a microphone, you must exercise even greater control over volume to avoid the impression of shouting at the audience. Placing the microphone about two to three inches from your mouth typically works best. Other challenges occur in an auditorium darkened for purposes of delivery. In that situation, eye contact becomes virtually impossible. In outdoor settings, echo effects can create havoc for the speaker who does not know how to control for feedback from the amplification system. (See the Reflections box.)

Engaging the Audience

A well-seasoned speaker once told me that when he caught the eye of a member of his audience, the person looked immediately afterward at the people on either side to see if they had noticed the special attention.[23] I checked, on a few occasions, to confirm the validity of his observation. He was right. The fact is that audience

Reflections

Whose Voice Is This, I Ask?

The occasion was graduation night. As a teacher of drama and public speaking, I had been charged with presenting honors awards at high school graduation, held in an outdoor stadium. Confidently, I walked to the microphone, ready to deliver my speech. But I was barely into my introduction when I heard a loud, strange voice throwing my words right back at me a few seconds after I said them! I was horrified to realize that the voice echoing over the stadium's public address system was my own. I had never spoken over a public address system in such a large venue before and had no idea such a thing could happen. I was so flustered that I forgot my entire speech and ended up adlibbing the whole thing. To this day, I'm still not sure of what I said, but since the honor graduates did come forward to receive their awards, I assume that I at least called their names. I've never since had to speak in such a situation, but if the need arises, I will definitely be more prepared and *practice* in the location beforehand.

Desirée Devereaux

members like to be noticed. They want to catch the sweaty towel tossed by a rock performer or the bouquet at a wedding. They want others to see that they have been singled out for attention.

An opposite situation occurs when speakers orient not only their eyes, but also their entire bodies, to one side of the audience—virtually ignoring the other members of the audience. Numerous reasons explain this tendency to prefer one side of

a classroom or auditorium. Sometimes the people sitting on one side of the audience are more responsive to the speaker. They may be smiling, nodding, and offering encouragement. Friends may be sitting on the preferred side of the classroom. At other times, more of the seats may be filled on one side than the other. The reasons for choosing to present to one side of the room are usually personal in nature. But whatever the reasons, you should always try to maintain eye contact with all parts of the audience—first one section, then another. Otherwise, you will fail to engage your audience.

Like performers in the Broadway musical *Cats*, you can leave the stage and walk among the audience. You can pass a microphone around the audience and request feedback or invite audience members to join you on the stage. You can call for a volunteer willing to participate in the demonstration of a back massage. If you are showing how to make candles, create a card for an anniversary, or read tarot cards, you can ask for larger-scale participation from the audience. In that case, you might hand out supplies to the entire group or to selected members, who work along with you in performing the task. You can ask the audience to join you in practicing a salsa step. If you are teaching visualization techniques, you can request that the audience members close their eyes and imagine a spoken scenario. Creative and dynamic speakers find ways to engage their audiences. Speaking at a graduation exercise, alternative theater director David Diamond asked three-hundred gowned students, faculty, and their families and friends to participate with him in the spontaneous construction of a "theatrical moment." Afterward, he asked twenty audience members to join him on stage to "complete the image" of graduating.[24]

Immediacy behaviors
Things we do to get literally or figuratively closer to our audience while speaking

When you walk among the audience or invite listeners to join you onstage, you are engaging in what Albert Mehrabian called *immediacy* behaviors.[25] This term refers to the extent to which we perceive ourselves as being physically and/or psychologically close to other people. As will be discussed in a subsequent section on sociability, large numbers of studies have pointed to the importance of using nonverbal immediacy behaviors in speaking. Kenyans employ these kinds of strategies in their speechmaking, as do most African-American preachers: "Members of the audience at a public speech are not spectators, they are participants coming together to construct a shared communal meaning. . . . Audience response is part of that process."[26] A common strategy is to leave the ends of sentences unfinished, waiting for an audience response. For an example of a student speech that employed audience engagement, see the Sample Speech.

TRUSTWORTHINESS

Trustworthiness
The quality of being safe and reliable

Speakers can establish trust through eye contact and consistency between verbal and nonverbal elements in delivery.

Creating Trust Through Eye Contact

Another important dimension of source credibility is *trustworthiness*, also termed *character* or *safety*.[27] In the United States, the most visible indicator of trustworthiness is willingness to look someone in the eye. An important factor in source credibility, the maintenance of direct eye contact tells the audience that the speaker is

Sample Speech

International "Talk Like a Pirate" Day

With each passing year, an increasing number of people overlook an important day in our history. A day when the world can come together and speak a unified language: one of acknowledgment and appreciation. I'm talking of course about September 19th: International "Talk Like a Pirate" Day. Ahoy ye scurvy landlubbers! I'm Cap'n Wagthorn the Mahogany of the Delirious Granny, an' I be here to tern ye all into tip top pirates for the tenth annual International Talk Like a Pirate Day. Arrr! This day, though officially inaugurated by Dave Barry in 2002, actually be existin' in 1995, an' it be about time that ye all be familiarzin' yerselves w'it.

Now. There be three key elements t'ward enterin' piratehood. The first be yer name. The second be yer speak. An' the last be yer dress.

When pickin' a pirate name, it be most important ta pick a name that be colorful. Violent words an' ugly descriptors be excellent tools for accomplishin' this task. Werds like *creep*, *dead*, *cold*, *bloody*, *lumpish*, and *smutty* be great, grand werds for comin' up w' your names.

Yer speak be the second key element t'ward enterin' piratehood. **Can everybody say Ahoy?** This be your landlubbin' equivalent o' *hello*. **Now look 'cross the room to someone, and yell to 'em, Ahoy! Again! Again! Again!** Avast! Another important term to know be *Arrr!* **Can everybody here say Arrr!?** This be your landlubbin' equivalent o' *Yes* or *I agree* or *I were her first.* **Now everyone look 'cross the room and say Arrr! Now say Ahoy! Now say Ahoy! Then Arrr!** Not too shabby for a bunch o' scallywags!

The last element be yer dress. And by dress, me means not dress as in wench's garb, but your accoutrements. An eye patch or hook be quite appropriate. Also a parrot on yer shoulder, or a hat w' skull an' cross bones on the front be quite suitable. Now where be mine accoutrements, ye ask? Well, I fergot me eyepatch in me other pants.

Once ye have got these three elements down, ye be well on yer way ta becomin' a bonafide pirate! Now off w' ye! Go get some grog or ta buckle yer swashes! Find some booty, but let me not catch ye speakin' no landlubber talk, or it'll be the gallows meat for ye! Arrr!

Sebastian Samur

---

open, honest, and trustworthy. A number of Arab, Latin American, and southern European countries are also comfortable with direct gaze. In some other countries, however, direct eye gaze signals a lack of respect for the listener or an overly aggressive personality. The Chinese, Japanese, Indians, Pakistanis, and people in northern Europe look only peripherally (or not at all) at their conversation partners in interpersonal situations. (See the Reflections Box.)

Building Trust Through Consistency Between Verbal and Nonverbal Behaviors

In speaking, we strive to achieve a fit between what we say and how we say it. When former President George H. W. Bush announced allied military action in the Persian Gulf on January 16, 1991, he smiled as he spoke. Commentators later criticized the president for lack of consistency between the seriousness of the words (verbal content) and the manner in which he delivered the speech (nonverbal content). President George W. Bush has the same tendency as his father to speak about

Consistency between verbal and non-verbal behaviors
Using expressions and gestures that match our spoken message

Reflections

When Cultures Clash

I taught in an isolated community in northern Manitoba, Canada. My class was fifteen Cree students studying to become teachers. Having taken public speaking courses, I was excited to incorporate what I had learned into my teaching. At the beginning of the course, I focused on good voice projection, eye contact, hand and body gestures, as well as audience participation. I thought that my classes were great, as I asked questions that engaged my students to think and interact with the material being presented. One day, however, one of my students asked to see me. I suspected he wanted to tell me how inspired he was to be in the course. Instead, his question confused me.

"Why are you so rude?" he asked. "Rude?" I asked in return. He then explained that Crees always lower their eyes as a sign of respect for the person to whom they are speaking. Natives consider both direct eye contact and questions to be extremely aggressive. When a Cree knows you are ready to listen to his or her words, the words will be spoken. To ask questions as to what one is thinking is an invasion of that person's private space. From that day forth, I changed my classroom techniques and became less dependent on my acquired public speaking expertise.

Murray Smith

serious subjects with what often seems to be a half smile or smirk. Even if unintentional, the effect is diminished credibility in the eyes of those who expect consistency between the verbal and nonverbal elements in delivery.

Fiorello La Guardia, multilingual mayor of New York City from 1933 to 1945, was a master at achieving congruency in verbal and nonverbal language. A study of old newsreel footage of La Guardia's campaigns found that the body language of La Guardia reflected the language of the discourse. Even without sound, researchers could identify the language in which La Guardia was speaking. If La Guardia spoke in Italian, his gestures were broad and expansive. When speaking in English, his gestures were much more constrained, conforming to an American tendency to restrict broad gestures to situations of anger, frustration, excitement, and emotional arousal. If speaking in Yiddish, La Guardia's gestures were short and choppy.[28]

We transmit as much as 93 percent of our meaning through nonverbal communication.[29] Used effectively, *illustrators* (i.e., nonverbal acts that accompany speech) reinforce what we say in words.[30] Gestures, in particular, serve to clarify, reinforce, and add emphasis to points made in our presentations. When confronted with inconsistencies between verbal and nonverbal, people tend to believe the nonverbal.

Illustrators
Nonverbal acts such as gestures that amplify points we are making verbally

SOCIABILITY

Sociability
Likeability

Audiences like speakers who are *sociable*. Immediacy behaviors enable speakers to create the perception of sociability. Although originating with the study of teacher-student interactions,[31] the concept of immediacy holds relevance for all types of public speaking. Many studies have found that nonverbal immediacy, in particular, can have a positive effect on liking of a speaker or interest in enrolling in subsequent classes with an instructor.[32]

Immediacy behaviors could include adopting a conversational delivery, wearing clothing that communicates warmth in colors and design, and using physical proximity and body orientation to connect with the audience.

Creating a Sense of Immediacy Through Conversational Delivery

I learned the importance of *immediacy* in speaking at the age of seventeen when my debate partner and I reached the next-to-last round of a state competition. We were both experienced speakers, accomplished at delivering in a fast staccato style. We were accustomed to meeting each argument raised by the opposition in a cold analytical fashion before proceeding without pause to the next point. Logic was our forté. And as late as the 1950s, speaking at a rapid rate was considered to be the best way to persuade.[33] But on the day that we met Amy, I learned a valuable lesson. (I no longer recall her last name, but I will always remember her first name.) Amy was a member of the opposing team; and when she rose to speak, everyone listened. She smiled at the judge and at my partner and me. She paused before beginning her speech to be certain that she had the attention of the audience. Then she spoke in a friendly and personal fashion. Her unhurried and sociable way of speaking surprised me. (You have to be a speed listener to keep up with most debaters, and the typical American debater sounds pretty upset and angry.)

Amy was a different kind of speaker. She spoke in a warm and conversational way, explaining each point in some detail, unlike the usual scattergun approach. And even though she covered far fewer points than we had covered, the audience knew what she had said when she finished. She created a sense of immediacy with her audience by smiling, maintaining a relatively relaxed posture, and proceeding at a slower pace than the typical debater. She left her position behind the speaker's podium in order to stand closer to the audience, and she used examples to which the audience could relate. At the end of the day, Amy and her less remarkable partner walked away from the competition with the first place trophy; and my teammate and I had to be satisfied with third place.

After that experience, I began to change my style of speaking. I smiled more often. I concentrated on making my gestures more natural. I spoke more slowly. I left the speaker's podium more frequently, and I stopped talking "at people." Instead I concentrated on speaking "with people." I began to see my audience, no matter the size, as a collection of individuals with a need to be recognized. In short, I tried to engage in *immediacy* behaviors and to establish a greater sense of personal contact and closeness with my audience.

Some mannerisms in delivery achieve the opposite results from immediacy; they detract from perceptions of sociability. A few years ago, I taught a student with a near flawless manner of delivery. She was an experienced debater—fluent and confident. She had good volume and clear enunciation, and she exuded confidence. In short, even to an experienced judge of speechmaking, she seemed like a role model. But something was wrong. I searched at length to identify the reason that the audience did not respond warmly or enthusiastically to her speeches. On the final day of class, I asked for some help with diagnosing the problem; and one student pointed, without hesitation, to the nature of the problem. He said that Connie had a tendency to tilt her head slightly backward as she spoke, giving the impression that she was talking down to the group. To audience members, this nonverbal element conveyed the feeling that Connie had a patronizing and condescending attitude toward her audience. Following this comment, I also thought about the fact that Connie's verbal style was probably closer to that of a debater, thus reinforcing the nonverbal impression of someone who is performing in a contrived situation rather than connecting with her audience. At other times, I have noted that this tendency to hold the head too high can lead to a second problem with delivery. The speaker may appear to have half-closed eyes. The unnatural tilt to the head creates a situation where the speaker must look down at the audience.

In concluding this section, it is important to observe that, even though few contemporary public speaking occasions require that we wear a tuxedo or evening gown, exceptions do happen. A friendly and smiling demeanor may not be appropriate in all circumstances. The family of a deceased member may expect pomp and ceremony in the memorial service, and some cultures require a high level of decorum and formality in the celebration of marriages. When these formal rites of passage occur, we must customize our delivery to fit the expectations of the audience and the occasion.

Note especially that *informal* and *natural* do not mean *unrehearsed*. "Naturalness" does not come easily or spontaneously to most people. The tension felt by many speakers translates into the most unnatural gestures, awkward body postures, and lack of vocal control. Most speakers have to work hard to acquire the ability to present in a spontaneous and conversational way. They move along a continuum in developing this kind of skill. The continuum involves, first, eliminating distracting habits; second, acquiring new skills; and third, practicing the new skills so that they appear unrehearsed and natural.

Conversational style
Speaking as if you are talking one on one, but to entire audience

Finally, the term *conversational* does not imply that speakers should abandon the physical or psychological space that separates speakers from their audience. As in the classroom situation, the audience should always know who has the floor. A fine (albeit) invisible line always separates a speaker from the audience. If the speaker crosses that line, the audience becomes uncomfortable and the speaker loses her privileged platform. To identify the proxemics of space accorded to any speaker, an instructor need only ask the speaker to roam the room and address the class from different positions. Members of the audience will be able to identify, very easily, when speakers have crossed the invisible line.

Creating a Sense of Immediacy Through Hair and Dress

An interesting example of manipulating speaker immediacy through dress and hair relates to the case of Marcia Clark, lead prosecutor in the O. J. Simpson trial. Clark underwent a major transformation in image after she tested unfavorably with mock jurors in the period leading to the trial. One mock juror claimed, for example, that Clark came across as a tough female lawyer. Media consultants feared that her cold and hard veneer could alienate the jurors. They advised that she should alter her image in verbal and nonverbal ways. She should chat with the press about such "female" topics as shopping and children. She should wear lighter-colored clothing, softer fabrics, and additional jewelry to soften her appearance. They advised her to change her hairstyle to achieve a more feminine effect.[34] "Dress for Success" books counsel that women should wear darker colors such as black and navy to create a more professional appearance and to convey a sense of power and authority.[35] In the instance of Marcia Clark, however, the consultants wanted to deemphasize the power and authority dimensions and close the psychological distance separating speaker and audience.

The rules for men are not so different from those for women. On one occasion, the president of a teachers' union told a professor to wear slacks, a dress shirt, and sweater to an appeals hearing, instead of a suit. The lawyer told him that his peers would respond more warmly if his dress were not so stiff and formal. Dress can convey warmth and humanity or formality and coldness. Whether the reason for a positive decision was the quality of his argumentation or his sweater, the professor won his appeal. Politicians often use the same technique to convey the impression of having the "common touch." (See the Keep in Mind box for general advice on delivery.)

As with all other aspects of communication, culture influences audience perceptions of both dress and hair. Some audiences might perceive a shaved head or long hair as antisocial, and they might be reluctant to approach the person. Others, however, might see the same individuals as highly approachable. In general, source credibility studies tell us that appearance has an impact on audience responses. As superficial as it may seem, the level of a person's attractiveness influences audience receptivity to messages.

Speakers need to observe one other important rule of a pragmatic nature. They should never style their hair so that it can fall into their eyes. One of the most common tendencies of novice female speakers is to push back or flip their hair while they speak. Hair should be pulled away from the face and secured with a hair clip,

Keep in Mind

General Delivery Tips

- Position yourself so that everyone can see you.
- Wait until you have everyone's attention to begin.
- Watch your posture; don't lean on the podium.
- Don't be afraid to leave the podium, but don't wander purposelessly.
- Use note cards for most speeches; avoid full-sized sheets of paper.
- Be natural, and don't be afraid to smile.
- Don't apologize or thank the audience for listening to your speech.
- When appropriate, acknowledge a mistake with humor.
- Be enthusiastic and dynamic in your presentation.
- Don't rush your speech.
- Keep eye contact with the audience.
- Speak loud enough to be heard.
- Vary rate and volume to maintain interest.
- Avoid a condescending or patronizing attitude and posture.
- Control extraneous movements.
- Keep an eye on the time.
- Prior to delivery, practice your speech before a friend and/or in front of a mirror.

scrunchie, hair comb, elastic band, or headband. In the same way, all speakers (men and women) should avoid clothing that draws the attention of the audience away from the message. Excessive or dangling jewelry, busy scarves, tops that expose too much skin, tight pants, and wild mixes of color in clothing can create more interest in the speaker than the speech. (Although the solutions may vary, the same cautions apply to men with long hair, flashy clothing, or distracting visuals on T-shirts.)

Creating a Sense of Immediacy Through Physical Proximity and Body Orientation

Peggy Noonan, political analyst for MSNBC and speechwriter for former President Ronald Reagan, talked about the importance of eliminating physical barriers between speakers and audiences. She quoted Senator Slade Gorton as saying:

> There's something I learned unconsciously, and then I was told. If you can possibly do so, speak without having something between you and the audience. Don't have a podium, don't be at a table. . . . The more exposed you are to an audience the more connected you will be, the more attention they'll pay. . . . When you speak without a barrier you can say exactly the same thing you'd say behind a podium, and you get twice the impact.[36]

Kenneth E. Bickel, a preacher with the Grace Theological Seminary, recounted an experiment conducted by a practicing minister.[37] The minister (a doctoral student) hired a professor of communication from a local college to observe the congregation from behind a one-way glass during ten Sunday morning sermons. In the experiment, the minister varied certain elements of his delivery. He stood away from the pulpit for the introduction of each sermon. Then, as he made the transition into the main body of the sermon, he moved behind the pulpit to speak. The 100 percent listener attentiveness that he enjoyed during the introduction quickly dropped to about 30 percent attentiveness. When he moved to the second major section of his speech, he stepped away from the pulpit once again to stand closer to his audience. The observing professor noted that the minister recaptured a significant amount of audience attention with this change of position. The observer also noted that, when the minister moved to the right side of the sanctuary, larger numbers of that side of the congregation paid better attention; and when he moved to the left side, the situation reversed itself. After repeating the experiment ten times, the minister became convinced that remaining behind a pulpit represented a significant impediment to listener attention.

A number of studies of the physical environment have demonstrated the impact of putting any sort of physical barrier between speaker and listener. One study of patient-doctor communication demonstrated, for example, that patients felt almost five times more at ease after the researchers removed the desks that separated them from their doctors.[38]

Over many years of teaching, I have noted that audiences respond more warmly in classrooms where they feel physically close to other audience members, as well as physically close to the speaker. For events of limited duration, they are usually happier in a small inadequate classroom than in a large room where they feel lost in space. This principle has its limitations, however. Lengthy stays in crowded

(particularly overheated) environments can generate negative effects. Hitler applied this principle in an extreme and unethical way, crowding people together in small places to get a unified reaction. Obviously, taking the idea to its extreme is unethical. However, when the intent is to foster a good classroom dynamic and the duration of the speech event is limited, the principle seems appropriate.

STATUS

Listeners attach greater credibility to speakers with higher status.[39] Speakers convey status through dress; vocal cues (including accents and dialects); movement, posture, and stance; and the physical environment. A related concept is power, which speakers acquire through stance, body language, dress, and a strong clear delivery.

Conveying Status Through Dress

"One time I wore what I thought was this very cool outfit—a muumuu-type dress with pants underneath and super high sandals," quipped actress Kathleen Robertson (Theo in *Scary Movie 2*). "*The National Enquirer* ran a photo of me with a caption saying, 'Would you be caught dead in this outfit?' I was thrilled!" Not everyone shares Kathleen's zest for bad publicity, however; and most speakers seek to build their credibility through positive perceptions of their dress. A classic study manipulated dress to achieve "attractive" and "unattractive" female speakers. They found that the "attractive" female speakers (as judged by subjects) experienced more success than the "unattractive" female speakers in changing the attitudes of male students.[40] In the view of many, a speaker's dress conveys professionalism (or lack of professionalism), judgment (or lack of judgment), and respect (or lack of respect) for the audience.[41]

Studies have gone further to identify a relationship between clothing and judgments of status,[42] and the use of terms such as "blue collar" and "white collar" workers confirms this perceived relationship.[43] Norms in dress vary over time, but some such as John T. Molloy (*Dress for Success*) counsel that speakers should always dress in relatively formal attire. Others have concluded that many people are intimidated by formal dress; but if increased status is more important than increased immediacy, the person may want to choose more formal attire.[44] This advice may be particularly applicable to women and minorities, who face more barriers than do Caucasian male speakers in garnering credibility:

> Just last year, the *Wall Street Journal* cited Executive Coach Dee Soder's survey of male CEOs. She asked about what the CEOs considered to be "barriers to female advancement." They said women who had weak handshakes or who couldn't wear stiletto heels without wobbling weren't seen as strong leaders.[45]

Despite these rather extreme reports, which one hopes are not representative of the larger population of CEOs, the rules are probably less fixed than they have been in the past. A 2002 article in the *Wall Street Journal* reported that 88 percent of U.S. companies adhere to a business casual dress code.[46] Also, a group of youth volunteers, high school dropouts, or street youth may relate more easily to someone in casual dress. Expectancy violation theories also suggest that we are sometimes more successful when we violate expectations. A group of high school students, for example, may be pleasantly surprised when a scheduled speaker shows up in jeans and running shoes to deliver a talk on high-risk behaviors.

Sometimes audiences have set expectations for how speakers should dress—expectations that diminish the significance of immediacy concerns and work against the speaker who violates those expectations. Some audiences may perceive "dressing down" as an insult, a transparent attempt to identify for reasons of self-gain. One politician learned this fact when he arrived in jeans and lumberjack shirt for a meeting with blue collar workers. The audience thought that the politician did not show sufficient respect for the group by dressing in such informal clothing.

Given the conflicting opinions, it is my personal belief (based solely on observation) that the best advice may be to dress *one level above* how you anticipate your audience will dress. In other words, if you think that the audience will wear jeans and casual dress (e.g., on a retreat), wear the equivalent of slacks with a sports shirt if you are a man or the equivalent of a skirt or pants with casual top if you are a woman. If you think that male members of your audience will wear slacks with dress shirts and that females will wear the equivalent of dresses or pants with tailored tops, consider wearing a suit and tie or dress slacks with a sports jacket if you are a man. A woman in the same situation might choose a classical style of dress, suit, or pants suit.

Conveying Status Through Accents and Dialects

Audiences also judge the status of speakers on the basis of vocal cues, including accents and dialects. The term *accent* refers to the phonetic sounds of language. The term *dialect*, on the other hand, implies the patterns of speech in a particular region

Status
A sense of power and social position

or part of a country—syntax, idiom, and accents. The classic story of Eliza Doolittle in *My Fair Lady* (a musical adaptation of *Pygmalion* by George Bernard Shaw) illustrates how dialects can define status. In response to a challenge, the arrogant and aristocratic Professor Henry Higgins undertakes the daunting task of turning Eliza into a "lady." In order to present her as a duchess at a high-society ball, he must rid her of a lower-class Cockney accent. A more recent version of the Eliza Doolittle story is *The Princess Diaries*. In this film, an American teenager learns that she is next in line to inherit the throne of Genovia, a small Monacolike country in Europe. Before assuming her new role, however, Mia Thermopolis must learn how to speak and behave like a princess. She accomplishes this task with the assistance of her grandmother, Queen Clarisse Renaldi. Like Eliza, Mia makes many mistakes as she undertakes the learning process.

The basic premise of *The Princess Diaries* is not totally unrealistic in the sense that accents and dialects continue to carry meanings associated with status, even in modern contexts. French Canadians visiting France often complain that native Parisians refuse to speak to them in French, addressing them instead in English. Not surprisingly, they interpret this refusal as a statement of status. Yet, within Canada, the same kinds of status distinctions manifest themselves. Some Quebecers, for example, regard their accents to be superior to those of northern Ontario or New Brunswick, and some francophones in Ottawa regard their accents as superior to those of their neighbors across the river in Gatineau. In the same way, some French-speaking Canadians consider their accents to be superior to those of the Acadians in southern Louisiana. In short, people still read status into vocal cues; and some studies have found that listeners can make status judgments on the basis of single words, without even taking grammatical context or fluency into account.[47]

As a speaker, what can you do about accents and dialects? The answer is "very little on a short-term basis." Unless you are truly adept at dialects, like some actors and stand-up comics, you may not be able to adopt the dialect of your audience. (And there could be an ethical risk if you chose to try.) But you can use good grammar, practice pronouncing difficult words in advance of the speech occasion, and enunciate clearly. A common fault of beginning speakers is mumbling and dropping of sounds at the ends of sentences. Yet effectiveness of delivery probably hinges more on clarity of speech than on accent or dialect. Audiences are often intrigued by accents and dialects different from their own. Although the Southern accent was politically incorrect in the 1960s and 1970s, it enjoyed a renaissance in the 1980s with television shows such as *Designing Women* and *The Golden Girls*. In the same way, the Kennedy family popularized the Massachusetts accent in the late 1950s and early 1960s.

Conveying Status Through Movements, Posture, and Stance

One aspect of status is power, which we convey in part through body stance and movement.[48] Expansive movements, erect posture, feet placed slightly apart, and a relaxed and sociable demeanor carry inferences of power.[49] So if speakers want to be perceived as confident and powerful, their stance and mannerisms must convey this impression. (See the Question of Ethics box.)

A Question of Ethics

Larry arrived early for his speaking engagement. He positioned the podium so that he could move close to the audience at strategic points in the speech. He had read that speakers can be more persuasive if they invade the personal space of listeners, encouraging an emotional response. For the same reason, he placed the chairs close to each other and raised the temperature to a slightly uncomfortable level.

The purpose of the speech was to encourage the audience of corporate executives and local businessowners to support local sports groups. To enhance his credibility with the audience, Larry had brought some slides of his family attending sports events. One photo showed him shaking hands with the coach of the team. Another slide showed him interacting with the players and crowd at a baseball game. He also showed photos of himself at an awards ceremony where he had been honored for his financial contribution to a local baseball team. Realizing that this particular audience would find his regional accent unattractive, Larry planned to speak with an accent that would be more acceptable to his audience. After reading a book on how to dress for success, he had purchased an expensive dark navy suit and gold tie. He chose colors and styles known to communicate power and influence.

Just before people began entering the auditorium, Larry dimmed the lights and turned up the sound system, which was playing soft music, hoping to create a warm personal atmosphere for the speech. He hoped that these added effects would encourage his audience to support local sports teams. He had also planned the content of his speech to focus on the teams with the best records—the ones that had won the most games in the last season.

How do you feel about Larry's preparations for his speech? Where do you draw the line between ethical and unethical approaches to delivery? Between adapting to your audience and seeking to manipulate them? Should the motivations of a speaker influence your reactions to strategies of the above variety? What if Larry were trying to persuade his audience to give money to a children's hospital? Would your evaluation be different than if he is trying to persuade them to purchase a life insurance policy or to become involved in a get-rich-quick real estate scheme?

Using the Physical Environment to Convey Status

The environment also can affect audience perceptions of speaker status. A plush and comfortable environment can lend an air of credibility to a speaker. In the same way, the number of people who attend the event, (as well as the number who remain to the end of the speech) can enhance or lower credibility.

COMPETENCE

Competence
A sense of being capable

Another aspect of source credibility is the perceived competence of a speaker.[50] How does a speaker convey competence? Studies suggest that we perceive communicators as competent when they are assertive, responsive, and versatile.[51] We also read fluency as an indicator of competency.[52]

Displaying Competence Through Assertiveness, Responsiveness, and Versatility

Assertiveness displays itself in the posture and voice of speakers. The voices of assertive speakers are strong and animated. To Americans, the lowering of the voice at the end of sentences also connotes assertiveness. Rising inflection, on the other hand, suggests uncertainty (associated with the asking of questions), lack of confidence, and insecurity. But different cultures use language in different ways. Pakistanis raise their inflection for statements and lower their inflection for questions.[53] Americans who know little about the Pakistani language might interpret the upward inflection as an indicator of hesitancy and a request for validation. And as the example of Ethel Blondin (discussed earlier) indicates, we are not always right in our interpretation of the meaning of inflection patterns.

The responsive speaker looks for cues that the audience may be bored, tired, or alienated by the speech. He also looks for nonverbal signs that the audience understands the content of the speech and accepts his message. When speakers sound bored or disinterested or speak in a monotone voice, they project the impression of nonresponsiveness. If the attention of the audience appears to be flagging, the versatile speaker will use an attention-getting strategy, catch the eye of disinterested individuals, or strive for a more animated delivery to recapture and refocus attention on the speech. In question-and-answer sessions, the responsive and assertive speaker will answer the questions of the audience in a direct, confident, and energetic fashion.

Demonstrating Competence Through Expertise

Competent speakers know their material. Their expert knowledge enables them to avoid excessive reliance on note cards and manuscripts and to maintain direct eye contact with their audiences. Less competent speakers tend to overrely on their written speeches and to lose eye contact when they read their material. Speakers should not, however, scan the audience like a rotating fan. In auditorium settings, speakers will not be able to catch the eye of every individual, but if they look in the general direction of different segments of the audience, members will perceive that they have been targeted for attention. Student speakers should avoid a fixed gaze on the instructor when they are speaking.

OBJECTIVITY

A final dimension of credibility that merits discussion is objectivity.[54] While you establish objectivity predominantly through your spoken text, you have some opportunities to communicate objectivity through delivery as well. The perceived objectivity of the person performing your introduction, for example, can influence perceptions of you. If a member of the Marxist Leninist Party introduces you, the audience will conclude that you are biased in favor of certain principles.

Audiences also assign attitudes to speakers based on their dress or body ornaments. Rightly or wrongly, the audience may assign significance to the number of earrings in your nose, mouth, and ears or—at the other extreme—to highly

Objectivity
Dealing with facts, not emotions or opinions

conservative dress or lack of makeup. They may believe that they know your attitudes and values before you utter a single word. How we express ourselves, volume, and tone of voice can also communicate objectivity (or lack of objectivity).

As noted earlier, audiences read higher levels of conviction into emotional modes of delivery. However, risks can accompany this association. When ex-Democrat Zell Miller delivered a highly passionate address against presidential candidate John Kerry at the 2004 Republican national convention, even the Republicans backed away from an association with Miller.[55] Audiences saw the denunciation of Kerry as a "rant" rather than rational discourse. When speakers become red-faced, scream at their audiences, and use vituperative language, they run the risk of being rejected by those whom they seek to influence.

Meeting Technical Challenges

Speakers face a special kind of challenge when cameras televise their speeches. They face the need to accommodate both the audience that is physically present in the speaking environment and the physically remote television audience. Gestures and movements that appear natural in one environment may look contrived and unnatural in the other. And an audience that feels ignored will resent having made an investment in attending the speech event.

On one occasion, I can remember feeling alienated from a speaker who chose to focus on the television cameras at the expense of his audience. I had looked forward to hearing an address by First Nations Chief Phil Fontaine, as I felt a strong empathy with the Native cause.[56] But after reaching the speaker's rostrum, Fontaine turned the podium to face the television cameras, which were positioned away from the majority of his immediate audience. Throughout the speech, Fontaine spoke to the camera, rarely looking in the direction of his audience. In a similar fashion, prior to his speech, he had distanced himself physically from his audience. While audience members can understand, on a logical level, why speakers sometimes choose the thousands—or even millions—of television viewers over the scores who may be present in the room, they may nonetheless feel resentful that they have taken the time to dress, prepare for the occasion, and make their way through traffic to the speaking location. They wonder why they did not just stay at home instead of becoming wallpaper for the speaker.

As noted in Chapter One, the intimate style of delivery that characterizes television speeches is ill-suited to an auditorium audience, who expect a more animated delivery with larger gestures and greater expressiveness. The problem is analogous to that experienced by early film stars, who had to adjust to a new close-up medium when they moved from the stage to movies. Actors found that the familiar conventions no longer applied, and the exaggerated movements and larger-than-life facial expressions of the stage no longer worked. Actors had to learn a new style of communicating with their audiences. Imagine if they had been forced to act for two audiences at the same time (stage and film)—how difficult it would have been to perform simultaneously for the two media!

Yet speakers often face the challenge of deciding which audience is more important—the immediate or remote audience.[57] Advanced microphone technologies can help to bridge the two situations, allowing the speaker to reach her immediate audience without having to raise her voice. Gesture and movement are more difficult to reconcile.

Setting Realistic Goals

Many novice speakers believe that successful speaking depends upon a near-flawless presentation. But audiences do not expect speakers to be perfect; and they can identify more readily with people who are human, who make mistakes on occasion.[58] When I taught the introductory communication course, typically I asked my students to name the politicians whose speaking styles they liked and disliked. Invariably, they named one politician in particular whose style they disliked. They thought that he dressed well and that he was physically attractive. They also thought that he was an accomplished speaker—too accomplished. They said that his delivery was too confident and his style too polished and flawless to be credible. Studies confirm that we do not assign credibility to a speaker who stumbles and stammers through a speech; but we tolerate (and sometimes even prefer) the occasional hesitancy or blip in composure, as long as the speaker appears competent overall.

Visualizing the ideal presentation (see Chapter Two) is one way to improve delivery, and this chapter suggests additional strategies. But realistically, for most of us, the critical variable in improving our delivery is time. Practice translates into comfort at the podium and into improved delivery.[59] We do not become better dancers or skaters or hockey players by sitting in the audience. We have to engage both our bodies and our minds in many processes in order to acquire the skills. The same is true of speaking.

The more often we speak, the better we get. Our gestures become more natural as we gain practice. We stop fidgeting and tugging at our hair and clothes. We cease to sway and prop ourselves against the nearest physical object. We do not race through our speeches, run out of breath, pace like restless lions, or glue our gaze to our note cards. Certainly, we can expect some notable changes in the speechmaking that occurs over the course of a semester, but we must be realistic in what we ask of ourselves and others. We should identify our weaknesses and set small goals to be achieved in each speech. We should realize that some members of the group will have had much more practice at speechmaking than others, and we can learn from their efforts.[60] We should not, however, judge our progress against their standards. Let the skills of others inspire but not demotivate us.

Also, do not lose heart if you have a problem that challenges your ability to be the next Anthony Robbins, Deepak Chopra, or Peggy Fleming (top-billed motivational speakers). Bret Eastburn has no arms or legs; yet he is also a motivational speaker, in great demand. One of the most accomplished speakers in the U.S. presidency was Franklin D. Roosevelt; yet he spoke from a wheelchair. Some highly accomplished speakers are blind, while others deal with the challenges posed by dyslexia, stuttering problems, or lisps. Even people who are "vocally challenged" can succeed if they have sufficient energy, initiative, and personality to compensate for their deficiencies. Abraham Lincoln had a rasping, high-pitched voice that became shrill and squeaky when he was excited.[61] Heather Whitestone McCallum, the winner of the 1995 Miss America competition (a position that requires extensive speechmaking), was deaf when she was selected for that honor. Our ability to succeed as speakers or performers in general is bound only by the limits that we set for ourselves.

In addition, despite the perceived significance of delivery, audience concerns about the quality of a speaker's delivery rarely take first place in a situation where vital issues are at stake. So yes, delivery is important, but no one should underestimate the ability of a weak speaker to persuade on matters of vital importance to the audience. And from an ethical point of view, that ordering of criteria seems most appropriate.

Finally, no one type of delivery fits everyone, just as no one style in clothing suits everyone. We may admire the slender tall or muscular model or the prepubescent teenager who wears the latest Moschino, Calvin Klein, or Baby Phat fashions; but we cannot necessarily expect the styles to fit our frames or personalities. An older man, teenage boy or plus-size woman will choose according to their body builds and comfort level. The same is true of speakers, who have different kinds of voices, personalities, and experiences, and who speak to different kinds of audiences. Martin Luther King, Jr., was one of the most accomplished speakers of the twentieth century, but his style came from a unique era (the 1960s), context (civil unrest), country and region (the southern United States), and cultural tradition (Southern Baptist sermon). The most important point to remember is that audiences are most accepting of speakers who radiate sincerity and who reveal some elements of their own personality when they deliver a speech. The speaker who comes too close to our stereotype of the smooth-talking used car salesperson sometimes generates extreme suspicion and distrust in audiences.

Conclusion

In this chapter, the one-point speech provides an opportunity to practice delivery strategies aimed at building credibility. In addition, this chapter has looked at technical challenges in public speaking and the importance of setting realistic goals.

Questions for Discussion

1. Describe some situations that require impromptu speaking. What are some of the ways in which speakers prepare for these kinds of impromptu speaking situations?

2. Describe some elements of delivery that you would like to improve. What are the filler words upon which you most often rely?

3. How do you react when speakers pause to take a breath, slow their pace to emphasize a point, or look down to identify the next thought? Are you comfortable with the silence? Are you equally comfortable taking pauses when you speak?

4. Are you comfortable with emotional displays in speaking? Can you think of any speakers who are excessively emotional in their speaking styles, to the point that you are "turned off?"

5. What do you find most annoying in the delivery of poor speakers? If you were to offer advice to someone on delivering a speech, what would you stress?

6. Some of you come from different cultural backgrounds. Compare and contrast acceptable delivery (movement, gestures, eye contact, etc.) in that culture with preferred modes of delivery in mainstream or other cultures.

7. In terms of delivery, what causes us to trust or not to trust a speaker?

8. What are some of the ways in which speakers can create a sense of immediacy or psychological closeness with audiences?

9. Think of some high-status speakers. How do they dress? Do you believe that one standard exists for appropriate dress in today's environment?

10. Do you think that accents and dialects are always perceived negatively? Give examples to support your point of view.

Outline

VISUAL AIDS AND OTHER SOFTWARE PRESENTATIONS

The Computer-Assisted Presentation

Learning Objectives

- To understand the purposes of using visual aids to complement a speech
- To become acquainted with the principles governing the use of visual aids
- To learn about the different kinds of visual supports
- To find out about the visual presentation of statistical data
- To learn about computer-generated presentations

I recall a story from the early 1960s, a time when the arms race was in full swing. People worried that someone in Russia or the United States could inadvertently push a button that would end in a nuclear holocaust. Against that backdrop, then Premier Nikita Krushchev and President John F. Kennedy decided to establish a hotline to allow instant communication between the two heads of state. A problem arose, however, because the two leaders could not agree on the nature of the hotline. Kennedy wanted a telegraph system, whereas Khrushchev preferred the telephone. These preferences reflected cultural differences in the two societies, with the United States valuing the visual and Russia the oral tradition. Scholars in intercultural communication have long stressed the importance of recognizing such cultural preferences. Kennedy would only believe what he could see in writing, and Khrushchev wanted an oral commitment.

In the years since those events, television and the Internet have created even stronger preferences for visual content among people in technologically advanced societies.[1] People like and expect visual content in presentations of all varieties. Moreover, high-quality visual aids have an impact on the perceived expertise and authority of a speaker.[2] Thus, this chapter examines purposes of visual supports, general principles governing the use of visual aids, different kinds of visual supports, visual presentation of statistical data, and PowerPoint and other software presentations. A sample PowerPoint appears at the end of this chapter.

Purposes of Visual Supports

Visual supports/aids

Materials such as video, Power Points, flip charts—anything that can be seen by the audience—that a speaker uses to add to the speech to improve its impact

Visual aids accomplish several major purposes. First, they meet the needs of visual learners (described in Chapter Thirteen). People with visual intelligence learn best from videos, films, photographs, and other materials that appeal to this sensory mode.[3] Because visuals bypass language filters, they are especially appropriate in presentations to multicultural groups. In addition, visual aids give speakers something to do with their hands and deflect the attention of the audience from signs of tension. They allow the speaker a chance to feel less conspicuous. Visual aids also help listeners to understand statistics and other complex material. They add color and interest to presentations. People retain visual information better than verbal information.[4] This ability of people to recall pictures more easily than words is known as *pictorial superiority effect*. Finally, visual supports increase the perceived quality of speeches.[5] We are living in a time when people expect sophisticated presentations. Television has created a generation of people who want to be entertained as well as taught, and computer technologies have fostered expectations of interactive and dynamic content, filled with images. We judge the professionalism of speakers by their visual aids.

With PowerPoint presentations, speakers often have a tendency to duplicate their words on the screen rather than use the PowerPoint presentation as a visual support. When giving a five or ten minute speech to inform or persuade, presenters should not place outlines of their speeches on PowerPoint. Instead they should use the PowerPoint to highlight a key term or idea, to display a chart or graph, or to complement their spoken discourse with an interesting image.

Overview of General Principles

Some general principles apply to the choice, preparation, and use of visual supports. *First, exercise judgment in your choices of visual supports.* You would not want, for example, to bring a pit bull to class; and even the most innocuous pets have rarely learned the rules of classroom behavior. James C. McCroskey recounts a humorous story about the risks involved with using animals in demonstration talks:

> The story is told at Purdue, a university with noted programs in agriculture, that an instructor heard some unusual sounds in the hallway just prior to class. Investigating, he found four students trying to herd a Holstein cow up the stairs and into the classroom. The cow was to have been the visual aid for one of the student's speech on dairy production. While indeed authentic, the novelty of the cow, not to mention the possibility of the cow's by-products, would be so distracting that the point of the speech would probably be lost. One hopes the instructor had the presence of mind to tell the students that their choice of visual aid was *udderly* wrong.[6]

Always take your audience and speaking environment into account when you choose visual supports. A few years ago, a student asked to bring a rifle to class to demonstrate proper shooting postures. (His hobby was competitive shooting.) Of course,

I said "no." Given the environment set in place by Columbine and other incidents of school violence, I could only imagine the reaction of the class and the university's security officers to the presence of a gun in a classroom. (See the Reflections box.)

Follow some basic rules that extend to the preparation of most visuals. Be sure that your visuals are uncluttered, simple, colorful, and sufficiently large to be seen. Apart from the visibility issue, larger visuals produce more learning than smaller visuals.[7] Use appropriate fonts and lettering (see details in the Different Kinds of Visual Supports section.) Always acknowledge the sources on which you have relied in developing visual elements in your presentation. The credits may appear in a corner of visuals such as photographs or charts.

Plan ahead for equipment and technical needs. Book all equipment, not present in the speaking environment, well in advance. At educational institutions, you may need to secure signatures and provide identification to check out equipment. Be sure that your equipment is functioning properly and that you have the necessary extension cords and access codes for media consoles. Practice in advance of the presentation. If you ask someone else to help with equipment—for example, to turn lights *on* or *off*, or to operate audio players, VCRs, or media consoles—provide them with a marked script of your speech. Practice coordinating slides, overhead transparencies, and video and audio clips prior to the speaking occasion.

Prepare the speaking environment prior to beginning your speech. If someone speaks before you, remove any leftovers from the previous presentation before beginning your presentation. Erase the chalk board and eliminate distracting features in the speaking environment. Your visuals should not war with photographs or charts still hanging on the walls from earlier speeches. You also need to organize your own materials so that you do not create clutter. When giving a demonstration speech, do not leave paper bags lying on the floor within view of the audience or unnecessary papers and other items on tables. Leave items covered or hidden from sight until you are ready to use them. Have them sufficiently accessible, however, that you are not bent over, digging in bags, to locate them. When you have finished with the visual aid (whether placed on the table or projected on a screen), remove

Reflections

Dead or Alive?

I was giving a demonstration speech on how to make sushi. I'd read that Hawaiians make sushi by ripping the shell off a live shrimp, putting a bit of lemon juice on it, then quickly making and serving the sushi. As I described the process, I held the shell of a large dead prawn in my hand. When I put it down, the prawn rolled a bit. At that point, a woman jumped up and started toward the front with some animal rights comments. Then reconsidering, she turned back and wandered to the back of the room, mumbling to herself. She figured the prawn was alive, but most people saw it for what it was—a playful prop. Still it's hard to tell when such dramatic bits distract too much from the overall effect.

Vic Williams

the visual or hide the image from the sight of audience members. You can, for example, use the shutter on remotes that operate data projectors, turn off the overhead projector, or use a paper to hide the upcoming points on a transparency. If you do not take such measures, the audience will continue to focus on the visual rather than on your speech.

Follow a few basic rules of delivery. Display visuals long enough for audiences to absorb the material. A common mistake of novice speakers is to change the slide or transparency before the audience has a chance to comprehend the content. Do not rush your presentation. Stay open and visible to the audience at all times when you are presenting. Speak loud enough to be heard over the sounds of projectors.

Different Kinds of Visual Supports

Speakers have a choice of a number of different visual supports, including three-dimensional objects and models; chalkboards, white boards, and flannel boards; flip charts; handouts; posters; overhead and data projectors; slides; and audio and videotapes. When delivering a motivational talk, a speech of introduction or welcome—or even informative and persuasive speeches—these traditional visual supports are often quite effective. The following discussion lays out principles governing the use of each of these visual supports. Although classroom instructors, business executives, and trainers make heavy use of PowerPoint and other software presentations, students must be careful in using computer software with five- to ten-minute speaking assignments. (See the Keep in Mind box.)

THREE-DIMENSIONAL OBJECTS AND MODELS

Be sure that three-dimensional objects are sufficiently large to be visible to all audience members. If an object is too small, too large, awkward, or inappropriate to bring to class, you can construct a model—or you can bring a photograph of the object to class. Locomotives will not fit in the classroom, and the Smithsonian is not likely to offer the Hope Diamond on loan. But you can construct models or locate photographs of such items. If you choose the alternative of the photograph, you can make an enlargement at a print shop and mount it on a poster board. You can copy the photograph to a transparency to display on an overhead projector, scan the photograph into the computer for display, or make a slide of the photograph to show on a projector. Check the equipment available to you before deciding upon one of these options.

Never circulate objects or photographs among the audience during the course of your speech. When you are ready to talk about the object, position it between yourself and the audience. Sometimes speakers place multiple objects at various locations in the room, sufficiently close for the audience to see the objects without straining. In a demonstration speech, for example, the speaker can ask five or six members from a class of twenty students to work along with him in undertaking a task. If the participating class members are seated in different parts of the room,

Keep in Mind

Tips for Using Visual Aids and Equipment

Presentation Software

· Print should be large. Don't copy from books.
· Don't put more than eight lines on a page or six words per line.
· Use upper- and lower-case instead of all capitals.
· Use dark colors (black, blue, green, red, etc.) rather than light.
· Don't overuse pictures and icons; do use enough to add interest.
· If possible, personalize by using photos of class or local scenes.
· Use short video clip (no more than thirty seconds for a short speech) to add interest to presentation.
· Explain purpose of video or audio clips prior to playing them. If there is anything objectionable in the clip, mention it and explain why you chose to use it anyway.

Three-Dimensional Objects

· If you use an object, make it sufficiently large to be seen throughout classroom.
· If the object is too small to be seen, construct a model. Make a poster. Use felt or flannel shapes on the chalkboard. Use magnetic means of attaching materials.

Equipment and Lighting

· If you are using equipment, get someone to perform these tasks. The speaker should not run back and forth to a VCR or audio player.
· Do the same with lighting. If lights require adjustment during presentation (on, off, or dim), assign this task to a group member. Cues should be noted in a script.
· Don't keep the group in the dark for too long.
· If you use music, don't play it too loud.
· When working in a new location, be sure you have an extra extension cables for use with TVs, VCRs, overhead projectors, slide projectors, and so on.

Delivery

· Know your material.
· Maintain eye contact with the group.
· With presentation software, look at projected image; don't tie yourself to a podium.
· Use a remote control to switch slides.
· If necessary, use note cards—not pieces of paper—for additional support.
· Arrange for someone to help you with lights and equipment.
· Avoid clutter; hide any materials that you are not using.

everyone will feel a greater part of the process than if the speaker demonstrates the task on his own.

One student used this approach in demonstrating how to make decorative candles. She gave pieces of wax to about a third of the class. The others were able to observe and follow the process. In another instance, a speaker showed how to make favors for a wedding. She distributed supplies to everyone in the class. Class members worked with her from their desks. Sometimes, speakers walk around the room to display an object. At other times, they wait until the conclusion of the speech to display the object at close range or to pass it around the room. As mentioned, speakers should never circulate visuals while delivering a speech.

If you take an object apart during a demonstration speech, be sure that you can put it back together again. Also if you plan to construct an object in class, you should bring a finished product with you. The finished product (e.g., floral

arrangement or transformer) enables you to retain a measure of credibility even if something goes wrong, and you do not need to worry if you do not have time to complete the process of construction.

Sometimes your models are life size. On one occasion, a student brought a dummy to class to demonstrate resuscitation of cardiac patients. Your models can also be live. That is, sometimes students use other individuals in their demonstrations. If you use another person, you should give careful instructions to the individual prior to delivering the speech. The assistant should maintain a serious demeanor before the group. You can ask the person to carry out some action in slow motion (e.g., a self-defense or dance move) while you talk about the action. You should practice with the person prior to delivering the speech, so that the individual knows exactly what to do. Both the speaker and the person who is the visual prop should be visible to the audience. You also need to stay open to the audience, just as stage performers keep themselves open to the theater audience. Side-by-side positions are often good, as they allow both the presenter and demonstrator to be visible. Assisting individuals should sit down when you no longer require their involvement.

CHALKBOARDS, WHITEBOARDS, AND FLANNEL BOARDS

To the extent possible, speakers should avoid the use of chalkboards. The writing is typically too light to be seen clearly, the board is often dirty, and few people have a clear legible writing style when they are rushing to put information on the board. Moreover, the speaker must turn away from the audience in order to write on the board. Whiteboards are easier to see, cleaner, and often mobile, so you can move them closer to the audience. Nonetheless, some of the same problems exist. Other

Whiteboards
Synthetic board, which is cleaner and easier to read than a chalkboard

kinds of visual supports—ones that can be prepared in advance—are usually superior. On occasion, however, speakers may want to record comments by audience members, or they may want to conclude a speech by writing a web or e-mail address, telephone number, or postal address on the board. In those instances, the whiteboard works better than the chalkboard. If you do use a chalkboard or whiteboard, you should try to talk as you write and limit the amount of material placed on the board.

Flannel boards
Board on which felt objects can be added and subtracted

Another visual aid is the flannel board, often used by elementary school teachers. The flannel board offers possibilities to speakers who want to add or subtract material as they go along. One student employed the flannel board, for example, in giving a speech on proper dining etiquette. As she spoke, she placed felt representations of the tableware on the flannel board. The display was colorful, easy to see, and appropriate to the topic of the speech. On other occasions, a person could use a flannel board with felt cutouts to explain moves in a football or hockey game or stages in constructing a model airplane. Alternatively, the speaker could use this aid to show the locations of people in a building at the time that some event occurs. In a speech on the subway bombings in London, for example, the speaker could show the movement of the perpetrators of violence from one part of the subway system to another.

As with other visual aids, speakers must be careful not to turn their backs to the audience in using the flannel board, and they must not fall silent as they position pieces on the board. An alternative to felt pieces and flannel boards could be magnetic pieces on a metallic board.

FLIP CHARTS

Flip charts, or oversized writing pads, work well in locations that lack electricity or screens. Sometimes groups have retreats in isolated settings, or businesspeople travel to remote locations for their annual meetings. The easels that hold flip charts are inexpensive and easy to construct on location.

Flip charts
Large writing pad, on an easel

If you plan to use a flip chart, check the paper supply prior to the time of delivery. In writing on the pad, use the upper third of the page and never include more than five lines on a sheet. Some flip charts have light blue grid lines that help to align writing. No line should include more than five or six words. Abbreviate long words and use acronyms whenever possible. Use dark-colored markers; yellows and oranges do not work well. You can alternate colors as you make lists, but you should avoid using more than three colors on a page. Repeat and summarize the ideas out loud as you record them.

If you prepare the materials in advance, you can put your speaking notes on the back of the pages. If you position the flip chart to the side and slightly in front of your speaking position, you can refer to the notes without anyone realizing that you are relying on them. When working in a spontaneous situation (e.g., recording reactions from audience members), you can tape the pages (torn from the chart) to walls for easy viewing. At the conclusion of the exercise, you can provide audience members with stickers to use in prioritizing the most important points.

HANDOUTS

As noted earlier, you should avoid distributing visuals during a speech. If you want to use a handout, place copies (face down) on the desks or seats of audience members prior to speaking. Ask the group not to turn over the handout until you reach the point that you want to use it. Otherwise, they will read the handout while you are speaking. Alternatively, you can distribute the handout at the conclusion of the speech. You may want to color code handouts with multiple sections to facilitate reference to the handout. You can also include information that audiences can use to follow up on your ideas. When students give food demonstration speeches, for example, they often distribute copies of their recipes at the end of the speeches. When students give persuasive speeches, they distribute sheets with phone numbers, websites, and mailing addresses for information sources and advocacy groups.

POSTERS

Because few people are highly skilled at creating poster displays, poster presentations are rarely professional in appearance. Even when people have abilities in art, they may not know how to generate exhibition materials. Nonetheless, posters may be the only way to display certain kinds of information, especially if the setting does not include equipment. If you plan to prepare a poster, aim for a display with prominent lettering and graphics that are easy to see from the back of the room. Ask friends to tell you if they can see the lettering, graphics, or photographs from the distance that will separate the speaker from the rear of the audience. Most of the time, the audience cannot see the materials on posters. Check the speaking location to ensure that you have a way to hang the poster; if not, bring tape to secure the poster to some surface. Easels for flip charts can also hold posters, but you need a clip to attach the poster to the flip chart.

OVERHEAD, SLIDE, AND DATA PROJECTORS

In low-technology environments, transparencies offer a way to display major talking points and visual material—graphs, charts, and images. You have several alternatives for producing transparencies. (1) You can photocopy material onto a transparency, which you magnify through projection. (Photocopy machines require specific kinds of transparencies, so be sure that you purchase the right variety.) (2) You can scan an image from a book or other source into your computer and then print a copy on a transparency. (3) You can locate an image on the Internet or in your computer files, which you then print on a transparency. (4) You can download an image, make a hard copy, and then use a photocopier to transfer the image to a transparency. Do not copy charts or tables from books. They will rarely be sufficiently large or clear to use on a transparency. Redo the chart on the computer. Number your transparencies and store them in plastic covers for protection. Business supply stores sell clear plastic sheaths with holes that allow transparencies to be stored in notebooks. Remove the transparencies from their jackets to display them. The plastic sheaths lower the visibility of the transparencies.

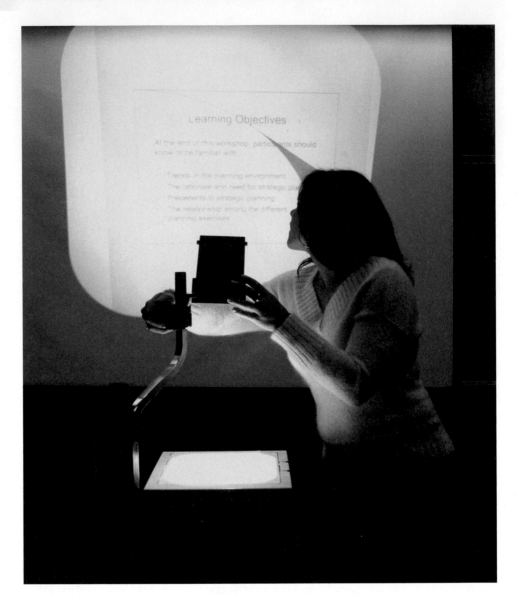

Prior to beginning your presentation, check the overhead projector to be sure that the lightbulb works. (They give out on a regular basis, but most projectors have a storage place for spare bulbs.) Ensure that the images and print on the transparency can be easily seen when projected. As with other visuals, do not include more than five or six lines on a page or more than six words on a line. Use 30- to 36-point type font for headings, 24-point for subheadings, and 18-point for text. No more than one major idea should appear on a page. Eliminate extra words, including adjectives such as *the* and *an*. For aesthetic purposes, allow the same space at the bottom and top of the transparency. When making your presentation, you may want to cover part of the page in order to reveal points one by one. You can use an opaque sheet to cover points not yet addressed. If you use a transparency to record impressions from the group, stay open to the audience when you are writing and speaking. Avoid looking down unless you are writing.

Another low-technology aid, slide projectors are useful when you do not have access to media consoles, laptop computers, or other sophisticated technologies. Before the advent of digital cameras and software programs, presenters often used slide projectors in speeches about geography, art, and history. When using this technology aid, you should test the slides before the presentation to be sure that they are not upside down. You also need to know the speech extremely well because the low lighting levels required in slide shows make it difficult to read note cards. You should practice the timing of your speech in advance so that you know how long to spend on each slide. Most slide projectors have remotes, which permit you to change the slide from various positions in the room.

In high-technology environments, data projectors are the norm. Before begin ning your presentation, check for basics such as image projection. If you see a wedge-shaped image on the screen (wider at the top than at the bottom), refocus the projector to correct the "keystoning." When using a data, overhead, or slide projector, maintain eye contact with your audience. Position yourself so that you can glance, from time to time, at the projected image—without turning your back to the audience. You may need to dim the lighting to ensure the visibility of projected images. You may also need to speak louder to overcome the noise from a projector. When you are not discussing an image, turn off the overhead projector and raise the lighting level in the room. With data projectors, you can use the shutter function on the remote control to hide the image. More information on the use of data pro jectors appears in the PowerPoint and Other Software Presentations section.

AUDIO AND VIDEO TAPES

You should edit audio and video materials to facilitate ease of use. Edited clips pre vent loss of time and unnecessary searching for places on a tape. Clips should be brief, often no more than fifteen or twenty seconds in length. The length of the speech determines the number of clips and the amount of time that can be given to each clip. Short clips allow the speaker to illustrate specific points or behaviors, such as a negotiation between two people, a gymnastics move, or the dress adopted by trial lawyers. You can use audio recordings in a speech about the characteristics of rap music, bird calls, or noise pollution. Speakers should always check audio or video equipment prior to the speech.

Audio and video clips should supplement and clarify rather than merely repeat points in the speech. If you use music, do not play it too loud. Tell the audience the length of the recording and explain the rationale for using the clip prior to playing it. If you think that the video contains any objectionable material (e.g., old films often contain conversations with sexist and politically incorrect language), mention your reservations and explain why you chose to use the clip anyway. Remain attentive during the playing of the tape. Do not try to talk over a tape with audio content.

Visual Presentations of Statistics

Pie charts
Graphs in which values appear as slices in a pie

Visual formats make statistical data more comprehensible. This discussion introduces the reader to the most common ways of presenting statistics: simple breakdown tables, pie charts, complex breakdown tables, line graphs, bar graphs, and multiple line graphs.

Simple breakdown tables (Figure 7.1) and *pie charts* (Figure 7.2) show frequency distributions, such as monthly household expenditures on gambling or the allocation of income from gambling. The information in simple breakdown tables and

Simple Breakdown Table: Sources of Annual Casino Income

Amount Gambled Annually by Players	Percentage of Annual Income of Casino
Less than $100	45.3
$100–$500	22.2
$100–$1,000	10.8
$1,000–$5,000	13.7
$5,000–$10,000	4.6
More than $10,000	3.4

Source: Report of the National Gambling Impact Study Commission, April 14, 1999. Survey administered by the National Opinion Research Center, University of Chicago. http://www.norc.uchicago.edu.

Figure 7.1

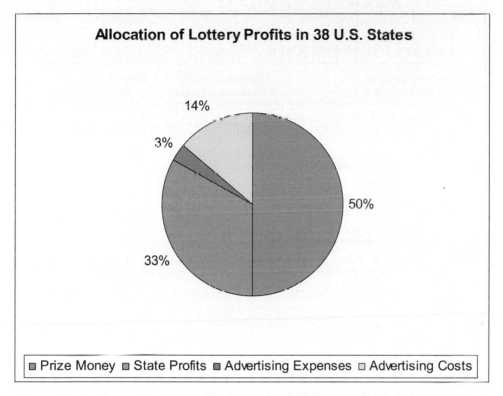

Figure 7.2 Pie Chart

pie charts appears in the form of numbers or percentages. *Complex breakdown tables*, on the other hand, break down the information according to factors such as gender, age, region, and income bracket. A complex breakdown table might look at how many men versus women engage in the different forms of gambling or the income levels of people who engage in the different forms of gambling. Figure 7.3 compares the activities preferred by female and male problem gamblers.

Sometimes the speaker wants to show changes over time—that is, trends. Both *bar* and *line graphs* are useful formats for presenting trends. *Bar graphs* are more appropriate when you want to show changes over a short period of time or to focus on a few specific points in time (see Figure 7.4). Line graphs, on the other hand, are useful when you want to show the progress of changes over an extended period of time. With line graphs, you are more interested in the overall profile of the trend—the rise and fall of the line over time (see Figure 7.5). Multiple line graphs compare trends between or among two or more sets of data (see Figure 7.6).

Another type of graphical representation is the pictograph. Pictographs use images of objects to show numbers and percentages in bar graphs. The software program Excel has a number of interesting examples of pictographs. One pictograph shows the levels of antioxidant activity in different fruits and vegetables. The bar graphs appear in the colors of the fruits and vegetables that they depict (blue for blueberries, green for spinach, red for strawberries, etc.). A bar graph that shows the popularity of chili pepper consumption uses four chili peppers to represent

Bar graphs
Graphs in which values appear as bars of varying lengths, good for showing change over short period of time

Line graphs
Graphs in which values appear as points on a continuum, good for showing change over longer periods

Pictographs
A visual that uses images of the objects themselves as values in bar graphs

Complex Breakdown Table

Percentage Who Bet on Activity	Current Female Problem Gamblers	Current Male Problem Gamblers
Instant or scratch tickets	92%	88%
Lotto-type games	78%	86%
Bingo	76%	24%
Raffles and fund-raising tickets	70%	74%
Video lottery terminals	41%	46%
Card games with family or friends	41%	64%
Break-open, pull-tab, Nevada tickets	41%	40%
Local casinos	37%	46%

Source for statistics: National Council of Welfare, http://www.ncwcnbes.net/htmdocument/reportgambling/Gambling_e.htm#_Toc522256759, accessed on July 7, 2005.

Figure 7.3

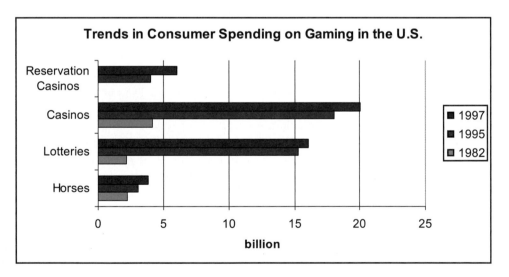

Figure 7.4 Bar Chart

40 percent and seven chili peppers to represent 70 percent. In the third example, dollar bills substitute for the bar graphs. The dollar bills represent the rates charged by different companies for fifteen-minute weekday calls from New York to Los Angeles.[8] Figure 7.7 shows the relative amounts of money spent by problem gamblers on four popular forms of gambling: lotteries, casinos, video lottery terminals (VLTs), and slot machines.

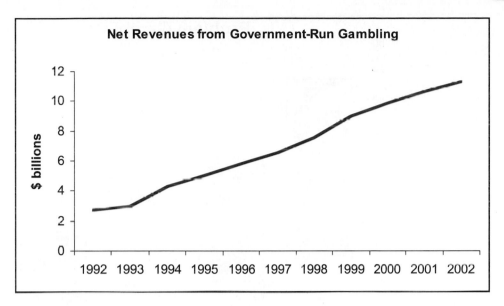

Figure 7.5 Line Graph

Source: Statistics Canada, "Perspectives on Labour and Income: Fact Sheet on Gambling," http://www.statcan.ca/english/studies/75-001/00403/fs-fi_200304_01_a.pdf, p. 2, accessed on July 7, 2005.

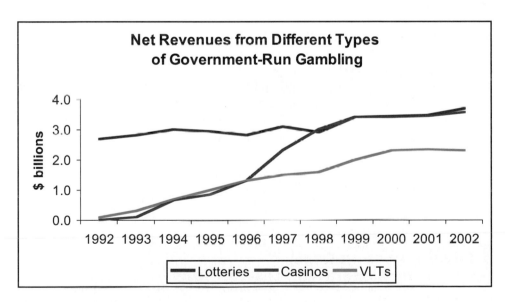

Figure 7.6 Multiple Line Graph

Source: Statistics Canada, "Perspectives on Labour and Income: Fact Sheet on Gambling," http://www.statcan.ca/english/studies/75-001/00403/fs-fi_200304_01_a.pdf, p. 2, accessed on July 7, 2005.

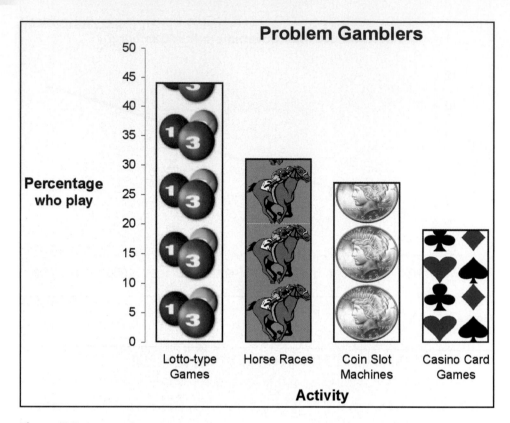

Figure 7.7 Pictograph

When presenting statistics in a speech, remember that the audience must be able to grasp and understand the material within the time frame of your discussion. In a short nontechnical speech, complex breakdown tables present too much information. In a speech delivered to a group of experts or businesspeople, on the other hand, the situation may be different. Also, you should use strong colors for your line, bar, and pie graphs—sufficiently dark to be seen easily. Present the lines and bars in different colors for maximum clarity and effectiveness. Avoid too many lines, too much clutter, and too many different colors. Include only the most necessary data and clearly label axes and data lines on graph. Make the bars wider than the space that divides them.

PowerPoint and Other Computer-Generated Presentations

In the corporate world, the standard for computer-assisted presentations is high. Communication staff members, trained in graphics and design, create most of these presentations for higher-level managers and executives. They put together "decks" that are highly professional in appearance, and organizational members

come to expect quality in the presentations. An ill-prepared or technologically un-sophisticated presentation can create major credibility problems for the speaker-whether she comes from inside the organization or enters the organization as a consultant. And sometimes, of course, technological difficulties can pose what seem to be insurmountable problems. As the Reflections box indicates, it is always important to be well-prepared.

Project proposals, sales talks, and debriefings are typical instances where pre-senters must demonstrate their ability to deliver finely honed and technologically sophisticated presentations. These presentations most often employ PowerPoint, Corel, Apple Works, or other software programs. Different software programs work in different ways, and "help" files come with the software. To elaborate on the details of one out of many software choices would be inappropriate. Also, the programs are updated on a regular basis; and by the time this book is on the mar-ket, the programs may have changed. Nonetheless, certain principles apply in using all of the programs; and studies have found that user guides can be as good as hands-on training in learning how to use the presentation software.[9]

The following discussion includes suggestions related to mixed media presenta-tions, aesthetic considerations, considerations related to continuity, use of contrast and colors, typeface and font size, grammar and structure, formatting, and presen-tation techniques.

PowerPoint
Commonly used computer-generated slide program

Reflections

I recently had the opportunity to make a presentation at a national academic conference. I diligently prepared my PowerPoint presentation and practiced my comments for each slide. The time arrived, and I began my presentation before a room filled with forty to fifty of my peers, college faculty from around North America.

Before I finished with the third slide (of twenty-four), the power to the building went out, plunging everyone into near darkness. After waiting several minutes to see if the power would return (it didn't), I decided to continue with my presentation . . . without the Power-Point. My laptop computer was on battery power, but I couldn't project the slides onto the screen without power to the projector. I thought about turning my computer around so the audience could see the screen, but I realized it would be too small to be seen by anyone but those who were sitting right in front of it. I panicked!

But I knew that, despite the power outage, we had a schedule to keep; so I abandoned the laptop, left the safety of the lectern to stand closer to the audience, and delivered my presentation the "old-fashioned way," without technology . . . and in the near dark.

Luckily, I had prepared *very* well for the presentation and had provided participants with a folder of handouts, including a handout of my original PowerPoint presentation. I have since discovered that session evaluations showed that my presentation was one of the best received of the entire conference (even those delivered in rooms with lighting!). It pays to be prepared for the unexpected.

Desiree Devereaux,
e-learning coordinator,
Sowela Technical
Community College

Communicating in a Brazilian Business Environment

BREW Consulting

Erika Adams
Rebecca Cook
Cathy Daoust
Wendy Sandles
Becky Zettl

11/04/2003   BREW Consulting   1

Agenda

10:00 – 10:10	Welcome, introduction, & overview
10:10 – 10:25	Warm-up: Brazilian Trivia Jogo
10:25 – 10:35	Brazilian society and people
10:35 – 10:45	Your experience
10:45 – 11:00	Corporate culture
11:00 – 11:15	Storytelling
11:15 – 11:25	Business and corporate practices
11:25 – 11:35	Saúde pausa (health break)
11:35 – 11:55	Negotiation and role of expediters
11:55 – 12:05	Nonverbal interactions
12:05 – 12:20	Role playing
12:20 – 12:30	Fish bowl
12:30 – 12:40	Successful entertaining
12:40 – 12:50	Quiz and recap

11/04/2003   BREW Consulting   2

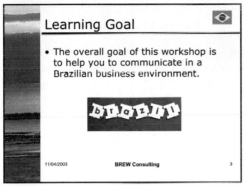

Learning Goal

- The overall goal of this workshop is to help you to communicate in a Brazilian business environment.

11/04/2003   BREW Consulting   3

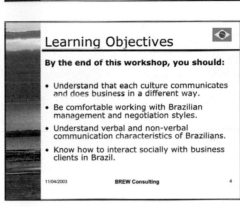

Learning Objectives

By the end of this workshop, you should:

- Understand that each culture communicates and does business in a different way.

- Be comfortable working with Brazilian management and negotiation styles.

- Understand verbal and non-verbal communication characteristics of Brazilians.

- Know how to interact socially with business clients in Brazil.

11/04/2003   BREW Consulting   4

Let's PLAY

11/04/2003   BREW Consulting   5

brazilian TRIVIA

11/04/2003   BREW Consulting   6

Brazilian Society

- Portuguese - national language

- Dominant religion - Roman Catholic

- Personal values – family, education, & achieving socioeconomic status

11/04/2003   BREW Consulting   7

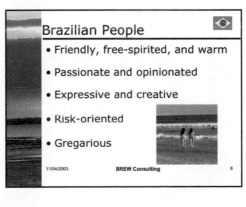

Brazilian People

- Friendly, free-spirited, and warm

- Passionate and opinionated

- Expressive and creative

- Risk-oriented

- Gregarious

11/04/2003   BREW Consulting   8

Your Experience

Have you had an interesting cultural experience in another country?

Tell us about it.

11/04/2003   **BREW Consulting**   9

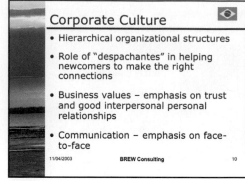

Corporate Culture

- Hierarchical organizational structures
- Role of "despachantes" in helping newcomers to make the right connections
- Business values – emphasis on trust and good interpersonal personal relationships
- Communication – emphasis on face-to-face

11/04/2003   **BREW Consulting**   10

Storytelling

Sailing through the Brazilian business style

11/04/2003   **BREW Consulting**   11

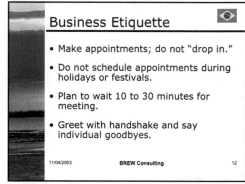

Business Etiquette

- Make appointments; do not "drop in."
- Do not schedule appointments during holidays or festivals.
- Plan to wait 10 to 30 minutes for meeting.
- Greet with handshake and say individual goodbyes.

11/04/2003   **BREW Consulting**   12

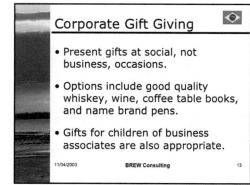

Corporate Gift Giving

- Present gifts at social, not business, occasions.
- Options include good quality whiskey, wine, coffee table books, and name brand pens.
- Gifts for children of business associates are also appropriate.

11/04/2003   **BREW Consulting**   13

Saude Pausa

Enjoy your brigadeiros!!

- Sweets made with condensed milk and chocolate
- Named after Brigadeiro Eduardo Gomes, an Air Force commander from the 1940s

11/04/2003   **BREW Consulting**   14

Negotiation Styles

North Americans adopt a direct approach to negotiations.

What is the most common negotiation style in Brazil?

11/04/2003   **BREW Consulting**   15

Negotiations

- North Americans are more direct; Brazilians are more wordy.
- Brazilians use personal touch to break down barriers.
- Trust comes before negotiations.

11/04/2003   **BREW Consulting**   16

The Nitty-Gritty

- "Hype" & casual conversation at onset
- Hard negotiation style
- Emergence of facts over time
- Written agreements at conclusion
- Assistance with contract issues by local accountants and lawyers

11/04/2003   **BREW Consulting**   17

The Role of Expediters

- Practice of bribery encouraged by bureaucratic inertia
- "Expediters" hired by multinationals to "grease the wheels"
- Bribery or "jeitinho" seen as acceptable

11/04/2003   **BREW Consulting**   18

Nonverbal Interactions

Body Language

- Physical contact - part of everyday communication
- Touching – sign of friendship and concern
- Eye contact – more intense than in Canada

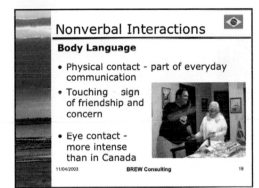

11/04/2003   **BREW Consulting**   19

Nonverbal Interactions

Dress

- For men: Conservative dark suits, shirts, and ties
- For women: Feminine, more "sexy" than North America
- For both: Overall stylish appearance Stylish, polished, and well-kept shoes

11/04/2003   **BREW Consulting**   20

Role Playing

Your experience and mine

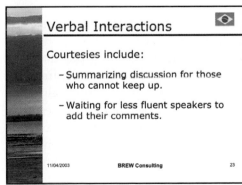

11/04/2003   **BREW Consulting**   21

Verbal Interactions

Brazilians:

- Speak more loudly than Canadians.
- Accept interruptions.
- Are comfortable with verbal confrontation.
- Respond quickly.
- Provide many details when offering info.
- Treat others with courtesy.

11/04/2003   **BREW Consulting**   22

Verbal Interactions

Courtesies include:

- Summarizing discussion for those who cannot keep up.
- Waiting for less fluent speakers to add their comments.

11/04/2003   **BREW Consulting**   23

Fish Bowl

"Muddy Waters"

11/04/2003   **BREW Consulting**   24

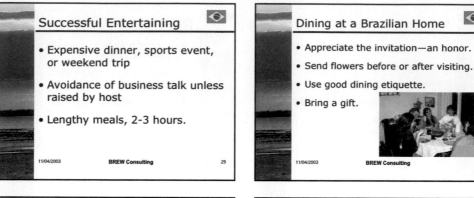

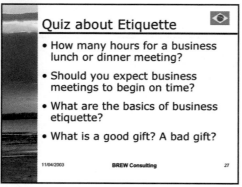

Source: http://www.cprs.org/confhandouts2004/Res-- Statistics_Can Lie Handout.pdf

MIXED MEDIA PRESENTATIONS

PowerPoint, Corel, AppleWorks, and other software programs allow speakers to create integrated presentations, involving a mix of text, visual images, and audio content. The programs enable the users to generate charts, graphs, and tables with the click of the mouse. With a few keystrokes, they can download images or video clips from the Internet, a digital camera, or camcorder. They can scan materials from books into the computer for download, and they can use programs such as PhotoShop to enhance the quality of the images.

These audio and visual aids add a dynamic quality to presentations. In a speech on feng-shui (the ancient Chinese art of achieving balance in one's environment), for example, a speaker can display graphs that show the growing popularity of this approach to home construction and design. Video clips can demonstrate options in room layouts and ways of arranging furniture and plants. Audio clips can include testimonials from individuals who have had positive experiences with feng-shui. In a similar way, a PowerPoint presentation on cross-cultural communication could include text on business etiquette, video clips showing nonverbal transgressions, and audio clips involving conversations between inept communicators.

AESTHETIC CONSIDERATIONS

To achieve an aesthetically pleasing presentation, speakers should adhere to a visual theme. On my website, I use a Ferguson plaid to represent my company. My PowerPoint presentations apply the same theme. You can establish a common look by repeating colors, fonts, shapes, and lines of similar width.

Computer-generated presentations allow for many special effects. While variety is interesting, some novice users overdo the effects. You do not want too many flying images, clanging shutters, or loud zips to distract the listeners. Aim for professionalism rather than entertainment. Use clip art and photographs to add interest to the presentation. Do not be tempted, however, to clutter the slide with an excessive number of visuals. When I first learned to use PowerPoint, I used two or three pieces of clip art on every slide. In retrospect, it was far too much!

Clip art
Free art, commonly available in word processing and graphics programs, used as visual supports

CONSIDERATIONS RELATED TO CONTINUITY

To achieve continuity in the presentation, you can continue the wallpaper, which appears as background on the introductory slide, as a sidebar on all subsequent slides. You can also repeat an icon or visual image on slides that talk about the same concept. In a presentation on interview strategies, for example, several slides may discuss techniques for identifying likely employers. The next set of slides may talk about telephone techniques for getting an interview. The third set of slides may talk about dress codes. And the final set of slides may address interview strategies. A new visual image will introduce each new idea cluster: a computer monitor to represent research, telephone for discussion of securing the interview, item of clothing for dress codes, and two people interacting for interview strategies. The audience can only see one slide at a time; consequently, it is easy for them to lose a sense of organization when attending a lengthy PowerPoint presentation.

USE OF CONTRAST AND COLORS

Presentations require contrast—either a light font on a dark background or a dark font on a light background. White typeface works well against deep purple or dark blue backgrounds, and dark blue typeface looks nice against a yellow background. In one PowerPoint presentation, I use gold headings and white text against a green backdrop. A swath of purple on each page adds a splash of extra color without overwhelming the reader. For simplicity and clarity, you can use white against black or black against white, although audiences typically prefer color. People respond emotionally to colors, and some studies show that they learn better from presentations that employ color.[10] Avoid backgrounds with patterns or detail that could distract. You should not use more than three or four colors in a presentation.

TYPEFACE AND FONT SIZE

Users of computer-generated software presentation packages have a choice of *serif* or *sans serif* typefaces. Serif typefaces have short lines or curls at the tips of letters. Examples include Times, Garamond, and Palatino Linotype. Sans serif typefaces have letters with straight lines. With electronic projection, sans serif typefaces are more readable than serif typefaces. The most common varieties are Arial, Verdana, and Tahoma. They will work with every kind of printer and operating system. Some designers, who say that variety is desirable, suggest using sans serif typeface for headings and serif typeface for text. (See the Question of Ethics box.)

Whatever the eventual choice on font size, presenters should avoid highly ornate fonts such as Brush Script MT and Gigi, which are difficult to read; fonts such as Broadway and Audience, which are too wide and dark for presentations; and Agency FB, which is a bit anorexic and compressed. Speakers should also avoid too much variety in typefaces (no more than two or three) and font sizes. Most

A Question of Ethics

Scanners and computer software programs allow us to edit the words of other people, doctor the images that we present in PowerPoint presentations, and alter photographs to suit our ends. It is possible to put the head of one person on another or omit parts of headlines, changing the meaning of the caption. We can bold, highlight, or lighten selected passages to give them more or less emphasis. Can you think of any examples where communicators have abused the potential of the new technologies?

Daryl Huff wrote a much publicized book in 1954 titled *How to Lie with Statistics* (New York: W.W. Norton). Many speakers have followed his advice since that date. At one conference, for example, speakers made a presentation titled "Statistics Can Lie: How to Create Charts That Help to Show Your Program in a Positive Light." They advocated the use of bold dark colors in pie charts. More compelling than pale pas-

tels, dark colors also appear larger. The speakers suggested making selective choices on what to include and exclude in bar graphs. Placing the highest values in charts on the right side of the frame creates the impression that they are greater since the eye reads from left to right. Photographs involve the audience on an emotional level. A presenter could depict an increase in soccer participation but omit the declining interest in basketball.

How do you feel about this kind of advice? The presenters were just trying to help cities to improve their participation rates in recreational activities. Their advocacy efforts supported the public interest. Would you feel differently if someone were using these same strategies to persuade you to buy new exercise equipment from their company? Does the end ever justify the means? How do speaker motives figure into the ethics equation?

experts agree that you should use a mix of upper- and lower-case letters. Upper-case by itself is hard to read.

Most experts say that the font size should never go below 14 points. The following recommendation appears often in discussions related to formatting of computer presentations: 36 points for major headings, 24 points for subheadings, and 18 points for text. The appropriate size of font depends, in large measure, on the typeface, the distance between speaker and audience, and whether or not boldface is used. Some typefaces are larger or more readable than others, even when they indicate a smaller font size. The space consumed by words written in different typefaces can vary dramatically.

GRAMMAR AND STRUCTURE

Too often, PowerPoint presentations lose their integrity by sloppy use of grammar. Each slide should support a single idea, such as the spread of HIV among different demographic groups, behaviors to implement in the event of fire, or rules for conducting business in Latin America. Also, you should avoid mixing phrases and sentences on the same slide, and you should aim for parallel sentence structures. The following list illustrates these problems:

- Running a business without a goal
- Wants profits more than clients
- Lost a large percentage of the business
- In trouble with shareholders and customers
- He's ready to give up.

In this example, the speaker combines a gerund phrase (*running a business*) with phrases beginning with a present tense verb (*wants profits more than clients*) and a past tense verb (*lost all perspective*). Then she uses a prepositional phrase (*in trouble with shareholders and customers*) and ends with a sentence (*He's ready to give up.*) Even though one central thought is probably present on this slide, the presentation of the ideas creates confusion. When the grammatical structures keep shifting, you have to work harder to figure out what the person is saying. In aiming for parallel sentence structure, you can begin each bullet with an infinitive, as in the following case:

- To promote the rights of children
- To encourage new child abuse legislation
- To enforce existing laws to protect children

A second example of parallel structure would be verb phrases used as nouns:

- Answering the telephone
- Responding to walk-in clients
- Doing the paperwork

Alternatively, you could use a series of phrases such as the following:

· European reactions to war in Iraq
· Domestic reactions to war in Iraq
· Latin American reactions to war in Iraq

A final example would be the following:

· Spread of HIV in African and Caribbean countries
· Spread of HIV among heterosexuals
· Growing number of women with HIV

To the extent possible, use phrases rather than sentences. Avoid unnecessary words such as *the*, *a*, or *an*. If you use sentences, they should be short, as in the following example:

Desirable Behaviors in the Event of Fire

· Identify the nearest exit.
· Avoid elevators.
· Do not panic.
· Walk; do not run.
· Avoid pushing and shoving others.

FORMATTING

Do not try to crowd too much on any slide. Allow sufficient "white space"—space that does not contain text or visuals. Begin the text at approximately the same place on each slide. Allow the same amount of room on the top and bottom of the slide. Software programs such as PowerPoint assist with this process because they do not allow you to go below a certain point on the slide. Use bullets to designate the different points. Note that you always capitalize the first word in a bullet. Place a period at the end of sentences or the last phrase in a series. As with flip charts, limit the material to five or six lines on a slide and do not exceed forty characters on a line.

PRESENTATION TECHNIQUES

When delivering from PowerPoint, stand to the side of the screen so that you do not block the view of your audience. Refer as necessary to the screen but do not depend too much on it. Do not peer down at your laptop computer screen. Keep yourself open to your audience and use a remote to change the slides. Some remotes have a shutter device that allows you to hide the image while you are talking about some other point. When you are ready to continue, you can renew the image on the screen by pressing the button a second time. If you

require additional note cards for quotations or amplification of points on the screen, limit the number of cards and learn the material prior to presenting. (See the Keep in Mind box.)

Most software programs allow you to introduce one point at a time, which works well with certain kinds of content. With cartoons, for example, you can introduce one frame at a time. You can progressively add content to bar, line, or pie graphs in the same fashion.

In a formal business presentation, delivered to an executive audience, the speaker typically previews the major points to be covered but avoids displaying a detailed outline of the presentation. In a classroom lecture, on the other hand, students expect and need the notes for purposes of studying for examinations. So instructors present a detailed outline of what they will cover during the lecture. Even in that situation, however, speakers are wise to distribute the materials *after* the lecture or presentation. When audience members have a complete set of notes, they do not bother to listen so closely. Some leave the classroom mentally; others walk out the door. The remaining listeners may read the notes rather than listen to the more detailed explanations, reducing their attention to important supplementary material. In that situation, the two media (aural and visual) compete, rather than complement, each other. A rule of television production is that a visual should never repeat the script. The two should always work in concert with each other. That same principle applies to the use of visuals in speaking contexts. Visual aids (also audio) should complement and highlight, rather than repeat, the content of a spoken presentation.

Keep in Mind

Tips for Using PowerPoint

- Use mixed media (audio and clip art) to add interest.
- Achieve a common look by repeating colors, fonts, shapes, and lines.
- Acquire continuity by repeating icons on slides that pertain to the same idea cluster.
- Limit the amount of clip art on any slide.
- Use contrasting colors.
- Avoid backgrounds with patterns or excessive detail.
- Avoid distracting noises—clanging and banging of shutters.
- Use *sans serif* typefaces; avoid highly ornate fonts.
- Keep font size between 18 and 36 points.
- Each slide should support a single idea.
- Limit the material to 5 or 6 lines on a slide.
- Do not exceed 40 characters on a line.
- Don't mix sentences and phrases on the same slide.
- Use parallel grammatical structures.
- Allow sufficient white space on slides.
- Use bullets to designate different points.
- When presenting, stand to the side of the screen; stay open to audience.
- Refer to the screen but maintain eye contact with your audience.
- Use a remote to change the slides.
- Use the shutter device to hide an image and talk about the ideas.

Bring backup copies of your presentation—on CD and hard drive—to your speaking event. Some speakers bring an extra copy of their presentations on transparencies; however, updating the transparencies on a regular basis can be costly.

A final suggestion is to take principles of audience adaptation into account in your presentation. Involve the audience to the extent possible. You can, for example, include photographs of group members among your slides. You can invite comments or questions from the audience at appropriate points during or after the presentation.

Conclusion

This chapter has expanded upon the channel component in the CCM model, introduced in Chapter One. Topics included the functions served by visual aids, the choices of visual aids, and principles governing their use. In this chapter, I also discussed how to present statistical data and computer-generated presentations.

Questions for Discussion

1. How important are visual supports to you as an audience member? Do you find that they enhance your learning?

2. Have you ever had a bad experience using a visual aid in an oral presentation? Discuss your experiences.

3. What do you like about PowerPoint and other computer-assisted presentations? What do you dislike about these presentations? Describe one that you found to be very effective. How was it different from one that you found to be ineffective?

4. Discuss some ethical considerations related to the use of visual supports.

Outline

RESEARCHING AND SUPPORTING YOUR IDEAS

The Informative Speech

Learning Objectives

- To learn about different kinds of informative speeches
- To learn how to prepare an informative speech

The purpose of all informative speaking is to impart memorable information that expands and reinforces the knowledge base of the listener. In achieving that end, the informative speech may explain or clarify an idea, concept, or term; talk about a person, place, or event; or demonstrate a process or procedure. Topics to be reviewed in this chapter include taking audience interests into account in choosing your topic, writing purpose and thesis statements, organizing your speech and writing preview and linking statements, writing introductions and conclusions, using visual aids and delivering extemporaneously. The following new concepts will allow you to continue expanding your knowledge base: researching your topic and supporting your ideas. The major headings of this chapter draw the reader to consider types of informative speaking, steps to be followed in preparing an informative speech, and a review of major structural elements in speeches to inform.

Different Types of Informative Speaking

Informative speeches have several main functions. They can explain *ideas or concepts*, such as time travel, the history of modern comic strip characters, slang used by college students, conspiracy theories, or the legacy of rap music. Sometimes informative speakers explain *terms* such as *channeling*, *roller rapper*, or *homeboy*.

Informative speeches can also introduce the audience to *people, places, and events*—historical or contemporary. A speaker could talk, for example, about a historical figure such as the legendary world wrestler Eddie Guerrero or event such as the first basketball game in North America. Alternatively, informative speeches can look at contemporary figures such as Steven Spielberg or events such as the threat posed by the avian flu. Some current happenings, such as the Iraq war, have their roots in history. In those cases, you may want to bring historical perspectives to bear on the discussion of contemporary events. Informative speeches can also discuss places such as the Holocaust Museum in Washington, DC; the "Old West"; or the infamous prison Alcatraz, a prime attraction for visitors to San Francisco. A speaker could talk about the rainforests of Brazil, the Great Barrier Reefs of Australia, or the barren beauty of the Alaskan wilderness.

Informative speeches can also describe or demonstrate a *process or procedure*. These speeches give instruction on how to make or to do something such as how to prepare sushi, build an electric go-cart, see Australia on a budget, or use martial arts techniques to protect yourself in the event of an assault. These instructional talks identify a series of steps that lead to a desired result. In these examples, the desired results could be the following: sushi, a go cart, an inexpensive trip to Australia, or a new response set for defending yourself.

Steps in Preparing an Informative Speech

Thirteen steps in preparing an informative speech include (1) choosing your topic, (2) framing a purpose statement, (3) writing a thesis statement, (4) researching your speech, (5) identifying points of possible confusion, (6) choosing an organizational pattern, (7) developing an outline, (8) writing a preview statement, (9) writing an introduction, (10) developing your outline with supporting materials, (11) linking the parts of your speech, (12) adding interest with visual aids, and (13) concluding your speech. The preferred mode of delivery for informative speaking is extemporaneous, discussed in Chapters Four and Six.

STEP 1: CHOOSING YOUR TOPIC

When planning your informative speech, think back to what you learned in Chapter Five on audience adaptation. Consider audience interests, levels of knowledge, and possible attitudes toward your topic. If your audience is young and female, choose a topic that would appeal to a young female audience. If you are delivering the speech in Indianapolis, choose a subject to which audiences in central Indiana can relate. Avoid subjects that are overworked or provide little opportunity for novel input. Avoid topics where you would risk boring your audience with details that they already know. If the subject matter is too trivial, your audience may not pay attention.

The most popular choices with students are speeches of demonstration, where they describe some process or procedure. Examples of such process-oriented topics include how to choose an imaginative gift for your partner, make decorative candles or dried floral arrangements, prepare a table centerpiece for parties, interpret dreams, read someone's palm, or travel safely in foreign countries. One of my students delivered a speech on how to travel lightly. As she removed the items—one by one—from her backpack, she talked about the purpose of each item and the ways in which she had economized on space by choosing that particular item. Some of the most popular speeches cater to the limited budgets of students: how to plan a low-budget trip to the Caribbean for winter break, prepare an inexpensive but attractive meal for two, shop for bargains at clothing stores, or decorate one's apartment on a shoestring budget.

Topic
Theme or main idea for the speech

Speech of demonstration
A speech in which the speaker teaches the audience how to do or make something

If the topics are light or humorous in nature, students may wear special clothing to establish a mood. One student gave a speech, for example, on how to listen to '70s music. He came to class in retro clothes—bell-bottom pants, wide tie, and a loud shirt that he had purchased at a second-hand clothing store. He set up an old phonograph player, along with records from the 1970s, in the front of the classroom. His demonstration speech detailed the steps required to listen effectively to music from the 1970s. Another wore his Star Trek uniform when speaking on the legacy of *Star Trek*.

Students often adapt to the season by selecting topics with holiday or seasonal themes. The themes selected for demonstration speeches in February sometimes relate to Valentine's Day. Students talk about how to prepare homemade

Valentine candies or cookies for their friends or how to plan for the perfect Valentine evening. One student, dressed as Cupid, spoke about ideas for how to meet and interact with members of the opposite sex. Another spoke on how to identify potential problem dates. With winter close at hand, students often talk about winter activities (skiing, snowboarding, hockey, or figure skating). In the fall, they select subjects such as how to prepare for an outdoor camping trip, decorate apartments for Halloween parties, or make apple cider. In the spring, when the sap is running, the students give speeches on how to prepare maple syrup muffins, select and plant vegetable seeds for the beginnings of a summer garden, establish an herb garden, take creative approaches to looking for summer employment, or guard against pickpockets when traveling abroad. Students enrolled in summer classes prepare demonstration speeches on topics such as mountain hiking, rock climbing, boating, or activities that can be enjoyed on rainy days at the cottage.

For students who choose to inform audiences about ideas, people, places, and events, the choices are endless. Speakers might educate their listeners on the growth of radio talk shows, G.L.O.R.Y. wrestling, peacemakers in the twenty-first century, girl power and roller derbies, or the increasing popularity of New Zealand as a vacation destination. The criteria for topic selection are the same as with more process-oriented speeches.

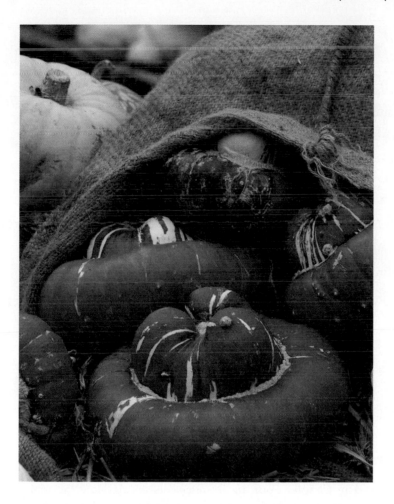

STEP 2: FRAMING A PURPOSE STATEMENT

After choosing a topic area, you must decide upon a purpose for the speech. The
following examples constitute *purpose statements* for selected topics:

Purpose statement
A specific statement
about the intent of a
speech

· To explain the benefits of yoga.
· To show how to prepare sushi.
· To demonstrate some basic tai chi moves.
· To educate the audience on the threat posed by bacterial infections in hospitals.
· To describe how to build a home radio receiver.
· To explain why the Sahara Desert is disappearing.

Notice that the purpose statements are extremely specific. For that reason, the desired results are obvious. At the conclusion of a successful informative speech, the
audience will know more about some person, idea, place, event, or process. Informative speeches increase the knowledge of listeners; they result in cognitive learning. Sometimes you will want to revise your purpose statement after conducting
in-depth research on the topic. However, you should have some purpose in mind
when you begin your research, even if that purpose later shrinks, expands, or
changes in focus.

STEP 3: WRITING A THESIS STATEMENT

Thesis statement
A statement that summarizes the main idea of the speech

As discussed in Chapter Four, *thesis statements* encapsulate the major idea of a speech. Every other point in the speech should relate back—and support—the thesis statement. Thesis statements can be quite detailed or more general, as in the following instances:

- Yoga takes us to a quiet place in our minds.
- Sushi is popular, healthy, and easy to prepare.
- Tai chi is a low-impact exercise with high benefits.
- Antibiotic-resistant "super bugs" are thriving and multiplying in American hospitals.
- Building a home radio receiver is fun and easy.
- Recent scientific studies have indicated that the Sahara Desert may be retreating.

STEP 4: RESEARCHING YOUR SPEECH

Once you have decided upon the topic and framed tentative purpose and thesis statements for your informative speech, you must research the topic. You can draw from a variety of sources—your own knowledge and background, interviews with others who have had firsthand experiences with the subject matter, and secondary sources available in the library and on the Internet. After researching the topic, you may decide to modify your purpose and thesis statements.

Personal Experience

One source of information is your own background. Your experience can make you an expert. In the following example, the student sought to bolster her credibility by pointing to her personal experience with the topic:

> I have consulted numerous government reports, newspaper articles, and websites dedicated to aiding those who live with debilitating disorders and disease. Many of these sources recommend the use of marijuana to alleviate the effects of these disorders and diseases. However, none of my library research gave me the insights gained by watching my grandmother battle throat cancer. When the cancer left my grandmother unable to eat, the doctor offered medicinal marijuana to increase her appetite and help with the side effects of the chemotherapy. After my grandmother began to use the marijuana, the difference was remarkable. She was able to eat small amounts of food, and the side effects of the chemo became manageable. She found some relief and comfort for her final weeks.[1]

When you combine your own knowledge with information acquired from other sources, you gain credibility with your audience. Do not make the mistake, however, of relying totally on your own experience. To appear knowledgeable *and* objective, you should be able to bring multiple points of view to bear on your topic.

Firsthand Experiences of Others

To adapt your topic to your local audience, include some local sources. Some of the best sources are experts in your city, whose views are available to you through interviews. Assume, for a moment, that you would like to speak on the topic of crisis help lines. The best place to begin your search for information is a local help center that assists victims of violence and people suffering from depression. These centers are listed in the yellow pages of phone books, as well as on the Internet. Volunteers

with these organizations can provide firsthand information to you and can direct you to other sources of information. Similarly, if you want to speak on the rising cost of college tuition, you might want to go to someone in your university administration or to a state representative. For anecdotal evidence, you can talk with other college students. Good sources of information on conflict resolution are practitioners with local mediation centers. Supplement these firsthand sources with newspaper and magazine articles, Internet sources, and recent books on the topic.

A few tips on interviewing can help you to obtain required information. Identify the right people to interview. Plan sufficiently in advance to obtain appointments with these sources, and, if possible, go directly to their offices to make the appointments. Extremely busy people will not be able to grant last-minute interviews. Do not rule out people whom you know. They are often the most accessible and interested in helping you.

Members of nonprofit organizations, politicians, and government employees are usually most willing to grant interviews. They serve the public interest and depend on the good will of the community to sustain their organizations. If politicians cannot meet personally with you, staff members will be available. Business executives and personnel may be more difficult to access because their first obligations are to shareholders and clients. Nonetheless, the most forward-looking organizations assume a responsive posture and support local initiatives. So your chances of gaining cooperation from these organizations are greater than your chances with less civic-minded firms. Your chances of getting an interview are greatest if you are seeking information on an uncontroversial topic and you know where to go in the organization for expertise on your topic.

Conduct as much library or Internet research as possible before the interview and prepare your questions in advance of the meeting. Open-ended questions such as "What are the most important aims of this program?" are better than questions that call for *yes* or *no* answers. Questions to which you can find answers on the web or in the library should not appear in an interview. Also avoid expressing your personal opinion on the topic. Remember that the purpose of the interview is to access the knowledge and insights of the other person. When you voice your own opinions, you consume valuable interview time and risk alienating the interviewee who does not share your point of view. Avoid leading questions such as "You do believe that we should have a Department of Homeland Security, don't you?" or hostile questions such as "Don't you think that your organization has gone a bit overboard with its cuts to arts programs?" If you decide to ask more controversial questions, save them for the latter part of the interview, after you have covered less controversial areas. You do not want your interview to end prematurely.

Leading question
A question that unfairly prompts a desired answer

To the extent possible, frame controversial questions in a neutral way. Assume that you are interviewing the local police chief about several recent deaths from police use of taser guns. You might introduce the interview in this way: "The media has reported fifty deaths from taser guns. Journalists report that stun guns appear to have the most deadly effects on individuals who are in a weakened physical state or under the influence of drugs. How accurate is this statement, in your opinion?" A follow-up question on the topic of taser guns could ask about the reasons for using the guns: "I understand that the police have adopted the use of tasers to protect both the individual and the police officers involved in difficult arrests. Could you describe a typical situation in which you might decide to use a taser rather than some other method of subduing the person?" You could also ask, "What were the alternatives to the stun guns in these particular cases?" Even though the subject area is highly sensitive (as well as controversial), the calm, reasoned approach and the neutrality of the phrasing creates the possibility that the police chief will respond to your questions. (See the Question of Ethics box.)

Had you worded the question in the following way, the interviewee would probably have bolted: "I've read about two deaths in the last two weeks from the police shooting victims with taser guns. Two deaths in two weeks. That's pretty scary. Don't you think that you should reconsider your position on this issue?" The interviewer has committed several offenses. She has used loaded language (*police shooting victims*, *scary*). She has also expressed a personal opinion: "Two deaths in two weeks. That's pretty scary." Finally, she has asked a leading question: "Don't you think that you should reconsider your position on this issue?" The question

Loaded language
Words that tend to suggest bias

A Question of Ethics

Candace was researching the topic of toxic emissions for an informative speech. She was especially interested in this topic because she suspected that the local chemical plant might be releasing unsafe levels of chemicals into the air. A number of people had complained that they could smell the chemicals in the air late at night. They believed that the plant might be waiting until people were asleep to release the toxins into the air. Others said that they had seen heavy smoke coming from the plant stacks at the same time that the air had a smell of noxious gases.

Candace also knew about three employees who had died from a rare form of cancer after working for the plant. The three were only in their mid-thirties; and two were nonsmokers, without a history of physical problems. For those reasons, Candace felt strongly about the importance of investigating the topic.

She had already conducted an extensive search of the literature. She had read a large number of newspaper and magazine articles and explored the subject on the Internet. But she wanted some firsthand information from people who worked at the plant. More specifically, she wanted an interview with senior management. She believed that the interview would allow her to ask questions to which she did not have answers, and the interview would give added credibility to her speech.

Candace did not believe, however, that a plant manager would grant an interview if he knew the subject of her speech. So she decided to tell the manager that she wanted an interview on a different topic. She said that she wanted to learn more about charitable activities undertaken by the company, such as the sponsoring of a local golf tournament and a run for charity. With this introduction to her research purposes, the public relations person at the plant agreed to arrange an interview for Candace.

Candace did not believe that she was doing anything wrong. She felt that the company's responsibility to the community outweighed any ethical concerns in the situation. Also, she wanted to become an investigative journalist, and she had read about how journalists sometimes misrepresented their purposes initially in order to secure an interview. Then once on the premises, they revealed their real purpose. Do you think that Candace was right? How do you feel about the ethics of her research methods?

also calls for a *yes* or *no* response, not allowing for grey areas. These kinds of statements will probably result in a defensive response and a premature end to the interview.

After preparing your questions, you should arrive at the interview on time, dressed appropriately. Your dress should reflect professionalism and seriousness of purpose. After introducing yourself, you should set up any equipment—computer, tape recorder, or notebook. With the permission of the interviewee, you can record the interview. However, many people are not comfortable being recorded. So if the person says *no*, do not argue. If two people attend the interview, one can take notes while the other asks the questions.

Flexibility should be your guide in interviewing. At the beginning of the session, remind your interviewee of your goals in the interview. Be prepared for the person to go off track from time to time and to answer some questions before you have asked them. The order in which the person answers the questions is less important than the fact that he answers them. Do not try to hold the interview to its original course if you are getting interesting information. The person may raise some points that you have not considered. At the same time, you should be aware of the time so that, if some important questions remain unanswered, you do not lose the opportunity to ask the questions. Gently steer the interview back on course at an appropriate moment. Ask for clarification when you do not understand a point or ask probing questions if you need more information on a topic.

If you interview a high-level executive, expect the person to take control of the interview. Studies demonstrate that executives like to take the lead and set the direction of interviews. If that happens, do not interrupt. Listen to see how many of your questions are answered during the course of the interview. If the time allotted to the interview nears an end, thank the person for her contribution and say that you have several additional questions that you would like to ask before concluding. Do not exceed the time limits set for the interview unless the person is clearly willing to give more time. Review and transcribe your notes as soon as possible after the interview, before you forget the details.

Libraries (On-site and Online Facilities)

Libraries are the repository of the most solid and reliable information of a secondary nature. You can obtain access to most secondary sources through your university and local libraries. *Secondary sources* include books, journals, magazines, newspapers, yearbooks, and other published materials. The authors communicate to you through their publications, not in person. You can visit your library *in person* or *on the web*. If you go to the physical facility, you can obtain the help of your reference librarian. Every library has fact sheets on its services, and most offer orientation tours to new students. Unanswered questions can be addressed directly to the librarian on duty. Computerized catalogues list books, videos, and other library holdings by author, title, key words, and subject. If you are in the library, you can use a computer to access this database and look up call numbers for books and other library materials. As long as you hold a valid permit to use library facilities, you can also access relevant databases from a variety of other locations—home, office, hotel room, or even another country.

If you do not know the author or title, the online search function in the computerized catalogue allows you to locate materials by inputting key words or subjects. An increasing number of libraries allow you to reserve books online. If books, videos, or other materials are checked out of the library, you can put them on hold; and the library will notify you upon their return. If your library does not hold a book, journal article, or video, you can often order the book through interlibrary loan services, a special library unit that helps patrons to secure books from other

libraries. To retrieve a book from the shelves, reserve the book, or order the book through interlibrary loan services, you need to know the author, title, and call number.

Most libraries have special rooms where they keep current magazines, newspapers, and other periodicals. A few years back, libraries bound and shelved the older periodicals. As binding became too expensive, libraries began to put the older magazines and journals on microfilm or microfiche. Some library floors are still dedicated to these microfilm and microfiche collections, as well as to government publications. However, increasingly, libraries have moved to online subscriptions, where users can access current and archived periodicals via the Internet. Like libraries, government departments also are moving to web publication.

Why should you go to your university or other library website as a point of access for information? Libraries pay institutional fees that allow users to access the information without paying for it. They also reference materials that have been reviewed and approved as legitimate sources of information. If you use search engines such as Alta Vista, HotBot, Lycos, and Yahoo, on the other hand, you will encounter a much more fluid environment. These search engines do not differentiate between websites with accurate and inaccurate information. Some web masters have their own political or social agendas; and they seek to proselytize, not to represent unbiased information to web visitors. Other web sources are simply inaccurate or out of date, or they do not list the sources of the information. For that reason, the following discussion introduces you to databases that are usually available through university and other library websites. Legitimate users can access these sites free of charge. (See the Keep in Mind box.)

Search engines
Electronic program for the retrieval of data

A number of indexes are available online to help you to locate popular magazines, academic and trade journals, and newspapers. The oldest and most often consulted index for popular literature, *The Readers' Guide to Periodical Literature*, can

Keep in Mind

Online Library Resources

- *AccessScience*—encyclopedia of science and technology
- *American National Biography*—portraits of more than 17,400 men and women
- *American Women's History*—biographies of American women, historical and topical entries, speeches, maps, timelines, tables and charts, and photographs
- *Ancient History & Culture*—coverage of Africa, Egypt, Greece, Rome, Mesoamerica, and Mesopotamia, spanning the period from three to five million years ago through 1522 C.E.
- *Bartleby.com Great Books Online*—full text of a number of standard reference books, fiction, nonfiction, and poetry
- *Bartlett's Familiar Quotations*—1901 edition of this popular book of quotations
- *Contemporary Authors*—biographies of more than 100,000 writers
- *CQ's Electronic Encyclopedia of American Government*—articles and illustrations on the three branches of U.S. government
- *Dictionary of Literary Biography*—information on literary figures from all time periods in genres such as fiction, nonfiction, poetry, drama, history, and journalism
- *Encyclopaedia Britannica*—the complete encyclopedia, as well as *Merriam-Webster's Collegiate Dictionary* and the *Britannica Book of the Year*
- *Encyclopedia Americana*—online encyclopedia with an added news database
- *Grolier Online*—*Encyclopedia Americana, Grolier Multimedia Encyclopedia, The New Book of Knowledge, Nueva Enciclopedia Cumbre en Línea, New Book of Popular Science, Lands and Peoples*
- *Information Please Almanac*—full text of the *Information Please Almanac*, as well as an online dictionary and an online encyclopedia
- *Literature Resource Center*—information on literary figures from all time periods in the genres of fiction, nonfiction, poetry, drama, history, and journalism
- *Oxford Classical Dictionary*, 3rd ed.; *Oxford English Dictionary (OED)*, 2nd ed.
- *Webster's Third New International Dictionary*, unabridged
- *World Book Online Reference Center*—encyclopedia articles, web links, periodical articles, videos, maps, and more
- *World Fact Book*—maps, current issues, history, geography, people, government, economy, communications, transportation, military, and transnational issues

be found in the reference room of some libraries. However, a new *Reader's Guide Full Text, Mega Edition* and *Select Edition* are now available online. These new databases contain the full text of magazine articles back to 1994 and abstracts back to 1983. They also reference popular newspapers such as the *New York Times*. Subjects include science, business, arts, entertainment, health, sports and fitness, current happenings, and many more. *The Reader's Guide Retrospective: 1890–1982* indexes articles that have appeared in 375 leading magazines over more than a century.

Other sources specialize in news. *NewsLink*, for example, connects the reader to newspapers, broadcasters, and magazines. *News and Newspapers Online* also contains worldwide linkages to news sources. The *Newspaper Association of America* references many U.S. dailies, local newspapers, weeklies, business papers, and alternative press papers. *Ethnic News Watch* is a full-text collection of the newspapers, magazines, and journals of the ethnic, minority, and Native press. *LexisNexis*

Academic contains mostly full text entries from major newspapers (U.S. and international), as well as magazines, journals, newsletters, trade magazines, and abstracts. The specialty of this database is law.

Other commercial databases, available in many electronic library collections, include *ProQuest*, *EBSCOhost*, *PsycINFO*, *MEDLINE*, and *Info Trac College Edition*. *ProQuest* is an electronic collection of millions of articles originally published in magazines, newspapers, and journals. The *Educational Resource Information Center* (ERIC) database includes citations for journal articles and original research on all aspects of education. An increasing number of publishers are also putting their academic journals and excerpts from books online. Many professional associations, which lack complete collections of their early journals, are asking members to share the missing issues with the associations so that they can put them on the web. A number of encyclopedias, dictionaries, yearbooks, and other resources—traditionally found in the reference areas of libraries—are now available online.

While this discussion has emphasized computerized databases as information sources, you should not overlook the physical library facility. Sometimes the best way to begin a project is to peruse the bookshelves. After locating a few call numbers in the computerized catalogue, skim through the books on shelves holding those call numbers. Many older documents will never be available online even though some are important resources, and you can miss them if you do not input the right key words in the computer.

Search Engines on Internet

Although libraries (on-site and online) are the most reliable information sites, web researchers are relying increasingly on the larger Internet. Popular Internet search

engines include Google, Alta Vista, HotBot, Go.com, Lycos, Metacrawler, Webcrawler, Magellan, Infoseek, Excite NetSearch, Ask.com, and Yahoo. On a day-to-day basis, people use the Internet to research a host of topics from health to current issues to recreational sites, hotels, and airfares. Most news organizations, as well as many magazines, host websites with current news and feature items. If you are looking for an interesting parable or colorful story, the general search engines can lead you to many personal websites that include quotations and stories. Unfortunately, these sources do not always identify the authors of the quotations or stories; and sometimes the wording is inaccurate. In other situations, you may need to identify the meaning of a word, find the name of the person who won a sports event, research tourist attractions, or locate a recipe. The general search engines offer multiple sources of information on these kinds of topics. However, you should use the criteria discussed earlier to determine the validity and worth of the information that you intend to use in speeches.

Certainly, cautions are in order when you rely on the general search engines. As noted earlier, many sources are biased, inaccurate, and/or outdated. So ask yourself the following kinds of questions before you decide to use information from a website accessed with a general search engine: Does the source appear to be an expert in the field? Is the author of the material affiliated with an advocacy organization (e.g., gun control, animal rights, abortion, tobacco, or other)? Is the source missing altogether? (Usually the credentials of the author will appear on more credible websites.) If the author is not listed, does the information appear on a website hosted by a credible organization (e.g., reputable market research firm or broadcasting corporation)? Does the author cite statistics, objective facts, and evidence to back up his point of view? Does he include a bibliography of sources on which he has relied? The literacy of the writing may indicate the accuracy of the material. Careful researchers avoid grammatical and typographical errors. Their material is edited and, in the case of academics, subjected to peer reviews. Sloppy writing is a good indicator of sloppy research. Look for the last revision date for the material included on the website. If no dates appear with the material, you should check its validity by going to other sites for confirmation. If you are using Netscape, you can check the date by going to the *file* menu, selecting *document* information, and selecting *last modified*.

Some of the search engines are now adding specialized functions. Google, for example, has inaugurated a new search engine for scientists and academic researchers called Google Scholar. Another new service is Google Print, which locates books with text to match your search terms. Links take the reader to the referenced text and to publishers and libraries that hold the book. The new service references scientific citations and peer-reviewed papers, abstracts, books, and technical reports available in digitized form in libraries. It also suggests ways to locate materials at libraries that are not online. Google Uncle Sam is another search engine developed at Stanford University, which indexes U.S. government websites. The Amazing Picture Machine locates images that can provide visual support for speeches.

In addition, many university websites include links to credible sources of information on the Internet; and a growing number of professors include course syllabi, along with bibliographies and lecture materials, on their websites. They also link their sites to other websites. A more limited number of professors have begun to put their published articles or abstracts of their work on personal websites. Many universities now publish guidelines for writing academic papers, referencing sources, and creating bibliographies. The University of Wisconsin–Madison website, for example, includes examples of the American Psychological Association (APA) format, used by many communication programs. The Humanities Department and the Arthur C. Banks Library at the Capital Community College, Hartford, Connecticut, have generated a comprehensive guide to the Modern Languages Association (MLA) format. These are just two of many university websites that include examples of formats employed in popular style guides.

As mentioned earlier in this chapter, you can also find references to commercial databases such as *Pro-Quest* on the Internet. However, you will be required to pay for much of this information if you do not go through the library where you hold a membership. The same is true for many of the articles referenced on Google Scholar and Google Print. The fees for journal membership can be prohibitive for the average student budget. So if you happen to run across an interesting resource when you use the Internet search engines, check your library holdings before you pay for the material.

STEP 5: IDENTIFYING POINTS OF POSSIBLE CONFUSION

Speakers should anticipate the parts of an informative speech that are likely to create confusion or resistance in the mind of the listener. The speaker should ask: What could be confusing to audience members? Has their past experience led them to believe something different from the information that I will present to them? Does my information war with common conceptions of reality? Will they accept my explanation if I do not explicitly recognize their preconceived notions on the topic? Your research should assist you in identifying points of possible confusion. Responding to these questions requires a strategic approach to informative speaking.[2]

Sometimes audience members will be convinced that their interpretations or understanding of an event or concept is the right one. Imagine that you were informing an audience on the topic of immunizations. Some common misconceptions could influence audience acceptance of your speech. People may believe, for example, that the diseases for which we vaccinate children no longer exist in the United States. They may suspect that vaccines cause autism in children or trigger infant death syndrome (SIDS). They may be convinced that the DTP vaccine overloads the immune system, pushing the health of people over the brink. They may believe that the risk from vaccines is greater than the risk from some diseases such as chickenpox. If people genuinely believe that immunizations are dangerous, they may tune out much of the information that you provide.

People have confused or inadequate understanding of many topics. In fact, when you input the term *misconceptions* into Google search engine, you obtain over three million references. It would appear that people hold misconceptions about Buddhism, climate change, evolution, dinosaurs, tornadoes, contraception, hearing disabilities, Day of the Dead celebrations in Mexico, quackery, night people, Islam, Florida prisons, depression, Africa, and a range of other subjects too vast to mention. So the person who intends to deliver an informative speech must take areas of confusion into account.

At other times, we speak on topics about which the subject matter is counterintuitive.[3] Many people believe, for example, that chairs are constituted of solid matter; but physicists tell us that they are mostly empty space. Physicists tell us that, if we could eliminate emptiness from the entire planet, the earth would be reduced to the size of an orange even though its weight would remain constant. Wayne State professor Moti Nissani concluded, "This tells us that common sense and intuition are not infallible guides to reality."[4]

Other hurdles in preparing an informative speech may relate to the difficulty of the material. In explaining a highly complex concept such as string theory, the speaker must arrive at a strategy to make the material more understandable to the audience. Even physicists have difficulty understanding this theory, which talks about the timeless nature of the universe and parallel existences. A speech on the topic of string theory would need to use many examples and analogies, such as comparisons with the resonating strings of a guitar, to explain the theory.

STEP 6: CHOOSING AN ORGANIZATIONAL PATTERN

When choosing an organizational pattern, speakers must consider what they learned from audience research about levels of understanding of the topic. Speeches to inform typically rely on *chronological*, *spatial*, and *topical* patterns of organization; but they may also use *comparative*, *narrative*, *myth response*, or *transformative* patterns of organization. Where audiences hold misconceptions or have limited understanding of a complex topic, the speaker may need to take a more strategic approach to choosing the organizational pattern.[5] For purposes of contrast, I have used the same topic, child pornography, to illustrate each of these seven patterns of organization.

Chronological organization
Time-based

Chronological patterns of organization are time-based. That is, a time sequence governs the development of the speech: first to last, last to first, past to present, present to past, past to future, future to past. A speech about painting an apartment could rely, for example, on a time-sequenced (first-to-last) pattern of organization. The major ideas could be deciding on a color scheme (first step), choosing paints that fit your budget (second step), preparing the apartment (third step), and using special techniques in painting (fourth step). In Figure 8.1, a speaker uses a chronological ordering to trace the development of legislation governing child pornography. Note that the outline employs phrases, rather than full sentences.

Spatial organization
Focused on the relationship of parts in space, often geographical

The *spatial* pattern organizes content according to the relationship of the parts in space. Often we are talking about some kind of geographical ordering. In the case of a speech on child pornography, for example, you could talk about initiatives in different countries, such as the United Kingdom, Sweden, and the United States. Spatial order implies location, such as different parts of a shopping mall (first level, second level, top level), different regions in a country (eastern, southern, central, midwestern, western), different parts of a city (Manhattan, Queens, Westchester, Brooklyn, and the Bronx in New York City), or different parts of a page (top of the page, center of the page, bottom of the page). Figure 8.2 demonstrates the use of

Legislating Child Pornography

I.   Passing of Protection of Children Against Sexual Exploitation Act in 1978

    A.   Outlawed the use of children in the production of obscene materials

    B.   Enhanced the penalties for transmission or receipt of obscene materials containing depictions of children

    C.   Rejected any measures that would have exceeded the scope of existing obscenity laws

II. Passing of Child Protection Act in 1984

    A.   Changed the meaning of sexual conduct to include certain nonobscene pictures of children

    B.   Raised the age of "children" for purposes of the law from sixteen to eighteen, thereby extending the scope of "child pornography"

    C.   Increased the maximum fines tenfold

    D.   Removed the requirement that the transmission or receipt of child pornography have a profit motive

III. Amendment of Child Protection Act in 1986

    A.   Banning of advertising for any type of exchange of child pornography

    B.   Banning of advertising that solicits participation in any sexually explicit conduct for the purpose of creating child pornography

IV. Passing of Child Protection Restoration and Penalties Enhancement Act in 1990 (amended in 1996)

Figure 8.1 Chronological Pattern of Organization

spatial order in discussing international initiatives to control child pornography. Like the first example, this outline uses phrases, instead of full sentences.

A *topical* scheme of organization groups ideas according to some rational ordering. That is, the speaker places the major points in an order that makes logical sense. The following points could constitute major headings in a speech on identity theft: increases in numbers of people who are targeted, nature of the problem, a profile of people who are most vulnerable, and ideas for protecting your identity. In this example, related ideas cluster under different subject headings. In the case of child pornography, speakers using a topical form of organization could examine the ways by which traffickers find their way around the laws, the pros and cons of different approaches to solving the problem, the provisions in the UN Convention on Rights of the Child, the different manifestations of child pornography, or the effects of pornography on children. Figure 8.3 illustrates a topical organizational pattern in a speech about the effects of pornography on children. Note that this outline uses full sentences—a variation on the earlier examples.

Topical organization
Based on a rational ordering of ideas

International Initiatives to Address the Problem of Child Pornography

I. Recent initiatives in the United Kingdom
 A. "End Child Exploitation" campaign
 B. Establishment of hotlines and the INHOPE forum
 C. Participation in Childnet International

II. Recent initiatives in Sweden
 A. Hosting of the Stockholm Congress on Commercial Child Exploitation
 B. Participation in the UN Convention on Rights of the Child
 C. Joint funding of the UNESCO International Clearinghouse on Children and Media Violence on the Screen
 D. Establishment of the Swedish Save the Children hotline

III. Recent initiatives in the United States
 A. Efforts to produce the Communications Decency Act
 B. Passing of Child Protection Restoration and Penalties Enhancement Act
 C. Establishment of the cyber tip line by the Center for Missing and Exploited Children

Figure 8.2 Spatial Pattern of Organization

Comparative organization
Placing two things (ideas, events, concepts) next to one another in order to shed light on both

A *comparative* scheme of organization places two ideas, concepts, or events side by side—using one to illuminate the other. For example, a speaker could compare views of women as expressed in the Torah and the New Testament. Sometimes the comparison becomes an extended analogy. In the case of child pornography, for example, a speaker might compare the challenges of dealing with child pornography to the challenges of dealing with the heroin trade. By learning more about the successes and failures of the justice system in dealing with heroin addicts, we can gain greater understanding of the challenges we face with child pornography addicts. (See Figure 8.4.)

Narrative pattern
Using stories and examples

A *narrative* pattern of organization simply introduces and defines a term or concept such as *tolerance* and then supports the definition with a number of examples, stories, and analogies. Some of the supporting materials will be "nonexamples."[6] In semiotics, we often define concepts and terms by *what they are not*. Bravery is not being afraid. Quiet is the absence of noise. Complacency is not caring. We can learn much about the definitions of many words or the meaning of concepts by looking at what they are *not*. By looking at examples of intolerance, for instance, we can better understand tolerance. (See Figure 8.5.)

Effects of Pornography on Children

I. The availability of pornography increases the chances that molesters will commit acts of sexual violence against children.

   A. Child molesters use child pornography to stimulate themselves prior to committing rape and other sexual acts against children.

   B. Child molesters use photographs to encourage children to believe that the activities are acceptable and to gain compliance.

II. Exposure to pornography may lead children to act out sexually with younger children in their families and communities.

   A. Children imitate what they see, hear, and read in the media.

   B. Curiosity could lead children to experiment with younger siblings and friends.

III. Exposure to pornography may interfere with a child's psychological development.

   A. Children are not psychologically ready to deal with sexual relationships.

   B. Children may develop feelings of shame and guilt that inhibit their development into healthy adults.

   C. Children may develop the inability to experience sexual feelings independent of viewing pornography.

Figure 8.3 Topical Pattern of Organization

Similar to the claims pattern (applied in persuasive speeches), a *myth response* scheme of organization involves identifying and negating the misconceptions on some topic. A speech on child pornography, for example, could counter the following five myths: (1) Anti-pornography legislation violates First Amendment rights to free speech. (2) Pornography is a victimless crime. (3) The prevalence of pornography suggests that many people support it. (4) No one has the right to impose his or her morality on another person. (5) Opponents of pornography are ultraconservative and reactionary. This organizational pattern would entail identifying the myths one at a time, followed by a clarification and explanation of the real situation. (See Figure 8.6.)

Finally, the *transformative pattern*, advocated by Katherine Rowan, applies to situations where the new information violates our intuitive understanding of science or other systems of knowledge. The speaker, in that case, should adhere to the following sequence: (1) identify common belief structures on the topic, (2) recognize the seeming plausibility of these beliefs, (3) discuss their shortcomings, and (4) introduce the new information, using examples that are within the experience of the audience and that demonstrate the plausibility of the information.[7] (See Figure 8.7.)

Myth response
Identifying and clarifying misconceptions on a topic

Transformative pattern
A pattern that causes the listener to examine and reconsider long held beliefs

Challenges in Dealing with Child Pornography, Not Unlike Heroin

I. Challenges in dealing with heroin

   A. Addictive

   B. Profitable

   C. Easily accessible

   D. Difficult to control

   E. Expensive in costs to society

II. Challenges in dealing with child pornography

   A. Addictive

   B. Profitable

   C. Easily accessible

   D. Difficult to control

   E. Expensive in costs to society

III. Learning from our mistakes

   A. Lessons to be drawn from how we have dealt with heroin users in legal contexts—how we have tried to legislate away the problem

   B. Lessons to be drawn from how we have dealt with heroin users in family contexts—how we have tried to ignore the problem

   C. Lessons to be drawn from how we have dealt with heroin users in school contexts—how we have tried to understand the problem

   D. Lessons to be drawn from how we have dealt with heroin users in psychological contexts—how we have tried to transform the problem

IV. Provisions of the new legislation—educating the public

   A. Where we've been

   B. Where we are now

   C. Where we are going

Figure 8.4 Comparative Pattern of Organization

STEP 7: DEVELOPING AN OUTLINE

Figure 8.8, which depicts standard levels of organization, offers a review of first-level headings (I, II, III, etc.), second-level headings (A, B, C, D, etc.), third-level headings (1, 2, 3, etc.), and fourth-level headings (a, b, c, d, etc.). As mentioned in Chapter Four, speakers should limit the number of major and supporting points in speeches. A speech that is five to six minutes long does not usually allow time for more than three major points and three levels of supporting detail under those

Child Pornography—Stories About Victims

I.   Introduction of myth that child pornography is a "victimless" crime

II. Meeting some victims through stories about their experiences

    A.   Story of Nancy, who became pregnant at thirteen after being molested by an uncle, who admitted to trafficking in child pornography

    B.   Story of Timothy, still haunted by dreams of his molestation by a minister, whose computer contained images of children in sexual positions

    C.   Story of Jennifer, raped and murdered by a pedophile, who possessed a large store of illicit magazines

    D.   Story of Mark, unable to have a healthy relationship with a woman after years of abuse by a neighbor (a child pornography user)

    E.   Story of Kevin, a teenager who abused his younger sister after viewing pornography on a long-term basis

    F.   Story of Elizabeth, who turned to drugs on the street after long-term abuse by her father, who admitted to being addicted to child pornography

III. Arriving at a new definition of *victim*

Figure 8.5 Narrative Pattern of Organization

points. You should place your most important points either first or last. Research suggests that audiences have the best recall of material that appears at the beginning of speeches (termed *primacy effect*) and end of speeches (termed *recency effect*).[8]

As previously discussed, five rules govern the generation of an outline. First, you should use *either* complete sentences or phrases in developing your outline. Do not mix the two formats. Second, every major point requires at least two supporting details. If you have only one supporting point, the single point should become part of the heading that it supports. So if you have only "A," you should combine "A" with the Roman numeral that it supports. If you have only "1," you should combine "1" with the letter that it supports (A, B, C, etc.) If you have only "a," you should combine "a" with the number that it supports (1, 2, 3, etc.). The third rule in outlining is to use parallel construction. The ideas that appear at each level or under the same heading should reflect the same organizing principle. The fourth rule requires *indenting* each new point and *capitalizing the first word* in the statement or phrase. The fifth and final rule obligates you to include only one major idea in each point. If you have any questions on these points, review the detailed examples and sample outlines in Chapter Four.

Myths About Child Pornography and Obscenity Laws

I. Anti-pornography legislation violates First Amendment rights to free speech.

    A. The Supreme Court has consistently held that some forms of speech, including child pornography, are not protected.

    B. Criminal elements control the child pornography trade.

II. Pornography is a victimless crime.

    A. Studies have shown that many rapists feed on pornography.

    B. Pedophiles use pornography to encourage their victims to engage in sexual activities of an illicit nature.

    C. Some children molest other children after being exposed to pornography.

III. The prevalence of pornography suggests that many people support it.

    A. National polls show that most people oppose child pornography.

    B. You cannot judge community standards by the people who frequent pornography sites or visit adult book stores.

IV. No one has the right to impose his or her morality on another person.

    A. No one has the right to engage in illegal activities.

    B. The activities of child pornography traffickers and users threaten others in society.

V. Opponents of pornography are sexually repressed and reactionary.

    A. Dislike of child pornography has nothing to do with sexual interest in adult relationships.

    B. The pornography business subverts healthy loving relationships into illegal products that degrade the victims.

Source: "Myths About Child Pornography and Obscenity Laws," Morality in Media, Inc. (MIM), http://www.moralityinmedia.org/index.htm?obscenityEnforcement/cliches2.htm, accessed on August 19, 2005.

Figure 8.6 Myth Response Pattern of Organization

STEP 8: WRITING A PREVIEW STATEMENT

Preview strategies
Letting an audience know what you are about to discuss

Preview or orientation statements (also called statements of structural progression) tell the audience where you are going in the speech. In five- to six-minute speeches, such statements are often no more than one sentence in length. These orienting statements point to the organizational pattern of the speech, as in the following examples:

- In explaining the benefits of tae kwon do, I will introduce you to the philosophy underlying tae kwon do, its history and origins, and major styles associated with this martial art.

Countering the Perception That Child Pornography Abounds on the Worldwide Web

I. Most people believe that child pornography abounds on the worldwide web.

II. Because we see so many links to adult pornography sites, this belief seems highly plausible.

III. The problem with holding this belief is that we look in the wrong places to find the real offenders.

    A. The real offenders use e-mail more than the web to share images.

    B. Criminal organizations are using other means to distribute their products.

    C. Parents are monitoring the wrong activities, thus putting their children at risk.

IV. In truth, child porn is almost nonexistent on the worldwide web.

    A. Most photos of children on the web are not sexually explicit; the children pictured are riding bikes, swimming, or engaging in some other innocent activity.

    B. Family albums, placed innocently on the web, contain many of the nude photos of children that exist on the web.

    C. Some photos, intended to entrap child pornography offenders, come from police; but those are not sexually explicit.

    D. Other photos come from girls and young women with exhibitionist tendencies, who place photos of themselves on the web; in this situation, the victim is also the offender.

Source: Points I, II, and IV are based on the research of Judith Levine, *Harmful to Minors: The Perils of Protecting Children from Sex* (Minneapolis: University of Minnesota Press, 2002).

Figure 8.7 Transformative Pattern of Organization

- In the next ten minutes, I will acquaint you with the cultural origins of sushi, the required ingredients, and the steps to follow in preparing this delicious meal.
- In this speech, I will describe four steps in building a home radio receiver: deciding upon the frequency of the signal, choosing a circuit, selecting and assembling the components, and testing the reception.
- In this presentation, I will share some recent statistics on the retreat of the Sahara Desert, talk about the reasons for the rejuvenation of these desert lands, and consider the implications of these environmental shifts for the people of Africa.

I.
   A.
   B.
      1.
      2.
      3.
         a.
         b.
         c.
      4.
   C.
II.

Figure 8.8 Levels of Organization

STEP 9: WRITING YOUR INTRODUCTION

The next step in the preparation process involves writing your introduction. Since most people feel creative at the beginning of the speechwriting process, it is a good time to undertake that task. If you know what you hope to accomplish in the speech, you can also write your conclusion before you add flesh to your outline. In fact, some people write their conclusions before they write their introductions. For organizational purposes, however, I will discuss the writing of conclusions later in this chapter.

A good introduction is extremely important. Audience members form first impressions of speakers when they arrive at the podium and confirm these impressions as they listen to the first words of the speaker. Either they like you or they dislike you. They think that you are competent or incompetent. They conclude that you have spent time on the speech or thrown it together. These first impressions can help or hinder you in achieving your speech purposes.

In addition to providing statements of purpose, thesis, and structural progression, the introduction to an informative speech should accomplish three goals: (1) capture the attention of your audience, (2) give the audience a reason to listen to your speech by explaining the benefits that will come from listening to the speech, and (3) establish your credibility to speak on the topic. Why should they listen to you? What qualifies you to speak on the topic? (Sometimes you will not need to include an explicit purpose statement in your introduction.)

Attention-Getting Strategies for Informative Speaking

The first step is to grab the notice of your audience. Attention-getting strategies used in informative speaking include immediacy strategies; references to the novel; suspense and shock techniques; description; quotations and expressions; activity, drama, and conflict; and humor. Some speakers use gimmicks to gain attention, but these strategies carry heavy risks. The following discussion will review these attention-getting techniques, which the speaker can use in the introduction, body, and conclusion of the informative speech.

Immediacy Strategies. As discussed in Chapter Four, immediacy techniques help to close the psychological distance between speaker and audience. The speaker may make a *reference to someone in the audience*, extend a *personal greeting or compliment*, mention *the occasion or surroundings*, self-disclose by *sharing personal information*, ask a *question*, use *conversational language*, or *translate a general statistic* into one that applies to this specific audience. References to the *vital* interests of the audience and the *familiar* also add a sense of immediacy to the occasion. Whereas this chapter focuses on how speakers use language to bridge the divide between themselves and their audiences, Chapter Six discussed immediacy techniques from the perspective of delivery.

When rock musician and song writer David Bowie delivered the commencement address at the Berklee College of Music on May 8, 1999, he began his speech by making *reference to a recent event* and *complimenting his audience*: "Thank you. Thanks very much. Rockers . . . Jazzers . . . Samplers . . . That was a fantastic concert last night. I think both Wayne and myself were just so moved to hear our compositions coming back at us through your ears and abilities. It was dynamite. You don't know how much we appreciate it."[9]

The second example represents an effort to *recognize the person* who has introduced the speaker and *acknowledge the demographics of the audience*:

> Thank you for the kind introduction, William. I truly enjoyed reading your book *Boom or Bust*. Whenever William and I get together, we seem to find ourselves comparing notes on our lives as baby boomers. You know, we are the ones born between 1947 and 1966. We often wonder when our children will leave home—for good. And wonder if we could be fired—again. Not a concern. After our third layoff, we know that we can survive inflation, deflation, recession, and depression. We've lived through all of them. And we are still here to talk with you about our hopes for America's future—your future. After all, most of you are under 30. So you don't need happy pills to make you optimistic. The future is yours.[10]

The third example illustrates the immediacy strategy of *self-disclosure* or sharing of personal information. On December 10, 2004, in Oslo, Norway, Wangari Maathai concluded her Nobel Peace Prize lecture with the following personal story:

> As I conclude I reflect on my childhood experience when I would visit a stream next to our home to fetch water for my mother. I would drink water straight from the stream. Playing among the arrowroot leaves I tried in vain to pick up the strands of frogs' eggs, believing they were beads. But every time I put my little fingers under them they would break. Later, I saw thousands of tadpoles: black, energetic and wriggling through the clear water against the background of the brown earth. This is the world I inherited from my parents. Today, over 50 years later, the stream has

dried up, women walk long distances for water, which is not always clean, and children will never know what they have lost. The challenge is to restore the home of the tadpoles and give back to our children a world of beauty and wonder.[11]

Questions can also be used to involve the audience. Some require the audience to respond by raising their hands or offering verbal feedback. Others only require the listeners to ponder the question. Here the speaker employs rhetorical questions that do not demand a visible or vocal response:

> Do you become bored easily? Find yourself moving from task to task without completing anything? Are you chronically late and disorganized? Forgetful and unable to stay focused on tasks? Do you become distracted easily? Do you procrastinate? If you have answered "yes" to these questions, you may have an undiagnosed attention deficit disorder (ADD).

As noted in earlier chapters, speakers tend to overrely on questions in introducing their speeches. Often they ask questions when they have not spent adequate time to arrive at a more creative introduction. They throw in a few questions so that their instructors can give credit for including an attention-getting strategy. But attention-getting strategies should be judged not only by their inclusion in a speech, but also on their interest value, the way that the speaker integrates the question(s) into the fabric of the speech, and their combination with other strategies. As noted in Chapter Four, a Rutgers University study found that one out of three amateurs began their essays with rhetorical questions, whereas no professionals used this writing strategy.[12]

References to the *vital*—facts and statistics that relate to our health and well-being—also bring a sense of immediacy to a speech. In the following example, the speaker informs his audience on the problem of poverty in the United States:

> Poverty is the most pressing domestic problem of the twenty-first century. It has been said that, if poverty were a state, it would be the second largest in our country, with "more people than the combined populations of Connecticut, Kentucky, Maryland, Michigan, New Jersey, and Nevada!"[13] This statistic affects all of us in terms of increased health care costs, higher crime rates, and longer commuting times for those who flee the cities.

Conversational language can also convey the feeling that the speaker is relating to the audience on a personal level. The following excerpt from a speech by Ray Bradbury illustrates this point:

> I went to New York with all of my short stories. I went on the Greyhound bus—four days and four nights to New York City. No air conditioning. No toilets. We've had many improvements in the last few years. But traveling to New York on the Greyhound bus and then arriving at the YWCA, where I stayed for $5 a week. With a stack of manuscripts in my lap, hoping to conquer the editorial field, I met with all these editors. They rejected me. On my last night in New York—defeated by my encounters—I had dinner with the editor of Doubleday, who said to me, "What about all those Martian stories you've been writing? If you tied them together and made a tapestry of them, wouldn't they make a book called *The Martian Chronicles*?"[14]

Another immediacy strategy involves references to the *familiar*, which can draw the listener into the speech:

> We've all heard about DNA—how scientists use DNA to learn more about diseases, how criminologists use DNA to free innocent prisoners from jails, and how families

use DNA to confirm parentage. But few of us would suspect that our knowledge of DNA may soon be used to fight spammers. Using knowledge acquired in DNA research, scientists at TJ Watson Research Center have developed a new and highly effective anti-spam filter. Using pattern recognition, this filter enables computers to identify patterns or character sequences in spam mail that are not present in legitimate mail. The new tool is 96.5 percent effective.

References to the Novel. Although the familiar can capture audience attention, the *novel* holds the attention. One student gave a speech, for example, about ways to save money in planning and booking cruises. She was able to offer many innovative suggestions based on her own extensive travel experience—about the best rooms for the money, ways to work your way around the world on cruises, and how to save money in booking cruises. She said, for example, that builders rarely meet their deadlines in building new cruise ships. So if you request a ship under construction, you have a relatively good chance of getting a free trip. When the ships are not ready to sail on time, companies offer free voyages or significant reductions to passengers who have been inconvenienced by having to delay their travel plans.

> **References to the Novel**
> Using an example that is unexpected, to hold attention

Use of Suspense and Shock Techniques. The next example illustrates the use of suspense to gain and hold audience attention:

> **Suspense/shock techniques**
> Using examples that are deliberately mysterious or even disturbing, to gain and hold the interest of the audience

> Audrey. Hugo. Eloise. Floyd. Hazel. Carla. Andrew. Do any of these names sound familiar? They should, because they are the name of mass murderers. Their nationalities are English, French, and Spanish. Cumulatively, they have killed hundreds of people. It may surprise you to learn that the females in this list have killed as many innocent people as the males. I met Audrey in 1957, when I was a child; and I will never forget her. Who are these dangerous offenders? They are seven of the most notorious hurricanes to originate in the Atlantic Ocean—infamous for the damage that they have wreaked and the numbers of lives they have claimed. When an outstanding athlete retires from sports, his team often withdraws his jersey or number, out of respect for the person. In the world of hurricanes, the names of the worst storms are retired from the lottery of names available to meteorological organizations. Audrey, Hugo, Inez, Floyd, Hazel, Carla, and Andrew wreaked so much damage that the most affected countries requested the withdrawal of their names, along with forty-one others. The World Meteorological Organization can no longer use these forty-eight names. The latest offender, Katrina, will also appear on this list of banned names.

This passage could be used to introduce an informative speech on hurricanes.

Activity, Drama, and Conflict. Activity, drama, and conflict also pull audiences into speeches; and 60 percent of professional writers begin their work with stories.[15] In an acclaimed address to the graduates of Wellesley College, former First Lady Barbara Bush used this technique:

> Wellesley, you see, is not just a place, but an idea, an experiment in excellence in which diversity is not just tolerated, but is embraced. The essence of this spirit was captured in a moving speech about tolerance, given last year by the student body president of one of your sister colleges. She related the story by Robert Fulghum about a young pastor who, finding himself in charge of some very energetic children, hits upon a game called "Giants, Wizards and Dwarfs." "You have to decide now," the pastor instructed the children, "which you are: a giant, a wizard or a

dwarf?" At that, a small girl tugging at his pants leg asked, "But where do the mermaids stand?" The pastor told her there are no mermaids. "Oh, yes there are," she said. "I am a mermaid." Now this little girl knew what she was, and she was not about to give up on either her identity or the game. She intended to take her place, wherever mermaids fit into the scheme of things. Where do mermaids stand—all those who are different—those who do not fit the boxes and the pigeonholes? "Answer that question," wrote Fulghum, "and you can build a school, a nation, or a whole world."[16]

This example also demonstrates an effective application of audience adaptation principles because historically Wellesley was an all-girls preparatory school. In a school with feminist roots, the story of the assertive little girl seems particularly appropriate.

Description. Effective speakers rely heavily on descriptive language to capture and hold listener attention.[17] The following description by Andrea Ball exemplifies the use of strong sensory-drenched language, which appeals to sight, touch, hearing, and smell.

> Each country I've visited has left a lasting, sensual impression on me. In Hong Kong, it was standing on a hill overlooking a lush valley below and listening to the sounds of the wind rustling the bamboo scaffolding of a nearby building. In Bermuda, it was the feeling of being completely surrounded by turquoise water while sitting on the edge of the battlements of an old British fort. And in England, it was Stonehenge, my favorite place. When we pulled into the parking lot of the

tourist centre, a storm was brewing, reminiscent of Macbeth. And by the time we got to the henge itself, the storm felt like a full-fledged hurricane. But for me, the weather only served to make the experience that much more memorable. I slowly walked around the henge, obeying the role boundary and examining the stones, in awe of their size and power. By the time I was halfway around, everyone else in our group had gone inside; but I remained—in the thrall of nature, with the wind buffeting me and the rain washing over me. The dampness filled my nostrils. I was alone, surrounded only by nature, history, and magic. And then, out of the sheets of rain, figures appeared across the stone circle from me. In their dark clothes, huddled together in groups, they looked like druids performing some ancient ritual. I stood breathless as these figures, which appeared to have jumped out of history and fantasy, walked towards me.[18]

The speaker also builds a feeling of suspense as she proceeds with the description.

Quotations
Citing words of others

Quotations and Expressions. Motivational speakers often rely heavily on *quotations or sayings* such as the following to capture the attention of audiences and inspire listeners: "Life should not be a journey to the grave with the intention of arriving safely in a pretty and well preserved body, but rather to skid in broadside, thoroughly used up, totally worn out and loudly proclaiming, 'Wow . . . What a Ride!'"[19] Before the proliferation of content on the Internet, speakers drew their quotations from sources such Barlett's *Familiar Quotations* and *Chicken Soup for the Soul*. In the current environment, almost every quotation appears on the Internet. Identifying the sources is more problematic, as they are often cited as anonymous or attributed to multiple sources.

Cliché
An overused expression

Speakers should avoid worn clichés and tired overused expressions such as "murdered in cold blood," "clear as a bell," "take the bull by the horns," "sadder but wiser," and "better late than never." (See the Keep in Mind box.) To demonstrate the lack of content in clichés, professors sometimes give an assignment that involves using as many clichés as possible.

Keep in Mind

Clichés—Avoid Them!

- If you can't beat them, join them.
- Live and learn.
- No pain, no gain.
- Cool as a cucumber.
- All is fair in love and war.
- It's what's on the inside that counts.
- Time will tell.
- There are more fish in the sea.
- Busy as a bee.
- Haste makes waste.
- Shoot from the hip.
- It happens to the best of us.
- You can't judge a book by its cover.
- Rome was not built in a day.
- No news is good news.
- He put himself on the line.
- Every cloud has a silver lining.

Humor. Speakers also use humor to capture attention, make the material more interesting, and improve learning.[20] The most appealing humor is often gentle—the phrase that provokes an unplanned smile rather than the joke that precipitates forced laughter. Former President Ronald Reagan was well-known for witticisms such as the following: "We were told four years ago that seventeen million people went to bed hungry each night. That was probably true. They were all on a diet!"[21] In the speech referenced earlier, Ray Bradbury brought smiles to his audience when he said: "When I got married, all of my wife's friends said, 'Don't marry him. He's going nowhere.' But I said to her, 'I'm going to the moon, and I'm going to Mars. Do you want to come along?' And she said, 'Yes.' She said yes. She took a vow of poverty, and married me."[22] Humor that builds on the experiences of people is often better received than the stock joke. Chapter Twelve talks more about sources of humor in speeches.

Giving the Audience a Reason to Listen

Introductions to speeches should include a reason to listen to the speech. In other words, the knowledge gained from a speech should be translatable into tangible benefits for the audience. A speaker may promise that the audience will save money if they follow advice given in the speech. Alternatively, speakers may promise rewards such as a sense of satisfaction, a higher grade in school, an adventurous experience, or better relationships. For maximum impact, at least some of the benefits should be ones that listeners can realize in the short term—the immediate future. The speaker may say, for example: "If you listen to this speech, you will know how to get the best bargains on airfares when you take your next spring vacation." "If you pay close attention, you will make a better grade on your next examination." "Listening to this speech will translate into money in your next big job interview." Or you may say, "If you want a better behaved dog or cat, you might want to pay attention for the next five minutes." The benefit of listening could be more sleep, a better relationship, or fewer annoyed neighbors.

Building Your Credibility

Credibility
Believability

The third function of introductory comments is to establish personal credibility—to explain why you are competent or qualified to speak on the topic. Do you have a personal stake in the issue? Have you worked in the business about which you are speaking? Do you know someone who has experienced the situation that you are describing or derived the benefit that you attribute to the product? The concept of source credibility will be explored in much greater depth in other chapters. However, for the purposes of this assignment, you need to build credibility on three dimensions in particular: *competency*, *trust*, and *composure*. The following example illustrates how a speaker can establish his *competency* to speak on the topic by making reference to his previous experiences: "During my ten years in the U.S. Air Force, I had the opportunity to work with the Thunderbirds, a world-class precision-flying team. Today I want to tell you something about what those experiences taught me." In the next example, the speaker builds credibility on the *trust* dimension by talking about experiences shared in common with the audience:

Competency
Established ability or credential

Trust
A belief in the reliability of a person (or thing)

> I face the same challenges as you in trying to make my student bursaries and summer jobs pay for my education. Like you, I paid $300 more this semester than I paid last year in tuition fees. My rent increased by five percent. And after buying eight textbooks for five courses, I had to cancel my plans to go to Daytona on spring break. Some months I eat a lot of Kraft dinners, and I am very familiar with the merchandise at the retro stores. I don't shop at the malls until the sales hit 50 percent off. Yes, going to university can be a poverty-inspiring experience. But in this speech, I want to tell you about everything that you will gain from your sacrifices—the long-term financial and psychological rewards of a college or university education.

If you have no firsthand knowledge of the subject, your audience needs to know that you have acquired competency through secondhand knowledge. In the following example, the speaker uses this strategy to gain credibility:

> Since beginning research into this speech topic, I have spoken to a dozen students who have participated in our university's Co-op program. I have reviewed the statistics on job placements with our Co-op office. And I have spoken with several professors who have worked with the Co-op program. This research has given me some very good insights into how the program functions, its benefits, and its shortcomings. I would like to share highlights of that information with you in the next five minutes. After hearing this speech, you should be more qualified to make an informed decision on whether to apply to our university's Co-op program.

Note that the speaker also points, in the concluding sentence, to the benefits of listening to the speech.

Composure
A sense of being in control, which increases your credibility in the eyes of audiences

The final example relates to *composure*. In Chapter Six, we considered composure at length, a credibility factor that some regard as a subset of *competency*. *Composure* refers to the fluency of a speaker and the ability to appear calm and in control.[23] Speakers build credibility on this dimension predominantly through a capable and polished delivery. However, a few points can be mentioned in regard to the message. Source credibility studies tell us, for example, that we may prefer a speaker who makes an occasional mistake. So if you experience some moment that threatens your composure, a creative recovery can build your credibility on the composure dimension.

A speaker should never apologize. An apology seriously undermines perception of a speaker's competency and draws attention to possible shortcomings—weaknesses that the audience might not otherwise notice. Speakers should never make statements such as "I am not an expert on the topic" or "I am not an accomplished public speaker" or "I hope you will bear with me. Speaking is not my forté." They should avoid statements that suggest lack of preparation or time invested in the speech such as, "I haven't had much opportunity to do reading on this topic." In the same way, a speaker should never make reference to being nervous or intimidated by the occasion. While speakers often feel as if every nervous gesture is highlighted in bold, the audience may be so interested in the ideas that they pay little attention to nervous gestures or shaky knees.

STEP 10: DEVELOPING YOUR SPEECH

In developing your speech, refer back to your research on audience awareness and attitudes. How much does the audience know about the topic? If you assume too little knowledge, you risk boring audience members with information that they already know. But if you judge their level of knowledge to be too high, you may lose them. Will you need to define some terms? Will the audience understand specialized language or jargon specific to this topic area?

Supporting materials clarify, explain, and add flesh to the information in your skeleton outline. They offer proof of the validity of your claims. Authors categorize supporting materials in many different ways. Some use such broad categories as *examples*, *statistics*, and *testimony*. Others become more specific, including *analogies*, *quotations*, *stories*, *explanations*, and various kinds of *instances* (e.g., personal or business). As in so many other areas of communication, the terminology varies from author to author; however, the ideas are constant. For organizational purposes, the following discussion uses these categories: *historical and other facts*; *comparison and contrast*; *analogies*; *proverbs* and *quotations*; *narratives*; *legends*, *fables* and *parables*; *poems*, *ditties*, and *songs*; *statistics*; *examples*; *description*; *explanation and amplification*; and *expert testimony*.

Historical and Other Facts

Facts add interest to a speech. Speakers can provide details about the culture that created the recipe for an ethnic dish; traditions associated with Hanukkah, Ramadan, or the Chinese Lunar New Year; or the history of Halloween or Valentine's Day. If you talk about karate, you should include details about the Japanese culture that produced karate—who, why, and when. If you talk about mountain climbing, you can introduce the topic by mentioning some of the most famous American climbers. You can tell one or more stories about crises confronted or journeys that ended unexpectedly. If you give a demonstration speech on how to prepare several Greek appetizers, you can talk about the Greek culture, their love of good food and good times, and the origins of the individual dishes. Detailing the steps to be followed in preparing the appetizers is not sufficient. When appropriately referenced, the myths of a culture can be interesting additions to speeches. The following example, which talks about the history of the croissant, illustrates this point:

> Food historians debate the origins of this buttery, crescent-shaped puff pastry, but several date it back to the late 1600s when Vienna came under attack by the Turks. According to the legend, the Turks tunnelled under the walled city in the dead of night for a surprise attack. Bakers, who worked in underground kitchens, heard noises and sounded the alarm, thereby thwarting the enemy forces. To commemorate the victory, the bakers made a small roll in the shape of a crescent moon, a symbol on the Turkish flag, to signify that the Austrians had eaten the Turks for lunch. One hundred years later, Marie Antoinette (the Austrian princess who married French king Louis XVI) introduced the croissant to the French aristocracy. However, some food historians dismiss these tales as romantic legends and assert that the croissant is a French creation (the word itself is derived from the French for "crescent"). They contend that the croissant didn't appear until 1850 and that the first recipe wasn't published until 1891. Still others argue that the recipe didn't produce a true croissant, and that such a pastry did not emerge until 1905.[24]

In speeches of demonstration, speakers should avoid presenting a series of "what to do next" steps. An interesting speech will do much more.

Comparison and Contrast

Comparisons
Weighing the similarity of various things

Comparisons look at the similarities in different ideas or objects. One journalist compared the odds of winning a national lottery to a number of other possible scenarios. He said that you are fourteen times more likely to die from a flesh-eating disease and ten times more likely to die from a poisonous snake bite. In an extended comparison, he said: "Say you're standing on a football field. You're blindfolded and holding a pin. A friend has released an ant on the field. Your chance of piercing that ant with your pin is about the same as winning a Lotto 6/49 jackpot. One in 14 million."[25]

Contrasts
Weighing the differences of various things

Contrasts, on the other hand, entail looking at differences, as in the following example:

> A few months ago, on a visit to the Women's Health Care Centre . . . , a top doctor offered me a fascinating, but disturbing, explanation of why more women are dying of heart disease (as opposed to cancer) than men. When a man gets a chest pain, she explained, he assumes he's having a heart attack due to stress or over work, immediately rushes off to a hospital, and is told to relax, etc. But when a woman gets a chest pain, she'll often dismiss it as a bit of indigestion, a bit of neurosis, nothing serious. She'll take a pill and go on because she can't afford to relax, so her actual condition is not discovered until much later and, by then, it's more acute and often fatal.[26]

Analogies
Comparing partially similar ideas, objects, or situations by transferring the qualities of one to other

Analogies

An analogy is a comparison of two basically dissimilar concepts or objects that share some common characteristics. The comparison of the two concepts or objects allows us to use the familiar concept to learn more about the less familiar concept.

In the following example, the train analogy helps to explain why you should not pursue someone who "just isn't into you":

> If a train comes to your stop and doesn't stop, IT'S NOT YOUR TRAIN. Would you try to run after it and make it stop? NO. If someone passes you by and doesn't stop, then they don't want to be with you in the way you deserve. Let them go. They aren't your train. When the right person comes along, they will stop for you.[27]

Proverbs and Quotations

When used to support points in speeches, proverbs and quotations should be relevant to the topic of the speech. A proverb such as the following, for example, can apply to many different topics: "A society grows great when old men plant trees whose shade they know they shall never sit in." An Internet search for references to this Greek quotation reveals applications in the following topic categories: wilderness living, nature, society, service, liberty and patriotism, importance of children, woodworking, landscaping, and change management, among others. Speakers can also find many different applications for a single quotation.

When citing the words of someone else, you should always mention the person's title, position, or other identifying information: "Comedian Tom Green"; "Bo Dice, runner-up in the 2005 *American Idol* competition"; or "radio personality Glenn Beck." If the reference is clear, the descriptor can be short: "Walter Gretsky, the father of hockey legend Wayne Gretsky, once commented, 'You miss 100 percent of the shots you don't take.'" If the individual is little known or the contribution requires explanation, however, more details about the person may be appropriate or necessary.

Proverb
A short saying containing a general truth

Narratives

Effective speakers tend to be good storytellers, and some of the most interesting stories are true ones. The following story, told by social anthropologist Bronislaw Malinowski, illustrates this point:

> I once talked to an old cannibal who, hearing of the Great War raging in Europe, was most curious to know how we Europeans managed to eat such huge quantities of human flesh. When I told him the Europeans did not eat their slain foes, he looked at me with shocked horror and asked what sort of barbarians we were, to kill without any real object.[28]

This story could serve as an introduction to speeches about Western habits of consumption, the environment, the warlike tendencies of "civilized" societies, or a number of other topics. In Gold River, British Columbia, federal fisheries officials eventually abandoned a two-year effort to capture and relocate a killer whale named Luna. A speaker could use this example in a speech on beliefs about the afterlife, Native culture, or whales, among other topics.

Narratives
Stories

> A four-year-old killer whale named Luna has won the right to remain, at least for the time being, off the coast of northern Vancouver Island. The 1,400-kilogram whale left her pod almost two years ago to journey 400 kilometres to the coastal waters off Gold River, British Columbia, an area inhabited by a small community of

Native Canadians. Fisheries officials have been worried about the increasingly friendly behaviour of Luna, who bumps against boats and stays close to land. But the local Native residents have intervened to thwart efforts to capture and relocate Luna. Whenever the fishery officials set a capture pen, the Natives (led by their chief) lure Luna away from captivity. The Mowachaht-Muchalaht tribe believes that the spirit of their late chief, Ambrose Maquinna, inhabits the body of Luna. A few days before his death, Maquinna promised that he would return, in the form of a whale, after he died. Within days of his death, Luna appeared in the Gold River area.[29]

Speech theory suggests the effectiveness of self-disclosing and sharing stories about our own experiences. A number of studies have found, for example, that students react positively to teachers who use humor, self-disclosure, and narrative (stories) to clarify course content.[30] Nevertheless, you should never reveal details in personal stories that you will regret having divulged after the speech has ended. Also you should limit stories and anecdotes to a paragraph in length (maximum of a half page of double-spaced, 12-point Times Roman font).

Parables, Fables, and Legends

Parable
Imagined story used to provide a moral lesson

Fable
A story, often supernatural and involving animals, which provides a moral lesson

Legend
A traditional story, unproven—a myth

Many parables, fables, and legends circulate on the Internet. *Parables* are moral, philosophical, or religious stories, such as the parable of the prodigal son, which appears in the Bible. *Fables* are short moral stories, usually populated by animal characters. Unlike fables, parables do not typically have animal characters. *Legends*, on the other hand, are stories or historical accounts presumed to be true, but unverifiable.

Some parables and fables provide interesting ways to begin speeches, although you must be careful not to rely on material that has circulated too widely. If you have received a story more than once on the Internet, you should probably avoid using it in a speech. The following *parable* (paraphrased from an unknown source) has doubtless been used in many motivational speeches and religious sermons since its first appearance on the Internet:

> An elderly carpenter told his employer of his plans to retire. Sorry to learn that he was losing such a reliable worker, the contractor asked the carpenter, as a personal favor, to build one last house. The carpenter agreed, but he was tired and unmotivated to do his usual good work. So he economized on materials and labor; he took the easiest and cheapest path to finishing the house. At the end of the project, the employer came as usual to inspect the carpenter's work. But this time, before leaving, he handed a key to the carpenter, "This key, this house is yours, dear friend. It is my gift to you." In deep regret and embarrassment, the carpenter hung his head, unable to look at his long-time employer. Like so many of us, the carpenter realized—too late—the consequences of his choices.

Following the telling of the parable, the speaker draws a moral from the story. She might relate the building of the house to how we construct our relationships or live our lives—how we sometimes fail to do our best, not realizing that we are ultimately the real losers.

An example of a *fable* comes from *Aesop's Fables*, from the sixth century B.C.E. The fable goes like this: A hungry fox comes into a vineyard where he sees delicious clusters of ripe grapes. His mouth waters when he looks at them. But they are growing so high on a trellis that, no matter how hard he tries, he cannot reach a single grape. At last, in frustration, he gives up. "Let someone else have them," he mutters, "I don't want them at all. Anyone can see they are sour." A speaker could use this fable to illustrate the tendency of people to rationalize their failures. Alternatively, he could use the fable to launch the idea that we should not limit ourselves to one approach—that jumping higher only results in failure and disillusionment. Instead of jumping higher or trying harder, we should look for more creative ways to reach our goals. This last interpretation could be used in many different contexts, since the idea relates to creative approaches to problem solving.

If we were talking about the worst fires in history, we could begin our speech with a *legend* about the origins of the Great Chicago Fire of 1871. Although the truth of the story is suspect, people around the world recount the tale, which goes like this:

> According to popular legend, a cow is responsible for the Great Chicago Fire. The cow's mistress, Catherine O'Leary, operated a neighborhood milk business out of her barn. One evening, she accidentally left a kerosene lantern in the barn. When one of her cows kicked over the lantern, the hay on the floor caught fire. The results are history. On October 8, 1871, Chicago became a city in flames.

Poems, Songs, and Limericks

Speakers often use short stanzas from poems or popular songs to support points made in speeches. Sometimes speakers use limericks—humorous and nonsensical verses—such as the following to introduce an idea:

> There was a young lady of Niger
> Who smiled as she rode on a tiger.
> They returned from the ride
> With the lady inside
> And the smile on the face of the tiger.
>
> —Anonymous

To cite one possible application, this limerick could appear in a speech on the importance of recognizing dangers and taking appropriate precautions against risks. Speakers should avoid long recitations or content that is not tightly tied to the subject of the speech.

Statistics

The following discussion examines the function of statistics and rules to observe in citing statistics. In Chapter Seven, we looked at ways to present statistics in visual formats. In terms of functions, statistics allow the speaker to generalize to larger numbers of cases—to express the magnitude of a problem or situation: "The Center for Children of Incarcerated Parents estimates that at least 10 million American children have parents who have been incarcerated. Three out of four female prisoners and two out of three male prisoners are parents. On any given day, over two million minor children have parents in jail."

Statistics
The use of numerical data to support an argument

Second, statistics facilitate comparisons and contrasts. The figure of 600,000 Americans killed or wounded in the Civil War means more, for example, if you compare the figure to the combined casualties of World War I, World War II, and Vietnam. (The two figures are roughly comparable.) A second example follows:

> According to some sources, Michael Eisner, the CEO of Disney, pays himself $133 million a year. That works out to about $63,000 per hour. By way of contrast, the Bangladesh workers who sew Disney clothing earn 12 cents an hour. That means it would take those workers nearly 210 years to earn what Mr. Eisner earns in an hour.[31]

In citing statistics, you should observe certain rules. *First, gear your discussion of statistics to the level of the audience.* Not everyone is an expert in statistical terminology. The following explanation, for example, would be confusing and incomprehensible to anyone but specialists such as engineers, mathematicians, and statisticians: "The chi-square goodness-of-fit test can be applied to discrete distributions such as the binomial and the Poisson."[32]

Second, translate the statistics into terms that are meaningful to your audience. On one occasion, former President Ronald Reagan translated the incomprehensible figure of $146 billion into recognizable outcomes: "We spend $146 billion. With that money, we bought a 2-million-dollar yacht for Haile Selassie. We bought dress suits for Greek undertakers, extra wives for Kenya government officials. We bought a thousand TV sets for a place where they have no electricity!"[33]

You can practice converting statistics into concrete examples by putting the figure into the Internet to see what pops up. I used this technique to convert a statistic on deaths from HIV into terms with which a young audience could identify:

> Thirty-three million is an important number. Do you have any idea what it represents? Since it's hard to imagine such a large number of anything, let me give you some examples. Thirty-three million is half the population of Iran. It is the number of foreign-born citizens living in the U.S. It is also the number of people who subscribed to AOL in 2001. It is the number of people who watched the funeral of Princess Diana, the last episode of *Joe Millionaire,* and the average number of people who watched the winter 2004 season of *American Idol.* Thirty-three million is 70 percent of the forty-seven million Americans who would like to quit smoking and the number of people who live under the poverty line in the United States. And last but not least, thirty-three million is the number of people in the world with HIV. In short, there are thirty-three million reasons to find an answer to the Black Plague of this century.

Third, discuss the statistic in terms that have immediacy for the audience—the potential to make a difference to their lives. For many years, speakers at orientation exercises for freshman students made the following kind of statement to their young audiences: "Look at the person on your right. Now look at the person on your left. One of you won't be here next semester. The failure rate for first year college students is one out of three." Not only did the speakers translate the statistic into terms that had relevance for their audience, but they also articulated the statistic in terms that were immediate.

Fourth, round off numbers to make them easier to deliver and for the audience to comprehend and remember. Rather than saying 3,422 people, say "3,400 people." Rather than saying 15,203 pounds of steel, say "more than 15,000 pounds of steel."

Fifth, always include the source of the statistic; and if you think that the audience will be unfamiliar with the source, give the qualification. Say, for example, "According to the U.S. Department of Justice, partners and other intimate acquaintances commit an average of more than 600,000 rapes, robberies, and assaults each year."

Sixth, to add credibility to your speech, include the size of the population from which a statistic is taken. A 20 percent increase in a population of 5,000 means much more than a 20 percent increase in a population of 10. Say, for example: "The Great Plague of London killed almost 69,000 people out of a population of 460,000. Out of a population of 1.8 billion people, the influenza epidemic of 1918 incapacitated 1 billion people and killed 20 million."

Seventh, ensure that the statistics are representative of the larger picture. After September 11, 2001, some studies placed firemen ahead of doctors and policemen in terms of respected professions. If you looked only at this period in time, you might say, "Firefighting is the most respected occupation." But that increase may have been an unusual spike in credibility, not representative of the months leading to—or following—9/11.

Finally, use statistics sparingly and (when feasible) present them in graphical form. Reciting a long list of statistics bores an audience.

Examples

Examples can be brief or extended, real or hypothetical, and personal or reflective of the experience of others. The following excerpt from a commencement address by musician Billy Joel illustrates the use of a number of one-line examples, as well as an extended personal example:

> And still we hear the same question: So when are you going to get a real job? How many times have you been asked this question or some incarnation thereof? Beethoven heard it. John Lennon heard it. Milli Vanilli heard it. Bob Marley heard it. Janis Joplin heard it. Tschaikovsky heard it. Charlie Parker heard it, Verdi, Debussy. When I was 19, I made my first good week's pay as a club musician. It was enough money for me to quit my job at the factory and still pay the rent and buy some food. I freaked. I ran home and tore off my clothes and jumped around my tiny apartment shouting "I'm a musician, I'm a musician!" It was one of the greatest days of my life.[34]

Example
Using a specific instance to illustrate an idea or concept

A catalogue of brief examples generalizes a situation, much as statistics do. They make the listener realize that the example is typical—not unique. The extended example, on the other hand, enables the listener to identify emotionally and cognitively with the material in a way not possible with the brief example. The following detailed example illustrates this point:

> My work with a very large corporation brought me into intimate contact with the life of a sweatshop worker. In one of our shipments, I found two pairs of scissors. At least three inches of thread was wound around the handles of each pair. I could tell that the worker had collected the thread for some time, because the little scraps of thread were tied together. As well, because the thread was wound so thickly, I knew that the worker needed that material to protect her knuckles from the metal handle. This experience reminded me that, although these sweatshops exist across the ocean, they are still very close to home.[35]

Hypothetical
A fictitious scenario used to illustrate a point

These examples are drawn from real life. Other examples, developed by speakers, can be *hypothetical*. That is, the speaker creates a fictitious example to illustrate a point. To be valid, however, the hypothetical example should reflect a situation that has happened or could happen in the future:

> Imagine the following scenario. You have just arrived at university. Your bags are still unpacked. The doorbell rings, and you quickly move to the door to greet your new roommate. You met Kim over the Internet. You were very excited to learn that she was beginning classes at the same university. You seemed to have a lot in common. So you made immediate plans to share an apartment. But when you open the door, you find that *she* is a *he*, and *he* is a 6-foot-tall, middle-aged man! He smiles and extends his hand while you reach out to steady yourself. Another Internet adventure gone awry!

Like examples based on real experiences, hypothetical examples can be brief or extended. When examples are hypothetical, the speaker should give notice by using terms such as *imagine, picture this situation*, or a *future scenario could be*. Sometimes audiences become irate when they realize that a speaker has duped them. In 1992, students in a law class at the Australian National University made a formal complaint about their professor's use of hypothetical examples concerning sexual assault.[36]

Relevance
Importance

In all cases (hypothetical or real), you should ensure the *relevance* of the examples; and the connection should be explicit, not implied. In a speech on the rights of adopted children, for example, you could state:

> We talked about the case of Joan and Margaret, two young women who lived on opposite sides of the country—one in Vermont and one in California. They never imagined that they had a sister until, one day, they discovered that they shared something very important: DNA. Their example reflects the experience of many people who face life-threatening illnesses. They learn carefully guarded facts and secrets—information about their genetic and personal past. But Joan and Margaret should not have had to wait until they faced a serious health crisis to learn that they had surviving biological family. The laws have changed to allow greater access to personal family history, but children without knowledge of their past cannot take advantage of these new rights.

Be sure that the example is typical of the larger picture. Using atypical examples breaches ethical norms. To emphasize the representative nature of the example, you can tie the example to a statistic: "You may think that the case of Joan and Margaret is an unusual one, a rare occurrence. In fact, statistics reveal that at least one-third of adoptive parents try to hide their children's past—sometimes for the sake of the children, at other times because they fear being replaced at some point in the future." The most effective speeches rely on more than one form of supporting evidence.

As with statistics, you should ensure that the audience can understand and identify with your examples. The language should not be above the level of the group. If you are talking to an audience of nurses, your examples should be ones that are within their range of experiences. If you are talking to a young audience about investing for their future, you should use an example with which they can identify—saving for their college educations, for example, instead of saving for retirement.

Description

Just as speakers can use evocative language to capture audience attention, they can use vivid description to support points in their speeches. The following description employs concrete language replete with details and appeal to multiple senses:

> Christmas, for most, is a season of memories. We remember the sights, the smells, and the sounds of Christmas past. Strings of colored lights and holly on the mantle. The smell of pumpkin and mincemeat pies set out to cool. The crackling sound of logs about to burst with warmth. And the arrival of people we love, wrapped in wool parkas and scarves, cheeks and hands still cold to the touch as they close the door against the howling snow and wind. These memories, drawn from our childhood, serve as backdrops for later Christmases. But some years we cannot recapture the perfect Christmases of our youth. Something or someone is missing. Maybe we don't have the money to fly home for Christmas. Perhaps we have too many assignments to complete over the holidays to afford the time away from our books. Or by chance we have just broken up with a partner and have no special place to go. On those occasions, we may be prone to give in to feelings of loneliness and depression. And untreated, those feelings can lead to unhappy consequences. Statistics tell us that more people commit suicide over the Christmas holidays than at any other time of the year.

Explanation and Amplification

Explanation
A statement in a speech, intended to expand, clarify, and contribute to understanding

Explanations respond to questions such as "Why?" and "How?" An explanation that responds to the question *how* follows:

> How do you locate an apartment in a city as large as New York? The process can be scary and intimidating. If you follow my instructions, however, you will greatly increase your chances of finding a suitable place without succumbing to undue emotional stress. First, you need to place ads in community newspapers. Locals read these small neighborhood newspapers. Second, you need to post advertisements in desirable apartment buildings and in local supermarkets and variety stores. Third, you should contact churches and community groups who keep lists of homeowners willing to rent rooms or apartments. Fourth, you should ask your employer for help. Universities are another source of information, since turnover is high in the university community. Finally, many people use an apartment finder service.

If you wanted to add an example to this explanation, you could continue in the following way: "To better understand how the process works, let's look at the hypothetical case of Elizabeth." Demonstration speeches always respond to the question *how*. Demonstration speeches explain how to juggle, create floral arrangements, spend money wisely, windsurf, or use PowerPoint. They explain how hot air balloons function, how builders create energy efficient houses, and how culture jamming works.

The next explanatory passage responds to the question *why*. The explanation concerns the causes of forest fires:

> Forest fires occur for a variety of reasons. Studies suggest that between 67 percent and 99 percent of all fires are set by people. Campers leave fires unattended. Smokers throw cigarettes into the brush, or children play with matches in dry areas. Earth moving equipment, chain saws, and torches also ignite forest fires. Arsonists set more than 50 percent of all fires. In a smaller number of cases, nature is the perpetrator. Lightning strikes a tree or ignites a bush, or, more astoundingly, thunder causes a fire. On July 30, 2004, the China Net reported that thunderstorms ignited two forest fires. The percentages on causes of forest fires vary because some regions are more susceptible than others to wildfires.

Amplification
Details added to support a point in a speech

You need to be careful, however, that explanations are not too long and tedious or too general. Explanations are most effective when combined with concrete examples and details. The term *amplification* refers to the details that are added to any speech.

Expert or Personal Testimony

We can use testimony from experts or our own personal experience to add credibility to our arguments. If we speak on a medical topic, we cite doctors and other members of the medical community. When speaking on a legal topic, we look to the views of lawyers. Sometimes we cite people who have become experts by virtue of their interest in—or experience with—the subject matter. Erin Brockovich became an expert on water quality when she investigated practices of the Pacific Gas and Electric Company. Princess Diana became an expert on landmines and HIV research through her advocacy efforts. Martha Stewart became an involuntary expert on life in the American penal system in October 2004.

We can quote experts in our speeches, or we can paraphrase their views. We might introduce a quote by the activist mother of a U.S. Marine in the following way:

> On August 22, 2005, Gilda—mother of a U.S. Marine stationed in Iraq—raised her voice in protest against the war. Gilda spoke on behalf of an organization called "Military Families Speak Out," dedicated to bringing an end to the war in Iraq. In the following excerpt from that speech, reported in the online edition of *The Independent*, Gilda proclaimed: "We, [the] . . . mothers, will not let you 'move on with your life,' Mr Bush. We hold you accountable for their deaths and injuries. And we call now for an immediate withdrawal of our troops from Iraq. Now. Not next year. Not in 10 years!"[37]

Notice that several different things happen in this use of expert testimony. The speaker gives the name of the expert (a woman known simply by the name of "Gilda"), her position (mother of a U.S. Marine and member of an antiwar organization), the source of the quotation (speech reported in the online edition of *The Independent*), and the date of the comment (August 22, 2005). The speaker also explains why Gilda is qualified to speak on this particular topic (she has a son in Iraq).

> **Expert testimony**
> Using the words of those who have special skills or knowledge about the subject matter

STEP 11: LINKING THE PARTS OF THE SPEECH

As discussed in Chapter Four, transitions, signposts, and internal summaries help speakers to see the relationship among different parts of the speech. The next step in writing the speech is to ensure that you have used effective linking devices and created effective summaries to guide your listeners through the speech.

Transitions

Transitions help the listener to follow a speech from one point to the next. They connect thoughts, establishing the relationship between different parts of the speech. Sometimes they are single words or short phrases such as *in addition to, also, moreover, however,* or *next*. At other times, they are full sentences: "*The next topic* that I want to discuss is the feeding habits of exotic pets." Or "*Now that we have considered exotic pets,* I would like to talk about domestic pets." Sometimes transitions serve a secondary function of emphasizing points: *Among the exotic animals that we have discussed, the most dangerous pet is the lion.* This transition can lead the speaker from a general discussion of exotic pets to a consideration of the most dangerous. A second example of a transition that places emphasis is the following: *More important than anything else,* you need to understand that exotic pets require a great deal of work.

> **Transitions**
> Verbal cues that alert an audience to a shift in the speech

Signposts

Like bookmarks, *signposts* position the listener in the speech. Often they are just numbers, as in the following example: *The first exotic pet* that I would recommend is. . . . *The second exotic pet* that I would recommend to apartment dwellers is . . . Finally, as the speaker reaches the last part of the discussion, he says, "*My third and*

> **Signposts**
> Devices that re-connect the audience to the structure of the speech

final recommendation on exotic pets is. . . ." An alternative way of signposting is to ask questions as you enter each new area of discussion. For example, a speaker may introduce the first section of the speech by asking, "What happened in the past?" Once she reaches the next part of her speech, she asks, "What is the current situation?" She approaches the final section of the speech by asking, "What can we expect in the future?" Like transitions, signposts act as connectors. They alert the listener to major divisions or headings in the speech; therefore, speeches have fewer signposts than transitions. Signposts refer back to the divisions suggested in the statement of structural progression.

Internal Summaries

Internal summaries
Brief recaps within the body of the speech, keeping the audience focused

Internal summaries also help to ensure the continuity of a speech. Especially important to longer speeches, internal summaries remind the audience of the progress of the speech. The following example illustrates this point:

> *In short*, adopting an animal should imply a lifelong commitment. *As I have explained, however*, not everyone understands the importance of that commitment. People continue to abandon their cats near farmhouses, leave their dogs behind when they move to a new apartment, flush lizards down the toilet, and return birds and fish to pet stores. So how can we create a more enlightened and committed public?

Notice that the internal summary, in this instance, is relatively brief. In extremely short speeches, the summaries may be briefer or even omitted. (See Figure 8.9 for a review of the basic structural components in speeches.).

STEP 12: ADDING INTEREST WITH VISUAL AIDS

After writing your speech, you should consider the possibility of creating visual supports. Visual aids add interest and color to presentations. In preparation for a speech on the topic of drunk driving, for example, one student went to the local police station. She borrowed a pair of goggles used in instructional talks on drinking and driving. The goggles allow the users to experience the changes in vision that occur when they consume alcohol. At the conclusion of her speech, the student passed the goggles around the classroom, allowing the class to observe the differences for themselves. People were surprised to see that, after even one drink, a difference occurred in the quality of their vision. After two drinks, the difference was marked. The visual aid was highly effective in making the point that driving and drinking do not mix.

In another instance, a young man brought a mask to the front of the class for his speech of introduction. He said that, for many years, he had hidden behind a mask such as this one, not revealing his true self to people. The mask, he said, had helped him to hide a secret from the world. But it had also kept him from developing open and honest relationships with people. He said that he did not want to hide any more behind masks, and he revealed the secret that he had kept for many years—that he was gay. When the young man held the white mask to his face in the beginning of the speech, it conveyed a sense of the surreal, much like the mask worn by the stage character in *Phantom of the Opera*. The visual aid captured the

Attention: Our highway system can be compared to the veins and arteries in our bodies. Like our circulatory system, highways bring food, medicine, and other life-sustaining supplies to the places where they are needed. As biological beings, we are able to function because we receive the necessary nutrients through our circulatory system. Our cities are able to function because extensive highway arteries connect supply sources with end users. And if either of these two critical circulatory systems breaks down, the whole system crashes. *Thesis statement*: A well-functioning highway system is critical to the viability of our cities. *Preview of organization of speech*: Today I will talk to you about the pressing need to improve our toll roads, bridges, and city freeways and update you on some short-term and long-term plans to address the situation. *Signpost*: First, I will review some studies on the existing state of our toll roads, bridges, and freeways. [*The development of the section on studies pointing to needed improvements occurs at this point.*] *Signpost*: Second, I will consider short-term plans to improve our highway system. [*The development of the section on short-term construction plans occurs next.*] *Signpost*: Finally, I will consider some long-term ideas for improvement. [*The development of the section on a long-term vision occurs next.*] *Internal summary*: In summary, we can see that research demonstrates the importance of planning for the future at this time. *Example of transition statement*: Now that we have seen the statistical picture, let's consider the human dimension of the situation. [*A discussion of the human costs of the crisis occurs at this point in the speech.*] *Conclusion*: When the arteries to our bodies become clogged, we go to the doctor to request a bypass. While the cost may be high, we consider the investment to be worthwhile. When the arteries to our highways become clogged, we must go to the people who are capable of solving the problem, our highway planners and our politicians. Complaining about the problem to our friends and neighbors accomplishes nothing. The only solution is action, and in this case, major surgery is required. My purpose today was to inform you about what state and municipal authorities are doing to correct these problems. I hope that you have acquired a better understanding of where matters stand at this time, where we plan to be in another year or two, and where we hope to be in ten years' time.

Figure 8.9 Structural Elements

attention of the audience and helped the speaker to make the point that he was not a real person when he was wearing the mask. Like the revelers who participate in a carnival, he was hiding his true identity.

Demonstration speeches, in particular, rely heavily on visual supports such as models (live and constructed), charts, photos, and other materials. For a detailed discussion of visual supports and PowerPoint, see Chapter Seven. The preferred mode of delivery for informative speeches is extemporaneous, discussed in Chapters Four and Six. For tips on speaking from note cards, refer to the Keep in Mind box.

STEP 13: CONCLUDING THE SPEECH

Conclusions should provide closure and leave the audience with a memorable thought. In a five- to six-minute informative speech on why people turn to

Closure
In speech, a sense that the end is near

Keep in Mind

Tips for Delivering from Note Cards

· Use 3″ × 5″ or 5″ × 8″ cards—never regular paper!
· Write clearly and legibly, large enough to see easily.
· Write out quotations and statistics; note sources.
· Limit the number of points per card to five or six.

· Highlight or underline hard-to-remember points.
· Avoid using more than five cards.
· When you deliver, hold the cards with one hand.
· Maintain eye contact; do not read from cards.

cremation as an alternative to traditional burial, a concluding summary could bring closure:

> In this speech, we have looked at four reasons behind the shift to cremation as a preferred alternative to embalming: the shortage of available land in highly populated areas; environmental concerns related to cemeteries; the high costs of traditional burial; and finally, shifts in cultural beliefs regarding methods of body disposal.

A second way to provide closure is to refer back to an example or point made in the introduction—a hypothetical or real story, for example, or a shocking statistic. In the following case, the speaker began with a story about her grandmother:

> When I was seventeen, I went to see my grandmother for the last time. Although she would not pass on for another three years, I found visiting so frustrating. It didn't seem worth the effort for someone whom I had never known. You see, my grandmother suffered from early Alzheimer disease. I never knew the real person; and toward the end, she rarely put the right name with the right family member. In fact, she thought that she lived in a different decade. Though I can never get to know what my grandmother was like before Alzheimer stole her identity, I can help to support awareness of the disease.[38]

In closing, the speaker returned to the initial idea with this brief statement:

> I never got to know my real grandmother, only her disease. Our time with her was brief. There is a myth that only the old are affected by Alzheimer disease; but in my family, we know that is not the reality. The painful reality is that all of us are at risk. And we must all work to give researchers the money and tools that they need to find a cure.

In terms of support materials, conclusions typically employ quotations, proverbs, or a few lines from a poem. A number of the attention-getting strategies used in introductions are inappropriate in conclusions. For a five- to six-minute speech, a conclusion that is one-third of a page in length should be sufficient.

Conclusion

This chapter has expanded your knowledge base in areas such as researching your topic and supporting your ideas. The chapter has reviewed the following concepts: taking audience adaptation into account in choosing your topic, writing purpose and thesis statements, choosing an organizational pattern, developing your outline, writing preview statements, writing an introduction and conclusion, linking the parts of your speech, and adding interest with visual aids. See the Sample Speeches for examples of informative and demonstration speeches.

Sample Speech

Informative Speech

Have you ever blown all of your money in one giant shopping spree, only to return later and find that everything you bought had been slashed in price? Have you ever winced when one of your friends talked about a great deal on some item that you had just purchased at full price?

You may attribute your friends' spectacular deals to being in the right place at the right time. However, these people may be what *Seventeen* magazine calls "super shoppers"—people who have learned the strategic art of sleuthing deals. And today you are in luck, because I have just learned that my long-term obsession for shopping has a name! So hold on, you're in for a treat, because I am going to let you venture into my closet. I am going to explain how to get great service, save a buck (or much more), and know when the next sale is around the corner. In case you are one of those people who dread even the thought of buying something new, pay attention. These tips are for you.

First, you need to ensure that you will receive the kind of service that you deserve. Achieving this goal means that you must dress up a bit more than you might normally plan to do. Ever notice a pattern to the people who get the best service? That's right, the ones with the shirts that match the pants that match the belts that match the shoes. These people convey the message that they are serious shoppers, and salespeople respond to these nonverbal cues. So if you pull on sneakers and your beer-stained T-shirt from last night's bar hop, you may find that you are closely watched, but for the wrong reasons.

Second, you should select an outfit that represents your taste in clothes. Don't pull out the Christmas sweater that grandma gave to you unless it reflects the style that you like in clothes. And always ask questions. Most shoppers only have a vague idea of what they want; so when the salesperson asks, "Can I help you?" they are almost certain to say "no." At minimum, you should indicate that you would like to take a look first. Or if you know what you want, ask the clerk to help you. They know the store better than you, and they can save time and point to specials.

Assume that you have passed the first two tests for getting great service. You look like a shopper, and the sales clerk is ready to help you. Now you want to move on to your next objective—getting the best buys. To accomplish that goal, you should begin your search at the back of the store, not the front. Stores tend to place their newest merchandise near the front of the store and their sales racks at the back. The newest

(Continued)

Sample Speech

Informative Speech—cont'd

inventory is generally full price. As super shoppers, you do not want to pay full price for anything.

Another rule in looking for the best buys is to note the items that appear to be in excess. When you see twenty-five of the same shirt, you should wait to buy that item. It is probably destined for the sales rack in the coming days. Since the store may have additional items in the stock room, you might want to ask if they have a large stock that is not yet on display.

I have also managed to save money by getting discount cards at the stores where I shop the most often. I own a Suzy Shier prestige card that allows me to save 10 percent, even on sales items. By using my card, I bought this skirt (the one that I am wearing) for $5 last summer.

Finally, in terms of getting the best buys, you need to be a regular at the mall. I find that prices change every two weeks. You also have to pay attention to the times of year. Prices will be highest at the beginning of every sales season. Avoid shopping during these periods. You won't lose anything because the new spring line never follows the weather outside. Why not wait to buy those summer shirts until the weather actually allows you to wear them? By then they will be on sale.

How do you know when the next sale is around the corner? Watch for sales patterns and learn when to expect them. There are always sales at the end of seasons and before holidays. I rarely buy things that are brand name. I almost never buy things that are regular price, and lately I have been using the Internet to find better bargains.

With that said, I would like to bring your attention to a few examples of my best bargains. Look at what I am wearing right now. Would you believe that my entire outfit cost less than $20? If you have the patience to dig, you can find remarkable buys at your local chain store outlets. My shirt was $12 before I used my prestige card at Suzy Shier. I bought another $5 skirt on December 23rd, which I wore on New Year's Eve. [*Display skirt.*] I got the boots for $30 at half off. [*Point to boots.*] I snagged this sweater off the sales rack for $20 [*Display sweater.*] Paying regular price, I bought its clone in black last year for $45.

So if you feel as if your dollar isn't going very far, take my advice and follow these simple steps. After listening to my speech, you should have a better idea of how to get great service, save money, and shop at the right times of the year. Hopefully, you will all become super shoppers with full closets of inexpensive clothing like myself. See you at the malls!

Magdalen Dabrowski

References

Debbie Rigaud, "Are You a Super Shopper?" http.//www.seventeen.com/quizzes/qu.fa.ssh.question1.epl, accessed on February 7, 2004.

Sharon Shaver, "Money-Saving Tips to Bargain Hunt your Way to Top Style," http://www.focusonstyle.com/shoppingsecrets.htm, accessed on February 7, 2003.

Sample Speech

Demonstration Speech

After living at home for the summer, I was happy to be back in my own apartment, accountable only to myself. You know that feeling. But after a few weeks, I began to miss my mom's cooking. Don't get me wrong. I actually like to cook, but I missed the foods that were uniquely mom—mashed potatoes, homemade macaroni and cheese, and pie! So what did I do? I got out the recipe book that I hadn't touched since my mom gave it to me in my first year of university. And I looked for a recipe that would satisfy my taste buds.

My roommate's family owns a fruit farm, and she had brought a whole bunch of apples with her when she moved in. So it seemed that the best idea was to bake an apple pie. Now as students, you can understand that I had a dilemma at this point. Not only was I inexperienced at making pies, but also I didn't have a kitchen equipped with any special baking utensils. I was pretty much broke, unable to go out and buy the missing items. So I decided to improvise.

When it was all over, I decided that baking a pie is a skill that everyone should learn. In the next few minutes, I will explain why you should learn this skill, and I will go through the entire process with you, giving some tips on how to improvise when your kitchen is as ill-equipped as mine.

All right, so I bet you are all wondering why you should know how to bake an apple pie. There are three important reasons. First of all, how impressed people will be when you can whip up a pie on demand! If you live at home with your parents, think about how happy your mom will be when she comes home from work to smell a wonderful aroma coming from your oven. Plus, if you are short on money for books, baking your dad a pie will put him in a good mood, making it easier to ask him for a loan. If you have already moved away from home, you can impress your family with your growth and maturity when they come to visit. Or you can just describe the pie that you just made in your next telephone conversation.

But what about the reaction of your friends? Baking a pie can put people in your debt. Negotiate a trade with your roommates where, if you bake a pie, they will do the dishes for three or four days. In my opinion, this is a pretty fair trade-off, because there is nothing that I hate so much as washing dishes. Last, when you finish your first pie, you will feel a sense of accomplishment. A beautiful latticed pie is like a piece of art. You admire it and then you get to eat it!

Now let's talk about the supplies that you will need to make the recipe. For the crust, you will need flour, shortening, baking powder, and milk. If you are anything like me, you might not have measuring cups, which can pose a problem when adding the ingredients. If you are lacking in this department, you will just have to eyeball the ingredients and improvise. You can take a mug (like this one), for example, and fill it almost to the top. This mug is pretty close to one cup in size.

Now that you have a way of measuring your ingredients, you will need to locate a bowl.

(Continued)

Sample Speech

Demonstration Speech—cont'd

During my first semester in university, we did not have a single bowl that was larger than cereal size. But after looking everywhere, I found a large ice cream bucket, which became my mixing bowl. Use whatever you have in your kitchen.

To make your crust, you will need to combine your dry ingredients—5½ cups of flour and 1 teaspoon of baking powder—with one pound of shortening. If you don't have a pastry blender, use two knives to cut the shortening into tiny bits. Finally, add approximately one cup of milk, just enough to moisten the flour. Mix everything thoroughly together. No utensil works so well as clean hands.

Now that you have made the pastry, you will need to shape the pie. Spread some flour on a clean countertop. Place a ball of dough in the middle of the flour. You will need to find some way to roll the pastry into a pie crust. If you don't have a rolling pin, use a cylinder shaped glass or soft drink bottle. Roll the dough into a circular shape so that you can lay it in your pie pan. Allow some excess to hang over the edges. Then put the pastry aside for the moment.

Arguably, the best part of your pie will be the apples, and I am going to go over a few easy steps for a killer filling. You will need to peel and cut up three and a quarter cups of apples—the equivalent of about seven or eight medium-sized apples. I use a potato peeler to remove the skin, but a small paring knife works equally well. Put the apples aside. Mix together two-thirds of a cup of brown sugar, 2 tablespoons of flour, and if you have some spices, ½ teaspoon of cinnamon and ¼ teaspoon of nutmeg. Sprinkle the flour and spices over the apples, coating each one. Put the apples into the pie shell.

The final step is to roll the top pie crust and finish off the pie. Basically, do the same that you did for the bottom crust, rolling it into a circular shape with your glass or rolling pin. Fold the crust in half, lift it carefully, and place it on top of the apples, unfolding as you go. You will need to poke holes in the top with a knife or cut shapes so that the steam can escape while the pie is cooking. Finally, roll up the sides of the crust to give the pie an edge. Voila, you're done!

Put the pie in a 375 degree heated oven and forget about it for 45 minutes while you are studying. Enjoy the smell of cinnamon wafting from the oven as you watch your favorite rerun of *Seinfeld* or *Friends*. Congratulations, you have just made your first pie!

Despite all of the stereotypes, it is not only moms who know how to bake. Anyone can learn how to make an apple pie, and if you lack utensils or ingredients, you can be creative and improvise. I did it, and I know each of you can, as well. So the next time that you are feeling lonesome for a taste of home, or you need to impress your partner or family member, bake a pie. Forget about your problems and just enjoy the moment.

Leslie Revere

Sample Speech

Demonstration Speech

Today is a very spooky day, sandwiched between two of the spookiest days of the whole year. Yesterday was Halloween (or all Hallows Eve), and tomorrow is All Souls Day. What better day to sharpen skills that will allow us to answer impossible questions, uncover hidden truths, and transcend barriers of mortality? That's right, folks, welcome to a five-minute seminar on contacting the dead. For the next few minutes, I am going to demonstrate some tricks of the trade in "mediumship" and divination; and hopefully, we'll all come out alive.

First, when deciding how to approach making contact with the deceased, you have to consider your objective. Do you simply want to want to know whether or not your professor will give you an "A" on your next speech? Or do you want to get some pointers from famous speakers of the past that will blow your professor away?

For a simple *yes* or *no* answer, you may not need to bother the deceased at all. You can cast dice, with even numbers meaning *yes* and odd numbers meaning *no*. Or you can cut a regular deck of cards, designating red cards for *yes* and black cards for *no*. For example, "Will I get an A+ on this speech?"

One of my personal favorites for simple answers is pendulum dowsing, which relies on the interaction between the body and hidden forces in the environment. This technique requires attaching some form of weight to a cord. You can use a necklace with a heavy stone or locket, a ring strung through a chain, or even a thimble tied to a string. After asking the pendulum to give you a sign for "yes," you watch which way it moves—either back and forth or in a circle. Alternatively, you can ask for the sign for "no." That's all it takes. And if you feel that you may be subconsciously tempted to influence certain answers, might I suggest closing your eyes while you ask your questions.

Now, if you're after a more thorough interaction with great aunt Bertha, you'll have to use more sophisticated means. Since I doubt that most of you know a live medium, able and willing to be filled with dead spirits at a séance, I recommend a form of talking board. Ouija boards are a classic example, although you can achieve the same effect with paper letters and a drinking

(Continued)

Sample Speech

Demonstration Speech—cont'd

glass. The idea is that spirits use human energy to move the pointer, spelling out words and sentences. I've found this method to be terrifyingly effective, and I'd like to offer a few words of caution. Approach talking boards as you approach Internet chat rooms; you never know to whom you are talking and whether they're going to be friendly. If you're encountering a less than personable spirit, stop immediately. Or if you're determined to proceed, rub a piece of silk across the board to neutralize the negative energy.

Beyond the wonder of Ouija, I find automatic writing to be particularly intriguing. Although this method requires a great deal of patience and practice (and I've never had much luck with it), I wanted to try it out for you today. Basically all you do is hold a pen to a piece of paper and let your mind drift. Supposedly, with your conscious mind suspended, spirits will be able to use your arm to write messages. You should try to forget that you're holding a pen at all; and when the pen starts to move, don't look down.

Let's see, grocery list: eggs, milk, butter, beer . . . WHOA! Okay, I did that on purpose, but apparently this technique really can work. Handwriting analysts even testify that the writing styles of some people change entirely when they engage in automatic writing.

Now, if you're really committed to that conversation with Elvis and none of these methods have worked, you can always try table levitation.

This complicated technique involves a number of people sitting at a round table with their fingers gently resting under the tabletop, like so. In response to simple questions, the table is supposed to tilt, lift, or thump. If things really get hopping, the table can thump out whole sentences through some sort of complex table language. Again, I would leave this method as a last resort.

Well, friends, this nearly concludes our adventures in the paranormal. But I'd like to offer a few general pointers that I've found helpful. When dealing with spirits, remember that there's no reason to become freaked out. After all, they're people too—they just happen to be dead. This means that they may be privy to some information we are not, and conversing with them in a respectful and responsible manner could prove beneficial. Secondly, avoid using spirits or the paranormal for personal material gain. For example, don't ask your dead grandfather for the winning lotto numbers. That's bad karma and a bad idea. You don't know how messing with the spirit world could come back to haunt you. And finally, it's all about attitude. When approached with an open yet rational mind, anything from drops of candle wax to patterns in egg yolks might just provide you with answers from beyond the grave.

Joanna Mennie

Questions for Discussion

1. Brainstorm some topics for informative speaking that could reflect seasons of the year, holidays, or other special occasions.

2. Identify topics that you would consider to be inappropriate for presentation to the group. Why would you find these topics inappropriate?

3. Identify topics that could be appropriate and interesting but difficult to explain. Can you think of any topics on which the audience would have preconceived and inaccurate perceptions?

4. What are some of the risks and benefits of using web sources?

5. How could you make use of e-mail in preparing for an informative speaking assignment?

6. Discuss some ethical considerations related to informative speaking. Refer to the Question of Ethics sidebar.

Outline

THE BUILDING BLOCKS OF PERSUASIVE DISCOURSE

A Debate Involving Minority Voices

Learning Objectives

- To learn how to identify and use source credibility appeals (*ethos*)
- To understand the role of emotional appeals in persuasive discourse (*pathos*)
- To learn how to identify and use logical appeals (*logos*)

Keep in Mind

Issues Relevant to Minority Populations or Disadvantaged Americans

- Panhandling
- Illegal immigrants
- Unemployment
- Accessibility issues for people with disabilities
- Language rights of Hispanics
- Rising cost of education
- Deployment of National Guard to Mexico/ United States border and related issues
- Glass ceiling for women
- Migrant labor
- Fraud perpetrated against seniors
- Ghetto housing
- Invisible disabilities
- Violence in low-income communities
- Racial profiling
- Substance abuse on reservations
- Rejection of immigrants on the basis of health issues
- Denial of insurance on the basis of DNA testing
- Mandatory retirement
- Social benefits for people without income
- Catalogue brides
- Minimum wage
- Smoking in public places
- Same-sex marriage
- Right to carry handguns
- Affirmative action laws

- Poverty in single-parent families
- Affordable health care
- Rights of victims of violence
- Native land rights
- Homelessness
- Singing the national anthem in a language other than English

Successful persuasive speaking draws on the Aristotelian concepts of *ethos*, *logos*, and *pathos*. This chapter will discuss how speakers build their source credibility (*ethos*), use emotional appeals in persuasive speaking (*pathos*), and use argumentation and reasoning (*logos*). Chapters Ten and Eleven talk more about emotional appeals in the context of discussions of language (ethical and unethical). (See the Keep in Mind box.)

Ethos as a Persuasive Strategy

Ethos
Source credibility

From the Socratic period to the present day, rhetoricians have studied the concept of *ethos*—the credibility that audiences attach to speakers. Aristotle looked at how speakers establish their credibility (or *ethos*) through the speech itself.[1] For

Cicero, a good orator was not simply a man of skill, but also a man of personal integrity;[2] and Quintilian placed still more stress on the idea of a good man speaking well.[3]

Beginning in 1949, scholars subjected the classical concepts of source credibility to tests in laboratory settings. By the 1950s, Harvard psychologists Carl I. Hovland, Irving L. Janis, and Harold H. Kelley had begun to publish their findings on the factors that constitute source credibility.[4] In the 1960s, Kenneth E. Anderson joined with Theodore Clevenger, Jr., to publish a summary of current research on the topic.[5] Soon after, James C. McCroskey published the results of his efforts to uncover the dimensions of source credibility,[6] and others followed suit in 1970.[7] McCroskey, whose efforts continued over a number of years, became one of the leading authorities in this area.

True, the terms used in talking about source credibility vary from study to study, and the factors cluster in different ways in different studies. Some researchers refer to the *trustworthiness* dimension of source credibility, whereas others use terms such *safety* or *character* to refer to the same idea. Some use the term *competency*, while others talk about the *qualification* or *expertise* dimension. *Likeability* is another term used to refer to *sociability*, and the term *dynamism* often substitutes for *extroversion*. Some researchers have identified only two dimensions to source credibility: *trustworthiness* and *competency*.[8] Others have identified *competence*, *trustworthiness*, and *dynamism*.[9] Still others have located four dimensions: *trustworthiness*, *competency*, *dynamism*, and *objectivity*.[10] Some studies include *charisma* as a source credibility factor.[11] Others regard *composure* and *status* as components of *competency*, rather than independent variables.[12] So the terms and the organization of the concepts vary, but the basic ideas surface in many studies. For instance, even when *composure* does not appear as a separate factor, discussions about composure appear under other headings. Chapter Six described how speakers can influence their credibility through delivery. This chapter focuses on building credibility through speech content.

CONSTITUENTS OF CREDIBILITY

Trustworthiness

Most agree that the most important dimension of source credibility is *trustworthiness*. Audiences tend to trust speakers who violate expectations by taking a position that puts them at risk. Questioned in August 2004 about a speech she had delivered on the erosion of civility in politics, Teresa Heinz Kerry (wife of U.S. Senator John Kerry) responded abruptly to the reporter, "Shove it!" Although her comment made headlines, her willingness to stray from the safety of a politically correct response got positive press. Beuenia Brown (delegate to the 2004 Democratic convention) said that she found Heinz Kerry's candor to be disarming: "I think that when a person is outspoken, I think of them as honest. I don't see them as having to connive. They're speaking from the heart."[13] In the same way, audiences *distrust* those who are "wishy-washy" or who change their point of view to match the situation. Senator Kerry faced no end of ridicule for making the statement "I actually did vote for the $87 billion before I voted against it" in reference to a vote on funding the Iraq war. (See the Reflections box.)

Homophily
Similarity

Audiences also trust speakers who are "one of us"—who share our background, our experiences, and our likely fate. For that reason, speakers often point to similarities with their audiences. Behavioral scientists refer to this phenomenon as *homophily*.[14] When U.S. Senate candidate Barack Obama of Illinois addressed the Democratic national convention in Atlanta, Georgia, in the summer of 2004, he spoke of his own humble beginnings, a background shared by many audience members: "Tonight is a particular honor for me because, let's face it, my presence on this stage is pretty unlikely. My father was a foreign student, born and raised in a small village in Kenya. He grew up herding goats, went to school in a tin-roof shack. His father, my grandfather, was a cook, a domestic servant."[15] Had Obama shared the privileged upbringing of Nelson Rockefeller, this assertion might have had the ring of insincerity. Someone living in the ghettos of Chicago or Atlanta might have found his words to be unconvincing. But because Obama's family came from humble beginnings, like many members of his audience (immediate and virtual), his pronouncement of oneness with his audience was credible. Sincerity is a very important part of trustworthiness. In a quote that became a catchphrase in the 1990s, Bill Clinton told an unemployed man in a town hall, "I feel your pain."

To establish credibility on the trustworthiness dimension, speakers should acknowledge divergent points of view, speak in respectful terms of opponents, remind audiences of shared experiences and common values, speak in concrete terms in order to avoid an impression of wishy-washiness, be willing to take a stand on controversial issues, and demonstrate consistency in belief structures over time. Some studies in classroom settings have found that instructors can lose credibility when they engage in sarcastic put-downs of students or make verbally abusive comments.[16]

Reflections

Speaking with Conviction

It is a very different Mr. [Anderson] Cooper who has captivated CNN viewers in the two weeks since Hurricane Katrina crashed ashore. . . . Mr. Cooper's heart-on-his-sleeve demeanor has been anything but slick and packaged. The 38-year-old anchor has dressed down officials in interviews with polite righteous indignation in behalf of hurricane victims. At least twice he choked up on air, once abruptly stopping his commentary about lost homes and waving away the camera as he looked about to burst into tears. . . . Mr. Cooper's Sept. 1 interview with Senator Mary L. Landrieu, Democrat of Louisiana, marked a turning point in the tone of hurricane coverage as he snapped when she began thanking federal officials for their recovery efforts. "Excuse me, Senator, I'm sorry for interrupting," Mr. Cooper interjected. "I haven't heard that, because, for the last four days, I've been seeing dead bodies in the streets here in Mississippi. And to listen to politicians thanking each other and complimenting each other, you know, I got to tell you, there are a lot of people here who are very upset, and very angry, and very frustrated. And when they hear politicians slap—you know, thanking one another, it just, you know, it kind of cuts them the wrong way right now, because literally there was a body on the streets of this town yesterday being eaten by rats because this woman had been lying in the street for 48 hours." . . . "When you travel with him, he's no joke . . . He's really intense. He could care less how he looks, his hair and makeup. If there's no cameraperson, he grabs the camera."

Source: Elizabeth Jensen, "An Anchor Who Reports Disaster News with a Heart on His Sleeve" (September 12, 2005), www.nytimes.com/2005/09/12/arts/television/12coop.html, accessed on September 12, 2005.

Competence

The second most frequently acknowledged factor in source credibility is *competency* or expertise.[17] Audience attitudes change more dramatically when the information source has expertise related to the topic under discussion.[18] In order to establish credibility on the competency dimension, speakers can refer to previous experience, knowledge of the topic, or positions held in the past. References to personal acquaintance with experts or earlier encounters with similar audiences support the impression that the speaker is not a novice to the topic area.

If you have no firsthand knowledge of the subject, your audience needs to know that you have acquired competency through secondhand knowledge. In the following example, the speaker uses this strategy to gain credibility:

> You may wonder how an eighteen-year-old can identify with the plight of an older worker. First, I can identify because I have a father who was laid off from his work at a major industrial plant at the age of forty-four. He never got another job that paid as well or offered the same benefits. Our entire family experienced the consequences of my father's layoff. Second, I have done extensive research to learn more about a problem that has created untold distress for millions of Americans. Statistics, case studies, and personal instances all paint the same bleak picture. In the context of modern technological society, many older workers face discrimination and unfair competition to maintain their jobs.

The next example comes from a speech by television and screen actor and director Alan Alda, delivered on May 25, 1979, to the graduating class of the Columbia

University College of Physicians and Surgeons.[19, 20] Alda had achieved fame for his role as a field doctor in *M*A*S*H*, a long-running TV show about the Korean war. In this speech, Alda faced the challenge of building credibility with audience members who knew far more than he did about the technical and scientific aspects of doctoring. The following excerpt illustrates how he accomplished this end:

> Ever since it was announced that a non-doctor, in fact an actor, had been invited to give the commencement address at one of the most prestigious medical schools in the country, people have been wondering—why get someone who only pretends to be a doctor when you could get a real one? Some people suggested that this school had done everything it could to show you how to *be* doctors and in a moment of desperation had brought in someone who could show you how to act like one. It's certainly true that I'm not a doctor. I have a long list of non-qualifications. In the first place, I'm not a great fan of blood. I don't mind people having it. I just don't enjoy seeing them wear it. I have yet to see a real operation because the mere smell of a hospital reminds me of a previous appointment. And my knowledge of anatomy resides in the clear understanding that the hip bone is connected to the leg bone. I am not a doctor. But you have asked me, and all in all, I think you made a wonderful choice. I say that because I probably first came to the attention of this graduating class through a character on television that I've played and helped write for the past seven years—a surgeon called Hawkeye Pierce. He's a remarkable person, this Hawkeye, and if you have chosen somehow to associate his character with your own graduation from medical school, then I find that very heartening. Because I think that it means that you are reaching out toward a very human kind of doctoring—and a very real kind of doctor.[21]

Rather than compete with the knowledge of the audience, Alda talked about the personal qualities of the character that he played for so many years, Dr. Hawkeye Pierce. Since Pierce was allegedly modeled after Dr. Keith Keemtsma, a professor

Keep in Mind

Improve Your Credibility!

- Ask a well-respected person with status to introduce you.
- Refer to members of the audience.
- Mention your experience with—or expertise in—the topic.
- Demonstrate objectivity by giving both sides of the issue.
- Use solid evidence and reasoning to support your position.
- Mention your commitment to shared audience values such as family.
- Use examples that show that you are "one of us."
- Use strong colorful language; avoid weak nonassertive language.

- Be consistent; do not shift from one position to another.
- Do not be afraid to put your views on the line; audiences respect people who are willing to stand up for their views.
- Give examples that show your commitment to change and progress.
- Do not demean anyone; demonstrate respect for your audience and those who oppose your position.
- Do not apologize for mistakes.
- Do not thank the audience for attending the speech.

and chairman of surgery at the College of Physicians and Surgeons from 1971 to 1994,[22] this approach was especially appropriate.

Speakers can also transmit a sense of authority and competency by using a variety of support materials —statistics, examples, and expert testimony. When speaking to an audience of experts, speakers gain credibility by using the terminology of the field. Guest speakers gain additional credibility in the competency dimension when the introductions by others are complimentary. (The speaker often provides this biographical information, thus making an active contribution to the building of his own *ethos*.) (See the Keep in Mind box on p. 284.)

Speakers lose credibility on the expertise dimension when they do not know their material, make statements that cannot be supported with evidence, and make poor choices with regard to language and grammar. Studies have found that these same factors can affect instructor credibility.[23]

Status

A related concept, which many include under the category of competence, is *status*. If we perceive the speaker to have an elevated place in society and to be respected, we are more likely to see the person as credible. We typically derive our impressions of status from the reputation, appearance, and occupation of the speaker. Chapter Six described how speakers use dress to establish status. This chapter discusses how they use references to reputation and occupation to construct status.

A number of years ago, the U.S. Public Health Service published a study that suggested a causal relationship between smoking and lung cancer. The release of the study had little influence on the attitudes of the public until 1964, when the

Surgeon General called a press conference to publicize the findings of the study. Subsequently, many Americans claimed that they had stopped smoking. Communication researchers concluded that the status of the source had a significant impact on the receptivity of the audience to the second release of the information.[24] As studies have proved, scientists have enormous credibility with audiences. In a classic experiment by Stanley Milgram, the most compliant subjects in the experiment administered what they believed to be dangerous (even lethal) electric shocks to others.[25] They did so upon the orders of a man in a white laboratory coat, whom they believed to be a scientist—an authority figure.

Speeches of introduction often talk about awards or recognition received by the person. The endorsement of high-status individuals adds to credibility, while the endorsement of low-status individuals detracts from credibility. Speakers attempt to build their own credibility when they talk about affiliations with people or organizations with status.

Hesitations such as "*Well, uh,* I suppose" and "I wish that you—*er*—would be more considerate" strip language of its power and speakers of their status and composure. Speakers also dilute language when they use *hedges* such as "*I think* that I would like to spend tomorrow at the beach" or "*I guess* that you can use the car." More powerful language would be "I would like to spend tomorrow at the beach" or "You can use the car."[26]

Disclaimers give wiggle room to speakers. The person makes an excuse before making the assertion. "I really shouldn't admit that I wrote the essay, but . . ." or "I know that I shouldn't have gone to the show after hearing the bad reviews, but. . . ."[27] *Qualifiers* such as *maybe, perhaps,* and *possibly* achieve the same purpose, removing the edge in the event that the listener disagrees. Excessive politeness also strips the speaker of power.[28]

Tag questions are powerless because they demonstrate uncertainty on the part of the speaker. The speaker makes an assertion and then questions her own statement: "That movie is wonderful, *don't you think*?" "Sally should have won that award, *shouldn't she*?" "You do want to go, don't you?" To be more assertive, the speaker could have said, "That movie is wonderful" or "Sally should have won that award." Tag questions add a negative to the end of sentences: "isn't it?"; "don't you think?"; "shouldn't she?"; "wasn't it?"; "didn't it?"[29]

Intensifiers achieve the opposite of what the term implies. Rather than strengthening a thought, they weaken it. Examples of intensifiers are "I am *so* anxious to go," "I *really* want to see her," and "I am *so* angry that he broke his promise."

In informal communication, people may deliberately strip language of some of its power in respect for norms of social interaction. They may use *polite forms* such as "Forgive me, sir, but would you be willing to change seats so that I can be close to my grandchild?" The tone is beseeching, and the language is powerless. Phrases such as "forgive me, sir" and "would you be willing" convey the impression that the speaker has little power or status in the situation.

When you deliver a speech, you should use powerful language—language that is strong and assertive rather than weak and unassertive. In his book *Influence: Science and Practice*, Robert B. Cialdini tells us that people are influenced by those whom they perceive to have power.[30] *Nonverbally*, speakers convey an impression of power through the clothes they wear and through vocal characteristics, stance,

Hesitations
Vocal fillers such as "uh" or "er", which often undermine audience confidence in a speaker

Hedges
Use of weak phrases such as "I think" or "I guess"

Disclaimer
An excuse that a speaker makes about an assertion, usually before the assertion is made

Qualifiers
Words such as *maybe, perhaps,* and *possibly*

Tag question
A question such as "don't you think?" or "isn't it?" that follows an assertion, usually undermining its strength

Intensifiers
Words used with the intent to strengthen a statement (***really** want to, **so** anxious*) that often weaken it

posture, and gestures. *Verbally*, speakers communicate power through strong and assertive language. It should be noted, however, that behaviors viewed as assertive in men are sometimes seen as aggressive in women.

Dynamism

American audiences also assign credibility to speakers who are *dynamic*—bold, energetic, and assertive. It is easy to recall examples such as Bill Clinton playing the saxophone on the Arsenio Hall television talk show in 1992, prior to his election as president. Speakers can build credibility on the dynamism dimension by using forceful, active language. To establish themselves as members of today's generation, politicians can speak about change and progress, new ideas, and current legislation and policies. Barack Obama's speech to the 2004 Democratic convention, in which he issued a call for action and change, illustrates the use of strong, powerful, and dynamic language:

> Democrats, Republicans, Independents—I say to you tonight: we have more work to do. More to do for the workers I met in Galesburg, Illinois, who are losing their union jobs at the Maytag plant that's moving to Mexico, and now are having to compete with their own children for jobs that pay seven bucks an hour. More to do for the father I met who was losing his job and choking back tears, wondering how he would pay $4500 a month for the drugs his son needs without the health benefits he was counting on. More to do for the woman in east St. Louis, and thousands more like her, who has the grades, has the drive, has the will, but doesn't have the money to go to college.[31]

At other times during this keynote address, Obama talked about having "energy" and "urgency" and pursuing and defeating enemies.

> **Dynamic**
> Bold, energetic

Sociability

The rise of William Hung to cult fame, after being featured as one of the worst singers to try out for the first season of *American Idol*, demonstrates the weight that audiences put upon the sociability dimension. Both judges and global audiences responded to the warmth, humility, and sincerity of the young man with the engaging smile and whimsical demeanor. While the top ten finalists were selected on the basis of talent, the top ten "worst" performers were chosen on the basis of audience appeal. They were entertaining—and none more so than William, whose name has become synonymous with "She bangs, She bangs!"

Studies of student-teacher interactions have found that students like friendly instructors who know their names, use a number of examples to explain concepts, recount interesting stories, use a conversational tone and rate of speech, have an expressive voice and dramatic manner, use humor that is spontaneous and relevant to the course content, encourage students to talk, address the issues raised by students, and show openness and a willingness to disclose personal information.[32] When instructors are warm, expressive, involved, and articulate, students also perceive them to be more competent.[33] Most scholars believe that we can apply these findings to speaking in general.

When politicians fail to show signs of sociability, they become the objects of severe criticism. When running for the presidency, John Kerry was sometimes criticized for being too stiff and aloof. Interviews with southern Democrats in October 2004 confirmed the importance of being able to connect with people on a personal level.[34] After interviewing supporters of John Kerry, the television correspondent concluded, "The good news is that Kerry is not Bush. The bad news is that he is not Bill Clinton." The response of one southern barber summed up the reaction of many people. When asked, "Could you see Bill Clinton sitting in your barber chair?" the man responded that he could easily imagine Bill Clinton dropping into his barber shop for a haircut. Asked if he could imagine John Kerry in the same chair, the man smiled and shook his head. He said, no, he couldn't see John Kerry in his chair. And that may be an important reason that John Kerry lost the presidency. Southerners could not see John Kerry sitting in their barber chairs. Americans want to feel a sense of connection with the real person when they choose their leaders. In speakers, they expect the same qualities.

Speakers use strategies of *immediacy*, discussed in earlier chapters, to build rapport with audiences and enhance their credibility on the sociability dimension. The term *immediacy* refers to the extent to which we feel physically or psychologically close to another person.[35] To build this sense of closeness, speakers may refer to someone in the audience, extend a personal greeting or compliment, mention the occasion or surroundings, or ask a question of the audience. Showing respect for the audience and pointing to similarities in background also enhance credibility on the likeability dimension. A major characteristic of speeches given by science fiction writer Ray Bradbury, for example, was his conversational quality and lack of pompousness. One has a sense of meeting the real person in accounts such as the following:

> I had a thing happen to me when I was 9 years old, which is a great lesson. That was in 1929—the start of the Great Depression. And a single comic strip in the newspaper sent me into the future. The first comic strip of Buck Rogers. In October 1929 I looked at that one comic strip, with its view of the future, and I thought, "That's where I belong." I started to collect Buck Rogers comic strips. And everybody in the fifth grade made fun of me. I continued to collect them for about a month, and then I listened to the critics. And I tore up my comic strips. That's the worst thing I ever did. Two or three days later, I broke down. I was crying, and I said to myself, "Why am I crying? Whose funeral am I going to? Who died?" And the answer was, "Me." I'd torn up the future. And then I sat down with myself, and I was crying, and I said, "What can I do to correct this? And I said, "Well, hell, go back and collect Buck Rogers comic strips!" . . . And that's what I did. I started collecting Buck Rogers again.[36]

Objectivity

A final dimension of credibility that merits discussion is *objectivity*.[37] When you cite statistics, expert testimony, specific instances, and illustrations, you avoid the appearance of relying strictly on personal opinion. You appear unbiased and objective.

SHIFTS IN CREDIBILITY DURING A SPEECH

Variations in the level of credibility from the beginning to the end of a speech lead researchers to talk about *initial*, *derived*, and *terminal* credibility.[38] *Initial* credibility refers to audience perceptions of the speaker at the moment that he starts to speak. *Derived* credibility refers to the ways by which the speaker gains credibility during the process of delivering the speech. *Terminal* credibility concerns audience perceptions of the speaker at the end of the speech.

Initial credibility
Audience impressions of a speaker when the speaker begins

Derived credibility
The gaining of believability in the course of a speech

Terminal credibility
Audience impressions of a speaker at the end of the speech

Audience reaction to a controversial speech by former congressman and four-time Louisiana Governor Edwin Edwards illustrates how speakers can dramatically alter initial audience perceptions. In 1969, at a time of great controversy over the busing of children to other school districts, Edwards spoke to members of the Louisiana Education Association on this contentious issue. His stance was moderate—favored by neither blacks nor whites. J. K. Haynes, a verbal spokesman for the African-American educators, introduced Edwards as "a former friend" of the black community. Jim Baronet, a television news broadcaster, described the dilemma confronted by Edwards in the following way:

> It was a hairy type of situation. He [Edwards] knew that there was nothing he could say that would please them [the audience], without cutting his own throat. Yet he impressed the group—gave a particularly good speech. He was very blunt. He said in essence that everyone was going to have to be fairer. . . . Not in the particular way that most politicians usually have about them, trying to slice up the pie so that everyone can have a piece. He somehow managed to say things bluntly, almost brutally, and I suppose in mere relief, they appreciated it to the point that they gave him a standing ovation for about six or seven minutes.[39]

This example demonstrates how a speaker can move from low initial credibility to high terminal credibility. Initially, the audience distrusted him; and the introduction by Haynes only worsened the situation. But audience perceptions changed when they began to see the speaker as sincere, willing to risk his popularity for his personal convictions. One audience member made the following observation, "Well, he may be stupid, but at least he's honest."[40] On another occasion, Edwards received a standing ovation from "a ballroom full of journalists whom he had just castigated for over an hour for what he saw as their habitual unfairness, sloppiness, bias, sleaziness, and sensationalism."[41] Edwards is presently in federal prison, convicted on extortion and bribery charges; however, thousands of Louisiana residents have signed petitions for his release, and many supporters would still vote for him if his name appeared on a ballot. (See Tips from a Professional.)

As noted already, many factors can influence audience views of a speaker's credibility. The audience may have prior knowledge of the speaker, which determines their initial perceptions. The actions or behavior of the speaker in the moments leading to the speech can mitigate these initial perceptions. Introductory comments can also influence the initial credibility of the speaker. The quality and relevance of the speech, as well as the speaker's delivery, can lead to higher levels of derived credibility. The terminal credibility of the speaker results from the interaction of initial perceptions with the immediate experience.

Pathos as a Persuasive Strategy

Pathos
Emotional appeals

Speakers must appeal not only to the rational thought processes of their audiences but also to their emotions. Aristotle applied the term *pathos* to the use of emotional appeals in speaking. Like later rhetorical scholars, he considered emotional

TIPS FROM A PROFESSIONAL
Sincerity Matters

George Orwell, author of 1984, said that the great enemy of communication is lack of sincerity. Comedian Groucho Marx agreed when he observed, "Sincerity is everything." But Marx added, jokingly, "If you can fake that, you've got it made." In the realm of public speaking, sincerity is everything—but you cannot fake it. It is the key to communicating with an audience—a necessary condition of connecting with listeners.

What does it mean to say someone is "sincere"? The dictionary gives various definitions: free from pretense or deceit; earnest, genuine, honest, frank. I like this one: the same in reality as in appearance. Think about a speaker whose words touched or moved you at some time. I am willing to bet that you experienced him or her as sincere. I remember one speaker who often appeared on public television at fund-raising time. Leo Buscaglia would tell the most amazing stories about his big, wacky Italian family. He talked about life, love, and learning. He was passionate. He was real. And he cared. Audiences adored him—sometimes staying hours after a lecture for one of his famous hugs.

Now think of a speaker who turned you off—a politician, marketer, motivational speaker, or a particular television evangelist. What bothered you about the speaker? Again, I am willing to bet that it related to your perception of that speaker's sincerity. Audiences know a phony when they see one. I recall attending a speech contest a few years back. The speaker gave, in technical terms, a flawless performance. The eye contact was there. The organization and gestures. The vocal variety. But he was not communicating "in the moment." Rather, he was play-acting for our benefit, reciting a text from his head. In fact, he didn't seem to know—or care—that an audience was present. His speech felt fake. Not surprisingly, he didn't win. The reality is that we can have all the "technicals" right. But if we are not believable, we are finished.

How can we "speak with sincerity"? In keeping with the earlier definition, one of the most basic ways is simply to be ourselves—to appear to be who we really are. Being the same in appearance as in reality implies being true to our values and beliefs and not putting on airs, play-acting, or throwing in big words in an attempt to impress others. We also communicate sincerity when we speak on subjects about which we genuinely care. After all, if we don't care about our subject, why should our listeners? As I heard one speaker put it, "I'll believe how much you know when I see how much you care."

One of the best ways to communicate sincerity is to speak from personal experience. We show that we have a stake in the issue, that our interest is not purely academic. Indeed, who is better placed to speak about something we have lived than we are? At times, this means daring to appear vulnerable before an audience, even looking emotional or sentimental. Risking vulnerability by sharing our personal stories is often the price we must pay to connect emotionally with an audience. Our listeners need to be able to see themselves in us. The clearer and more intimate the picture we paint, the more they can identify with our plight.

Of course, it is not easy to share a moving story or difficult experience. This lesson was brought home to me very poignantly a few years ago. A brother was diagnosed with terminal cancer. The experience of being with someone through the dying process was difficult and new to me. Nonetheless, I decided to share my story in a speech. I spoke about how he and I had

(Continued)

Sincerity Matters—cont'd

struggled with our emotions to connect with one another in the hospital one day—a process that was not easy for either of us. After writing the first draft of the speech, however, I had reservations. I feared my account might be a bit too personal or overly sentimental. And as I often do, I shared my misgivings with a trusted friend. Her advice was simple, "Leave it in." So when the time came to deliver the speech a few days later, I trusted her advice and ignored my misgivings. After I had spoken, a woman in the audience came to me to say that she had been very moved by my speech. She said that she was particularly touched by the story of my brother's and my struggling to connect with one another that day in the hospital. Her reaction reinforced in my mind a powerful lesson: We must be willing to share and risk ourselves as speakers. We must be willing to put ourselves on the line if we wish to connect with an audience. When we do, our listeners sense and see that we are genuine.

Communicating sincerity also means focusing on the audience. How can they grow or benefit from our knowledge or experience? Public speaking is not about the speaker. It is about the audience. If our talk is all about us, we will almost certainly fail. By asking for examples or input from the audience and making time for questions, we show that we care and that our presentation is real—not canned.

Finally, to speak sincerely is to say what we mean and mean what we say. This implies, first and foremost, taking responsibility for our language. How many times have you heard prominent public figures avoid responsibility for taking action by speaking in the passive voice? Notice the difference between these two statements: "It is important that action be taken" and "I will act." Speaking in the passive voice undermines our sincerity because it conveys an impression of distance. We say something must be done without saying who will do it. The active voice leaves no doubt as to where the responsibility for action lies. We respect people who are clear about where they stand on an issue. We experience them as sincere, even if we do not personally agree with their point of view.

Some speakers avoid responsibility for their words by using roundabout or vague phraseology. Notice the difference between one company's pledge to "reduce environmental pollutants" and another's promise to "work toward reducing" such pollutants. Other examples of vague terminology are "in due course" and "at the proper juncture." Listeners are familiar with such gobbledygook, and they sense that speakers who use such language are not leveling with them. Speaking with sincerity means eliminating the "wiggle room" that leaves doubt about our motives and our intent.

Sincerity does matter—probably more today then ever. In an age of information overload, audiences have little time for speakers who are less than genuine. Technical competence is not enough. Audiences relate to real human beings who show that they care—about their subject and their audience. Speakers must mean what they say and say what they mean.

Brian Creamer is an experienced speaker and speech coach. He is the author of *Successfully Speaking: Seven Keys to Unlock Your Speaking Potential*, 2002. He can be reached through his website, www.successfullyspeaking.ca.

appeals to be not only ethical but also necessary to the achievement of speaker goals. Speakers seek to invoke feelings in listeners such as compassion, anger, fear, pride, empathy, guilt, humility, and respect.

When we react emotionally to an event or person, we experience physiological changes. Minute alterations in blood chemistry affect our breathing, digestive processes, heartbeat, and muscle control. But what causes an emotional response in one person may create no reaction in another. Mohawks, for example, are known for their abilities as high steel workers. They are able to walk across small beams, hundreds of feet above the ground, without experiencing the sort of transformed physical state or fear that most of us would find debilitating. The same person, however, might sweat uncontrollably if confronted with the need to address an audience of twenty students.[42]

Many Americans, who learn to control their emotions in public settings, consider overt emotional responses to be a sign of weakness. They think of such emotional arousal as an unnatural and undesirable state of being. In reality, feeling is a prerequisite to understanding and acting; and most scholars recognize the importance of touching people emotionally with our words. Moderate emotional appeals help to hold the attention of audience members, focus on their needs, motivate them to think seriously about a topic, improve understanding, and encourage intelligent behavior. If we have no feelings, we will not act—intelligently or unintelligently.[43] At the same time, our emotions should not overwhelm our ability to think rationally about a topic. Unethical speakers seek to arouse emotions to an extreme that inhibits intelligent decision making. Ethical speakers try to achieve

a balance by using appeals that are sufficiently strong to facilitate intelligent responses but not so intense that listeners react without thinking. We tend to react emotionally when we perceive that a speaker is meeting our needs in some way, and surely that should be the aim of every speaker.

The most arresting examples of emotionally compelling rhetoric occur in periods of war, conflict, and great tragedy—World War I, World War II, the Cold War, Vietnam, the Gulf War, and most recently, the war in Iraq. Many of our most powerful literary pieces (novels, poems, and other works) have come from the pain of individuals and societies at war with themselves or others. In the film *The Third Man* (scripted by Graham Greene in 1949 and later made into a radio series and television production), character Harry Lime (played by Orson Welles) delivered these famous words: "In Italy, for thirty years under the Borgias, they had warfare, terror, murder, bloodshed—they produced Michelangelo, Leonardo da Vinci and the Renaissance. In Switzerland, they had brotherly love, five hundred years of democracy and peace, and what did that produce? The cuckoo clock."[44] This tongue-in-cheek comment holds some truth for rhetoric also. If the examples in this chapter appear to be loaded in favor of wartime rhetoric, the reason has been stated here.

The rhetoric related to the terrorist attacks on September 11, 2001, and the "war against terrorism" also reflects this need to connect with emotionally laden values such as love of country and the most deep-seated need for security. On September 11, 2004, President George W. Bush commemorated the victims of 9/11 in his weekly radio address from the Oval Office:

> Three years ago, the struggle of good against evil was compressed into a single morning. In the space of only 102 minutes, our country lost more citizens than were lost in the attack on Pearl Harbor. Time has passed, but the memories do not fade. We remember the images of fire, and the final calls of love, and the courage of rescuers who saw death and did not flee.[45]

Speeches of this nature are compelling because they speak to vital issues and reflect shared values. Health-related concerns such as HIV/AIDS and issues such as drunk driving also produce rhetoric with strong emotional appeals. Speakers use vivid and concrete language, balanced and parallel sentence structures, antithesis, repetition, alliteration, first and second voice, rhythmic triads and quads, comparison and contrast, metaphors, similes, personification, analogies, and rhetorical questions to evoke powerful emotions in their audiences. Chapter Ten will discuss these strategies.

Fear appeals
Attempting to persuade by scaring an audience

A final area of consideration concerns the use of fear appeals in persuasive speaking. Most scholars argue that mild or moderate fear appeals work better than strong fear appeals since people tune out overly gruesome statistics and images.[46] A few studies suggest, however, that when persuaders succeed at creating high levels of fear in audiences, the persuasive effect is greater than would otherwise be the case.[47] They say researchers are unable to document the effectiveness of strong fear appeals because university ethics boards prohibit studies that employ strong appeals. (See the Question of Ethics box.)

A Question of Ethics

Brian presented a speech on the topic of political fraud and corruption. He spoke, in particular, about a recent scandal involving a number of high-profile public officials. He decided to name the guilty officials, all of whom belonged to the same political party. Brian realized that not all members of this party were dishonest, and he knew that his speech would offend audience members who belonged to the political party accused of wrongdoing. In addition, his instructor had told him to avoid topics such as politics and religion. Still, Brian believed that public officials have a special responsibility to behave in an ethical way. He also believed that public servants have an obligation to answer to their publics. Brian agreed with his professor that students should avoid topics such as religion in speeches, but he believed that politics was a different matter.

Moreover, in researching his topic, Brian had uncovered information to suggest that these same officials might have commissioned shoddy work on some high-rise structures, highways, overpasses, and bridges in order to save money for inflated personal budgets. Although he had no proof that the shoddy work would result in the collapse of buildings or highways, he worried that it could. As a result, he felt justified in using strong emotional and fear appeals. He warned his audience that the cost of the corruption might be more than monetary losses—that lives might also be lost if they did not elect an official who was more committed to the common good.

Another factor played into this situation, as well. Brian did not tell the audience that his cousin was running for political office against the candidate that he was accusing of wrongdoing. Brian did not think that this information was relevant since he believed that the candidate was guilty and that he would not have supported him under any circumstances. Still he did want his cousin to win the election, and he hoped that his speech would make a small contribution to that end.

How do you feel about discussing political topics in a classroom speaking environment? Religious topics? Should speakers be allowed to attack the credibility of public figures? How do you feel about Brian's use of emotional and fear appeals? Is name calling ever justified in a speech?

Levels of anxiety and age can influence the effectiveness of a fear appeal. Already anxious audience members may respond more negatively to fear appeals than less anxious members, whereas teenagers react less to threats of bodily injury than to threats of rejection or social embarrassment. Researchers concur that speakers should provide audiences with explicit instructions on how to reduce the fear appeals.[48] In a speech on the prevalence of thyroid cancer in young people, for example, the speaker could assure the audience that the cancer can be safely and easily removed. In a speech on the risks of smoking, the speaker could advise the audience on specific places to go to seek help.

Fear appeals appear to have the greatest impact in the following three conditions: when speakers are highly credible, when they discuss the problem in very specific terms, and when they offer ways to alleviate or eliminate the threat.[49] The audience should be in a position to take immediate action to reduce the state of anxiety, since the effects of persuasive appeals disappear within twenty-four hours.[50]

Logos as a Persuasive Strategy

Logos
Use of argumentation and reasoning

The term *logos* refers to argumentation and reasoning—the use of logical appeals in persuasion. The following discussion describes the processes of reasoning from example, reasoning from generalization, causal reasoning, reasoning from sign, and analogical reasoning. I also discuss common flaws or fallacies that occur in these reasoning processes. (See the Keep in Mind box.)

REASONING FROM EXAMPLE

Reasoning from example
Reaching a conclusion based on a number of specific instances

With reasoning from example, the speaker reaches a general conclusion on the basis of a number of specific instances. President Franklin D. Roosevelt's declaration of war on December 8, 1941, illustrates the process of inductive reasoning:

> Yesterday, the Japanese government also launched an attack against Malaya. Last night, Japanese forces attacked Hong Kong. Last night, Japanese forces attacked

Keep in Mind

Tips for Using Evidence

- Does the evidence come from a credible and unbiased source?
- Is the evidence up to date?
- Is the evidence representative of other findings on the topic?

- Does the evidence support the points that you are making?
- Have you given sufficient evidence to support your ideas?

Guam. Last night, Japanese forces attacked the Philippine Islands. Last night, the Japanese attacked Wake Island. This morning, the Japanese attacked Midway Island. Japan has, therefore, undertaken a surprise offensive extending throughout the Pacific area.[51]

The speaker lists specific instances that lead to the conclusion that the Japanese have launched a surprise offensive extending throughout the Pacific region. In a radio broadcast on the following evening, Roosevelt again reasoned from examples to support his claim that the actions of Hirohito in Asia, Hitler in Germany, and Mussolini in Italy confirmed a pattern of active collaboration among fascist forces in the three countries:

In 1931, ten years ago, Japan invaded Manchukuo—without warning. In 1935, Italy invaded Ethiopia—without warning. In 1938, Hitler occupied Austria—without warning. In 1939, Hitler invaded Czechoslovakia—without warning. Later in 1939, Hitler invaded Poland—without warning. In 1940, Hitler invaded Norway, Denmark, the Netherlands, Belgium, and Luxembourg—without warning. In 1940, Italy attacked France and later Greece—without warning. And this year, in 1941, the Axis powers attacked Yugoslavia and Greece and they dominated the Balkans—without warning. In 1941, also, Hitler invaded Russia—without warning. And now Japan has attacked Malaya and Thailand—and the United States—without warning. It is all of one pattern.[52]

Some cautions are in order with reasoning from example. The following line of argumentation illustrates typical risks.

Hurricane Charley targeted Florida.
Hurricane Frances targeted Florida.

Hurricane Ivan targeted Florida.
Hurricane Jeanne targeted Florida.
Therefore, all hurricanes will target Florida.

Of course, as hurricanes Katrina and Rita illustrated, an insufficient number of examples can lead to the wrong conclusion, a hasty generalization. We often develop fears on the basis of events that appear frequently on the news. We worry that our children will be kidnapped, that we will become victims of violent crime, or that our identities will be stolen. In reality, however, these kinds of events may be featured on the news because they are rare or unusual. Another problem arises if we deliberately or inadvertently select examples that support our claim and disregard examples that call our claim into question.

REASONING FROM GENERALIZATION

In the case of deductive reasoning, the speaker reasons from the general to the specific, as in the following: All people are created equal. I am a person. Therefore, I was created equal. For a second example, look at the following argumentation:

College students eat too much fast food.
Janet is a college student.
Therefore, Janet eats too much fast food.

Reasoning from generalization
Making an argument from a limited or inadequate number of instances

Several problems can occur with reasoning from generalization. If the basic premise (college students eat too much fast food) is inaccurate, any conclusions drawn from the statement will also be inaccurate. Other problems with reasoning from generalization occur if Janet is an exception to the rule. Even if the basic premise is true, it may not apply to Janet, who is conscientious about her diet. This fallacy in reasoning is particularly problematic when we ascribe general characteristics of a culture to every member of the culture: All Italians are emotional. Antonio is Italian. Therefore, Antonio is emotional. At other times, our definition of terms influences the validity of the argumentation. There may be basic disagreement on what is meant by the term emotional. Do we mean waving one's arms and talking in an animated fashion? Do we mean crying easily? Does the term *emotional* imply that the person expresses his feelings easily to others or admits vulnerability?

In brief, problems arise when the basic premise is flawed (all Italians are emotional). Problems also arise if you do not recognize the possibility for exceptions to the rule (Antonio might not be like all Italians). Finally, problems may occur if the terms are ambiguous, where not everyone has the same meaning for the term *emotional*.

CAUSAL REASONING

Causal reasoning
An argument that takes an effect and looks for the cause

With cause-effect reasoning, speakers observe effects and look for the causes. If we have an increase in violent crime (effect), we may seek to identify the causes of the increase. If we see that more people are unemployed (effect), we may look for the causes of the unemployment. If we find that more students are dropping out of school (effect), we may seek to uncover the causes. We ask, "What generated this effect?" Often we face the dilemma of having to identify the relationship between causes and effects. Does poverty create crime in the inner city, or does crime create poverty by causing merchants to flee inner-city neighborhoods?

When seeking to identify the causes of problems or other conditions, we must be careful to establish clear and compelling connections between effects and their causes. Former President Ronald Reagan used the following colorful example to point to flaws in people's reasoning processes: "We have so many people who can't see a fat man standing beside a thin one without coming to the conclusion that the fat man got that way by taking advantage of the thin one!"[53]

The most common error is to attribute all of the blame to one cause, but that kind of reasoning is too simplistic. Most conditions result from the interaction of many different variables. Cancer, for example, has been linked to many different causes—both environmental (e.g., smoking, dietary habits, and exposure to chemicals in the air and water) and genetic. Insomnia has been linked to stress, lifestyle, consumption of caffeine, and the use of certain medications, as well as many other influences. Dropouts in school result from emotional, financial, and intellectual factors. Because so many factors can influence any of these situations, we must be careful not to make the wrong connections or to attribute undue influence to one cause.

REASONING FROM SIGN

With reasoning from sign, you see a visible indicator—or physical manifestation—of a condition. You try to figure out what the sign means. Does someone with a cough, high fever, and headache have the flu? Possibly. You may see bruises, fractures, and bumps in a child. Has the child been abused? Maybe. You see a fellow student with expensive designer clothing. Does the person have money? Perhaps. But reasoning from sign can be problematic. The person with the previously named symptoms may or may not have the flu. He may have pneumonia or other serious lung condition. The child with bumps, bruises, and fractures may be abused or may be accident prone. The student with designer clothes may have money or may invest all of his income from a part-time job in his clothing budget. Grey hair is usually a sign of aging; but Taylor Hicks from *American Idol* has grey hair, and he is under thirty years of age.

> **Reasoning from sign**
> Taking a visible indicator and constructing an argument that explains it

An example of flawed *reasoning from sign* is the following. I have a headache. Since headaches can be a sign of encephalitis, I conclude that I have encephalitis. In fact, headaches are a sign of many different illnesses. The least common is encephalitis. So I may or may not have encephalitis. The conclusion is not supportable on the basis of such limited information. It has been said that first-year medical students develop every illness that they study—at least, according to their own first diagnosis! Once they have learned the symptoms of certain serious and rare diseases, they tend to interpret the appearance of similar symptoms in themselves as manifestations of these dread diseases. Yet, in more cases than not, the symptoms are indicators of much less serious conditions. In other words, the medical students engage in fallacious reasoning from sign.

ANALOGICAL REASONING

Analogical reasoning
Taking the characteristics of one thing and applying them to another

When you use analogical reasoning, you extrapolate the characteristics of one situation to a second situation. You infer that what is true for one situation also is true for the second situation. Let us say that you are good at skateboarding, and you have decided to try your skills at snowboarding. You assume that the two situations are analogous—that your skills in skateboarding will transfer to snowboarding. But traveling downhill on a snowboard may be quite different from skateboarding on city sidewalks. In argumentation, you attempt to convince the audience that two cases share enough similarities that the model is transferable between cases.

The difficulty, of course, with reasoning from parallel cases derives from the fact the characteristics or demands of the two situations may be more dissimilar than similar. My husband taught for a time at a West African university. He said that, on one occasion, agricultural experts from a midwestern U.S. university arrived in the region with high ambitions of establishing agricultural systems similar to those in the United States. One of their first experiments involved asking the natives to cut down the tropical forest and to plant rice in the areas that had been cleared. Although the Africans looked a bit confused at this advice, they complied with the request of the "experts." They chopped down the tropical wood and planted the fields with rice. Then the monsoon season arrived; and all of the top soil from the cleared land washed away—top soil that had taken centuries to accumulate. The rice went with the top soil. Too late, the scientists realized their mistake. In fact, the Africans had been growing crops among the trees for centuries. They knew that the trees held the soil in place. The newcomers had assumed that their models would work equally well in Africa, but they relied on a false analogy. The price of their learning was high for the African community.

Conclusion

Looking back to the CCM model, the focus in this chapter has been upon the message. We have examined how the speaker achieves persuasive affect through the use of credibility, emotional, and logical appeals.

Questions for Discussion

1. In analyzing your own source credibility, what do you consider to be your strengths and weaknesses as a speaker? Do you think that your credibility would vary from topic to topic? Give examples to illustrate this point.

2. Do you think that male and female speakers face different challenges when building their credibility? Are audience expectations the same for men and women?

3. How can a speaker with initial low credibility improve her credibility?

4. Why does war produce some of our greatest speeches and novels? Do you think that the kind of rhetoric produced during war would be deemed as overly emotional in times of peace?

5. What are some examples of jargon from various professions (law, medicine, academia, government, and other)? Does such language ever serve a useful purpose? Is it ever appropriate?

Outline

ARGUING ELOQUENTLY AND CONVINCINGLY

Speech to Convince, Stimulate, or Actuate

Learning Objectives

To learn how to prepare and present a persuasive speech, including:

· Selecting a topic

· Identifying a tentative position statement and defining a general purpose and desired outcome

· Researching and identifying levels of audience knowledge and attitudes

· Choosing an organizational pattern

· Developing and adapting materials to your audience

· Using evocative language to express your ideas

· Speaking from memory or note cards with memorable passages

· Responding to questions from your audience

Speaking to convince

Attempting to persuade an audience to *change* a point of view

Speaking to stimulate

Attempting to *reinforce* the beliefs and attitudes of an audience

Speaking to actuate

Attempting to get an audience to *act* on their beliefs

The persuader may have three potential purposes: to *convince* (change existing attitudes or effect a shift in position), to *stimulate* (reinforce existing attitudes or stances), or to *actuate* (move audience members to act on their beliefs or to eliminate an unwanted behavior). In this chapter, we will discuss how to prepare a persuasive speech that seeks to convince, stimulate, or actuate. That process involves (1) selecting a topic, (2) writing a tentative position statement, (3) translating your belief into a thesis statement, (4) defining a general purpose, (5) researching and identifying levels of audience knowledge and attitudes toward your position, (6) deciding upon a desired outcome, (7) choosing an organizational pattern, (8) writing an introduction, (9) developing the body of your speech, (10) researching and adapting to your audience, (11) writing transitions and internal summaries, (12) choosing evocative language, (13) writing your conclusion, (14) memorizing and delivering your speech, and (15) responding to questions at the conclusion of your speech.

Please note that a final genre of persuasive speaking—the speech to inspire—is discussed with special occasion speeches (Chapter Eleven), since most speeches of this variety tend to be sermonlike discourses. Speeches to inspire, which fit broadly under the heading of speeches to stimulate, encourage people to act on their beliefs; however, they utilize a format quite different from the ones discussed in this chapter.

Step 1: Selecting Your Topic

Your initial task is to select a topic that is meaningful to you *and* relevant to your audience. To achieve this goal, think about causes that matter to you, policies and laws that you would like to change, or policies and laws that may be at risk. Also consider the relevance of the topic for your audience. Persuasive discourse aims to *change* or *reinforce* existing attitudes and practices. In your deliberations, take ethical considerations into account.

THINK ABOUT CAUSES THAT MATTER TO YOU

Cause

A goal or principle to which one is committed

Advocacy

Support or argument for a cause

In selecting a topic, think about causes that matter to you. A *cause* is a goal, principle, or practice to which you are strongly committed. You might seek to convince listeners, for example, that vegetarianism will save the environment, that the arts should receive greater funding, or that students should use public transportation in preference to automobiles. Thinking in terms of political and social activism, you arrive at causes that matter to large numbers of people. Tree-huggers would say that their cause is environmental sustainability. People for the Ethical Treatment of Animals (PETA) argue for animal rights. Victims of Violence stand for the rights of victims of violent crime. Other social and political activists have causes that relate to the rights of women, men, grandparents, children, gays and lesbians, and various minority groups. Since most causes find their voice in advocacy groups, use key words such as *advocacy* to search causes on the Internet.

Values such as the following, identified by Milton Rokeach, are at the heart of causes: *achievement, activity, competence, compassion, generosity, obedience, freedom, imagination, independence, intelligence, logic and intuition, a comfortable life, honesty, a world at peace, a world of beauty, responsibility, sociality,* and *family orientation*.[1] Other researchers have added *individualism, patriotism, progressiveness, optimism,* and *efficiency* to the list. Many persuasive speeches address questions that relate to values.

THINK ABOUT POLICIES OR LAWS THAT MAY BE AT RISK

Policies and laws put values into action. They emerge from decisions made by governments (federal, state, municipal), schools, businesses, sports and recreational organizations, fraternities and sororities, churches, the courts, and other organized groups. Whereas policies emerge from administrative decisions, laws result from legal decisions. Policies are often formalized and usually recorded in print; that is, they appear in a document (legislative acts, charters, and operating rules of organizations). At other times, they are unwritten, but everyone knows that the rule or regulation exists. Laws are always formalized, emerging from the legal structures of governments and subject to interpretation by courts in democratic societies.

A persuasive speech can address policies, laws, or practices that are at risk of being discontinued or eliminated. A university, for example, may be considering whether to eliminate its program in classical studies or to rezone a student parking area. A government may be contemplating changes to family law. Opposition to a change in any one of these policies could become the subject of a persuasive speech in which you argue to support the *status quo*.

THINK ABOUT POLICIES OR LAWS YOU WOULD LIKE TO CHANGE

At other times, persuasive speakers disagree with a policy decision or law. They may call for stiffer penalties for white collar crime or lighter sentences for youth offenders. They may demand the abolition of hazing practices in military academies, bonfires on university campuses, or drinking competitions in fraternities. They may object to "no-fly" lists or strip searches at airports or the use of animals in cosmetic research.

Imagine that someone said to you, "You have the power to change any policies or laws with which you disagree. Which ones would you change?" What would you say? I would say, "I do not believe that governments should allow tobacco companies to operate. I do not believe that gambling should be legalized. I believe that governments should place stronger restrictions on violent or pornographic content on the Internet." If I were a political or social activist, several of these would be my causes; and I would argue to change or strengthen the laws that allow these policies and practices to continue. Of course, not everyone would agree with me. Some people would say, "No, I believe that smoking is a personal choice." "I enjoy gambling; I don't agree that we should ban it." "No, we should not regulate content on the Internet; freedom of expression is more important." So issues would arise from my choices, and values would be at the foundation of both of our arguments.

Values reside in policy questions, just as they are at the center of causes in general. When the military argues its case for increased funding, it says that troops will be at risk if the government does not allocate the necessary funds (*sanctity of human life*). The millitary says that troops are fighting to secure a *world at peace*. The military invokes the values of *compassion* and *humanitarianism* when it says that it will secure the rights of others against authoritarian and despotic regimes. Advocates for increased funding of the military also call upon the value of *patriotism*. See Keep in Mind for additional examples of topics that give birth to issues.

Sometimes people accept the basic concept of a policy or law but disagree on the definition of terms. They may support tax credits for families, for instance, but disagree on the definition of *family*. They may disallow the possibility for brothers and sisters, overage children, aunts and uncles, or same-sex partners to participate in pension and other benefits, saying that they are not family in the legal sense. The late Pope John Paul II argued that the term *spouse* should not include a same-sex partner and that the term *marriage* should refer only to the union of a man and woman. A persuader may argue for a change in how we define a term or, alternatively, for the preservation of a definition that may be at risk.

In other cases, people may agree with the *intent* of legislation or policies but disagree with how governments or other organizations interpret, implement, or enforce the policies. They may agree, for example, that refugees should be allowed to enter the country but disagree on implementation of the legislation, believing immigration authorities to be too lenient or too strict in their interpretation of the law. Alternatively, they may disagree with criteria set in place to determine who qualifies for refugee status.

Keep in Mind

Sample Topics for Persuasive Speeches

Legalized gambling

Costs of health care

Proliferation of street gangs

Motorcycle gangs

Cosmetic surgery

Panhandling

Violence in schools

Addiction to video games

Climate change/global warming

Establishment of government spy agencies

Surveillance practices by the government

Child trafficking

Poverty

Custody laws

Risks of inoculations

"Super bugs" (antibiotic-resistant bacteria)

Biological terrorism

Polluted water

Land rights for Natives

The role of the courts in deciding laws

Street racing

Eating disorders (anorexia, bulimia, obesity)

Consumption as a way of life

Medical errors

Protection of animals

Endangered species

Exotic pets

Sexually transmitted diseases (STDs)

Overpopulation

Criminalization of drugs

Cost of being a drug "mule"

Medical uses of marijuana

Violent sports

Spousal violence

Gun control

Suicide rates among undercover police

Cost of wars (human, financial)

Costs of insurance (car, house, etc.)

Violence on the Internet

By-products of video games

Male-female roles in society

Costs of legal suits

Insurance fraud

Identity theft

Internet scams

White collar crime

Dangerous pets

Disposal of hazardous wastes

The costs of a plastic society

Increasing problem of allergies

Costs of aging society

Equity in health care for the elderly

Giving official status to illegal immigrants

Costs of conformity/loss of individuality

Congested highways

Pollution in cities

Risks associated with travel abroad

Risks associated with domestic travel

Use of stun guns in law enforcement

Full-time student, full-time employee

Risks associated with amusement parks

Costs of partying in universities

Children who kill their parents

Date rape

Internet predators

Airline safety

Racial profiling

Employment practices

Sexual harassment

Branding of society/designer society

Polygamy

Suicide in teenage populations

THINK ABOUT CONTROVERSIAL CLAIMS YOU WOULD DEFEND OR DISPUTE

Many people and groups make claims that cannot be definitively proved. Because the claims have not been proved, they are subject to controversy. Scientists speculate, for example, that the virus associated with AIDS originated in the rainforests. A number of communication scholars claim an association between violence on television and criminal behavior. Members of groups interested in UFOs claim that aliens visit our planet on a regular basis. You may choose to speak in defense of—or against—one of these controversial claims. In other words, you may address a *question of fact* in your persuasive discourse.

TAKE ETHICAL CONSIDERATIONS INTO ACCOUNT

On some occasions, you may want to reconsider your choice of topics for ethical reasons. Imagine that you have decided to deliver a speech supporting a French law, passed in 2004, that bans the presence of religious symbols in schools. Banned

symbols include Christian crucifixes, Jewish skull caps, and, most contentiously, Muslim headscarves. At the time that you plan to deliver your speech, extremists are holding two French hostages and demanding that France rescind its law. The situation is tense and emotional, and the lives of two individuals are at stake in the debate. You learn that some students have expressed anger toward your position statement. Views appear to be polarized along religious lines. Some do not believe that you should use classroom time to promote a point of view that trespasses upon their religious convictions. In a case such as this one, you might consider selecting another topic. Where levels of hostility are too strong and latitudes of rejection are too large, you must ask yourself whether you can accomplish any purpose in a short speech delivered to a captive audience.

Step 2: Framing a Tentative Position Statement

After choosing a topic for your speech, you should frame a tentative position statement—your position on the question on which you have chosen to speak. You could say, for example, *I believe that governments should do more to protect the rainforests. I believe that large-scale consumption of beef is destroying our environment. I believe that fashion television contributes to the prevalence of eating disorders. I believe that gambling should be illegal.* Some of these position statements concern policies and laws; others concern values and personal choices.

Tentative position statement
A statement of the argument you intend to make in your speech

Step 3: Translating Your Position Statement into a Thesis Statement

After framing a position statement, you should convert that statement of personal belief into a thesis statement for your speech, such as:

· Governments should pass new laws to protect the rainforests.
· Large-scale consumption of beef is destroying our environment.
· Fashion television contributes to eating disorders such as anorexia and bulimia.
· Gambling destroys families.

Note the conversion from position statement to thesis statement in the following example: [I believe that] video games contribute to violence in society.

Thesis statement
A single declarative sentence that expresses the main point of your speech

Step 4: Researching Your Audience

After framing a thesis statement, research audience *demographics* (e.g., level of education, occupation and income, age, gender, race, ethnicity, and prior experience with the topic), *psychographics* (beliefs, attitudes, and values), *personality* (e.g.,

Demographics
Data about the age, gender, ethnicity, income, education, etc., of an audience

Psychographics
Data about the beliefs, attitudes and values of an audience

open- vs. closed-minded, high or low esteem), and *situation* (e.g., environmental constraints). This information will allow you to generate a profile of your audience and situation, so that you can better meet audience needs and achieve your purposes. As a student in a speech course, you can keep a weekly journal in which you make notes about the interests, abilities, and experiences of your classmates.

Persuasive speakers face audiences with four potential attitudes on any topic: supportive, undecided, apathetic (not caring one way or the other) or hostile. Audiences are at different places on the persuasion continuum. Some are ready to be persuaded. Others have not received the necessary preparation to understand the speech. They may lack information or awareness of the significance of the topic. They may not be able to see how the topic applies to their lives. A final group may be highly resistant. A well-kept journal can give valuable clues to audience attitudes on topics. A second way to learn about audience attitudes is to administer a questionnaire. See Chapter Five for a review of some of these concepts.

Step 5: Defining Your General Purpose

After articulating position and thesis statements and researching audience views on the topic, the speaker defines a general purpose to be achieved in the speech. Informative speaking aims to increase the *knowledge or awareness* of audiences. Persuasive speaking, on the other hand, aims to influence *beliefs*, *attitudes*, and *actions* of audiences. Despite the popularity of a long-standing distinction between informative and persuasive purposes, many believe that changes in awareness, attitudes, and actions tend to occur on a continuum:

> **Speech → Change in awareness → Change in attitude → Change in behavior**

That is, higher levels of awareness are necessary before changes in attitudes or actions can take place.

What does this finding mean for the persuader? *First, the existence of a continuum means that the persuasive speaker will often need to include a strong informative element in the speech.* This informative element typically appears in the problem or need and solution steps. The less informed the audience, the more complex and controversial the issue, the more information will be required to bring about changes in beliefs or attitudes. Attempting to effect changes in audiences with low knowledge levels is unrealistic.

Second, the necessity to move audiences along a continuum means that the speaker will need to be flexible on purposes. Speakers who confront a well-informed audience will have a choice of speech purposes: to reinforce existing attitudes, convince the audience to change attitudes, *or* move the listeners to action. If the audience holds *positive attitudes* toward the position of the speaker, the persuader can choose to reinforce those attitudes or encourage the audience to act on their beliefs. If the audience is *relatively neutral* or *noncommitted*, the persuader may aim to shift their anchor positions in the direction of acceptance. If the audience is *hostile* to the position advocated, the speaker may want to convince audience members to change their opinions. Realistically, however, the speaker should expect little change with hostile listeners. At best, the speaker can hope to move the hostile person closer to the noncommitment zone. Until attitudes move into the zone of acceptance, the speaker will be unable to effect shifts in behavior. Aiming for behavior change in this situation is unrealistic.

Step 6: Framing a Desired Outcome

To frame a desired outcome, change the wording of your position statement to reflect what you would like your audience to believe or to do at the conclusion of your speech. Examples include: *I want my audience to understand why charity organizations should not spend their money on publicity targeted at existing donors. I want the audience to agree that governments should ban gambling. I want my audience to send letters to their congressional representatives, demanding better protection of children against Internet predators. I want the audience to demand that states ban the dumping of toxic wastes in populated areas.* These outcome statements will embody the general speech purposes, aimed at informing, convincing, or moving audiences to action. They will, however, become more specific in nature, reflecting the content of the speech.

Latitudes of acceptance
When the listener's views are likely to be aligned with the speaker

A number of influences mediate the ability of persuaders to achieve their desired outcomes. As discussed earlier, listeners fall at different places on the persuasion continuum. They also have different latitudes of acceptance, hold different beliefs and values, and have personality characteristics that influence their willingness to learn, change their attitudes, and adopt new behaviors. As mentioned in Chapter Five, you are unlikely to convince pig farmers to become vegetarians. Their latitude of rejection is too large. You may aim, however, for some more realistic outcome, such as a commitment to treating their animals well.

Latitudes of rejection
When the listener's views are likely to be opposed to those of the speaker

A need for flexibility in framing desired outcomes derives from an understanding of audience composition and psychology. The statement of desired outcomes should reflect the results of audience research—an identification of how much audience members know about a topic, their opinions on the topic, the values that could influence the persuasion process, and personality characteristics of the audience. Setting and other environmental influences can also affect outcomes.

Step 7: Matching Purposes and Audiences with Organizational Patterns

Persuasive speeches to stimulate or convince can follow one of several organizational schemes: problem and solution, reflective thinking, causal, criteria-satisfaction, comparative advantages, or claim. Speeches to actuate should follow Monroe's motivated sequence.

CHOICES OF ORGANIZATIONAL PATTERN

Problem speech
A speech that describes a condition needing change

Solution speech
A speech that offers answers to a perceived need

Problem-solution speech
A speech that explores a problem and then offers a solution

Here we will consider the problem and solution, reflective thinking, causal, criteria-satisfaction, comparative advantages, claim and motivated sequence patterns.

Problem and Solution Patterns

A *problem* speech limits itself to the description of a condition requiring change—in other words, a perceived need. A *solution* speech offers answers to perceived need(s). A *problem and solution* speech, on the other hand, both explores the problem confronted by a group *and* proposes a viable solution to the problem. The problem section of a speech on obesity could include the nature of obesity, its causes, and its effects. If included, the solution step could describe how the solution will alleviate or eliminate the problem, refer to the practicality of the solution, and identify the benefits of adopting the solution. As in Figure 10.1, some speeches substitute an action step for the benefits step.

I. *Introduction:* A steady increase in the numbers of overweight and obese Americans has been occurring in men and women of all age groups.

    A. Affected populations include non-Hispanic whites, non-Hispanic blacks, and Mexican Americans.

    B. According to the *Journal of the American Medical Association*, two out of three Americans are overweight.

    C. One out of three Americans is obese.

Figure 10.1 Problem and Solution Pattern of Organization

II.   *Nature of the problem:* Obesity causes serious health risks to individuals.

    A.   People who are obese have a high risk of cardiovascular disease.

    B.   Obese people are at higher risk of diabetes.

    C.   Obese people have more back, hip, and foot problems as a result of the strain that obesity places on the body; they also have more varicose veins.

    D.   Obese people have a greater chance of getting colon or breast cancer.

III. *Causes of the problem:* The causes of obesity are numerous.

    A.   People are overeating.

    B.   People are eating too much fast food.

    C.   People are not exercising.

IV.   *Effects:* Obesity has serious implications for individuals, our health care system, and our social fabric.

    A.   People are dying.

    B.   The health care system is faltering under the burden imposed by people in poor health as a result of obesity.

    C.   The military does not have an adequate pool of people from which to draw its recruits.

    D.   Airlines are concerned about tragedies resulting from excessive weight in planes, and transportation providers in general have to provide special accommodations for the growing number of overweight clients.

    E.   Young people who are obese sometimes suffer poor self-image.

V.   *Solution:* Since the problem is complex, any solution must be multifaceted.

    A.   Governments need to regulate the fast-food industry.

    B.   Schools need to include mandatory exercise programs in their curricula.

    C.   Schools should remove candy and soft drink machines from their premises.

    D.   Schools should not allow advertisements for fast foods in bathrooms, halls, or cafeterias.

    E.   Restaurants should serve smaller portions and eliminate "all-you-can-eat" buffets.

    F.   Health services and clinics need to make educational materials on healthy lifestyles readily available to the public.

    G.   Advertisers should not place fast-food commercials in proximity to children's TV programs.

VI.   *Benefits:* The benefits of solving the problem are obvious.

    A.   People will live longer, healthier lives.

    B.   The costs of health care and other social services will decrease.

    C.   The cost of restaurant meals will decrease if owners serve smaller portions.

    D.   Our military system will have a larger pool of fit applicants.

    E.   Young people will have a better self-image.

VII. *Practicality of the solution:* The solution makes sense because no one group in society will bear all of the costs or responsibility for alleviating the problem.

Figure 10.1—cont'd

The problem and solution pattern can be used with an audience of any disposition. The quality of the supporting evidence will doubtless determine the effectiveness of this pattern with undecided audiences. When facing disinterested audiences, a speaker may want to include a discussion of the benefits in order to rouse the audience from a state of apathy. As noted earlier, not all problem speeches include solution or benefit steps. Alternatively, a speaker may present only a brief needs step and focus *almost exclusively* on solutions.

Reflective Thinking Pattern

Reflective-thinking pattern
A five-step sequence that is a variation on the problem-solution speech

Philosopher John Dewey developed a variation on the problem and solution pattern of organization: the *reflective thinking* pattern.[2] This organizational pattern follows a five-step sequence: defining the problem, analyzing the problem, establishing criteria for a solution, identifying possible solutions, and selecting the best solution based on the criteria. Using the earlier example of obesity, the outline could look like Figure 10.2.

I. *Introduction:* A steady increase in the numbers of overweight and obese Americans has been occurring in men and women of all age groups.

   A. The problem includes non-Hispanic whites, non-Hispanic blacks, and Mexican Americans.

   B. According to the *Journal of the American Medical Association*, two out of three Americans are overweight.

   C. One out of three Americans is obese.

II. *Definition of the problem:* Obesity, a condition that results from an excess number of fat cells in the body, causes serious health risks to individuals.

   A. People who are obese have a high risk of cardiovascular disease.

   B. Obese people are at higher risk of diabetes.

   C. Obese people have more back, hip, and foot problems as a result of the strain that obesity places on the body; they also have more varicose veins.

   D. Obese people have a greater chance of getting colon or breast cancer.

III. *Nature of the problem:* The problem results from the actions of individuals, advertisers, institutions, and the food industry.

   A. The lifestyles of individuals contribute to the problem.

      1. Overeating adds billions of fat cells to the body.

      2. A diet of fast food also contributes to the fat cell count.

      3. People are not exercising, which is one way to keep the fat cell count in check.

   B. The advertising industry contributes to the problem.

      1. Advertisers often promote unhealthy food choices.

      2. Advertisers place their commercials at times in the evening when people should not be eating carbohydrates and sweets.

      3. Advertisers put promotional materials in schools.

Figure 10.2 Reflective Thinking Pattern of Organization

C.   Institutions contribute to the problem.

    1.   Schools allow the placement of soft drink, candy, and other vending machines on their premises.

    2.   Governments have done little to regulate the advertising or fast-food industries.

D.   The fast-food industry and restaurants contribute to the problem.

    1.   Hamburger, pizza, and other fast-food chains offer too much volume and too few healthy choices.

    2.   Some restaurants economize by offering fries with every meal.

IV.   *Criteria for solution:* Any solution must meet the following criteria.

A.   The solutions must not put the person's health at risk.

B.   The solutions must be sustainable over time.

C.   The solutions must be practical in terms of cost.

D.   The solutions must be realistic in terms of implementation.

V.   *Possible solutions:* Below are possible solutions; some are better than others.

A.   Individuals with long-term and serious problems of obesity may want to seek medical help with reducing the number of fat cells.

    1.   Medications are available.

    2.   Surgery is an option for some people.

B.   Advertisers should adopt self-regulatory policies.

    1.   Agencies should advise their clients to place ads for high carbohydrate foods in daytime and early evening hours.

    2.   Advertisers should adopt ethical guidelines related to fast-food clients.

C.   Parent and other advocacy groups should insist that schools prohibit advertisements and vending machines, promote healthy food in cafeterias, and build mandatory exercise programs into their curricula.

    1.   Advocates for healthy eating should insist that local candidates build this issue into their platforms.

    2.   Advocates should seek to gain representation on school boards.

D.   Governments should regulate the advertisement and fast-food industries.

    1.   Federal departments of agriculture and health should get involved.

    2.   States should adopt new regulatory policies.

    3.   Governments should sponsor campaigns for healthy eating and exercise.

E.   Consumer groups should promote and monitor the fast-food and restaurant industries.

    1.   Consumer groups should approach local restaurants and fast-food outlets to request help with solving the problem.

    2.   Consumer groups should establish checklists and monitor the situation.

    3.   Local food consumer groups should publicize the results of their efforts and make recommendations to youth on where to eat.

    4.   Consumer groups should urge advertisers to educate their clients on the negative impact of some choices.   *(Continued)*

Figure 10.2—cont'd

VI. *Best solution:* The following solution will meet the criteria of being safe, sustainable over time, practical, and realistic.

A. Individuals should consult with their doctors about appropriate medical and exercise options.

B. Parent groups should become more active in promoting healthy foods in cafeterias, insisting on the removal of vending machines and urging school boards to include mandatory exercise programs.

C. Governments should sponsor campaigns for healthy eating, just as they sponsor antitobacco campaigns.

D. Local consumer groups should monitor progress on the part of local restaurants, schools, and advertisers; and on that basis, they should make recommendations to city councils and others with regulatory powers.

Figure 10.2—cont'd

Like the problem and solution model, the reflective thinking model applies to most audiences. While no one can guarantee a positive response from a hostile audience, this organizational scheme may be more effective than others in reaching well-educated listeners. If the speaker also provides sound supporting evidence, she may have some opportunity to effect change of a limited nature, even with those who are fundamentally opposed to her position.

Causal Pattern

Causal pattern
The linking of causes and effects

Speeches that employ *causal* patterns of organization are concerned with linking causes and effects. Like the problem and solution and reflective thinking models, this organizational pattern looks at problems. The causal pattern does not, however, concern itself with solutions—only with looking at the relationship between the causes of problems and their resulting effects on people, institutions, and systems. Perhaps the speaker sees an *effect* or manifestation of a problem in society, such as violence, increasing suicide rates among teenagers, or growing numbers of homeless people. Then she asks the question "Why?" *Why* do we have violence in society? *What explains* the increases in suicide rates among young people? *Why* do we have so many homeless people?

In the case of a speech on homelessness, the speaker could begin with *effects* such as growing numbers of people on the streets of large urban centers, deaths from harsh cold winters, and rootless families. Next he talks about the causes of homelessness such as underfunding, lack of subsidized housing, legislation that limits the stay of mental patients in institutions, and the overcrowded conditions in psychiatric facilities. These overcrowded conditions push people onto the streets before they are able to take care of themselves. Alternatively, a speech on homelessness could begin by talking about the *causes* of homelessness, followed by the *effects*. A speech on obesity, which employed a causal pattern, could concentrate on parts III and IV of the problem and solution outline that appears in Figure 10.1.

Persuasive speakers employ causal patterns with audiences who question the basic premises of a position—people who do not accept the causal relationships in an issue. Some people, for example, attribute homelessness to lack of motivation on the part of homeless people. They may not know about the large numbers of homeless people with mental problems. They may not understand the relationship between unemployment and homelessness. Discourse that employs causal patterns is well suited to less informed, skeptical, and hostile audiences, who need to understand and be convinced of the source of problems before they will take action.

Comparative Advantages

Whereas the causal pattern focuses on the problem, the *comparative advantages* pattern focuses on the solution. This model is appropriate in situations where most audience members would agree that a problem exists. They would not, however, necessarily agree on the best solution. For this reason, speeches that employ the comparative advantages pattern of organization concentrate on solutions and make only passing reference to the problem. With this model, the speaker looks at the advantages of one solution over the others, as in Figure 10.3.

Comparative advantages pattern
Focusing on the advantages of one solution over another one

Criteria-Satisfaction

Like the comparative advantages model, the criteria-satisfaction pattern of organization focuses on solutions and makes only passing reference to problems. With this model, the speaker examines a solution against a set of criteria. You will recall that the reflective thinking model also includes a criteria-satisfaction component.

Criteria-satisfaction pattern
Relating the solution to a set of standards

I.   The problem manifests itself in a steady increase in the numbers of overweight and obese Americans.

   A.   The problem occurs in men and women of all age groups.

   B.   Affected populations include non-Hispanic whites, non-Hispanic blacks, and Mexican Americans.

   C.   According to the *Journal of the American Medical Association*, two out of three Americans are overweight.

   D.   One out of three Americans is obese.

II. Medical solutions are not the answer to obesity.

   A.   Medical solutions are costly.

   B.   Medical solutions pose health risks to some individuals.

   C.   Medical solutions focus on the symptoms rather than the underlying causes.

III. Lifestyle changes are a better answer to the problem of obesity.

   A.   The results are long-term.

   B.   Lifestyle changes carry no risks, only benefits.

   C.   Lifestyle changes get at the root of the problem, which may be psychological as much as physical.

Figure 10.3 Comparative Advantages Pattern of Organization

The comparative advantages and criteria-satisfaction models are appropriate patterns to use with well-informed audiences who understand the problem but disagree on solutions. While listeners may not need to be convinced that a problem exists, they may hold various views on solutions. See Figure 10.4.

Claims

Claims
Assertions

Alternatively, the speaker may choose to argue a series of *claims*, which she supports with reasoning and evidence. The organizational format would be as follows: attention, claims, and supporting material (logical, credibility, and emotional appeals). Alternatively, the speaker may counter the claims of another party. In the last scenario, the speaker follows the articulation of claims with counterclaims and supporting material. See Figure 10.5.

Motivated Sequence

Motivated sequence
From communication scholar Alan Monroe, five steps of a speech including attention, need, satisfaction, visualization, and action

The *motivated sequence*, developed in the 1930s by Alan H. Monroe, goes beyond the problem and solution speech in its inclusion of visualization and action steps.[3]

I.   Offer a brief introduction to the problem.
   A.   A steady increase in the numbers of overweight and obese Americans has been occurring in men and women of all age groups.
   B.   The problem includes non-Hispanic whites, non-Hispanic blacks, and Mexican Americans.
   D.   According to the *Journal of the American Medical Association*, two out of three Americans are overweight.
   C.   One out of three Americans is obese.
II. Set criteria for solutions to solve the problem of obesity.
   A.   The solutions must not put the person's health at risk.
   B.   The solutions must be sustainable over time.
   C.   The solutions must be practical in terms of cost.
   D.   The solutions must be realistic in terms of implementation.
III. Evaluate solutions against criteria; propose lifestyle changes as optimum solution to the problem of obesity.
   A.   Lifestyle changes do not put the person's health at risk.
   B.   By definition, lifestyle changes involve the long term.
   C.   Individuals can tailor their diets and exercise regimes to their budgets.
   D.   Individuals control what happens; they do not have to depend on others to change laws or policies.

Figure 10.4 Criteria-Satisfaction Pattern of Organization

I.   Get the attention of the audience.

   A.   Mention the opening of the first school for obese high school students.

   B.   Ask for a definition of obesity.

   C.   Introduce position that the problem of obesity is overstated.

   D.   Preview four common claims about obesity.

II. Statistics related to deaths from obesity are overstated. (response to claim #1)

   A.   The *New England Journal of Medicine* (January 1998) says that data supporting a link between weight and mortality is weak.

   B.   So many factors interact in the case of premature deaths that it is impossible to contribute the deaths to any one cause.

   C.   A study reported in the *Gerontologist* says that the risks of dying from obesity have been exaggerated fifteen-fold.

   D.   The Centers for Disease Control says that the problem has been overstated.

III. Some measures of obesity are flawed. (response to claim #2)

   A.   The body mass index (BMI) is flawed because it fails to distinguish between weight from body fat and weight from muscle.

   B.   Using body mass index, many fit athletes and weight lifters would fall into overweight categories.

IV. Obesity does not cost Americans $117 billion each year. (response to claim #3)

   A.   Only one source supports this figure: the *Obesity Research Journal*.

   B.   Reliance on the wrong body mass index number added ten million Americans who should not be included in the total.

   C.   The data is inconclusive.

V.   Older Americans are no more likely than young Americans to die from obesity. (response to claim #4)

   A.   A study by the *Gerontologist* found that obese seniors are less likely than nonobese seniors to die prematurely.

   B.   Since older Americans often die from a combination of factors, one cannot attribute their deaths to any one cause.

VI. Conclude with the observation that obesity is not as serious a problem as the pharmaceutical industry, lawyers, and animal rights groups would have us believe.

Source: This information came from websites such as The Heartland Institute (http://www
.heartland.org/Article.cfm?artId=15400) and The Center for Consumer Freedom (http://www
.consumerfreedom.com/news_detail.cfm/headline/2863). David Martosko is the author of
the first article, which appeared in *Health Care News*, August 1, 2004. The article is based on
Martosko's testimony to the Food and Drug Administration on October 23, 2003.

Figure 10.5 Claims Pattern of Organization

The motivated sequence pattern includes *attention, need, satisfaction, visualization,* and *action* steps.

The *attention* step captures the interest of the audience. The *need* step defines the problem, discussing weaknesses or risks in the present situation. The *satisfaction* step proposes a solution and describes how the solution will meet the need. To this point, the speech is like the problem and solution speech, which includes introduction, problem, and solution phases. The next two steps, however, extend the problem and solution model. The *visualization* step asks the audience to imagine a future with or without the preferred solution. The speaker uses vivid (but not unrealistic) language to describe this possible future. Some speeches include positive and negative visualization steps—painting a future with the preferred solution and a second future without the preferred solution. Others employ one or the other. The following example illustrates a negative visualization:

> But what will happen if we do nothing, if the situation persists? Imagine the following scenario, an alternative future. You walk down the streets of your town. Two out of three pedestrians are seriously overweight, and the bicycle paths are almost deserted. You see fewer people over sixty. A friend notes that many of his older acquaintances have died from heart attacks, strokes, and diabetes—conditions aggravated by their weight problems. You try to get an appointment with a doctor, but you learn that no one can see you for months. The health system is overloaded. There are fewer sports teams, fewer athletes to represent the country in Olympic competitions, and fewer people who are fit for military service.

In the *action* step, the speaker summarizes the main points of the speech and appeals to the audience to take action. She offers specific, concrete suggestions. Sometimes the speaker also states personal intent to take action and challenges the audience to do the same. The speaker may say, for example: "In the last five minutes, I have discussed the serious nature of the shortage of blood in our community. When I leave this class, I intend to go to the on-campus blood clinic to give my blood. If any of you are willing to join me, I will be pleased to offer you a ride."

Theories related to social learning suggest that messages should specify the exact nature of the behaviors expected from audiences, especially in fear-arousing situations.[4] They also say that audiences are most likely to act if communicators make suggestions that they can follow in the near future. In other words, the speaker should suggest actions that listeners can perform in the days and weeks immediately following the speech. Persuaders should also encourage people to find a visible means to show their commitment to these behaviors—wearing a button or making a speech to support the new behaviors.[5] If a persuader fails to specify actions, the audience will usually do nothing.

Figure 10.6 illustrates the development of a speech using the motivated sequence. Please note that, in practice, the attention-getting step for all speeches (problem and solution, reflective thinking, causal, motivated sequence, and others) is only one part of a larger introduction, which includes statements of position, purpose, reason to listen, credibility, and orientation or structural progression.

The motivated sequence works well with topics where the audience is not polarized with passionate feelings on the subject. The existence of an action step implies that the speaker can realistically hope for action on the issue. The position of

---

Attention step
Capturing the interest of the audience

Need step
Definition of a problem

Satisfaction step
Presentation of a solution that speaks to need

Visualization step
When the audience is asked to imagine the future with or without the satisfaction of the need

Action step
An appeal to the audience to do something specific

I. *Attention:* A steady increase in the numbers of overweight and obese Americans has been occurring in men and women of all age groups.

    A. Affected populations include non-Hispanic whites, non-Hispanic blacks, and Mexican Americans.

    B. According to the *Journal of the American Medical Association*, two out of three Americans are overweight.

    C. One out of three Americans is obese.

II. *Need:* Obesity is creating serious health problems for Canadians.

    A. People who are obese have a high risk of cardiovascular disease.

    B. People who are obese are at higher risk of diabetes.

    C. Obese people have more back, hip, and foot problems as a result of the strain that obesity places on the body; they also have more varicose veins.

    D. People who are obese have a greater chance of getting colon or breast cancer.

III. *Satisfaction:* Solutions require partnerships among all levels of government, schools, parents, the restaurant industry, advertising firms, and individuals.

    A. Governments need to regulate the fast-food industry.

    B. Schools must include mandatory exercise programs in their curriculum.

    C. Schools should remove candy and soft drink machines from their premises.

    D. Schools should not allow advertisements for fast foods in bathrooms, halls, and cafeterias.

    E. Restaurants should serve smaller portions and eliminate "all-you-can-eat" buffets.

    F. Health services and clinics need to make educational materials on healthy lifestyles readily available to the public.

    G. Advertisers should not schedule fast-food commercials in association with TV programs for children.

IV. *Visualization (positive):* Imagine a future in which we return to the past; visualize the return of a time when . . .

    A. Young and old alike lead active lives.

    B. Seniors are able to remain in their own homes for most of their lives, since they are healthy and fit.

    C. School cafeterias offer a healthy array of foods instead of providing vending machines.

    D. School hallways showcase the artwork of students and teachers instead of the advertisements of the jean companies.

    E. Families and communities get together on the weekends for picnics, swimming, and outdoor activities that require active engagement.

    F. Our military has a large pool of fit applicants and recruits.

    G. Our health care system is able to channel funds to treat those most in need.

V. *Visualization (negative):* But what will happen if we do nothing, if the situation persists? Imagine an alternative future without my solution.

    A. Four out of five Americans are seriously overweight.

    B. The waiting list for hip replacements is five years.   *(Continued)*

Figure 10.6 Motivated Sequence Pattern of Organization

C. You see fewer people over sixty on the streets because many have died from heart attacks, strokes, and diabetes—conditions aggravated by their weight.

D. Getting an appointment with a doctor requires months of waiting because the health care system is seriously overtaxed.

E. There are fewer sports teams, fewer athletes to represent our country in Olympic competitions, and fewer people who are fit for military service.

VI. *Action:* The solutions rest with you.

A. Do not give business to restaurants that offer only unhealthy options.

B. Tell the managers of restaurants how you feel about their menus when asked to fill out comment cards.

C. Demand that school boards enact new policies; attend local meetings and make your views known.

D. Protest the presence of vending machines and advertisements in schools.

E. Run for office on school boards and press for changes once in office.

F. Ask your local health clinics to distribute materials on the problem; get doctors involved.

G. Petition governments for more research funds to identify the causes of obesity.

H. Ask community centres to sponsor more recreational events for families.

Figure 10.6—cont'd

the speaker, in other words, probably falls within the latitude of acceptance of the audience if he selects this organizational scheme. Perhaps the speaker is asking for more people to sign organ donation cards, vote in elections, or participate in a walkathon for charity. If the speaker can realistically expect both compliance and action to result from the speech, the motivated sequence may be the right organizational choice. The inclusion of need and solution steps, on the other hand, implies that the audience may need to know more about the topic.

CONSIDERATIONS IN DEVELOPING AND ORDERING ARGUMENTS

Within the chosen organizational framework (problem and solution, reflective thinking, causal, criteria-satisfaction, comparative advantages, motivated sequence, or claim), you must make decisions on how to develop and order your arguments.

Presenting the Opponent's Argument

Two-sided argumentation
Presenting both sides of a question

Two-sided argumentation (presenting both sides of a question) is the most ethical form of persuasion. Research also demonstrates that two-sided arguments are more effective than one-sided arguments in gaining audience compliance.[6] That is, the most ethical *and* persuasive messages present both points of view but refute the opposing arguments. If you seem flexible and balanced, audiences are more likely to listen to your arguments. One dimension of speaker credibility is objectivity. You can also improve your credibility in areas such as expertise and trustworthiness when you show a broad understanding of a topic. Well-educated audiences and well-informed audiences, as well as those who disagree with your position, are particularly responsive to messages that acknowledge both points of view before stating a biased perspective.[7] Although one-sided argumentation has been found to be more effective with less educated audiences, this conclusion only applies when listeners are not hostile to your message.

Two-sided argumentation also "inoculates" your audience against the opposing arguments that they may hear in the future.[8] Some legal analysts claim that the prosecuting attorneys in the highly publicized Scott Peterson murder trial presented not only their own case but also the defense case. After presenting the defense arguments, they answered them. In essence, they inoculated the jury against the arguments, preparing them with counterarguments. In the same way, political candidates often warn voters of strategies their opponents might use to damage their credibility.[9]

Reviewing the organizational patterns, we can see that the reflective thinking, motivated sequence, causal, and comparative advantages models allow the possibility for two-sided argumentation. The reflective thinking and motivated sequence patterns, in particular, allow the speaker to present alternative solutions before proposing an optimum solution. The causal pattern allows the speaker to explore various possible causes or effects before reaching conclusions. The comparative advantages model enables the speaker to argue the advantages of one solution over another.

Ordering Arguments

When offering both perspectives, which side should you present first? *Primacy* research suggests that listeners are more likely to remember arguments appearing early in the discourse.[10] Other studies suggest that arguments appearing early in discourse have a greater influence on audience attitudes than those appearing later.[11] Adhering to these principles, you would present your side first, especially when audiences do not know much about the topic or disagree with you. Then you would present and refute the opposing arguments. Since some audience members always leave early, some say that the strongest arguments should appear early in the discourse in order to reach the maximum number of listeners. Although you may present both sides of the argument, you will place more emphasis on your position.[12]

Recency research concludes, on the other hand, that audiences are most likely to recall arguments appearing at the end of speeches. Still others say that it does not matter—that the findings are inconclusive.[13] Some scholars say that the response to questions of order depends upon the *initial attitudes* of audience members (their orientation toward the topic) and the *importance of the topic* to audience members (level of concern that they feel); however, they have been unable to reach agreement on whether the stronger or weaker arguments should come first in the different circumstances.[14]

Primacy research
Research that suggests that the first argument raised is the most easily retained by—or has the greatest influence on—a listener

Recency research
Research that suggests that the last argument raised by the speaker is the most easily retained—or has the greatest influence on—a listener

Whatever their disagreements, most studies concur that arguments appearing in the middle of a discussion have less impact. And the weight of most experts appears to come down more heavily on the side of sooner rather than later for the strongest arguments. Thus, in most circumstances, you would do best to proceed from strongest to weakest argument.

Getting Explicit

Although some studies indicate that speakers achieve maximum opinion change when they draw explicit conclusions for their audience members, others suggest that more educated and better-informed audience members prefer to draw their own conclusions.[15]

Step 8: Writing Your Introduction

After deciding upon an organizational pattern, you should write the introduction to your speech. The following five elements appear in the introduction: attention, purpose, position, reason to listen, and basis of credibility. Sometimes an explicit statement of purpose is not necessary. You should, however, always have the purpose firmly in mind as you write the speech. The other components are mandatory.

REMEMBERING ATTENTION-GETTING STRATEGIES

Whatever organizational scheme you adopt, attention-getting strategies constitute the first step in preparing your introduction. The strategies most often used in persuasive speeches are immediacy; personalization; references to the novel; suspense and shock techniques; activity, drama, and conflict; and quotations. The following discussion will briefly review attention-getting techniques discussed in previous chapters, as well as add a discussion of personalization strategies, often employed in persuasive discourse.

Immediacy Strategies

The persuasive speech is often more dramatic and less conversational than informative speeches. A less chatty tone characterizes the introductions and conclusions of these speeches, and immediacy strategies focus more strongly on establishing the vital nature of the subject matter. References to the *vital* interests of the audience—their health and well-being—characterize most persuasive speeches.[16] The following example illustrates this immediacy strategy:

> Kidnappings for profit are on the rise in many countries. Members of the Chinese community say that they are common in some Asian countries. They are also on the rise in Mexico, a favorite destination for many college students on spring break. The high-profile case of Natalee Holloway, missing in Aruba, reminds us that even

the most tranquil tropical locations can be risky. And this next fact may surprise you. On a list of ten countries that share this problem, the United States ranks in seventh place, ahead of Venezuela, India, and Ecuador! So take care on your next trip, whether hiking in the Himalayas, windsurfing in Cancun, or sunning on the beaches of Miami.

Another immediacy strategy involves asking *questions* of audiences. In the following example, the question is rhetorical, not demanding a visible or vocal response of the listeners:

> Have you ever noticed the skid marks on the highway that runs through Acadia National Park? They usually come in close proximity to signs that warn about moose and deer crossings. Or maybe you haven't noticed the signs either? I never used to notice. The warning signs were invisible to me until one night when our headlights showed a twelve-foot moose standing directly in the path of our fast-moving vehicle. Space and time collapsed, and we were upon the moose before we knew what had happened. At the last minute, we swerved in time to avoid catastrophe—hitting the rear, rather than the side, of the moose. And the next day, when we returned to the scene, we noticed the now familiar remains of tire marks etched into the highway—our tire marks. We also noticed the large warning sign.

For maximum effectiveness, speakers should usually combine questions with some other attention-getting strategy. In this case, the speaker builds action and drama into the story.

Personalization

Another often employed technique in persuasive speaking is *personalization*. When we personalize accounts, we use the experiences of people (real or hypothetical) to humanize the dry facts and statistics. In one highly emotional speech, a student brought a stuffed animal to the front of the classroom. The topic of her speech was suicide among young people, and the stuffed animal was the last treasured gift from a high school friend who had killed himself. The following excerpt from a speech by Sonia Genovesi illustrates how another student used personalization to persuade her audience on the highly controversial issue of abortion:

> Many of you would shrink at the idea of murder, killing a person. But when does one become a person? Is it at conception? Two weeks? Three months? Six months? At birth? *There are things I never saw, and these are the things I miss: her first smile, her first words.* Some would argue that personhood emerges at conception—the time, in their view, when the soul meets the body for the very first time. Others consider that personhood has occurred when a clearly distinctive DNA code appears in the mother's womb, a few hours after conception. Does life begin when the heart starts beating at eighteen days or at three months when the fetus starts to resemble a baby? Or is it simply at the materialization of thought or measured brain wave patterns? *These are the things I never saw, and these are the things I miss: seeing her ride her bike for the first time, consoling her when she scraped her knee.* In the first three months after conception, we can observe the baby sucking his thumb, swimming around in the amniotic fluid, even grasping at the umbilical cord. At two months after conception, if you tickle the baby's upper lip with a hair, it can move its entire body to avoid the stimulation. Is it possible to assume the baby can experience sensation? *These are things I never saw and these are the things I miss: her first day of school, helping her with her homework.*[17]

Personalization
Using the experiences of real or fictitious people to give life to an argument

Instead of using the most common shock techniques, Genovesi spoke of the simple pleasures of being a mother—pleasures that will be missed if a woman gives up the opportunity to experience motherhood. She attempts to evoke an emotional response from the audience by relying upon the strategy of personalization. In the later development of the speech, she talks about how she will miss making Halloween costumes and trick-or-treating with her child, attending piano recitals and ballet rehearsals, and watching her daughter blossom into a young woman who falls in love.

References to the Novel

The most effective persuasive speeches include *novel* information, as in the following example:

> Did you know that kidnapping for profit is one of the leading domestic industries in Columbia? It generates millions in revenues. The major group that carries out the kidnappings is the Revolutionary Armed Forces, or FARC for short. Last year FARC kidnapped over 3,700 wealthy landowners, prominent government officials, *and* foreign tourists. In a typical scenario, victims are seized from airports or hotel rooms and held in hiding while the kidnappers extort a ransom payment from relatives. Kidnapping has become so much a business that there are set ransom fees. You might be interested to know, for example, that our instructor's value as a kidnap victim is approximately $8,000, the standard ransom for university professors.

Use of Suspense

In the next example, the speaker uses suspense to gain and hold audience attention:

> A killer is now in our community. When last seen, the strangler was moving along Highway 105, headed toward Chelsea. The risk to the community is high, because no one has any idea how to control this murderous *dog-strangling vine*. Does this sound like the old movies about giant man-eating tomatoes or lizards that have taken growth hormones? Unfortunately, the threat is much more real. Dog-strangling vines *do* exist, and they *are* a real threat to our national parks and gardens, if not to dogs.

Use of Shock Techniques

The persuasive speaker often hopes to shock the audience into recognizing a problem or acting on a solution. Johanne Gelinas (the Canadian Commissioner of Environment and Sustainable Development) made use of this strategy when she asserted: "Livestock operations in Ontario and Quebec generate enough manure to equal the sewage from over 100 million people."[18]

At other times, understatement can be more effective than overstatement in making a point. New York lawyer Moe Levine was prosecuting a case for a man who had lost both arms. All parties to the trial expected a long summation from Mr. Levine, detailing the extreme difficulties of living with such a handicap. Instead his closing comments were of the following order:

> Your Honor, eminent counsel for defense, ladies and gentlemen of the jury: as you know, about an hour ago we broke for lunch. And I saw the bailiff came and

took you all as a group to have lunch in the jury room. And then I saw the defense attorney, Mr. Horowitz, and his client decided to go to lunch together. And the judge and the court clerk went to lunch. So, I turned to my client, Harold, and said, "Why don't you and I go to lunch together?" And we went across the street to that little restaurant and had lunch. [*Significant pause.*] Ladies and gentlemen, I just had lunch with my client. He has no arms. He eats like a dog! Thank you very much.[19]

This summation resulted in one of the largest monetary awards ever rendered to that point in time in a New York court.

Activity, Drama, and Conflict

Persuasive speeches often include strong elements of drama and conflict that build to a climax. In the following instance, the speaker describes such an event:

The police arrived at 2:00 A.M. They tried to get the man to open the door, but he did not respond. Others had gathered in the hall, drawn by the commotion. The scene was chaotic. When the police finally broke down the door, the man rushed at them, holding a knife in one hand and a baseball bat in the other. One of the police officers tried to subdue the man with pepper spray, but his efforts were unsuccessful. The man was high on cocaine. With no other clear alternative, the officer responded by

shooting the man with a taser gun. Stunned, the man fell to the ground. When the police checked his pulse, they realized that he had stopped breathing. They called an ambulance to come to the rooming house, but it was too late. The man was dead, and the media took the story and ran with it. Fifty men, they reported, have died in the last year from the use of stun guns by police.

Quotations

Quotations, proverbs, and poems are also used to gain audience attention in persuasive speeches. When citing the words of someone else, you should always mention the person's title, position, or other identifying information: "astronaut John Glenn," "well-known author Carol Shields," or "late-night talk show host David Letterman." If the reference is clear, the descriptor can be short. An example follows:

> Crime and poverty. Poverty and crime. Which one comes first? Criminologists argue that poor neighborhoods breed crime, but economists say that the opposite is true—that crime creates poverty. Their argument goes as follows. When people are afraid, they leave the city; and when they leave the city, they take their money and businesses with them. James K. Stewart, the former director of the National Institute of Justice, agrees with this point of view. He said that "crime is the ultimate tax on enterprise. It must be eliminated before poor people can fully share in the American dream."

REVIEWING OTHER ELEMENTS IN THE INTRODUCTION

After getting the attention of your audience, you should state your purpose and position, give the audience a reason to listen, establish your credibility to speak on the topic, and give a preview statement. The ordering of these elements is flexible. Since we have already discussed these points in a previous chapter, I will offer a review in the form of an example. Look at the following excerpts from a persuasive speech, intended to get the audience to contribute to the work of a local heart institute:[20]

> Attention strategy (personal story): In March of 1986, my grandfather had a heart attack. I was not quite two years old. The hospital in my hometown of Beaumont transferred him to the Texas Heart Institute, where he could receive more specialized care. Here the doctors determined that his only hope for a healthy life was a valve replacement. As a result of this successful procedure, my grandpa was in my life for another twelve years. I was able to get to know him and still have memories of him.
>
> Credibility to speak on the topic: Heart problems run in my family, and so the Texas Heart Institute has played an important role in the health of some of my closest relatives. For this reason and others, this topic is important to me; and I have done extensive research to provide you with credible and reliable information.
>
> Reason to listen (why should you care): Many of you—I suspect all of you—also have a friend or relative who has experienced heart problems. Listening to my speech will give you important information on how to help this person by contributing to the activities of the Arizona Heart Institute.
>
> Purpose and position statements: At the conclusion of my speech, I hope that you will take some of the actions identified in my talk. I believe that we can reduce the deaths and disabilities from heart disease if we put our minds, pocketbooks, and bodies into the effort.

Preview statement: In the next few minutes, I will give you some facts about heart disease, discuss the research efforts of the Heart Institute, and tell you what you can do to help the Institute in their fight against cardiovascular disease.

Step 9: Developing the Body of Your Speech

Chapter Eight on informative speaking discussed the importance of conducting primary and secondary research on your speech topics. That chapter also described the range of support materials available to a communicator. Those supports include *historical and other facts, description, comparison and contrast, analogies, proverbs* and *quotations, stories* and *legends, fables* and *parables, poems* and *songs, statistics, examples, explanation* and *amplification,* and *expert testimony.* Like informative speakers, persuasive speakers often translate their statistics into *visual supports.* The speaker uses these various support materials to build the main body of the speech.

Studies have found that some kinds of supporting materials are better than others in effecting attitude change. Examples, illustrations, and case histories, for instance, have a greater impact on attitudes than statistical or other data summaries do.[21] Most difficult to refute is argument by example. A personal instance or story can have a greater impact than the most exhaustive statistics. In addition, attitudes formed on the basis of examples and case histories are more stable over time than attitudes stimulated by data summaries.[22]

The most eloquent and acclaimed speeches (e.g., Martin Luther King, Jr.'s, "I Have a Dream" and John F. Kennedy's inaugural address) often contain no statistics or hard data. Yet the speeches consistently appear on every "Top Speech" site. In some countries, such as Kenya, personal testimonials are regarded as the best and most reliable form of evidence.[23] Nonetheless, statistics and other forms of evidence enable the speaker to generalize a particular incident or event to the larger population. Moreover, few people enjoy the credibility of Martin Luther King, Jr., or John F. Kennedy—credibility that extends the parameters of the permissible.

Even though current wisdom suggests that speakers should rely more heavily on narration, self-disclosure, and visual supports,[24] many inexperienced speakers still overrely on statistics. They spout a series of numbers that have little meaning for the audience. If they took more time to convert the numbers into examples, to present them in visual formats, and to support them with personal instances, they could be far more effective. (See Chapters Eight and Ten for more detailed discussions of statistics.)

The necessity to prove your case means that you must use a variety of support materials, and expert sources should be highly credible and unbiased. Your materials should be current, representative of other findings on the subject, relevant to the points in question, and sufficient in numbers. You should be specific in citing your sources. Because persuasive speaking is serious business, you employ less humor than you might use in an informative or special occasion speech. For a review of the full range of support materials, refer to Chapter Eight on informative speaking.

In addition to logical supporting materials, such as those described here, you should use emotional appeals in a strategic fashion. That means thinking about the needs, beliefs, values, and attitudes of your audience as you write your speech. In addition, when you seek to persuade, you must establish your credibility early in the speech. Why are you qualified to speak on this topic? And why should we believe what you have to say?

Step 10: Considering Your Audience

Speakers adapt to their audiences through strategies that recognize audience demographics, psychographics, needs, and personality profiles.

DEMOGRAPHICS

Audience demographics such as level of education, occupation and income, age, gender, race, ethnicity, and prior experience with the topic should influence your approach. Without being condescending, you should gear your language to the educational level of your audience. You should include more definitions, explanations, and examples with audiences that are less familiar with the subject. You should include more evidence to support your case with hostile audiences. To capture and hold the attention of apathetic audiences, you should emphasize the benefits of listening to the speech. You can use jargon with people who share your profession but not with those who do not share a common language.

Age affects our knowledge of—and perspectives on—issues. Many older adults have difficulty understanding the language and value sets of young Americans. They may think, for example, that words such as *dating* have the same meaning as when they were young. They may anticipate that living together implies the same commitment as marriage. People within bracketed age groups also share some life experiences. People who lived through the Great Depression of the 1920s, the civil unrest of the 1960s, the fall of the Berlin Wall in 1989, the destruction of the World Trade Center in 2001, and the death of Pope John Paul II in 2005 have accumulated some shared life experiences (even if their perspectives on these events vary). When presenting to these audiences, speakers can make brief references to such events without having to offer supporting details. They can assume general knowledge of the events and sometimes shared perspectives, as well.

In addition, speakers can assume some shared concerns among people in the same age group. Young adults are often worried about getting an education, finding a partner, locating suitable employment, purchasing an automobile, and finding reasonable housing. Middle-age adults are more concerned about paying off their mortgages, getting promoted at work, helping their children through college, building their pensions, and finding ways to lower their taxes as they move toward their peak earning years. Older adults tend to be most concerned about issues such as health care, transportation, and housing. An overriding concern is to find ways to maintain their independence for as long as possible.

Women have some issues and interests that are not equally important to men—and vice versa. Women experience the loss of ability to conceive children much earlier than men. They confront diseases such as ovarian and uterine cancer, not experienced by men. They enjoy individual sports more than men, and they converse more than men about personal relationships. In conversations, men tend to focus more on sports, finances, and business. Of course, many exceptions exist, and sexual stereotyping is always risky.

The same kinds of considerations apply to demographic groupings based on income, ethnicity, race, occupation, and other areas. People from certain racial and cultural groups, for example, may feel more strongly than the general population does about issues such as racial profiling and equity legislation. People in particular occupations or income groups often look at arguments from the perspective of self-interest. How will this proposed policy affect me? Will I lose my investment or savings? Will I have a reduced pension when I retire? Will I be able to continue to afford my present lifestyle? At other times, audience members may perceive the information to be irrelevant to their circumstances. So speakers need to identify ways to answer objections based on self-interest and to clarify the relevance of the proposals for other audiences.

PSYCHOGRAPHICS

Often speakers have to move argumentation to the level of values—to appeal to the patriotism, altruism, generosity, competitiveness, or other value orientation of audience members. To the extent possible, speakers should look for values that they hold in common with the audience—a place where the two can meet and connect.

When seeking to persuade, speakers also need to consider the potency of values at the foundation of their argumentation. The abortion debate illustrates this point. Prolife advocates base their arguments, for example, on the sanctity of life. Sanctity of life is a high-priority value for Americans. If prochoice advocates are to argue their position successfully, they must base their argumentation on equally potent values. Right to self-determination, although extremely important in individualistic cultures, is not as potent as right to life. But when prochoice advocates place coat hanger decals on their T-shirts, they make the statement that lives are also at risk when legislation takes away the rights of women to an abortion.

NEEDS

As discussed in Chapter Five, audience members look for ways to satisfy their basic physiological, safety, love, esteem, and self-actualization needs. When persuasive speakers can convince audience members that their ability to meet those needs has been compromised or when they can demonstrate that their solutions will overcome the obstacles, audiences will listen to the speakers. As discussed in an earlier chapter, speakers sometimes use fear appeals to persuade audiences. Those fear appeals may involve threats to the safety, security, esteem, or other audience needs. Inciting fear is not enough, however, to accomplish persuasive aims. The speaker must also offer the listeners explicit advice on how to reduce or eliminate the threats. Most experts agree that mild to moderate fear appeals are more effective than strong fear appeals and that teenagers are likely to react more to threats to their ego and self-esteem than to safety.[25] Teenagers tend to respond to peer influence and to seek role models among their own reference groups. So persuaders should consider these factors when framing persuasive strategies.

If audiences stand to lose from the proposed stance or solutions (e.g., to receive a lower pension with changes to social security), speakers need to explain how the long-term benefits outweigh the short-term costs. In other words, speakers need to identify a strategy for persuading the audience such as mentioning the benefits of the charges to grandchildren. But the first step is to recognize audience feelings on the topic. Audience members may feel insecure, threatened, or even angered by the proposed policy. They will reject the arguments of anyone who does not recognize their situation. So the argumentation must include recognition of audience sentiments on the topic.

PERSONALITY

Other considerations, raised in an earlier chapter on audience research, include factors such as personality. One can speculate, with some degree of certainty, that audiences populated by CEOs, Olympic athletes, and successful entrepreneurs probably do not suffer from low self-esteem. Thus, these audiences are likely to prefer messages that leave the choices open to them, not limiting their options or giving high levels of direction. They are more likely to respond to arguments based on logic and sound evidence than on loose opinions, since they do not depend on outside authorities to the same extent that low-esteem individuals do. They do not tend to be conformists who seek the approval of others. They are more likely to respond to optimistic than pessimistic messages. The task of persuading an audience of high-esteem individuals can be a formidable one.[26] When speaking to a group of low-esteem individuals (e.g., recovering drug addicts or teenagers with weight problems), the persuader may want to adopt a different strategy—involving more directive messages and greater use of role models drawn from peer populations. The program Alcoholics Anonymous (AA), run by alcoholics for alcoholics, exemplifies this approach. The speakers at AA meetings are themselves recovering addicts.[27] Reliance on pessimistic content would raise ethical questions with groups that already experience low self-esteem.[28]

Some of the same persuasion strategies that work with high-esteem audiences apply to open-minded audiences. Open-minded audiences tend to be more optimistic than close-minded audiences. They see problems in a larger context, and they look for ways to accommodate the new information within their existing belief structures. Thus, persuaders can feel more comfortable introducing new and controversial ideas to an audience populated by open-minded individuals. They can rely more on expert opinions and less on authority figures to support their position.[29] With more closed-minded audiences, on the other hand, persuaders must work harder to gain acceptance for controversial or new ideas. The audience may be pessimistic in the first place toward proffered solutions, and speakers may need to rely more strongly on sources trusted by the audience to gain acceptance and compliance. (See the Question of Ethics box.)

A Question of Ethics

William was strongly in favor of gun control. One of his cousins had died in an accidental shooting several years previously. Nonetheless, he decided to argue against gun control in his persuasive speech. His decision resulted from the feedback that he had received on his speech topic. A number of his classmates expressed annoyance when they learned that he planned to argue for stricter gun control legislation. Living in a rural area, many students were hunters. They believed that they knew how to use guns in a responsible way and that they had the right to purchase guns for recreational use. Worried that he would offend his classmates if he took such a controversial position, William decided to argue a position that he did not believe to be morally right. Evaluate the decision of this speaker to abandon his original position.

Meredith, on the other hand, delivered a persuasive speech on the topic of overpopulation. She decided that the speech would be more interesting if she generated a hypothetical example in which she described the likely consequences of uncontrolled population growth. Her hypothetical example involved a country in western Africa. She also generated statistics to support her example. She did not inform her audience that the example and statistics were fictitious or exaggerated, generated to dramatize the worst possible effects of overpopulation. She also said that the negative consequences were not just likely, but certain, if people did not act. And she presented two alternatives: support her solution or face disaster.

After Meredith sat down, a young man from Africa questioned her statistics and conclusions. When he learned that the example was hypothetical, created to provoke interest in the topic, he was extremely angry. He said that the speaker had falsified information rather than taken the time to research actual cases and gather valid statistics. Meredith defended her speech on the grounds that her motives were honorable. She said that many people would die in the future if nothing happened to change the situation. Moreover, she argued that the country chosen for the example was the most likely to experience problems and that the statistics reflected patterns that were already developing. Was Meredith justified in using a hypothetical example in this way? Was she justified in creating or exaggerating statistics to support her claim? Was she justified in simplifying a complex situation, presenting only two alternatives, and pretending to be certain about the outcome of failure to act? Discuss the ethics of Meredith's approach.

GENERAL CONSIDERATIONS

Speakers should realize that a single speech will do little to effect major changes in audiences. Often the speech only stimulates the audience to think more seriously about the topic under consideration. In line with principles of political communication, politicians tend to target their communications to those most likely to be persuaded—the undecided. They also seek to reinforce the positive perceptions of audience members who favor their point of view and to energize those who are apathetic. Typically, they pay less attention to those who are hostile to their point of view, recognizing that change is highly unlikely in the "decided" population. Persuaders, in general, face the same decisions. To what extent should they target their communications to some audience segments and ignore others? Wanting to reach every audience member is a laudable objective; however, it is rarely realistic. For that reason, most persuasive speakers direct their speeches to those audience members with whom they can have the greatest impact. To identify those audiences and aim for realistic outcomes, they must conduct research.

Step 11: Choosing Evocative Language

Evocative language
Using words that inspire feelings and/or memories

Evocative language allows the speaker to appeal on an emotional level to the audience. Speakers use literary techniques such as vivid and concrete language, balanced and parallel sentence structures, antithesis, repetition, alliteration, first and second voice, "the rule of threes and fours," comparison and contrast, metaphors, similes, personification, analogies, rhetorical questions, and religious references to evoke powerful emotions in their audiences.

CONCRETE AND VIVID LANGUAGE

Concrete language
Translating abstract ideas into tangible realities

When speakers use concrete language, they translate abstract concepts into more tangible realities—ones that we can see and touch in our own lives. Instead of saying "one of my supporters," they say "Tom." Instead of saying "A bird chirped," they say "A yellow finch chirped." A house is ranch or Victorian or adobe. In the early 1970s, civil rights lawyer and activist William J. Kunstler presented a powerful antiwar speech to 3,900 audience members (mostly students), who packed the Indiana University auditorium in Bloomington, Indiana. The following excerpt demonstrates the power of using specifics in a speech:

> Wherever you go, wherever discussions are heard, people are going to say, "What about violence on campus? How can you condone the destruction of a building in which a man died, and people are going to forget that every day B-52's go out over South Viet Nam; people are going to forget what happened to the demonstrators on Lower Wall Street in New York; people are going to forget who was responsible for the defoliation of millions of acres in Vietnam. . . . People are going to forget My Lai 4 and the bayoneting of grandmothers and babies. . . . And when people tell you that students are violent, ask them if it's students who pilot the B-53's, ask them if students started the war in Vietnam or invaded Cambodia; ask them if students killed Fred Hampton and Mark Clark; ask them if students shot down the Kennedy brothers, Martin Luther King, Medgar Evers, Malcolm X and others. . . . Ask them if students killed *themselves* at Kent State on the Commons or killed *themselves* in Alexander Hall at Jackson State. Did students gun down the six in Augusta, Georgia?[30]

BALANCED AND PARALLEL SENTENCE STRUCTURES

Eloquence of spoken language relies on the balancing of sentence structures, so that one part of the sentence "weighs" the same as the other part. The following statement demonstrates the principle of balanced sentence structure: "She was not so much confident as determined; not so much fearless as committed." Sometimes, the balance occurs in adjacent sentences, as in the eulogy delivered by Republican House leader Dennis Hastert at the funeral of former President Ronald Reagan: "While others worried, President Reagan persevered. When others weakened, President Reagan stood tall. When others stepped back, President Reagan stepped forward. And he did it all with great humility, with great charm and with great humor."[31]

We use this kind of language most often in highly formal and ceremonial speeches. In conversational language, we do not try to achieve an equal weighting for the different parts of a thought or sentence.

ANTITHESIS

One type of balanced sentence structure is antithesis. Antithesis employs *not*, *not/but*, and *never/but* to offer a contrast between two ideas. John F. Kennedy was an acclaimed master in the use of antithesis with passages such as "Ask not what your country can do for you . . . ask what you can do for your country" and "Let us never negotiate out of fear, but let us never fear to negotiate."[32]

In 1984, speaking at the U.S.-French ceremony at Omaha Beach on the fortieth anniversary of D-Day, President Ronald Reagan employed antithesis in a moving tribute to veterans of World War II:

> When men like Private Zannata and all our Allied forces stormed the beaches of Normandy 40 years ago they came not as conquerors, but as liberators. When these troops swept across the French countryside and into the forests of Belgium and Luxembourg they came not to take, but to return what had been wrongfully seized. When our forces marched into Germany they came not to prey on a brave and defeated people, but to nurture the seeds of democracy among those who yearned to be free again.[33]

Antithesis
The direct opposite; in speech, using balanced sentence structures including *not*, *not/but*, *never/but*

REPETITION

Repetition is another key linguistic strategy. In a eulogy delivered in June 2004, President George W. Bush spoke of former President Ronald Reagan's courage: "It

Repetition
In speech, to emphasize a point by using the same words or word patterns over and over

is the faith of a boy who read the Bible with his mom. It is the faith of a man lying in an operating room, who prayed for the one who shot him before he prayed for himself. It is the faith of a man with a fearful illness, who waited on the Lord to call him home."[34]

Experienced speakers use various techniques to induce variation into speeches that employ repetition. In an emotionally compelling address, delivered in the House of Commons on June 4, 1940, Winston Churchill spoke of the commitment of the British to fight to the end in World War II. The passage is well known for its cadence and rhythm, as well as its eloquent use of repetition. In this example, Churchill achieves variation by using different endings to sentences that begin with a repetitive phrase:

> We shall not flag or fail. We shall go on to the end, we shall fight in France, we shall fight on the seas and oceans, we shall fight with growing confidence and growing strength in the air, we shall defend our Island, whatever the cost may be, we shall fight on the beaches, we shall fight on the landing grounds, we shall fight in the fields and in the streets, we shall fight in the hills; we shall never surrender.[35]

Sometimes, speakers build variety into adjacent sentences or paragraphs that separate the repetitious chant. In June 1963, President John F. Kennedy illustrated this strategy in a speech delivered at the wall that separated East and West Berlin:

> There are many people in the world who don't understand, or say they don't, what is the great issue between the free world and the Communist world. *Let them come to Berlin.* There are some who say that communism is the wave of the future. *Let them come to Berlin.* And there are some who say in Europe and elsewhere we can work with the Communists. *Let them come to Berlin.* And there are even a few who say that it is true that communism is an evil system, but it permits us to make economic progress. Lass'sie nach Berlin kommen. *Let them come to Berlin.*

This final example by a student speaker shows how a small variation in the repeated phrase can be effective:

> I regret to inform you that I am the bearer of bad news. *The bad news* is that an organization exists, whose policies threaten the jobs of over 30,000 members of our community. *The bad news* is that these policies threaten to eliminate nearly 1.3 billion dollars from our local economy. And the *worst news of all* is that these same policies put the lives and safety of nearly 175,000 snowmobilers at risk.[36]

Beginning speechwriters often tend to overuse repetition; when strategies become too obvious to an audience, they lose their effectiveness. The audience sees the strategies as transparent attempts at manipulation.

ALLITERATION

Alliteration
In speech, using a repetitive sound to begin words, usually two or three

Alliteration involves repetition of a letter or sound, usually at the beginning of words, as in "She slid down the slippery slope at Sedona." Unlike poets, who sprinkle alliteration throughout their work, speakers often limit alliterative passages to two words in a phrase. In 1961, newly elected President John F. Kennedy delivered a farewell address to the people of Massachusetts, whom he had served as U.S. senator. In this speech, he used a number of literary devices, including alliteration:

> And so it is that I carry with me from this state to that high and lonely office, to which I now succeed, more than fond memories and fast friendships. The enduring

qualities of Massachusetts—the common threads woven by the Pilgrim and the Puritan, the fisherman and the farmer, the Yankee and the immigrant—will not be and could not be forgotten in this nation's executive mansion.[37]

Note the alliteration in the passages "fond memories and fast friendships," "Pilgrim and the Puritan," and "fisherman and the farmer." He also used alliteration with great impact in his 1961 inaugural address when he said:

> Let the word go forth from this from this time and place, to friend and foe alike, that the torch has been passed to a new generation of Americans. . . . Let every nation know, whether it wishes us well or ill, that we shall pay any price, bear any burden, meet any hardship, support any friend, oppose any foe, in order to assure the survival and the success of liberty.[38]

If not overdone, alliteration enhances the aesthetic quality of speeches. The technique adds a rhythmic quality to the speech.

FIRST AND SECOND VOICE

The importance of audience adaptation means that speakers typically make limited use of first person singular voice (*I*) in a speech. Instead they use first person plural (*we*) and second person (*you*) to involve the audience. On occasion, however, speaking in the first person can have a powerful impact on an audience, especially in a situation where the speaker has high credibility and a strong desire to assert responsibility for his words and actions. Those variables were at work on April 20, 1964, when a young Nelson Mandela spoke from the prisoner's dock in the Pretoria, South Africa, Supreme Court building. The 1990s would see Mandela assume the leadership of South Africa, but not before he had spent twenty-seven years in prison. On this day in 1964, Mandela faced the possibility of death if convicted of the crimes with which he was charged. You can see his acceptance of responsibility in his opening statement to the courtroom:

> I am the First Accused. I hold a Bachelor's Degree in Arts and practised as an attorney in Johannesburg for a number of years in partnership with Oliver Tambo. I am a convicted prisoner serving five years for leaving the country without a permit and for inciting people to go on strike at the end of May 1961. At the outset, I want to say that the suggestion made by the State in its opening that the struggle in South Africa is under the influence of foreigners or communists is wholly incorrect. I have done whatever I did, both as an individual and as a leader of my people, because of my experience in South Africa and my own proudly felt African background, and not because of what any outsider may have said.[39]

Some speak in the first person to give voice to some historical person or group or to achieve dramatic effect. In 1960, I wrote a speech for the Voice of Democracy competition, in which I spoke from the perspective of those who have died in defense of their country:

> I am the Voice of America—her past, her contemporary, her future. And I speak with a deep conviction, because I am the Voice of Democracy. I am a Son of Liberty. The bonfires of revolt blaze heavenward about me. The times are troublesome and tumultuous. . . . I have heard the cries of injustice swell upward in torrents toward the overcast skies. The voice of Patrick Henry echoes through the House of Burgesses and resounds through the colonies amid cries of treason. His rebuttal is,

First person voice
Using "I", or more typically, "we" constructions

Second person voice
Using the "you" construction

"If this be treason, then make the most of it." . . . . I left my blood on the slopes of Bunker Hill, in the icy waters of the Delaware River, and in the snows at Valley Forge. . . . I lie in Flanders Field. Above my grave there stands a small white cross. The sky overhead spreads a canopy of azure over me; and the poppies, rippling in the summer breeze, form a crimson cover over my bed. . . . I fought on the slopes of Iwa Jima. The blood of my comrades stained the countryside and flowed in rivers to the valleys below. Mine were the hands that planted the Stars and Stripes in the soil of our enemy. . . . I am a pioneer of the space age. I can hear the roar of the jet planes over my head and feel the quivering rebellion of the earth beneath my feet. I cringe before the reverberating echoes of exploding atoms. I wonder at the satellites that probe the heavens. Yes, I am bound by the universe, but I am free to explore it. I am free because I am an American, and mine is the Voice of Democracy.

More commonly, speakers employ first person plural (*we*) or second person (*you*)—inclusiveness strategies that bring the audience into the speaker's frame of reference, as in the below eulogy to former President Ronald Reagan. President George W. Bush delivered these words on June 11, 2004:

When the sun sets tonight off the coast of California, and we lay to rest our 40th President, a great American story will close. The second son of Nell and Jack Reagan first knew the world as a place of open plains, quiet streets, gas-lit rooms, and carriages drawn by horse. If you could go back to the Dixon, Illinois of 1922, you'd find a boy of 11 reading adventure stories at the public library, or running with his brother, Neil, along Rock River, and coming home to a little house on Hennepin Avenue. That town was the kind of place you remember where you prayed side by side with your neighbors, and if things were going wrong for them, you prayed for them, and knew they'd pray for you if things went wrong for you.[40]

RULE OF THREES AND FOURS

Writers and speakers tend to use clusters of three or four words, phrases, or sentences (rhythmic triads and quads) to achieve lyrical effect in language. Former President Jimmy Carter demonstrated the *rule of threes* in this excerpt from a July 27, 2004, speech to the Democratic National Convention: "The United States has alienated its allies, dismayed its friends, and inadvertently gratified its enemies by

proclaiming a confused and disturbing strategy of 'preemptive' war." Earlier in the same speech, Carter delivered the words for which he became so well known: "I believe tonight, as I always have, that the essential decency, compassion, and common sense of the American people will prevail."

Sometimes speakers use a variation on the rule of threes—*the rule of fours*. The following statement—drawn from a July 12, 1976, speech by Barbara Jordan—likewise illustrates this popular variation. Barbara Jordan was the first African-American woman from the South to serve in the U.S. Congress.

> We are a people in a quandary about the present. We are a people in search of our future. We are a people in search of a national identity. We are a people trying not only to solve the problems of the present: unemployment, inflation . . . but we are attempting on a larger scale to fulfill the promise of America.[41]

The following colorful statement from a speech by Winston Churchill also illustrates the rule of fours: "We have not journeyed across the centuries, across the oceans, across the mountains, across the prairies because we are made of sugar candy."[42]

COMPARISON AND CONTRAST

As in the following example, *comparison* reveals similarities between ideas or concepts:

> Like kleptomaniacs, people with addictive-compulsive disorders cannot resist the urge to steal. And like kleptomaniacs, they may have absolutely no need for the shoplifted objects. Nonetheless, they feel a sense of relief and pleasure at the time that they commit the act of theft. Neither the kleptomaniac nor the addictive compulsive thief is a bad person, in the sense of being uncaring or antisocial. Most are good, otherwise law-abiding citizens.

Contrast, on the other hand, involves looking at differences. In the next example, the speaker compares the number of cancer-related deaths to losses from airline

Comparison
Weighing the similarity of various things

Contrast
Weighing the difference of various things

crashes and then contrasts the way in which we treat airline companies and tobacco companies:

> If 800 fully loaded jumbo jets crashed each year, killing all 400,000 passengers, would we take action against the company that made the planes? The answer is *yes*. Yet the same numbers of people die each year from lung cancer, and we do nothing to close down the companies or seize their profits. What is the logic behind such contradictory behavior?

METAPHOR

Metaphor
Comparing two ideas or things by asserting that the one *is* the other

A *metaphor* is a highly compressed comparison. It compares two ideas or concepts by saying that one *is* the other. In a rallying speech that followed the collapse of France in World War II, Winston Churchill asserted:

> Hitler knows that he will have to break us in this Island or lose the war. . . . If we fail, then the whole world, including the United States . . . will sink into the abyss of a new Dark Age made more sinister, and perhaps more protracted by the lights of perverted science. Let us therefore brace ourselves to our duties, and so bear ourselves that if the British empire and the Commonwealth last for a thousand years, men will still say, "This was their finest hour."[43]

Many consider the final line of this passage to be one of Churchill's two most memorable rhetorical moments. Metaphors in this passage include "the abyss of a new Dark Age" and "the lights of perverted science."

On April 3, 1968, Martin Luther King, Jr., spoke to an audience gathered at the Mason Temple in Memphis, Tennessee. In this speech, King's journey to the top of the mountain is a metaphor for the realization of his hopes for a just society. The reference to the mountaintop also evokes the biblical account of Moses, who went to the top of Mount Sinai to receive the Ten Commandments from God. Moses led his people to the promised land but never got there himself. As with his other speeches, King (a Southern Baptist minister) delivered this talk in the manner of a sermon, with predictable rising and falling cadences.

> Well, I don't know what will happen now. We've got some difficult days ahead. But it doesn't matter to me now. Because I've been to the mountaintop. And I don't mind. Like anybody, I would like to live a long life. Longevity has its place. But I'm not concerned about that now. I just want to do God's will. And He's allowed me to go up to the mountain. And I've looked over. And I've seen the promised land. I may not get there with you. But I want you to know tonight, that we, as a people, will get to the promised land. And I'm happy, tonight. I'm not worried about anything. I'm not fearing any man. Mine eyes have seen the glory of the coming of the Lord.[44]

The day after delivering these prophetic words, King died at the hands of an assassin, shot to death on the balcony of his Memphis motel at the age of thirty-five.

SIMILE

Simile
Comparing two ideas or things by asserting that the one *is like* the other

A metaphor, as we have seen, states that "this is that." *Similes*, on the other hand, are explicit comparisons that use terms such as *like* or *as*. In a speech presented as part of the Take Back the Night program at Rutgers University, Suzanne Stutman said that those who have been abused are "like the phoenix rising from the ashes," with a responsibility to make life better for others. Speaking on the risks of deregulating the media, television journalist Bill Moyers said that deregulating the media is "like turning out searchlights on dark and dangerous street corners."[45]

PERSONIFICATION

Personification entails attributing human characteristics to an abstract idea or concept. In the following excerpt from a speech delivered to the Republican national convention, activist Mary Fisher personified the problem of AIDS:

> The AIDS virus is not a political creature. It does not care whether you are Democrat or Republican. It does not ask whether you are black or white, male or female, gay or straight, young or old. Tonight I represent an AIDS community whose members have been reluctantly drafted from every segment of American society.

Personification
Giving human qualities to an abstract idea or concept

ANALOGY

An analogy uses a known concept to explain an unknown or less familiar concept. Although analogies are like similes and metaphors in comparing two different ideas, they are more extended and involve a reasoning process. That is, an analogy seeks to establish the logic in the relationship between the two dissimilar ideas. One speaker translated the statistics on deaths from cigarette smoking into the following strong, compelling analogy:

> If, in the year 2020, we were to stack each person who died a smoking-induced death one atop the other, we could build a column of bodies reaching 180 km into the sky. If we would continue to pack these bodies one atop the other for just one more year, a warning light would have to be placed at the apex of this column to prevent the International Space Station from ploughing into this grotesque metaphor.[46]

Analogy
Comparison of partially similar things or ideas by transferring the qualities of one to the other

In the historic address "I Have a Dream," Martin Luther King, Jr., develops an equally powerful analogy in which he compares the treatment of African Americans to the predicament of someone given a check for insufficient funds.

> In a sense we have come to our nation's capital to cash a check. When the architects of our republic wrote the magnificent words of the Constitution and the Declaration of Independence, they were signing a promissory note that all men, yes black men as well as white men, would be guaranteed the inalienable rights of life, liberty, and the pursuit of happiness. It is obvious today that America has defaulted on this promissory note insofar as their citizens of color are concerned. Instead of honoring this sacred obligation, America has given the Negro people a bad check, which has come back marked "insufficient funds." But we refuse to believe that the bank of justice is bankrupt. We refuse to believe that there are insufficient funds in the great vaults of opportunity of this nation. So we have come to cash this check—a check that will give us upon demand the riches of freedom and the security of justice.[47]

RHETORICAL QUESTIONS

Asked at the beginning of speeches, rhetorical questions are a crutch for the novice speaker. However, rhetorical questions are powerful tools in the hands of accomplished persuasive speakers. In the latter case, they appear in the middle or toward

Rhetorical question
Question posed by a speaker, who does not expect an answer, used to provoke interest in the audience

the conclusion of speeches. When a speaker asks a rhetorical question, he does not expect the audience to respond in an audible or visible way—only to answer the question in their heads. When lawyers use rhetorical questions in their closing arguments, they lead the audience to a preferred conclusion. In a similar fashion, African-American Sojourner Truth applies this strategy in a historical speech delivered to a woman's convention in Akron, Ohio, in 1851. Her speech protests the discrimination experienced by African Americans, women in particular:

> That man over there says that women need to be helped into carriages, and lifted over ditches, and to have the best place everywhere. Nobody ever helps me into carriages, or over mud-puddles, or gives me any best place! And ain't I a woman? Look at me! Look at my arm! I have ploughed and planted, and gathered into barns, and no man could head me! And ain't I a woman? I could work as much and eat as much as a man—when I could get it—and bear the lash as well! And ain't I a woman? I have borne thirteen children, and seen most all sold off to slavery, and when I cried out with my mother's grief, none but Jesus heard me! And ain't I a woman?

RELIGIOUS REFERENCES

The most common marker of presidential rhetoric is the invocation of religious references. Few presidents end their speeches without asking for a blessing upon the country. When the space shuttle *Challenger* was lost on January 28, 1986, former President Ronald Reagan delivered the following words of sympathy: "The crew of the space shuttle *Challenger* honored us by the manner in which they lived their lives. We will never forget them, nor the last time we saw them, this morning, as they prepared for their journey and waved goodbye and 'slipped the surly bonds of earth' to 'touch the face of God.'"[48] When the space shuttle *Columbia* fell from the skies on February 1, 2003, President George W. Bush drew upon religious references to express his grief and condolences to the families of crew members:

> In the skies today we saw destruction and tragedy. Yet farther than we can see there is comfort and hope. In the words of the prophet Isaiah, "Lift your eyes and look to the heavens. Who created all these? He who brings out the starry hosts one by one and calls them each by name. Because of His great power and mighty strength, not one of them is missing." The same Creator who names the stars also knows the names of the seven souls we mourn today. The crew of the shuttle *Columbia* did not return safely to Earth; yet we can pray that all are safely home.[49]

For the average person, the use of biblical references holds some risks. Increasingly, the United States is a mix of people from many parts of the world. Not all are Christian in background, and some consider religious references to be inappropriate in speeches by their national leaders. Also, some international audiences are offended when American presidents end their speeches with "God bless America." They interpret the reference as a request for the deity to favor America over other countries. American speakers should be sensitive when they journey to other countries to deliver their speeches. The world in which we live is increasingly smaller, and the international distribution of communication products means that audiences are no longer exclusively regional or national.

Step 12: Linking Your Ideas

As discussed in Chapters Four and Eight, *transitions*, *signposts*, and *internal summaries* help speakers to see the relationship among different parts of the speech. These linking devices and summaries guide the audience through the speech. Listeners cannot go back to confirm the organization of the speech, as they can do when they read a book or article. So they must depend on the speaker to give orienting signals as he progresses through the speech. Figure 10.7 reviews the role of transitions, signposts, and internal summaries within the larger speech structure.

Attention: Justice has a face. The children of Napakiak tell me the face is white. Justice has a home. The children of the Arctic say that they have never seen the home. It must be far away. Justice has a job—to see that all of us are safe from those who err and lose their way. The children of the Yukon say that they do not feel safe when they do not feel close to those who aim to judge. For many Native Alaskans, justice is a "Southerner," who wears spiked heels in New York City, pinstriped suits in Washington, and strapless evening wear in L.A. Justice wears Armani to work, Versace to play, and Calvin Klein to sleep. Justice does not wear the dress of those who live in Arctic Village or hunt caribou on frozen tundra. *Thesis statement*: The protection of culturally appropriate models is required to ensure justice for Native Alaskans. *Preview statement*: In this speech, I will identify biases in the mainstream justice system, especially as they relate to Native Americans. Then I will suggest the need for the new federal commission to ensure continuing tribal control of the native justice system in Alaska. Finally, I will suggest some specific actions that you can take to ensure that the commission considers this point of view. *Signpost*: First, let us consider biases in the mainstream justice system. [*A discussion of biases will comprise the first part of the body of the speech.*] *Internal summary*: Let us pause for a moment to reiterate what we have just said. First, we have seen that our justice system does not effectively protect every American. Some groups such as our Native population "fall through the cracks." We have also seen that the design and operation of our penal institutions are culturally biased against Natives. *Transition*: Moreover, we can conclude that the situation will only worsen if tribes are consolidated into one unified justice system. *Signpost*: Proceeding to the second part of my speech, let us look at solutions involving changes in the federal penal system. [*Discussion of required changes comes next.*] *Signpost*: What can you do as an individual to better the situation? [*Discussion of personal actions comes next.*] *Conclusion*: Thus, you can see that we must be flexible to ensure that every American has the same access to justice. We can work toward ensuring that our prisons are not populated by the poorest in our society. We can change the conditions that nurture crime in our northern communities. We can ensure that every American has equal access to competent legal counsel. We can strive to establish penal systems that are based on culturally appropriate models, whether that system be healing circles or modern correctional facilities. And we can act as individuals to ensure that these changes take place. The key to solving the problems are the two words *We can*. In an interview following the exposure of Clinton's affair with Monica Lewinsky, Larry King asked Bill Clinton why he had the affair with Monica Lewinsky. Clinton responded, "For the worst of all possible reasons—because I could." Conversely, I challenge you today to commit yourself to ensuring justice for the people who live in the Aleutians and the Kobuk Valley and all of the other northern communities—for the best of all possible reasons—because *you can*.

Figure 10.7 Structural Elements

Step 13: Writing Your Conclusion

In addition to leaving the audience with a memorable thought, conclusions should provide closure. They often include a brief summary, as in the last example, or refer back to some example from the introduction. The conclusions of speeches to actuate (e.g., the motivated sequence) suggest specific actions to be taken by the audience. Speeches to actuate often include a challenge to the audience, as well as a quotation, proverb, or poem. Sometimes speeches to actuate ask the audience to visualize a future with or without the desired solution. The conclusions of speeches to convince, on the other hand, do not include an action component. The following conclusion summarizes the major points in the speech and challenges the audience to make difficult choices:

> I hope I've succeeded in explaining what the government intends to do on the health care issue and in describing your options as a consumer of health care services. Mark Twain said, "The only way to keep your health is to eat what you don't want, drink what you don't like, and do what you'd rather not." Well, I say that the only way to fix our health care system is to accept that our choices may not always be what we *want* to do, *like* to do, or would *prefer* to do. But they can lead us to a solution with long-term and sustainable results. In this case, three negatives can lead to a positive.

For a six- to eight-minute speech, a conclusion that is half of a page in length is sufficient.

Step 14: Delivering Your Speech

Extemporaneous speaking from note cards is the preferred form of speaking for most occasions. Exceptions occur, however, when speakers compete in oratory contests, deliver addresses at ceremonial events, or aim to capture a place in the annals of history. In those situations, the speakers will create a manuscript speech, carefully worded and refined, which they read or deliver predominantly from memory. Eloquence of language is very important in those circumstances. The speeches that we study as examples of great oratory were not improvised. The speakers knew, in advance, exactly what they were going to say. Either they or their speechwriters had spent hours on the wording of the speeches.

The difference between an extemporaneous speaking event and a memorized presentation should not be the presence or absence of note cards. Rather, the difference between the two kinds of delivery should be the extent to which you strive for spontaneity in wording. With an extemporaneous delivery, you vary your wording from practice to practice so that you will appear to be totally "in the moment." With a more memorized delivery, you strive to remember each word as you have written it. Your aim is eloquence of expression and a finely honed delivery.

Some speaking competitions, which demand that speakers rely totally on recall, prohibit the use of note cards. Most occasions, however, allow speakers to bring whatever memory devices they choose to the podium. So even if you plan to deliver a memorized speech, you may feel more comfortable bringing a few notes to the stand with you. Should you forget your speech, you can refer to the note cards. Finding your place in the full manuscript would be much more awkward and difficult. The challenge for most speakers is to refrain from going to the note cards when it is unnecessary. For that reason, you should restrict your notes to the major points and wording of hard-to-recall passages. Bring the cards with you as a reminder, should you need them; or use the cards for long quotations or stories that may be difficult to remember. Above all, the goal of memorized delivery is to respect the exact wording of the speech. In practicing the speech, think about the sequence of ideas. Memorize the sequence and then memorize the wording. When delivering the speech, focus your attention on your purpose in speaking and on your audience so that you do not sound robotic. If you forget a part of the speech, stop and find your place. If necessary, improvise until you are back on track.

Step 15: Responding to Questions

The question-and-answer session following the speech is an opportunity to demonstrate the breadth and depth of your research. You should listen carefully to the questions, restate them before responding, and then answer clearly and succinctly. You should never dismiss any question as unworthy, and you should try to engage a maximum number of people. If you cannot answer a question, offer to get back to the person with a response. Do not pretend to know something that you do not know. Finally, you should respect the time period that is assigned for responding to questions from your peers. For additional information on how to manage question and answer sessions, refer to Chapter Thirteen.

Conclusion

As noted in the introduction to this chapter persuasive speeches may aim to convince (change existing attitudes or effect a shift in position), stimulate (reinforce existing attitudes or stances), or actuate (move an audience to act on their beliefs or to eliminate an unwanted behavior). The process of writing such a speech involves selecting a topic and defining a general purpose, writing a tentative position statement, translating that position statement into a thesis, researching and identifying levels of audience knowledge and attitudes toward your position, deciding upon a desired outcome or specific speech purpose, choosing an organizational pattern, writing an introduction, developing supporting materials for your outline, adapting to your audience, choosing evocative language, writing transitions and internal summaries, writing your conclusion, memorizing and delivering your speech, and responding to questions at the conclusion of your speech. Sample Speeches appear at the end of this chapter.

Sample Speech

Persuasion Speech—Problem and Solution Pattern of Organization

Introduction

*James Murray Davidson, beloved husband of Eliza-
beth and the late Evelyn. Cherished father of Jane,
Cathy, Martha, David, Nancy, and Angus. Much
loved stepfather of Pat, David, Paul, and Judy. Missed
terribly by his daughters and sons-in-law. Beloved and
respected grandpa of thirteen. Memorial donations to
the cancer society.*

What I just read to you was my grandfather's
death announcement. On May 3, 2004, cigarettes
killed my grandfather, who died of lung cancer.
Cancer did not just end my grandfather's life. It
also took away a husband, a father, and a grandfather. My grandfather survived the Great Depression. He was shot twice during World War II.
And in his career as a civil engineer, supervising
some of the country's most northern highways,
he was no stranger to danger. But what ended up
killing him was cigarettes.

I am not here today to preach to you about the
dangers of smoking. You've all heard that message many times. Rather, I would like to share
with you the reality of smoking. I would like to
suggest that a decision you make today affects
not only you, but also everyone connected to
you. And I would like to remind you of the benefits of not smoking.

Nature of Problem

Lung cancer has acquired the reputation of being
a silent killer. By the time you realize that it has
claimed a space in your life, you have little hope
of a cure. When I was home for winter break in
late February, my grandpa was making his own
wine and snowblowing his neighbors' drive-
ways. By the time that I returned home for Easter
break, they had given him weeks to live. The

rapidity of his decline was hard to accept and part
of the reason that I am so passionately against
smoking. My grandfather had lived a long and
productive life, but it did not ease the pain of
watching him struggle in the months preceding
his death. I understand how difficult it is to quit
smoking. I've watched countless family members
struggle to quit in the months after my grandfather's death. But you know what, watching a
loved one die of lung cancer is not easy either.

Causes

The fact is that 99 percent of all deaths from lung
cancer are smoking-related. Notice the word related. Not everyone who dies from lung cancer is
a smoker. Exposure to secondhand smoke holds
the same hazards as smoking, but the myth persists that only smokers get lung cancer. So if you
have been sitting here, comfortable that this
speech does not apply to you, you should take
notice.

The overall rates of death from cancer are
twice as high among smokers as nonsmokers,
with heavy smokers having rates that are four
times greater than those of nonsmokers. More
people die from smoking than from traffic accidents, AIDS, and suicide combined. The government invests millions of dollars in cancer research each year, but we all know that the major
cause of cancer is sitting in the coat pockets of
Americans, including some members of this
class.

Effects

An article in *Men's Health Magazine* predicts that,
on average, smoking removes fifteen years from
an expected life span—a large chunk of your life

for the pleasure of a few puffs a day. Recent statistics also tell us that lung cancer has now replaced breast cancer as the leading cause of cancer-related deaths in women. So why don't we have runs and special charities for lung cancer victims?

Solution

A depressing picture, yes, but change is possible. According to national statistics reported by the Arizona Department of Health services, the number of people smoking peaks at age twenty and then declines steadily. By age thirty, the percentages have dropped from a high of 44 percent to 31 percent. By age sixty-five, only 10 percent of the population will be smoking. But . . . not everyone lives to age sixty-five.

For the smokers in this class, you have two choices. You can quit or you can continue smoking. I realize that the decision is yours. My aim is simply to put a human face on cancer—to expose the problem and to suggest the benefits of quitting.

Benefits

What are the benefits? You may be able to add another fifteen years of life to your lifespan. With the money that you spend on smoking, you may be able to afford that vacation trip that you've been postponing. You may have more money to spend on recreation or a down payment on some valued purchase. And you may be able to watch the antitobacco ads on television without leaving the room or switching to another channel because you feel so uncomfortable.

Practicality of Solution

So the next time you consider your options, remember that fifteen years is a long time to lose and cancer is no way to die. We can't change what happened to our grandparents, but we can change what happens to our grandchildren. It is possible.

Conclusion

My grandfather died of cancer, and I miss him terribly. Cigarettes accomplished what the Great Depression, a world war, a stressful career, and ten children could not. To the smokers in this class, I ask you: Sixty years from now, do you want your grandchild to be standing in front of her peers, uttering the words, "My grandparent died of lung cancer"?

Emily Goucher

References

Balance TV, "Tips for Talking to Your Kids About Smoking Day," http://www.balancetv.ca/balancetv/client/en/Wellness/DetailNews.asp?idNews=542.

CDC TIPS Tobacco Information and Prevention Source, "Health Effects of Smoking Among Young People," http://www.cdc.gov/tobacco/stspta5.htm, accessed on April 2, 2005.

"Smoking Facts and Smoking Statistics on Dangers of Smoking Hazards," *Men's Health* magazine, online edition, http://www.men-health-magazine-online.com/smoking-facts.html.

S. Sussman, C. W. Dent, D. Burton, A. W. Stacy, & B. R. Flay. *Developing School-Based Tobacco use Prevention and Cessation Programs* (Thousand Oaks, CA: Sage Publications, 1994).

Tobacco Education Prevention Program, Arizona Department of Health Services, www.azdhs.gov/phs/tepp/pdf/disparate_populations.pdf, accessed on April 2, 2004.

Sample Speech

Persuasion Speech: Comparative Advantages Pattern of Organization

Introduction

Archeological data tell us that the burial of bodies dates back to the Stone Age, or about 3000 B.C. This practice occurs in countries around the world, including Asia, North America, and Europe. Our ancestors saw burial as returning to the elements, with everyone sharing the same eventual destiny. Churches filled catacombs with the deceased and layered the dead in cemeteries. The practice of layering bodies on top of each other occurred because, even several hundred years ago, space was limited in some parts of the world.

Nature of the Problem

But even the layering of bodies has not solved the bigger problem—what to do with the remains of a growing world population. Environmentalists argue that we should be making better use of space in our cities and populated areas of the world. Health experts declare that many cemetery spaces are carriers of disease. Some studies have found that bodies from the eighteenth century still contain bacteria from diseases such as the Bubonic Plague. Celebrities are often entombed in concrete structures to avoid ravaging of their grave sites. Burials have become extravagant affairs, involving the purchase of expensive plots of land, caskets, and head stones. Many families cannot afford this kind of expense.

In short, most people would agree that traditional forms of burial carry significant risks, but not everyone understands the advantages of alternative methods of disposal. In this speech, I will compare the advantages and disadvantages of five kinds of body disposal, including city graveyards, garden cemeteries, transfer of bodies to other locations for burial, cremation, and woodland burials. By the accounts of many people, the best alternatives are cremation and woodland burials. What are the advantages and disadvantages of these various methods of burial?

City Graveyards—A Solution

Obviously, city graveyards are convenient, easy to access for purposes of funerals, and easy to visit. Many people like to know that loved ones are close at hand. City cemetery plots come with many disadvantages, however. They are often relatively shallow, making it easy for thieves to snatch bodies from their graves and leave bones scattered about the graveyard. Two hundred years ago, numerous rundown cemeteries in Europe were closed after being declared a magnet for disease and delinquency. The closing of some cemeteries, however, only made the problem more serious for those that remain open for burials.

In cities such as London, England, archeologists are stymied by the inability to conduct archeological digs in areas where bodies are buried—a significant problem since the ancestors of the Londoners did not pay a great deal of attention to where they placed the bodies of their family members. To relocate the bodies involves huge expenditures of money, generally not seen as worth the investment.

Garden Cemeteries—A Solution

In some communities, residents have moved cemeteries outside city boundaries in order to prevent the spread of disease. Their solution was to create garden cemeteries—sprawling landscaped areas, replete with benches, monuments, and yes, the deceased. We can find such communities close to most towns and cities. They are certainly attractive, and like parks, they allow people to stroll in quiet spaces. But these garden cemeteries consume large amounts of space that cannot be used for other purposes. Consider the following statistics. Approximately 6,400 people die each day in the United States. If each person has a traditional interment (6.5 feet × 6.5 feet), they will consume about 64 square miles of space each day. This calculation does not take into account the space between grave sites. That is the size of Staten Island, three times the size of Manhattan.

Moreover, once a tract of land has been declared as a burial site for human remains, no building can be zoned for that area. In more senses than one, this space has become a "dead" zone, claimed by the dead for the dead, impossible to be employed for the purposes of the living. While in the 1920s, many people took Sunday strolls in these garden cemeteries, they no longer spend their Sundays in this way. In short, the creation of garden cemeteries has not proved to be a good solution. The cemeteries could be put to better use as farm land for crops and the grazing of animals, wild life preserves, or residential areas.

Transportation of Bodies to Other Locations—A Solution

In cities such as Hong Kong, families have solved the space problem by transporting the bodies of their loved ones to the mainland. But this solution is only a temporary one. With the continuing growth of populations in countries such as China, available spaces for burial will become scarce over time.

Cremation—A Better Solution

What are the alternatives to these city and garden burial sites? The first alternative is cremation. Ashes to ashes, dust to dust. Cremation returns you to the elements immediately. With cremation, you do not decompose slowly over time. A box or coffin containing the body is placed in an oven structure. The crematorium burns the body at 1,000 degrees centigrade, reducing the body and its container to ashes and small bone fragments. The bone fragments are later crushed into a fine powder. The remains, which weigh about four pounds, are placed in an urn, which can be buried in a small plot or placed in niches above ground. Alternatively, family members can spread the ashes in a location desired by the deceased. It is important to check with local officials before proceeding with the spreading of ashes in public domains.

More than a half million people are cremated each year in North America. Despite some minor problems, such as the potential for mixing of ashes with the bodies of other cremated individuals, many people choose this alternative to traditional burials. Some religious groups also choose cremation over other alternative methods of burial. Cremation requires no services by others if the family retains the urn.

Woodland Burials—A Better Solution

If cremation violates the religious beliefs of a person or group, however, a second alternative exists. Woodland burials involve placement of a body in a biodegradable casket, which is buried in the ground. Caskets can be made of bamboo, wicker, or pine. Instead of a head stone, the family plants a tree above or beside the plot. In time, the box will decompose, as will the body, fertilizing the tree. Although the lands still qualify as cemeteries, they could be designated as wildlife preserves. Once full, they could become woodlands. Instead of having tracts of wasted land, void of vegetation, the cemeteries would be preserves of nature.

Woodland burials make sense not only from an environmental point of view, but also from a financial perspective. Woodland burial caskets are more economical than traditional ones. They cost an average of $1,000 less than other kinds of coffins. Neither cremation nor woodland burials require the purchase of head stones, which can cost upwards of $400. Cemeteries also require constant upkeep, and the families of the interred must pay for these services. Woodlands do not require the same level of maintenance.

Conclusion

In a world where the land mass is limited and the population is expected to rise to nine billion, we cannot afford to allocate so much space to the deceased. In a world where ancient rainforests are destroyed to support cattle, we cannot afford to waste grazing land on the dead. With space becoming scarcer in cities and cemeteries encroaching upon rural communities, we cannot afford to waste more time before shifting to alternative methods of body disposal.

One reason for the popularity of traditional burials was to ensure that the deceased really were deceased. That argument no longer holds, since most bodies are embalmed prior to burial. We no longer have to bury people with communication devices to ensure that they can alert us if they happen to awaken after being buried. We know when brain activity has ceased. The old excuses for traditional burials no longer work, and we must abandon a past bogged down with foolish superstitions and land wasting traditions. Add your voice to the growing numbers of those who care about our environment and our present and future needs. Reclaim our land for the living.

Crystal Cuthbert

References

J. B. Bradfield. *Green burial: The "D-I-Y" Guide to Law and Practice (New York: Hyperion Books, 1993).*

E. Hallam & J. Hockey. *Death, Memory and Material Culture* (New York: Oxford University Press, 2001).

B. A. Robinson. *Cremation vs. Burial*, www.religioustolerance.org/crematio.htm.

M. Salisbury. *From My Death May Life Come Forth: A Feasibility Study of the Woodland Cemetery in Canada.* www.earthartist.com/research/thesis, accessed November 24, 2004.

A. Taylor. *Burial Practice in Early England* (London: Tempus Publishing Limited, 2001).

Sample Speech

Persuasion Speech—Claims Pattern of Organization

Attention

They pass you on the street. They are in your classes. They may be sitting next to you or standing right in front of you. They are people with learning disabilities—people like me. No, I am not slow or stupid. Nor do I have a disease. I am dyslexic, and I am not alone. According to the International Dyslexia Association, 15 percent of Americans have a language-based learning disability. That statistic means that three of you can identify personally with what I am saying.

People like me are not less intelligent than other people. In fact, we can be academically gifted and highly motivated achievers. But we are unable to communicate our intelligence because we learn in a different way. That is, a person with a learning disability experiences a large gap between personal strengths and weaknesses. I am very good, for example, at problem solving and oral expression. But when it comes to reading and writing, as well as spelling and math, I am below average. These weaknesses sometimes make it impossible for me to communicate my strengths.

At times, I have felt hopeless, as if I were climbing a hill covered in ice, fighting to keep my grip. My successes have come from getting help and accommodations from teachers and peers. *Accommodations*—this word is a vital part of my success, but a misunderstanding of its importance has also made my journey very difficult at times.

Today I will educate you on why these accommodations do not give me an upper hand or constitute abuse of the system. I will explain why people with learning disabilities, including myself, need these accommodations in order to accomplish our personal learning goals. And I hope to dispel the myth that accommodations constitute an unfair practice. More specifically, I will respond to claims that accommodations are available to anyone who asks, they give some students an unfair advantage over others, and they constitute hand-holding. None of these claims are true.

Response to Claim #1: Anyone Can Get an Accommodation.

Some people have the confused impression that accommodations are easy to secure. My university offers a range of vital services to students with disabilities, including note-takers, taped texts, and testing accommodations. These services are not accessible to everyone. You cannot just walk in and say, "I have a learning disability and I need accommodations." You must have a valid assessment. An assessment is a series of tests that evaluate the learning abilities and outline the needs of the individual. By law, the person with the learning disability must receive the accommodations suggested by that needs assessment.

I can tell you, however, that the matter is rarely that simple. This assessment does not ensure willing compliance. No matter where I go, I find that I must fight and stand up for myself. I must argue to receive the accommodations that help me to succeed. In my case, I require extra time, access to a computer, and carbon paper. At times, I also need certain kinds of technical assistance.

Response to Claim #2: When Professors Grant Accommodations, It Is Unfair to the Other Students.

Some professors think that it is unfair to grant accommodations. On one occasion, I almost had a panic attack when a professor gave a pop quiz in class. I knew that, despite my understanding of the subject, I would not be able to communicate my knowledge in writing. Yet I had no choice; so I wrote the quiz. When I got the results, I was not surprised to see that I had failed the quiz. I did what I always do. I went to the professor's office to explain my need for special accommodations. Without hesitation, she said, "Well, I can't do anything about it. If I give special treatment to you, I will have to give special treatment to everyone and that's not fair."

Let's talk about fair. Do you believe in equal opportunity? Well, accommodations give me equal opportunity. They make life a little fairer for me. When talking about learning disabilities, accommodations, and the concept of fairness, the following example comes to mind. If Danielle were to fall unconscious, would I say, "I can't give her CPR because if I do, I would have to give CPR to Mike and Adrienne and Ashley"? Does that seem logical to you? It doesn't to me. I know that this example is a bit extreme, but that's how I feel when a professor says, "I can't do this for you because it's not fair to others."

Well, it is fair. It is fair to have someone read an exam to you if you can't decipher the questions. It is fair to have someone read your answer out loud when you cannot differentiate what is on the page from what is in your mind. And it is fair and reasonable to expect access to a dictionary that allows you to check for spelling errors. These kinds of supports do not give an unfair advantage to a student with dyslexia. Rather, they put us on the same playing field as the rest of you.

Please, can someone tell me what this says? Dis ri p the co ns e bt of he j m o n y? Sabrina? Imagine this gibberish was an exam question.

This is how people with dyslexia sometimes see things when they are trying to read. In doing this short exercise, you put yourself in their shoes. How do you feel? I don't have quite this much difficulty reading, but it is still tough. I expend as much energy reading the question as writing the answer. By the time I have finished one question, I'm exhausted. That's why the accommodation of time and a half is so important to me. In order to have the proper time to answer the question, I must have more time to read the question.

Claim #3: It Is Unfair to Ask for Help from Other Students.

The same principle applies to taking notes. I have to concentrate so much on spelling the words that I miss information. For this reason, I often ask classmates for a copy of their notes. But many of my peers are hesitant to share. I always get the same response, "Why don't you just take notes? It's not fair that I have to take them for you, while you just sit there." In response I ask, "Is it fair that I will miss half the lecture trying to figure out how to record a thought? Is it fair that, even if I get most of the lecture, when I go home to review it, it is so misspelled that I cannot read my own hieroglyphics? Is that fair?

Conclusion

Today, I have given you some clear examples of why accommodations given to students with learning disabilities are crucial for their success. Everyone has the right to learn. Everyone who expends the effort has the right to succeed. Shouldn't everyone have the opportunity to become productive and contributing members of society? I hope that today I have opened your mind and dispelled the ignorant claim that accommodations offered to students with learning disabilities are a type of hand holding, a freebie. Because nothing I have done has been easy. Achieving an education has been a battle for me, and everyday I confront the enemy.

I hope that the next time someone asks you for a special accommodation, you will remember this speech and consider the possibility that *fair* can have different meanings in different contexts. And if you look around our classroom and say, "We do not have five members of this class who are dyslexic; the statistics must be wrong," consider the possibility that the other 15 percent may have grown tired of coping with the mantra "I can't help you because it would be unfair."

Carly Fridman

References

J. M. Fletcher, W. A. Coulter, D. J. Reschly, and S. Vaughn. "Alternative Approaches to the Definition and Identification of Learning Disabilities: Some Questions and Answers," *Annals of Dyslexia* 54(2) (2001), 304–331.

International Dyslexia Association, http://www.interdys .org, accessed on March 21, 2005.

Shirley Kurnoff. *The Human Side of Dyslexia* (London: London Universal Publishing, 1995).

Maria Shivers. *Practical Strategies for Living with Dyslexia* (London, England: Jessica Kingsley Publishers Ltd, 2001).

The Dyslexia Institute, http://www.dyslexia-inst.org .uk, accessed on March 20, 2005.

Sample Speech

Sample Persuasion Speech—Motivated Sequence Pattern

Attention

Every two seconds, someone in North America requires a blood transfusion to save his or her life. By the time that I finish this speech, blood donations will have saved 240 lives. By the time we finish this class, 5,400 lives will have been saved by blood donations. By the end of the day, these acts of caring will have saved the equivalent of the population of this university. It takes less than one hour to donate your blood, and one donation can save up to four lives. Blood donations make a difference.

I am, unfortunately, not eligible to give blood because I have iron deficiency anemia. Nonetheless, I think that giving blood is a very important cause about which people should be educated. And I have done extensive research in order to share some of the most important facts on the topic. In this speech, I will talk with you about the importance of donating blood, tell you how to donate, and explain who benefits from donated blood.

Need

At the moment, America's blood reserve is in decline. Since at least 1999, the American Association of Blood Banks has been issuing emergency calls for blood in January and summer months. Five percent of Americans donate blood each year, but double that amount is required to keep the supply at an acceptable level. Many blood banks maintain only a one- or two-day reserve of certain blood types, when they require a five-day reserve. The aging population will create a situation of even greater need in the coming years.

Blood donations may not affect you personally right now, but statistically speaking, one in ten people will need a blood transfusion in a lifetime. That means that at least two people in this class will require donated blood to stay alive. But even if the person receiving the blood is a stranger to you, he or she is someone else's mother, child, best friend, or partner.

Sixty percent of Americans are eligible to give blood, but as mentioned, only five percent donate their blood. People use excuses such as, "I don't want to feel weak afterwards" or "I don't have enough time." In reality, the entire process of giving blood takes less than one hour. It is a simple procedure, which responds to a serious problem.

Satisfaction

To qualify as a donor, you must be between the ages of seventeen and seventy-one and weigh at least 110 pounds. It can be dangerous to give blood if you are not in good health. This requirement protects the donor, not the recipient. Nor can you have had any piercing or tattoos in the last year. Since tattoos and piercing can transmit HIV, the blood foundations ask you to wait a year to be sure that you are not carrying a virus unknowingly. This requirement protects the recipient.

A nurse will ask a few confidential questions, intended to screen donors to be sure that they are not at risk and that the recipients of the blood will not be at risk. Some sample questions include, "Are you taking medication? Have you had the flu in the last two days?" Following the interview, the actual donation process will take less than ten minutes. In less than one hour, you can save up to four lives with your blood. The donated blood will be taken, tested, and put into a blood bank, to be distributed to hospitals.

Visualization

Unlike the U.S., Britain is presently working with an acceptable level of blood donations. Blood is readily available to all people in need—accident victims, surgery patients, and those with anemia and leukemia.

Imagine that we were working at the same level in the United States as Britain. We would have more than enough donated blood in our system. No one would have to postpone surgery because of an inadequate blood supply. Hospitals would always have enough blood on hand. Patients at risk of dying would not have to wait for it to be shipped from central donation banks. A different future could occur, however, if the donation rate continues to decline. Hundreds of thousands of Americans could die needlessly. The baby boomers, our parents' generation, will suffer the most from the depletion of our blood supplies.

Action

We can ensure a different scenario if we donate and encourage others to do the same. This university is holding a blood donation clinic this Wednesday, November 19, at 550 Cumberland. You can arrive without an appointment, or for more information, you can call 1-888-2-DONATE. As students, you may not have extra funds to give to charities, and you may not have the time to volunteer for food banks or at homeless centers. But you can save lives by donating one hour of your time and giving the most precious gift of all—your blood.

Only a couple of months ago, my best friend's father made a successful recovery from prostate cancer because he was able to receive donated blood following his surgery. He harvested his own blood before surgery, but complications required him to receive more blood than originally anticipated. The hospital used donated blood to save his life. Without that donation, my friend would have lost her father. The next person in need could be your father, your brother, or your best friend. "Blood—it's in you to give" (www.bloodservices.ca).

Elizabeth Buryk

References

Abbott Laboratories, *The Use of Blood* (Chicago: Abbott Laboratories, 1961).

Piet J. Hagen, *Blood: Gift or Merchandise: Towards an International Blood Policy* (New York: A.R. Liss, 1982).

Denise M. Harmening (ed.), *Modern Blood Banking and Transfusion Practices* (Philadelphia: F.A. Davis, 1999).

"Hospital Waiting Times/List Statistics," www.doh.gov.uk/waitingtimes/2002/q2/qm08r_s_821.html, accessed on November 9, 2003.

"Numbers," *Time* 162 (2003): 29.

Melvin Weiner, *Personal and Social Consequences of Blood Donors and Non-Donors* (Ottawa: National Library of Canada, 1980).

Sample Speech

Persuasive Speech—Variation on Motivated Sequence Pattern of Organization

Attention

As some of you may have noticed, I am wearing a green ribbon today. Do you know what the ribbon represents? For those who don't know, the ribbon symbolizes organ donation, the topic of my speech. For the next several minutes, I will share with you the benefits of organ and tissue donations. I will lay to rest some of the fears or concerns that you may have regarding organ donation. And finally, I will let you know how you can help to save lives.

Need

I have been a supporter of organ donation for over ten years now. Let me explain why. In the early nineties, my brother was diagnosed with an unknown lung disease. He was twenty-two years old, the same age as some of you. Before his diagnosis, he was very active. Throughout high school, he was a cadet, going to army training camps every summer. He loved to play hockey and worked out regularly at the gym. While manual labor wasn't his first love, he knew the value of a hard day's work. One of his jobs involved working on a farm, where the doctors think that he contracted the lung disease.

While there is no name for his disease, it is common among people who work with animals. The symptoms are similar to cystic fibrosis, where fluid builds up in the lungs. Doing the simplest tasks, such as climbing the stairs in our home, became unbearable for my brother. My family spent so much time at the hospital that the doctors and nurses knew our family members by name, and my brother rarely had to wait in the ER. He would walk into the emergency room, find a vacant bed, and hook himself to the oxygen machine while we checked him into the hospital. After several years and many surgeries, the doctors decided that he required a lung transplant. After a year on the waiting list, my brother's condition deteriorated seriously. At that time, I was only sixteen. I didn't realize that, if he had not received his lung when he did, he would not have survived the following twenty-four hours.

As of this minute, 89,000 Americans are waiting for an organ—a heart, lungs, kidney, liver, or pancreas, just to name a few. By this time next year, 2,300 of those people will have died. Two thousand three hundred families will have lost a mother, father, sister, son, or daughter, because only twenty-three out of every one million people have chosen to become a donor. I would like to translate this statistic into something more real for you. The following statistics come from a Quebec, Canada, website. My brother was one of these numbers:

Number of Quebec Patients Waiting for a Transplant in 1996

Kidney	Kidney/pancreas	Pancreas	Liver	Heart	Heart/lungs	Lungs	Total
471	16	5	32	24	1	28	577

In 1996, he was one of ten people who received a lung donation:

Number of Transplants in Quebec in 1996

Kidney	Kidney/pancreas	Pancreas	Liver	Heart	Heart/lungs	Lungs	Kidney (live)	Total
184	1	2	95	37	0	10	14	341

And my family thanks God that he was not listed on the next chart, the number of people who died while on this list. The total number of deaths is unknown, since no data are available in some categories:

Number of Quebec Patients Who Died on the Waiting List in 1996

Kidney	Kidney/pancreas	Pancreas	Liver	Heart	Heart/lungs	Lungs
N/D	N/D	N/D	14	11	0	7

Unfortunately, many families are not as lucky as my family.

Satisfaction

What can be done to change these statistics? The number one solution is for more people to become organ donors. Some of you may be asking: Exactly what does becoming a donor entail? To answer your question, there are two kinds of donors—living and dead. The most common organ donation by living donors is the kidney. Economically, it makes much more sense for someone to receive a kidney transplant than to be on dialysis for years. The cost of a transplant can be as low as $25,000. The cost per year for someone to stay on dialysis is $50,000—a saving of $25,000 to our health care system in the first year alone. Not only that, the transplant allows for a person to resume normal activities, while dialysis is only a temporary fix.

The second type of donation can be made when you die. While this topic of conversation may not be pleasant, an uncomfortable conversation at this time can save up to seven lives, if not more, in the future. Some people are hesitant about donating their organs because they don't know the facts. That is why I am here today, to set the record straight. The perfect donor candidates are those with severe head trauma, who have been declared brain dead. These traumas may be the result of a car accident, a gun shot, a lack of oxygen to the brain, or cerebral bleeding.

Everyone can become a donor, regardless of health. In fact, the oldest donor is over ninety years of age. Most religions support the concept of organ donation, including Judaism, Christianity, Buddhism, even Quakers. Most of the other religions leave it up to the individual to decide.

Willing your organs does not mean that doctors will deliberately let you to die to increase their organ bank. On the contrary, every attempt will be made to save your life; and the doctors who care for you will have nothing to do with the transplant. Their primary concern will be preserving your life. They will only ask about your status as an organ donor after they have made every effort to save you.

Others may not want to donate for fear the recipients of their organs are smokers or alcoholics. While every concern is valid, one must ask: Is the life of a smoker any less important than the life of a nonsmoker? What if it were your mother or your uncle? Most of us have some family members who became addicted before cigarettes were declared deadly. In addition, being on a transplant list requires adherence to strict rules. If you are waiting for a liver, for example, and you have even one drink, you are kicked off the list indefinitely. The same applies to smoking of cigarettes.

My family has been on the giving, as well as the receiving, end of a donation. My cousin had a burst blood vessel in his brain. While he lived for several months, medical science could not save him. After his death, his mother donated his organs. Not all were healthy enough to use in transplants, but those that were helped to save and improve the lives of recipients. And a year after my brother received his new lung, I was involved in a serious car accident. I was unable to move for months, confined to the house for a year. Without the generosity of one person and his family, my brother would not have been there to help me recover.

Action

You are now better prepared to decide whether you want to become an organ donor. If you have decided to give the gift of life, you must take several actions. First, take out your medical card. On the back of the card is a place for a signature. If you sign the card, the doctors will ask your family for permission. If your family declines, your organs will not be taken.

To register to be a donor, go to the following website: http://www.organdonor.org/register .html. Individual states have additional locations for registration on the web. Registration ensures that doctors will not need permission from your family. Another alternative to secure your gift of life is to make a living will. If you prefer this al-

ternative, go to http://www.uslivingwillregistry
.com/register.shtm.

Visualization

Think of it this way. The heart, lung, or kidney
that you donate today could help to save the life
of the doctor who cures cancer or AIDS or lung
disease tomorrow. Imagine a future without
these diseases. Imagine a future in which the figures in this second chart outnumber those in the

third chart—if the number of organ donations
was not twenty-three people out of every million
but one-hundred or two-hundred out of every
million. Imagine the reduced suffering and the
savings to the health care system that could result
from a higher percentage of Americans sharing
their most precious gift of life with someone else.
Just imagine . . . and then give.

Lee-Ann Cass

References

A. Cline, "Ethics of Organ Transplants. Agnosticism/
Atheism," http://atheism.about.com/library/
weekly/aa052302a.htm, accessed March 21, 2004.

Emory Healthcare, Kidney Transplant Program, http://
www.emoryhealthcare.org/departments/
transplant_kidney/patient_info/faqs.html, accessed
on March 21, 2004.

A. J. Langone and J. H. Helderman, "Disparity Between
Solid-Organ Supply and Demand," *New England
Journal of Medicine* 349 (2003):704–706.

Nation Foundation for Transplants: Organ/Tissue Donation, www.transplants.org/OrganTissueDonation
.php, accessed March 21, 2004.

Quebec-Transplant, http://www.quebec-transplant.qc
.ca/anglais/public_e.htm, accessed on March 21,
2004.

E. Sheehy, S. L. Conrad, L. E. Brigham, R. Luskin, P.
Weber, M. Eakin, L. Schkade, and L. Hunsicker, "Esti-
mating the Number of Potential Organ Donors in the
United States," *New England Journal of Medicine* 349(7)
(2003):667–674.

S. Smith, "Organ Donation at the Crossroads," www
.chfpatients.com/tx/txrules.htm, accessed on March
21, 2004.

U.S. Department of Health and Human Services,
www.organdonor.gov, accessed on March 21, 2004.

Questions for Discussion

1. If you had to choose some cause to which you would leave your inheritance,
   what would it be? How does this cause represent values of importance to you?

2. Have you ever been held responsible for breaking a law that you thought should
   be eliminated? How could you use this idea in a speech to persuade? Practice
   forming a position statement on the issue. How would your audience feel about
   your position on the issue? Are they likely to be supportive, undecided, hostile,
   or apathetic? How could you approach your topic so that you could overcome
   any hostility or apathy?

3. How is social judgment theory relevant to persuasive speaking?

4. Do you think that any modern speakers can compete with the rhetorical talents
   of speakers such as Martin Luther King, Jr., and John F. Kennedy? If so, who?
   What are the characteristics of that speaker in terms of language usage? Does
   the person speak in eloquent terms or use more conversational language?

Outline

THE LANGUAGE OF PROPAGANDA

A Coffee-Shop Discussion on Ethics

Learning Objectives

- To learn both classical and modern definitions of *propaganda* and *demagoguery*
- To find out about the toolbox of the propagandist
- To understand fallacies in reasoning
- To learn about the problems related to improper use of statistics
- To discover the application of the critical communication model to questions of ethics

This chapter looks at classical and modern definitions of *propaganda* and *demagoguery*. The chapter also examines the toolbox of the propagandist—strategies used to manipulate audiences—and improper use of statistics.

Defining Propaganda

Propaganda
Information used to spread a doctrine or belief

The word *propaganda* has acquired different meanings over time. Until the seventeenth century, *propaganda* simply meant "the dissemination of ideas and information." But the term lost some of its neutrality when the Roman Catholic Church attached the label to the activities of a committee of cardinals responsible for opposing Protestantism and disseminating the Church's word in the colonies.[1] By the late nineteenth century, governments around the world had begun to use the term *propaganda* to refer to their efforts to promote political ideologies such as socialism, communism, or democracy. The growth of mass society and new media fueled this expansion of propagandistic activity. Any remaining hint of neutrality in the term disappeared with the establishment of the German Ministry of Propaganda in the years leading to World War II.[2]

DEFINING PROPAGANDA IN THE CONTEXT OF WORLD WAR II

Jacques Ellul, a contemporary of Adolf Hitler, defined propaganda in the following way: "[Propaganda is] a set of methods employed by an organized group that wants to bring about the active or passive participation in its actions of a mass of individuals, psychologically unified through psychological manipulation and incorporated in an organization."[3] In further discussion, Ellul says that groups engaging in propaganda will manipulate the truth in any way necessary to achieve their ends.

According to Ellul, these propaganda efforts can only succeed when the audience has an internal need for the propaganda—that is, when people feel vulnerable. While awaiting trial at Nuremberg, Vice-Führer Hermann Göering (head of the Gestapo in Nazi Germany) explained why people are willing to act on the rhetoric of propagandists in periods of uncertainty and conflict:

> Naturally, the common people don't want war; neither in Russia, nor in England, nor in America, nor for that matter in Germany. That is understood. But, after all, it is the leaders of the country who determine the policy and it is always a simple matter to drag the people along, whether it is a democracy, or a fascist dictatorship, or a parliament, or a communist dictatorship. . . . Voice or no voice, the people can always be brought to the bidding of the leaders. That is easy. All you have to do is tell them they are being attacked, and denounce the pacifists for lack of patriotism and exposing the country to danger. It works the same in any country.[4]

Demagogue
A speaker who capitalizes on the biases and fears of an audience, manipulating them in order to control them

Removing the idea of the audience as innocent victims of propaganda, Ellul sees society as participating in acts of propaganda. (See the Question of Ethics box.)

An associated term is *demagogue*. In the WordNet dictionary, a *demagogue* is "an orator who appeals to the passions and prejudices of his audience."[5] The 1913 *Webster's Dictionary*, on the other hand, defines *demagogue* as "one who attempts to control the multitude by specious or deceitful arts" and "an unprincipled and

A Question of Ethics

An army recruiter delivered a speech to a group of high school students, urging the young men and women to make a career in the armed forces. She included almost no facts in her speech. Instead she relied on patriotic appeals, talking about the vastness and greatness of the country, the pride of being American, and the influence of the U.S. in the world. She spoke in abstract terms and glittering generalities about the importance of serving one's country and being loyal to American values. In other words, she "waved the flag." How do you feel about this kind of speech strategy? In times of war, should speakers be able to use patriotic appeals to strengthen the resolve of troops and people at home?

Another speaker gave an antiwar speech with strong fear appeals for his persuasive assignment. Part of the speech involved graphic descriptions of the injuries suffered by some veterans of the Iraqi conflict. He also described, in detail, the kinds of torture undergone by prisoners of war and showed photographs of injuries sustained by the prisoners. Prior to giving his speech, the speaker had learned that some members of the class had relatives currently on duty in Iraq. Feedback forms also told him that other students faced the possibility of being sent to Iraq when they completed the school year. Several of his peers suggested that he should choose

a different speech topic. They thought that the antiwar content was disrespectful to their relatives and friends who were serving in Iraq. Others worried that the graphic descriptions of injuries and torture could create high levels of stress and anxiety in some audience members, who faced the prospect of going themselves to Iraq. They argued that their attendance was a class requirement; thus, they did not voluntarily choose to be subjected to the speech. The speaker chose nonetheless to present the speech, believing that the topic was sufficiently important to justify making people feel uncomfortable. He believed that support for the war would only flag when enough people realized the human cost of the war. Whose point of view do you support? Why?

A third speaker accused a politician of involvement in a scandal. She said that the politician had dined with one of the parties accused of fraud. She also said that the politician had received a thank-you letter from the person at a later date. She did not, however, offer any evidence to support the alleged link between the breakfast meeting, the correspondence, and the acts of fraud. But the audience was led to infer that a link existed. Based on your chapter reading, what was the speaker's strategy? Was the strategy ethical?

fractious mob orator or political leader."[6] Putting these definitions together, the demagogue gains power by appealing to the emotions and prejudices of listeners, and he seeks to control the masses by manipulating the truth. The rise of Adolf Hitler to power in Germany imbued the term with many additional layers of meaning. As practiced by Josef Goebbels, Minister of Propaganda for Adolf Hitler, the language of demagoguery came to be synonymous with *propaganda*.

PROBLEMS WITH DEFINING PROPAGANDA IN A MODERN CONTEXT

Some scholars claim that definitions of *propaganda* are problematic. In a modern context, communication scholars ponder the distinction among the terms *information*, *persuasion*, and *propaganda*. Every democratic government, for example, has a mandate to educate its citizenry on affairs of state. This task involves the distribution of information. At the same time, democratic governments must persuade their constituencies to accept their policies and programs if they are to remain in power. Without consensus, political parties soon lose their mandates to govern; and without a mandate, individual politicians do not remain long in positions of authority.[7] So the information and persuasion functions work together. In the same way, health communication campaigns seek to inform the public on health risks and best practices; but they also seek to persuade us to follow their suggestions:

> While health communication researchers and practitioners prefer to call their work "health education interventions" or "public health campaigns," the truth is that their ultimate goal is to manipulate people into practicing healthy behaviors. For example, doctor-patient researchers study how to make patients feel satisfied with medical encounters (i.e., manipulate patients into feeling a certain way about a medical interaction) or how to make patients comply or adhere to medical advice (i.e., manipulate patients into doing what physicians want them to do).[8]

Persuasion
An attempt to influence

Persuasion, in this context, is simply an attempt to influence public perceptions, attitudes, and/or behaviors. In common usage, persuasion can imply a friendly

effort to prod someone to action—or, at the other extreme, to coerce or bribe the person. So the term itself is neutral, although a persuader may employ ethical or unethical means to achieve personal ends. Those ends may benefit the persuader or the audience or both.

According to one definition, *propaganda* is the "deliberate and systematic attempt to shape perceptions, manipulate cognitions, and direct behavior to achieve a response that furthers the desired intent of the propagandist."[9] Thus, like persuasion, propaganda becomes an activity aimed at influencing publics and achieving the purposes of the propagandist. This modern definition of *propaganda* sounds pretty much like definitions of *persuasion*. With the proliferation of mass media and advertising, many believe that propaganda has become an institutionalized part of modern society. They claim that we are subjected daily to huge doses of propaganda from commercial organizations, governments, and even nonprofits.

Whether the terms *propaganda* and *demagogue* are in fashion or out of fashion is not very important in the context of this discussion. What is important is that some speakers (whether you call them *information providers, persuaders, propagandists, ideologues,* or *demagogues*) use unethical means to achieve their ends. Such speakers employ a number of strategies to confuse and unfairly influence the opinions of their audience.

Despite the difficulty that academics experience in defining terms such as *information, persuasion,* and *propaganda,* the average person uses the term *propaganda* in a negative context. If you happily proclaimed to your family, "I've just taken a job as a propagandist!" they would look with surprise upon your pronouncement. The word has acquired values associated with unethical efforts to manipulate the public, even though contemporary definitions of propaganda do not require this negative interpretation.

If modern concepts of propaganda teach us little that allows us to differentiate between ethical and unethical attempts to persuade, perhaps we can learn from the practices of men such as Adolf Hitler and his colleagues. Few would claim that these persuasion efforts fell within the boundaries of ethical communication. Unfortunately, Hitler does not stand alone in his efforts to motivate people to act solely on emotional (as opposed to rational) grounds. Just as the rhetoric of war provides examples of some of the most eloquent discourse, the language of war also offers examples of the most questionable in ethical terms.

The Toolbox of the Propagandist

The following discussion looks at common strategies for gaining compliance, which many would categorize as propaganda: eliciting signal responses, manipulating the truth, softening the truth, oversimplifying complex issues, relying on generalities and patriotic platitudes, stating the obvious, speaking in the third person, using extreme fear appeals, pretending to be someone that we are not, getting on the bandwagon, engaging in name-calling, and labeling people as guilty by association.

ELICITING SIGNAL RESPONSES

In the effort to shape perceptions and manipulate cognitions, unethical speakers rely to a heavy extent on emotional appeals. As noted in Chapter Nine, emotional appeals are important in persuasive discourse. Winston Brembeck and William Howell made a distinction, however, which helps us to understand the difference between ethical and unethical use of emotional appeals. They talked about the difference between *signal* and *symbol* responses. *Signal responses* are "immediate, unthinking, largely automatic, uncritical responses." *Symbol responses*, on the other hand, are, at least to some degree, "deliberate and discriminating."[10] They cited the work of linguist S. L. Hayakawa, who taught a chimpanzee to drive an automobile. The chimpanzee handled mechanical operations with ease. When he came to a red light, he stopped; and when he approached a green light, he continued without stopping. One significant difference, however, separated the actions of the chimpanzee from those of human drivers. When the light turned green, the chimpanzee accelerated, whether or not the way was obstructed. He did not modify his response to take his environment into account.[11] Instead his response was "automatic and uncritical, exemplifying the pattern of the signal response." When speakers aim for such an uncritical response from listeners, they engage in communication behavior that characterizes the kind of unethical persuasion that we often call *propaganda*. The aim of the propagandist (as defined in the context of World War II) is to bypass our reasoning processes and gain immediate access to the emotions.

Signal responses
Immediate responses —gut reactions

Symbol responses
Thoughtful responses, more deliberate

Emotional appeals are not in themselves unethical, as they stimulate an audience to think seriously and to care about a topic. They can move an apathetic audience to action. To use an analogy, water is necessary to survival; but consumed in excess, it drowns us. The same is true of emotional appeals. Used in excess, they overpower rational thought processes and encourage listeners to respond without thinking. In *Mein Kampf*, Hitler advocates the exclusive use of emotional appeals to reach his listeners, and the orators of the Third Reich used various strategies to accomplish this end:

> They complemented their rhetoric [at rallies] with flamboyant displays of pageantry, dramatic lighting, and martial music at rallies. They used posters, slogans, and symbols such as the swastika and military dress to encourage displays of patriotism to the motherland. Hitler also identified enemies of the state for censure, picked out one enemy in particular for vilification, and played on stereotypes.[12]

Believing that life is a struggle where the fittest survive, Hitler also advocated vehemence of expression. In short, the orators of the Third Reich engaged in a form of persuasion that relied almost completely on emotional appeals, without concern for rationality, truth, or common concepts of morality.[13] All of these rhetorical strategies came to be associated with the language of demagoguery, the most unethical manifestation of propaganda.

MANIPULATING THE TRUTH

They say that the first casualty of any war is truth. In the aftermath of World War II, analysts looked at the ways in which Hitler had manipulated the truth through means such as "the big lie," failure to qualify statements, and offering only one side of any argument. Hitler adhered to the view: The bigger the lie, the more likely it is to be believed. During the Gulf War, I was watching television with my husband. To my dismay, I heard a young Kuwaiti woman explaining that the Iraqi military had come into the nursery where she worked, taken infants from incubators, and thrown them on the floor. I expressed my feelings to my husband, who had been a fighter pilot in the Royal Air Force during World War II. He responded with a simple caution, "It may not be true. In war, people lie." Two years later, the story was proclaimed to be untrue, manufactured by an organization calling itself Citizens for a Free Kuwait. An account in the British press described the incident in this way:

> Take the Kuwaiti babies story. Its origins go back to the first world war when British propaganda accused the Germans of tossing Belgian babies into the air and catching them on their bayonets. Dusted off and updated for the Gulf war, this version had Iraqi soldiers bursting into a modern Kuwaiti hospital, finding the premature babies ward and then tossing the babies out of incubators so that the incubators could be sent back to Iraq. The story, improbable from the start, was first reported by the *Daily Telegraph* in London on September 5, 1990. But the story lacked the human element; it was an unverified report, there were no pictures for television and no interviews with mothers grieving over dead babies. That was soon rectified. An organization calling itself Citizens for a Free Kuwait (financed by the Kuwaiti government in exile) had signed a $10m contract with the giant American public relations company, Hill & Knowlton, to campaign for American military intervention

to oust Iraq from Kuwait. The Human Rights Caucus of the US Congress was meeting in October and Hill & Knowlton arranged for a 15-year-old Kuwaiti girl [later revealed to be a relative of the Kuwaiti ambassador to the U.S.] to tell the babies' story before the congressmen. She did it brilliantly, choking with tears at the right moment, her voice breaking as she struggled to continue. The congressional committee knew her only as "Nayirah" and the television segment of her testimony showed anger and resolution on the faces of the congressmen listening to her. . . . In the Senate debate on whether to approve military action to force Saddam out of Kuwait, seven senators specifically mentioned the incubator babies atrocity and the final margin in favour of war was just five votes.[14]

SOFTENING THE TRUTH

Transfer
Using words that deliberately evoke a positive association

Transfer involves using words or images that evoke associations of a positive nature. In the debate over cloning and stem cell research, both sides use this strategy to argue their causes. *Supporters* of cloning and stem cell research use terms such as *therapeutic cloning*, *somatic cell nuclear transfer*, and *nuclear transplantation* to transfer the positive values of medical research to cloning. The term *ethnic cleansing* became popular during the Serbo-Croatian conflict. Originators of the term sought to transfer the positive associations of the word *cleansing* to acts of genocide.

Euphemism
A word or phrase that substitutes for harsher (though often more accurate) words or phrases

Euphemisms are words or phrases such as the ones just mentioned that we substitute for more offensive or less comfortable words. We use euphemisms to soften the impact of death, war, and other unpleasant phenomena. Euphemisms for death include *passed away*, *crossed over*, *kicked the bucket*, *cashed in his chips*, and *went to his final reward*. Euphemisms related to firing and layoff practices include *downsizing*, *rightsizing*, *streamlining*, *outsourcing*, *repositioning*, *transitioning*, *reengineering*, *restructuring*, and *personnel enhancement*.

In times of war, people often use euphemisms to distort or hide the truth behind words. George Orwell, for example, wrote about the kinds of euphemisms that characterized the rhetoric of World War II.[15] When military forces invaded Grenada, they spoke of the attack as a *predawn vertical insertion*, meaning an early morning invasion. During the Vietnam war, the Military Assistance Command Office used similarly obtuse terms in their press releases. Then the Gulf War generated a whole new set of terms to talk about war. With a twist on Orwell's references to *newspeak*, William Lutz refers to this phenomenon as *doublespeak*—language that is deceptive, contradictory, and evasive. His examples include terms such as *terminate with extreme prejudice* (to kill) or *negative patient care outcome* (death of patient). These examples illustrate the language of nonresponsibility.[16] (See Figures 11.1, 11.2, 11.3, and 11.4.)

OVERSIMPLIFYING COMPLEX ISSUES

Polarization
Oversimplifying an argument to make it seem either-or

Polarization involves oversimplifying complex issues and concepts so that only two positions appear possible: "You are either for me or against me." The most recent example of this strategy appeared in the rhetoric of George W. Bush when he proclaimed, "You're either with the terrorists, or you're with us." This type of

Military Terminology in World War II

- **Pacification** (bombing and destruction of villages)
- **Orderly retreat** (running from the enemy)
- **Elimination of unreliable elements** (imprisonment, execution, and exile of political enemies)
- **Rectification of frontiers** (forcing people to abandon homes and possessions)

Figure 11.1 Examples of "Doublespeak"

Military Terminology During the Vietnam War

- **Accidental delivery of ordinances** (we bombed our own troops)
- **Incendiary jelly** (napalm)
- **Friendly fire** (accidentally firing upon one's own troops)
- **Mobile maneuvering** (trying to retreat in the face of enemy confrontation)
- **Free fire zone** (everything is a military target)
- **Civilian irregular defense unit** (mercenaries)
- **Search and clear** (search and destroy)
- **Rallier or returnee** (deserter)
- **Redeployment** (strategic retreat)
- **Combat emplacement evacuator** (shovel)
- **Protective reaction air strike** (bombing that involves aircraft)
- **Greenbacking** (paying mercenaries)

Figure 11.2 Examples of "Doublespeak"

Military Terminology During the Persian Gulf War

- **Delivered ordinances** (dropped bombs or missiles)
- **Dropped their payload** (dropped bombs)
- **Collateral damage** (civilian casualties)
- **Incontinent ordinance** (bomb or missile that misses target and kills civilians)
- **Repositioning assets** (relocating troops and equipment)
- **Gave an official assist** (CF-18s from Canada helped the United States to stop Iraqi vessels)
- **Targets of opportunity** (the enemy)
- **Shock and awe** (massive bombing with resulting fireworks displays)
- **Nonoperative personnel** (dead soldiers)
- **Servicing the targets** (killing the enemy)
- **Surgical strike** (bombing or shelling)

Figure 11.3 Examples of "Doublespeak"

Military Terminology in Iraq War

- **War against terrorism** (rationale for invading Iraq)
- **Embeds** (journalists who travel with the troops to cover the war)
- **Coalition of the willing** (countries who back U.S. position in Iraq)
- **Targets of opportunity** (any spot selected for attack or bombing)
- **Security contractors** (mercenaries)
- **Servicing targets** (attacking selected targets)
- **Collateral damage** (civilian casualties)
- **Softening up** (dropping bombs in anticipation of an invasion)

Figure 11.4 Examples of "Doublespeak"

statement leaves no middle ground for those who oppose terrorism but also question the decisions of the government. Early studies of propaganda termed this process as "two-sided orientation." With two-sided orientation, persuaders describe people as saints or sinners, good or bad, intelligent or stupid.

The language of polarization makes use of *god terms* and *devil terms*, a concept attributed to Richard Weaver.[17] Language used to characterize one's own position is always positive, while language depicting the other party's position is always negative. The debate over cloning illustrates this point. *Supporters of cloning* use god terms such as "therapeutic cloning," "tools of medicine," "wonders of discovery," "saving human lives," and "a range of choices" to characterize their position. In speaking of the opposition, they employ devil terms such as "radical antiabortion right," "closed-minded intolerant religious fanatics," and "muzzling our minds." *Opponents of cloning* use god terms such as "prolife, "dignity of human procreation," "human dignity," "strong ethical verdict," and "respect for human life" to speak of their position. They apply devil terms such as "Nazis," "a race of supermen," "eugenics," "clone-and-kill bill," "spare body parts," "genetic cocktails," "Frankensteinian research," and "the dead unborn" to the position of the opposition. As you can see, the typically loaded language of polarization often involves name-calling. Yet democracy depends upon the ability of citizens to voice their concerns and to engage in lively public debate over issues.

RELYING ON GLITTERING GENERALITIES AND PATRIOTIC PLATITUDES

Sometimes speakers cross the boundaries of ethical communication in their over-reliance on abstract words that sound virtuous but lack concreteness. They are "feel-good" words with which everyone can agree, such as *freedom, justice,* and *fatherland.* The rhetoric of Adolf Hitler was filled with these kinds of glittering generalities and platitudes, as illustrated in the following passage: "He [the Aryan] is the Prometheus of mankind from whose bright forehead the divine spark of genius has sprung at all times, forever kindling anew that fire of knowledge which illumined the night of silent mysteries."[18]

Generality
A word, phrase or idea that lacks specificity

The lack of specificity and concreteness in this kind of rhetoric raises ethical questions. The audience cannot be sure what the speaker means or what he is asking them to accept, sanction, or undertake. Many of the *god terms,* discussed earlier, also fall into the category of the glittering generality, as do *patriotic platitudes* (waving the flag to arouse the emotions of the audience). The speaker seeks to get the audience to act by making references to the greatness of the country, its moral strength, and its potential for victory over its enemies.

Platitude
A lofty but empty word, phrase or idea

Many international audiences find patriotic platitudes, usually uttered by politicians, to be superior and alienating. In some situations, however, speakers must use ambiguous language to bridge cultural gaps. In the United Nations, for example, speakers often use highly metaphorical language to reach people from many different social, economic, religious, cultural, and political backgrounds. Common in UN rhetoric are terms such as the "icy winds of change," "seeds of life," "flowers of peace," "tides of self-determination," and "fruits of aggression."[19]

STATING THE OBVIOUS

When a speaker uses tautological language, she states the obvious, as in the following examples: *Life is for the living. Nothing succeeds like success. Victory is enjoyed by those who win. Our future lies in front of us. If we don't succeed, we run the risk of failing.* Like platitudes, tautological language is bereft of meaning.

SPEAKING IN THE THIRD PERSON

Sometimes speakers remove themselves from responsibility for their actions by referring to themselves in the third person. This strategy has become more common in the last few years with athletes and politicians. Brigadier-General Janis Karpinski exemplified this strategy in August 2004 when she claimed that a conspiracy had prevented her knowing about prisoner abuse at the U.S. military prison at Abu Ghraib in Iraq. "From what I understand . . . it was people that had full knowledge of what was going on out at Abu Ghraib who knew that they had to keep Janis Karpinski from discovering any of those activities."[20] In a July 2004 court appearance in Iraq, Saddam Hussein also spoke of himself in the third person. For less clear reasons, Robert Dole made repeated references to himself in the third person in the 1996 presidential campaign. Whatever the motivations, the result is that the person assumes the status of a third party or a product. A disconnect occurs between the individual and the act.

USING EXTREME FEAR APPEALS

Extreme fear appeals are not only questionable on ethical grounds, but they also prove ineffective most of the time. Cancer patients say that they do not remember anything after the doctor says, "You have cancer."[21] In the same way, we often switch the television channel when we see images of the human victims of famine, drought, and war; and we throw away the pamphlet that depicts a badly abused animal. The images are too strong. In the case of health issues, we may rationalize by concluding that the claims are exaggerated; and we dismiss the arguments.

PRETENDING TO BE SOMEONE WE ARE NOT

Another persuasive strategy has been dubbed *plain folks*. In essence, the person says, "I'm just a simple country boy." This "plain folks" or "common folks" strategy appeals to many Americans, who respect those who have achieved success by hard work and perseverance. Typical of the plain folks strategy is the following from a speech by former Louisiana governor Edwin Edwards:

> You see, my father had a third grade education, and my mother had a seventh-grade education. We were cotton sharecroppers in rural Avoyelles Parish. I was seventeen years old before electricity came into my home. So I know better than most Americans and as well as any what opportunities are available in America.[22]

No matter his subsequent accomplishments, in the minds and hearts of many Americans, Jimmy Carter will always be a peanut farmer from Georgia, a man in jeans with a warm folksy smile. His campaign for president was highly successful in promoting this image of a man who, in reality, was far more complex and sophisticated. In the same way, many recall the images of Bill Clinton jogging to McDonald's for breakfast, images that warred with the reality of a Rhodes Scholar. And Ronald Reagan was every American's grandfather during his years in the presidency. The images of Reagan on his ranch presented a reality that was only a partial truth. And that is why some question the use of the "plain folks" strategy. They believe that a speaker should not rely too strongly on this kind of emotional appeal, particularly if the person is not really a "simple country boy." Nonetheless, many speakers do use this strategy as a means of identifying with their audiences; and some consider the strategy to be legitimate if, in fact, the representation of the person is genuine rather than contrived.

"Plain folks" strategy
When speakers (usually well-known) try to convince an audience that they are "just like them" in an effort to connect

GETTING ON THE BANDWAGON

The bandwagon argument seeks to convince listeners that they should accept an idea or join a movement because everyone else is doing it. "Get on the bandwagon. Join the crowd of supporters." This line of argumentation seeks to impress the listeners by pointing to the number of people who agree with your position. Following the declaration of allied military action in the Persian Gulf on January 16, 1991, then President George H. W. Bush proclaimed: "Tonight, 28 nations—countries from 5 continents, Europe and Asia, Africa, and the Arab League—have forces in the Gulf area standing shoulder to shoulder against Saddam Hussein." Similarly, Blogspot.com recently urged web visitors "join 60 other cities and pass a resolution to bring our troops home."[23] Political parties often use the results of polls to encourage voters to get on the bandwagon for their candidates.

Bandwagon argument
An argument that attempts to convince by suggesting that many others already agree

CALLING NAMES AND LABELING BY ASSOCIATION

Name-calling involves a verbal attack on a person using terms considered to be derogatory, such as *hawk*, *wimp*, or *pansy*. The attack sometimes involves the use of

Labeling
Name-calling

Guilt by association
Connecting a person
with another person
or idea that holds a
negative image in
order to encourage
the audience to make
the same connection

sexist or racist language, such as *pig* or *slut*. The most often cited example of name-calling comes from the period of McCarthyism, when labeling someone as a "Commie" carried strong negative connotations.

Guilt by association, on the other hand, involves bracketing the person with another person or concept that could raise questions in the minds of the audience. In one attack on presidential hopeful John Kerry in September 2004, Vice President Dick Cheney said that terrorist Osama bin Laden wanted Americans to elect Kerry as president of the United States. By saying that Kerry had the support of the country's number one enemy, Cheney used the strategy of "guilt by association." Kerry countered by referring to the sexual orientation of Cheney's daughter Mary. Although Kerry claimed that the association was intended to be positive, many believed that Kerry was trying to say that the Bush administration was not unified on the question of gay and lesbian rights. By bracketing Cheney with the gay and lesbian movement, Kerry could demonstrate this lack of unity. One of the most common applications of "guilt by association" involves bracketing the person with elite monetary interests. On a number of occasions, the Democrats have bracketed the Bush family with monetary interests associated with the war in Iraq.

Sometimes the results of guilt by association can be tragic, as in the case of the young Brazilian electrician shot eight times by London police in July 2005. The Brazilian had been labeled as a terrorist because he emerged from a building in which suspects lived.

GOING DOWN THE SLIPPERY SLOPE

When people use slippery slope reasoning, they argue that one step will lead to the next. That step, in turn, will create its own set of predictable consequences and so on. The process is similar to the argumentation that emerged during the Cold War when politicians claimed that if one government fell to communism, another would follow. When that government fell, a third would follow suit and so on. To prevent the worldwide spread of communism, the United States must prevent the first country from falling into the hands of communists. That reasoning process became known as the "domino effect." In other words, if you push down one domino, it will cause all of the others to fall. One event inevitably leads to a second, the second to a third, and the third to a fourth.

People who smoke sometimes engage in slippery slope reasoning. Before my sister gave up smoking, she argued: If I stop smoking, I will gain weight. If I gain weight, I will be more likely to have a heart attack. If I have a heart attack, I may die. Therefore, the best way to protect my health is to continue smoking. Logical? Of course not. Dying of a heart attack is not the inevitable consequence of gaining weight. Moreover, the amount of weight that one gains is under the control of the individual. The person can exercise more and pursue a healthier lifestyle.

Slippery slope reasoning
An argument that suggests that one step will inevitably lead to an eventual unfortunate outcome

PULLING OUT THE RED HERRING

In interpersonal communication, we use the term "gunnysack issues" to refer to unrelated issues that we pull out of our bag (or gunnysack) whenever we get into an argument. A couple may argue, for example, about the amount of overtime that one of the parties is working. But the argument soon encompasses a much wider range of issues—choice of friends, spending habits, dress, and family relationships. The couple may even completely abandon the original issue as they enter the territory of other emotional concerns. These issues are red herrings, not relevant to the main topic under discussion. Like a coronary bypass, the red herring diverts discussion into a different and unrelated vein.

Gunnysack issues
Unrelated issues that we work into our arguments even when not relevant

Red herring
An irrelevant point or argument, used intentionally to avoid a more relevant one

Politicians receive media training to learn how to divert questions from one area to another. The reporter asks, "What do you intend to spend this year on health care?" The politician answers, "Health care is important, but reducing our deficit is more important. I plan to introduce a three point plan for reducing the national debt." Suddenly, the topic has switched from expenditures on health care to a plan for reducing the national debt. Alternatively, the politician might say, "I'm glad that you raised that point. The cost of health care is spiraling out of control with increases in insurance rates." In both cases, the responses have little to do with the questions asked by the reporter. They are red herrings, designed to set the media agenda and distract the reporter into preferred topics of discussion.

ENGAGING IN CIRCULAR REASONING

A university department wanted to establish a graduate program. When the chair and committee members went to higher-level administrators, they were told that they needed more professors to establish a graduate program. But when they asked to hire more professors, they were told that they could not hire more professors because they did not have a graduate program. The departments with existing programs had priority. In short, they could not have a graduate program because they did not have a graduate program. It took many years for the department to escape from this circular pattern of reasoning. Usually, this kind of reasoning is employed to support the *status quo*. Circular reasoning entraps parties so that they cannot escape without breaking the pattern. With circular reasoning, the argument used to support the main premise is a restatement of the premise: "Smoking is dangerous because it hurts you" or "Give to good causes because they are worthy of support."

Circular reasoning
Using an argument whose premise is merely a restatement of the premise

LYING WITH STATISTICS

Stacking the cards occurs when the speaker does not offer complete information. Sometimes this technique characterizes the use of statistics. Governments often tell us, for example, that crime is going down. If you consider all categories of crime (vehicle theft, burglary, robberies, theft identity, forgery, etc.), the statement is true. However, *violent* crime (murder, conspiracy to murder, and serious assault) has increased dramatically in many of the countries where governments talk about lowered crime rates. Sometimes the increases are as high as 15 percent. One writer expressed the situation in this way:

Stacking the cards
A misleading argument that withholds or exaggerates key information

> We've never had it so good, but we've also never had it so bad. The latest crime statistics paint different pictures of Britain. There were nearly 6 million crimes recorded by police last year, one percent up on the previous year. For the first time, over a million of those were violent crimes, up 12 percent, but the British Crime Survey paints a rosier overall picture. So who's right? Is it up or down? First the gospel according to the British Crime Survey. Since a peak in 1995 crime in England and Wales has fallen by 39 per cent, fuelled mainly by drops in vehicle crime and burglary, that's a fall of 5% in the past year. But in the separate data for recorded crime, the statistics suggest that the most serious type of violent offences have gone up by 15% in the past year. That figure includes attempted murder up 8%, conspiracy to murder up 23% and serious wounding which endangers life—up 8 per cent on last year.[24]

If you give only the statistics or other data that supports your position, you are "stacking the cards."

Visual presentations of statistics also can give an erroneous impression. A classic book, *How to Lie with Statistics*, explained how the elongation of a boxed graph, in one direction or the other, can cause the statistics to look more or less impressive. (See Figure 11.5)

Conclusion

As noted in the critical communication model (CCM), you must look at a number of different factors in assessing any speech event. More specifically, you must consider *intent* (speaker motives and purposes), *means* (strategies, language, and modes of delivery), *environment* (economic, technological, political, social, and

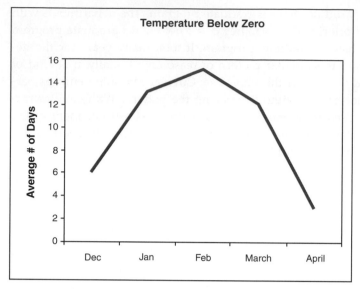

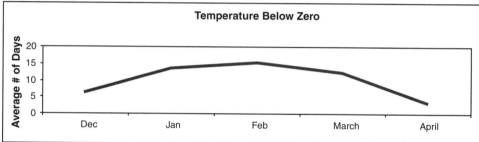

Figure 11.5 Visual Presentations that Distort

cultural factors within which the speech event occurred), *impact*, and *ethical costs of achieving one's purposes*. This chapter has concentrated largely on rhetorical strategies—that is, one aspect of *means*. However, other chapters in the book present other questions, dilemmas, and exercises related to ethics.

Judgments in some cases seem clear-cut. Hitler would clearly fail on all categories—intent, means, impact, and ethical costs. In other cases, however, the judgments may not be so clear-cut. The moral borderline in the spectrum of persuasion depends, in large measure, on the interpretation of the individual. People frequently push this borderline around on the basis of "the end justifies the means." The risks in accepting this sort of fluidity in defining the limits of ethical persuasion are high.

Questions for Discussion

1. What does the word *propaganda* mean to you? Does the term carry negative connotations? How would your family feel if you told them that you intended to pursue a career in propaganda?

2. In what contexts do we typically use euphemisms? In talking about what kind of topics? Do you think that euphemisms serve a purpose? Is that purpose ethical or unethical?

3. Can you think of any modern speaker who uses the "plain folks" strategy to his advantage?

4. Are you familiar with anyone who speaks of himself in the third person? An example would be hockey legend Wayne Gretsky saying, "Wayne Gretsky does not agree with that position."

5. When thinking about the war on terrorism, what are some of the god terms used by politicians? Devil terms? What is the potential impact of using these kinds of labels? Do you think that the rhetoric surrounding the war on terrorism tends to become extreme in the reliance on fear appeals?

6. Do you think that Americans tend to use more patriotic platitudes in their speechmaking than people in other countries? If so, does this mean that Americans are more patriotic?

7. How do you react to politicians who engage in name-calling? Do you think that this strategy is effective with audiences? Is it ethical?

8. Give some examples to illustrate problems with circular and slippery slope reasoning. Reasoning from sign. Reasoning from generalization. Can you think of an example to illustrate a red herring?

9. Have you noted any examples of flawed reasoning in the rhetoric of contemporary politicians? If so, what were they?

Outline

SPEAKING IN SOCIAL CONTEXTS

A Speech for Special Occasions

Learning Objectives

- To learn about the speaking requirements for various kinds of social occasions—after-dinner, roast, wedding toast, graduation, award and acceptance, tribute, eulogy, and introduction to another speaker

- To learn about strategies, cautions, and delivery techniques for using humor

A best man presents a toast to the bride and groom. A statesman rises to present a eulogy to a fallen leader. Friends and fellow workers gather to roast a retiring member of their organization. The soccer coach presents an award for most valuable player. An invited speaker delivers a speech following the annual banquet for members of a social club. An actress accepts an award for best performance in a dramatic film. A student delivers a graduation address at spring convocation. A motivational speaker delivers a talk at the local public library. Special circumstances call for special kinds of speeches, customized to meet the demands of that occasion. Most of us will deliver a social occasion speech at some point in our lives; and collectivist cultures, in particular, have a heavy reliance on ceremonial speaking of this nature.[1] The first part of this chapter describes some of the most common social contexts in which people deliver speeches. The second part of the chapter discusses strategies and cautions in using humor, as well as delivery techniques.

Types of Special Occasion Speeches

Outside of the workplace, the most common special occasion speeches are the following: after-dinner, roast, wedding toast, graduation, award and acceptance, tribute, eulogy, introduction, sermon, and motivational talk.

AFTER-DINNER SPEECHES

The after-dinner speaker aims to entertain her audience. Most often, she presents this kind of address in a banquet environment. The speech rarely exceeds twenty minutes in length. While the person speaks, others are often finishing the last of their desserts and coffee.

After-dinner speech
A brief speech to entertain, often in a banquet setting

Although the majority of after-dinner speeches aim to entertain, the speaker may have a secondary purpose of equal importance. She may offer information to her audience. She might, for example, talk about the history of tsunamis, haunted museums, or the economic forecast for the coming year. Most after-dinner speeches include some humorous or whimsical content, even with the most serious of topics. (See the Sample Speech.)

The organizational pattern for after-dinner speeches is generally narrative. The speaker supports the semiserious or humorous theme with a series of examples to illustrate the point. One speaker, for example, delivered a talk on "senior moments." His topic was forgetfulness. He illustrated the subject with a series of humorous anecdotes about times when he had been forgetful.[2]

Roast
A tribute comprised of a series of short speeches making good-humored fun of the honoree

ROASTS

Another social occasion speech is the roast, where work colleagues, family members, and friends pay tribute to an individual who is retiring, leaving his position in the organization, or being recognized for some accomplishment. Roasts have a

Sample Speech

Speech to Entertain

Picture this. The morning sun is just edging over the horizon, splashing the dew-covered lawns with the bright yellows and oranges of a new day. Robins and sparrows are perched outside my window, chirping a friendly welcome to the dawn. The air is crisp and fresh. The sounds of my favorite radio station, playing my favorite songs, chime from the alarm clock near my head. And I swing at it with all of my might, hoping to dislodge it from the wall outlet! Cause long-term damage, if I can.

The birds, thank you Lord, are long since gone. Their incessant and obscenely cheery chirping goes to someone else's window. You see, I hate mornings. A lot. I know that some of you are probably what we call "morning people," or what I like to call "weird." But I'm certainly not one of you. Nothing can drag me out of bed in the morning. Nothing, that is, except for a grandpa breakfast. Actually it's one of only two things that can get me out of bed in the morning—the other being a house fire. But even that isn't as effective as a grandpa breakfast.

What is a grandpa breakfast, you ask? Well, it's a breakfast made by grandpa. But not just any grandpa . . . *my* grandpa. You see, he's been in the breakfast business for a long time, serving tens upon tens of family, and . . . well, mostly family. But he's been making them for as long as I can remember. A grandpa breakfast is not spectacularly complicated. It's not fancy or frilly. A grandpa breakfast is not a gourmet meal. But a grandpa breakfast is made from the heart. It is served with a smile and a laugh. A grandpa breakfast is simply the best breakfast that I've ever eaten. Picture this. Eggs, over easy. Enough to cover the entire flat iron skillet a few times over. Pancakes, their outsides grilled to a golden brown, their insides light and fluffy. Thick maple-sweetened bacon—I've only ever tasted bacon this good at grandpa's.

Now it's usually at about this time that the scent of breakfast cooking wafts down the hall at grandma's and grandpa's place and plays tricks on my brain. It makes me think that I like mornings. It makes me think that I look good enough to wander out into the kitchen without first doing something to my bed head. This is pretty powerful stuff.

Now comes the big moment. . . . Grandpa brings everything over and . . . starts digging in himself. I'm lucky if I can get the pancakes before he does. Not to mention the fact that grandma has already commandeered the eggs and will only pass the bacon if you hand her the syrup. For a grandpa breakfast, not only do I have to get up early. I've got to be at the top of my game to fend off senior citizens who are surprisingly quick. It takes them twenty minutes to answer the door, but for breakfast, they'd make Donovan Bailey look like slow maple syrup.

Now that I've mentioned grandma, you may be wondering how she fits into a grandpa breakfast. Well, grandma happens to be a breakfast architect. I learned from grandma at an early age that the only way to eat a grandpa breakfast is to stack everything strategically—starting with the pancake on the bottom, then the egg, then the bacon, and then, of course, cover the whole construction with syrup. The beauty of this method is that, when you go for seconds, you can never get just one more thing. If you want to eat another pancake properly, then you've got to get another egg and a slice of bacon. That grandma . . . she's a genius.

When breakfast is finished and I've put away all of the dishes and cleared the table (grandma and grandpa aren't so quick now, are they?), the whole day waits ahead. I'm up, I'm fed, and I'm extremely satisfied. The sun has arched its way westward for what's bound to be a warm, sun-filled day. So what better to do than go back to bed? Picture this. One happy kid.

Tim Mowrey

mistress of ceremonies (MC) or roast master, who introduces the speakers. Preselected members of the audience take turns presenting short speeches that poke fun at the person. Usually the speeches target and exaggerate some distinguishing characteristics or eccentricities of the person. So if the person is often late for appointments, one or more speeches might center on past instances of missed appointments. Each five- to ten-minute speech has a theme, based on idiosyncrasies identified by the speaker, family members, colleagues, or friends.

Research may be required (e.g., interviews with friends and family members) to identify the most humorous stories that relate to this eccentricity. Sometimes the speakers present little gifts that make fun of this personality characteristic. If the person's distinguishing characteristic is being late for appointments, for example, the speaker might present the person with a watch or a time clock, calendar, or an ostentatious watch. The gifts are often inexpensive and humorous in nature.

Roasts employ many of the same humorous strategies as the after-dinner speech. Incongruity and unexpected twists characterize these speeches. A speaker might say, for example, "Although late for most events, Bill was always on time for the really important occasions—the office Christmas party, union votes for salary increases, and Friday afternoon dart challenges at Rosie's Pub. Is that true, Bill?"

At the end of a retirement or resignation roast, at least one person delivers a more serious address that pays tribute to the past contributions of the person, expresses regret about the impending departure, and wishes the person well in future experiences. Sometimes, however, roasts celebrate a birthday or an accomplishment, rather than the impending departure of a person. After six years of being urged by church members to complete her ordination paper, Ashley Claire Smith was officially consecrated as minister of the First Baptist Church of Pittsfield, Massachusetts. To celebrate the long anticipated and much delayed event, her congregation roasted her at an official gathering that followed the church service. One of the speakers wrote a rhymed poem, in which she used a Dr.–Seuss style of storytelling to poke fun at Ashley. At that event, the focus was on the characteristic of procrastination.

No one organizational pattern applies to speeches that roast individuals. The speaker can order the content chronologically (time-ordered), logically (topic-ordered), or with other scheme. Typically, the organizational scheme is narrative, with one main point and a number of stories to support the point. Whatever the choice of organizational patterns for the individual speeches, a series of narrative accounts dominate the event. That is, the speakers tell stories about the person.

WEDDING TOASTS

Toast
A brief set of remarks made as a tribute

Wedding toasts offer a mix of serious and humorous moments. As with many other kinds of social occasion speeches, the speaker reflects on past memories and offers a toast to the future happiness of the bride and groom. The typical order of wedding toasts follows: best man, father of the groom, father of the bride, groom, bride, friends and relatives, maid or matron of honor, groom's mother, bride's mother, and miscellaneous others. (See the Sample Speech.)

Speakers should wait to begin speaking until everyone has received a drink to be used in the toast. Since not everyone will know the speakers, they should introduce themselves and explain their connection to the bride and/or groom. Because a number of people present toasts, each speech should be short, no more than three or four minutes in length. Less is appropriate. Some toasts may be only one line in length, such as, "May your problems be as far away as yesterday and your happiness as close as tomorrow." Others may include rhyme: "May the sun eclipse the shadows, may your friends outwit your foes, may your hopes cast out your fears, and may your love outlast the years." One of my favorite Irish toasts is, "May the road rise to meet you, may the wind be always at your back." Another simple but eloquent toast says, "May the strength of three be in your journey." One of the most popular wedding toasts, of unknown origins, is the following: "If you cheat, may you cheat death. If you steal, may you steal one another's heart. If you fight, may you fight for each other. And if you drink, may you drink with me." Other examples include, "To the newlyweds, I say: 'May *for better or worse* be *far better than worse*'" and "Today I wed my best friend."

Longer wedding toasts usually include some light, as well as sentimental, moments. The lighter moments will involve humorous accounts of experiences involving the bride and groom—a time when one partner brought the wrong load of laundry back from the laundromat, a weekend without luggage in New York City, or confusion arising from having the same last names before marriage. Other moments will be more inspirational, talking about the love shared by the couple, sacrifices made to be together, or the significance of the bride and

Sample Speech

Roasting a Friend: Eulogy to a Bride

Dear family and friends. We are gathered today to remember and celebrate the life of Anna. Anna was beautiful, youthful and energetic. But sadly, Anna's life as we know it is no longer. As her best friend, I remember her favorite pastimes. She loved hanging out with her girlfriends and going to the bar on weekends. She loved shopping and cruising around the town with her friends in her cute convertible. She liked watching funny romantic films and taking long hot baths in her impeccable bathroom. I remember how excited she was when she first fell in love.

I remember how much she loved moving into her own apartment—the time she danced atop the counter at the Lebanese shwarma place. I remember all the hours we spent doing each other's hair and gossiping. I remember our weekly girls' night watching *Friends* and *Will and Grace*. I recall the road trips we would take every summer. But sadly all of this has come to an end, and we must say goodbye to Anna. Anna has left the world of singletons to be joined in holy matrimony, and some would say that a wedding is a funeral where a woman smells her own flowers.*

It is always sad when such a thing comes to someone so young and with so much ahead of her. Anna always dreamt of backpacking in Europe and learning to surf in Australia. She thought for sure that she would have the opportunity to become a model. But Anna was unable to escape the vice grip that love had on her. Shackled, she carried these chains with her for years, desperately seeking a means of escape; but after a long struggle, she could not fight any longer.

Sometimes we ask ourselves, "Why has this happened? Why is she being taken from us?" But we must remember that fate works in mysterious ways and that Anna will always be with us in spirit and in memory. Even if she can no longer fly to Vegas with us for Christmas, we will think about her at home with her new husband and mother-in-law.

And many new experiences await Anna. Instead of going out to lunch with the girls, she can accompany her husband to the pub for wings and beer. Instead of enjoying her clean bathroom, Anna can enjoy scrubbing the bathroom clean. Instead of driving in her convertible, Anna can watch her husband spend countless hours trying to fix it without success. Instead of wearing lingerie to bed, she can wear earplugs. Instead of watching romantic comedies with Julia Roberts, she can watch action films with Arnold Schwarzenegger. Instead of watching *Friends* and *Will and Grace*, she can search for the humor in Jimmy Kimmel and *The Man Show*. Road trips will be replaced by fishing trips, girls' night by poker night, and her little black book by babysitting numbers.

And so while we may be feeling sorry for ourselves for losing Anna in our everyday lives, we should really be feeling sorry for Anna. Being a carefree single girl is not something you can easily get back. Let us take the time to say goodbye. Goodbye to girls' night out, goodbye to clean bathrooms. Goodbye to lingerie and to road trips. Goodbye to the little black book. Goodbye Anna. For a woman may be incomplete until she is married, but after that, she is finished.†

Rosalind Marchut

*Tom Haibeck, *The Wedding MC* (Vancouver: The Haibeck Group, 2002), p. 68. The original quote was, "A wedding is a funeral where a man smells his own flowers."
†The original quote, by Zsa Zsa Gabor, was "A man is incomplete until he is married. After that, he is finished."

groom having found each other. Like the humorous moments, many of these serious thoughts will appear in the guise of stories (e.g., a story about how the couple met or how one spontaneously flew to Paris to spend a weekend with the other person). In planning the wedding toast, each speaker draws on his or her repertoire of past experiences with the bride and groom. The longer wedding speeches often conclude with a one-line toast. Whether lengthy or brief, wedding toasts should always steer away from vulgar language and stories that involve other partners. The stories should make the couple smile, not blush with embarrassment.

The organizational pattern is generally narrative, involving a series of stories linked to some central theme. The style of language and presentation should be conversational, warm and friendly in tone. You are speaking to a room of friends, people united in their desire to wish the couple a healthy and happy marriage.

GRADUATION SPEECHES

Keynote speakers or invited commencement speakers have three major goals: to congratulate the graduates on their past accomplishments, offer some advice in the present, and wish them well in future undertakings. If a speaker follows this pattern, she is pursuing a chronological pattern of organization—past, present, future. Although the overall structure of the talk is chronological, within this larger pattern, the speaker may use a secondary order such as topical or narrative. (See the Sample Speech.)

Conceivably, a champion of activist causes could adopt one of the persuasive patterns of organization; however, graduation speeches are almost always inspirational in nature. When universities and colleges select commencement speakers, they choose them on the basis of some life accomplishment. The keynote speaker will have excelled in some career area or made a notable contribution to society. Sometimes the person will be a noted political figure, a writer, or a celebrity. Not infrequently, commencement speakers have special ties to the university, college, or town in which the educational institutions are situated. The person may be a former graduate or a native of the community, or their daughters or sons may attend the school. The university or college typically awards an honorary degree at the graduation ceremonies to the keynote speaker(s). Exceptions occur on rare occasions. On June 11, 1999, Mumia Abu-Jamal delivered a thirteen-minute audio-recorded speech from his jail cell to the graduating class of Evergreen State College, Olympia, Washington. Abu-Jamal is a convicted killer (regarded by supporters as a political prisoner), presently facing execution on death row in the Pennsylvania prison system. An activist student organization promoted this highly controversial event to bring awareness of what they regarded as institutionalized racism in the criminal justice system. In 1992, Evergreen students had selected another controversial figure, Leonard Peltier, as commencement speaker. Convicted on circumstantial evidence for the murder of two FBI agents, Peltier was the national leader of the American Indian Movement (AIM). Organizations such as Amnesty International have called for the retrial of both men. A student member of the Mescalero tribe read the commencement address for Peltier.[3]

Sample Speech

Mock Commencement Address

In the now famous speech, the class of 1997 was advised to "Wear Sunscreen." Tonight, friends and fellow students of the class of 2003, I would like to tell you to "lose your bra"!

Most of you are probably saying to yourselves right now, "What is she smoking?" and "Where can I get some?" I would like to share a little story from my university career to demonstrate what I mean when I say, "Lose your bra."

As for many of you, my first year of university was one of adjustment. I arrived at our university not knowing a soul. I questioned my sanity at going so far from home, into a new and alien environment. In high school, I had been rather quiet and shy. The thought of public speaking or being in the spotlight froze me with fear. I would rather have written a thirty-page paper than talk in front of a classroom of my peers.

One night during frosh week, a group from my floor went down to Faculty Hollow to hear the Philosopher Kings. In the middle of one song, the lead singer said to the audience, "If you give a little, we'll give a little." I guess this request appealed to Chloe, the bad angel who sits on my right shoulder, because—all of a sudden—my bra was sailing through the air. It landed squarely on stage in the glaring spotlight. I felt free—in more ways than one!

In later years, I have come to view that moment as the symbolic gesture of throwing off my adolescence, overcoming my fears of expressing myself, and growing up a little. Today, instead of asking ourselves where we would like to go to university, we are asking ourselves, "What do I want to do with the rest of my life?" The answers are scary. We are leaving the comfort and routine of university life to go out into the "real world."

Basically, the bra—and I'm not trying to be feminist here—represents all of our fears and inhibitions that we have regarding the unknown and the novel.

So I urge you tonight, when the bra is restricting your movements, too tight to be comfortable, lose it. Take all those fears and doubts and throw them away. And when you ask yourself, "Should I take that job in California?" Lose the bra. "Do I want to move in with my boyfriend or girlfriend?" Lose the bra. "Do I want to do my master's?" Lose the bra. Even if things turn out badly, everything (as our parents have often told us)—good or bad—is experience. And everything happens for a reason.

I expect to be throwing my bra many times this year. Not only am I about to receive my diploma, signifying my freedom from nineteen years of educational drudgery, but my parents are moving halfway across the country. I will be sharing a house with my friends and hoping that they will not turn into my enemies. I have no clue what type of career appeals to me, nor do I have a permanent job, unlike some of my peers who have already established themselves in various organizations.

Back in first year, we had to lose the bra in order to mature. Today we need to lose the bra in order not to fear what the future holds. Over at our sister institution, the valedictorian has just spent a half hour talking about how much he will cherish his university experience and how his education has prepared him for the workforce. I just spent five minutes telling you to get naked. Guess who lucked out?

Christine Gravelle

Unlike keynote speakers, valedictorians, salutatorians, and class speakers are members of the graduating class. These individuals will have achieved a position of status within their class by virtue of academic achievements. The salutatorian speaker typically has the second highest average in the graduating class; the valedictorian has the highest average. Salutatorians greet the graduating class, and valedictorians bid the class farewell. Both recall the highlights of shared school experiences, note the accomplishments of their classmates, and wish their classmates well in future endeavors. Following this pattern, the overall structure of the talk is chronological; however, within this larger pattern, the speaker may use a secondary order such as topical or narrative.

Salutatory and valedictory addresses are part of long-established rituals with symbolic significance and emotional impact on the participants. The speeches may, nonetheless, contain moments of humor. Conforming to historical traditions, salutatorians at Princeton University deliver the salutatory address in Latin. Only the news media receive an English translation of the address. The graduating students, for their part, receive a copy in Latin, which indicates appropriate places to laugh, applaud, groan, or otherwise react to the speech. To attending members of the audience, it appears that the students have a complete grasp of Latin, whereas in reality, the planners have manipulated the occasion for humorous effect. Unless they are scholars of Latin, the audience members (constituted of families and friends) will have no idea of what is said in the salutatory address.[4]

AWARD AND ACCEPTANCE SPEECHES

The presenter of an award must accomplish the following. He must give the name of the award, the reason for its establishment, and criteria for granting the award. Subsequently, he must identify the winner of the award and talk about how the person meets the criteria for award winners. When speaking of the qualities of the winner, the presenter should be specific and concrete, giving examples or anecdotes to illustrate the points. If the audience includes competitors who lost, the speaker should also acknowledge the quality of the competition. The presenter may conclude by talking about feelings of pride associated with being selected to give the award. Speeches of presentation rarely exceed four or five minutes in length. The most common organizational scheme is topical, using the aforementioned categories.

In accepting an award, speakers should express appreciation for the award and acknowledge those who played a contributing role. They should thank both the donor(s) of the award and the presenter. The speeches should be short, to the point, and humble in tone. Being acquainted with the history of the award (its establishment and former winners) will allow the person to comment on what the award means in personal terms. Recipients of awards should avoid saying that they do not deserve the award. Such statements degrade the choices of the committee that selected the individual and diminish the credibility of the speaker. The speaker may say that he will try hard to represent the values of the organization that selected him. (See the Sample Speeches.)

Sample Speech

Sample Acceptance Speech

It is an honor to accept this basketball trophy, most valuable player, on behalf of Stephane Nkakibirerero, who cannot be here tonight. I've known Stephane since he arrived in this country from Burundi, and I would like to share with you guys how much this award means to Stephane. From grade 9, Stephane and I have been a part of this team, contributing our skills and talent. But it wasn't easy, as I'm sure you remember. We had to work really hard to improve our basketball skills. Well, there wasn't much that I could do because I was too short. And it didn't really help to have a little belly that slowed me down.

But you guys don't know Stephane's story. How did Stephane go from the basketball player who ran with the ball instead of dribbling it to the all-star player that he is today? Well, I know, because I was there every step of the way. You really have to put yourselves into Stephane's shoes to understand how this great transformation came about. First, picture a tall African high school kid who just came straight from his homeland. Then remember that Burundi is all about soccer, not basketball.

When Stephane first picked up a basketball, he could neither dribble nor shoot the ball. And he always played by his own rules. He ran with the ball every time that it was passed to him. After seeing him play for the first time, I was certain that there was no hope for him in basketball. Maybe soccer, but not basketball. Stephane was definitely *not* a good basketball player when he first started five years ago. But no matter how embarrassing his skills, he always loved the game and never stopped trying. I remember in grade 10, Stephane and I spent almost every day playing basketball after school, so that we could improve for the coming season. Even when it started getting cold, we continued playing in our winter coats and gloves. Now when you hear that two Africans are outside playing in the winter, you automatically know there's a problem. Stephane was allergic to the cold New England winters. His thin body had not adjusted to the horrible conditions. But he still managed to practice in the freezing cold because of his love of the game.

Over the years that I've known Stephane, I have come to realize what a great achiever he is. When he first started playing for this school, he sat on the bench most of the games—right next to me. And for three straight years, Stephane and I sat together on the bench, watching instead of being a part of the game. Remember, I had an excuse for being on the bench. I was too short, and my little belly slowed me down! It wasn't my fault. I loved hamburgers and hot dogs back then. I'd never eaten such foods in Burundi.

But Stephane made no excuses for himself. He wanted to play. He was tired of entering the game with only a minute left, giving a break to those who had played most of the game. I said to him: "Stephane, this coach is never going to give us a chance. It's embarrassing to be on the bench all of the time. Let's just quit and go have a burger." He looked me in the eyes (like this) and told me, "Arcade, I won't quit and eventually I will be the best!" Stephane surely proved me wrong. He did become the best the following basketball season. He averaged over fifteen points a game and went from playing two minutes to playing the whole game. He proved himself to everyone who thought that he would never be a good basketball player. And he definitely proved himself to me. Stephane turned a dream into reality through his hard work, determination, and spirit. This is a man we should all respect for his achievements—and not only on the basketball field. But academically and as a person. Once again, let's give a round of applause for this year's most valuable basketball player.

Arcade Kakunze

Sample Speech

Spoof Acceptance Speech

Thank you! Thank you so much! Wow, this is such an honor. I am truly shocked. I never expected to be Employee of the Year at Bob's Burger Barn—such a great place to work and be part of. It is an honor that I truly accept graciously.

You know, I can still remember the first day I walked through the Bob's Burger Barn doors. It was my first shift, and Daddy had got me the job because Momma is actually Bob's fifth cousin by marriage—or is it seventh just plain cousin? Oh well, never mind, you all know how everyone in this town just seems to be related somehow.

Anyway, I was a nervous wreck that first day on the grill, let me tell you. I was putting bacon on the Barneriffic mushroom melt (which we all know should just have cheese) and Barn BBQ sauce on the Bawk Bawk Barn chicken burger, which of course only requires mayonnaise. Man, what a day! I was so down, really having lost all hope of succeeding in this place. And as the orders piled in front of me, I thought, "I can never be a grillin' girl. Look at this. I'm messing up right and left." And that's when my now best friend Bobby Jane got beside me on that grill, told me to pull myself together, stand tall, and turn my frown upside down, because I was a Triple B girl now.

She told me that, as a Bob's Burger Barn employee, I had to strive for perfection and be composed at all times. It was now my duty to make sure that every man, woman, and child's order was a-okay so that they too could have a Barneriffic day and walk out of here with a smile on their faces. I watched her, completely mesmerized by her quickness; learned from her; and soon mastered my grilling skills. To this day, I live by the words she said to me on that first shift. And I never forget my purpose here. I would like to give a very special thank you to Bobby Jane for helping me on that one fateful day and for nominating me for this prestigious award. Without you, I would not be standing here right now.

Next I would like to thank another colleague, one who helped me to push the envelope and exceed the Triple B employee standard, setting a new record. Tommy Rae, I will never forget that cold, blustery night last month when those two buses pulled into our parking lot. They were old folks, headed down to Las Vegas, looking for food to fuel them up before they gambled their pensions away. I can still picture Tommy Rae's face as he yelled, "Code Red, Code Red, man your stations," as dozens of hungry seniors came bursting through the Barn doors. I turned and told him not to worry: We were ready and trained, and we would do this together. And do it we did. And as most of you know, that night I broke the record for the most perfect orders served in one hour. The previous record was 68, and that night I put out 162 perfect orders in sixty minutes. What a complete rush that was, and Tommy Rae, I could not have done it without you, buddy. You manned that cash like a pro, taking those orders without missing a beat. Thank you so much.

Next month will be my seventh year here at this wonderful place, and I truly feel it is my second home. The Triple B staff have become like a family to me. You are all assets to this company in your own ways—and an inspiration to me personally. And next week, when I am promoted to Barn Supervisor #2, I will strive to continue the Burger Barn tradition of teamwork, exceeding customer expectations. I will push even harder for perfection with each and every order.

Lastly, I would also like to thank my general manager Jimmy Henkle and Barn Supervisor #1 Marilee Sauvé for choosing me for this award. This is a dream come true, and I am truly honored to be accepting it today. But most of all, I am proud to be a part of this great team and proud to say that I am a Bob's Burger Barn employee. Thank you all again, and wow, this has just been the most Barneriffic day ever! Thank you!

Jennifer Pierce

On most occasions, the language of the acceptance speech will be relatively formal and dignified in tone. The organization is topical, reflecting the aforementioned categories. The speaker may tell a story to illustrate a point. Any humor should be gentle, evoking smiles rather than guffaws. Sometimes speakers accept awards for others who are absent. The same rules apply to those speakers. Speeches should not exceed several minutes in length.

At times in past years, winners of Academy Awards have chosen to use the award ceremony as a platform for expressing their political views. In 1973, Marlon Brando asked an unknown Native American, Sacheen Littlefeather, to speak on his behalf at the awards ceremony. Forced by show producers to abandon her plans for a fifteen-minute speech, Littlefeather appeared in full Apache dress to say that Brando would not accept the award for best actor in *The Godfather*. The refusal was in response to the film industry's poor treatment of American Indians. Some audience members clapped, but many booed.

In 2003, amid hisses and boos, best documentary film winner Michael Moore invited the other documentary nominees on stage to denounce President George W. Bush. Moore proclaimed, "We are against this war, Mr. Bush! Shame on you, Mr. Bush, shame on you!" The audience did not appreciate his actions. In such a situation, audiences are often resentful. They feel that the person has taken advantage of a position of privilege, a gift. Speakers who choose to promote their personal agendas must accept the risks associated with these actions.

TRIBUTES

Tribute
Speech that celebrates a person or commemorates an event or cause

Speeches of tribute celebrate the life of a person, recall an event of significance, or commemorate a cause. Tributes to *people* are often emotional and personal. The speaker uses language to paint a portrait of the person. Rather than just say that the person is generous, the speaker describes actions performed by the person— the time that the person sent a bag of groceries to the home of someone without money, drove two hundred miles to assist someone whose car had broken down on the highway, or took meals on a weekly basis to homebound seniors. The specifics allow us to obtain an understanding of why the person should be admired. No one organizational format exists for speeches of tribute about people. The speaker may build a metaphorical comparison, construct a series of stories about the person, or simply detail characteristics with supporting examples. Whatever the organizational pattern, the speaker should pursue a central theme. The nature of the occasion dictates the length of the speech. (See the Sample Speech.)

Other tributes honor *events* or *causes*. A speaker might deliver a speech, for example, on the anniversary of a decisive battle in World War II or civil rights event such as the march through Selma, Alabama, on "Bloody Sunday." Numerous speeches mark the anniversary of September 11, 2001. Other tributes are delivered in remembrance of causes. In the following address, University of Calgary professor Leslie Tutty remembered the massacre of fourteen young women in Montreal, Quebec. For forty-five minutes on December 6, 1989, deranged gunman Marc Lepine roamed the halls of Montreal's École Polytechnique in search of female victims. In one classroom, Lepine separated the men from the women and screamed, "I

Sample Speech

Speech of Tribute

She stands a symbol of virtue. A symbol of strength. A symbol of resilience. She is a homemaker, a dressmaker, a shoemaker, a baker, and a tailor. She is a disciplinarian, a teacher. She is a psychologist, nurse, wife, and a compassionate friend. Her mother called her *Eula*, her friends call her *Galy*, others call her *Mother*. But I call her *Mama*. I stand here today to pay tribute to a lady who gives her all in expectation of nothing in return. I stand in recognition of my mother.

My mother has ten children. Her life has been one of self-sacrifice in the rearing of the ten of us. As a child, I was amazed at the fact that she was always the last to go to bed at night and the first to wake in the morning. She just had to make sure that we were all safe and accounted for in the home. *This is Mama the protector*.

There were times when we were sick with the cold or the flu. This lady would be up at 2 A.M., preparing a hot poultice and rubbing a back or chest with eucalyptus oil. The warmth of her hands and her gentle touch of love never failed to speed our recovery. *This is Mama the nurse*.

One of Jamaica's famous dishes is the traditional rice and peas. The main ingredients are kidney beans, rice, and coconut. Anyone who knows anything about rice and peas knows that the best rice and peas are cooked over a slow fire until all the rice grains split. Mama knows this—and almost everything else there is to know about cooking and serving a meal. This was how she earned the name *Galy*, as she is always found around the fireplace, or galie, at weddings, parties, church, and community functions. She is famous—not only among us, but throughout the community—for her cooking. *This is Mama the cook*.

My mother is a devoted Christian. She believes that God placed her on this earth to be of service to others. For this reason, she has always adopted an elderly person in the community who does not have any relatives. She performs household chores for this person and ensures that they have a warm meal every day. *This is Mama the social worker*.

My mother is a firm believer in the phrase, "It takes a village to raise a child." Every child was her child. For this reason, our home was a place where every child was welcomed. And she treated them as she treated us. She was a strict lady, but even the most rebellious child in the community gravitated toward her. *This is Mama the caregiver*.

As a family, we saw rough times. Money was not always available. But we were always clean and fed, and she ensured that we all went to school, no matter what. She believed that a good education was important if we were to get the most out of life. She was always encouraging not only us, but also our friends, to get good grades and to become involved in extracurricular activities. *This was Mama the motivator*.

The wise man Solomon said, "Who can find a virtuous woman? For her price is above rubies. The heart of her husband doth safely trust in her. She seeketh wool, and flax, and worketh willingly with her hands. She riseth also when it was yet night and giveth meat to her household. Her children shall rise and call her blessed. Many women have done well but thou excelest them all." *Mama, you have truly excelled them all.*

Claude Pike

hate feminists!" before opening fire on the women. In this speech, Tutty responds to the question, "Why do we remember the fourteen young women murdered in Montreal?" Her answer to this question extends beyond the deaths of fourteen women. In that sense, the speech is more of a tribute to a cause than a eulogy to the victims, who died eleven years earlier:

> *We remember* because they might have been our daughters, sisters, friends. This was the first incident in Canadian history, perhaps in recent world history, when a group of people were targeted and murdered simply because they were women. This must not happen again. *We remember*, not to punish men for the violence that other men perpetrate against women, but to appreciate the men who do advocate for women's rights—the men who create white ribbon campaigns and join us today in memoriam. . . . *We remember*, because of the seldom-heard voices of other Canadian women who live every day with the threat of violence and even death. . . . And so, *we remember* the fourteen young women because it reminds us that countless Canadian women live with violence every day and we need to do something to address this sad fact. *We remember*, so we can channel today's grief into action, to read, do research, advocate and protest any act of violence against others, but for today, especially, violence against women. . . . Finally, *we remember*, because it would be dishonourable to the memory of the fourteen young women killed in the Montreal Massacre, to forget.[5]

Our most central values lie at the heart of speeches of tribute. We talk about what matters most to us in terms of personal qualities, causes, and events of significance. We identify our heroes and talk about the ideals for which they stand and for which we should strive. Some are collective tributes to veterans of foreign wars or the "unknown soldier." Others remember distinguished people such as Martin Luther King, Jr., or celebrities such as Elvis Presley or Marilyn Monroe. Many speeches of tribute explicitly acknowledge the shared nature of the values held by speaker and audience. These speeches are inspirational in nature, encouraging the audience to stretch its goals and extend its reach.

EULOGIES

Eulogy
Tribute spoken at a funeral or memorial service honoring the deceased

Eulogies are speeches of tribute to those who have died recently. Ministers, family members, and close friends deliver such tributes at funerals and memorial services. A Greek derivative, the term *eulogy* means "good word."

Audiences anticipate that eulogies will pay respect to the person who has died by praising his good qualities and contributions while living. More specifically, eulogies recognize the death of the person, establish the relationship of the speaker to that person, talk about the impact of the deceased on the speaker and others, and offer consolation to the family and friends of the deceased. Eulogies do more than talk about the accomplishments of an individual; they also talk about how the person lived his life. They usually have a spiritual dimension, where speakers reassure the audience that life continues beyond the moment of death. If the eulogy does not contain such a religious bent, the speaker will reassure the audience that the good deeds of the eulogized will continue to live in the memories of those who knew them. (See the Sample Speech.)

Sample Speech

Eulogy

Last week my Grandma died. This past weekend I returned home to remember her and to say good-bye. Her death was a moment of clarity and reflection for me. It was an opportunity for the reality of mortality to truly sink in and manifest itself within me. Thoughts that had been contemplated over and over again in my head throughout the summer returned and have been revisited. Just over four months ago, my Grandpa passed away. The odd juxtaposition of their deaths is comforting, in a sense, as they blend together in my mind as one event.

It was somehow easier this time around, as I could trust in the closure that Grandpa's death had provided me. I would like to speak a bit about my relationship with Grandpa, as he and I were a little closer than Grandma and I. My journey home was an opportunity to say one final farewell to both, who have joined each other somewhere, if only in my mind.

On Saturday, I had an eight-and-a-half hour drive home from university. And on that trip, I spent a great deal of time thinking about Grandpa—about his life, his accomplishments, his ethics and morals, his faith, his genuine nature and gentle approach. I thought about crocano (a favorite pastime), buckets of lawn mulch in the garage (I never knew the reason for the mulch), the woodshed behind their house (a great place to play), rhubarb (Grandma made him pies from a huge rhubarb patch), the rub of his whiskers across my face when I was a child, and his quiet little chuckle. He was always "pretty fair." The seasons went in cycles (some years being dry and hot, others being wet and cold). The weather has always been hotter and always been colder.

On that trip, I thought about my grandparents, the things I have thought and never said. I thought about the letter I never wrote. And let me tell you, I often thought about writing it, just never did.

It was after I graduated from high school that Grandpa and I became really close. On my trips home from university, I always tried to reserve an afternoon, with at least an hour and a half, so that I could visit with Grandpa and Grandma. We talked about a lot of things. Among others were politics, history—American history, world history, and family history. His past, my future, and God. It was a rare moment when Grandpa wasn't familiar with a topic, but when he wasn't, he was upfront about it and we moved on.

It is important that I express a little of what Grandpa taught me during our many conversations about God. For a little background, I come from a Quaker family. Quakers are pacifist Christians who believe in the good in everyone and in the ability of everyone to have a personal relationship with God. Our services do not have preachers or pastors. The service is conducted in silence until someone feels touched to say something. It could be a poem, a scripture, or just a thought. Funerals are conducted in the same way.

Grandpa showed me that God is accessible, visible, active, and loving. Most of my faith has found root both in what Grandpa has told me and in who Grandpa is. In life, he was a profoundly good person because of his relationship with God. Whenever he explained to me a virtue from his faith, I saw that virtue in him. Patience. Kindness. Selflessness. Humility. Peace. Generosity. Inclusiveness. Tenderness. Love. Compassion. Commitment. Forgiveness. Understanding. Work ethic. All of these traits that Grandpa wore so easily found their origin in his understanding of God.

As his grandson, who falls short in so many of these categories, I am overwhelmed by the magnitude of this man's spirit. And I recognize how

(Continued)

Sample Speech

Eulogy—cont'd

fortunate I am to have been able to spend time with him—learning, sharing, and growing. In my mind, Grandpa is the epitome of Christianity. In my mind, he personifies what Jesus was trying to tell us over two thousand years ago. How wonderful it is for a message to be so fresh—and alive—and accessible to us here today.

There has been a powerful feeling that has been constantly invading me over the past few days. My grandparents are together and young again.

I love my grandparents very much and will miss them dearly. And this is the letter that I wish I had sent. These were the words I wish I had said.

Adam Brown

When offering a eulogy, speakers should take care not to overextend their praises so that the eulogy rings false. Most people have faults; they are not perfect. Therefore, eulogies should concentrate on the strengths that will be recognized by audience members—love of family, dedication to hard work, or generosity of spirit, for example. The speaker should bolster the assertions with stories that demonstrate the best qualities of the person. Eulogies should address a limited number of character or personality traits. If you talk about too many qualities of the person, you will not have time to develop the ideas with stories and examples. The language of eulogies should be simple but eloquent. A beautiful example of such a eulogy comes from Edward Kennedy, speaking at the funeral of Robert F. Kennedy:

> My brother need not be idealized, or enlarged in death beyond what he was in life, to be remembered simply as a good and decent man, who saw wrong and tried to right it, saw suffering and tried to heal it, saw war and tried to stop it. Those of us who loved him and who take him to his rest today, pray that what he was to us and what he wished for others will some day come to pass for all the world. As he said many times, in many parts of this nation, to those he touched and who sought to touch him: "Some men see things as they are and say why. I dream things that never were and say why not."[6]

When offering a eulogy, the speaker shares his profound sense of loss, his sadness, with the audience. At the same time, he recognizes in specific terms that the pain is not his alone—that the audience shares in the loss. Although some speakers inject gentle humor into eulogies, the overall tone is somber and dignified. Patterns of organization vary but always include much narrative content.

INTRODUCTION OF ANOTHER SPEAKER

Chapter Four discussed the demands of introducing oneself to an audience. The following discussion offers guidance to speakers who are introducing a second party. In such a situation, you greet the audience in a warm fashion, introduce

yourself if you are unknown to the audience, introduce the speaker and the topic of the speech, and talk about the qualifications of the speaker to present on this particular topic. In other words, your aim is to create a warm, friendly climate and to build the credibility of the speaker. You should also establish the importance of the topic for the audience. Why should they care about listening to the speech? What can they get from the occasion? You want to instill a sense of anticipation in the audience without overselling the speaker. Excessive praise can make a speaker feel unable to rise to the occasion and create unrealistic expectations in the audience.

Speakers usually provide biographical statements to those who will introduce them. The presenter should study the statement prior to introducing the speaker and integrate the comments into her presentation. Even though the practice of providing biographical details is necessary, the speaker does not want to focus audience attention on the prepared statement. Otherwise, it will appear that the person being introduced is promoting herself. Rather, the details in the biographical summary should appear to originate with the person who is offering the introduction. The presenter should emphasize those details that are most relevant to the occasion and topic and not feel obliged to include every point on the prepared statement.

The presenter should check with the speaker, prior to delivering the introduction, to verify details and check for acceptability of the comments. Also, the presenter should be certain that she can pronounce the speaker's name. In introducing presenters to the Los Angeles assembly, speaker Fabian Nunez mangled the names of two California Supreme Court justices. After mispronouncing the last name of

Justice Kathryn Mickle Werdegar, Nunez introduced Justice Ming Chin as "Ming Ching."[7] To make matters worse, Nunez had a reputation for giving a speech instead of an introduction.[8]

Statements of introduction should not exceed four to five minutes in length, even for a long speech. Prior knowledge of the speaker should dictate the length of the introduction. The more well-known the speaker to the audience, the less needs to be said. You can create a greater sense of drama when you withhold the speaker's name until the final moment.

Finally, you should be certain of the appropriate title to be used in the introduction. Many European and Canadian professors, for example, use the term *Professor* in preference to *Doctor*, while American professors tend to use the designation *Doctor*. Women may have a preference for *Miss*, *Mrs.*, or *Ms*.

As with other kinds of speeches, you must adapt speeches of introduction to the audience and occasion. Some speeches of introduction occur within business (as opposed to social) contexts. More formal occasions demand more formal introductions. Comments should be in the spirit of the occasion and never violate standards of good taste. Organizational patterns vary.

SERMONS

Sermon
Speech given in a religious context, usually one-point speech, intended to inspire

Sermons seek to instruct, inspire, and motivate; and they tend to be one-point speeches of a narrative nature. The minister, rabbi, or other spiritual leader, for example, uses a parable or story to introduce the main point or lesson of the sermon. He then proceeds to develop the point through a series of examples and stories. At the end of the sermon, he pulls together the narration with a concluding comment about its application to the lives of congregation members. Some of the most acclaimed speeches in political rhetoric use this same narrative pattern. The speeches of Martin Luther King, Jr., for example, were more like sermons than like the argumentative discourse advocated in classical persuasion textbooks. King did not follow a problem and solution, motivated sequence, or other persuasive format. Rather, he delivered sermons in speeches such as "I've Been to the Mountain Top" and "I Have a Dream." Through the technique of repetition, he pulled together disparate threads of thought.

MOTIVATIONAL TALKS

Like sermons, motivational talks fall into the category of speeches to inspire. They do not aim to instruct, as such. Outside of business settings, the most common motivational speeches dwell on personal relationships, fulfillment of personal goals, and financial gain. Speeches that address personal relationships and goals leave the audience with an inspired thought, a story, or a moral that they can take away with them. Other motivational talks focus on the materialistic, suggesting ways to achieve an easy fortune, succeed in the stock market, or save money.

Motivational talks tend to take place in service clubs, convention auditoriums, public libraries, and other social settings. The most credible motivational speakers have earned a reputation by performing altruistic deeds or contributing to society in some fashion beyond the rhetorical. This person might have overcome significant physical challenges to achieve personal goals, worked as an advocate for social justice causes, served with a group like Doctors Without Borders that helps impoverished children in developing countries, or made some significant contribution to world peace. We are inspired by the person. When we listen to the person speak, we know that the words are not empty shells. These are the motivational speakers who command the greatest respect from audiences.

Like sermons, motivational talks tend to be narrative in nature. The speaker introduces the main point of the talk and then amplifies the point with stories, personal experiences, examples, testimonials, and vivid descriptions. Unfortunately, less competent motivational speakers often sound more like preachers (in content and cadence of delivery), and audiences sometimes react with negativity to sermon like discourse delivered in lay settings.

The Use of Humor

Speakers use a number of strategies to build humor into their speeches. Those strategies include exaggeration or overstatement; understatement; incongruous and sometimes absurd comparisons; pairing personality characteristics with inanimate objects, events, or activities; playing on stereotypes; puns; irony; and oxymoron.

HUMOROUS STRATEGIES

Exaggeration
Making something larger or more significant than it is, often for comic effect

Speakers and comedians use *exaggeration* for humorous effect. "If you drove any slower, we would need to requisition the foot patrol for a walking permit." "Her fur looked so real that I offered to feed it." "It was so cold that a flea could have done a slalom run in my ear canal." Comedian Robin Williams used exaggeration for humorous effect with the following comment: "The only people flying to Europe will be terrorists, so it will be, "Will you be sitting in armed or unarmed?"[9] See the Sample Speeches for examples of exaggeration.

Understatement
Making something smaller or less significant that it is, often for comic effect

A second technique involves *understatement*. "In the event of a nuclear disaster, expect some delays in your mail service." "No, I'm not upset. Would you like to share a cup of Windex with me?" While waiting for surgery after a March 1981 assassination attempt, President Ronald Reagan looked at his doctors and said, "I hope you're all Republicans." See the Sample Speeches for additional examples of understatement.

Sometimes speakers use *comparisons* for humorous effect. "Forgetting your wife's birthday is like sudden death in tennis. The game's over." "Fighting for peace is like shouting for quiet." "A narcissistic personality is like a mummy—all wrapped up in herself."

Another technique involves *pairing personality characteristics with inanimate objects, events, or activities*. American Comedy Awards winner Margaret Smith once joked, "My uncle Sammy was an angry man. He had printed on his tombstone: What are you looking at?"[10] In this case, the speaker achieves humor by combining a common occurrence (people visiting gravesites) with a personality characteristic (anger). If you put together a different personality trait (slowness) with a common activity (swimming), you can see how it works: "Johnny liked to swim with his dog. But it was quite a job for the dog, paddling backward to keep up with him."

Stereotype
Popularly held belief or generalization about a type of person or group of persons that does not consider individual differences

Humor sometimes depends on audience acquaintance with *stereotypes*. Robin Williams once joked, "We had gay burglars the other night. They broke in and rearranged the furniture."[11] Comedian Chris Rock calls upon our acquaintance with a number of stereotypes in the following joke: "You know the world is going crazy when the best rapper is a white guy, the best golfer is a black guy, the tallest guy in the NBA is Chinese, the Swiss hold the America's Cup, France is accusing the U.S. of arrogance, [and] Germany doesn't want to go to war."[12] As I will discuss in the next section, those of us who do not qualify as comedians must take great care not to cross ethical boundaries with regard to evoking stereotypes.

Pun
A play on words

Speakers sometimes use *puns* or plays on words for humorous effect. Sometimes puns involve gaining humor from double meanings of words. The next example illustrates this point: "I used to work for a tow company, but it got to be too much of a drag." A second example could be: "My boyfriend has no trouble with commitment. Any hospital will take him." At other times, the humor comes from slight changes in the wording, as the following example illustrates: "Fullerton (California) divorce lawyer Linda Ross has a sign in her office that reads, 'Satisfaction guaranteed or your honey back.'"[13]

The next and final example demonstrates how plays on words can also involve mispronunciations:

A robbery took place at the home of an elderly immigrant woman. As the robbers ran from the house, her neighbors heard her frantic shouting, "The *bully's* coming.

Sample Speech

Speech to Entertain

Today is December 1, and it is indeed a special occasion. Only twenty-three more days to shop the malls, in search of that perfect Christmas gift—or let's face it, for some people, any gift at all. As consumers, we head to the malls, sharing Christmas cheer with throngs of other shoppers—shoppers who grow increasingly more desperate as the number of chocolates disappear from their Advent calendars.

As it happens, I am not just a consumer. Like many of you, I am also a student who earns extra money through part-time jobs. I earn that money working as a sales clerk at Pharma Plus, and this year will be my third retail Christmas. Because this is the first day of December, our last day of classes, I thought that I would share with you some of my favorite Christmas moments. This is our story, mine and yours, of a retail Christmas.

As we wander the malls, some of our favorite Christmas songs fill the air—"Jingle Bell Rock," "I Saw Mommy Kissing Santa Claus," and the seemingly endless "Twelve Days of Christmas," each day more riveting than the last. I know these songs well because as of the first of December, they will be the theme song of my life—repeated in sequence, every twenty minutes, for the next twenty-three days. The monotony of the soundtrack seems as endless as the streams of people lining up at the cashes.

I can still remember my first retail Christmas. It was December 1, 1999, about 9:45 P.M. I was sixteen and not nearly as jaded as I am today. The malls were busy that day. Customers were entering the store in hordes, ravaging our displays, leaving their coffees and soft drinks on our shelves, filling their hands with more junk than they would ever need at any other time of year. They came through our cashes with wrapping paper, gadgets, decorations, gift baskets, and chocolates.

We were four cashiers that evening, and I had already seen one fall. An angry woman cried vengeance on poor Nathalie when she discovered that we had run out of Planters peanuts—as if it was Nathalie's fault. Tears welled up in Nathalie's eyes as she fled the ever-expanding lines of shoppers for the solitude of the store bathroom. "Not me," I said, "I shall not fall."

The tension mounted as customers continued their campaign of pillaging with their credit cards and gift certificates. Another agitated shopper looked in my direction as she remarked loudly to her friend, "This is ridiculous. They should really open another cash." I wondered what she expected me to do—build one right there, out of the stack of empty coffee cups lining our stockroom desk? The sweat was beginning to bead down my face as we struggled to move faster and faster. Out of the corner of my eye, I noticed a man step out of line. He had a roll of wrapping paper and a travel-size bottle of Listerine. He glared at me, eyes wide open. His face, which under non-Christmas conditions would have been normal, had turned a bright red. As he drew nearer to the front of the line, I was sure that conflict was eminent. It was obvious that he intended to perform a "bud," and without the permission of the gentleman in front of him. In elementary school, we learn that the consequences of budding without permission can be dire. Were my vibes right? Was he about to commit this transgression?

Another customer called out, "Hey, that's not right!" pointing at the red-faced gentleman. He had been caught. He turned his glance toward me, demanding that I offer his very important person some special consideration. "I'm sorry, sir, but you'll have to follow the line," I said firmly. Then the Christmas spirit hit me, literally. It struck me in the form of a bottle of Listerine and a tube of wrapping paper, hurled toward my post. I turned to protect my head, but left my back exposed to assault from the travel-size

(Continued)

Sample Speech

Speech to Entertain—cont'd

Listerine. I bore many scars that night—and not just from the customer's choice of projectiles.

December 1 is an important day, you see. There are only twenty-three days left to shop. It is the first day of that wonderful soundtrack. Most importantly, it is a day when the consumer-retailer relationship enters its bitter transformation. I tell you this from the eyes of a retailer. And yet I know that I am not all that patient when I journey to those suburban jungles that we euphemistically call malls. This year, however, my theme song will not be of a partridge in a pear tree, but of John Lennon, as I ask myself, "And so this is Christmas and what have you done?"

Nicholas Kowbel

The *bully's* coming." Worried that the woman was unable to get a grip on herself, the neighbors rushed to her side. They pointed to the departing truck of thieves, "See they're going. We'll call the police." "No need, I called already," the woman replied in an agitated voice. "The *police* coming. The *police* coming."

Stories and anecdotes sometimes come with an *unexpected twist*. In a twist on the joke that typically relates to men, comedian Carol Leifer once commented, "I don't have any kids. Well . . . at least none that I know about."[14] This joke also relies on *irony*, which entails drawing a contrast between the expected and unexpected, as in the following example: "It is ironic that her desire for success led her to destroy everything and everyone that could have assured that end." Irony can involve saying the opposite of what we mean: "Sure, I can pay back my school loan in no time. I'll just live in my minivan, put myself on a no-calorie diet, and jog to work to save gas. No problem."

Irony
Using words that convey the opposite of their literal meaning

Sample Speech

Speech to Entertain

As some of you may have noticed, I have had my hair trimmed. Just a little bit off the top.

In one of my classes, we had a discussion about the possible motivations for cutting my hair. There were many suggestions—none of which were right. The real reason is a deep-seated psychological need that manifested itself as early as five years of age. In hopes of shedding some light on my internal motivations, I would like to describe an incident that occurred when I was in kindergarten.

It was arts and crafts time and—as all good children do—we were sitting around our table, eating paste and cutting paper to eat later. At that particular point, I had a thought—perhaps inspired by the paste, perhaps evidence of my struggling creativity. In this moment, I was inspired. The muses of art and beauty struck. I decided that I was going to create the greatest art the world had ever seen. That's right. I decided to cut my own hair. I knew that this inspiration would not last long; so I decided to cut my hair right there in the classroom. The rebel inside me was screaming for release. I was challenging the norms set down by our elders. My classmates were awe struck by my audacity. My friends tried to stop me, but I would not hear their arguments. I was breaking free. No more bowl cut for this kiddo!

But first I needed to test the scissors to ensure that they would make a clean cut. So I applied them to the bottom of my shirt. The large chunk of fabric that fell away before the awesome power of these shears was a testament to their designer and manufacturer. Having seen clear evidence that my tool of choice worked, it was time to select the canvas for the expression of my creative juices. I chose a swath of my hair an inch wide directly over my left eye. This would be an ideal location to showcase my talent and my struggle for independence. With the site chosen, I carefully removed the selected follicles, in a manner similar to the clear-cutting of a forest.

When I got home, my parents were not as impressed with my art as my friends had been. In fact, they saw it as some sort of vandalism. They demanded an explanation. I was cornered. I had to think fast. If my parents knew that I was a rebel at heart, I would never again be allowed to roam free. So I devised a tale so ingenious that not even the great detective Sherlock Holmes would be able to figure out what had happened.

My first tactic was denial. "What do you mean what happened to my hair? Nothing happened." It would seem that my parents were smarter than I had reckoned. They examined my hairline closely and demanded to know who had cut my hair. The piece missing from my shirt seemed to lend credibility to their theory that something had indeed happened, and they suspected that I had done it myself. I could see it in their eyes. Time for my backup plan. "Uhh, I didn't cut it off."

They demanded to know, if it wasn't me, then who was it? I chose the most logical answer I

(Continued)

Sample Speech

Speech to Entertain—cont'd

could. "Ummm . . . I was on the playground at recess and . . . uhhh . . . a kid came up to me with scissors and . . . attacked me, cut my shirt, and cut off my hair." The words tumbled out of my mouth.

My parents wanted to know more. Who was this crazed hairdresser? What did he look like? The interrogation was brutal, but I kept my cool. "Uhhh . . . I don't know his name, but I think he is in . . . umh . . . grade 6."

I gave the best description I could conjure. "He was wearing a jacket that was red and black and grey (the same colors as my own vest). And I think that he had a bowl cut." I was brilliant, a masterful storyteller. Someday I would be a player in the international game of espionage.

My parents looked concerned and puzzled. My dad tried to break me. He said, "Now look, Chris, you won't get in trouble if you just tell us the truth." Yeah, right. I'd heard that one before. I stuck to my story. It became a war of attrition, one that I was determined to win.

The next day, my parents again tried to force me to reveal my secrets. They tried to convince me of the value of being honest. But I had carefully evaluated the situation and developed several scenarios. I was prepared for every possible tactic that they could use to tame my wild nature and regain their hold over me. Soon it would be time for me to strike out on my own, and this situation had become a way for me to break free of my parents' mind control.

On the third day, my dad came to my school and pulled me out of class. We went down the hall to the sixth grade classroom to identify the culprit. My emotions were riding a stand-up looping rollercoaster. I imagine the feeling was somewhat similar to what a death row inmate feels on his way to the execution chamber.

This was not an action I had anticipated. I gave the only answer I could. "Nope, I don't see him."

Now for those of you who remember the size difference between a kindergarten student and a grade sixer, you can well imagine my terror at facing a whole classroom of giants. I was stunned that my daddy would try something so evil to force my hand.

Later that night, at dinner, my father informed me of the actions to be taken. He told me that, since I was unable to identify the barbarian, the entire grade 6 class would lose their recess privileges until the guilty party came forward.

"Oh, the humanity of it all!" If my parents were willing to go to such lengths and punish others to force my confession, I was obviously in a battle I could not win. I had underestimated my parents and their desire to crush my spirit. I had fought a hard battle, but I could not allow others to suffer for the actions of a heroic freedom fighter such as myself.

Of course, the other consideration was that the grade 6 class would eventually discover who was behind their loss of privilege. This would no doubt result in some serious bloodletting. And since I was a fat little kid, I was convinced the blood would be mine.

I confessed, but I still managed to strike a blow for posterity. Class pictures were the next week, and the evidence of my fight against conformity was center stage.

And so, for those of you still wondering about my motivations for cutting my hair this time, it should be obvious that it was simply a manifestation of my desire to be a heroic freedom fighter. Or maybe I was just having paste flashbacks?

Chris Ratcliffe

Sometimes speakers use *oxymoron* for humorous effect. An oxymoron contains a contradiction. A speaker could say, for example, "She had a genuine fake fur" or "It was real imitation leather." Other examples are "paid volunteer," "virtual reality," and "small crisis."

Oxymoron
A phrase that contains a contradiction—*jumbo shrimp*, for example

CAUTIONS IN USING HUMOR

Humor should always bear a strong relationship to the content of a speech. Even with after-dinner speeches, the linkages should be obvious and explicit, as in this example: "As Jerry learned when he leapt from the top of the Eiffel Tower, our perspective changes as we get closer to the ground." Otherwise, the speaker runs the risk of appearing to be a standup comedian, moving from one joke to the next.

Speakers must also recognize the ethical limits of using humor—not the same as those that govern comedians. Because comedians operate in the theater of the absurd, we allow them a wider margin and special privileges. On March 3, 2005, a Santa Barbara judge ruled in favor of Jay Leno's right to make satirical comments on the Michael Jackson child molestation trial. Comedians such as Jay Leno and David Letterman earn their living by making fun of human frailties and weaknesses. The assaults on character are often strong; and no one is safe, especially politicians and celebrities. Speakers, for the most part, are held to more rigid standards than comedians. In general, speakers must shy away from ethnic and sexist jokes, as well as character slurs. (See the Question of Ethics box.)

Research suggests, however, that members of oppressed groups (as defined by gender, race, politics or religion, economics, physical characteristics, or sexual orientation) tend to use more *self-deprecatory* humor—humor directed at themselves—than do members of other groups.[15] Generally speaking, we can poke humor at groups in which we hold membership, but we cannot use humor at the expense of groups in which we do not hold membership. Lawyers can make jokes about lawyers, and doctors can make jokes about doctors. Lesbians and gays may refer to themselves as *queers* or *dykes*, but they will take offense if others use the terms as a source of humor. But there are limits even with self-deprecating humor. Some feminists resent the use of stereotypes in jokes about women, even if the remarks come from comediennes. Comedian Bill Cosby argues that the use of derogatory labels is unacceptable, whether coming from black or white performers.[16] We can laugh at ourselves in some situations, but not in others. Speakers must evaluate the tolerance of the audience and the larger society for humor that is self-deprecating. They must assess the potential costs of the humor.

Self-deprecatory humor
When speakers gently poke fun at themselves

As will be discussed in Chapter Fourteen on ghostwriting, differences also exist between males and females in terms of their appreciation and use of humor. Men tend to enjoy jokes with a punch line more than women, whereas both men and women appreciate anecdotal humor.[17] Men also like to tell stock jokes.[18] Women, on the other hand, have a hard time telling a stock joke without forgetting or messing up the last line. They tend to be much more comfortable with experiential humor, telling stories about themselves and their families (extensions of themselves).[19] More than is the case with men, their humor tends to be self-deprecatory and aimed at power structures and figures.[20]

A Question of Ethics

Asked to speak at a roast honoring Willard, a work colleague, Charlie, thought at length about what he could use as focal points for the speech. He thought about Willard's habit of triple checking everything. Willard also mumbled to himself when he was upset with someone, especially his boss. A third habit involved making appreciative comments about an attractive female employee. Charlie decided to use these traits as the basis for his speech. On the night of the roast, Charlie strode confidently to the podium. He began the speech by talking about Willard's admiration of female employees, especially Barbara.

Out of the corner of his eye, Charlie saw Barbara stiffen; her husband looked angry. Willard's wife didn't look too happy either. Caught off guard, Charlie fumbled over the next several sentences before reaching the part about his colleague's triple checking everything. He glanced in the direction of Willard, as the room grew quiet. No one was laughing, and Willard's face now matched the color of his burgundy tie. Charlie didn't know what to think, and he wanted to be anywhere but in front of this audience. Only afterward did someone tell him that the couple had been having marital difficulties related to jealousy, and Willard struggled with an obsessive compulsive disorder that involved repeating actions multiple times. Willard's boss laughed when Charlie talked about his employee's tendency to complain about his requests, but Willard did not look happy.

Ellen had a similar experience. She delivered a wedding toast to her best friend, Melanie. In the toast, she talked about Ellen's efforts to hide her relationship from her family and their friends in the months leading to her engagement. Living secretly with her boyfriend, Melanie was afraid to tell her family, whose religion did not sanction intimacy outside of marriage. When Ellen talked about Melanie's efforts to deceive her family, a hush fell over the room. Melanie blushed in shame and her family looked shocked and upset. Ellen thought, "Oh no, what have I done?"

What can we learn from the mistakes of Charlie and Ellen? Have you ever been witness to—or made—a similar mistake?

DELIVERING HUMOROUS CONTENT

In terms of delivery, humorous speeches call for a more theatrical presentation than other kinds of speeches. You can use larger and more exaggerated arm and hand gestures and broader facial expressions. You can move your eyes in ways designed to get a humorous reaction or drop your jaw, as if in astonishment. Like the comedian, you should insert pauses after punch lines. After-dinner speakers, who aim to entertain, use more extreme inflections of the voice, mimic sounds, or impersonate a person or animal. Often they leave the podium and employ the entire body in the presentation. As noted previously, however, the speakers must take care not to offend any individual or group.

Conclusion

Most of us will present a social occasion speech at some point in our lives because social occasion speeches celebrate the highs and lows of life. Although some (e.g., eulogies) are more formal and somber in nature, others (e.g., retirement roasts) focus on the light and whimsical. But even when the speeches are light in tone and whimsical in spirit, they usually have some inspirational moments.

Questions for Discussion

1. Have you ever delivered one of the kinds of speeches discussed in this chapter? If so, what was your experience?

2. Have you ever attended a social occasion such as a wedding or shower where the speaker offended the person he was supposed to be honoring? How did the audience react to the derogatory comments? How did the subject(s) of the jokes react? Were they embarrassed? Offended? Hurt?

3. Can you recall an eloquent speech delivered at a funeral or other somber occasion? What made the speech memorable and special?

4. As a speaker, are you comfortable using humor? Do you prefer to tell jokes with a punch line or to recount stories with humorous content? As a listener, what kind of humor do you prefer?

5. Is it acceptable to poke fun at groups in which you hold membership? What if the jokes enter the public arena?

Outline

SPEAKING IN CLASSROOM CONTEXTS

A Team Presentation

Learning Objectives

· To understand what is involved in preparing and presenting a successful team presentation, including choosing a theme, establishing teaching and learning objectives, and determining an agenda for learning activities

· To learn how to manage group dynamics, including drawing the audience into question-and-answer and other interactive activities

· To find out how to integrate the various components of a team presentation

Imagine the following scenario. The course instructor has assigned Nancy, Jim, Belinda, and Rodney a group presentation on risk management. The four students meet to discuss their strategy for the presentation. Nancy volunteers to deliver a lecture on current health and environmental risks such as mad cow disease, bioterrorism, and possible mutations of the avian flu virus. Jim offers to research and present a discussion on current theories related to managing health and environmental risks. Belinda assumes the task of putting together a presentation on how to engage in planning for risk management. Rodney says that he will research and discuss the efforts of several major corporations in the area of risk management. Having allocated tasks successfully, the four leave the meeting with a sense of confidence that they have achieved a credible plan. Sound familiar?

The day arrives for the group presentation. Each member rises and makes a fifteen-minute PowerPoint presentation to the class. The quality varies from one to the next presentation, depending upon the skills of the presenter. At the end of the four lectures, the members sit down, satisfied that they have fulfilled the requirements of the assignment. Certainly, they have achieved the most basic goal of delivering an oral presentation on a selected topic. Chances are that presentations by the other students will look and sound much the same. But a learning theorist might have some questions: What were the teaching and learning objectives for the presentation? Did the group choose the right strategies and use its time wisely? Did the audience learn anything from the group presentation? What do audience members remember? Could the class answer content-based questions at the end of the presentation?

Too often, the response to these questions is *no* because the presentations do not reflect broadly accepted design, learning, teaching, and oral presentation strategies. Rather, the group has relied on the most common teaching technique, the lecture; and they have equated hearing with learning. The selected process to transmit knowledge has been one-way, offering little opportunity for feedback outside of possible questions and answers at the end of the presentation. This scenario is repeated again and again in classrooms around the country, on a range of subjects from business to engineering to communication.

As the numbers of students in classrooms increase, instructors find that time often does not permit individual presentations of material; and they call on their students more and more frequently for small group presentations. Oral presentations by groups create new challenges, different from the requirements for individual presentations or speeches. At the same time, group presentations offer new teaching and learning opportunities for students. The classroom becomes an exciting forum for learning when students exercise creativity and strategy in their oral presentations, engaging their audiences through active learning techniques.

This chapter seeks to introduce the basic principles of how to design and deliver an effective small group presentation—one that will depart from the expectations associated with other speaking genres. More specifically, we will examine how to choose a theme for the presentation, establish teaching and learning objectives, decide upon an agenda of learning activities, manage the group dynamics, and deliver the presentation. The material in this chapter is geared to students interested in teaching, training, and interactive team presentations of all varieties.

Choosing a Theme

First, the group meets to decide upon a theme for the presentation. A presentation on communication planning can focus, for example, on the relationship among different kinds of planning—strategic, operational, and work—to show how everything fits together. This focus governs the organization of the presentation. When designing a presentation on cultural differences in communication, you could have a theme such as "different but equal." Your theme for a talk about e-mail communication could be "e-mail etiquette." If you have titled your presentation, you have probably selected a theme for the presentation. If ideas are too scattered, your presentation will seem confused and disorganized. So choosing a theme, early in your planning, prevents a disoriented approach to the subject matter.

Theme
The main focus of a presentation—often, its title

Setting Teaching and Learning Objectives

The next step in the process is to establish teaching and learning objectives. These objectives flow directly from the theme of the presentation and define what a group wants to achieve in the presentation. For example, in a presentation on risk management, group members might decide upon this *teaching* objective or goal: "To convey the importance of risk management in the current business environment and to identify strategies for dealing with high-risk situations." Teaching goals are written from the perspective of teachers or, in this case, small group presenters.

Teaching objectives
The ideas a speaker or group wants to get across to their audience

The group should also write *learning* objectives, which they frame from the perspective of the listeners.[1] Learning objectives are audience-centered. They tell the listeners what they will acquire from the presentation in the way of information and/or skills. What will the listeners take with them when they leave the room? In framing learning objectives for their presentation on risk management, Nancy, Jim, Belinda, and Rodney can say that (at the end of the group presentation) the class should be able to:

Learning objectives
Intended outcome of a presentation, from the perspective of the audience

1. Discuss at least three reasons that risk management has become a current topic of importance to those who work in health and environmental spheres.
2. Identify four current threats to our health and environment.
3. Reflect in writing upon several contemporary theories of risk management.
4. Pinpoint six common elements that appear in the strategies of corporations noted for successful risk management practices.
5. Generate at least two statements that could appear in each section of a risk management plan and explain how these statements reflect current theories and best practices.

In addition to being audience-centered, the objectives should be specific, unambiguous, measurable, positive, and realistic,[2] although some learning theorists disagree on the desired level of specificity.[3] If you wanted to add a behavioral component to objective 2 (in the previous list), you could write, "In a role play, you should be able to demonstrate knowledge of several contemporary theories of risk management." Even if not explicitly stated, the means to measure the achievement of a learning objective should be immediately obvious. In this example, the presenting group could test for knowledge of risk management theories by giving a quiz or could test for ability to apply the theories and best practices by asking the class to generate a skeletal risk management plan.

The *teaching goal* for a presentation on assertiveness training could be "to provide skills in assertiveness." The *learning objectives*, written from an audience perspective, could be the following:

At the end of the session, audience members should be able to:

· Analyze their own communication styles.
· Diagnose situations that call for more assertive behaviors.
· Identify the techniques for communicating assertively.
· Apply assertiveness techniques in interactions with aggressive personalities.

As you can see, these earning objectives are audience-centered. They are also clear and specific in wording. They are measurable in the sense that the presenters could test the ability of the audience to analyze their own communication styles, diagnose situations that call for assertive responses, identify assertive communication behaviors, and apply the techniques in a simulated situation. The objectives are positive in wording, and they are realistic and achievable.

Most theorists believe that the framing of learning objectives contributes to the reduction of anxiety,[4] focuses audience attention on relevant concepts,[5] and increases learning.[6] Stating and reiterating these learning objectives in opening and closing the group presentation is important. If you put the teaching and learning objectives on transparencies or PowerPoint, they will be most clear to the audience.

Agenda
A list of things to accomplish

Learning styles
Ways in which different people understand concepts

Deciding upon an Agenda of Learning Activities

Decisions on the agenda should be based on application of sound learning theories and principles of audience adaptation. The agenda should include a variety of activities that take different learning styles into account.[7] (See the Keep in Mind box.)

Keep in Mind

Activities

· Icebreakers
· Energizers
· Guided fantasies
· Storytelling
· Gallery exercises
· Read arounds

· Timelines
· Card sorting
· Case studies and scenarios
· Fishbowl exercises
· Role plays
· Artwork and other visuals

TAKING LEARNING THEORIES INTO ACCOUNT

Studies have demonstrated that learners retain 10 percent of what they read, 20 percent of what they hear, 30 percent of what they see, 50 percent of what they see and hear, 70 percent of what they say, and 90 percent of what they say and do.[8] In classroom situations, a retention rate of 10 percent is common,[9] probably in large part because of heavy reliance upon lectures as a dominant method of conveying information. What does this finding imply for the design of group presentations?

First, learning theory suggests that oral presenters should actively engage their audiences in the learning process.[10] This necessity conforms to current trends in society and in educational theories. Stand-alone lectures violate the principles of engagement. Lectures offer a fast, efficient way of transmitting large quantities of information, but the results in terms of learning are often questionable. Some say that, instead of trying to "cover" the content, instructors should aim to "uncover" the material by using a number of interactive demonstrations and problem-solving activities that engage the learners.[11] Instructors should draw more on the ideas and experiences of the students, especially in the case of older adults and professionals. Older and professional audiences want facilitators and coaches, not lecturers. They like to share information within a structured framework, and they like group exercises.

A *second* principle relates to organization of course content. Educators have learned that lectures should be broken into no more than fifteen-minute learning "chunks."[12] My own experience has demonstrated that, in a one-hour presentation by students, groups should limit lecture components to five-minute chunks for maximum effectiveness. In a three-hour presentation, the students should adhere to ten-minute "mini-lectures." Lacking the experience of their instructors, student presenters have a harder time holding attention in lectures, especially if they select relatively dry facts for presentation. Other more interactive parts of a small group presentation can, however, be longer than five or ten minutes.

A *third* principle in learning theory asserts that individuals vary greatly in how they prefer to learn. Some people may prefer to learn new material by listening (auditory), by reading or viewing (visual), by touching (tactile), or by doing (kinesthetic).[13] Auditory learners might get the most out of hearing an audiotape of a speech or listening to music while they work. Visual learners might want to examine photographs, see graphical depictions of the material, or watch a film or television show. Those with a preference for the tactile might like to work on the computer, use their hands in some way, or take notes. The kinesthetic learner likes to practice the skill.

A *final* principle relates to priorities. Professionals in training situations, for example, want to acquire the information, learn how to apply it, and move to the next point.[14] They enjoy the stimulation of discussing ideas; but at the end of the day, they want to know how they can use the ideas. Time is important to the professional. Lack of organization and failure to respect learning agendas can seriously undermine the credibility of an instructor. Older learners are also less interested than younger learners in being entertained, and they place less importance on liking the instructor.[15]

Close to twenty years of teaching workshops to professional communicators allows me to validate the aforementioned points. And in 1983, Howard Gardner, professor of education at Harvard University, developed a comprehensive theory of multiple intelligences that explains and amplifies these ideas.[16] This popular theory advocates the existence of nine potential pathways to learning (originally Gardner proposed seven avenues to learning):

Multiple intelligences
Theory that suggests that people have nine possible pathways to learning

- Linguistic intelligence (ability to understand, use, and appreciate words)
- Logical-mathematical intelligence (ability to think in logical terms, to reason abstractly, and to see numerical patterns)
- Visual-spatial intelligence (ability to think in images and pictures and to discern visual and spatial patterns)
- Bodily-kinesthetic intelligence (ability to exercise control over body movements and to handle objects with agility)
- Musical intelligence (ability to produce and appreciate melody, rhythm, pitch, and timber)
- Interpersonal intelligence (ability to interact easily with others, to understand their socioemotional needs, and to respond in a way that furthers the relationship)
- Intrapersonal intelligence (ability to connect with one's inner feelings, motivations, and values)
- Naturalist intelligence (ability to appreciate and relate to the world of nature)
- Existentialist intelligence (ability to ponder and enjoy contemplating deep questions about the meaning of life and human existence)

According to Gardner, all human beings possess the totality of the nine intelligences; however, people vary in the extent to which they possess any single intelligence. Therefore, one person may be very good at calculating the distance of stars from earth (logical-mathematical intelligence) but limited in the ability to play soccer (bodily intelligence) or to feel comfortable in a social setting (interpersonal in-

telligence). Another person might win accolades for musical intelligence but have a difficult time creating images on paper (visual-spatial intelligence). A third person might have the ability to survive in an arctic environment under the harshest of winter conditions (naturalist ability) but be unable to articulate his feelings to himself or others (intrapersonal and linguistic intelligences). See Figure 13.1 for a multiple intelligence questionnaire developed by Walter Mckenzie.[17]

When oral presentations by groups depend strictly on words, some audience members may be unable to relate to—or learn from—the presentation. The bodily-kinesthetic learner may grow restless and anxious to find a way to express herself in a more dynamic way. The visual learner may want to see pictures and photographs that illustrate the ideas being discussed. The interpersonal learner may become bored with one-way communications that disallow the opportunity for interaction. In order to satisfy this need, she may write notes to the person sitting next to her in the classroom, while the musical learner quietly slips a listening device into one ear. The logical-mathematical learner may drift into his own reverie, wondering if he could create a chart that compared and contrasted the ideas in some more quantitative fashion; and the naturalist learner may pay more attention to the squirrels on the lawn outside the classroom than to the speakers. In such as a situation, the linguistic learner may be the only person whose needs are recognized and met.

Learners also vary in whether they like to work alone, in dyads, or in small groups.[18] Some people prefer to learn from their peers and coworkers, while others

Multiple Intelligences Survey

Part I

Complete each section by placing a "1" next to each statement you feel accurately describes you. If you do not identify with a statement, leave the space provided blank. Then total the column in each section.

Section 1

____ I enjoy categorizing things by common traits

____ Ecological issues are important to me

____ Classification helps me make sense of new data

____ I enjoy working in a garden

____ I believe preserving our National Parks is important

____ Putting things in hierarchies makes sense to me

____ Animals are important in my life

____ My home has a recycling system in place

____ I enjoy studying biology, botany and/or zoology

____ I pick up on subtle differences in meaning

____ TOTAL for Section 1

Section 2

____ I easily pick up on patterns

____ I focus in on noise and sounds

____ Moving to a beat is easy for me

____ I enjoy making music

____ I respond to the cadence of poetry

____ I remember things by putting them in a rhyme

____ Concentration is difficult for me if there is background noise

____ Listening to sounds in nature can be very relaxing

____ Musicals are more engaging to me than dramatic plays

____ Remembering song lyrics is easy for me

____ TOTAL for Section 2

Section 3

____ I am known for being neat and orderly

____ Step-by-step directions are a big help

____ Problem solving comes easily to me

Figure 13.1 Multiple Intelligences Survey.

_____ I get easily frustrated with disorganized people

_____ I can complete calculations quickly in my head

_____ Logic puzzles are fun

_____ I can't begin an assignment until I have all my "ducks in a row"

_____ Structure is a good thing

_____ I enjoy troubleshooting something that isn't working properly

_____ Things have to make sense to me or I am dissatisfied

TOTAL for Section 3

Section 4

_____ It Is important to see my role in the "big picture" of things

_____ I enjoy discussing questions about life

_____ Religion is important to me

_____ I enjoy viewing art work

_____ Relaxation and meditation exercises are rewarding to me

_____ I like traveling to visit inspiring places

_____ I enjoy reading philosophers

_____ Learning new things is easier when I see their real world application

_____ I wonder if there are other forms of intelligent life in the universe

_____ It is important for me to feel connected to people, ideas, and beliefs

_____ TOTAL for Section 4

Section 5

_____ I learn best interacting with others

_____ I enjoy informal chat and serious discussion

_____ The more the merrier

_____ I often serve as a leader among peers and colleagues

_____ I value relationships more than ideas or accomplishments

_____ Study groups are very productive for me

_____ I am a "team player"

_____ Friends are important to me

_____ I belong to more than three clubs or organizations

_____ I dislike working alone

_____ TOTAL for Section 5

Figure 13.1—cont'd

Section 6

_____ I learn by doing

_____ I enjoy making things with my hands

_____ Sports are a part of my life

_____ I use gestures and non-verbal cues when I communicate

_____ Demonstrating is better than explaining

_____ I love to dance

_____ I like working with tools

_____ Inactivity can make me more tired than being very busy

_____ Hands-on activities are fun

_____ I live an active lifestyle

_____ TOTAL for Section 6

Section 7

_____ Foreign languages interest me

_____ I enjoy reading books, magazines, and websites

_____ I keep a journal

_____ Word puzzles like crosswords or jumbles are enjoyable

_____ Taking notes helps me remember and understand

_____ I faithfully contact friends through letters and/or e-mail

_____ It is easy for me to explain my ideas to others

_____ I write for pleasure, puns, anagram, and spoonerisms are fun

_____ I enjoy public speaking and participating in debates

_____ TOTAL for Section 7

Section 8

_____ My attitude affects how I learn

_____ I like to be involved in causes that help others

_____ I am keenly aware of my moral beliefs

_____ I learn best when I have an emotional attachment to the subject

_____ Fairness is important to me

_____ Social justice issues interest me

_____ Working alone can be just as productive as working in a group

_____ I need to know why I should do something before I agree to do it

_____ When I believe in something, I give more effort toward it

_____ I am willing to protest or sign a petition to right a wrong

_____ TOTAL for Section 8

Figure 13.1—cont'd

Section 9

_____ I can visualize ideas in my mind

_____ Rearranging a room and redecorating are fun for me

_____ I enjoy creating my own works of art

_____ I remember better using graphic organizers

_____ I enjoy all kinds of entertainment media

_____ Charts, graphs, and tables help me interpret data

_____ A music video can make me more interested in a song

_____ I can recall things as mental pictures

_____ I am good at reading maps and blueprints

_____ Three dimensional puzzles are fun

_____ TOTAL for Section 9

Part II

Now carry forward your total from each section and multiply by 10 below:

Section	Total Forward	Multiply	Score
1		×10	
2		×10	
3		×10	
4		×10	
5		×10	
6		×10	
7		×10	
8		×10	
9		×10	

Figure 13.1—cont'd

Part III

Now plot your scores on the bar graph provided:

	Sec 1	Sec 2	Sec 3	Sec 4	Sec 5	Sec 6	Sec 7	Sec 8	Sec 9
100									
90									
80									
70									
60									
50									
40									
30									
20									
10									
0	Sec 1	Sec 2	Sec 3	Sec 4	Sec 5	Sec 6	Sec 7	Sec 8	Sec 9

Part IV

Now determine your intelligence profile!

Key:

Section 1–This reflects your Naturalist strength

Section 2–This suggests your Musical strength

Section 3–This indicates your Logical strength

Section 4–This illustrates your Existential strength

Section 5–This shows your Interpersonal strength

Section 6–This tells your Kinesthetic strength

Section 7–This indicates your Verbal strength

Section 8–This reflects your Intrapersonal strength

Section 9–This suggests your Visual strength

Remember:

    Everyone has all the intelligences!

    You can strengthen an intelligence!

    This inventory is meant as a snapshot in time–it can change!

    M. I. is meant to empower, not label people!

Figure 13.1—cont'd

like to draw their knowledge from authority figures. Some studies have identified differences between introverted and extroverted learners.[19] Introverted learners prefer activities such as questionnaires, handouts, worksheets, gallery exercises (discussed later in this chapter), and computer exercises that they can do at home or in some quiet setting. Extroverted learners like activities that bring them into contact with other people. Examples include icebreakers, brainstorming, games and simulations, read-arounds, role plays, discussions, and psychodramas. Extroverts are not shy about expressing their points of view, and these activities enable a dynamic exchange with other people.

Gender, personality, and age variables also intervene to influence learning preferences. Women in general prefer a wider variety of activities than men do, and they have stronger needs for collaborative sharing of ideas. Men in general (especially younger men) prefer a more analytical and active experimenter style of learning. But . . . it's not that simple. More apprehensive women also like the more analytical and active experimenter style of learning—that is, "watching and doing"; less apprehensive women prefer innovative approaches to learning.[20] Less flexible personalities favor a more direct and formal teaching style (e.g., lectures), and more optimistic personalities appreciate a wide variety of learning activities.[21] In short, people have many different preferences as to how they want to learn, which creates the need for flexible and eclectic approaches to classroom instruction.

With the trend toward lifetime learning, more professionals and older adults are returning to the classroom. Almost one out of eight Americans is sixty-five years of age or older. In addition, the focus on "just-in-time" learning sends many professionals back to the classroom to retool and learn new skills. In comparison with their younger cohorts, these older adults and professionals have more and different kinds of experiences. Moreover, they may have organized the experiences differently.[22] These seasoned adults almost always prefer an interactive classroom that allows them to share their life and work experiences and to learn from each other. They want to know how they can apply what they learn inside and outside

of the classroom. They adhere to a philosophy articulated by noted psychologist Carl Rogers: "Experience is, for me, the highest authority. The touchstone of validity is my own experience. No other person's ideas, and none of my own ideas, are as authoritative as my experience. It is to experience that I must return again and again."[23]

APPLYING THE LEARNING THEORIES

Group presenters should establish an agenda that recognizes the learning profiles of all members of the class and seeks to engage them in active learning. A "something-for-everyone" approach means that the presentation must include diverse kinds of activities.[24] Examples of activities that appeal to different senses include the following: auditory (lecture, discussion, music, read-arounds, storytelling), visual (handouts, overheads, gallery exercises, maps, timelines), tactile (worksheets, card sorting, artwork), and kinesthetic (movement/sorting, practice role-plays, psychodrama).[25]

A presenting group can use music, art, role plays, multimedia, and other techniques to appeal to sensory preferences in learning. They may ask the listeners to reflect upon a passage from a poem (individual learning), then to discuss the passage with another classmate (learning in dyads), and finally to share their findings with the larger group (learning through group interactions). Using videotaped interviews with experts or quoting authority figures can appeal to the learners who prefer to get their information from experts or people in positions of influence or power.

In a recent classroom presentation on the nine intelligences, a group fabricated a dialogue that could have occurred between Microsoft CEO Bill Gates and rapper Enimem. They used a rapper dialogue, along with body movements, to transmit the idea of multiple intelligences. The contrast between the personalities of Gates and Enimem allowed for the incorporation of humor in the presentation. It would be hard to imagine that any member of the audience would not remember the musical interaction or the lesson that was transmitted. On other occasions, class members have used games such as *Jeopardy* to test the knowledge of class members on topics discussed in the presentation. As you plan your activities, ask yourself which intelligences are required to carry out the activities. If the activities seem to be too linguistically based, restructure for diversity. For example, if you plan to make a presentation on television reality shows, consider the following kinds of activities:

- Lecturing on the popularity of current reality shows (appeal to linguistic intelligence)
- Asking the class to guess the ratings for five of the top shows (appeal to logical-mathematical intelligence)
- Presenting a graph showing the rise of reality shows over time, concurrent with the fall in popularity of other types of shows (appeal to visual-spatial intelligence)
- Showing a video clip from one of the *Amazing Race* episodes (appeal to naturalist, bodily-kinesthetic, and visual intelligences)
- Asking the class to reflect on whether they would consider trying out for a show such as *Big Brother*, where they would have little privacy, or *Survivor*, which requires lying and deception (appeal to intrapersonal intelligence)
- Requesting that students act out an episode of a reality show such as *American Idol*, in which they depict the ways that contestants show empathy for other contestants (interpersonal intelligence)
- Asking the class to create a plot line for a new reality show (linguistic intelligence), to create the spirit of the new reality show through a group painting (visual-spatial intelligence), and to choose the music for the show (musical intelligence)

TAKING AUDIENCE ADAPTATION THEORIES INTO ACCOUNT

As noted in Chapter Five, audiences should be the starting point for designing the presentation. Presenters need to be sensitive to levels of knowledge held by different audiences, as well as variations in beliefs, attitudes, and values. An older audience may know more about environmental disasters that occurred in the 1980s and the work of Ralph Nader, but a younger audience may know more about contemporary celebrity crusaders such as Bono or Angelina Jolie. Women may know more about some topics than men (e.g., current styles in women's clothing or the history of the feminist movement), but men may be more acquainted with other topics (Major League baseball players or the financial news).

We need to take care, however, not to stereotype audiences. Some women are heavily into baseball history and memorabilia, and some of the top fashion stylists are men. The meaning of being a feminist has acquired different interpretations over the years; so the knowledge gap between women of different ages may be almost as wide as the gap between men and women. In the same way, hair and dress as indicators of values can be deceptive. I recall an experience with one student in the early 1980s. The young man had a short crewcut, which I identified with a very conservative period in history—the 1950s. His "A+" status in the class lent credibility to my diagnosis of his personality as serious and probably conservative in nature. However, the final project submission from the student included lyrics to a song that he had written. The lyrics contained many obscenities, not unlike those of Enimem; and I learned that the young man played in a hard rock band. Not only was he *not* conservative, but he was at the vanguard of a movement that soon swept the country, as the military cuts gave way to pink hair and shaved heads. When his uniquely adorned girlfriend came to collect one of his papers at the end of the semester, I became even more convinced of the inaccuracy of my initial perceptions. In short, I learned that the meanings that I had attached to hair conventions and other symbols of behavior had changed dramatically since the 1950s and even the 1960s. Crewcuts had assumed a very different meaning over the intervening decades between 1950 and 1980.

To the extent that we can identify the knowledge levels, values, opinions, and beliefs of the audience on any given topic, however, we will be in a better position to achieve our teaching goals. When people do not agree with positions presented by speakers, they tend not to hear, to tune out, or to forget the information. As in the case of audiences with different learning preferences, group presenters can seek to bridge the differences or adopt a "something-for-everyone" approach in the design of their oral presentations. The next section will discuss the options in more detail.

CHOOSING YOUR LEARNING ACTIVITIES

In determining the agenda, the presenting group needs to consider the appropriate mix of lecture and other activities. They also need to establish appropriate and realistic timelines for the activities. The following discussion identifies activities that appeal to different kinds of learners and audiences: icebreakers, energizers, guided fantasies, storytelling, gallery exercises, read-arounds, timelines, card sorting, case studies and scenarios, fishbowl exercises, role plays, and artwork and other visuals. For the purpose of deemphasizing the role of presenters as "instructors of learning," I will use the term *facilitator* in the following section of the chapter. A facilitator frames and guides the process of learning. The role is dynamic, interactive, and two-way.

Facilitator
Someone who frames and guides a group

Icebreakers

Icebreakers
Activities geared to put group members at ease

The first item on any agenda should be an icebreaker, an activity designed to warm the climate of the group, eliminate inhibitions, and establish a frame of mind that is conducive to active participation in the presentation. The icebreaker may be tied directly to the theme of the presentation, or it may be unlinked, since the major purpose of the activity is to "break the ice" and establish a strong group dynamic.

Examples of icebreakers abound. One icebreaker asks members of the audience to remove their shoes and to place one shoe on the floor in the middle of the classroom. Afterward everyone takes a shoe from the pile and attempts to locate its owner. After identifying the owner, the person collects enough information to introduce the person to the larger group. A second individual, in turn, introduces that person. In another icebreaker, members of the group receive balloons. Inside each balloon is a question that the person must answer after popping the balloon. A favorite icebreaker with students involves asking the class to pull pieces of toilet paper from a roll passed around the group. They are not told how much paper to pull. Afterward, the members of the class must answer as many questions about themselves as the numbers of articulated paper that they hold. A fourth icebreaker requires class members to describe a favorite childhood game.

Some icebreakers have a largely physical component. They may require group members to tangle and disentangle themselves. The "Mill Mill" exercise, similar to the floor game *Twister*, requires that participants assume difficult body positions

that bring them into close physical contact with other group members. The common ingredient to all icebreakers is that they take participants to a higher level of familiarity with other members—either by requiring that they disclose personal information or come into close physical proximity with other members of the group.

One caution is in order. People from more reserved or formal cultures, which place strict limits on cross-gender interactions, may resist participating in high-contact icebreakers. Older individuals may also feel uncomfortable participating in some of the more physical exercises. People who feel sensitive about their weight may be uncomfortable with the balloon exercise described earlier. Before selecting an icebreaker, group presenters should assess the appropriateness of the activity and the probable level of acceptance by participants. In one class, an icebreaker required students to sit on the laps of other students. Some students were clearly uncomfortable with the exercise, even though no one complained. The exercise might have worked well with young children, but it was marginally appropriate in a university classroom, and I cannot imagine that an older audience would have agreed to participate.

After placing the icebreaker on the agenda, the presenting group should establish the order of lectures and other activities. They should set limits on the time to be spent on any single lecture or activity. As mentioned earlier, presenters should adhere to five-minute lecture segments in order to allow time for a variety of other activities in a one-hour presentation. A sample agenda appears in the PowerPoint presentation located in Chapter Seven. This agenda demonstrates how varied activities can illuminate and expand upon the concepts introduced in the lectures.

Depending on their nature, icebreakers hold appeal for many different kinds of learners. The more physical icebreakers appeal to bodily-kinesthetic learners and those who enjoy tactile experiences. Icebreakers that require listing of personal qualities appeal to learners with intrapersonal and linguistic intelligences. People with interpersonal intelligence enjoy icebreakers that require interacting with other people; and people with musical intelligence respond well to icebreakers that require singing, dancing, or chanting. For more information on the function of icebreakers, energizers, and other educational strategies that involve the speaker on a kinesthetic level, refer to material developed by the Ontario Institute for Studies in Education, University of Toronto.[26]

Energizers

Energizers
Activities geared to give group members a mental break by involving them in something physical

During a presentation of three or more hours, facilitators should make use of energizer activities. Energizers engage a group in some kind of physical activity that allows a break from concentrating on a demanding mental task. A popular energizer with university students is "shoot the rabbit." The learners divide into two groups. Among themselves, members of each group decide upon which of three postures they will choose: wall, rabbit, or arrow. On cue, the two groups show their posture to the other group. The following criteria determine the winner:

· An arrow beats a rabbit, since the arrow can kill a rabbit.
· A wall beats an arrow, since it can stop the arrow.
· A rabbit beats a wall, since it can jump over the wall.

Other energizers require participants to move about the room, talk to other people, sing, or dance. Songs accompanied by actions, such as clapping or stomping, are especially dynamic. Applauding latecomers in the morning or after lunch also activates a sleepy group and adds a touch of laughter to the classroom environment.[27] Some games require that people keep balls or balloons in the air, much as they would do in a volleyball game. To make the exercise more difficult, facilitators can ask participants to sort the balloons into color clusters as they work to keep them in the air.[28]

Obviously, in a one-hour presentation, energizers have limited use. However, professional facilitators and trainers rely heavily on energizers in longer presentations. They understand that audiences lose focus if they do not have the opportunity to move about from time to time. Energizers have particular appeal to learners with bodily-kinesthetic intelligence, as well as those with interpersonal and musical intelligence. Learners who enjoy tactile experiences also enjoy many of the energizers.

Guided Fantasies

Guided fantasies ask participants to relax, close their eyes, and visualize scenes and experiences. The facilitator talks the group through a visualization experience such as the following:

Guided fantasies
A group visualization activity

> I want all of you to close your eyes. Think of yourself walking down a dirt road. All around you are valleys and hills, and the sun is shining down upon you. The sky is blue and the wind blows lightly against your face, whishing your hair back and forth. The sun gets hotter as you walk, and you begin to sweat. You stop by the side of the road to get a drink of water from a nearby stream. As you bend down, you notice that the water is a bright chemical green. You see an oily black substance, almost like gasoline, floating on top of the water. Looking deeper, you notice dead fish floating just beneath the surface. Suddenly you realize that the plant life around you looks twisted and gnarled, and the weeds are coated with the same black substance as the water. Startled, you turn to run back to the road but stumble over something. You realize that a dead cow is just one of many animals and birds strewn about the field. Escaping back to the road, you run until you see a farm. Relieved and still thirsty, you look for some sign of life to remind yourself that you have not been transported to another planet. In the near distance, you see a farmer looking across his fields. You look too and see a large truck dumping material into a land fill located about a half mile away. When you reach the farm, you ask the man what the trucks are dumping. He replies, "Death."[29]

In a presentation to medical students, a facilitator could ask a group to imagine a day in the life of a medical doctor in 2020:

> You get up at your usual time—7:30 A.M. You take a cup of strong black coffee into your office to begin your workday—at home, of course. Your office is bright and cheerful. Large windows overlook a lake, and the sun is arching higher in the morning sky as you look out over the glistening water. A few geese alight a nearby pond. You feel comfortable, sitting with a pair of slippers and light robe in a comfortable easy chair. A breeze wafts through the room and rustles a few papers on your large mahogany desk. Checking the calendar, you notice that the date is January 15, 2020. But you don't feel the cold because you are in a "cocooned" office. Last night, before you went to bed, you programmed your office for mid-April. The computer

program set the temperature, images that you see outside the windows, and the general ambiance for a beautiful spring day. You can hear the flapping of the wings of the geese from time to time. To alert your staff to the fact that you are now on duty, you press a button, embedded in your wrist. Promptly, you receive a mental image of your schedule for the day, set to run until about 5:30 P.M., with an hour for lunch. Before switching to an interactive screen, you program your internal computer for a business day. That means that you will not appear in a robe and slippers to your patients. You will appear in a light grey business suit with a red tie. No need for uniforms in this virtual world! Finally you switch to an interactive screen on your computer, which shows a hologram of your first patient. She sits at a table with her child. Her dress has a pleasant floral pattern. (She was able to discern the fact that your office was set for spring, and she wanted to dress for the occasion.) You switch the audio to interactive mode. "Hello there. I see that (oops, need a name, another button to push) Jimmy is having some problems with his (ah, another button, virtual scan of body) throat. I'll order the prescription (push another button). Have a good evening. Must be late in Finland."

Guided fantasies need not be futuristic. You could, for example, conduct a guided fantasy that leads people through a desired response to an assault or a guided fantasy that asks people to imagine the life of someone who lived in the eighteenth century. Alternatively, you could lead a group through a visualization exercise that would help them to enter a meditative state. Learners with linguistic intelligence, as well as those with visual-spatial intelligence, enjoy guided fantasies. Depending on the nature of the visualization, other intelligences such as the naturalist may also come into play. Those who like auditory experiences and imaginative learners are receptive to guided fantasies.

Storytelling

The facilitator can use a story (real or metaphorical) to generate reflection on a given topic. The following legend of the dream catcher, for example, could lead into a discussion of dreams, mythology, Native culture, or any one of a number of other topics:

> A long time ago, the clans of the Ojibway nation lived in a place known as Turtle Island. To ensure that the babies of the tribe enjoyed peaceful sleep, Spider Woman wove little dream catchers on the tops of their cradle boards. Bad dreams stuck in the spiderlike webs, while the good dreams slipped through the openings. Each morning, with the first rays of dawn, the bad dreams died. In later years, Spider Woman found it hard to make her way to all the cradle boards. So others in the clan—the grandmothers, mothers, and sisters—began to help to weave the magical webs. They used hoops from willow trees, sinew from animals, and cords from plants to make the dream catchers. In honor of ancient traditions, they connected the web to the hoop at seven or eight points. The number 7 represents the Seven Prophecies, and the number 8 represents Spider Woman's eight legs.[30]

Storytelling as a teaching strategy offers a way of reaching out to imaginative learners and to those with linguistic intelligence. People who enjoy auditory experiences also like storytelling.

Storytelling
Use of a narrative to initiate reflection

Gallery Exercises

Gallery exercises use pictures to stimulate discussion on a topic relevant to the theme of the presentation. Assume, for example, that you want to sensitize

Gallery exercises
The use of pictures to stimulate discussion

managers to behaviors that could be construed as sexual harassment. You could include a series of slides in your presentation that depict inappropriate behaviors. One slide could show a male manager with a hand on the shoulder of a female subordinate. Another slide could show a manager who has invaded the personal space of an employee by leaning over his shoulder as he sits at his desk. A short video clip could depict employee reaction to an off-color joke by an employer or an invitation to go for drinks at a local bar. Seek some degree of balance in showing slides and video clips on a topic such as sexual harassment. That is, attempt to show members of both sexes in uncomfortable positions. Gallery exercises appeal, in particular, to learners with visual-spatial and linguistic intelligences.

Read-Arounds

Read-arounds
A group activity involving reading a passage selected by a facilitator

Read-arounds are similar to tryouts in theatre. Participants take turns reading aloud from material provided by the group facilitators. The material in a read-around could come from a poem, play, story, travelogue, book, or other material. Imagine that you are making a presentation on superstitious behaviors. The following material from a Japanese website would work well for a read-around. Proceeding around the circle or room, each person from the group reads one point. The facilitator prefaces the read-around with the following kind of statement: "In Japan, you avoid certain actions because they bring bad luck."

· Avoid the number 4. The number 4 is pronounced the same as *shi*, the word for *death*. Therefore, you should not give presents with four pieces. [*first person in read-around*]
· Avoid the number 9. The number 9 rhymes with *ku*, the word for *pain*. Some hospitals do not have fourth or ninth floors. [*second person in read-around*]
· Do not stick your chopsticks upright in a full rice bowl. At funerals, chopsticks are stuck into rice that is placed on the altar. [*third person in read-around*]
· Do not transfer food from chopstick to chopstick. This practice only occurs at funerals with the bones of the cremated body. [*fourth person in read-around*]
· Do not sleep toward the north because bodies, in Buddhist funerals, are laid in a northward-facing direction. [*fifth person in read-around*]
· If a funeral car passes, be sure to hide your thumb. [*sixth person in read-around*]
· If you cut your nails at night, you will not be with your parents when they die. [*seventh person in read-around*]
· Do not stare at anyone over your rice bowl, lest you become increasingly ugly in appearance. [*eighth person in read-around*]
· If you whistle in the night, a snake will come to you. [*ninth person in read-around*]
· You will have bad luck if you break a comb or a wooden shoe. [*tenth person in read-around*]
· If your ear itches, you will hear good news. [*eleventh person in read-around*][31]

Read-arounds appeal to the auditory learner and to the learner with linguistic intelligence.

Timelines

One kind of activity calls upon participants to develop a calendar of activities. If you were making a presentation on crisis communication planning, for example, you might ask participants to construct a timeline of when things tend to go wrong in their organization. Afterward you could discuss their examples. The timeline activity would appeal to learners with logical-mathematical intelligence.

Card Sorting

With card-sorting activities, you ask participating group members to sort and order cards in terms of priorities, time sequence, or some other organizational scheme. The cards may pertain to duties that have to be performed, the component parts of some task, or the distinguishing features of some situation. If you are making a presentation on change management, the card-sorting exercise could involve establishing the order for undertaking various change management activities. The facilitators use this information as a takeoff point for discussion. Card sorting will appeal to tactile learners, as well as logical-mathematical and linguistic learners.

Case Studies and Scenarios

Case studies describe some incident that has occurred in the past. If you are making a presentation on airport security, for example, you could develop a case study that points to inadequacies in the system. Then you ask the class to divide into small groups to review the case and to arrive at solutions to the problems. Afterward you facilitate a discussion of the findings. Your introduction to the case study could read something like the following: "Imagine that you have been charged with making recommendations on enhanced airport security. Review the scenario that describes what happened in several recent breaches of airport security. Then identify possible solutions to the problem. Suggest measures that could better ensure the safety of flyers." Organizations often develop case studies of best practices and worst practices, from which their members can draw lessons. (See Keep in Mind box.)

Whereas case studies concern the past, scenarios offer a glimpse into a possible future. Typically, scenarios depict a situation that could occur at some future date, such as a natural disaster or a terrorist event. They ask participants to answer the question "What if?" What if an earthquake struck California? What if terrorists attacked the New York City subway system? What if insufficient rain caused power shortages in western states, an ice storm wreaked havoc in Detroit, or a computer virus shut down air traffic control at O'Hare International Airport in Chicago?

Scenarios offer participants the chance to test their response systems and practice their skills in a simulated environment, thus ensuring a faster and more effective response in an actual threat situation. Public schools conduct fire drills; emergency preparedness teams conduct simulations based on scenarios of potential future disasters. In the late 1980s, for example, federal agencies in Detroit, Michigan, and Windsor, Canada, acted out a scenario that entailed terrorists overtaking a barge in the Detroit River. In the scenario, the terrorists threatened to release toxic gases into the atmosphere. The toxic gases would have affected both Detroit and

Timelines
Activities that involve the development of a schedule

Card-sorting
An activity involving putting cards in order to help organize a task or establish priorities

Case studies
Incidents that occurred in the past, used to illustrate

Scenarios
Proposed outcomes set in the future

Keep in Mind

Customer Care Scenario

Imagine that you have been asked to set up a new customer response policy at your restaurant. Review the problems associated with earlier policies. (See the following list of problems identified by previous employees of the restaurant.) Design a new policy that overcomes these problems.

· Failure of employees to solicit feedback from discontented customers

· Inability or unwillingness of employees to respond to negative customer feedback

· Lack of employee support from supervisors, who fear admonishment

· Tendency of employers to punish, not reward, employees

· No monetary incentives for employees to perform better

· No monetary or other incentives to encourage business

· Inability to handle fast customer turnover when restaurant is busy

Windsor residents. The two governments (the U.S. and Canada) coordinated their responses to the simulated threat. A second example, often used in presentations devoted to small group dynamics or teambuilding, follows:

> You and your companions have just survived the crash of a small plane. Both the pilot and co-pilot were killed in the crash. It is mid-January, and you are in northern Michigan. The daily temperature is 25 below zero, and the night time temperature is 40 below zero. There is snow on the ground, and the countryside is wooded with several creeks criss-crossing the area. The nearest town is 20 miles away. You are all dressed in city clothes appropriate for a business meeting. Your group of survivors managed to salvage the following items: a ball of steel wool; a hunting rifle; a can of Crisco shortening; newspapers (one per person); a cigarette lighter (without fluid); an extra shirt and pants for each survivor; 20 × 20 ft. piece of heavy-duty canvas; a sectional air map made of plastic; one quart of 100-proof whiskey; a compass; and family-size chocolate bars (one per person). Your task as a group is to list the above 12 items in order of importance for your survival. List the uses for each. You *must* come to agreement as a group.[32]

Both case studies and scenarios are attractive learning tools for people with logical-mathematical, linguistic, and interpersonal intelligences. The exercise itself appeals to those with logical and linguistic intelligence, whereas the small group interaction appeals to those with interpersonal intelligence. If you include visuals (maps, photographs, etc.) with the exercise, then you can also appeal to those with visual-spatial intelligence. Tactile learners will also like dealing with objects, papers, or other tangible items. Case studies and scenarios consume too much time for short classroom presentations; however, a three-hour presentation may be able to employ limited versions of such narratives.

Fishbowl exercises
A structured exercise in which participants alternate between speaking and listening roles

Fishbowl Exercises

A fishbowl is a structured discussion, usually fifteen minutes in length, that allows class members to rotate between speaking and listening roles. A few

participants (fish) take seats in the middle of the larger group. They discuss their views on some assigned topic, while the others listen quietly. Whenever observers are ready to join the fishbowl discussion, they signal their interest by standing at their seats. Once a speaker has finished her turn making a statement and interacting with other members of the fishbowl, she surrenders her seat to a member of the listening audience. So the rotational process continues as various members join and leave the fishbowl discussion. Speaking is restricted to the four or five people in the fishbowl at any given time.

Facilitators prepare the group for the exercise by defining any relevant terms, identifying key concepts, and asking for questions about the exercise. Handouts with terms, background information, and questions are helpful in stimulating an organized discussion. The facilitators prepare responses in advance for the large group discussion to follow the fishbowl exercise.

Sometimes facilitators divide groups along gender, occupational, ideological, or other lines in order to allow for the expression of minority or less popular views. The females in the group, for example, could be asked to conduct a fishbowl discussion of a topic such as division of responsibilities in the home. In that situation, the males are asked to listen without interrupting. Once the females have finished their discussion, the males replace them to present their views on the topic. Then the females listen, without responding, to the male perspectives. Afterward, the facilitators (who act as note takers in the discussions) lead the whole group in a discussion.

With a topic such as discrimination in workplace environments, multiple groups could be formed. One group might represent the interests of women; another might reflect the interests of a linguistic minority; still another group might form to represent the views of ethnic or cultural minorities in the workplace. One by one, the members of the various groups would take their places in the fishbowl

and express their points of view on the topic of equity in the workplace. The group would rely on discussion guidelines distributed by the facilitators.

Fishbowl activities hold a strong appeal for learners with linguistic, bodily-kinesthetic, and interpersonal intelligences. The activity is also compatible with a bias toward auditory learning. Because the activity requires thoughtful consideration, learners with logical-mathematical and intrapersonal intelligences would respond favorably, as well.

Role Plays

Role plays
Activities in which participants act out different parts in order to understand emotional motivation or appropriate behavioral responses

In 1956, Benjamin Bloom identified three aspects of learning experiences: cognitive (knowledge), psychomotor (skills), and affective (beliefs).[33] The role play taps into the *affective* or emotional domain of learning. Role plays are used to convey concepts related to human interactions such as doctor-patient, male-female, and manager-employee. In a presentation on management theories, facilitators could ask participants to assume the role of employees in an organization with a scientific management philosophy or a human relations philosophy. In a presentation on intercultural variables in negotiation, facilitators could ask students to assume the roles of business executives from two different cultures who are trying to negotiate an agreement. With some role plays, facilitators ask participants to model an effective behavior such as assertiveness, or to demonstrate an ineffective response such as aggressiveness or passivity. Role plays are attractive to learners with linguistic, bodily-kinesthetic, and interpersonal intelligences.

Artwork and Other Visuals

Facilitators might give finger paints to members of the audience and ask them to create individual or group paintings that illustrate their perceptions of some topic, group, philosophy, or institution. Afterward, they lead the group in a discussion of the meanings and feelings behind their paintings. Tactile learners and those with visual-spatial, bodily-kinesthetic, and interpersonal intelligences would enjoy this activity. Most groups also like presentations that include the use of slides and video and film clips. When the latter are used in presentations, facilitators must limit the time given to the clips. For three-hour presentations, I suggest limiting video clips to five-minute segments. No group should use more than one five-minute video clip or several two-minute audio or clips in a one-hour presentation.

Managing Group Dynamics

Early in the project, the group needs to set regular meeting times, establish ground rules, and allocate tasks. Ground rules for meetings typically require that members inform others if they cannot attend a meeting, arrive on time, come prepared, make constructive suggestions, and treat team members with respect. Some groups write a contract, in which they agree to assume certain responsibilities and to meet deadlines. They may even take a group picture to accompany the signed contract, as a sign of their commitment to the team. Ground rules can also set out procedures for dealing with conflict.

Tasks
The jobs a group needs to do

Task-oriented roles
Instrumental roles that relate to the accomplishment of group tasks

Initiators
Group members who propose new ideas

Information givers
Group members who support their ideas with evidence

Information seekers
Group members who look for explanations

Opinion seekers
Group members who elicit ideas from others

Elaborators
Group members who build on the ideas of others

Integrators
Group members who synthesize the ideas of many

Orienters
Group members adept at keeping the group focused

Energizers
Group members adept at keeping the group active

To facilitate the group process, course instructors can use student presentation tools such as Blackboard or WebCT. These computer software programs allow students to upload and share files and create group presentations. All group members are able to access a folder that contains the work of the members, but they cannot access the work of other groups. The software also enables instructors to establish discussion forums for exchange of ideas among group members. The discussions remain in the online file so that members can review comments from other group members as time allows. That is, group members are not bound by the time schedules of the other members. They can participate on their own time schedules. The instructor can also monitor the progress of the group. After the group has completed and delivered its presentation, members can allow public access to the file by transferring the information to a web page. The software enables this transfer process.[34]

A group's success depends upon the ability of its members to work together as a team. While division of tasks works relatively well for the research phase of a group project, members must engage in higher levels of interaction as the work progresses. Ideally, group members will take the roles for which they are best suited. Every group needs a leader, who can assign tasks and ensure that the group meets its deadlines. A person with good writing and editing skills should assume the role of editor for the entire project so that the final product has stylistic integrity. Another group member may be good at interacting with people. That person could be charged with tasks such as interviewing or making telephone calls. Someone with artistic skills could prepare the visuals for the presentation, and the individual with technological skills could prepare the PowerPoint presentation and video or film clips. Someone should be in charge of equipment and ensuring that the group has backup computer disks for the presentation. The person with the best organizational skills could take care of miscellaneous tasks such as purchasing the supplies required for the presentation, making name tags, purchasing refreshments, and locating appropriate music for break periods in the presentation.

A classical study in group dynamics classified common participant behaviors under the categories of group task roles, group building and maintenance roles, and self-centered and dysfunctional roles.[35] According to this study, group members act out one or more of these roles during the course of a group discussion. Awareness can help people to assume more positive roles in group discussions and avoid the more dysfunctional roles.

When members assume *task-oriented roles*, they act as initiators, information givers, information seekers, opinion givers, opinion seekers, elaborators, integrators, orienters, and/or energizers. *Initiators* propose new ideas, directions, and solutions. *Information givers* support their opinions with evidence, whereas *opinion givers* contribute only their personal views on a topic. *Information seekers* look for information and explanations, and *opinion seekers* ask others to provide and explain their ideas. By offering examples, stories, and explanations, *elaborators* clarify and build on ideas presented by others. *Integrators* act as synthesizers of ideas contributed by others. *Orienters* keep groups focused on goals by summarizing and clarifying group contributions at different stages in the process. *Energizers* encourage members to participate more fully in the group process.

Those acting in *maintenance* roles nurture the interpersonal relationships in groups and try to increase group cohesiveness. They act as encouragers, harmonizers, tension relievers, gatekeepers, and/or followers. The *encourager* compliments the contributions of others. The *tension reliever* uses humor to achieve a more informal and relaxed atmosphere, and the *harmonizer* mediates conflicts by proposing compromises to the group. The *gatekeeper* uses body language and eye contact to encourage balanced participation from group members. The *follower* allows others to decide her stance on issues.

Dysfunctional roles inhibit the achievement of group goals and threaten interpersonal relationships. Members who assume the roles of blockers, aggressors, recognition seekers, "anecdoters," distracters, dominators, confessors, and special-interest pleaders can derail a discussion or cause friction and disruption. The *blocker* complains and offers negative feedback when others try to move the discussion forward. The *aggressor* insults, criticizes, and points to the mistakes of group members. *Dominators* monopolize proceedings by interrupting or flattering others, whereas *recognition seekers* focus group attention on their own achievements. The "*anecdoter*" takes the group on side trips with irrelevant stories and personal experiences; and the *distracter* (originally labeled as *playboy/playgirl*) uses antics, jokes, and irrelevant comments to divert a group from task-oriented goals. The *confessor* talks about personal problems, revealing fears and perceived inadequacies. The *special-interest pleader* seeks favors for someone who is not present.

Maintenance roles
Roles that relate to the nurturing of group cohesiveness

Encouragers
Group members adept at affirming others

Tension relievers
Group members adept at keeping the group loose

Harmonizers
Group members adept at mediating conflicts

Gatekeepers
Group members adept at encouraging balanced participation, preventing domination by one or two members

Followers
Group members tending to allow others to decide their stances

Blockers
Group members who tend to thwart group process by complaining

Aggressors
Group members who insult and criticize other group members

Dominators
Group members who monopolize the group

Keep in Mind

Tips for Using PowerPoint

- Use mixed media (audio and clip art) to add interest.
- Achieve a common look by repeating colors, fonts, shapes, and lines.
- Acquire continuity by repeating icons on slides that pertain to the same idea cluster.
- Limit the number of visuals on any slide.
- Use contrasting colors.
- Avoid backgrounds with patterns or excessive detail.
- Avoid distracting noises—clanging and banging of shutters.
- Use *sans serif* typefaces; avoid highly ornate fonts.
- Keep font size between 18 and 36 points.

- Each slide should support a single idea.
- Limit the material to five or six lines on a slide.
- Do not exceed forty characters on a line.
- Do not mix sentences and phrases on the same slide.
- Use parallel grammatical structures.
- Allow sufficient white space on slides.
- Use bullets to designate different points.
- When presenting, stand to the side of the screen; stay open to the audience.
- Refer to the screen but maintain eye contact with your audience.
- Use a remote to change the slides.
- Use the shutter device to hide an image and talk about the ideas.

Recognition seekers
Group members who always need to have their achievements acknowledged

"Anecdoters"
Group members who waste time by telling stories

Distracters
Group members who act out and keep the group from accomplishing its tasks

Confessors
Group members who talk about their own personal issues

Special-interest pleaders
Group members who ask for consideration for a group member who is not present

If every group has some members operating in maintenance roles, the group will have an easier time negotiating conflict situations. Early in the life of the group, members may want to consciously adopt certain maintenance roles. Not only in group meetings, but also on the day of presentation, the group will need to function as a team. So every group needs to conduct a dry run prior to the day of presentation, preferably in the same physical setting. Those who are responsible for technical matters such as changing slides in the PowerPoint presentation or operating lights and sound will need to coordinate their efforts with the presenters. Successful group presentations are team efforts. Videotaping the presentations allows the opportunity for the group members to review their performance after class hours. (See the Keep in Mind box.)

Making the Presentation

On the day of the presentation, team members should arrive early to prepare the room, check equipment, organize materials, and share last-minute concerns or newly acquired information with team members. Next we will consider the requirements for setting up the room, making an impression through dress, sharing responsibilities for the presentation, interacting with other team members and the audience, communicating "outside the kite," managing the feedback process, and distributing materials.

SETTING UP THE ROOM

Presenting group members should always arrive early enough to adjust for unexpected problems—microphones that do not function, missing lecture podiums, cassette players that malfunction, multimedia consoles that become like alien pieces of machinery when you need them the most, or a room in disarray. Whenever possible, the arrangement of seating should be appropriate for the type of presentation that you plan to make. If you are in a setting with bolted chairs, flexibility is not possible. Nor are adjustments possible in a room with theater seating or an auditorium. In other more flexible situations, you may be able to relocate chairs or tables into a U-shaped or more friendly arrangement. Comfortable seating is always a plus. The experts do not agree on whether windows act as a positive or negative force in presentations. People can become more easily distracted, but they are also happier in rooms with windows. Some studies show, for example, that employee turnover rates are much higher in physical settings that lack windows. Presenters should also check the temperature settings and ensure that doors are not locked so that latecomers can enter without major disruptions.

In Chapter Six, we discussed the fact that intimate settings (small rooms that allow for maximum eye contact and a sense of closeness to others) work best for short presentations. If you are making a half-day or longer presentation to a group, however, you should try to arrange for a room with ample space for milling and talking, stretching, and moving about the room for small group work. As a facilitator, you need sufficient space to conduct icebreakers and energizers. Sometimes group presenters are able to relocate the group to another setting that is more conducive to learning and conducting interactive exercises. If you do relocate to a different room, you need to announce the change and post signs to the new location for those who are not present for the announcement or who arrive late.

If the cost is not prohibitive, group members (involved in a presentation of three or more hours) might consider sharing the cost of refreshments for the break period—coffee, juice, and doughnuts or finger foods that conform to the theme of your presentation. If you are making a presentation on business etiquette in Brazil, for example, you could provide coffee and brigadeiros (a chocolate candy of Swiss origins that is common to Brazil, inexpensive, and easy to prepare). If you are making a presentation on yoga, you might provide fruit and juices or bottled water.

MAKING AN IMPRESSION THROUGH DRESS

The manner of dress will vary from one group presentation to the next. Team members often choose to dress in a more formal manner than they would normally dress. Sometimes they color coordinate their dress in order to appear more professional, wearing the same colors of shirts, skirts, and/or slacks. The most frequent choices are colors that the students already have in their closets, such as black and white. Occasionally, students choose to wear costumes that reflect the theme of their presentation. If they are speaking on the topic of dealing with difficult customers in a restaurant setting, they might wear waiter/waitress or host/hostess type clothing. If they are talking about cross-cultural communication in a tropical setting like Hawaii, they might wear leis or floral shirts or dresses.

SHARING RESPONSIBILITIES

Group members should plan to greet their classmates as they enter the room and distribute names tags (if appropriate), a copy of the agenda, and materials required to conduct small group exercises. Sometimes presenting groups give a copy of the PowerPoint presentation. Many groups like to establish a mood by playing background music as the audience enters the room. If audience members are scattered in a large room, presenters should suggest that they move closer to the front of the room.

The presentation itself should be a cooperative effort, with tasks distributed evenly among the group members. The mantra should be "different but equal." One person will act as moderator for the presentation, introducing the other members and introducing each new item on the agenda. The moderator should announce the topics to be covered by each new presenter. The same person should summarize and conclude the discussion in order to give a sense of continuity to the presentation.

If some members are better at interacting spontaneously with the audience, those members could facilitate question-and-answer sessions or follow-ups to exercises. Members with less ability in impromptu speaking could prepare the lecture portions of the presentation. Sometimes two group members cofacilitate a part

of the presentation, with one fielding questions and the other recording comments on the chalkboard or whiteboard. Facilitators with good interpersonal skills can move among small groups, formed to participate in exercises. They answer questions about assigned exercises, while others use the time to ready for the next part of the presentation. When one person makes a PowerPoint presentation, an assistant should handle the console, relieving the presenter of the task of technical responsibilities—operating lights, sound, PowerPoint, and other tasks. The focus should always be on the presenter.

INTERACTING DURING THE PRESENTATION

Interaction among presenting members during the presentation also conveys a feeling of cooperation and team spirit. While interruptions during lectures are not recommended, interjections from different team members during discussions or question-and-answer sessions add dynamism to the presentation. They also make the team look knowledgeable and interested and comfortable with each other. Uninvolved members should sit (as a group) in locations that do not draw attention from the presenters. Their listening postures should convey interest in the presentation. They should not be scanning the room during the presentation or slumping in a bored posture, especially if they are within view of the audience. Speakers should also refer to presenters who came before them and note how their contribution will relate to other topics in the team presentation, including those that will come later on the agenda.

When members of the class are engaged in small group activities, presenting team members should circulate among the groups to be sure that they understand the exercise. Leaders will generally emerge from every small group; however, if a group seems to be struggling with an exercise, members of the presenting team should move to their aid to respond to questions and assist in organizing the group.

To ensure good group dynamics and to save class time, you should place people in groups prior to the day of the presentation. If you assign colors, numbers, or names to teams, you can include the team identities in introductory materials that you give to the class. Varying the membership of groups for different activities is a good idea. In that situation, you can present a grid or other visual that depicts the assignments.

COMMUNICATING OUTSIDE THE KITE

In an earlier chapter, we noted that speakers tend to communicate in a kite-shaped pattern, ignoring people seated in front and rear corners. In a theater-style or straight-row seating arrangement, speakers must take care to maintain eye contact with all of the audience, not just those who are sitting in the "action zone." If the audience is large, speakers can create the perception that they are communicating with everyone by catching the eye of some individuals in all parts of the room.

As with other kinds of presentations, extemporaneous delivery works best. When members are delivering a lecture, they should use the PowerPoint slides as their guide and use note cards for supplementary materials. Because PowerPoint is a relatively formal instructional tool, speakers can close some of the psychological distance that separates them from the audience by moving away from the podium. They can rely on a team member or use a remote control to change slides. (See Chapter Seven for additional discussion of PowerPoint.)

Earlier chapters have discussed the importance of *immediacy* behaviors in stimulating feelings of affinity for instructors and other speakers. Some of those behaviors include use of humor, vocal expressiveness, smiling, relaxed body postures, warmth, sustained eye contact, dynamism in gestures and movement, and high levels of approachability. Most studies have also found a relationship between immediacy behaviors and student learning.[36] In fact, in a review of eighty-one studies, researchers found a striking relationship between nonverbal immediacy and reported student learning.[37] These findings apply to multicultural classrooms, as well as more homogeneous ones.[38] They also apply to distance learning in televised situations.[39]

MANAGING THE FEEDBACK PROCESS

Managing the feedback process involves knowing how to ask questions, acknowledge and respond to questions and comments, and reframe and redirect questions.

Asking Questions

When asking questions, facilitators should observe certain rules. Questions should be prepared in advance. They should be open-ended, answerable, clearly worded, significant, and thought-provoking. Rhetorical questions do not require a response, only consideration by the audience.

Questions should be *planned in advance*, and they should be *open-ended*. Open-ended questions call for unstructured responses: What are the most important issues in the debate over regulation of the Internet? How do you feel about the new gun control legislation? If I asked you to name the three most important steps in preparing for an exam, what would you say? Open-ended questions do not anticipate a response. Rather, they give people the freedom to generate their own answers, and they encourage in-depth responses. Open-ended questions can also probe to find out why a person answered in a certain way: "What did you mean when you said that governments are invading our privacy?" "Why did you say that the border control policies discriminate against some ethnic groups?"

Unlike open-ended questions, *closed-ended* questions ask respondents to choose from the alternatives provided. Examples of closed-ended questions are multiple-choice questions and those that ask for "yes-no" or "agree-disagree" answers. Compared to open-ended questions, closed-ended questions require little time or effort to answer. The responses, which are often "top-of-mind," provide little information. If you do choose to ask a closed-ended question, you should be prepared to follow with an open-ended probe. An example follows: Do you prefer less directive or more directive styles of leadership? (closed-ended question) Why did you choose less directive? (follow-up open-ended question)

Facilitators should ask *questions that the audience can answer*. If you ask questions that are too controversial, too complicated, or too technical, you may get no response. People do not like to give politically incorrect answers, even if their belief structures vary from the accepted social norms of the day. Questions should not have multiple parts. You should not ask two-part or three-part questions such as the following: "What do you like and dislike about the new company logo? Do you think that the logo represents the mission and mandate of the company? Why do you think that people have been protesting against the new design?" If you want to ask multiple questions, you should ask the additional questions as follow-up after people respond to the first question. Alternatively, you can put the three questions on a PowerPoint slide and ask for the group to consider one point at a time. Finally, questions should not require expertise that is lacking in the audience. If you ask lower-level employees, for example, to respond to a question that requires management experience, they will have no idea of the appropriate answer. In the same

Open-ended question
Questions not able to be answered by *yes* or *no*

Closed-ended questions
Questions able to be answered by *yes* or *no*

way, questions that call for highly technical expertise are inappropriate in some cases.

Questions should be *clearly framed, significant, and thought-provoking*. Facilitators should plan alternative ways to ask the same questions in the event that the group does not understand the original question. The questions should be significant enough to demand the consideration and time of the group. When an answer is too obvious or a concern too trivial, people will be reluctant to answer the question.

Some questions are rhetorical, intended only to provoke thought, not to get actual responses. Facilitators might ask the following question, for instance: "Consider for a moment. What do you think could happen next if we don't change direction—if we don't stop the incremental takeover of our civil liberties? Civil liberties, once lost, can become fugitives from justice."

Facilitators can direct questions to the entire audience or to specific individuals or subgroups. Or they can go from one to another class member in the manner of a relay. If a group has generated a response to some problem, for example, the facilitator could say the following: "John, I know that your group has arrived at a pretty creative answer to this problem. Could you share your ideas with the group?" Group presenters must take care, however, not to embarrass people by calling upon individuals who may not have an opinion or information on a topic. Usually, when people do not know the answer to a question, they avoid the eye gaze of the interrogator. When participants close the lines of communication in this way, facilitators should look elsewhere for a respondent.

Acknowledging and Responding to Comments and Questions

Give the group time to respond to questions and do not let silence unnerve you. If you think that the group has not understood your question, rephrase it. Do not continue asking the same question using the same wording. If the same people answer every question (not uncommon), find a way to involve more people. You may want to direct your eye gaze away from the persons who respond quickly and look in the direction of those who have been silent. You might need to say, "I've received some really interesting responses from some of you, but I would like to know the opinions of others as well." Then you catch the eye of several people who have not yet responded. If they close the communication channel by looking away, locate other respondents.

In another case, you could say: "Jennifer has offered one perspective to us. But I would like to get at least three or four other views. I'll give you a couple of minutes to think about the question." Some people are slower to respond to questions because they like to give thoughtful measured responses. If you go consistently to the first person who answers, you may miss the input from people who like to think through problems before answering. Different people have different personalities. Giving that extra time for thought can result in wider involvement among group members.

Always acknowledge the responses of those who answer a question and (whenever possible) find a way to integrate the ideas into summaries and conclusions. Rephrase the thoughts to show that you are listening and understanding.

Rephrasing can also help to clarify the responses for the larger group. Try to position the idea within the framework of your discussion. If you do not understand a response, ask for clarification.

If a response reveals lack of understanding, do not put down the respondent. If you undermine the contribution of even one person in a group, others will be reluctant to offer their ideas. Audience members are often as nervous as presenting group members. They fear looking unintelligent or uninformed in front of their peers (class members or work colleagues). In work situations, they often fear that they might be overlooked for a job transfer or promotion if they seem incompetent in a group situation. For that reason, responses from some group members will be timid and tentative. Facilitators must offer encouragement and (when warranted) compliments to those who make themselves vulnerable. If responses are not on target, you can still thank the person for contributing to the discussion or acknowledge points of interest in the remark.

Often a person will raise an idea or ask a question about something that you plan to discuss later in the presentation. In that case, you might want to say: "That's a really interesting idea, and we will be discussing it later. Perhaps you could hold comments on this point. But you've definitely raised a point of relevance to our topic. You're just a bit ahead of the rest of us." When you do reach the point where you planned to discuss the topic, make reference back to the question and acknowledge the individual who raised the point. If you decide to respond to a question that takes the discussion off track, take the time after answering to reposition the discussion by giving a brief review of what you had covered to that point. If you do not know the answer to a question, say that you will check and get back to the group with the answer. If you need more time to think about the question, ask the person to repeat it, or say that you will come back to the point later in the presentation. A sample response follows: "To be honest, I haven't given much thought to that question. But it is an interesting one, and I will get back to you before the end of the period." Alternatively, you might want to write the question on the board to allow more time to consider it before responding to the person.

Notice the kind of language that one uses in facilitation. Effective facilitation is courteous, sensitive to the feelings of participants, and encouraging in tone. When you employ "we" language as a facilitator, you assume more of the responsibility for what does not work in the presentation. Mistakes and problems become "our" mistakes and problems—not "your mistakes" and "your confused understanding." Body language should also be supportive and encouraging. Qualifiers such as *a bit*, *a little*, and *somewhat* soften the impact of less positive responses. If you say, "There appears to be *some* misunderstanding on this point," you have avoided saying, "You have misunderstood this point." The first statement is less *bare*. Adding some flesh softens the impact of the statement. Women tend to use this kind of language more frequently than men do.

Using the same example, we can also observe some other points about appropriate language to use in group facilitation. When you use *indirect language*, you soften the impact. If you say, for example, "*There* appears to be some confusion on this point," you have avoided saying "*You* are confused." This kind of language serves the function of allowing those who are among the confused to "save face." In addition, this example illustrates a third point. If you say, "There *appears to be*

Indirect language
Words used to soften impact, to prevent offense

some misunderstanding," you sound less dogmatic than when you say "There *is* some misunderstanding." While you should avoid this kind of indirect and powerless language in speeches, the language is appropriate in group facilitation, where you are encouraging audience participation and offering feedback.

Reframing and Redirecting Questions

Redirecting questions
Turning a question around on the audience to open up discussion

Sometimes facilitators redirect questions to the larger group. In a session on retirement planning, someone might ask about the best savings plans. The facilitator could redirect the question to the larger group: "What are your experiences with some of the savings plans? Which ones would you recommend?" In a presentation on the increasing costs of automobile insurance, an audience member might ask for more information about specific plans. Again the facilitator could say: "Most of you are in the same age and risk group as the person who asked the question. What do some of you pay for insurance?" At other times, you might want to redirect a question to the person who asked it: "That is a good question. Do you have any ideas on the topic?"

PROVIDING HANDOUTS AND OTHER SUPPLEMENTARY MATERIALS

Materials provided to the class should be professional in appearance. Handouts should be neatly packaged or bound, preferably with cerlox or spiral binding. As mentioned earlier, these handouts typically include the agenda, materials for group exercises, copies of the PowerPoint presentation, and references. Instead of binding the materials, some groups provide folders to each class member. If the group does not distribute name tags as people enter the room, the folders may also include name tags, pens, and small favors. Whenever possible, the facilitators should give transparencies and markers to the groups to record any responses to be shared with the larger group. (See the Keep in Mind box.)

Keep in Mind

Tips for Using Supplementary Materials

- Avoid distributing handouts to class during a talk.
- Staple or bind handouts—cerlox or spiral for maximum appeal.
- Leave room on pages for people to write on handouts.
- Ask the group not to look ahead in their handouts or manuals.

- If you refer to a book, bring a copy to show the group.
- Provide bibliographical information on sources used in lectures.
- Provide transparencies and markers to groups to record their group responses.

Keep in Mind

Tips for Using Flip Charts

- Use flip charts to gather audience reactions.
- If you plan to use a flip chart, be sure it is available and ready to use, with sufficient paper.
- Put notes on the back of the flip chart and position yourself several feet behind the chart to deliver.

- Use the upper two-thirds of each page; restrict to five lines of no more than five words per line.
- Abbreviate long words and use acronyms when possible.
- Tape charts, once torn off, to walls for easy viewing by participants.

If flip charts are available, the groups can profit from having individual flip charts at their disposal for collecting and recording ideas. If you make reference to a book, you should have the book with you. Visual aids are highly desirable in long presentations. To review the requirements for visual aids, refer to Chapter Seven. (See the Keep in Mind box.)

Taking Ethics into Account

In classroom settings, where audience are held in relatively captive situations (unable to come and go at will), speakers have a strong responsibility to adhere to ethical norms of conduct. The idea that a professor or student presenter can express any viewpoint—no matter how extreme—has come under attack in courtrooms in recent years. Those who want to preserve the principle of academic freedom, however, argue that censorship of ideas in classrooms can result in the kind of draconian control exercised in authoritarian societies. The debate is an animated one. (See the Question of Ethics box.)

Conclusion

This chapter has looked at the requirements for preparing and presenting a successful team presentation, including choosing a theme, establishing teaching and learning objectives, and determining an agenda for learning activities. To achieve their goals, the team must learn to work together and manage group dynamics. On the day of presentation, the group must set up the room, make an impression through dress, share responsibilities and interact during the presentation, communicate clearly and effectively, manage the feedback process, and provide necessary handouts and other supplementary materials to the class. Finally, presenters must take ethics into account in interacting in classroom settings.

A Question of Ethics

A major concern in academia relates to the right of professors to teach what they please, without being subjected to the normal rules of legal society. That is, traditionally professors have enjoyed *academic freedom*—the right to express their views freely without fear of being disciplined or fired for their beliefs. The aim of this principle has been to protect the rights of professors to disseminate knowledge without worrying about being challenged in courts of law or imprisoned for their teachings. In many countries in the world, academics can teach only the doctrines that are acceptable to political or religious authorities. Democratic countries have not believed, in past years, in these forms of censorship.

In recent years, however, this principle of academic freedom has been challenged in the courts. Accusers claim that professors are as responsible as anyone else in society for their words. Several recent cases have highlighted the murky and often disputed nature of academic freedom. In the first instance, a high school instructor taught that the Holocaust never took place—that it was a conspiracy created by people of Jewish descent to justify aggressive actions against Palestinians.

In a second instance, a university professor publicized research demonstrating that some racial groups (e.g., the Chinese) are more intelligent than other racial groups. In a third instance, a prominent researcher made a presentation that accused pharmaceutical firms of hiding results that do not support their products. Representatives of the pharmaceutical firms attended the speech event. Threatened with potential loss of funding from the pharmaceutical companies, the university canceled the employment contract of the researcher. (The university did not, however, admit that the dismissal of the researcher was related to this speech.) What if a professor were to urge his students to boycott Walmart or Home Depot and give their business to local merchants?

What are the similarities and differences in these examples? Do you believe in the principle of academic freedom? If so, do limits exist? What are they? When state-funded institutions employ professors, should they be as accountable as politicians for their words? Should they be able to promote their own political views in a classroom setting? What are the risks of failure to protect the principle of academic freedom?

Questions for Discussion

1. Have you ever made a team presentation in a classroom or other context? What problems did your group experience, if any, in preparing and delivering the talk? What were the strengths of your presentation? Do you prefer individual or team presentations? Why?

2. What are some weaknesses that you have observed in team presentations by others?

3. What is the difference between teaching and learning objectives?

4. What is your preferred method of learning (auditory, visual, tactile, or kinesthetic)?

5. Multiple intelligence theory tells us that there are seven to nine pathways to learning, including linguistic, logical-mathematical, visual-spatial, bodily-kinesthetic, musical, interpersonal, intrapersonal, and naturalist. Which pathways work best for you?

6. What are some popular icebreakers? Some popular energizers?

7. What are some of the differences in the priorities of older adults and professionals who return to the classroom? How do their expectations about the learning experience differ from those of their younger and less experienced peers?

8. Analyze the dynamics of some small group in which you have held membership. What were the roles played by different people? Do they conform to the discussion in the text?

Outline

THE BUSINESS OF SPEECHWRITING

A "Ghostwritten" Speech

Learning Objectives

- To understand the history of ghostwriting as a presidential function
- To learn about the steps required to produce a ghostwritten speech
- To understand the techniques for preparing a manuscript for delivery
- To discover the importance of relinquishing ownership
- To find out how to evaluate your efforts as a speechwriter
- To learn about finding work as a speechwriter
- To gain an appreciation of the debate over the ethics of ghost writing

Because of the multitude of occasions at which politicians, bureaucrats, and CEOs speak, they often call upon professional speechwriters and staff members to write speeches on their behalf: The grueling schedules of presidents, captains of business, or senior figures in any institution rarely allow them time to draft long speeches or construct articles for the media. Relying on trusted members of one's press office, communications department, or private office is the only logical solution.[1] At one point in time, these speechwriters were anonymous, unknown to the public. In fact, their anonymity resulted in their being titled *ghostwriters*. For many years, politicians protected the names of their speechwriters, concerned that they could appear less sincere if the public knew that someone else was putting the words in their mouths.

This chapter will examine (1) the history of presidential speechwriting, (2) steps in producing a ghostwritten speech, (3) techniques for preparing a manuscript for delivery, (4) the importance of relinquishing ownership of the speech, (5) evaluating your efforts, (6) getting work as a speechwriter, and (7) the debate over the ethics of ghostwriting.

History of Presidential Ghostwriting

Historical accounts reveal that a number of early presidents, including George Washington, used prominent individuals to assist with at least some of their speeches.[2] Alexander Hamilton, for example, assisted George Washington; and Mark Twain wrote on occasion for Ulysses S. Grant.[3] Warren Harding was the first president to put a ghostwriter (Justin Welliver) on the official payroll of a government department. Welliver did not, however, hold a title that suggested his true responsibilities—assisting the president in drafting speeches and other communication products.[4] Franklin D. Roosevelt was the first president to create a position that recognized the writing function in any real way. Roosevelt appointed Samuel

Ghostwriter
A professional speechwriter or aide who writes a speech for another to give

Rosenman to a newly created post of "counsel to the president." Playwright Robert Sherwood later teamed with Rosenman, and the two worked in close collaboration with another Roosevelt adviser and with Roosevelt himself.[5] By the time John F. Kennedy entered the presidency, the American people knew and accepted the presence of speechwriters in the Oval Office. Theodore Sorensen enjoyed immense prestige as Kennedy's principal speechwriter and senior adviser. Sorensen also assisted other members of the Kennedy family with major addresses.

Past presidents have varied greatly in the extent to which they have participated in the drafting and editing of their speeches. Historians believe that Thomas Jefferson, Abraham Lincoln, and Woodrow Wilson can take full credit for the writing of their own speeches.[6] Roosevelt participated actively in the development and editing of the speeches. The involvement of his advisers in the policy process made it possible for the speeches to have a unified theme and feel.[7] Dwight Eisenhower, Lyndon Johnson, Richard Nixon, and Ronald Reagan, on the other hand, probably had a much lower level of engagement. Harry Truman, Gerald Ford, and Jimmy Carter are believed to have delegated primary responsibility for their speeches to others.[8]

Presidents and political figures also have varied greatly in the extent to which they are willing to acknowledge the contribution of their speechwriters. As late as 1952, Democratic presidential candidate Adlai Stevenson worried about admitting that he hired speechwriters. On one occasion, Stevenson restricted speechwriter John Kenneth Galbraith to his hotel room for an entire day before allowing the noted economist to emerge and join Arthur M. Schlesinger, Jr., as a visible member of his team of advisers.[9] When Richard Nixon took the helm in 1969, presidential speechwriting took a backseat under the "wider umbrella of 'outreach and communications.'"[10] Presidential speechwriters would not find full recognition again until the administrations of Ronald Reagan and Bill Clinton.[11] Reagan supposedly had thirteen ghostwriters.[12] In discussing the role of speechwriters in the administration of former President Bill Clinton, reporter Tracy Jan (American Society of Newspaper Editors) explained:

> After Washington shuts down for the night and the players return home to warm beds, a few dedicated "ghostwriters" are crafting President Clinton's next speech into the wee hours of the morning. They wear their beepers religiously. They have to. When the president comforts the nation after an emergency, such as the Oklahoma City bombing, his team of speechwriters provides those words. These devoted writers help the president speak as a leader, a consoler and a man of vision.[13]

Along with Terry Edmonds, June Shih and another writer, Carolyn Curiel (former editor at the *Washington Post* and *New York Times*), performed the domestic speechwriting tasks for President Clinton. Shih also assisted Hillary Clinton with her speeches. Three other writers tackled the job of writing speeches for delivery to foreign audiences. Clinton's speechwriting teams were ethnically diverse, reflecting the cultural diversity of the country and allowing for a better understanding of foreign audiences.[14] He employed the first female Hispanic writer.

Sometimes presidents employ writers on the basis of specific expertise. Lyndon Johnson, for example, called upon different people to write about health, education, and welfare from those who wrote about civil rights, military affairs, and Vietnam. Sometimes presidents also take ideologies into account when they employ speechwriters.[15]

Steps in Producing a Ghostwritten Speech

The large majority of speeches delivered by government and corporate leaders fall into the category of *good will*, speeches that allow the speakers to build rapport with the audience, establish credibility, and transmit the strategic messages of the organization. In a guide prepared for the U.S. Congress, Thomas H. Neale described the role of the good will speech in the following way:

> [These] speeches may be solemn in nature, such as a Memorial Day address or celebratory, at the opening of a new school, library, or child-care facility. They remind citizens of their joint identity as members of a community; these events, seemingly everyday, or even trite, are actually vital expressions of civic life. The Member's role as a community leader and spokesperson on these occasions should not be underestimated; it is a great honor for him or her to deliver remarks at these community rites; and a congressional speechwriter should devote talent and originality to them.[16]

The work of crafting the speech involves gathering background materials, structuring and developing the speech, recycling content, and making choices on language.

GATHERING BACKGROUND MATERIALS

If the speechwriter is not a member of the organization, the person will usually meet with some organizational representative (often a staff assistant, press secretary, or communication officer) to discuss the requirements for the speech. This representative will oversee the development of the speech by setting up meetings with relevant individuals, providing background material, responding to questions from the speechwriter, setting deadlines for speech drafts, circulating the drafts for comments from relevant policy executives, and editing and approving the final product. Background material, usually acquired from the organization, will include information on the speaker and the organization, speech purpose, occasion, audience, and messages to be conveyed.

Researching the Speaker

If you are not personally acquainted with the person for whom you are writing the speech, your job will be more difficult. You can, however, take steps to learn more about the speaker. Ask to meet and interview the person. If the speaker is not available to you, interview other individuals within the organization who have an intimate knowledge of the speaker. Ask for a biographical statement on the speaker if one is not available on the organization's website. Most political figures and CEOs have these kinds of statements. If they do not, their chiefs of staff, assistants, communication advisers, or other close associates will have the information. Does the organization have a videotape of an earlier speaking engagement? Transcripts of what the person has said on the topic in radio or television interviews?

Gather information on the speaker's background—where the person was raised and has resided, cultural and travel experiences, knowledge of languages, education, and family. The best speakers make references to their own background and experiences as a means of identifying and cultivating a relationship with their audiences. If you are writing the speech, you should be able to draw on the background of the speaker to personalize and add color to the speech.

Learn as much as you can about the person's attitudes toward speaking—stylistic preferences and commonplaces that the person likes to use in speeches (e.g., references to certain experiences or affiliations)—and words that he or she might have difficulty pronouncing. Attend a press conference or other occasion where the speaker is interacting with a group. Note patterns of speech and preferred expressions. Review press clippings on the speaker to learn more about the person and about audience reactions to previous speaking experiences.

Ask for copies of previous speeches that the speaker felt comfortable giving. Study the speeches for content, style, and other cues to understanding the speaker. These speeches can be valuable in identifying the linguistic style preferred by the speaker. On some occasions, I was told, for example, "This is a speech that the person liked." Organizations often tell speechwriters to use excerpts from these earlier speeches or to use the speeches as models. You can find examples of preferred speeches on the websites of many organizations. Just as we throw away photos that are not flattering, many speakers discard speeches that did not suit their style and personality. This action may have nothing to do with the inherent quality of the speech, but it may have everything to do with the fact that the person writing the speech was a stranger to the person delivering it. See the Keep in Mind box for a review of the major points in researching the speaker.

Researching the Organization

You also need to know as much as possible about the organization. The mission, mandate, and priorities of most organizations—as well as current and archived press releases—are available on the web. The strategic plans of many public institutions appear on their websites. The communication plans (in which messages appear), however, are not usually available. Speechwriters must request those documents from organizational representatives.

Keep in Mind

Researching the Speaker

- Ask to meet and interview the speaker.
- If the speaker is not available, interview close associates.
- Request copies of previous speeches.
- Attend a speech or press conference.

- Ask for a biographical statement.
- Locate information on the Internet and in newspapers and other media—bio, speeches, and articles.

Researching the Speech Purpose

Find out what motivated the speaker to accept this particular occasion. What does he or she wish to accomplish with the speech? The best way to think of purpose is to think of the *response* that the speaker wants from the audience. What does the speaker want the audience to think, understand, say, feel, know, value, or dislike?

The four most commonly acknowledged purposes of speeches are: (1) to inform (increase the knowledge or awareness of the audience on a particular topic), (2) to persuade (reinforce or change opinions and attitudes held by the audience or to encourage the audience to think, believe, feel, or act in a certain way), (3) to entertain (amuse or give pleasure, with no particular concern that the audience learn a great deal or adopt a definite attitude or belief), or (4) to inspire (encourage the audience to set lofty goals).

The following purposes will rarely be articulated but will be as important as the stated purposes: (1) to generate good will, (2) to leave a favorable impression of the organization and a positive image of the individual, and (3) to transmit the messages of the organization (usually found in the strategic plans of the organization).

The most common speech crafted for government officials and CEOs will "look like" a speech to inform. The ostensible purpose of the speech will be to tell the audience what the organization is doing in the way of programs, services, and research. The unspoken purpose of the speech will be to create good will, to leave a favorable impression of the speaker and his or her organization, and to transmit the strategic messages and themes of the organization. The speaker will probably be seeking support not only for himself as an individual but also for the organization. The person who made the initial contact will probably be able to respond to your questions on purposes of the speech.

Researching the Occasion

Occasion governs the content and style of a speech. Veterans' Day and Memorial Day call for serious and somber speeches that dwell on themes of "commemoration, service, and sacrifice."[17] Other occasions call for motivational or informative speeches. Every occasion is unique. The physical environment can place constraints on the speaker or can contribute to the ability of the speaker to achieve his or her purposes. Settings can also diminish or enhance the status of the speaker. As a means of adaptation, speakers will often make references to the region, city, or building in which they are speaking. This is especially the case if the building has historical or other significance. Sometimes a speaker is dedicating a building or participating in opening ceremonies. As a speechwriter, you should learn as much as possible about the occasion. Some useful questions to ask are the following:

· Is the occasion formal or informal? Just as speakers wear different types of clothing for different speaking occasions, they use a different kind of language for different occasions.
· Will your speaker be delivering a keynote address? Or are you preparing a panel presentation for the speaker, a situation where different individuals address different aspects of a topic? Again, the style and content of speeches will vary, depending upon the answers to these questions.

- Will someone else introduce your speaker? If so, he or she may need to acknowledge the introductory comments.
- Will your speaker be the only speaker? If not, how many other speakers are involved in the event?
- In the event of multiple speakers, will your speaker begin or end the session? Who will precede and follow your speaker? You may wish to insert references to the earlier speeches. If the other speakers come from your organization, you may want to find out what they are saying to avoid overlap and repetition. Try to complement rather than reiterate what other speakers say; work with other speechwriters in the same organization to negotiate content areas.
- What time of the day will the speech be delivered? Will the speech precede or follow a dinner? Humor or other strong attention-getting devices may be critical if your speaker follows a meal or comes late in the agenda. Audiences get tired and sleepy.
- Has a period been set aside for questions during or after the speech? Additional briefing notes may be necessary if questions are expected.
- Will the speech be televised? If so, who will be the first audience? The live audience or the television audience? References to the immediate occasion and audience may be inappropriate in some situations. Both linguistic style and content may have to change if the speech is to be broadcast.
- What are the time limits for the speeches? The attention span of audiences varies from the first to the last speaker, from the beginning to the end of the day, and before and after dinner. Audiences become restless when speakers exceed their time limits, and the last speakers pay for failure of the first speakers to observe time requirements.

Most of the time, event or conference organizers give specific instructions on time requirements for speaking, and the decision regarding the length of the speech does not reside with the speaker. The more prestigious the speaker, however, the higher the level of control. Event planners may suggest a time, but they are likely to be flexible if a high-status speaker asks for more or less time. In the latter case, it can be useful to the ghostwriter to understand the expectations of audiences. Whatever time is allotted, you may decide to adjust the length of the speech to accommodate the realities of audience attention spans. According to the congressional speechwriting guide (and my own experience), few speeches exceed twenty minutes in length in today's environment.[18] The appropriate time for speaking at many events ranges from five to ten minutes.

Researching the Audience

The ultimate success of a speaker will depend, at least in part, upon his or her ability to achieve empathy with the audience—that is, to project himself or herself into the position of the other person. To achieve empathy, a speaker must be familiar with the audience and its situation.

Factors such as age, gender, ethnicity, education and income level, occupation, and regional and political affiliations influence the receptivity of audience members to the message. What is their level of knowledge on the topic under discussion? Will audience members know a great deal or little about the topic? What are

Researching the audience
Getting to know more about the group to which the speech will be delivered

their affiliations in terms of associations and reference groups? What are their religious, economic, and political biases? What beliefs, attitudes, and values bring this audience together as a group? Does the audience meet on a regular basis, or will it be gathering for a special occasion? Will the audience perceive your speaker as an insider or an outsider? What is the anticipated size of the group? What are group members' goals and purposes in attending the meeting? Will they consider the topic to be important and relevant to their special needs and preoccupations or peripheral and inconsequential? Will audience members be friendly, interested, hostile, or apathetic? What are possible sensitivities of this audience? Should the speaker avoid some subjects or take particular care in wording some parts of the speech? How open is the audience to change? Research can provide you with the answer to many of these questions.

Speechwriters must tailor their messages to take these and other variables into account. Knowing whether the speech will be delivered to members of a large heterogeneous audience, a small group of business leaders or municipal officials, a seniors' organization, or an activist group is very important. The references and examples must be appropriate to the audience. More knowledgeable publics require less explanation than less knowledgeable publics do. You can use professional jargon with specialists that you cannot use with the lay public. Educated listeners look for balanced presentations, where the speaker acknowledges more than one point of view on controversial topics. Apathetic audience members will not listen unless you give them a reason to listen. You must stress the takeaway value of the speech. If the audience sees the speaker as an insider, you can employ humor that would be inappropriate if the person is perceived as an outsider. When viewed as an outsider, the speaker must point to areas of commonality—shared experiences, values, and/or acquaintances. When audience members know each other in advance, the atmosphere is likely to be warmer and more social. Speakers can use that kind of climate to their benefit.

To obtain information of this nature, speechwriters need to make direct contact with the host organization or request the information from the organization that commissioned the speech. Local constituency or congressional offices can obtain this information for political speeches. These offices have a wealth of information on grassroots organizations. Many voluntary groups, professional associations, and charitable organizations have websites. Information is also available on the websites of political figures.

Identifying the Strategic Messages of the Organization

Strategic messages
Statements about the strategic direction or policies of an organization, often appearing in "good will" speeches

Does the organization want to highlight some areas more than others? Does it want to give an overview of activities undertaken in recent weeks or months? Or does it simply have several messages that it wants to convey? Most speeches have a central overriding theme, as well as a series of organizational "messages" that speechwriters build into the speech. Higher-level executives or bureaucrats agree upon the messages prior to giving them to speechwriters and public relations specialists. In the case of government, the messages must reflect the actual policies and directions of government. Otherwise, the government will be held accountable for not fulfilling its promises. Businesses can also lose credibility if they make promises that they cannot fulfill or do not want to fulfill.

In my experience, ghostwriters do not conduct a great deal of original research in preparing speeches for government. Typically, communication and political staff prepare a package of material for use by the speechwriter. Governments employ large numbers of people in policy areas who do nothing but research the issues of the organization. The demand for original research is greater, however, in corporate and business environments. When asked to conduct original research, speechwriters increase their fees significantly to accommodate the increased time demands. Undertaking research can be far more time-consuming than writing the speech. Supporting materials, nonspecific to the topic at hand, include collections of quotations, encyclopedias, and dictionaries. Most materials of this nature are available online. (See the Keep in Mind box.)

STRUCTURING AND DEVELOPING THE SPEECH

In a guide prepared for Congress, Thomas H. Neale explained the importance of preparing an initial outline for speeches, striving to maintain a central theme throughout the speech, and having a clear three-part structure (introduction, body, and conclusion). He urges speechwriters to save these outlines for future reference.[19]

Like other kinds of speeches, good will speeches require clear thesis and purpose statements. The thesis statement reveals the dominant theme of the speech, and the purpose statement usually has an informative component. A statement of

Keep in Mind

Online Resources for Speechwriters

Periodicals and Professional Publications for Speechwriters, http://www.executive-speaker.com/res_peri.html: resources for speechwriters, including references to such publications as *Executive Speeches* and *Canadian Speeches: A National Forum of Diverse Views*

On Speechwriting, http://www.thespeechwriter.com/ (website of American organization): free Internet newsletter with tips on speechwriting

TheSpeechWriters.com, http://thespeechwriters.com/ (website of speechwriter Garrett Patterson): tips on professional speechwriting

The Executive Speaker, http://www.executive-speaker.com/lib_spch.html: resources for speechwriters

Speechwriting Tools, http://www.gov.mb.ca/chc/leg-lib/vrd/speech.html: online resources for speechwriters

Washington Speechwriters Roundtable, http://www.washingtonspeechwriters.com: articles and exchanges about speechwriting experiences

SpeechTips.Com, http://www.speechtips.com: guide to speechwriting and delivery

Dave's Guide to Speechwriting, http://davegustafson.com/speech: tips on writing a variety of special occasion and other speeches, as well as PowerPoint presentations

Public Speaking and Communications Resources, http://www.danieljanssen.com/MainPagePublicSpeakingCommunicationResources.shtml: website with tips for speechwriting, sample speeches, and links to other resources

structural progression should introduce the main points to be covered in the speech. Within the first minute or two of the speech, for example, the audience should know the organizational scheme of the speech.

Most good will speeches begin with a fairly predictable opening. The speaker acknowledges the audience, as in Figure 14.1. Also see Figure 14.1 for a review of basic elements in the introduction and conclusion of this speech on elder abuse.[20] Most attempts at humor will appear early in the good will speech, along with other attention-getting strategies that the speaker may choose to use, such as stories, parables, or personal instances.

Attention: Thank you. I am pleased to be with you today, speaking on behalf of Elisha Winters, representative for seniors' issues. I am not unique this afternoon in representing the interests of someone absent from this room. Many of us at this meeting are, in one way or another, standing in for someone else. Some of you are here to give a voice to women who have been physically or psychologically battered, often by those they most trusted and loved. Others speak for the children, many of whom have likewise suffered the traumas of family violence. Acting on behalf of Ms. Winters, I am here to speak for the seniors— voices that, too often in the past, have not been heard in the noisy corridors of power. *Statement of purpose*: As a spokesperson for seniors, I would like to take the next several minutes to introduce you to some concerns specific to the area of elder abuse. *Thesis sentence*: Elder abuse is a problem to which all of us must pay attention, especially governments. *Preview statement*: I would like to discuss three points in particular that are relevant to a good understanding of this topic. *First*, I would like to acquaint you with what we believe to be a profile of the older victim. *Second*, I would like to suggest what appears to be emerging as a profile of the abuser. *Third*, I would like to focus your attention on what many are finding to be the most critical challenges in dealing with the problem of elder abuse. . . . *Finally*, I would like to talk about what my organization is doing to address these challenges. . . . *Conclusion*: International Women's Day is important because it gives us an opportunity to recognize the fact that violence against women knows no geographical, socioeconomic, or cultural differences. The problem is universal. It also knows no age boundaries. In the 1960s, child abuse was an emerging topic. In the 1970s, wife assault began to capture headlines. In the 1990s, the problems of older Americans are becoming more commonly recognized and discussed. Whether young or old, able or disabled, victims of violence have much in common. And those of use who have gathered today to represent their interests have much to share and learn from each other. The time has come to speak out against violence, to give a voice to those unable or afraid to speak for themselves. We must also learn to listen more carefully and to help the victims of violence to find their own voices.

Figure 14.1 Sample Introduction and Conclusion to a Good Will Speech

The strategic messages typically govern the organization of business and political speeches. If a U.S. congressperson speaks to an audience of Texas poultry farmers, for example, the theme of the speech could be federal actions to control the avian flu virus. The supporting messages might be the following: (1) The U.S. Department of Agriculture has set aside $10.8 million to develop a control and prevention program for avian flu. (2) The government is investing in research to find a vaccine capable of immunizing humans against the avian flu. (3) The National Poultry Improvement Plan is developing a monitoring system to identify different strains of the disease. (4) The depopulation of more than nine thousand birds in Texas will help to control the spread of avian flu. (5) The government is giving almost $3 million in subsidies to poultry farmers affected by the destruction of chickens.

If the politician speaks to an audience of educators, he might talk about what the government is doing in the arena of educational reforms. In that case, the major messages could be the following: (1) Educational reform is long overdue. (2) Educational reform implies finding new and better ways to provide quality education to our youth. (3) Educational reform does not imply throwing more money at an outdated system. (4) This government is committed to supporting efforts to undertake meaningful reform. (5) In partnership with states and institutions of higher learning, the federal government is supporting a number of research initiatives, designed to identify solutions to the challenges faced by higher institutions.

On a topic such as mad cow disease, the messages of the Food and Drug Administration could be the following: (1) The FDA regulates animal feed. (2) The FDA has implemented procedures to spot-check feed supplies in affected regions.

(3) The FDA has removed high-risk cattle tissues from the human food chain. (4) The threat to human life posed by mad cow disease is much less serious than originally perceived.

The messages for a fitness club, on the other hand, might be: (1) Our fitness equipment is state-of-the-art. (2) Our club provides affordable rates to its members. (3) The cost of annual membership is less than the cost of staying home from work for one minor illness. (4) We are a certified member of the Fitness Clubs of America.

When politicians, bureaucrats, and CEOs deliver good will speeches, they always talk about what they are doing to help their constituencies and stakeholders and to meet the challenges that they confront. Business and corporate leaders stress the positive aspects of their environment—their innovations, growing client base, competitive edge, and/or commitment to customers and employees or the community. In a good will speech, messages focus on accomplishments, not failures, and speakers stress their efforts to achieve solutions to problems.

As discussed earlier, good will speeches have an organizational structure different from that of other kinds of speeches. Speechwriters should put the most important messages of the speech early. In the event of time overruns by other presenters, the speaker may decide (or be confronted with the need) at the last minute to shorten the speech. Speechwriters also should avoid trying to cover too much territory in the speech. Audiences will be bored by speeches that are too broad and general in focus. The speechwriter should narrow the focus to allow more specificity and concreteness in the development of the topic. Instead of writing about economic trends in the new century, the speechwriter could focus on the buying patterns of older people or the trend toward private investments by young people.

Obviously, the time available for speaking influences the amount of content that you can include in the speech. Speaker variables will also influence the length of a manuscript. Different personalities speak at different rates. When engaged in ghostwriting for politicians and bureaucrats, I found that most speakers take two minutes to cover one typewritten page, double-spaced, 12-point Times New Roman font (i.e., approximately 250 words). That calculation translates into an average of 125 words per minute. Studies have found, however, that speaker rate can vary considerably, ranging up to 180 words or more per minute.[21] We speak more slowly when we deliver a speech in a second or third language. We speak faster when we are nervous. Some cultures are more ponderous in their speaking rhythms. Sometimes speechwriters have to prepare shorter or longer speeches for the allocated time slot, depending upon the personality, culture, and language of the client delivering the speech. The writer must assume that a slower speech rate will translate into less content.

The conclusion of a good will speech has familiar elements—usually a summary statement, challenge, request for support, or inspirational thought. The speaker might conclude with a quotation, poem, story, or some other memorable idea.

RECYCLING CONTENT

Recycling content
Using material in more than one speech

Politicians and executives with frequent speaking engagements tend to recycle content, using commonplaces that appear in multiple speeches. Since the messages of some organizations remain relatively constant, this recycling of content makes sense. If you write a speech for a politician or executive, the person may ask you to use excerpts from favorite passages in other speeches. Veteran speechwriter Frederick J. O. Blachly recounted an experience with this kind of recyling:

> When Thomas W. Wilson . . . and I were working for Averell Harriman, in the Executive Office of the President, we were asked to prepare a speech. We did. He gave the speech, not once, but over and over again. No matter what the occasion, or what the audience, he gave the same speech. However, since Harriman's usual style of delivery was a barely audible mumble, perhaps it didn't make any difference.[22]

Arthur M. Schlesinger, Jr.—speechwriter and special assistant to President John F. Kennedy—explained that people used to prepare different speeches for different occasions. However, over time, presidents (and others) began to give the same speech over and over again.[23] Given the number of speeches that must be given in a year by senators, members of congress, or CEOs, this practice should not be surprising. Ironically, the issues of plagiarism that plague university students do not apply in the context of professional speechwriting. If you pay for a speech, you typically acquire the rights to use that speech in whatever circumstances you wish—for that occasion or on future occasions.

Despite this tendency to be most comfortable with commonplaces (favorite passages used in multiple speeches), speakers usually want their writers to tailor the speech (at least to some extent) to specific audiences and occasions. So humor, acknowledgments, and linguistic style may vary even when the main body of the speech remains constant. The more important the speaking event, the higher the level of customization. Also, the more important the speaking event, the more people will look at the speech and the higher the likelihood that the speaker himself or herself will take a personal interest in the final speech product. Organizations with larger communication budgets will often invest more in original speeches than smaller organizations with lesser budgets will invest. Most presentations will have some elements of uniqueness, but the amount of original material will vary from presentation to presentation.

MAKING CHOICES ON LANGUAGE

In making choices on language, you must consider the speaker, the audience, and the occasion.

Speaker

The words should sound natural for the person for whom you are penning the speech. As mentioned earlier, you should study speeches given on earlier occasions by the speaker (and, if possible, videos of speaking occasions) to become acquainted with the person's style. Before writing her first speech for Maryland Governor Parris Glendening, speechwriter Samantha Kappalman spent her "first few weeks going to events . . . and watching the way the governor spoke, what his hand movements were and writing down phrases he liked to say."[24]

The speechwriter must consider the linguistic profile of the speaker. If the person does not speak English as a first language, the writer may need to consider the possibility that some words or phrases will be more difficult to pronounce.

Recent studies have demonstrated that computer programs are able to identify the gender of an author. A scan of key words and syntax yields 80 percent accuracy. Female writers make more frequent use of pronouns such as *I, you, she, their,* and *myself* in general. They have a more involved style of writing. When males use pronouns, on the other hand, they tend to use fewer personal pronouns such as *they* and *them*. Their style is more "informational."[25] What is the significance of this finding for speechwriters? If a speaker is to be credible, the speech should sound natural for that person. So ideally men should write for men, and women should write for women. When that is not possible or practical, however, the speechwriter should be aware of the need to temper writing style to reflect the gender of the client.

Men and women also differ in how they use humor. If you choose to include humor in the speech, you should ascertain the comfort level of the speaker with delivering jokes. Unlike their male counterparts, female speakers are often uncomfortable delivering stock jokes; they prefer humor that comes from the telling of personal experiences.[26]

Audience

As in other situations, writers must write for the ear of the listener. The best way to ensure that you are writing for the ear is to read the speech aloud as you write—to make adjustments whenever a sentence or cluster of ideas does not allow for the taking of a breath. Some experts say that the average length of sentences, written for the ear, should be eight to ten words in length.[27] However, I have found that the structure of ideas within the sentence (not the number of words) determines the comprehensibility of the speech. Consider the following statement: *The sound of the rain, the rush of the wind, the silence of the forest—all speak to us of the eloquence of nature.* This sentence has twenty-four words; however, a speaker could easily deliver the sentence, and audiences could just as easily grasp the meaning. In delivering this statement, the speaker pauses for effect after each phrase. Varying the length of sentences, inverting the order of words, and speaking in sentence fragments can also add variation and interest to speeches. Speechwriters often ask rhetorical questions, to which the speaker does not expect an audible response.

Writers should paint pictures by using concrete language and extended metaphors. They should listen for the sound of words and aim for cadence and lyricism in passages that they would like to be eloquent. The guide to congressional speechwriting mentioned earlier urges writers to use devices such as repetition (with variation), antithesis, alliteration, parallelism, and rhythmic triads (groups of three words, phrases, or clauses).[28] (See Chapter Ten for a detailed discussion of these linguistic strategies.) If you are not well schooled in literature and history, you may wish to purchase a few standard poetry, literature, and history books. Quotations are readily available on the Internet. Most of the other material is also available on the web, but you may not find what you need if you do not have a reference framework. Historical references are often interesting additions to speeches.

As noted earlier, speechwriting involves preparing a speech, not an essay. Admittedly, many of the same rules apply to both genres in terms of attention-getting strategies, thesis and purpose statements, summaries, and the need for clarity of organization and vivid concrete language. Because the writer of speeches must write for the ear, not the eye, he will sometimes write in incomplete sentences. Meaning is more important than grammar, although most "great" speeches are also grammatically correct.

To involve the audience, the speechwriter should use first-person collective (*we, us, our*) and second person (*you*) more often than *they, people, a person, the author*. Sometimes the use of first-person *I* can be important, if the speaker wants to take responsibility for some decision or action. When talking about a third person, speechwriters should make the person real to the audience. They should call the person by name (real or fictitious) and talk about the situation in concrete terms.

Political correctness is extremely important—whether writing for oneself or for a second party. Audiences will hold the speaker accountable for whatever is said, but the speechwriter will ultimately pay as great a price in loss of reputation and income. As noted in Chapter Five, speechwriters need to research the current terms used to refer to older people, those with disabilities, and ethnic and minority groups. In government, some terms are considered totally inappropriate, even when they are politically correct. Politicians and bureaucrats, for example, never include the word *problem* in any speech. Instead they substitute the term *challenge*. So governments face *challenges*, never *problems*. Examine any text by a political figure to confirm this point. An upbeat and optimistic style characterizes the good will speech.

At the same time that political correctness is important, speechwriters should avoid professional jargon when writing for lay audiences. They should avoid terms such as *portfolio, downsizing, rightsizing, prioritizing, branding, customer-calibrated, benchmarking, value-driven, debriefing, reflective modernity, contingency planning, need-to-know, stakeholders, reputation management, per-share growth, leveraging, facilitation, strategy, at-risk publics, buy-in, promise management, knowledge management, human capital performance, outcomes, paradigms, sunset clause, risk management,* and *balanced scorecard*.

Jargon
Terms often known only to insiders, generally to be avoided in speeches

Speakers should also avoid the use of acronyms such as *MREs* (meals ready to eat), *OD* (organizational development), *ADM* (Assistant Deputy Minister), *IT* (Internet technology), *MOU* (memorandum of understanding), *SAP* (simplified acquisition procedures), *WOSB* (women-owned small business), *RFP* or *RFQ* (request for proposal or quotation), and *LB* (large business), which confuse lay audiences.

Speechwriters should define terms that may be unfamiliar to the audience and explain concepts that may be alien to audience experiences, but they should avoid condescending language. *Uneducated* does not mean *unintelligent* or even *unlearned*. My father had a tenth grade education but never missed the nightly news reports. My husband did not return to school until he was forty, but he knew all the major historical and classical works and could recite Shakespeare and other favorites by heart. If the audience cannot understand what you are saying, it is probably because you are not saying it very well.

Sometimes writers must consider not only the immediate audience, but also remote audiences that may view the speech on television or listen to a radio broadcast. The speechwriter must take both audiences into account.

Reflections

Many female comedians draw their humor from self-deprecation—making fun of their homes, children, and husbands. When Jean Kerr writes that an expensive brown dress makes her look like a large bran muffin, she's relying on self-deprecation. When Erma Bombeck says her children won't eat anything that hasn't danced on TV, we see this comment as extended self-deprecation because children are an extension of their mothers.

Source: R. Barreca, *They Used to Call Me Snow White . . . But I Drifted: Women's Strategic Use of Humor* (New York: Penguin, 1991), pp. 1–37; at http://condor.depaul.edu/~mwilson/extra/humor/snowedt1.html, accessed January 18, 2005.

When making choices on the inclusion of humor in a speech, you should note some basic facts about how men and women respond to humor. Long anecdotal jokes tend to be popular with both men and women, but jokes with a punch line (as noted in other chapters) are less popular with women.[29] Women, on the other hand, enjoy humor that makes fun of the affectations and hypocrisies of people and pokes fun at the powerful in society. Many female humorists rely almost exclusively on self-deprecating humor—that is, humor that occurs at their own expense. See the Reflections box for a comment on how women use self-deprecating humor.

Occasion

Simplicity and clarity are the keys to a good speech. The direct and low-key approach, characterized by a casual and conversational quality, is the most acceptable style in contemporary North American rhetoric.[30] The more formal the occasion, however, the more formal the language should be. You must adapt your language to the nature of the event—a dedication or commemorative event, an after-dinner speech, a keynote address, or other.

Techniques for Preparing the Manuscript for Delivery

Many government, political, and business figures read their speeches from manuscripts. They rely on a written script to ensure the accuracy and specificity of statements. Public figures incur high risks for the organization when they speak loosely.

In most cases, their words are not a personal statement. They are an organizational statement. And the organization can become politically, financially, or legally responsible for promises made in public speeches or inaccurate presentation of facts. For that reason, governments in particular require multiple levels of approval for speeches with policy content.

To deal with the excessive number of speeches that must be given by governing politicians and bureaucrats, some organizations commission the creation of speech modules for use by departmental or agency representatives. A speech module contains prepared and approved statements on a specified topic, with paragraphs that can be cut and pasted together for different speaking occasions. These modules serve the same function as the canned statements used by correspondence units to respond to public inquiries. The more important the speaking event, however, the more likely the speech will have been written or customized for that particular occasion.

Speech module
Chunks of material that can be cut and pasted into different speeches as needed

Communication staff members also prepare speaker notes or talking points for top-level government officials and CEOs. These talking points allow the speakers to sound more spontaneous in their delivery. But important speaking occasions will almost always necessitate the preparation of a full manuscript. The speakers will want to take care in making assertions and promises. Some communication staff members have told me that they cringe when political figures move away from their manuscripts because they not infrequently make claims that do not reflect existing government policies. At that point, communication staff members have to lurch into damage control to recover the situation.

Appropriate formatting of manuscript speeches can facilitate the reading of the manuscript. The speechwriter should *triple space* the manuscript and *put slashes* between the phrases, as in the following example: "Jenny was tall/lean in build/and muscular and athletic in body type./ She gave every appearance of being healthy/ free of disease/and the most unlikely candidate for cancer./But cancer does not put broad markers on its early victims./ No/cancer is a silent stalker/moving easily among all classes and occupations./"

When marking the manuscript, the ghostwriter will want to make some word clusters shorter and others longer. Commas are unnecessary since the slashes define where pauses should occur. Reading the speech aloud facilitates the process of marking the manuscript. When I write speeches, I read the words aloud as I write. Only in that way can I obtain a true feeling for the lyricism of phrases and some idea of how to phrase the ideas for readability. Speechwriters should not adhere to rules of grammar when deciding where to place a pause. A pause may come before or after a comma.

A large font (14 to 16 points) creates a more readable manuscript, but the use of all capital letters creates a less readable manuscript. Other markings in the speech can be personal ones, intended to assist the speaker in delivering the speech. The ghostwriter may want, for example, to underline or highlight places of emphasis or to indicate length of pauses. She may want to leave a good deal of white space on the first page so that the speaker can add last-minute references to audience members or impromptu remarks about the occasion. The manuscript should be typed on one side of the page only. The pages should be numbered, in case the speaker should drop them. The weight of the paper should be sufficiently heavy that the pages will not rustle or bend when the speaker turns or slides them.

Relinquishing Ownership

Relinquishing ownership

In ghostwriting, when the writer acknowledges that the deliverer of the speech will usually receive credit for having written it

Those who choose to make a career of ghostwriting speeches must learn to relinquish ownership of the speech. Most obviously, as the previous discussion implies, this relinquishing of ownership means forfeiting of authorship. Clearly, when a writer pens a speech for money, the person will not deliver the speech, hear the applause, or receive compliments from the audience. In the majority of cases, the client will never acknowledge the writer; and in my experience, the ghostwriter rarely receives feedback on the speech event. The client has purchased the speech, and the writer has received compensation of a monetary nature for his work. In the eyes of the organization, nothing more is required.

For many speechwriters, however, the most difficult aspect of relinquishing ownership does not relate to the forfeiting of recognition. Most writers accept that they are being paid in money, not in accolades; however, they find it more difficult to accept perceived assaults on the aesthetics of the work. In government, in particular, large numbers of policy and program experts analyze every word that appears in major addresses. The higher the status of the person delivering the speech, the greater the level of scrutiny to which the organization subjects the speech. Legal experts pore over the manuscript, carefully replacing objectionable passages with legalese. Policy experts change the content or the wording, often without regard for the need to write for the ear. In cases where the speaker is talking about government programs, program experts have their say on what to include or exclude from the speech. These writers may have limited abilities (or interest) in producing a document that is "sayable." And as Clinton speechwriter Carolyn Curiel observed, "Everyone thinks that they can write."[31] Ironically, scientific and research organizations are the worst offenders because their highly educated members often think that they have better writing skills than communication staffers or outside consultants. They certainly possess the knowledge, but they are often unable to communicate their ideas to a lay audience.

Most writers place a great value on the written and spoken word. Many are English or linguistic majors; or they have specialized in speech or journalism. They appreciate language. Yet in their chosen profession of speechwriting, they must learn to accept critiques from those who may know little to nothing about speechwriting, and they cannot become defensive or argumentative. They must respond to the concerns of individuals who are more worried about the legal ramifications of the wrong phrase than the quality of the language. When enough different people edit a speech, it often loses its coherence and stylistic consistency; and the requested changes may destroy the cadence of the speech or the flow of ideas.

In the end, the product may bear little resemblance to the original draft, which can be a source of professional concern to speechwriters. They may fear that a poorly edited product will reflect on their abilities, since the speaker may unfairly attribute problems of flow or quality of language to the ghostwriter. But experienced speechwriters know that the client has the right to make the changes that he or she desires.

In August 2000, John Podhoretz wrote that the "pride of every speechwriter in the world is deeply wounded today because Democratic presidential nominee

Al Gore has claimed to be writing his acceptance speech himself."[32] In the view of most professional writers, this "wounded pride" would be out of place. Clinton speechwriter Terry Edmonds said that "unless the president credits us, we don't publicize what we've done. . . . You have to bury your ego entirely."[33] As reporter Jan Tracy noted, speechwriters such as Terry Edmonds "live by deadlines but do not write for bylines or public praise."[34]

Evaluating Your Efforts

Speechwriters require feedback to improve their ability to meet the needs of clients. *People within the organization* require feedback to discover if they have met their objectives with the speech. To improve, the *speaker* requires feedback on the performance. This feedback will reflect judgments on the artistic merits of the speech, quality of the delivery, value of the information, ethics, and whether the speaker ultimately swayed the audience to his or her point of view. (See Chapter Fifteen for further discussion of the grounds on which audiences and critics judge speeches.

FEEDBACK TO THE SPEECHWRITER

Organizational representatives should inform speechwriters of any changes made to the speech, either before or after the speech is given. Not uncommonly, advisers and staff members will make changes in content and style. Ideally, the speechwriter should be involved in these changes. The changes may disrupt the style and flow of the speech. A speech should appear to be the product of one person; it should not have the look or feel of a patchwork quilt. Input by many people makes the speech less coherent as a unit and less fluid.

The reality of bureaucracies, however, is that changes may occur at any stage of a speech's journey through the many layers of the organization that must approve it. All too often, the speechwriter will be excluded from any say in the finalizing of speech content and form. The speech suffers, and the individual slated to give the speech may blame the resulting nonfluencies on the speechwriter. Those who make their living as speechwriters will occasionally (but not usually) put clauses in their contracts, insisting that they be consulted when changes are made in content and wording. Some writers have been known to quit when such consultations do not occur. The reason for their concern is easy to understand, given the fact that the speaker (often an executive with influence) may not realize that the speechwriter lost ownership of the speech at some point before the final draft. Where teams of writers produce speeches, the speechwriters do not feel so much personal responsibility; however, they confront equally great challenges in producing a coherent final draft.

Where the writer is excluded from the editing process, he should secure copies of the different drafts of the speech to learn who made what changes. Sometimes, the changes reflect organizational sensitivities; and if a speechwriter does not see the revised copy, he will continue to make the same mistakes in future writing

Draft
Early versions of a speech

assignments. In other cases, the speaker will be uncomfortable with the content or language of the speech. Sometimes, organizational priorities will change at the last minute and involve shifts in emphasis or content. If the language of the speech is not the first language of the speaker, the person may have difficulty pronouncing certain words. Those whose first language is French, for example, sometimes have difficulty with the word *focus*, which can be a source of embarrassment. Again, it is important to learn from each speech effort. In that way, speechwriters can avoid making the same mistake a second or third time.

FEEDBACK TO SPEECH ORGANIZERS

Organizations should try to evaluate the results of their speechmaking efforts. The following discussion suggests questions that can be asked to determine whether a speech achieved its purposes. The discussion also identifies methods to carry out this evaluation.

Strategic Considerations

Did the audience demonstrate enhanced levels of awareness or knowledge of the topic as a result of the speech? Did their understanding of the organization's policies, priorities, and programs improve as a result of attending this speaking engagement? Did listeners leave with a better understanding of the organization's mandate and mission? Entrance and exit interviews can help the organization to respond to these questions.

Have opinions regarding policies, priorities, and programs changed as a result of the speech? Was the audience moved to action after attending the speech? Is the organization getting more requests for information or services, increased business, or fewer complaints in the period following a speaking tour? Entrance and exit interviews can solicit the answers to some of these questions. Follow-up reports by inquiries units, publication departments, and human resources personnel can assess the nature and content of subsequent relations with clients. On issues of particular importance, political parties, governments, and large corporations may hire polling firms to measure "before" and "after" public opinion.

Did the audience react favorably to the speaker at the time of the speech? Was the applause generous? Did audience questions demonstrate interest in the presentation? Did nonverbal reactions suggest positive attitudes toward the speech and speaker? Did audience members make favorable comments to the speaker, other audience members, or organizational representatives following the speech? Did anyone make follow-up requests for the speaker? What was the nature of the media comment on the speech? Observation, interviews, logs of telephone calls and other inquiries, and analysis of media clippings and transcripts can assist the organization in responding to these questions.

Were the "right" people in the audience (that is, the people that the organization wanted to reach, elite opinion leaders, or others)? Should this forum be regarded as a suitable vehicle for future efforts to carry the organization's messages? Could the target audience have been equally or better reached in some other way—a press release, brochure, talk show, or public service announcement? Did the attendance figures justify the time and money expended by the organization and the speaker? Would a failure to provide a speaker for future meetings of this group undermine the organization's ability to achieve its strategic objectives with respect to this target audience? Did the speaking engagement generate further opportunities for meeting this target public or produce other benefits (for example, new contacts, partnerships, or sources of information)? Will this target audience be more likely to cooperate with the organization in the future as a consequence of this engagement?

Was the environment for the speech event conducive to getting across the ideas? Was it noisy or chaotic? Did hostile groups disrupt the proceedings? What was the effect of these influences on achievement of the speech purposes? Follow-up interviews with advisers and bureaucrats who attended the speech event provide a way to gain insights into questions unanswered by other methodologies.

Tactical Considerations

The next questions deal with practical matters related to the planning and implementation of the speech event. Were arrangements for pre-event and postevent publicity adequate? Did other communication products (e.g., press releases, backgrounders, and advance interviews with the media) give adequate support to the event? Follow-up interviews with members of media organizations, analysis of media coverage, and the calculation of attendance can help the organization to respond to these questions. (See Tips from a Professional.)

Were the room arrangements satisfactory from the perspective of the speaker, the audience, and the media? Were the acoustics acceptable? Were the facilities adequate for recording the event? Did the events proceed on time? Observation and interviews provide appropriate ways to answer these questions. Were sufficient numbers of the speech available for distribution to the media, interested audience members, consumers of media coverage of the event, regional and branch offices, elite opinion leaders, associations interested in the topic area, and other

TIPS FROM A PROFESSIONAL
Briefing Your Speaker . . .

Especially in the political world, senior staff and political handlers often negotiate speaking invitations on behalf of their political masters; and in most cases, they inform the actual speakers, almost as an afterthought. Whether you are a press attaché, communication assistant, or media relations specialist, you must ensure that the speaker is well briefed—not only on the contents of the speech, but also on the event. Omitting a detail as mundane as what to wear (especially for women) can have a devastating effect on the speaker and his or her state of mind prior to delivering the speech. I recall a time when my boss, a politician, showed up for work on the day of an afternoon speaking assignment wearing a golf shirt. He had to return home to change when he learned the event warranted a suit and tie. I don't have to tell you how unimpressed he was by the forty-five-minute detour home to change.

Time with your speaker beforehand is crucial and often limited; so make the best of it. Speech rehearsal aside, the spokesperson counts on you to provide the following key details about the event:

· Why am I giving the speech? What is the tone of the event? The format?
· Where am I going? Is it outdoors or indoors? Am I speaking with a microphone? Podium? Will I use a data projector? Audiovisuals?
· To whom am I speaking? Are they content experts? How many people will be present?
· Will my audience be hungry, sipping coffee, or waiting to eat?
· Who will introduce me?
· Am I the only speaker? If not, who else? Who speaks before me? After me?
· How much time do I have?
· Are the media invited? Will there be a photo opportunity, ambush, or Q & A session?
· What should I wear?

As a communicator, you'll need to be prepared for everything! I carried a special "speaker's emergency kit" with me to events. The kit contained a hodgepodge of items, such as mirror, comb/brush, breath mints, cough drops, Tylenol (or your spokesperson's medicine of choice), microfiber cloth for cleaning eyeglasses, Kleenex, water, antacids, sewing kit, powder makeup, and, of course, an extra copy of the speech. Another helpful tip is to get your spokesperson to keep a few outfits at the office for any last-minute changes. When you are on site, don't forget to check your speaker for lipstick smudges, opened zippers, drippy noses, and other potentially embarrassing physical *faux pas*. Trust me, it does happen!

While textbooks emphasize the importance of lead time and rehearsing the speech with your speaker, the reality is that there are only twenty-four hours in a day. Whether it's a scheduled meeting a week before or five minutes in the car on the way to the event, preparation time with your spokesperson is precious. Use it wisely for best results.

Juline Ranger is director of communications for Cable Public Affairs Channel (CPAC). She is responsible for the promotion of the national channel to key audiences: viewers, elected officials, media, and affiliate members. She is also the general manager of Cable in the Classroom. In addition to her experience in the broadcast industry, Juline has worked in the field of politics and municipal affairs.

stakeholders? Attendance at the speech event yields the opportunity to observe the distribution of speeches, and the units that handle follow-up requests for information can provide further insights.

Were publishing and distribution deadlines respected? Were budgetary restrictions respected? If appropriate, did the organization follow up with other activities to maximize the impact of this event? The organization's communication plans should contain the information necessary to answer these questions, since they identify ways to sustain messages and allocate funding to different communication activities.

FEEDBACK TO THE SPEAKER

The speaker should receive some of the same feedback that the organization receives. In addition, someone in the organization (probably a speech adviser or chief of staff) should sit down with the speaker after the occasion to discuss strengths and weaknesses of the performance. While this feedback may require some diplomacy, many organizations put their executives through speech and interview training. So the executives are not unacquainted with this kind of feedback.

Evaluation of the speaker's performance entails looking at the following areas: Did the speaker use his or her voice (including volume, pitch, rate, and diction) to the best advantage? How effectively did the speaker use pauses and emphasis? Did gestures and movement add to—or detract from—the speech? Were these movements motivated? There is no magic formula for an appropriate number of gestures or movements; but unnecessary movements, especially repetitive ones, distract from the content of the speech. Did the speaker maintain (or appear to maintain, in the case of a large auditorium group) eye contact with the audience? Did the speaker have a natural and relaxed posture? Were visual aids used effectively? Was the speaker composed and articulate in responding to questions that followed the delivery of the speech? Did the speaker reinforce the organization's messages and themes in responding to audience questions?

CONCLUSION

In conclusion, it is useful to note that audiences judge speeches on many grounds. Some of these grounds, which will be discussed in more depth elsewhere, are the following. From an artistic point of view, was the speech well written? From the point of view of structure and language, was it a good rhetorical effort? Was the speech eloquent or moving? Did the speech achieve its purposes in terms of getting the audience to act or believe in a particular way? To accept a new policy? To like the speaker? To change behaviors? Did the speech make a contribution to the knowledge or awareness of the audience? Was the speech suited to the audience and the occasion? Was the performance credible and convincing? Did the speaker hold the attention of the audience from the beginning to the end of the speech? Was the speech ethical? Was the speaker an honest man or woman speaking the truth? Can you defend the speech on moral and ethical grounds? Most

Keep in Mind

Working as a speechwriter entails . . .

- Gaining experience
- Advertising your work
- Identifying and contacting potential clients
- Negotiating a contract and professional fees

- Establishing a schedule for completing work
- Counseling on delivery
- Evaluating your efforts

audiences evaluate speeches from an eclectic perspective, but some points are more important than others to particular groups. How will this particular audience evaluate your speaker's efforts?

If you are to evaluate the success of your speaker's efforts and your own speechwriting efforts, you must take these points into consideration. An eloquent speech delivered to a group of laborers who do not understand the language that the speaker is using may be ill received. The eloquence will be lost. Furthermore, audiences vary from country to country in their expectations of speakers. These expectations also vary depending on the nature of the occasion.

Getting Work as a Freelance Writer

Getting work as a freelance writer involves gaining experience, advertising your work, negotiating a contract and professional fees, and establishing a schedule for completing the work

GAINING EXPERIENCE

When securing work as a speechwriter within organizations, communication specialists often have to pass writing tests. Presidential speechwriter Carolyn Curiel secured her position by passing a "blind writing test" that involved the preparation of an inaugural address.[35]

Would-be speechwriters can gain experience in a number of different ways. Many freelance writers begin their careers in organizations, working in public relations (PR) capacities. Speechwriting is one job duty of most PR practitioners or public affairs officers. Others begin their careers as journalists, writing for newspapers or magazines. If you have published some of your work, you will have enhanced credibility when you apply for work as a speechwriter.

Another source of experience is delivering your own speeches to a variety of organizations. Most social clubs, libraries, and community organizations welcome speakers who volunteer their services. Local chapters of Toastmasters International also help speakers to gain experience in writing and delivering speeches.

ADVERTISING YOUR WORK

Getting work as a freelance writer is not unlike getting work of any kind. You need to create business cards, brochures, and a portfolio of your work. Even if websites do not generate that much work, they give you a place to direct potential clients, where they can view your portfolio, read your biography, and learn more about your speechwriting services and fees.

Markets vary greatly, depending on where you live. If you live in Washington, DC; Chicago; New York City; or a state capital, the demand is large. In small locales, however, the writer must reach beyond his or her own community to find more than the occasional writing assignment. With the growth of the Internet and the possibility for writers to work with clients who are geographically dispersed, these kinds of possibilities grow larger. In my experience, however, organizations still like that one-on-one contact with their writers. Municipal governments, large business enterprises, and chambers of commerce offer possibilities for speechwriting assignments in smaller towns.

NEGOTIATING A CONTRACT AND PROFESSIONAL FEES

Organizations may employ a speechwriter on a full-time regular basis or hire the person on a contract basis. In some cases, speechwriters have a standing offer with an organization, where they are on "call-by" status. This kind of arrangement eliminates the necessity to write a new contract each time that the organization requires the writers' services. At other times, the organization contracts for speechwriting services on a speech-by-speech basis.

Often writers get less than more specialized communication consultants for their services because they have significant competition. The numbers of freelance writers are significantly greater than the numbers of strategic planners, organizational development (OD) consultants, or crisis management experts. Nonetheless, the quality of writing services varies greatly, and better writers can command higher rates than their weaker colleagues can.

Rates also vary greatly from one community to another. Working in the nation's capital, writers have a more lively market than those working in smaller locales do. If you write for nonprofit organizations, you will make less than you make when you write for government. Governments, on the other hand, pay less than big business; but you never have to worry about being paid. You may prefer to ask lower rates and get more business or ask higher rates and obtain a more select clientele of those who are prepared to pay for quality.

Not all writers advertise their fees because some do not want to be locked into a rate. Many prefer to negotiate their fees with clients on a job-by-job basis. If you have any measure of flexibility with your rates, you may not want to advertise them. Some writers, for example, offer better rates to voluntary organizations than they offer to businesses and governments. Some government departments, however, have a policy that requires consultants and contractors to sell similar services to all clients at the same rate. You are not allowed to vary your rate from job to job and department to department.

Internet advertisements indicate that the going rate for speechwriters varies significantly. Some writers work by the hour or set minimum charges such as $750 for

a speech; others advertise by the spoken minute, the page, or the word. One writer advertised her services at $100 per minute or $100 per double-spaced page. Since most speakers take about two minutes—not one minute—to cover a double spaced page, the rates seem inconsistent. The writer is charging twice as much with one rate structure as the other. In my experience, the latter rate is inadequate for a reasonably experienced writer with some track record.

Other writers charge by the word. One indicated a rate of $1 per word or $250 per page. Since manuscripts typed in Times Roman font, double-spaced with one inch margins have about 250 words on the page, these two figures match.

Some advertise hourly rates. One experienced writer indicated that he had obtained $5,000 for forty hours' work ($125 per hour or $1,000 per diem). Another writer advertised an hourly rate of $75. *Writers Market* lists current rates in its "How Much Should I Charge?" section.

Since speechwriting is often done on short deadlines, involving late night and weekend work, freelance writers should avoid billing on an hourly basis. A writer should not get less for a speech that she has only three hours or a weekend to prepare. The mental effort will be similar but the stress factor will be significantly greater, given the compressed time frame for writing the speech. Nor should experienced writers be penalized for taking a shorter period of time to produce a speech. If billing on *per diem* or hourly basis, the beginning speechwriter could conceivably make more than the experienced writer. Professional speechwriters often bill according to the length of the speech (so much per page of text or minute of speaking time). In that regard, their practices are like the translator, who bills by the word or page.

Contracts should include a description of the writing project, specifics on deliverables (a term used by contractors to talk about the final products that they will deliver to the client), deadlines, milestones, number of drafts for which the writer will be responsible, and amounts and terms of payment. Service contracts often have standard terminology, which specifies rights of ownership to all materials generated under the contract (unless otherwise negotiated).

ESTABLISHING A SCHEDULE FOR COMPLETING THE WORK

Speechwriters typically work on tight deadlines. Samantha Kappalman said that she had two hours, for example, to prepare Maryland Governor Parris Glendening's victory speech.[36] When politicians are unsure of the likely election results, they often prepare two speeches—a victory speech and a speech of concession. In the case of major speech events (known and anticipated), speechwriters may receive a briefing several weeks in advance of the occasion. However, political communicators often find themselves in the situation of writing a speech in the course of a short afternoon or evening. Most governments and many large organizations perceive themselves in an ongoing state of crisis, and crisis calls for personal statements by organizational leaders.

To the extent possible, speechwriters attempt to establish schedules for working on speeches. Professional writers may be working on multiple communication products at the same time. They cannot afford to book only one contract at a time. See the Keep in Mind box for an example of a schedule sheet for completing a paid speech assignment.

Debate over the Ethics of Ghostwriting

Speechwriter Terry Edmonds (part of the Clinton administration) said that writers must commit themselves to articulating the philosophy of the person for whom they are writing. She explained that the job of a speechwriter is "not to push our own personal agenda . . . but to articulate a policy for someone else."[37] Carolyn Curiel agreed that speechwriters must be able to put on "someone else's thinking cap."[38] According to defenders of ghostwriting, conformity to this norm exonerates the ghostwriter from charges of unethical undertakings. They further assert that organizations, including the presidency, are aggregates of individuals or corporate entities. According to this view, individual spokespersons (whether president or CEO) do not speak for themselves. They speak for the corporation or government they were chosen to represent. Therefore, speeches reflecting the views of

Keep in Mind

TheSpeechWriters.com Checklist

Date _____

Client: Name: _____

Phone, Email _____

Title, Organization: _____

Address: Suite No., Street _____

City, State, Postal Code _____

Speaker: Name, Title: _____

Event: Organization/Audience _____

Date, Occasion, Venue _____

Topic, Length: _____

Objective: _____

Points to Cover:

1. _____

2. _____

3. _____

4. _____

Contacts:

1. Name, Title, Phone, Email _____

2. Name, Title, Phone, Email _____

3. Name, Title, Phone, Email _____

Research Sources (documents and their locations, websites):

1. _____   4. _____

2. _____   5. _____

3. _____   6. _____

<u>Schedule</u>: Enter nine production schedule dates for client (C) and speechwriter (SP) onto a calendar in reverse order:

- Speaking date _____   · Final draft—SW to C (1 week earlier) _____
- Rev of 2nd—C to SW _____   · 2nd draft—SW to C (1 week earlier) _____
- Rev of 1st—C to SW _____   · First draft—SW to C (1 week earlier) _____
- Rev of outline—C to SW _____   · Outline—SW to C (1 week earlier) _____
- Assignment—C to SW _____

© Garrett Patterson

the corporate body do not need to originate with one person.[39] Others argue that, as long as the public understands that the words are the creation of a second party, the speaker has not violated an ethical convention. Responding to critiques levied against former President Clinton, John Scalzi said:

> With politicians there's the accepted fact that their words are written for them all of the time—they have speechwriters. When a president goes up and gives a State of the Union address, no one in his right mind believes that he's written that speech himself. . . . However, news reports don't say "Tonight, President Bush, as written by David Frum, announced sweeping new tax proposals."[40]

In presenting her perspectives on the issue, Patricia J. Parsons points to the definition of plagiarism as "the unauthorized use or close imitation of the language and thoughts of another author and the representation of them as one's original work."[41] Using this definition, she says that only unauthorized words qualify as plagiarism. If the professional speechwriter is hired to produce speeches, then the speaker is clearly authorized to use the words.

Not everyone agrees, however, with these perspectives. Some say that the public grows cynical when they realize that they are being misled about authorship of speeches: "When politicians pay writers to tell their stories, they generate a perception of insincerity that dilutes the public trust so that citizens greet even the most upstanding politician with cynicism."[42] Others say that the average person would be surprised at the extent to which politicians and CEOs rely on communication staff and speechwriters to generate their communication products.[43] Politicians also place themselves at risk when they use ghostwriters whom they do not know well. In 1987, Delaware Senator Joseph Biden withdrew from the Democratic presidential primary after critics disclosed that "large portions of his closing statement at a debate were nearly identical to portions of speeches delivered earlier by a leader of Britain's Labour Party."[44] Massachusetts Senator John Kerry also faced charges of plagiarism from critics in 2004. One researcher claimed to have found eleven instances of passages, used without attribution, in Kerry's published writings.[45] Even if ghostwriters penned the problematic passages (a likely scenario), ultimately the speaker or apparent author had to bear the responsibility for the words. (See the Question of Ethics box.)

Responses to ghostwriting practices may also vary across countries and cultures. In countries that recognize group (as opposed to individual) efforts, questioning of ghostwriting practices is likely to be uncommon.

In the same way that the speaker faces the risk of unconscious plagiarism in an environment where words are regularly recycled, speechwriters face the same problem. As mentioned earlier, communication or political staff members give copies of archived speeches to ghostwriters. They anticipate that the speechwriters will draw passages from these earlier speeches and use the speeches as models. Yet these archived speeches may contain instances of plagiarism, unknown to the current writer. Sometimes the speeches may even come from an earlier holder of an office, who delivered the policy address on behalf of the organization. So the situation is very complex when both speakers and writers work in an environment of "institutionalized plagiarism"—a situation where people are accustomed to using words purchased from paid writers.[46] Since many ghostwriters are journalists, the "plagiarized" passages could even come from their own work. Speakers could

A Question of Ethics

A professional speechwriter, Jeremy Smith, received about $2,500 for a ten-minute speech and $5,000 for a twenty-minute speech. Last-minute requests or jobs involving evening and weekend work were more expensive. His speechwriting duties involved meeting with a representative of the organization to learn more about the speaker, audience, and occasion; receiving instruction on the messages that should appear in the speech; reviewing materials provided by the organization, including previous speeches on the same or similar topics; producing a first draft of the speech; and making the requested changes for a final draft. At the first meeting, Jeremy usually outlined his own expectations in regard to the desired client-consultant relationship.

After being contracted to write a speech for the CEO of a large home office firm, Jeremy met with Susan, head of public relations; Joe, the special events planner; and Hannah, the CEO's personal assistant. The three could not agree on the messages for the speech. Jeremy concluded that politics were at work in the situation, and eventually he followed the suggestions of Hannah, the personal assistant. When Hannah gave a set of former speeches to Jeremy, she asked him to use highlighted passages intact in the new speech. This request was not unusual, and Jeremy complied. He delivered the first draft of the speech to Hannah.

When Jeremy received a call a week later, it came from Susan (head of public relations), who was displeased by his failure to follow her advice. She demanded that he completely rewrite the speech, using the ideas that she had contributed. Moreover, she gave him twenty-four hours to produce a second draft. She told him that several drafts might be necessary. Susan also told him that the ghostwriter for the other speeches would be upset by the inclusion of his material. This speechwriter was known for demanding that the organization acknowledge his contribution if they used his material in a second speech. Given the conflicting instructions, Jeremy felt that he had done the best that he could. Also, recycling content was common; and speechwriters did not typically demand acknowledgment. He found the requests unreasonable and asked for an additional $1,000 to revise the speech. Susan balked at the demand. She said that she would revise the speech herself and dismissed Jeremy, cutting his pay by half since he would not agree to produce a final draft. Discuss the ethics in this situation from the point of view of the organization, Jeremy, and the earlier ghostwriter whose materials were being used without his explicit consent.

scarcely say to their publics, however, "I didn't actually plagiarize the words. They belong to my speechwriter, who just happened to have written an article last year on the same topic." A humorous example of one speechwriter's effort to secure the "original" words and views of his client comes from the account of Frederick J. O. Blachly:

> I decided to use the President's own words to put together a [UN] proclamation. Using sentences from various speeches by the former Representative, Senator, Vice-President, and now President Nixon, I stitched together a suitable text and submitted it to the front office. The text came back marked "Too liberal!" Try again. I resubmitted the same text, but after each sentence I gave the [original speech] source. . . . So there I was, a ghost living off the work of other ghosts! The text went to the White House and appeared over the President's signature just the way I had put it together.[47]

Conclusion

Unlike the early years, the ghostwriting function in government has become institutionalized. Speechwriters occupy prominent staff positions and write books about their careers. The Smithsonian Institute hosted a seminar in December 1998 titled "All the President's Words," which was attended by speechwriters from the Truman through the Clinton administrations. Although corporate speechwriters enjoy a less publicly acknowledged role, they are also highly visible within their organizations. And hundreds of thousands of freelance writers make a living by putting words in the mouths of others.

Those interested in making a career in the field of speechwriting have a host of possibilities from which to choose. The large majority will, however, combine their speechwriting career with other forms of writing. Within the organization, for example, speechwriters produce a multitude of public relations products. Most freelance speechwriters also ghost other kinds of products, including books, brochures, and magazine articles. Some are freelance journalists or technical writers.

Questions for Discussion

1. How do you feel about the ethics of ghostwriting? Did you realize that most prominent politicians, including presidents, employ speechwriters?

2. Some people say that representatives of governments and business are not really espousing their own views, but rather the views of their organizations—that their views represent the stance of the organization on issues. Therefore, the organization is justified in paying a ghostwriter to create the speeches. Do you agree?

3. Should speakers publicly acknowledge those who write their speeches?

4. To what extent should speakers be involved in the final editing of speeches written by a paid speechwriter? Should speechwriters have the final say?

5. Do you think that it is important for the speechwriter to get to know the person for whom she is writing the speeches? To what extent should a ghostwriter attempt to reflect the style of the speaker in the written speech? (Not all speakers have a natural eloquence.)

6. Do you think that it is ethical to "recycle" content from one speech to another? Is it ethical for an organization to ask a speechwriter to incorporate passages from a speech written by a different speechwriter? Who "owns" the rights to the speech—the speechwriter, the organization that paid for the speech, or the speaker who delivers the speech?

Outline

THE NATURE AND FUNCTION OF RHETORICAL CRITICISM

A Rhetorical Analysis

Learning Objectives

- To learn how to apply the critical communication model (CCM) to rhetorical analysis
- To understand how to approach a rhetorical analysis from the perspective of societal movements

Rhetorical criticism
The attempt to understand and pass judgment on the quality of written or oral discourse

In an academic sense, criticism implies trying to understand or pass judgment on some work. Rhetorical criticism refers to an attempt to understand and pass reasoned judgment on written or oral discourse.[1] In the process of making this judgment, the critic seeks to discriminate between what is better or worse in the discourse. Sometimes the judgments will be negative in tone and content; at other times, they will be positive.

This chapter applies the framework from the critical communication model or CCM (described in Chapter One) to the discussion of rhetorical analysis. A second approach, based on societal movements, is discussed briefly in the conclusion to the chapter.

CCM Approach to Rhetorical Analysis

The CCM returns us to our opening thoughts on public speaking—a conclusion that brings us full circle. In many regards, analysts are like forensic detectives. In our quest to understand the rhetorical event, we look for evidence—evidence of speaker motives and purposes in delivering the speech, environment or context for the speech, primary and secondary audiences for the speech, initial speaker credibility, message strategies and supporting materials used to achieve purposes (logical, emotional, and source credibility appeals), impact. And we decide upon criteria for judging the speech. Any search for answers must begin with the framing of questions.[2] For that reason, the following discussion often suggests questions that can lead to better understanding of the rhetorical event.

SPEAKER

When trying to analyze speeches, we talk about the *rhetorical imperative* or the driving force behind the speech. Did the speaker articulate some purpose in giving the speech? If not, is there an unstated purpose? Is the real purpose different from the stated purpose? When a politician comes to your local Rotary Club meeting to talk about what he has been doing lately, is he really seeking to inform you, or does he hope that you will vote for him in the upcoming election? What does he have to gain by giving the speech?

Speaker purposes could be "to convince an audience to support social security reforms," "to inspire an audience to put aside their fears of failure when they tackle new challenges," "to encourage the audience to give financial support to flood victims," "to pay tribute to the veterans of foreign wars," or "to entertain the audience with stories of strange places and people." Examples of unspoken purposes could be "to rebuild personal credibility after allegations of misconduct," "to persuade the audience to vote for me in the next election," or "to reinforce my image as a family man."

In a rhetorical analysis, you seek to identify and document stated and unstated speaker purposes. Some speaker purposes will be ethical; others may be unethical. The rhetorical analyst attempts to locate and judge speaker motives. Like any other researcher, you must support your ideas with evidence. That is, you select passages from the speech and secondary sources to support your assessment of speech purpose(s)—evidence to back up your assertions. Examples of secondary sources are newspaper accounts of the speech event, media or personal interviews with the speaker, correspondence, or other supporting data.

As discussed in Chapters Six and Nine, audiences judge speakers on the basis of source credibility factors such as perceived dynamism, trustworthiness, expertise, composure, status, sociability, and objectivity. Our perceptions may not, however, always be valid. Audience members may believe that a dishonest speaker is honest, or they may arrive falsely at the conclusion that an expert has no real knowledge of a situation. The idea of initial and terminal credibility is also relevant to this discussion. Speakers arrive at the podium or speaker's platform with an existing persona and image. That is their initial credibility. During the course of the speech, speakers can improve or worsen this image. *Terminal credibility* refers to the last impression of the speaker.

Dynamism

American audiences expect speakers to be energetic and dynamic in their choice of words and style of delivery. They perceive speakers to be dynamic when they use forceful and assertive language, when they portray themselves as active and involved in the social and political life of the community, and when they are progressive and innovative in their ideas. When speakers talk about the future, rather than the past, audiences see them as more dynamic. They also see speakers as more dynamic when they advocate change and when they appear in settings with young people.

Rhetorical imperative
The driving force behind the decision to give a speech

Stated purposes
The explicit aims of a speech: what a speaker says directly

Unstated speaker purposes
The implied goals of a speech

Speaker credibility
The believability of a speaker, based on perceived attributes, which affects audience acceptance of the message

Trustworthiness

Audiences expect speakers to be trustworthy. They perceive speakers to be trustworthy when they are willing to take a position on issues, even when they stand to lose from taking that position. They expect speakers to believe in what they say and to say what they believe. Audiences do not like speakers who vacillate, or "flip-flop," on issues. Audiences expect speakers to be dedicated to their families and jobs. They also expect them to be socially responsible and to support laudable causes. When speakers share a common fate with the audience (meaning that the speaker will suffer the same consequences as the audience), audiences are more likely to trust and accept the proposals of the speaker. They are also likely to feel safer with speakers who have similar backgrounds and goals.

Expertise

Audiences expect speakers to be qualified to speak on a topic. Audiences perceive speakers to be competent when they demonstrate a good knowledge of the subject matter and have relevant experience. Speakers should be able to argue their positions in a logical fashion and cite statistics and evidence in support of their arguments.

Composure

Audiences expect speakers to be relatively composed. They perceive speakers to be composed when they appear confident, articulate, and in control. North American audiences tend to view direct eye contact as a sign of both honesty and confidence. Speakers show control when they do not stumble over their words or stammer or behave in a confused fashion when someone questions their ideas. Audiences look for such verbal and nonverbal signs of composure. American audiences are willing, however, to tolerate occasional blips in composure because these occasional mistakes suggest that the speaker is human, "one of us." They also admire a speaker who recovers, with some degree of panache, from a difficult situation.

Status

Audiences tend to accord more credibility to speakers who enjoy a prominent status. Different audiences, of course, have different standards for interpreting status. To an audience of Wall Street brokers, status could derive from success in the business world, whereas members of Amnesty International might accord more status to someone who has earned a reputation as a peacemaker. In either case, the person enjoys a privileged position in the minds of the audience. Association with a prestige occupation, an influential authority figure, or a prominent family may give status to a speaker. Some speakers gain status by wearing designer clothing or executive suits. Others position themselves for major addresses before respected authority symbols (flag or crest-of-arms) as a means of drawing attention to their status as officeholders. Presidents often seek photo opportunities with charismatic figures or respected leaders from other countries as a means of enhancing their own status. An introduction by another person with status can also increase the status of the speaker.

Sociability

Audiences expect speakers to be sociable. They perceive speakers as sociable when they are friendly in demeanor and when they adopt a warm personal style of delivery. They also perceive them as sociable when they attend community meetings, speak at social gatherings, and make personal references to members of the audience. Audiences like speakers who share their values and aspirations.

ENVIRONMENT

It has been said that the task of a rhetorical critic is "reconstruction of public consciousness."[3] The accomplishment of that goal entails looking at the broader context within which a speech occurred—the political, economic, cultural, social, technological, and legal factors that gave rise to the rhetorical event; the conventions that govern the speech occasion; and the immediate physical setting. Many disciplines—including history, sociology, political science, psychology, religion, literature, and others—have insights to offer the rhetorical critic.[4] In writing the context statement for your rhetorical analysis, for example, you can go to historical accounts of the speech—books that talk about the speech, newspaper or magazine accounts, and websites that describe the setting and context. You should cite any sources that you use at the end of your analysis (as well as giving a reference within the text of your paper). (See the Keep in Mind box.)

You must locate yourself in the place in history in which the rhetorical event occurred. To analyze a speech about feminist rhetoric in the 1960s, for example, you must understand what was happening in that decade. Much has happened since the

Speech environment
The context in which a speech is delivered

Keep in Mind

Online Collections of Speeches: Selected Sites

http://www.americanrhetoric.com: index to and database for 5,000+ audio and video (streaming) versions of public speeches, sermons, lectures, and other rhetoric

http://gos.sbc.edu/byyears/old.html: collection at Sweet Briar College, Virginia

http://www.historicaldocuments.com/Top100AmericanSpeeches.htm: top 100 American speeches

http://www.udayton.edu/~dss/past_speakers.htm: archived speeches at the University of Dayton

http://library.albany.edu/reference/speeches.html: archived speeches at the University of Albany

http://dir.yahoo.com/Education/Graduation/Speeches: graduation speeches

http://douglassarchives.org: electronic archive of American oratory and related documents

http://www.historychannel.com/speeches: speeches from the most famous broadcasts and recordings of the twentieth century

http://www.executive-speaker.com/spchlist.html: speeches by business executives

http://www.presidency.ucsb.edu: public papers of the presidencies, including major speeches

http://www.historyplace.com/speeches/previous.htm: collection of great speeches by world figures

http://www.presidentialrhetoric.com: collection that includes contemporary speeches of presidents

http://www.wfu.edu/~zulick/340/COM340.html: collection associated with course at Wake Forest University, North Carolina.

http://www.yale.edu/lawweb/avalon/presiden/presiden.htm: the Avalon project, a collection of documents on U.S. presidencies from the eighteenth through the twenty-first centuries.

http://www.americanpresidents.org: video archive that includes speeches

http://www.freepint.com/gary/speech3.htm: transcripts and speeches from September 11, 2001, to October 22, 2001

http://www.electionspeeches.com: election speeches from 2004

http://www.feminist.com/resources/artspeech: articles and speeches by women

http://www.princeton.edu/WebMedia/lectures: archived lectures

http://www.whitehouse.gov: includes major addresses of the current administration

http://www.bartleby.com/124: inaugural speeches

http://mlkonline.net: speeches of Martin Luther King, Jr.

http://www.anc.org.za/ancdocs/history/Mandela: selected speeches and writings by Nelson Mandela

---

sexual revolution and the activism of women's rights advocates such as Betty Friedan and Germaine Greer. To understand the rhetoric surrounding AIDS in the 1980s, you have to place yourself within the fabric of the society at that time. People were gripped with fear and lack of understanding of the threat. Members of the New York and San Francisco gay communities attended funerals on an almost weekly basis. The public looked with wonder and surprise at celebrities like Princess Diana, who dared to put themselves in close contact with those who had contracted AIDS. Certainly audience members in the 1980s would have reacted differently from present-day audiences to public discourse on the topic of AIDS. Their level of knowledge would have been dramatically lower, as well. The environment statement should reflect the knowledge of the day not contemporary understanding.

If you are looking at religious discourse from the 1950s, you should not bring discussion of recent scandals involving Roman Catholic priests in the Boston diocese into your environment statement. In the 1950s, most audiences were deferential toward priests. Although abuses were occurring, the public was unaware of the problem. No scandals had been unearthed. So your consideration of the religious rhetoric of the 1950s must omit consideration of these later events. This idea—that you must place yourself in the virtual moment of the speech event in order to write an environment statement—dominates all other considerations.

In short, to analyze rhetoric from other periods, you must be a time traveler. You must move backward in time, identifying the spirit and climate of the times that generated the speech. You have to don the mind-set of audiences in that day and place. To accomplish that end, you must reconstruct relevant political, economic, cultural, social, technological, legal, and ethical contexts of the day. The rhetorical conventions of the day may also influence the unfolding of the speech event. Some contextual considerations will be more important than others in any given situation. (See the Keep in Mind box.)

Political Context

Political context provides a framework for understanding many of our most vital issues. Martin Luther King, Jr., delivered his historical speech "I Have a Dream" at a time of great civil unrest, with marches in the streets of Washington, DC, and Selma, Alabama, and nonviolent sit-ins in cities such as Nashville, Tennessee. Some of the more aggressive of the black leaders, such as Malcolm X and Stokely Carmichael, had denounced the nonviolent nature of King's approach. The black community was divided in the 1960s. These political factors are important to understanding King's motivations, his rhetorical strategies, and audience response. The rhetoric surrounding the invasion and occupation of Iraq and the war against terrorism takes place within the broader political context of the events of September 11, 2001. In later years, rhetorical critics will not be able to divorce an understanding of the political rhetoric of the early part of this century from those events.

> **Political context**
> The state of the government and its affairs

Economic Context

Economic factors can also be important. Periods of heavy layoffs, economic recession, and unemployment generate many issues to which speakers respond. The

> **Economic context**
> The state of supply and demand and its effect on the wealth of the audience

Keep in Mind

Analyzing the Environment

- Political
- Economic
- Cultural
- Social

- Technological
- Legal
- Rhetorical conventions
- Physical setting

end of the new technology boom, the soaring costs of health care, the high cost of oil, and the rise of China as a major economic power create a backdrop for much of the rhetoric of this century. A rhetorical analyst must identify relevant factors in the economic environment likely to influence speaker motives, as well as audience reactions to the public discourse. The factors must, of course, be relevant to the particular speech event that you have chosen to analyze.

Cultural Context

Cultural context
The customs and ways of a people

The rhetorical critic must place herself, as well, in the cultural context in which the speech event occurred. How would that particular audience have judged the argumentation and reasoning or the moral position of the speaker? Would the speech have achieved its purposes with that particular group? Taking culture and ethnicity into account, would the audience have accepted the presentation style of the speaker? Would a Japanese audience, for example, have appreciated a highly animated and dynamic mode of delivery, or would audience members have expected a more dignified and quiet presence in a speaker?

Social Context

The response of television audiences to comedian Ellen DeGeneres illustrates changing societal norms. In 1997, ABC yanked the television series *Ellen* from the air after both Ellen DeGeneres and her character "came out of the closet." Low audience ratings had followed on the heels of the episode where Ellen's character proclaimed her sexual preferences. By 2003, however, DeGeneres was able to launch a new syndicated daytime talk show, which won four Emmy awards in its first season. At the same time, however, the religious right has gained great strength, partly as a consequence of the gains by the liberal left. Consideration of the rhetoric surrounding these issues must take the social climate of the day into account.

Social context
Socially accepted norms of behavior

Technological Context

Technological factors govern the options available to speakers in terms of channels. Speakers have a choice of delivering face-to-face, without technical interventions.

Technological context
The various media that can be used to reach audiences

Alternatively, they may choose to present their messages over the radio or on television. Speakers may also present live addresses over the Internet or archive their addresses on websites. They may use avatars (virtual representations of themselves) to deliver the speeches. These new and old technologies place some restraints on the speakers, who must conform to the conventions of the medium of communication. Television requires a close personal style of delivery, for example, whereas auditorium situations may demand larger gestures, broader movements, and a more public persona. The use of microphones, on the other hand, allows the speaker to return to a more personal style of delivery. A rhetorical critic must look for the potential influence of technology on the situation, as well as the extent to which the speaker recognizes and adapts to these conventions.

Legal Context

Legal context
The effects of the law on a speech or speaker

Recognition of legal constraints can also be important. Speakers are not always able to say exactly what they want to say. They may be forced, on the advice of lawyers, to talk around points, to be deliberately vague or ambiguous. We live in litigious days, when a cup of spilled coffee or a fall in someone's front yard can be grounds for a costly monetary settlement—in or out of court. Spokespersons of organizations pay serious attention to these legal threats.

Rhetorical Conventions

Rhetorical conventions
Speaking norms, which change over time

The rhetorical conventions of a given period also exert an influence on the speech event. If you are judging a speaker from an earlier period, you must understand the requirements for delivering a speech in that period of time. To judge a speech delivered in the U.S. Senate, you must understand the norms that govern rhetoric in that chamber. Are the speakers allowed to make caustic comments? Are personal

attacks allowed? What is the unspoken limit to which speakers must adhere in terms of time? Are interruptions tolerated? Are speakers typically low key in their delivery or dramatic and accusatory?

Cultural and religious norms also influence rhetorical conventions. Some religious groups expect to be highly engaged in church ceremonies. They expect the preacher to shout and exhort them to come to the front of the church and repent their sins. They may clap and stomp their feet as their engagement in the church rituals heightens. Other congregations may have quite different expectations of what should happen in a church setting. They may expect to remain quiet in their seats, while their ministers speak in a conversational manner, telling stories and using humor to impart their messages. Roman Catholic priests, however, traditionally have had a more constrained style of delivery, and they expect the same level of decorum in their congregations.

Ethical Context

The ethical norms and moral tenor of any period also influence the rhetoric of political and social actors, as well as audience reactions to the speeches. In earlier decades, for example, Roman Catholics saw their priests as infallible representatives of God. Recent revelations of wrongdoing, however, have produced a new climate and new rhetoric. When you write an environment statement, you must ask yourself how the people of a particular historical period (not your period) would have judged the speech. What were the ethical norms of that period? What were the moral taboos?

Ethical context
The moral norms that affect both speaker and audience

Physical setting

The precise location where a speech takes place

Physical Setting

Rhetorical analysts also need to understand the *immediate* context within which the speech occurs—the location, time, and other relevant characteristics of the setting. These settings greatly influence the mode of delivery, the content of speeches, and the expectations of the audience. The settings influence our expectations of speaker and occasion. In some political settings, for example, the seating arrangements place the speakers within a particular context, setting limits on the interactions that can occur within that context. Conflict is often ritualistic. The presence of television cameras within a setting also can influence interactions between speakers and audience members. With the televising of House and Senate proceedings, speakers became more theatrical in their delivery.

In the same way, the introduction of television cameras to the courtroom has had a dramatic effect on speaking styles. Lawyers have felt the need to become more like the leading characters in television series such as *Boston Legal* and *The Practice*. As Marcia Clark (lead prosecutor in the O. J. Simpson trial) discovered, they have to look and act the role.[5] As in the O. J. Simpson trial, the proceedings often become high drama. The lawyers are judged on how well they perform.

A speech may take place in a large auditorium or a small meeting room. The acoustics may be good or bad, and the general ambience may be friendly or cold and intimidating. The audience may have expectations of what should happen in this setting. Therefore, as rhetorical analysts, we must ask ourselves the following kinds of questions: Was the occasion formal and ceremonial or informal and personal? Was the seating comfortable? Were audience members sitting in proximity to each other or widely dispersed in an auditorium seating arrangement? Did an overheated room encourage listeners to become sleepy and inattentive, or did activity in the outside hallway serve as a distraction? Could the audience hear the speaker?

AUDIENCE

All good or successful speeches will have been adapted to their audiences. You must identify all of the audiences targeted by the speech if you want to understand its possible impact.

You may have one audience or multiple audiences when you speak. Possible audiences for a presidential address may be the general public, lobby or other interest groups, legislators, foreign governments, or international organizations, among others. At an awards ceremony such as the Golden Globes or Academy Awards, a celebrity might be speaking to an auditorium full of directors, fellow actors, and producers; but the most important audience may be the fans watching the events on television.

The audience may be domestic or international. When the president delivers a speech on foreign policy, he has domestic audiences, but he also has international audiences. Some audience members may be located in Africa, Asia, Russia, or elsewhere.

The audience may be immediate or remote in space. That is, the audience can be physically present at the speaking event, listening to a speaker with whom they are

in physical proximity. Or the audience can be in some other location, physically removed from the speaking event in space and time. The remote television viewing audiences are often the largest and most important audiences to speakers. Sometimes the immediate audience is only "wallpaper" for the televised speaking event—a backdrop against which the speaker delivers his or her address.

The audience may be immediate or remote in time. Some audiences are virtual consumers of the speech event. They may not hear or read the speech for months or years after it happens. An increasingly large number of people are going to the Internet, at times of their choice, to read or listen to all or parts of speeches delivered by political and celebrity figures. Some go to virtual town halls to attend the speeches. Other audiences are remote in generational terms. As noted in an earlier chapter, Nelson Mandela spoke to future generations of South Africans when he delivered his famous courtroom address in the 1960s. Knowing that he could not achieve his speech purposes at that point in time, he wrote his speech for those who would follow. You can listen to inaugural speeches delivered decades ago or to graduation speeches delivered last month. Excerpts from a State of the Union speech can be heard for weeks after the event, as pundits ponder the words, dissect the meaning, and speculate about the significance of the event.

The task of a rhetorical critic is to identify and prioritize these audiences. Who are the primary or most important audiences for this speech? Who are the secondary or tertiary audiences that the speaker hopes to reach? The speech will hold clues as to whom the speaker regards to be his or her audience. As a rhetorical analyst, you must find these clues and use them to support your assertions about audiences. Rhetorical critics should respond also to the following additional questions about audiences: What do audience members know about the subject, and how do they feel about it? Would audience members have had any experiences that could influence their reactions? With what reference groups does the audience identify? How would these reference groups feel about the topic? Would the reference groups have an official stance on issues discussed in the speech? Would the age, gender, ethnicity, or other demographic variables influence the reaction of the audience to the speech? In what way could the values of audience members influence their reactions?[6]

Perception
Our belief in something, which may or may not be correct

While historians are concerned with what actually happened, rhetorical critics are concerned with *perceptions* of what happened. The perceptions may or may not be correct. As a rhetorical critic, you want to understand how audiences reacted to speeches. Sometimes, when you cannot know for certain how they responded, you can only speculate about how they *might* have reacted, based on your knowledge of the period in which the rhetoric occurred, audience composition, and other variables. Therefore, you make statements such as, "It is *likely* that . . ." or "The audience *probably* reacted with some skepticism. . . ." Again you could say, "The loud clapping *suggested* that the audience supported the views of the speaker." In situations where you cannot have absolute knowledge of audience reactions, you should be tentative in your statements. You should avoid making comments such as, "The audience did not like the speaker's approach" or "The audience would have wanted to leave almost immediately." Instead say, "The audience was *probably* anxious to leave, given the length of the speech and the time of day." The wording in the second case is speculative rather than dogmatic, and the writer should offer some support for her reasoning on the matter. Words such as *could, might be, perhaps, sometimes,* and *often* qualify and soften assertions.

MESSAGE

The next step in a rhetorical critique is analysis of message or text. At this point, the critic looks strictly at the words of the speaker—the written or spoken text. (When speakers abandon their manuscripts or add spontaneous comments, the spoken text will diverge from the written script.) The analyst looks for strategies used by the speaker to achieve his purposes, dominant themes in the speech, and choice of supporting materials.

First, the analyst identifies the strategies used to achieve the speech purposes. What was the speaker's plan for persuading or informing the audience? How does she attempt to get past the objections of her audience? How does she enhance her credibility without diminishing the credibility of her opponent? What are the major arguments that she uses to convince her audience? In achieving speech purposes, for example, the speaker may pursue a strategy that relies heavily on logic and reasoning. Alternatively, the speaker may appeal almost exclusively to the emotions of the audience in achieving his purposes. The analyst may assess the quality of the speech. Was it well crafted? Eloquently written?

In a short analysis, you cannot cover everything. As a consequence, you may want to identify an area on which to concentrate—in other words, a theme.[7] A thematic approach can look at how a speech reflects attitudes toward women in a particular time period, how the speaker uses the language of hip hop culture to get across his message to youthful audiences, or how a Native speaker establishes credibility by connecting with the spiritual traditions of his people. Another approach involves looking at the kinds of examples used to bolster a political position or the aesthetics of a particular speech—how the speaker uses metaphorical language to paint images in the minds of the audience.

The title of a rhetorical analysis often hints at the themes identified in a speech: "The Logical Fallacies of Bill Smith," "Failing Credibility: The Speaker's Downhill Run," "Grabbing Attention: The Antics of Speaker X," "Eloquence in Shorthand," or "Testing the Tolerance of the Audience: A Question of Ethics." The following titles, drawn from analyses conducted by first- and second-year communication students, illustrate the way in which themes can help to focus an analysis: "Reverend Churchill: Listening to God"; "The Five Audiences of John F. Kennedy's Commencement Address"; "On Trial in Front of the World: George W. Bush Addresses the United Nations"; "Raising Emotions: Analysis of Martin Luther King's 'I Have a Dream'"; "The Role of Imagery in Connecting Emotionally to the Audience: Presidential Address to Congress on September 20, 2001"; "The Use of Humor in Prince Charles' Address to the Conference on Tall Buildings"; "Patriotism, Nationalism, and Tradition: Tools of Persuasion"; "Determination and Eloquence: Winston Churchill Addresses the British Public"; "A Nation Divided: Unification Strategies in President Bush's Acceptance Speech"; "This Is Our Finest Hour: Churchill's Finest Speech"; "Humor and Severity: Bill Cosby Speaks to the NAACP"; "The Rhetoric of Today with a Message for Tomorrow: A Final Farewell"; "Grabbing the Audience: An Expressive Delivery"; "Wading in the Deep End: The Politics of Hip Hop"; "The Inaugural Address of J.F.K.: Right Speech, Right Time, Right Audience"; "Eulogy to Ronald Reagan: The Epitome of Artful Rhetoric"; "The Power of One: A Rhetorical Analysis of Motivational Speaker Erin Brockovich"; and "Bush Declares Victory in Iraq: An Exercise in Patriotic Super-Saturation." The rhetorical critic must allow the content of the speech to inform on the strategies of the speaker. (See the Keep in Mind box.)

After identifying the speaker's strategies and limiting the analysis of the message to one thematic area, the critic looks for support of these ideas. How has the speaker supported her claims or assertions? With examples? Statistics? Personal experience? For a discussion of logical, emotional, and credibility supports, refer to Chapter Nine. Give specific examples from the speech to back up your claims.

IMPACT

Potentially, speakers can achieve changes in awareness, attitudes, behaviors, or relationships. To the extent that they can be documented, the changes qualify as speech outcomes. At the conclusion of a speech, listeners may be more aware or knowledgeable. They may be more convinced of a position previously held, or

Keep in Mind

Selected University Web Sites with Links to Speech Collections

Wake Forest University, North Carolina, http://www.wfu.edu/~louden/Political%20Communication/ Class%20Information/SPEECHES.html: links to collections of political speeches, audio sites, individual presidential sites, political debates, specialized genre sites, and miscellaneous collections (e.g., campaign rhetoric)

Virginia Commonwealth University, Virginia, http://www.library.vcu.edu/guides/speeches.html: links to American rhetoric sites and to collections on Winston Churchill and Nelson Mandela

University of Iowa, http://www.uiowa.edu/%7Ecommstud/resources: links to large and diverse collections of speeches on variety of topics, U.S. and world rhetoric, sermons, and addresses by popes

McLennan Community College, http://www.mclennan.edu/departments/spch/speechcollections: links to Nobel acceptance speeches, Academy Award speeches, university collections, and others

Pennsylvania State University (Lehigh Valley), http://www.lv.psu.edu/library/guides/Speech100: links to sample speeches by business executives, history channel archives, political speeches, and others

---

they may have changed their opinions on a topic addressed by the speaker. In some cases, listeners may be moved to action. At other times, relationships may be bettered (or worsened) as a result of a speech. Rhetorical analysts will assess the extent and significance of these changes.

We cannot always judge the impact or outcomes of a speech in the short term. Lincoln's two-minute Gettysburg Address got scant mention in the papers of the day, but Edward Everett's less memorable (two-hour long) speech on the same occasion made headlines. If you judge the speeches on *immediate* impact, you would have to say that Everett's speech was more effective at achieving his goals. But if you judge the speeches on *long-term* impact, Lincoln's achieved greater results.

CRITERIA FOR JUDGMENTS

In assessing the quality of a speech, the analyst can take a *pragmatic* perspective, looking only at the impact of the speech. Did the speaker achieve his purposes? Did the audience react favorably to the speaker? Did listeners vote as the speaker asked that they vote, buy the product advocated, or change buying habits in the direction suggested by the speaker? Alternatively, the critic can look at outcomes of the speech in terms of *contribution*. Did the speaker make a contribution to the knowledge of the audience or offer new options for action? The analyst can assess the outcomes of the speech from an *ethical perspective*. What were the effects of the speech? Was anyone harmed by the speaker's words or actions? Did the person deal in superficial terms with the subject matter, address a trivial subject, or play unfairly on the emotions of the audience? Did the speaker act with integrity and effect positive changes in the environment? An *aesthetic perspective* involves assessing

---

Pragmatic perspective
In speech analysis, judging the speech solely on its impact

Contribution
In speech analysis, the extent to which a speech creates a new or fuller understanding of its topic

Ethical perspective
In speech analysis, judging the speech on its adherence to codes of right and wrong

Aesthetic perspective
In speech analysis, judging the speech on its craft and the effectiveness of the delivery

the speech on the basis of its attributes. Was the speech well-crafted and eloquently delivered?[8]

Many speeches succeed on some points and fail on others. Some of the most beautifully written speeches have failed to achieve their goals. The speaker has lost the election, failed to win a court victory, or eloquently championed a lost cause. At other times, a speaker may be highly successful in achieving his purposes, but society condemns and laments the ethics of the person's discourse and actions. The rhetoric of Adolph Hitler comes quickly to mind on this point. At the other extreme, a completely inarticulate speaker may make a significant contribution to the knowledge of her audience and adhere to the highest of ethical standards. So, judged on aesthetic or artistic standards of a particular time and place, the speaker may fail dramatically. But judged on criteria such as contribution and ethics, the speech may be considered a "good" one. A rhetorical critic can also ask, "In ethical terms, what was the cost of achieving the desired outcomes?" Did the speaker tell the truth as he or she knew it? Has the speaker assumed a position that is "morally right" by some standards of society? Are the argumentation and reasoning legitimate and honest?

Positioning the Speaker Within a Larger Movement

A second approach to rhetorical criticism involves positioning the speaker and speech within a larger societal movement. After World War I, for example, a peace movement developed. The rhetoric of Harry Emerson Fosdick, whose speech appears in the Appendix, is positioned within this movement. Similarly, you can examine the rhetoric of Germaine Greer or Betty Friedan within the context of the feminist movement of the 1960s and 1970s. Under the presidency of George W. Bush, we have seen a growing strength in the religious right. Much of the political rhetoric from the early part of the twenty-first century (e.g., the debate over same-sex marriage, abortion, and stem cell research) reflects this religious movement, which some have characterized as *evangelical*. The other dominant influence in political rhetoric in this century has come from the events of September 11, 2001, which gave rise to the rhetoric of terrorism and counterterrorism. In adopting this second approach to rhetorical analysis, the critic defines the societal movement, describes the characteristics of the rhetoric that typifies this movement, and then looks for these characteristics in the speech event selected for analysis.

Conclusion

This chapter has proposed a framework for undertaking a rhetorical analysis. This framework derives predominantly from the critical communication model (CCM), described in Chapter One. In this final chapter, I have posed a number of questions that can be answered by a rhetorical critic. The responses to these questions will help the student of rhetoric to pull together theories addressed throughout the book. This chapter serves as a review of major speech concepts: speaker motives and purposes, environment or context, speaker credibility, message strategies, supporting materials, impact, and cost of achieving impact in ethical terms. And so this book ends where it begins, with a consideration of the major elements that constitute a speech event.

Questions for Discussion

1. Do most speakers have unstated and multiple purposes in delivering speeches? Give some examples to illustrate your point.

2. Can you think of any speaking occasions where the immediate audience was less important than a remote audience?

3. When researching contemporary rhetorical events, the analyst goes to different kinds of sources than when analyzing rhetorical events from other time period. Why would you use different kinds of sources?

4. Explain the following statement: While historians are concerned with what actually happened, rhetorical critics are concerned with *perceptions* of what happened.

5. Your textbook has described Nelson Mandela's speech to a packed courtroom in South Africa in the 1960s. Mandela had little hope that his judge or jurors would consider his plea, and many would say that Mandela spoke to future generations of South Africans and to people outside the courtroom. Can you think of other examples to illustrate speakers talking to future generations more than to the present generation?

APPENDIX
MEMORABLE SPEECHES, HISTORICAL MOMENTS

Outline

Barack Obama

Democratic National Convention
Boston, Massachusetts
July 27, 2004

On behalf of the great state of Illinois, crossroads of a nation, land of Lincoln, let me express my deep gratitude for the privilege of addressing this convention. Tonight is a particular honor for me because, let's face it, my presence on this stage is pretty unlikely. My father was a foreign student, born and raised in a small village in Kenya. He grew up herding goats, went to school in a tin-roof shack. His father, my grandfather, was a cook, a domestic servant.

But my grandfather had larger dreams for his son. Through hard work and perseverance my father got a scholarship to study in a magical place: America, which stood as a beacon of freedom and opportunity to so many who had come before. While studying here, my father met my mother. She was born in a town on the other side of the world, in Kansas. Her father worked on oil rigs and farms through most of the Depression. The day after Pearl Harbor he signed up for duty, joined Patton's army, and marched across Europe. Back home, my grandmother raised their baby and went to work on a bomber assembly line. After the war, they studied on the GI Bill, bought a house through FHA, and moved west in search of opportunity.

And they, too, had big dreams for their daughter, a common dream, born of two continents. My parents shared not only an improbable love; they shared an abiding faith in the possibilities of this nation. They would give me an African name, Barack, or "blessed," believing that in a tolerant America your name is no barrier to success. They imagined me going to the best schools in the land, even though they weren't rich, because in a generous America you don't have to be rich to achieve your potential. They are both passed away now. Yet, I know that, on this night, they look down on me with pride.

I stand here today, grateful for the diversity of my heritage, aware that my parents' dreams live on in my precious daughters. I stand here knowing that my story is part of the larger American story, that I owe a debt to all of those who came before me, and that, in no other country on earth, is my story even possible. Tonight, we gather to affirm the greatness of our nation, not because of the height of our skyscrapers, or the power of our military, or the size of our economy. Our pride is based on a very simple premise, summed up in a declaration made over two hundred years ago, "We hold these truths to be self-evident, that all men are created equal. That they are endowed by their Creator with certain inalienable rights. That among these are life, liberty and the pursuit of happiness."

That is the true genius of America, a faith in the simple dreams of its people, the insistence on small miracles. That we can tuck in our children at night and know they are fed and clothed and safe from harm. That we can say what we think, write what we think, without hearing a sudden knock on the door. That we can have an idea and start our own business without paying a bribe or hiring somebody's son. That we can participate in the political process without fear of retribution, and that our votes will he counted, or at least, most of the time.

This year, in this election, we are called to reaffirm our values and commitments, to hold them against a hard reality and see how we are measuring up, to the legacy of our forbearers, and the promise of future generations. And fellow Americans, Democrats, Republicans, Independents, I say to you tonight: we have more work to do. More to do for the workers I met in Galesburg, Illinois, who are losing their union jobs at the Maytag plant that's moving to Mexico, and now are having to compete with their own children for jobs that pay seven bucks an hour. More to do for the father I met who was losing his job and choking back tears, wondering how he would pay $4,500 a month for the drugs his son needs without the health benefits he counted on. More to do for the young woman in East St. Louis, and thousands more like her, who has the grades, has the drive, has the will, but doesn't have the money to go to college.

Don't get me wrong. The people I meet in small towns and big cities, in diners and office parks, they don't expect government to solve all their problems. They know they have to work hard to get ahead and they want to. Go into the collar counties around Chicago, and people will tell you they don't want their tax money wasted by a welfare agency or the Pentagon. Go into any inner city neighborhood, and folks will tell you that government alone can't teach kids to learn. They know that parents have to parent, that children can't achieve unless we raise their expectations and turn off the television sets and eradicate the slander that says a black youth with a book is acting white. No, people don't expect government to solve all their problems. But they sense, deep in their bones, that with just a change in priorities, we can make sure that every child in America has a decent shot at life, and that the doors of opportunity remain open to all. They know we can do better. And they want that choice.

In this election, we offer that choice. Our party has chosen a man to lead us who embodies the best this country has to offer. That man is John Kerry. John Kerry understands the ideals of community, faith, and sacrifice, because they've defined his life. From his heroic service in Vietnam to his years as prosecutor and lieutenant governor, through two decades in the United States Senate, he has devoted himself to this country. Again and again, we've seen him make tough choices when easier ones were available. His values and his record affirm what is best in us.

John Kerry believes in an America where hard work is rewarded. So instead of offering tax breaks to companies shipping jobs overseas, he'll offer them to companies creating jobs here at home. John Kerry believes in an America where all Americans can afford the same health coverage our politicians in Washington have for themselves. John Kerry believes in energy independence, so we aren't held hostage to the profits of oil companies or the sabotage of foreign oil fields. John Kerry believes in the constitutional freedoms that have made our country the envy of the world, and he will never sacrifice our basic liberties nor use faith as a wedge to divide us. And John Kerry believes that in a dangerous world, war must be an option, but it should never be the first option.

A while back, I met a young man named Shamus at the VFW Hall in East Moline, Illinois. He was a good-looking kid, six-two or six-three, clear-eyed, with an easy smile. He told me he'd joined the Marines and was heading to Iraq the following week. As I listened to him explain why he'd enlisted, his absolute faith in our country and its leaders, his devotion to duty and service, I thought this young man was all any of us might hope for in a child. But then I asked myself: Are we serving Shamus as well as he was serving us? I thought of more than 900 service men and women, sons and daughters, husbands and wives, friends and neighbors, who will not be returning to their hometowns. I thought of families I had met who were struggling to get by without a loved one's full income, or whose loved ones had returned with a limb missing or with nerves shattered, but who still lacked long-term health benefits because they were reservists. When we send our young men and women into harm's way, we have a solemn obligation not to fudge the numbers or shade the truth about why they're going, to care for their families while they're gone, to tend to the soldiers upon their return, and to never ever go to war without enough troops to win the war, secure the peace, and earn the respect of the world.

Now let me be clear. We have real enemies in the world. These enemies must be found. They must be pursued and they must be defeated. John Kerry knows this. And just as Lieutenant Kerry did not hesitate to risk his life to protect the men who served with him in Vietnam, President Kerry will not hesitate one moment to use our military might to keep America safe and secure. John Kerry believes in America. And he knows it's not enough for just some of us to prosper. For alongside our famous individualism, there's another ingredient in the American saga.

A belief that we are connected as one people. If there's a child on the south side of Chicago who can't read, that matters to me, even if it's not my child. If there's a senior citizen somewhere who can't pay for her prescription and has to choose between medicine and the rent, that makes my life poorer, even if it's not my grandmother. If there's an Arab American family being rounded up without benefit of an attorney or due process, that threatens my civil liberties. It's that fundamental belief—I am my brother's keeper, I am my sister's keeper—that makes this country work. It's what allows us to pursue our individual dreams, yet still come together as a single American family. "E pluribus unum." Out of many, one.

Yet even as we speak, there are those who are preparing to divide us, the spin masters and negative ad peddlers who embrace the politics of anything goes. Well, I say to them tonight, there's not a liberal America and a conservative America—there's the United States of America. There's not a black America and white America and Latino America and Asian America; there's the United States of America. The pundits like to slice-and-dice our country into Red States and Blue States; Red States for Republicans, Blue States for Democrats. But I've got news for them, too. We worship an awesome God in the Blue States, and we don't like federal agents poking around our libraries in the Red States. We coach Little League in the Blue States and have gay friends in the Red States. There are patriots who opposed the war in Iraq and patriots who supported it. We are one people, all of us pledging allegiance to the stars and stripes, all of us defending the United States of America.

In the end, that's what this election is about. Do we participate in a politics of cynicism or a politics of hope? John Kerry calls on us to hope. John Edwards calls on us to hope. I'm not talking about blind optimism here—the almost willful ignorance that thinks unemployment will go away if we just don't talk about it, or the health care crisis will solve itself if we just ignore it. No, I'm talking about something more substantial. It's the hope of slaves sitting around a fire singing freedom songs; the hope of immigrants setting out for distant shores; the hope of a young naval lieutenant bravely patrolling the Mekong Delta; the hope of a millworker's son who dares to defy the odds; the hope of a skinny kid with a funny name who believes that America has a place for him, too. The audacity of hope!

In the end, that is God's greatest gift to us, the bedrock of this nation; the belief in things not seen; the belief that there are better days ahead. I believe we can give our middle class relief and provide working families with a road to opportunity. I believe we can provide jobs to the jobless, homes to the homeless, and reclaim young people in cities across America from violence and despair. I believe that as we stand on the crossroads of history, we can make the right choices, and meet the challenges that face us. America!

Tonight, if you feel the same energy I do, the same urgency I do, the same passion I do, the same hopefulness I do—if we do what we must do, then I have no doubt that all across the country, from Florida to Oregon, from Washington to Maine, the people will rise up in November, and John Kerry will be sworn in as president, and John Edwards will be sworn in as vice president, and this country will reclaim its promise, and out of this long political darkness a brighter day will come. Thank you and God bless you.

George W. Bush

Address to the Nation from the Oval Office
Washington, DC
September 11, 2001

Good evening. Today, our fellow citizens, our way of life, our very freedom came under attack in a series of deliberate and deadly terrorist acts. The victims were in airplanes or in their offices: secretaries, business men and women, military and federal workers, moms and dads, friends and neighbors.

Thousands of lives were suddenly ended by evil, despicable acts of terror.

The pictures of airplanes flying into buildings, fires burning, huge structures collapsing have filled us with disbelief, terrible sadness, and a quiet, unyielding anger.

These acts of mass murder were intended to frighten our nation into chaos and retreat. But they have failed. Our country is strong. A great people has been moved to defend a great nation.

Terrorist attacks can shake the foundations of our biggest buildings, but they cannot touch the foundation of America. These acts shatter steel, but they cannot dent the steel of American resolve.

America was targeted for attack because we're the brightest beacon for freedom and opportunity in the world. And no one will keep that light from shining.

Today, our nation saw evil, the very worst of human nature, and we responded with the best of America, with the daring of our rescue workers, with the caring for strangers and neighbors who came to give blood and help in any way they could.

Immediately following the first attack, I implemented our government's emergency response plans. Our military is powerful, and it's prepared. Our emergency teams are working in New York City and Washington, DC, to help with local rescue efforts.

Our first priority is to get help to those who have been injured and to take every precaution to protect our citizens at home and around the world from further attacks.

The functions of our government continue without interruption. Federal agencies in Washington which had to be evacuated today are reopening for essential personnel tonight and will be open for business tomorrow.

Our financial institutions remain strong, and the American economy will be open for business as well.

The search is underway for those who are behind these evil acts.

I've directed the full resources for our intelligence and law enforcement communities to find those responsible and bring them to justice. We will make no distinction between the terrorists who committed these acts and those who harbor them.

I appreciate so very much the members of Congress who have joined me in strongly condemning these attacks. And on behalf of the American people, I thank the many world leaders who have called to offer their condolences and assistance.

America and our friends and allies join with all those who want peace and security in the world and we stand together to win the war against terrorism.

Tonight I ask for your prayers for all those who grieve, for the children whose worlds have been shattered, for all whose sense of safety and security has been threatened. And I pray they will be comforted by a power greater than any of us spoken through the ages in Psalm 23: "Even though I walk through the valley of the shadow of death, I fear no evil for you are with me."

This is a day when all Americans from every walk of life unite in our resolve for justice and peace. America has stood down enemies before, and we will do so this time.

None of us will ever forget this day, yet we go forward to defend freedom and all that is good and just in our world.

Thank you. Good night and God bless America.

Earl Charles Spencer

Eulogy at the Funeral of Diana Princess of Wales
Westminster Abbey, London, England
September 6, 1997

I stand before you today, the representative of a family in grief, in a country in mourning, before a world in shock.

We are all united, not only in our desire to pay our respects to Diana but rather in our need to do so.

For such was her extraordinary appeal that the tens of millions of people taking part in this service all over the world, via television and radio, who never actually met her, feel that they, too, lost someone close to them in the early hours of Sunday morning. It is a more remarkable tribute to Diana than I can ever hope to offer her today.

Diana was the very essence of compassion, of duty, of style, of beauty. All over the world, she was a symbol of selfless humanity. All over the world, a standard bearer for the rights of the truly downtrodden, a very British girl who transcended nationality. Someone with a natural nobility who was classless and who proved in the last year that she needed no royal title to continue to generate her particular brand of magic.

Today is our chance to say thank you for the way you brightened our lives, even though God granted you but half a life. We will all feel cheated, always, that you were taken from us so young, and yet we must learn to be grateful that you came along at all. Only now that you are gone do we truly appreciate what we are now without and we want you to know that life without you is very, very difficult.

We have all despaired at our loss over the past week and only the strength of the message you gave us through your years of giving has afforded us the strength to move forward.

There is a temptation to rush to canonize your memory; there is no need to do so. You stand tall enough as a human being of unique qualities not to need to be seen as a saint. Indeed, to sanctify your memory would be to miss out on the very core of your being, your wonderfully mischievous sense of humor, with a laugh that bent you double.

Your joy for life, transmitted wherever you took your smile and the sparkle in those unforgettable eyes. Your boundless energy which you could barely contain.

But your greatest gift was your intuition and it was a gift you used wisely. This is what underpinned all your other wonderful attributes, and if we look to analyze what it was about you that had such a wide appeal, we find it in your instinctive feel for what was really important in all our lives.

Without your God-given sensitivity, we would be immersed in greater ignorance at the anguish of AIDS and HIV sufferers, the plight of the homeless, the isolation of lepers, the random destruction of land mines. Diana explained to me once that it was her innermost feelings of suffering that made it possible for her to connect with her constituency of the rejected.

And here we come to another truth about her. For all the status, the glamour, the applause, Diana remained throughout a very insecure person at heart, almost childlike in her desire to do good for others so she could release herself from deep feelings of unworthiness, of which her eating disorders were merely a symptom.

The world sensed this part of her character and cherished her for her vulnerability, while admiring her for her honesty.

The last time I saw Diana was on July 1, her birthday in London, when, typically, she was not taking time to celebrate her special day with friends but was guest of honor at a special charity fundraising evening. She sparkled, of course, but I would rather cherish the days I spent with her in March when she came to visit me and my children in our home in South Africa.

I am proud of the fact, apart from when she was on display meeting President Mandela, we managed to contrive to stop the ever-present paparazzi from getting a single picture of her—that meant a lot to her.

These were days I will always treasure. It was as if we had been transported back to our childhood, when we spent such an enormous amount of time together—the two youngest in the family.

Fundamentally, she had not changed at all from the big sister who mothered me as a baby, fought with me at school, and endured those long train journeys between our parents' homes with me at weekends. It is a tribute to her level-headedness and strength that despite the most bizarre-like life imaginable after her childhood, she remained intact, true to herself.

There is no doubt that she was looking for a new direction in her life at this time. She talked endlessly of getting away from England, mainly because of the treatment that she received at the hands of the newspapers.

I don't think she ever understood why her genuinely good intentions were sneered at by the media, why there appeared to be a permanent quest on their behalf to bring her down. It is baffling.

My own and only explanation is that genuine goodness is threatening to those at the opposite end of the moral spectrum.

It is a point to remember that of all the ironies about Diana, perhaps the greatest was this—a girl given the name of the ancient goddess of hunting was, in the end, the most hunted person of the modern age.

She would want us today to pledge ourselves to protecting her beloved boys William and Harry from a similar fate, and I do this here, Diana, on your behalf. We will not allow them to suffer the anguish that was used regularly to drive you to tearful despair.

And, beyond that, on behalf of your mother and sisters, I pledge that we, your blood family, will do all we can to continue the imaginative way in which you were steering these two exceptional young men, so that their souls are not simply immersed by duty and tradition but can sing openly, as you planned.

We fully respect the heritage into which they have both been born and will always respect and encourage them in their royal role, but we, like you, recognize the need for them to experience as many different aspects of life as possible to arm them spiritually and emotionally for the years ahead. I know you would have expected nothing less from us.

William and Harry, we all care desperately for you today. We are all chewed up with the sadness at the loss of a woman who was not even our mother. How great your suffering is, we cannot even imagine.

I would like to end by thanking God for the small mercies he has shown us at this dreadful time. For taking Diana at her most beautiful and radiant and when she had joy in her private life.

Above all, we give thanks for the life of a woman I am so proud to be able to call my sister—the unique, the complex, the extraordinary and irreplaceable Diana, whose beauty, both internal and external, will never be extinguished from our minds.

Hillary Rodham Clinton

Speech to the UN Fourth World Conference on Women
Beijing, China
September 5, 1995

Mrs. Mongella, Under Secretary Kittani, distinguished delegates and guests:

I would like to thank the Secretary General of the United Nations for inviting me to be a part of the United Nations Fourth World Conference on Women. This is truly a celebration—a celebration of the contributions women make in every aspect of life: in the home, on the job, in their communities, as mothers, wives, sisters, daughters, learners, workers, citizens and leaders.

It is also a coming together, much of the way women come together every day in every country.

We come together in fields and in factories. We come together in village markets and supermarkets. We come together in living rooms and board rooms.

Whether it is while playing with our children in the park, or washing clothes in a river, or taking a break at the office water cooler, we come together and talk about our aspirations and concern. And time and again, our talk turns to our children and our families. However different we may be, there is far more that unites us than divides us. We share a common future, and are here to find common ground so that we may help bring new dignity and respect to women and girls all over the world. By doing this, we bring new strength and stability to families as well.

By gathering in Beijing, we are focusing world attention on issues that matter most in the lives of women and their families: access to education, health care, jobs, and credit, the chance to enjoy basic legal and human rights and participate fully in the political life of their countries.

There are some who question the reason for this conference.

Let them listen to the voices of women in their homes, neighborhoods, and work-places.

There are some who wonder whether the lives of women and girls matter to economic and political progress around the globe.

Let them look at the women gathered here and at Huairou—the homemakers, nurses, teachers, lawyers, policymakers, and women who run their own businesses.

It is conferences like this that compel governments and people everywhere to listen, look, and face the world's most pressing problems.

Wasn't it after the women's conference in Nairobi ten years ago that the world focused for the first time on the crisis of domestic violence?

Earlier today, I participated in a World Health Organization forum, where government officials, NGOs, and individual citizens are working on ways to address the health problems of women and girls.

Tomorrow, I will attend a gathering of the United Nations Development Fund for Women. There, the discussion will focus on local—and highly successful—programs that give hard-working women access to credit so they can improve their own lives and the lives of their families.

What we are learning around the world is that if women are healthy and educated, their families will flourish. If women are free from violence, their families will flourish. If women have a chance to work and earn as full and equal partners in society, their families will flourish.

And when families flourish, communities and nations will flourish.

That is why every woman, every man, every child, every family, and every nation on our planet has a stake in the discussion that takes place here.

Over the past 25 years, I have worked persistently on issues relating to women, children, and families. Over the past two-and-a half years, I have had the opportunity to learn more about the challenges facing women in my own country and around the world.

I have met new mothers in Jojakarta and Indonesia who come together regularly in their village to discuss nutrition, family planning, and baby care.

I have met working parents in Denmark who talk about the comfort they feel in knowing that their children can be cared for in creative, safe, and nurturing after-school centers.

I have met women in South Africa who helped lead the struggle to end apartheid and are now helping build a new democracy.

I have met with the leading women of the Western Hemisphere who are working every day to promote literacy and better health care for the children of their countries.

I have met women in India and Bangladesh who are taking out small loans to buy milk cows, rickshaws, thread, and other materials to create a livelihood for themselves and their families.

I have met doctors and nurses in Belarus and Ukraine who are trying to keep children alive in the aftermath of Chernobyl.

The great challenge of this Conference is to give voice to women everywhere whose experiences go unnoticed, whose words go unheard.

Women comprise more than half the word's population. Women are 70% of the world's poor, and two-thirds of those are not taught to read and write.

Women are the primary caretakers for most of the world's children and elderly. Yet much of the work we do is not valued—not by economists, not by historians, not by popular culture, not by government leaders.

At this very moment, as we sit here, women around the world are giving birth, raising children, cooking meals, washing clothes, cleaning houses, planting crops, working on assembly lines, running companies, and running countries.

Women also are dying from diseases that should have been prevented or treated. They are watching their children succumb to malnutrition caused by poverty and economic deprivation. They are being denied the right to go to school by their own fathers and brothers. They are being forced into prostitution, and they are being barred from the bank lending office and banned from the ballot box.

Those of us who have the opportunity to be here have the responsibility to speak for those who could not.

As an American, I want to speak up for those women in my own country—women who are raising children on the minimum wage, women who can't afford health care or child care, women whose lives are threatened by violence, including violence in their own homes.

I want to speak up for mothers who are fighting for good schools, safe neighborhoods, clean air, and clean airwaves; for older women, some of them widows, who have raised their families and now find their skills and life experiences are not valued in the workplace; for women who are working all night as nurses, hotel clerks, and fast-food cooks so that they can be at home during the day with their kids; and for women everywhere who simply don't have time to do everything they are called upon to do each day.

Speaking to you today, I speak for them, just as each of us speaks for women around the world who are denied the chance to go to school, or see a doctor, or own property, or have a say about the direction of their lives, simply because they are women. The truth is that most women around the world work both inside and outside the home, usually by necessity.

We need to understand that there is no formula for how women should lead their lives.

That is why we must respect the choices that each woman makes for herself and her family. Every woman deserves the chance to realize her own God-given potential.

We also must recognize that women will never gain full dignity until their human rights are respected and protected.

Our goals for this Conference, to strengthen families and societies by empowering women to take greater control over their destinies, cannot be fully achieved unless all governments—here and around the world—accept their responsibility to protect and promote internationally recognized human rights.

The international community has long acknowledged—and recently affirmed at Vienna—that both women and men are entitled to a range of protections and personal freedoms, from the right of personal security to the right to determine freely the number and spacing of the children they bear.

No one should be forced to remain silent for fear of religious or political persecution, arrest, abuse, or torture.

Tragically, women are most often the ones whose human rights are violated.

Even in the late twentieth century, the rape of women continues to be used as an instrument of armed conflict. Women and children make up a large majority of the world's refugees. When women are excluded from the political process, they become even more vulnerable to abuse.

I believe that, on the eve of a new millennium, it is time to break our silence. It is time for us to say here in Beijing, and the world to hear, that it is no longer acceptable to discuss women's rights as separate from human rights.

These abuses have continued because, for too long, the history of women has been a history of silence. Even today, there are those who are trying to silence our words.

The voices of this conference and of the women at Huairou must be heard loud and clear:

It is a violation of human rights when babies are denied food, or drowned, or suffocated, or their spines broken, simply because they are born girls.

It is a violation of human rights when women and girls are sold into the slavery of prostitution.

It is a violation of human rights when women are doused with gasoline, set on fire, and burned to death because their marriage dowries are deemed too small.

It is a violation of human rights when individual women are raped in their own communities and when thousands of women are subjected to rape as a tactic or prize of war.

It is a violation of human rights when a leading cause of death worldwide along women ages fourteen to forty-four is the violence they are subjected to in their own homes.

It is a violation of human rights when women are denied the right to plan their own families, and that includes being forced to have abortions or being sterilized against their will.

If there is one message that echoes forth from this conference, it is that human rights are women's rights—and women's rights are human rights. Let us not forget that among those rights are the right to speak freely—and the right to be heard.

Women must enjoy the right to participate fully in the social and political lives of their countries if we want freedom and democracy to thrive and endure.

It is indefensible that many women in nongovernmental organizations who wished to participate in this conference have not been able to attend—or have been prohibited from fully taking part.

Let me be clear. Freedom means the right of people to assemble, organize, and debate openly. It means respecting the views of those who may disagree with the views of their governments. It means not taking citizens away from their loved ones and jailing them, mistreating them, or denying them their freedom or dignity because of the peaceful expression of their ideas and opinions.

In my country, we recently celebrated the seventy-fifth anniversary of women's suffrage. It took 150 years after the signing of our Declaration of Independence for women to win the right to vote.

It took seventy-two years of organized struggle on the part of many courageous women and men. It was one of America's most divisive philosophical wars. But it was also a bloodless war. Suffrage was achieved without a shot being fired.

We have also been reminded, in V-J Day observances last weekend, of the good that comes when men and women join together to combat the forces of tyranny and build a better world.

We have seen peace prevail in most places for a half-century. We have avoided another world war.

But we have not solved older, deeply rooted problems that continue to diminish the potential of half the world's population.

Now it is time to act on behalf of women everywhere.

If we take bold steps to better the lives of women, we will be taking bold steps to better the lives of children and families, too.

Families rely on mothers and wives for emotional support and care; families rely on women for labor in the home; and increasingly, families rely on women for income needed to raise healthy children and care for other relatives.

As long as discrimination and inequities remain so commonplace around the world—as long as girls and women are valued less, fed less, fed last, overworked, underpaid, not schooled, and subjected to violence in and out of their homes—the potential of the human family to create a peaceful, prosperous world will not be realized.

Let this Conference be our—and the world's—call to action.

And let us heed the call so that we can create a world in which every woman is treated with respect and dignity, every boy and girl is loved and cared for equally, and every family has the hope of a strong and stable future.

Thank you very much.

May God bless you, your work, and all who will benefit from it.

Mary Fisher

Democratic National Convention
Houston, Texas
August 19, 1992

Less than three months ago at platform hearings in Salt Lake City, I asked the Republican Party to lift the shroud of silence which has been draped over the issue of HIV and AIDS. I have come tonight to bring our silence to an end.

I bear a message of challenge, not self-congratulation. I want your attention, not your applause. I would never have asked to be HIV positive. But I believe that in all things there is a purpose; and so I stand before you and before the nation gladly.

The reality of AIDS is brutally clear. Two hundred thousand Americans are dead or dying; a million more are infected. Worldwide, forty million, or sixty million, or a hundred million infections will be counted in the coming few years. But despite science and research, White House meetings, and congressional hearings, despite good intentions and bold initiatives, campaign slogans, and hopeful promises, it is—despite it all; it's the epidemic which is winning tonight.

In the context of an election year, I ask you—here in this great hall, or listening in the quiet of your home—to recognize that AIDS virus is not a political creature. It does not care whether you are Democrat or Republican.

It does not ask whether you are black or white, male or female, gay or straight, young or old.

Tonight, I represent an AIDS community whose members have been reluctantly drafted from every segment of American society. Though I am white and a mother, I am one with a black infant struggling with tubes in a Philadelphia hospital. Though I am female and contracted this disease in marriage and enjoy the warm support of my family, I am one with the lonely gay man sheltering a flickering candle from the cold wind of his family's rejection.

This is not a distant threat; it is a present danger. The rate of infection is increasing fastest among women and children. Largely unknown a decade ago, AIDS is the third leading killer of young adult Americans today—but it won't be third for long. Because unlike other diseases, this one travels. Adolescents don't give each other cancer or heart disease because they believe they are in love. But HIV is different. And we have helped it along—we have killed each other with our ignorance, our prejudice, and our silence.

We may take refuge in our stereotypes, but we cannot hide there long. Because HIV asks only one thing of those it attacks. Are you human? And this is the right question. Are you human? Because people with HIV have not entered some alien state of being. They are human. They have not earned cruelty, and they do not deserve meanness. They don't benefit from being isolated or treated as outcasts. Each of them is exactly what God made: a person; not evil, deserving of our judgment; not victims, longing for our pity—people, ready for support and worthy of compassion.

My call to you, my party, is to take a public stand, no less compassionate than that of the president and Mrs. Bush. They have embraced me and my family in memorable ways. In the place of judgment, they have shown affection. In difficult moments, they have raised our spirits. In the darkest hours, I have seen them reaching not only to me, but also to my parents, armed with that stunning grief and special grace that comes only to parents who have themselves leaned too long over the bedside of a dying child.

With the president's leadership, much good has been done; much of the good has gone unheralded; as the president has insisted, 'much remains to be done.'

But we do the president's cause no good if we praise the American family but ignore a virus that destroys it.

We must be consistent if we are to be believed. We cannot love justice and ignore prejudice, love our children and fear to teach them. Whatever our role as parent or policymaker, we must act as eloquently as we speak—else we have no integrity.

My call to the nation is a plea for awareness. If you believe you are safe, you are in danger. Because I was not hemophiliac, I was not at risk. Because I was not gay, I was not at risk. Because I did not inject drugs, I was not at risk.

My father has devoted much of his lifetime guarding against another holocaust. He is part of the generation who heard Pastor Nemoellor come out of the Nazi death camps to say, "They came after the Jews, and I was not a Jew, so, I did not protest. They came after the trade unionists, and I was not a trade unionist, so, I did not protest. Then they came after the Roman Catholics, and I was not a Roman Catholic, so, I did not protest. Then they came after me, and there was no one left to protest."

The lesson history teaches is this: If you believe you are safe, you are at risk. If you do not see this killer stalking your children, look again. There is no family or community, no race or religion, no place left in America that is safe. Until we genuinely embrace this message, we are a nation at risk.

Tonight, HIV marches resolutely toward AIDS in more than a million American homes, littering its pathway with the bodies of the young. Young men. Young women. Young parents. Young children. One of the families is mine. If it is true that HIV inevitably turns to AIDS, then my children will inevitably turn to orphans.

My family has been a rock of support. My eighty-four-year-old father, who has pursued the healing of the nations, will not accept the premise that he cannot heal his daughter. My mother has refused to be broken. She still calls at midnight to tell wonderful jokes that make me laugh. Sisters and friends, and my brother Phillip, whose birthday is today, all have helped carry me over the hardest places. I am blessed, richly and deeply blessed, to have such a family.

But not all of you have been so blessed. You are HIV positive but dare not say it. You have lost loved ones, but you dare not whisper the word AIDS. You weep silently; you grieve alone.

I have a message for you. It is not you who should feel shame; it is we—we who tolerate ignorance and practice prejudice, we who have taught you to fear. We must lift our shroud of silence, making it safe for you to reach out for compassion. It is our task to seek safety for our children, not in quiet denial, but in effective action.

Someday our children will be grown. My son Max, now four, will take the measure of his mother; my son Zachary, now two, will sort through his memories. I may not be here to hear their judgments, but I know already what I hope they are.

I want my children to know that their mother was not a victim. She was a messenger. I do not want them to think, as I once did, that courage is the absence of fear; I want them to know that courage is the strength to act wisely when most we are afraid. I want them to have the courage to step forward when called by their nation or their Party and give leadership—no matter what the personal cost. I ask no more of you than I ask of myself or of my children.

To the millions of you who are grieving, who are frightened, who have suffered the ravages of AIDS firsthand: Have courage, and you will find support.

To the millions who are strong, I issue the plea: Set aside prejudice and politics to make room for compassion and sound policy.

To my children, I make this pledge: I will not give in, Zachary, because I draw my courage from you. Your silly giggle gives me hope. Your gentle prayers give me strength; and you, my child, give me the reason to say to America, "You are at risk." And I will not rest, Max, until I have done all I can to make your world safe. I will seek a place where intimacy is not the prelude to suffering.

I will not hurry to leave you, my children. But when I go, I pray that you will not suffer shame on my account.

To all within the sound of my voice, I appeal: Learn with me the lessons of history and of grace, so my children will not be afraid to say the word AIDS when I am gone. Then, their children and yours may not need to whisper it at all.

God bless the children, and bless us all.

Senator Edward M. Kennedy

Eulogy for Robert Kennedy
St. Patrick's Cathedral, New York, New York
June 8, 1968

On behalf of Mrs. Robert Kennedy, her children, and the parents and sisters of Robert Kennedy, I want to express what we feel to those who mourn with us today in this Cathedral and around the world. We loved him as a brother and father and son. From his parents, and from his older brothers and sisters—Joe, Kathleen, and Jack—he received inspiration which he passed on to all of us. He gave us strength in time of trouble, wisdom in time of uncertainty, and sharing in time of happiness. He was always by our side.

Love is not an easy feeling to put into words. Nor is loyalty, or trust or joy. But he was all of these. He loved life completely and lived it intensely.

A few years back, Robert Kennedy wrote some words about his own father and they expressed the way we in his family feel about him. He said of what his father meant to him: "What it really all adds up to is love—not love as it is described with such facility in popular magazines, but the kind of love that is affection and respect, order, encouragement, and support. Our awareness of this was an incalculable source of strength, and because real love is something unselfish and involves sacrifice and giving, we could not help but profit from it.

"Beneath it all, he has tried to engender a social conscience. There were wrongs which needed attention. There were people who were poor and who needed help. And we have a responsibility to them and to this country. Through no virtues and accomplishments of our own, we have been fortunate enough to be born in the United States under the most comfortable conditions. We, therefore, have a responsibility to others who are less well off."

This is what Robert Kennedy was given. What he leaves us is what he said, what he did, and what he stood for. A speech he made to the young people of South Africa on their Day of Affirmation in 1966 sums it up the best, and I would read it now:

"There is a discrimination in this world and slavery and slaughter and starvation. Governments repress their people; and millions are trapped in poverty while the nation grows rich; and wealth is lavished on armaments everywhere.

"These are differing evils, but they are common works of man. They reflect the imperfection of human justice, the inadequacy of human compassion, our lack of sensibility toward the sufferings of our fellows.

"But we can perhaps remember—even if only for a time—that those who live with us are our brothers; that they share with us the same short moment of life; that they seek—as we do—nothing but the chance to live out their lives in purpose and happiness, winning what satisfaction and fulfillment they can.

"Surely this bond of common faith, this bond of common goal, can begin to teach us something. Surely, we can learn, at least, to look at those around us as fellow men. And surely we can begin to work a little harder to bind up the wounds among us and to become in our own hearts brothers and countrymen once again.

"Our answer is to rely on youth—not a time of life but a state of mind, a temper of the will, a quality of imagination, a predominance of courage over timidity, of the appetite for adventure over the love of ease. The cruelties and obstacles of this swiftly changing planet will not yield to obsolete dogmas and outworn slogans. They cannot be moved by those who cling to a present that is already dying, who prefer the illusion of security to the excitement and danger that come with even the most peaceful progress. It is a revolutionary world we live in; and this generation at home and around the world has had thrust upon it a greater burden of responsibility than any generation that has ever lived.

"Some believe there is nothing one man or one woman can do against the enormous array of the world's ills. Yet many of the world's great movements, of thought and action, have flowed from the work of a single man. A young monk began the Protestant reformation, a young general extended an empire from Macedonia to the borders of the earth, and a young woman reclaimed the territory of France. It was a young Italian explorer who discovered the New World, and the thirty-two-year-old Thomas Jefferson who proclaimed that all men are created equal.

"These men moved the world, and so can we all. Few will have the greatness to bend history itself, but each of us can work to change a small portion of events, and in the total of all those acts will be written the history of this generation. It is from numberless diverse acts of courage and belief that human history is shaped. Each time a man stands up for an ideal, or acts to improve the lot of others, or strikes out against injustice, he sends forth a tiny ripple of hope, and crossing each other from a million different centers of energy and daring, those ripples build a current that can sweep down the mightiest walls of oppression and resistance.

"Few are willing to brave the disapproval of their fellows, the censure of their colleagues, the wrath of their society. Moral courage is a rarer commodity than bravery in battle or great intelligence. Yet it is the one essential, vital quality for those who seek to change a world that yields most painfully to change. And I believe that in this generation those with the courage to enter the moral conflict will find themselves with companions in every corner of the globe.

"For the fortunate among us, there is the temptation to follow the easy and familiar paths of personal ambition and financial success so grandly spread before those who enjoy the privilege of education. But that is not the road history has marked out for us. Like it or not, we live in times of danger and uncertainty. But they are also more open to the creative energy of men than any other time in history. All of us will ultimately be judged and as the years pass we will surely judge ourselves, on the effort we have contributed to building a new world society and the extent to which our ideals and goals have shaped that effort.

"The future does not belong to those who are content with today, apathetic toward common problems and their fellow man alike, timid and fearful in the face of new ideas and bold projects. Rather, it will belong to those who can blend vision, reason, and courage in a personal commitment to the ideals and great enterprises of American society.

"Our future may lie beyond our vision, but it is not completely beyond our control. It is the shaping impulse of America that neither fate nor nature nor the irresistible tides of history, but the work of our own hands, matched to reason and principle, that will determine our destiny. There is pride in that, even arrogance, but there is also experience and truth. In any event, it is the only way we can live."

This is the way he lived. My brother need not be idealized, or enlarged in death beyond what he was in life, to be remembered simply as a good and decent man, who saw wrong and tried to right it, saw suffering and tried to heal it, saw war and tried to stop it.

Those of us who loved him and who take him to his rest today, pray that what he was to us and what he wished for others will some day come to pass for all the world.

As he said many times, in many parts of this nation, to those he touched and who sought to touch him:

"Some men see things as they are and say why.

I dream things that never were and say why not."

George H. W. Bush

Declaration of Allied Military Action in the Persian Gulf
January 16, 1991

Just two hours ago, allied air forces began an attack on military targets in Iraq and Kuwait. These attacks continue as I speak. Ground forces are now engaged.

This conflict started August 2 when the dictator of Iraq invaded a small and helpless neighbor. Kuwait—a member of the Arab League and a member of the United Nations—was crushed; its people, brutalized. Five months ago, Saddam Hussein started this cruel war against Kuwait. Tonight, the battle has been joined.

This military action, taken in accord with United Nations resolutions and with the consent of the United States Congress, follows months of constant and virtually endless diplomatic activity on the part of the United Nations, the United States, and many, many other countries. Arab leaders sought what became known as an Arab solution, only to conclude that Saddam Hussein was unwilling to leave Kuwait. Others traveled to Baghdad in a variety of efforts to restore peace and justice. Our Secretary of State, James Baker, held an historic meeting in Geneva, only to be totally rebuffed. This past weekend, in a last-ditch effort, the Secretary General of the United Nations went to the Middle East with peace in his heart—his second such mission. And he came back from Baghdad with no progress at all in getting Saddam Hussein to withdraw from Kuwait.

Now the twenty-eight countries with forces in the Gulf area have exhausted all reasonable efforts to reach a peaceful resolution—have no choice but to drive Saddam from Kuwait by force. We will not fail.

As I report to you, air attacks are underway against military targets in Iraq. We are determined to knock out Saddam Hussein's nuclear bomb potential. We will also destroy his chemical weapons facilities. Much of Saddam's artillery and tanks will be destroyed. Our operations are designed to best protect the lives of all the coalition forces by targeting Saddam's vast military arsenal. Initial reports from General Schwarzkopf are that our operations are proceeding according to plan.

Our objectives are clear: Saddam Hussein's forces will leave Kuwait. The legitimate government of Kuwait will be restored to its rightful place, and Kuwait will once again be free. Iraq will eventually comply with all relevant United Nations resolutions, and then, when peace is restored, it is our hope that Iraq will live as a peaceful and cooperative member of the family of nations, thus enhancing the security and stability of the Gulf.

Some may ask: Why act now? Why not wait? The answer is clear: The world could wait no longer. Sanctions, though having some effect, showed no signs of accomplishing their objective. Sanctions were tried for well over five months, and we and our allies concluded that sanctions alone would not force Saddam from Kuwait.

While the world waited, Saddam Hussein systematically raped, pillaged, and plundered a tiny nation, no threat to his own. He subjected the people of Kuwait to unspeakable atrocities—and among those maimed and murdered, innocent children.

While the world waited, Saddam sought to add to the chemical weapons arsenal he now possesses, an infinitely more dangerous weapon of mass destruction—a nuclear weapon. And while the world waited, while the world talked peace and withdrawal, Saddam Hussein dug in and moved massive forces into Kuwait.

While the world waited, while Saddam stalled, more damage was being done to the fragile economies of the Third World, emerging democracies of Eastern Europe, to the entire world, including to our own economy.

The United States, together with the United Nations, exhausted every means at our disposal to bring this crisis to a peaceful end. However, Saddam clearly felt that by stalling and threatening and defying the United Nations, he could weaken the forces arrayed against him.

While the world waited, Saddam Hussein met every overture of peace with open contempt. While the world prayed for peace, Saddam prepared for war.

I had hoped that when the United States Congress, in historic debate, took its resolute action, Saddam would realize he could not prevail and would move out of Kuwait in accord with the United Nation resolutions. He did not do that. Instead, he remained intransigent, certain that time was on his side.

Saddam was warned over and over again to comply with the will of the United Nations: Leave Kuwait, or be driven out. Saddam has arrogantly rejected all warnings. Instead, he tried to make this a dispute between Iraq and the United States of America.

Well, he failed. Tonight, twenty-eight nations—countries from five continents, Europe and Asia, Africa and the Arab League—have forces in the Gulf area standing shoulder to shoulder against Saddam Hussein. These countries had hoped the use of force could be avoided. Regrettably, we now believe that only force will make him leave.

Prior to ordering our forces into battle, I instructed our military commanders to take every necessary step to prevail as quickly as possible, and with the greatest degree of protection possible for American and allied service men and women. I've told the American people before that this will not be another Vietnam, and I repeat this here tonight. Our troops will have the best possible support in the entire world, and they will not be asked to fight with one hand tied behind their back. I'm hopeful that this fighting will not go on for long and that casualties will be held to an absolute minimum.

This is an historic moment. We have in this past year made great progress in ending the long era of conflict and cold war. We have before us the opportunity to forge for ourselves and for future generations a new world order—a world where the rule of law, not the law of the jungle, governs the conduct of nations. When we are successful—and we will be—we have a real chance at this new world order, an order in which a credible United Nations can use its peacekeeping role to fulfill the promise and vision of the UN's founders.

We have no argument with the people of Iraq. Indeed, for the innocents caught in this conflict, I pray for their safety. Our goal is not the conquest of Iraq. It is the liberation of Kuwait. It is my hope that somehow the Iraqi people can, even now, convince their dictator that he must lay down his arms, leave Kuwait, and let Iraq itself rejoin the family of peace-loving nations.

Thomas Paine wrote many years ago: "These are the times that try men's souls." Those well-known words are so very true today. But even as planes of the multinational forces attack Iraq, I prefer to think of peace, not war. I am convinced not only that we will prevail but that out of the horror of combat will come the recognition that no nation can stand against a world united. No nation will be permitted to brutally assault its neighbor.

No president can easily commit our sons and daughters to war. They are the nation's finest. Ours is an all-volunteer force, magnificently trained, highly motivated. The troops know why they're there. And listen to what they say, for they've said it better than any president or prime minister ever could.

Listen to Hollywood Huddleston, Marine lance corporal. He says, "Let's free these people, so we can go home and be free again." And he's right. The terrible crimes and tortures committed by Saddam's henchmen against the innocent people of Kuwait are an affront to mankind and a challenge to the freedom of all.

Listen to one of our great officers out there, Marine Lieutenant General Walter Boomer. He said: "There are things worth fighting for. A world in which brutality and lawlessness are allowed to go unchecked isn't the kind of world we're going to want to live in."

Listen to Master Sergeant J. P. Kendall of the 82nd Airborne: "We're here for more than just the price of a gallon of gas. What we're doing is going to chart the future of the world for the next one hundred years. It's better to deal with this guy now than five years from now."

And finally, we should all sit up and listen to Jackie Jones, an Army lieutenant, when she says, "If we let him get away with this, who knows what's going to be next?"

I have called upon Hollywood and Walter and J. P. and Jackie and all their courageous comrades-in-arms to do what must be done. Tonight, America and the world are deeply grateful to them and to their families. And let me say to everyone listening or watching tonight: When the troops we've sent in finish their work, I am determined to bring them home as soon as possible.

Tonight, as our forces fight, they and their families are in our prayers. May God bless each and every one of them, and the coalition forces at our side in the Gulf, and may He continue to bless our nation, the United States of America.

Harry Emerson Fosdick

"The Unknown Soldier"
Riverside Church, New York, New York
November 11, 1933

It was an interesting idea to deposit the body of an unrecognized soldier in the national memorial of the Great War, and yet, when one stops to think of it, how strange it is! Yesterday, in Rome, Paris, London, Washington, and how many capitals beside, the most stirring military pageantry, decked with flags and exultant with music, centered about the bodies of unknown soldiers. That is strange. So this is the outcome of Western civilization. . . . The whole nation pauses, its acclamations rise, its colorful pageantry centers, its patriotic oratory flourishes, around the unrecognizable body of a soldier blown to bits on the battlefield. That is strange.

It was the warlords themselves who picked him out as the symbol of war. So be it! As a symbol of war, we accept him from their hands.

You may not say that I, being a Christian minister, did not know him. I knew him well. From the north of Scotland, where they planted the sea with mines, to the trenches of France, I lived with him and his fellows—British, Australian, New Zealand, French, American. The places where he fought, from Ypres through the Somme battlefield to the southern trenches, I saw while he still was there. I lived with him in his dugouts in the trenches and on destroyers searching for submarines off the shores of France. Short of actual battle, from training camp to hospital, from the fleet to No Man's Land, I, a Christian minister, saw the war. Moreover I, a Christian minister, participated in it. I too was persuaded that it was a war to end wars. I too was a gullible fool and thought that modern war could somehow make the world safe for democracy. They sent men like me to explain to the Army the high meanings of war and, by every argument we could command, to strengthen their morale. I wonder if I ever spoke to the Unknown Soldier.

One night, in a ruined barn behind the lines, I spoke at sunset to a company of hand-grenaders who were going out that night to raid the German trenches. They told me that on the average no more than half a company came back from such a raid, and I, a minister of Christ, tried to nerve them for their suicidal and murderous endeavor. I wonder if the Unknown Soldier was in that barn that night.

Once in a dugout which in other days had been a French wine cellar I bade Godspeed at two in the morning to a detail of men going out on patrol in No Man's Land. They were a fine company of American boys fresh from home. I recall that, huddled in the dark, underground chamber, they sang,

> Lead, kindly Light, amid th' encircling gloom,
>   Lead thou me on.
> The night is dark, and I am far from home, —
>   Lead thou me on.

Then, with my admonitions in their ears, they went down from the second- to the first-line trenches and so out to No Man's Land. I wonder if the Unknown Soldier was in that dugout.

You here this morning may listen to the rest of this sermon or not, as you please. It makes much less difference to me than usual what you do or think. I have an account to settle in this pulpit today between my soul and the Unknown Soldier.

He is not so utterly unknown as we sometimes think. Of one thing we may be certain: he was sound of mind and body. We made sure of that. All primitive gods who demanded bloody sacrifices on their altars insisted that the animals should be of the best, without mar or hurt. . . . The god of war still maintains the old demand. These men to be sacrificed upon his altars were sound and strong. Once there might have been guessing about that. Not now. Now we have medical science, which tests the prospective soldier's body. Now we have psychiatry, which tests his mind. We used them both to make sure that these sacrifices for the god of war were without blemish. Of all insane and suicidal procedures, can you imagine anything madder than this, that all the nations should pick out their best, use their scientific skill to make sure they are the best, and then in one mighty holocaust offer ten million of them on the battlefields of one war?

I have an account to settle between my soul and the Unknown Soldier. I deceived him. I deceived myself first, unwittingly, and then I deceived him, assuring him that good consequence could come out of that. As a matter of hard-headed, biological fact, what good can come of that? Mad civilization, you cannot sacrifice on bloody altars the best of your breed and expect anything to compensate for the loss.

Of one thing we may be fairly certain concerning the Unknown Soldier—that he was a conscript. He may have been a volunteer but on an actuarial average he probably was a conscript. The long arm of the nation reached into his home, touched him on the shoulder, saying, You must go to France and fight. If some one asks why in this "land of the free" conscription was used, the answer is, of course, that it was necessary if we were to win the war. Certainly it was. And that reveals something terrific about modern war. We cannot get soldiers—not enough of them, not the right kind of them—without forcing them. When a nation goes to war now, the entire nation must go. That means that the youth must be compelled, coerced, conscripted to fight.

When you stand in Arlington before the tomb of the Unknown Soldier on some occasion, let us say, when the panoply of military glory decks it with music and color, are you thrilled? I am not—not any more. I see there the memorial of one of the saddest things in American history, from the continued repetition of which may God deliver us!—the conscripted boy.

He was a son, the hope of a family, and the nation coerced him. He was, perchance, a lover and the deepest emotion of his life was not desire for military glory or hatred of another country or any other idiotic thing like that, but love of a girl and hope of a home. He was, maybe, a husband and a father, and already, by that slow and beautiful gradation which all fathers know, he had felt the deep ambitions of his heart being transferred from himself to his children. And the nation coerced him. I am not blaming him; he was conscripted. I am not blaming the nation; it never could have won the war without conscription. . . . If I blame anybody about this matter, it is men like myself who should have known better. We went out to the Army and explained to these valiant men what a resplendent future they were preparing for their children by their heroic sacrifice. O Unknown Soldier, however can I make that right with you? . . .

The Unknown Soldier, sound in mind and body—yes! The Unknown Soldier a conscript—probably! But be fair and add that the Unknown Soldier had a thrilling time in France. To be sure, he may have had. Listen to this from a wounded American after a battle. "We went over the parapet at five o'clock and I was not hit until nine. They were the greatest four hours of my life." Quite so! Only let me talk to you for a moment about that. *That* was the first time he went over the parapet. Anything risky, dangerous, tried for the first time, well handled, and now escaped from, is thrilling to an excitable and courageous soul. What about the second time and the third time and the fourth? What about the dreadful times between, the long-drawn-out, monotonous, dreary, muddy barrenness of war, concerning which one who knew said, "Nine-tenths of War is Waiting"? The trouble with much familiar talk about the lyric glory of war is that it comes from people who never saw any soldiers except for the American troops, fresh, resilient, who had time to go over the parapet about once. You ought to have seen the hardening-up camps of the armies which had been at the business since 1914. Did you ever see them? Did you look, as I looked, into the faces of young men who had been over the top, wounded, hospitalized, hardened up—over the top, wounded, hospitalized, hardened up—over the top, hospitalized, hardened up—four times, five times, six times? Never talk to a man who has seen that about the lyric glory of war. . . .

The glory of war comes from poets, preachers, orators, the writers of martial music, statesmen preparing flowery proclamations for the people, who dress up war for other men to fight. They do not go into the trenches. They do not go over the top again and again and again. . . .

Granted, then, that the Unknown Soldier should be to us a symbol of everything most idealistic in a valiant warrior, I beg of you, be realistic and follow through what war made the Unknown Soldier do with his idealism. Here is one eyewitness speaking:

"Last night, at an officers' mess there was great laughter at the story of one of our men who had spent his last cartridge in defending an attack. 'Hand me down your spade, Mike,' he said; and as six Germans came one by one round the end of a traverse, he split each man's skull open with a deadly blow." The war made the Unknown Soldier do that with his idealism.

"I can remember," says one infantry officer, "a pair of hands (nationality unknown) which protruded from the soaked ashen soil like the roots of a tree turned upside down; one hand seemed to be pointing at the sky with an accusing gesture. . . . Floating on the surface of the flooded trench was the mask of a human face which had detached itself from the skull." War harnessed the idealism of the Unknown Soldier to *that*!

Do I not have an account to settle between my soul and him? They sent men like me into the camps to awaken his idealism, to touch those secret, holy springs within him so that with devotion, fidelity, loyalty, and self-sacrifice he might go out to war. Oh war, I hate you most of all for this, that you do lay your hands on the noblest elements in human character, with which we might make a heaven on earth, and you use them to make a hell on earth instead. You take even our science, the fruit of our dedicated intelligence, by means of which we might build here the City of God, and, using it, you fill the earth instead with new ways of slaughtering men. . . .

O my country, stay out of war! Cooperate with the nations in every movement that has any hope for peace. . . . I will myself do the best I can to settle my account with the Unknown Soldier. I renounce war. I renounce war because of what it does to our own men. . . . I renounce war because of what it compels us to do to our enemies. . . . I renounce war for its consequences, for the lies it lives on and propagates, for the undying hatreds it arouses, for the dictatorships it puts in the place of democracy, for the starvation that stalks after it. I renounce war and never again, directly or indirectly, will I sanction or support another! O Unknown Soldier, in penitent reparation I make you that pledge.

NOTES

CHAPTER 1

1. K. Viner, "Hand-to-Brand Combat: A Profile of Naomi Klein." *The Guardian* (September 23, 2000). http://www.commondreams.org/views/092300-103.htm. Accessed July 24, 2004.
2. The National Conference for Media Reform, Millennium Hotel, St. Louis, Missouri, May 13–15, 2005.
3. E. Potter, "Anarchy Makes a Comeback," in S. D. Ferguson and L. R. Shade, *Civic Discourse and Cultural Politics in Canada: A Cacophony of Voices* (Westport, Conn.: Ablex Publishing, 2002), p. 91.
4. "The ACLU and the NRA: Compatible Bedfellows" (August 4, 2003). Online at Talkleft: The Politics of Crime. http://www.talkleft.com/new_archives/003355.html. Accessed on April 1, 2006.
5. Liza Featherstone, "Strange Marchfellows." *The Nation* (May 13, 2002). http://www.thenation.com/doc/20020513/Featherstone. Accessed April 3, 2006.
6. S. Devereaux Butler, "The Apologia, 1971 Genre," *Southern Speech Journal* 37 (1972): 281–289.
7. J. Leonard, "And a Picture Tube Shall Lead Them," in R. Atwan, B. Orton, and W. Vesterman, eds., *American Mass Media: Industries and Issues* (New York: Random House, 1978).
8. G. Cameron Grant (cameron313@aol.com), letter submitted to the *New York Times*. http://www.nola.com/forums/feedback/index.ssf?artid=673, posted on September 2, 2005. Accessed on September 5, 2005.
9. D. Froomkin, "Untangling Whitewater." Online at Washington Post.com, http://www.washingtonpost.com/wp-srv/politics/special/whitewater/whitewater.htm. Accessed October 15, 2004.
10. D. Froomkin, "Untangling Whitewater." Online at Washington Post.com, http://www.washingtonpost.com/wp-srv/politics/special/whitewater/whitewater.htm. Accessed October 15, 2004.
11. See N. Chomsky and E. S. Herman, *The Manufacturing of Consent* (New York: Pantheon Books, 1988).
12. N. Klein, *No Logo* (Toronto, ON: Knopf Canada, 2000).
13. K. Crawford, "Special Report: The Verdict on Martha," CNN/Money. Online at http://money.cnn.com/2004/07/16/news/newsmakers/martha_sentencing/?cnn=yes. Accessed July 25, 2004.
14. "CEO Pay Hikes Double," July 28, 2004. Online at http://money.cnn.com/2004/07/28/news/economy/ceo_pay/index.htm. Accessed July 28, 2004.
15. "Employment Class Actions: A Tool in Transition," online at http://www.littler.com/publications/classactions.PDF; also Consumer Affairs,"'Interest-Free' Isn't, Suit Claims," online at http://consumeraffairs.com/news04/home_depot_lowes.html; "Bank of America Loses Class Action Suit," online at http://consumeraffairs.com/news04/bofa.html. Accessed October 31, 2004.
16. U.S. Census Bureau, American Community Survey, "2003 Aata Profile." Online at http://www.census.gov/acs/www/Products/Profiles/Single/2003/ACS/Tabular/010/01000US1.htm. Accessed October 29, 2004.
17. The 2003 American Community Survey excluded people living in institutions, college dormitories, and other group quarters. The estimate is based on a sample of the population.

18. Versna Chuop, communication student, University of Ottawa, 2002.

19. Among the researchers who have contributed to this value profile are the following: Robyn M. Williams, Jr., "Change and Stability in Values and Value Systems: A Socio-logical Perspective," in M. Rokeach, ed., *Understanding Human Values* (New York: The Free Press, 1979), pp. 15–46; D. Yankelovich, *New Rules: Searching for Self-Fulfillment in a World Turned Upside Down* (New York: Random House, 1981); L. R. Kahle, *Social Changes and Value Change: Adaptation to Life in America* (New York: Praeger Publishers, 1983); R. W. Belk, "Materialism: Trait Aspects of Living in the Material World," *Journal of Consumer Research* 12 (1985): 265–279; M. Wallendorf and E. J. Arnold, "My Favorite Things: A Cross-Cultural Inquiry into Object Attachment, Possessiveness and Social Linkage," *Journal of Consumer Research* 14 (1988): 531–547; G. Ger and R. W. Belk, "Measuring and Comparing Materialism Across Countries," in M. E. Goldberg, G. Gorn, and R. W. Pollay, eds., *Advances in Consumer Research* 17 (Provo, UT: Association for Consumer Research, 1990), pp. 186–192; G. Hofstede, "Motivation, Leadership, and Organization: Do American Theories Apply Abroad?" *Organization Dynamics* 9 (1980): 42–53; S. M. Lipset, "The Value Patterns of Democracy: A Case Study in Comparative Analysis," American Sociological Review 28 (1963): 515–531; S. M. Lipset, "Canada and the United States—A Comparative View," *Canadian Review of Sociology and Anthropology* 1 (1964): 173–185; S. M. Lipset, "The Values of Canadians and Americans: A Reply," *Social Forces 69* (1990): 267–272; M. Rokeach, *Beliefs, Attitudes and Values* (San Francisco: Jossey-Bass Inc., 1968); M. Rokeach, *The Nature of Human Values* (New York: Free Press, 1973); M. Rokeach, *Understanding Human Values* (New York: Free Press, 1979); F. R. Kluckhohn and F. L. Strodtbeck, *Variations in Value Orientations* (New York: Row and Peterson, 1960); A. Mitchell, *The Nine American Lifestyles* (New York: Macmillan Publishing Co., Inc., 1983); D. E. Vinson, J. M. Munson, and M. Nakanishi, "An Investigation of the Rokeach Value Survey for Consumer Research Applications," in W. E. Perreault, ed., *Advances in Consumer Research*, Vol. 4 (Provo, UT: Association for Consumer Research, 1977), pp. 247–252; E. F. McQuarrie & D. Langmeyer, "Using Values to Measure Attitudes Toward Discontinuous Innovations," *Psychology & Marketing* 2 (1985): 239–252; E. D. Steele & W. C. Redding, "The American Value System: Premises for Persuasion," *Western Speech* 26 (1962): 83–91; L. A. Crosby, M. J. Bitner, and J. D. Gill, "Organizational Structure of Values," *Journal of Business Research* 20 (1990): 123–134; D. F. Alwin and J. A. Krosnick, "The Measurement of Values: A Comparison of Ratings and Rankings," *Public Opinion Quarterly* 49 (1985): 535–52; V. Prakash and J. M. Munson, "Values, Expectations from the Marketing Systems and Product Expectations," *Psychology & Marketing* 2 (1985): 279–298.

20. U.S. Census Bureau, "U.S. Department of Commerce News, March 21, 2003. Online at http://www.census.gov/Press-Release/www/2003/cb03-51.html. Accessed October 29, 2004.

21. C. Clemmensen, "A Guide for Determining the Ethos of Online Brand Mascots," November 1999–May 2000. http://www.filmtracks.com/home/mascots_thesis/index .html. Accessed July 24, 2004.

22. R. Givhan, "Dick Cheney, Dressing Down: Parka, Ski Cap at Odds with Solemnity of Auschwitz Ceremony," *Washington Post*, January 28, 2005, p. C01. http://www .washingtonpost.com/wp-dyn/articles/A43247-2005Jan27.html. Accessed on October 2, 2006.

23. Givhan, p. C01.

24. In the same way, today's students expect and want higher levels of engagement in the classroom situation. See P. Smagorinsky and P. K. Fly, "The Social Environment of the Classroom: A Vygotskian Perspective on Small Group Process," Communication Education 42 (1993): 157–171.

25. N. Postman, *Amusing Ourselves to Death: Public Discourse in the Age of Show Business* (New York: Penguin Books, 1985).

26. S. D. Ferguson, "Robespierre: High Priest of the Jacobins." *Central States Speech Journal* (1972): 246–253.

27. F. J. Macke, "Communication Left Speechless: A Critical Examination of the Evolution of Speech Communication as an Academic Discipline." *Communication Education* 40 (1991): 125–143. Macke also referenced several articles that appeared in a classical

collection by K. R. Wallace, ed., *History of Speech Education in America* (New York: Appleton, 1954): W. Guthrie, "Rhetorical Theory in Colonial America," pp. 48–59; M. Hochmuth and R. Murphy, "Rhetorical and Elocutionary Training in Nineteenth Century Colleges," pp. 153–177; and M. M. Robb, "The Elocutionary Movement and Its Main Figures," pp. 178–201.

28. J. Walker, "The Elements of Gesture," in W. Scott, *Scott's New Lessons in Reading and Writing* (Philadelphia: A. Walker, 1816); G. Austin, *Chironomia, or a Treatise on Rhetorical Delivery* (London: T. Cadell and W. Davies, 1806), reprinted in M. M. Robb and L. Thonssen, eds., *Chironomia, or a Treatise on Rhetorical Delivery* (Carbondale: University of Illinois Press, 1966).

29. M. L. Clarke, *Rhetoric at Rome: A Historical Survey* (New York: Barnes & Noble, Inc., 1968).

30. "Traveling Culture: What Is Chataqua?" Online at http://sdrc.lib.uiowa.edu/traveling-culture/essay.htm, p. 2. Accessed June 18, 2004.

31. "Traveling Culture," p. 2.

32. "Sheridan." *The 1911 Edition Encyclopedia*. Online at http://26.1911encyclopedia.org/S/SH/SHERIDAN.htm. Accessed June 18, 2004.

33. J. A. Winans, *Public Speaking* (Drummond, NY: The Century Company, 1915).

34. Macke, 1991, pp. 125–143.

35. N. Frye, *The Well-Tempered Critic* (Bloomington: Indiana University Press, 1963).

36. S. Ferguson and S. D. Ferguson, "Proxemics and Television: The Politician's Dilemma," *Canadian Journal of Communication* 4 (1978): 26–35.

37. M. McLuhan, *This Is Marshall McLuhan: The Medium Is the Massage*. Film produced by Ernest Pintoff and Guy Fraumini and aired on NBC, March 19, 1967.

38. Leonard, "And a Picture Tube Shall Lead Them," 1978.

39. K. Jamieson, *Eloquence in an Electronic Age: The Transformation of Political Speechmaking* (New York: Oxford University Press, 1988).

40. See D. Schwartz, "Interdisciplinary and Pedagogical Implications of Rhetorical Theory." *Communication Studies* 46 (1995): 130–139; T. S. Frobish, "Jamieson Meets Lucas: Eloquence and Pedagogical Model(s) in *The Art of Public Speaking*." *Communication Education* 49 (2000): 239–252; G. Sorensen, "The Relationships Among Teachers' Self-Disclosive Statements, Students' Perceptions, and Affective Learning." *Communication Education* 38 (1989): 259–276; M. Javidi, V. C. Downs, and J. F. Nussbaum, "A Comparative Analysis of Teachers' Use of Dramatic Style Behaviors at Higher and Secondary Educational Levels." *Communication Education* 37 (1988): 278–288.

41. E. S. Bogardus, "Television and Political Conventions," *Sociology and Social Research* 37 (1953): 119.

42. S. Waxman, "The Oscar Acceptance Speech: By and Large, It's a Lost Art." *Washington Post*, March 21, 1999. http://www.littlereview.com/. Accessed October 15, 2004.

43. "Putin Pledges to Fight Back," *Globe and Mail*, online edition (September 4, 2004). www.globeandmail.com. Accessed September 4, 2004.

44. Cicero, *De Oratore*, ii. 43.

45. C. G. Christians and E. B. Lambeth, "The Status of Ethics Instruction in Communication Departments," *Communication Education* 45 (1996): 236–243.

46. Quintilian, *The Institutio Oratoria*, 12.1.

CHAPTER 2

1. J. Tang, "Cracking under Pressure." *The Varsity Online*, University of Toronto (June 21, 2004). http://www.thevarsity.ca/news/2003/03/11/Science/Cracking.Under.Pressure-391211.shtml. Accessed July 17, 2004.

2. Tang, "Cracking under Pressure."

3. P. A. Broughton, "Communication Apprehension—Implications for a Communication Instructor: Twenty Years of Communication Research Published in Communication Education." Paper presented at the National Communication Association, Miami, Florida, November 2003.

4. J. C. McCroskey, "The Communication Apprehension Perspective," in J. C. McCroskey and J. A. Daly, eds. *Avoiding Communication: Shyness, Reticence, and Communication*

Apprehension (London: Sage, 1984), pp. 13–38; also S. F. Paulson, "Changes in Confidence during a Period of Speech Training," *Speech Monographs* 43 (1951): 260–265.

5. StarsWelcome.com home page. Online at http://www.starswelcome.com. Accessed November 13, 2003.

6. "Famous People, Funny Stories." http://www.anecdotage.com/index.php?aid= 12880. Accessed July 18, 2004.

7. McCroskey, "The Communication Apprehension Perspective," pp. 13–38. Also J. Ayres, "Perceptions of Speaking Ability: An Explanation for Stage Fright," *Communication Education* 35 (1986): 275–287; A. H. Buss, *Self-Consciousness and Social Anxiety* (San Francisco: W.H. Freeman and Company, 1980).

8. S. Bochner, "Culture Shock due to Contact with Unfamiliar Cultures," in W. J. Lonner, D. L. Dinnel, S. A. Hayes, and D. N. Sattler, eds., *Online Readings in Psychology and Culture* (Unit 8, Chapter 7), 2003. Center for Cross-Cultural Research, Western Washington University, Bellingham, Washington. Online at http://www.wwu.edu/~culture. Accessed July 18, 2004.

9. J. A. Daly, A. L. Vangelista, H. L. Neel, and P. D. Cavanaugh, "Pre-Performance Concerns Associated with Public Speaking Anxiety," *Communication Quarterly* 37 (1989): 39–53; McCroskey, "The Communication Apprehension Perspective," pp. 13–38.

10. J. L. Duda and L. Gano-Overway, "Anxiety in Elite Young Gymnasts: Part II—Sources of Stress," *Technique* (March 1996). Online at http://www.usa gymnastics.org/publications/technique/1996/6/anxiety.html. Accessed July 17, 2004.

11. J. A. Keaton and L. Kelly, "Disposition Versus Situation: Neurocommunicology and the Influence of Trait Apprehension Across Situational Factors on State Public Speaking Anxiety." *Communication Research Reports* 21 (2004): 273–283.

12. "Famous People, Funny Stories."

13. Keaton and Kelly, "Disposition Versus Situation."

14. McCroskey, "The Communication Apprehension Perspective," pp. 13–38; J. Jackson and B. Latané, "Stage Fright as a Function of Number and Type of Co-Performers and Audience," *Journal of Personality and Social Psychology* 40 (1981): 73–85.

15. P. D. MacIntyre and R. C. Gardner, "Language Anxiety: Its Relation to Other Anxieties and to Processing in Native and Second Language," *Language Learning* 41 (1991): 513–534. Also see N. F. Burroughs, V. Marie, and J. C. McCroskey, "Relationships of Self-Perceived Communication Competence and Communication Apprehension with Willingness to Communicate: A Comparison with First and Second Languages," *Communication Research Reports* 20 (2003): 230–239.

16. J. W. Chesebro, J. C. McCroskey, D. F. Atwater, R. M. Bahrenfuss, G. Cawleti, and J. L. Gaudino, "Communication Apprehension and Self-Perceived Communication Competence of At-Risk Students," *Communication Education* 41 (1992): 345–360; J. Ayres, "Perceptions of Speaking Ability: An Explanation for Stage Fright," *Communication Education* 35 (1986): 275–287.

17. "Bridget Fonda, Actress Gallery." http://www.actressgallery.com/bridgetfonda. Accessed July 18, 2004.

18. McCroskey, "The Communication Apprehension Perspective," pp. 13–38.

19. McCroskey, "The Communication Apprehension Perspective," pp. 13–38. Also J. A. Daly and A. H. Buss, "The Transitory Causes of Audience Anxiety," in J. A. Daly and J. C. McCroskey, eds., *Avoiding Communication: Shyness, Reticence, and Communication Apprehension* (London: Sage Publications Inc., 1984), pp. 67–78.

20. P. D. McIntyre, K. A. Thivierge, and J. R. MacDonald, "The Effects of Audience Interest, Responsiveness, and Evaluation on Public Speaking Anxiety and Related Variables." *Communication Research Reports* 14 (1997): 157–168.

21. J. Ayres, "Perceptions of Speaking Ability: An Explanation for Stage Fright," *Communication Education* 35 (1986): 275–287; McCroskey, "The Communication Apprehension Perspective," pp. 13–38.

22. A. Mehrabian, *Silent Messages*, 2nd ed. (Belmont, CA: Wadsworth, 1981), pp. 47–48, 61–62.

23. "Famous People, Funny Stories."

24. "Famous People, Funny Stories." Drawn from Gyles Brandreth, *Great Theatrical Disasters*.

25. J. C. McCroskey, "The Communication Apprehension Perspective," 13–38.

26. J. C. McCroskey, "Measures of Communication-Bound Anxiety." *Speech Monographs* 37 (1970): 269–277. The most recent version of the trait anxiety instrument is the PRCA-24.

27. T. E. Robinson, "Communication Apprehension and the Basic Public Speaking Course: A National Survey of In-Class Treatment Techniques." *Communication Education* 46 (1997):188–197.

28. D. W. Moore, "Firefighters Top Gallup's 'Honesty and Ethics List.'" *The Gallup Poll Monthly* (December 5, 2001): 46–48.

29. R. H. Bruskin, "Fears." *Spectra* 9 (1973): 4. Also D. Wallechinsky, I. Wallace, and A. Wallace, *The Book of Lists* (New York: Bantam Books, 1977), p. 469.

30. Jerry Seinfeld, monologue, *Seinfeld*, episode 61.

31. K. H. Bourdon, J. H. Boyd, D. S. Rae, et al. "Gender Differences in Phobias: Results of the ECA Community Survey." *Journal of Anxiety Disorders* 2 (1988): 227–241.

32. R. R. Behnke and C. R. Sawyer, "Anticipatory Anxiety Patterns for Male and Female Public Speakers." *Communication Education* 49 (2000): 187–195.

33. J. C. Hahner, M. A. Sokoloff, and S. L. Salisch, *Speaking Clearly: Improving Voice and Diction*, 5th ed. (New York: McGraw-Hill, 1997), p. 362.

34. There appears to be no agreement on who first made this comment: Edwin Newman, Edward R. Murrow, or Walter Cronkite. Possibly the three news anchors used variations on the same idea.

35. R. R. Rubin, A. M. Rubin, and F. F. Jordan, "Effects of Instruction on Communication Apprehension and Communication Competence." *Communication Education* 46 (1997): 104–114; W. S. Zabava Ford and A. D. Wolvin, "The Differential Impact of a Basic Communication Course on Perceived Communication Competencies in Class, Work, and Social Contexts," *Communication Education* 42 (1993): 215–223; W. Thompson, *Quantitative Research in Public Address and Communication* (New York: Random House, 1967): 175–176.

36. A. Mulac and A. R. Sherman, "Behavioral Assessment of Speech Anxiety." *Quarterly Journal of Speech* 60 (1974): 134–143.

37. A. M. Bippus and J. A. Daly, "What Do People Think Causes Stage Fright? Naïve Assumptions about the Reasons for Public Speaking Anxiety," *Communication Education* 48 (1999): 63–72. For further examination of the interaction between speech anxiety and preparation, see J. A. Daly, A. L. Vangelista, and D. J. Weber, "Speech Anxiety Affects How People Prepare Speeches: A Protocol Analysis of the Preparation Processes of Speakers," *Communication Monographs* 62 (1995): 383–397.

38. M. T. Motley, "Taking the Terror Out of Talk." *Psychology Today* (January 1988): 47.

39. T. Clevenger, "The Effect of a Physical Change in the Speech Situation upon Experienced Stage Fright," *Quarterly Journal of Speech* 45 (1959): 134–145.

40. J. Ayres, T. Hopf, and D. M. Ayres, "Visualization and Performance Visualization: Applications, Evidence, and Speculation," in J. A. Daly, J. C. McCroskey, J. Ayres, T. Hopf, and D. M. Ayres, eds., *Avoiding Communication: Shyness, Reticence, and Communication Apprehension*, 2nd ed. (Cresskill, NJ: Hampton Press, 1997), pp. 401–422; J. Ayres and T. S. Hopf, "Visualization: Is It More Than Extra-Attention?" *Communication Education* 38 (1989): 1–3; J. Ayres, "Coping with Speech Anxiety: The Power of Positive Thinking." *Communication Education* 37 (1988): 289–296.

41. J. Bauman, "The Gold Medal Mind." *Psychology Today* (May/June 2000). Online at www.psychologytoday.com, p. 1. Accessed November 10, 2003.

42. K. Paauw, "Are You an Olympic Thinker?" Online newsletter, October 2000. Online at http://www.orgcoach.net/newsletter/oct2000.html, p. 1. Accessed November 10, 2003.

43. T. Orlick and J. Partington, "Mental Links to Excellence." *The Sport Psychologist* 2 (1988): 105–130.

44. T. Orlick and J. Partington, Psyched: Inner Views of Winning," 1988, p. 112. Online at http://www.zoneofexcellence.com/Articles/psyched.htm. Accessed August 1, 2005.

45. Orlick and Partington, "Psyched: Inner Views of Winning," p. 112.

46. "Substances and Mental Training," NCAA. Online at www.drugfreesport.com/choices/athletes/training.html, p. 1. Accessed November 10, 2003.

47. Bippus and Daly, "What Do People Think Causes Stage Fright?"

48. Bauman, "The Gold Medal Mind," p. 5.
49. Nazzaro, "Interview with Peter Jenson," p. 1.
50. F. G. De Lacerda, "Applied Sport Psychology: Peak Performance," p. 2. Online at http://airsports.fai.org/sep98/sept9803.html. Accessed November 10, 2003.
51. Bauman, "The Gold Medal Mind," p. 2.
52. See M. Martini, R. R. Behnke, and P. E. King, "The Communication of Public Speaking Anxiety: Perceptions of Asian and American Speakers," *Communication Quarterly* 40 (1992): 279–288.
53. "Sports Performance: Tiger Woods." Online at www.sports-performance.biz/tiger.htm. Accessed November 10, 2003.
54. For additional insights on how visuals aids can increase speaker confidence, see J. Ayres, "Using Visual Aids to Reduce Speech Anxiety," *Communication Research Reports* (June/December 1991): 73–79.
55. T. S. Frobish, "Jamieson Meets Lucas: Eloquence and Pedagogical Model(s) in *The Art of Public Speaking*." *Communication Education* 49 (2000): 239–252.
56. For further discussion of this technique, see W. J. Fremouw and M. D. Scott, "Cognitive Restructuring: An Alternative Method for the Treatment of Communication Apprehension." *Communication Education* 28 (1979): 129–133.
57. Bauman, "The Gold Medal Mind," p. 5.
58. Bauman, "The Gold Medal Mind," p. 4.
59. Bauman, "The Gold Medal Mind," p. 5.
60. J. L. Van Raalte, B. W. Brewer, P. M. Riviera, and A. J. Petitpas, "The Relationship Between Observable Self-Talk and Competitive Junior Tennis Players' Match Performances." *Journal of Exercise Psychology* 16 (1994): 400–415.
61. P. Stalker, *The No-Nonsense Guide to International Migration* (London: New Internationalist Publications, 2001), p. 8.
62. L. A. Samovar and R. E. Porter, *Communication Between Cultures*, 2nd ed. (Belmont, CA: Wadsworth, 1995), p. 199.
63. M. Imhof, "The Social Construction of the Listener: Listening Behavior Across Situations, Perceived Listener Status, and Cultures." *Communication Research Reports* 20 (2003): 357–366.
64. R. B. Adler, N. Towne, and R. F. Proctor, *Looking Out, Looking In* (Belmont, CA: Wadsworth Thomson Learning, 2004).
65. For additional information, see J. Ayres and T. Hopf, *Coping with Speech Anxiety* (Norwood, NJ: Ablex, 1993).
66. For further discussion, see S. B. Butterfield and R. R. Cottone, "Ethical Issues in the Treatment of Communication Apprehension and Avoidance." *Communication Education* 40 (1991): 172–179.

CHAPTER 3

1. R. F. Verderber, *The Challenge of Effective Speaking*, 11th ed. (Belmont, CA: Wadsworth Thomson Learning, 2000): 36.
2. *The Power of Listening* [motion picture] (Scarborough, ON: CRM McGraw-Hill, 1978).
3. F. Wolff, *Perspective Listening* (New York: Holt, Rinehart and Winston, 1983).
4. G. Levoy, "Is Anyone Listening?" *The Toronto Star*, December 10, 1987.
5. S. Hite, *Women and Love* (New York: Alfred Knopf, 1987).
6. K. F. Muenzinger, *The Psychology of Behavior* (New York: Harper, 1942).
7. Lance Armstrong, quoted in "Olympic's Perfect Ten." http://www.sportinglife.com/olympics/perfect_ten/story_get.dor?STORY_NAME=others/00/08/31/manual_083643.html. Accessed July 15, 2004.
8. R. E. Crable, *One to Another: A Guidebook for Interpersonal Communication* (New York: Harper & Row, 1981).
9. C. Rogers and R. E. Farson, "Active Listening," in S. D. Ferguson and S. Ferguson, eds., *Organizational Communication* (New Brunswick, NJ: Transaction Publishers), pp. 319–334.
10. R. G. Nichols and L. A. Stevens, "Six Bad Listening Habits," in R. G. Nichols and L. A. Stevens, eds., *Are You Listening?* (New York: McGraw-Hill, 1957).

11. S. Ferguson and S. Ferguson, "High Resolution Vision Prosthesis Systems: Research after 15 Years," *Journal of Visual Impairment and Blindness* (1986): 523–527.

12. Moody Institute of Science, Sense Perception [videorecording], 2nd ed. (Whittier, CA: Science Institute, 1968).

13. B. A. Wright and M. B. Fitzgerald, "Sound-Discrimination Learning and Auditory Displays." *Proceedings of the 2003 International Conference on Auditory Display*, Boston, Massachusetts, July 2003.

14. A. Koestler, *The Act of Creation* (New York: MacMillan, 1964).

15. E. F. Loftus, *Eyewitness Testimony*, rev. ed. (Cambridge, MA: Harvard University Press, 1996).

16. ABC News, July 9, 2004. Online at http://abcnews.go.com/wire/US/ap20040625_1908.html. Accessed July 9, 2004.

17. S. E. Taylor and S. C. Thompson, "Stalking the Elusive 'Vividness' Effect." *Psychological Review* 89 (1982): 155–181.

18. L. J. Postman, J. S. Bruner, and E. McGinnies, "Personal Values as Selective Factors in Perception," *Journal of Abnormal and Social Psychology* 43 (1948): 142–154.

19. J. Senger, "Seeing Eye to Eye: Practical Problems of Perception," in S. Ferguson and S. D. Ferguson, eds., *Intercom: Readings in Organizational Communication* (Rochelle Park, NJ: Hayden Book Company, 1980): 144–145.

20. N. C. Schaeffer, "Hardly Ever or Constantly: Group Comparisons Using Vague Qualifiers." *Public Opinion Quarterly* 55 (1991): 395.

21. R. D. Wimmer and J. R. Dominick, *Mass Media Research: An Introduction*, 5th ed. (Belmont, CA: Wadsworth, 1997): 356–357.

22. C. Cannell and J. MacDonald, "The Impact of Health News on Attitudes and Behavior." *Journalism Quarterly* 33 (1956): 315–323.

23. L. Festinger, *A Theory of Cognitive Dissonance* (Stanford, CA: Stanford University Press, 1957).

24. E. M. Rogers and R. Agarwala-Rogers, *Communication in Organizations* (New York: The Free Press, 1976), p. 91.

25. "The Good Times Are Killing Me," [TVTV production (California and New York)], funded by Ford and Rockefeller foundations, aired on PBS in 1975.

26. "Mardi Gras." Online at http://www.folkstreams.net/context,43. Accessed July 7, 2004.

27. G. A. Miller, "The Magical Number Seven, Plus or Minus Two: Some Limits on Our Capacity for Processing Information," in R. C. Anderson and D. P. Ausubel, eds., *Readings in the Psychology of Cognition* (New York: Holt, Rinehart and Winston, Inc., 1965), pp. 241–267.

28. D. B. Orr, "Time-Compressed Speech—A Perspective." *Journal of Communication* 17 (1967): 223.

29. R. G. Nichols, "Do We Know How to Listen? Practical Helps in a Modern Age." *Speech Teacher* 10 (March 1961): 118–124.

30. A. D. Wolvin and C. G. Coakley, *Listening*, 2nd ed. (Dubuque, IA: William C. Brown, 1985), p. 15.

31. D. Grant, "Blind Students 'Speed Listen,'" *Globe and Mail* (January 10, 1983): 14.

32. A. H. Maslow and N. L. Mintz, "Effects of Esthetic Surroundings: I. Initial Effects of Three Esthetic Conditions upon Perceiving 'Energy' and 'Well-Being' in Faces." *Journal of Psychology* 41 (1956): 253. Also see N. L. Mintz, "Effects of Esthetic Surroundings: II. Prolonged and Repeated Experience in a 'Beautiful' and 'Ugly' Room." *Journal of Psychology* 41 (1956): 465–466.

33. E. Cohen and A. Cohen, *Planning the Electronic Office* (New York: McGraw-Hill, 1983): 183.

34. W. Griffitt and R. Veitch, "Hot and Crowded: Influences of Population Density and Temperature on Interpersonal Affective Behavior," *Journal of Personality and Social Psychology* 17 (1971): 92–98.

35. R. B. Adler and G. Rodman, *Understanding Human Communication*, 5th ed. (Harcourt Brace College Publishers, 1994), p. 186.

36. Wolff, *Perspective Listening*.

37. R. S. Adams and B. Biddle, *Realities of Teaching: Explorations with Video Tape* (New York: Holt, Rinehart and Winston, 1970).

38. L. B. Rosenfeld and J. M. Civikly, *With Words Unspoken: The Nonverbal Experience* (New York: Holt, Rinehart and Winston, 1976).

39. R. Sommer, *Personal Space: The Behavioral Basis of Design* (Englewood Cliffs, NJ: Prentice-Hall, 1969).

40. J. C. McCroskey and R. W. McVetta, "Classroom Seating Arrangements: Instructional Communication Theory Versus Student Preferences." Paper presented at the annual meeting of the International Communication Association, Chicago, IL, ERIC 154460, 1978. http://www.jamescmccroskey.com/publications/82.htm. Accessed July 15, 2004.

41. P. D. MacIntyre and J. R. MacDonald, "Public Speaking Anxiety: Perceived Competence and Audience Congeniality." *Communication Education* 47 (1998): 359–365.

42. Cited in R. H. Bolton, *People Skills: How to Assert Yourself, Listen to Others and Resolve Conflicts* (New York: Simon & Schuster, 1986).

CHAPTER 4

1. A. N. Miller, "An Exploration of Kenyan Public Speaking Patterns with Implications for the American Introductory Public Speaking Course," *Communication Education* 51 (2002): 168–182.

2. T. S. Frobish, "Jamieson Meets Lucas: Eloquence and Pedagogical Model(s) in *The Art of Public Speaking.*" *Communication Education* 49 (2000): 239–252; M. Javidi, V. C. Downs, and J. F. Nussbaum, "A Comparative Analysis of Teachers' Use of Dramatic Style Behaviors at Higher and Secondary Educational Levels." *Communication Education* 37 (1988): 278–288; K. Jamieson, *Eloquence in an Electronic Age: The Transformation of Political Speechmaking* (New York: Oxford University Press, 1988).

3. W. B. Pillsbury, *Attention* (New York: The Macmillan Company, 1908). See also M. Billings, "Duration of Attention," *Psychological Review* 21 (1914): 124–135.

4. W. D. Scott, *Psychology of Public Speaking* (New York: Noble and Noble Publishers, Inc., 1925).

5. N. Postman, *Amusing Ourselves to Death: Public Discourse in the Age of Show Business* (New York: Penquin Books, 1985).

6. B. E. Bradley, *Fundamentals of Speech Communication*, 3rd ed. (Dubuque, IA: W.C. Brown, 1981), pp. 205–206.

7. D. B. Orr, "Time-Compressed Speech—A Perspective." *Journal of Communication* 17 (1967): 223. An even wider gap is identified in studies cited by A. D. Wolvin and C. Gwynn Coakley, *Listening*, 2nd ed. (Dubuque, IA: William C. Brown, 1985): 15.

8. Excerpt from speech by Sebastian Samur, communication student, 2004.

9. Excerpt from speech by Versna Chuop, communication student, 2003.

10. Speech by Kristen Pidduck, communication student, 2004.

11. L. Crewe, "Rhetorical Beginnings, Professional and Amateur," *College Composition and Communication* 38 (1987): 346–350. Online at http://www.rci.rutgers.edu/~lcrew/pubd/rhetbegi.html. Accessed on May 5, 2006.

12. The statistics, which form the basis for this example, were discussed on the *Oprah Winfrey* show, July 15, 2004.

13. Excerpt from speech by Erin Priddle, communication student, 2004.

14. D. Nimmo and J. E. Combs, *Mediated Political Realities*, 2nd ed. (New York: Longman, 1990): 56.

15. L. Crewe, "Rhetorical Beginnings, Professional and Amateur," *College Composition and Communication* 38 (1987): 346–350. Online at http://www.rci.rutgers.edu/~lcrew/pubd/rhetbegi.html. Accessed on May 5, 2006.

16. B. W. Jenkins and R. G. Eakins, *Sex Differences in Human Communication* (Boston: Houghton Mifflin Company, 1978), pp. 75–76.

17. Excerpt from speech by Joanna Mennie, communication student, 2004.

18. Excerpt from speech by Mary Kathryn Roberts, communication student, 2004.

19. K. E. Menzel and L. J. Carrell, "The Relationship Between Preparation and Performance in Public Speaking." *Communication Education* 43 (1994): 17–26.

20. Menzel and Carrell, "The Relationship Between Preparation and Performance in Public Speaking," pp. 17–26.

CHAPTER 5

1. W. L. Schramm, "How Communication Works," in W. L. Schramm, ed., *The Process and Effects of Communication* (Urbana: University of Illinois Press, 1954), pp. 3–26.

2. T. Striphas, "A Dialectic with the Everyday: Communication and Cultural Politics on Oprah Winfrey's Book Club." *Critical Studies in Media Communication* 20 (2003): 297.

3. M. Rokeach, *The Nature of Human Values* (New York: Free Press, 1973).

4. A. H. Maslow, *Motivation and Personality*, 2nd ed. (New York: Harper & Row, 1954), pp. 80–92.

5. E. M. Rogers and F. F. Shoemaker, *Communication of Innovations* (New York: Free Press, 1971).

6. M. Rokeach, *The Open and Closed Mind* (New York: Basic Books, 1960).

7. E. P. Bettinghaus and M. J. Cody, *Persuasive Communication*, 5th ed. (Fort Worth, TX: Harcourt Brace College, 1994), p. 163.

8. E. Hoffer, *The True Believer: Thoughts on the Nature of Mass Movements* (New York: Harper & Row, Publishing, Inc., 1951).

9. See the following discussions of the relationship between esteem and persuasibility: J. Brockner and M. Elkind, "Self-Esteem and Reactance: Further Evidence of Attitudinal and Motivational Consequences," *Journal of Experimental Social Psychology* 21 (1990): 346–361; E. P. Bettinghaus and M. J. Cody, *Persuasive Communication*, 5th ed. (Fort Worth, TX: Harcourt Brace College, 1994); and H. Leventhal and S. I. Perloe, "A Relationship Between Self-Esteem and Persuasibility," *Journal of Abnormal and Social Psychology* 64 (1962): 385–388.

10. J. C. Nunnally and H. M. Bobren, "Variables Governing the Willingness to Receive Communications on Mental Health." *Journal of Personality* 27 (1959): 275–290.

11. Excerpted from speech by Heidi Shelton, communication student, 2004.

12. C. Hovland and M. Sherif, *Social Judgment Assimilation and Contrast Effects in Communication and Attitude Change* (New Haven, CT: Yale University Press, 1961). Also see C. Sherif, M. Sherif, and R. Nebergall, *Attitudes and Attitude Change: The Social Judgment Approach* (Philadelphia: W.B. Saunders, 1965).

13. G. J. S. Wilde, "Effects of Mass Media Communications on Health and Safety Habits: An Overview of Issues and Evidence." *Addiction* 88 (7): 983–996.

14. Rokeach, *The Nature of Human Values*.

15. Barack Obama, "Elections: Text of Obama's Address at Convention," AP Wire, *Seattle-Post Intelligencer*, July 27, 2004, http://seattlepi.nwsource.com/national/apelection_story, p. 4. Accessed August 15, 2004.

16. Speech to Standing Committee on Justice and Human Rights, Parliament of Canada, Ottawa, Canada, November 1, 2001.

17. K. Burke, *A Rhetoric of Motives* (Englewood Cliffs, NJ: Prentice–Hall, 1950), pp. 20–46.

18. George Bush, speech to the nation announcing allied military action in the Persian Gulf, January 16, 1991.

19. S. Lepley, "First Lady Gives Hope to Families of Flight 93." *Daily American* (September 11, 2002). Online at http://www.dailyamerican.com/disaster.html. Accessed September 30, 2002.

20. See discussions in T. S. Frobish, "Jamieson Meets Lucas: Eloquence and Pedagogical Model(s) in *The Art of Public Speaking*." *Communication Education* 49 (2000): 239–252; M. Javidi, V. C. Downs, and J. F. Nussbaum, "A Comparative Analysis of Teachers' Use of Dramatic Style Behaviors at Higher and Secondary Educational Levels," *Communication Education* 37 (1988): 278–288; K. Jamieson, *Eloquence in an Electronic Age: The Transformation of Political Speechmaking* (New York: Oxford University Press, 1988); and R. W. Norton, *Communicator Style: Theory, Application, and Measures* (Beverly Hills, CA: Sage, 1983), p. 238.

21. George Bush, address to the nation announcing allied military action in the Persian Gulf, January 16, 1991.

22. Hillary Rodham Clinton, speech to the United Nations Fourth World Conference on Women, Beijing, China, September 5, 1995.

23. Sarah Johnson, personal experience, e-mail correspondence, May 24, 2004.

24. "Are Chicanos the Same as Mexicans?" Movimiento Estudiantil Chicana/o de Aztlan (MECHA de Tejaztlan), student organization at the University of Texas at Austin,

posted on April 30, 1998. Online at http://studentorgs.utexas.edu/mecha/archive/chicano.html. Accessed April 18, 2006. Page maintained by Jorge Tapia.

25. *"Fag Hags*: Women Who Love Men." *The Passionate Eye*, Canadian Broadcast Corporation (CBC), September 29, 2005.
26. Milton Himsl, personal experience, e-mail correspondence, May 24, 2004.
27. A. Ballard, "Mandela: The Man, the Legend, the Hero."Online at http://wblsi.com/blk_history/mandela.htm. Accessed on June 2, 2002.
28. John F. Kennedy, inaugural address to the nation, Washington, DC, January 20, 1961.
29. Ronald Reagan, "Reagan's D-Day 40th Anniversary Speech to Vets," June 6, 1984. Reported on NewsMax Wires, June 6, 2004. Online at http://www.newsmax.com/archives/articles/2004/6/6/140623.shtml.

CHAPTER 6

1. A. H. Monroe, "Measurement and Analysis of Audience Reaction to Student Speakers' Studies in Attitude Changes." *Bulletin of Purdue University Studies in Higher Education* 22 (1937).
2. A. N. Miller, "An Exploration of Kenyan Public Speaking Patterns with Implications for the American Introductory Public Speaking Course." *Communication Education* 51 (2002): 168–182.
3. C. A. Braithwaite, "Sa'ah Naagháí Bik'eh Hózhóón: An Ethnography of Navajo Educational Communication Practices." *Communication Education* 46 (1997): 219–233.
4. K. Jamieson, *Eloquence in an Electronic Age: The Transformation of Political Speechmaking* (New York: Oxford University Press, 1988). Also see T. S. Frobish, "Jamieson Meets Lucas: Eloquence and Pedagogical Model(s) in *The Art of Public Speaking*." *Communication Education* 49 (2000): 239–252; M. Javidi, V. C. Downs, and J. F. Nussbaum, "A Comparative Analysis of Teachers' Use of Dramatic Style Behaviors at Higher and Secondary Educational Levels." *Communication Education* 37 (1988): 278–288.
5. K. E. Menzel and L. J. Carrell, "The Relationship Between Preparation and Performance in Public Speaking." *Communication Education* 43 (1994): 17–26.
6. J. C. McCroskey and R. S. Mehrley, "The Effects of Disorganization and Nonfluency on Attitude Change and Source Credibility." *Speech Monographs* 36 (1969): 13–21. Also K. K. Sereno and G. J. Hawkins, "The Effects of Variations on Speakers' Nonfluency upon Audience Ratings of Attitude Toward the Speech Topic and Speakers' Credibility." *Speech Monographs* 34 (1967): 58–64.
7. "Why My Brain Hates Your Mistakes." Reuters, April 26, 2004, Washington, D.C. Reproduced on Yahoo online news service, www.yahoo.com. Accessed June 3, 2005.
8. T. Freeman and R. R. Behnke, "Behavioral Inhibition and the Attribution of Public Speaking Anxiety." *Communication Education* 46 (1997): 175–187.
9. P. Ekman and W. V. Friesen, "Nonverbal Behavior and Psychopsychology," in R. J. Friedman and M. N. Katz, eds., *The Psychology of Depression: Contemporary Theory and Research* (Washington, DC: J. Winston, 1974).
10. J. K. Burgoon, T. Birk, and M. Pfau, "Nonverbal Behaviors, Persuasion, and Credibility." *Human Communication Research* 17 (1990): 140–169.
11. J. Mulholland, *The Language of Negotiation* (London: Routledge, 1991), p. 78.
12. J. C. McCroskey, T. Jensen, and C. Valencia, "Measurement of the Credibility of Peers and Spouses." Paper presented at the International Communication Association Convention, Montreal, 1973. Also J. L. Whitehead, Jr., "Factors of Source Credibility." *Quarterly Journal of Speech* 54 (February 1968): 59–63.
13. S. W. Littlejohn, "A Bibliography of Studies Related to Variables of Source Credibility," in N. A. Shearer, ed., *Bibliographic Annual in Speech Communication* (New York: Speech Communication Association, 1972).
14. P. Ekman, *Telling Lies: Clues to Deceit in the Marketplace, Politics, and Marriage* (New York: Norton, Norton, 1985), p. 107.
15. *Bridging the Culture Gap* [videorecording]. San Francisco, CA: Copeland Griggs Productions, 1983.
16. Monroe, "Measurement and Analysis."
17. *Webster's 1913 Dictionary*. Online at http://www.webster-dictionary.org/definition/rhythm. Accessed June 22, 2004.

18. Mulholland, *The Language of Negotiation*, p. 89.

19. S. E. Lucas, *The Art of Public Speaking*, 6th ed. (Boston: McGraw Hill), p. 298.

20. L. B. Rosenfeld and J. M. Civikly, *With Words Unspoken: The Nonverbal Experience* (New York: Holt Rinehart and Winston, 1976).

21. R. D. Albert and G. L. Nelson, "Hispanic/Anglo-American Differences in Attributions to Paralinguistic Behavior." *International Journal of Intercultural Relations* 17 (1993): 19–40.

22. S. E. Lucas, *The Art of Public Speaking*, p. 298.

23. Interview with Edwin Edwards, New Orleans, Louisiana, February 20, 1970. Reported in *Edwin Edwards: A Study in Ethos*, unpublished M.A. thesis (University of Houston, 1971).

24. D. Diamond, commencement speech, University College of the Fraser Valley. Online at www.headlinestheatre.com/honourdoc.html. Accessed November 5, 2003.

25. A. Mehrabian, "Attitudes Inferred from Non-immediacy of Verbal Communication." *Journal of Verbal Learning and Verbal Behavior* 6 (1967): 294–295.

26. A. N. Miller, "An Exploration of Kenyan Public Speaking Patterns with Implications for the American Introductory Public Speaking Course." *Communication Education* 51 (2002): 179.

27. E. Haley, "Organization as Source: Consumers' Understandings of Organizational Sponsorship of Advocacy Advertising." *Journal of Advertising* 25 (1996): 19–36. Also see Whitehead, Jr. "Factors of Source Credibility," pp. 59–63.

28. E. T. Hall, *The Hidden Dimension* (Garden City, NY: Anchor Books, 1969).

29. A. Mehrabian, *Nonverbal Communication* (Hawthorne, NY: Aldine, 1972).

30. M. L. Knapp, *Nonverbal Communication in Human Interaction* (New York: Holt, Rinehart and Winston, 1972), p. 5.

31. See J. F. Andersen, "Teacher Immediacy as a Moderator of Teaching Effectiveness," in D. Nimmo, ed., *Communication Yearbook* (New Brunswick, NJ: Transaction Books, 1979), pp. 543–559. Also Jane Gorham, "The Relationship Between Verbal Teacher Immediacy Behaviors and Student Learning," *Communication Education* 37 (1988): 40–53; J. Andersen, R. Norton, and J. F. Nussbaum, "Three Investigations Exploring Relationship among Perceived Communicator Style, Perceived Teacher Immediacy, Perceived Teacher-Student Solidarity, Teacher Effectiveness, and Student Learning," *Communication Education* 30 (1981): 377–392.

32. See Q. Zhang, "Immediacy, Humor, Power Distance, and Classroom Communication Apprehension in Chinese College Classrooms." *Communication Quarterly* 53 (2005): 87–108; J. S. Chesebro, "Effects of Teacher Clarity and Nonverbal Immediacy on Student Learning, Receiver Apprehension, and Affect." *Communication Education* 52 (2003): 135–147; K. D. Roach and P. R. Byrne, "A Cross-Cultural Comparison of Instructor Communication in American and German Classrooms." *Communication Education* 50 (2001): 1–14; R. G. Powell and B. Harville, "The Effects of Teacher Immediacy and Clarity on Instructional Outcomes: An Intercultural Assessment." *Communication Education* 39 (1990): 369–379; J. K. Burgoon and J. L. Hale, "Nonverbal Violations Expectancy Model: Elaboration and Application to Immediacy Behaviors." *Communication Monographs* 55 (1988): 58–79; J. Andersen and J. C. Withrow, "The Impact of Lecturer Nonverbal Expressiveness on Improving Mediated Instruction." *Communication Education* 30 (1981): 377–393.

33. C. I. Hovland, I. L. Janis, and H. H. Kelley, *Communication and Persuasion* (New Haven, CT: Yale University Press, 1953).

34. E. Stack, "Dressing Marcia: The Construction of Gender in the 1990s." Online at http://collection.nlc-bnc.ca/100/202/300/mediatribe95/marcia.html. Accessed June 26, 2004.

35. J. T. Molloy, *The New Woman's Dress for Success Book* (New York: Warner Books, 1996).

36. P. Noonan, *Simply Speaking: How to Communicate Your Ideas with Style, Substance, and Clarity* (New York: Harper Collins, 1998), pp. 183–184.

37. R. R. Douglass, *A Study of the Effect of the Introduction of Visual Communication Devices in a Sermon*. Unpublished doctoral dissertation, Grace Theological Seminary, 1997. Cited by K. Bickel, "Preaching to Listeners: Communicating with Contemporary Listeners," Evangelical Homiletics Society, 2002. Online at www.evangelicalhomiletics.com/Papers 2002/Bickel.htm. Accessed July 11, 2004.

38. R. B. Adler and L. B. Rosenfeld, *Interplay*, 4th ed. (Holt, Rinehart and Winston, Inc., 1989), p. 163.

39. L. S. Harms, "Listener Judgments of Status Cues in Content Free Speech." *Quarterly Journal of Speech* 47 (1961): 164–168.

40. J. Mills and E. Aronson, "Opinion Change as a Function of the Communicator's Attractiveness and Desire to Influence." *Journal of Personality and Social Psychology* 1 (1965): 73–77.

41. For more information on the importance of personal appearance in speechmaking, see R. M. Perloff, *The Dynamics of Persuasion* (Hillsdale, NJ: Erlbaum, 1993), pp. 149–152. Also see J. C. McCroskey, V. P. Richmond, and J. A. Daly, "Toward the Measurement of Perceived Homophily"; P. N. Hamid, "Style of Dress as a Perceptual Cue in Impression Formation." *Perceptual and Motor Skills* 26 (1968): 904–906.

42. H. I. Douty, "Influence of Clothing on Perception of Persons." *Journal of Home Economics* 55 (1963): 197–202. Cited in Lawrence B. Rosenfeld and Jean M. Civikly, *With Words Unspoken: The Nonverbal Experience* (New York: Holt, Rinehart and Winston, 1976), p. 73. Also see R. E. Bassett, "Effects of Source Attire on Judgments of Credibility." *Central States Speech Journal* 30 (1979): 282–285; and J. K. Burgoon, D. B. Buller, and W. G. Woodall, *Nonverbal Communication: The Unspoken Dialogue* (New York: McGraw-Hill, 1996).

43. M. J. Horn, *The Second Skin: An Interdisciplinary Study of Clothing* (Boston: Houghton Mifflin, 1968).

44. V. P. Richmond, J. C. McCroskey, and S. K. Payne, *Nonverbal Behavior in Interpersonal Relations* (Englewood Cliffs, NJ: Prentice Hall, 1991), p. 211.

45. E. J. Natalle and F. Bodenheimer, "Prop-er Attire." Presenters University, sponsored by InFocus. Online at http://www.presentersuniversity.com/delivery_Attire.php. Accessed July 11, 2005.

46. Natalle and Bodenheimer, "Prop-er Attire."

47. D. S. Ellis, "Speech and Social Status in America." *Social Forces* 14 (1967): 431–437.

48. N. Carr-Ruffino, *The Promotable Woman* (Franklin Lakes, NJ: Career Press), p. 251.

49. Carr-Ruffino, *The Promotable Woman*, p. 251.

50. C. I. Hovland, I. L. Janis, and H. H. Kelley, *Communication and Persuasion* (New Haven, CT: Yale University Press, 1953); Whitehead, Jr., "Factors of Source Credibility," pp. 59–63.

51. Richmond, McCroskey, and Payne, *Nonverbal Behavior in Interpersonal Relations*, p. 226.

52. J. K. Burgoon, T. Birk, and M. Pfau, "Nonverbal Behaviors, Persuasion, and Credibility," pp. 140–169; G. R. Miller and M. A. Hewgill, "The Effect of Variations in Nonfluency on Audience Ratings of Source Credibility." *The Quarterly Journal of Speech* 50 (1984): 36–44.

53. Mulholland, *The Language of Negotiation*, p. 89.

54. J. L. Whitehead, Jr., "Factors of Source Credibility," pp. 59–63.

55. "GOP Backs Away from Miller's Blast," September 3, 2004. Online at http://www.msnbc.msn.com/id/5897622. Accessed April 2, 2005.

56. Media conference on Aboriginal issues, Carleton University, December 10, 1998, Ottawa, Ontario.

57. S. D. Ferguson, *Communication Planning: An Integrated Approach* (Thousand Oaks, CA: Sage, 1999), pp. 140–143.

58. R. B. Adler and N. Towne, *Looking Out, Looking In* (New York: Holt, Rinehart & Winston, 1990).

59. K. E. Menzel and L. J. Carrell, "The Relationship Between Preparation and Performance in Public Speaking," *Communication Education* 43 (1994): 17–26.

60. L. D. Crane, *Six Rehearsal Techniques for the Public Speaker: Improving Memory, Increasing Delivery Skills, and Reducing Speech Stress*. Paper presented at SCA, Washington, DC, 1977. Cited by Menzel and Carrell, 1994, p. 18.

61. E. J. Kempf, "Abraham Lincoln's Organic and Emotional Neuroses." *A.M.A. Archives of Neurology and Psychiatry* 67 (1952): 419–433.

CHAPTER 7

1. See, for example, W. J. Ong, *Orality and Literacy: The Technologizing of the Word*, 2nd ed. (New York: Routledge, 2002).

2. W. J. Seiler, "The Conjunctive Influence of Source Credibility and the Use of Visual Materials on Communication Effectiveness," *Southern Speech Communication Journal* 37 (Winter 1971): 174–185.

3. H. Gardner, *Frames of Mind: The Theory of Multiple Intelligences* (New York: Basic Books, 1983). See also E. Dale, *Audiovisual Methods in Teaching*, 3rd ed. (New York: Holt, Rinehart, and Winston, 1969).

4. K. L. Alesandrini, "Strategies That Influence Memory for Advertising Communication," in R. J. Harris, ed., *Information Processing Research in Advertising* (Hillsdale, NJ: Lawrence Erlbaum, 1983). See also T. L. Childers and M. J. Houston, "Conditions for a Picture-Superiority Effect on Consumer Memory." *Journal of Consumer Research* 11 (1984): 643–654; D. L. Horton and C. B. Mills, "Human Learning and Memory." *Annual Review of Psychology* 35 (1984). 361–394; K. A. Lutz and R. J. Lutz, "Effects of Interactive Imagery on Learning: Applications to Advertising." *Journal of Applied Psychology* 62 (1977): 493–498; D. J. MacInnis and L. L. Price, "The Role of Imagery in Information Processing." *Journal of Consumer Research* 13 (1987): 473–491.

5. K. E. Menzel and L. J. Carrell, "The Relationship Between Preparation and Performance in Public Speaking." *Communication Education* 43 (1994): 17–26.

6. J. C. McCroskey, in J. A. Daly and J. C. McCroskey, eds., *Avoiding Communication: Shyness, Reticence, and Communication Apprehension* (Beverly Hills: Sage, 1984). http://64.233.161.104/search?q=ache:U64hHX_ZmPkJ:www.cla.purdue.edu/academic/comm/pdf_doc_etc/com_114/chap12.doc+James+C.+McCroskey,+Communication+Apprehension,+udderly&hl=en. Accessed August 1, 2005.

7. S. M. Kosslyn, "The Medium and the Message in Mental Imagery: A Theory." *Psychological Review* 88 (1981): 46–66.

8. Pictographs collected on a site by Elizabeth Brunner. Online at http://www.csc.calpoly.edu/~ebrunner/ExcelPictographs.html. Accessed October 2, 2004. The examples come from other sites, such as www.baddogcomputer.com/unidial/assoc.htm (dollar bill example); ClarisWorks Tutorial at www.rialto.k12.ca.us/frisbie/pictogram.html (chili pepper example); USDA studies reported in *Journal of Agricultural and Food Chemistry* 44 (1996): 701–705, 3426–3443; and USDA studies reported in *Journal of Agricultural and Food Chemistry* 46 (1998): 2686–2693 (fruit and vegetable pictograph).

9. J. Downing and C. Garmon, "Teaching Students in the Basic Course How to Use Presentation Software." *Communication Education* 50 (2001): 218–229.

10. D. R. Vogel, G. W. Dickson, and J. A. Lehman, *Persuasion and the Role of Visual Presentation Support: The UM/3M Study* (St. Paul, MN: 3M General Offices, 1986).

CHAPTER 8

1. Alyssa Jacobs, communication student, 2004.

2. K. E. Rowan, "A New Pedagogy for Explanatory Public Speaking: Why Arrangement Should Not Substitute for Invention." *Communication Education* 44 (1995): 236–250.

3. Rowan, "A New Pedagogy," pp. 236–250.

4. M. Nissani, "Retrospective Reflections on Atoms and Stars: The Counter-Intuitive Nature of Science." http://www.is.wayne.edu/mnissani/a&s/LESSONS.htm.

5. Rowan, "A New Pedagogy," pp. 236–250.

6. Rowan, "A New Pedagogy," pp. 236–250.

7. Rowan, "A New Pedagogy," pp. 236–250.

8. E. P. Bettinghaus and M. J. Cody, *Persuasive Communication*, 5th ed. (Fort Worth, TX: Harcourt Brace College, 1994). See also J. C. Jahnke, "Serial Position Effects in Immediate Serial Recall." *Journal of Verbal Learning and Verbal Behavior* 2 (1963): 284–287.

9. David Bowie, commencement address, Berklee College of Music, May 8, 1999. Online at http://www.berklee.edu/html. Accessed September 20, 2002.

10. Excerpt from speech by Anne Clairmont, communication student, 2004.

11. Wangari Maathai, acceptance speech for Nobel Peace Prize, Oslo, Norway, December 10, 2004. http://nobelprize.org/peace/laureates/2004/maathai-lecture-text.html.

12. L. Crewe, "Rhetorical Beginnings, Professional and Amateur." *College Composition and Communication* 38 (1987): 346–350. http://www.rci.rutgers.edu/~lcrew/pubd/rhetbegi.html. Accessed on May 5, 2006.

13. Editorial, "In the Richest Nation in World, 33 Million Live in Poverty." *The Emmitsburg Dispatch* 7 (July 2003): 1. http://www.emmitsburgdispatch.com/2003/July/editorial .shtml. Accessed July 8, 2004.

14. Ray Bradbury, commencement speech, California Institute of Technology, 2000. Online at http://pr.caltech.edu/commencement/00/c2kbradburyspeech.html. Accessed September 20, 2002.

15. L. Crewe, "Rhetorical Beginnings, Professional and Amateur," *College Composition and Communication* 38 (1987): 346–350. http://www.rci.rutgers.edu/~lcrew/pubd/ rhetbegi.html. Accessed on May 5, 2006.

16. Barbara Bush, commencement address, Wellesley College, Wellesley, Massachusetts, June 1990.

17. T. S. Frobish, "Jamieson Meets Lucas: Eloquence and Pedagogical Model(s) in *The Art of Public Speaking.*" *Communication Education* 49 (2000): 239-252.

18. Excerpted from a speech by Andrea Ball, communication student, 2004.

19. One Internet source attributed this quotation to author Stuart Wilde; the others listed the quotation as anonymous.

20. M. Javidi, V. C. Downs, and J. F. Nussbaum, "A Comparative Analysis of Teachers' Use of Dramatic Style Behavior at Higher and Secondary Educational Levels," *Communication Education* 37 (1988): 278–288; J. W. Neuliep, "An Examination of the Content of High School Teachers' Humor in the Classroom and the Development of an Inductivity Derived Taxonomy of Classroom Humor," *Communication Education* 40 (1991): 343–355; D. Zillmann and J. Bryant, "Uses and Effects of Humor in Educational Ventures," in P.E. McGhee and J.H. Goldstein, eds., *Handbook of Humor Research*, Vol. II: Applied Studies (Springer-Verlag: New York, 1983), pp. 173–195.

21. Ronald Reagan, "A Time for Choosing." a speech delivered in support of Barry Goldwater, October 27, 1964.

22. Bradbury, commencement speech, 2000.

23. J. C. McCroskey and R. S. Mehrley, "The Effects of Disorganization and Nonfluency on Attitude Change and Source Credibility," *Speech Monographs* 36 (1969): 13–21; also K. K. Sereno and G. J. Hawkins, "The Effects of Variations on Speakers' Nonfluency upon Audience Ratings of Attitude Toward the Speech Topic and Speakers' Credibility." *Speech Monographs* 34 (1967): 58–64.

24. "History of the Croissant." *Healthy Home News* 8 (2004), Chelsea, Quebec, p. 3.

25. "What Are the Odds? Not a Lotto Chance." CBC News Indepth: Gambling, CBC News Online, October 24, 2005. www.cbc.ca. Accessed on May 2, 2006.

26. Hilary M. Weston, "Stories and Reflections: My Five Years as Lieutenant Governor." The Canadian Club, Toronto, Ontario, December 10, 2001. www.lt.gov.on.ca/sections_ english/history_middle_frame/hweston_speeches. Accessed November 5, 2003.

27. Referenced on http://www.enotalone.com/forum/showthread.php?t=131708 and attributed to musician and photographer Justin Winokur, http://www.justinwinokur .com. Accessed on April 30, 2006.

28. Bronislaw Malinowski, cited on "Famous People, Funny Stories." Original source: M. Kranes, F. Worth, S. Tremarius, M. Driscoll, M. Kuanes, and F. L. Worth, eds., *5087 Trivia Questions and Answers* (New York: Black Dog and Leventhal Publishers, Inc.). Online at http://www.anecdotage.com/index.php?aid=12880. Accessed July 18, 2004.

29. D. Meissner, "Luna to Stay in Adopted Home." CP wire story, *Globe and Mail*, online edition (July 29, 2004). www.globeandmail.com. Accessed July 30, 2004.

30. M. Javidi, V. C. Downs, and J. F. Nussbaum, "A Comparative Analysis of Teachers' Use of Dramatic Style Behaviors at Higher and Secondary Educational Levels," *Communication Education* 37 (1988): 278–288; also R. W. Norton, *Communicator Style: Theory, Application, and Measures* (Beverly Hills, CA: Sage, 1983), p. 238; K. Jamieson, *Eloquence in an Electronic Age: The Transformation of Political Speechmaking* (New York: Oxford University Press, 1988); and T. S. Frobish, "Jamieson Meets Lucas: Eloquence and Pedagogical Model(s) in *The Art of Public Speaking.*" *Communication Education* 49 (2000): 239–252.

31. Excerpt from speech by Erin Priddle, communication student, 2004.

32. *NIST/SEMATECH e-Handbook of Statistical Methods.* Online at http://www.itl.nist.gov/ div898/handbook. Accessed August 16, 2004.

33. Ronald Reagan, Republican National Convention, 1964.

34. Billy Joel, commencement address, Berklee College of Music, May 1993. Online at http://www.berklee.edu/html. Accessed September 20, 2002.

35. Excerpt from speech by Erin Priddle, communication student, 2004.

36. B. Martin, "Defamation Law and Free Speech." Online at http://www.uow.edu.au/arts/sts/bmartin/dissent/documents/defamation.html. Accessed August 16, 2004.

37. Excerpt from speech by "Gilda," delivered at a Washington, DC, candlelight vigil, convened in support of Cindy Sheehan's demonstration outside Bush's Texas ranch, August 17, 2005. Reported in the online edition of *The Independent*. Online at http://comment.independent.co.uk/podium/article307444.ece. Accessed August 24, 2005.

38. Excerpted from speech by Kristen Pidduck, communication student, 2004.

CHAPTER 9

1. Aristotle, *Rhetoric*, II.1, trans. W. Rhys Roberts (New York: Modern Library), pp. 90–91. The term *ethos* refers to the credibility or character of a speaker.

2. P. A. Meador, Jr., "Speech Education at Rome." *Western Speech* 31 (1967): 14.

3. Quintilian, *The Institutio Oratoria*, 12.1.

4. C. I. Hovland, I. L. Janis, and H. H. Kelley, *Communication and Persuasion* (New Haven, CT: Yale University Press, 1953).

5. K. E. Anderson, *An Experimental Study of the Interaction of Artistic and Non-Artistic Ethos in Persuasion*. Unpublished Ph.D. dissertation, University of Wisconsin, 1961; K. Anderson and T. Clevenger, Jr., "A Summary of Experimental Research in Ethos." *Speech Monographs* 30 (1963): 59–78.

6. J. C. McCroskey, "Scales for the Measurement of Ethos." *Speech Monographs* 33 (1966): 65–72.

7. D. K. Berlo, J. B. Lemert, and R. L. Mertz, "Evaluating the Acceptability of Message Sources." *Public Opinion Quarterly* 33 (1969): 563–576. An earlier representation of their research appeared in Research Monograph, Department of Communication, Michigan State University, 1966.

8. J. C. McCroskey, "Scales for the Measurement of Ethos." *Speech Monographs* 33 (1966): 65–72.

9. Berlo, Lemert, and Mertz, "Evaluating the Acceptability of Message Sources," pp. 563–576.

10. R. G. Smith, "Source Credibility Context Effects," *Speech Monographs* 40 (1973): 303–309; also Jack R. Whitehead, "Factors of Source Credibility." *Quarterly Journal of Speech* 54 (1968): 61–63.

11. S. W. Littlejohn, "A Bibliography of Studies Related to Variables of Source Credibility," in N. A. Shearer, ed., *Bibliographic Annual in Speech Communication* (New York: Speech Communication Association, 1972).

12. Smith, "Source Credibility Context Effects," pp. 61–63.

13. "Teresa Heinz Promotes 'Women's Voices,'" July 27, 2004, Democratic National Convention, Boston, Massachusetts. Online at http://www.cnn.com/2004/ALLPOLITICS/07/27/dems.teresa/index.html. Accessed July 28, 2004.

14. E. M. Rogers and D. K. Bhowmik, "Homophily-Heterophily: Relational Concepts for Communication Research," *Public Opinion Quarterly* 34 (1970): 523–538; E. M. Rogers and F. F. Shoemaker, *Communication of Innovations* (New York: Free Press, 1971); J. C. McCroskey, V. P. Richmond, and J. A. Daly, "Toward the Measurement of Perceived Homophily in Interpersonal Communication." Paper presented to the International Communication Association Convention, New Orleans, April 1974; V. P. Richmond, J. C. McCroskey, and John A. Daly, "The Generalizability of a Measure of Perceived Homophily in Interpersonal Communication." Paper presented to the International Communication Association Convention, Chicago, April 1975; R. L. Atkinson, R. C. Atkinson, E. E. Smith, and D. J. Bem, *Introduction to Psychology*, 10th ed. (San Diego, CA: Harcourt Brace Jovanovich, 1990), p. 713.

15. Barack Obama, "Elections: Text of Obama's Address at Convention," AP Wire, *Seattle-Post Intelligencer*, July 27, 2004. Online at http://seattlepi.nwsource.com/national/apelection_story, p. 2. Accessed August 15, 2004.

16. K. S. Thweatt and J. C. McCroskey, "The Impact of Teacher Immediacy and Misbehaviors on Teacher Credibility." *Communication Education* 47 (1998): 348–358.

17. E. Haley, "Organization as Source: Consumers' Understandings of Organizational Sponsorship of Advocacy Advertising." *Journal of Advertising* 25 (1996): 19–36.

18. F. S. Haiman, "The Effects of Ethos in Public Speaking." *Speech Monographs* 16 (1949): 192; C. I. Hovland and W. Weiss, "The Influence of Source Credibility on Communication Effectiveness." *Public Opinion Quarterly* 16 (1961): 635–650.

19. Alan Alda, commencement speech, University of Columbia, College of Physicians and Surgeons, New York, May 25, 1979, reprinted in *Physicians and Surgeons Journal* (summer 1979).

20. E. Enochs (compiler and editor), "Columbia-Presbyterian Medical Center 128-2004: 75 People, Events, and Contributions Worth Remembering." Online at http://cumc .columbia.edu/news/journal/journal-o/fall-2003/75years_2650.html. Accessed September 25, 2004.

21. Alan Alda, commencement address.

22. Enochs, "Columbia-Presbyterian Medical Center."

23. Thweatt and McCroskey, "The Impact of Teacher Immediacy and Misbehaviors on Teacher Credibility." Pages 348–358.

24. E. P. Bettinghaus, *Persuasive Communication*, 2nd ed. (New York: Holt, Rinehart, and Winston, Inc., 1968).

25. S. Milgram, *Obedience to Authority* (New York: Harper & Row, 1974). See also M. Karlins and H. Abelson, *Persuasion: How Opinions and Attitudes are Changed* (New York: Springer Publishing Company, 1970).

26. See discussions by B. W. Eakins and R. Gene Eakins, *Sex Differences in Communication* (Boston: Houghton Mifflin, 1978): 38–49; P. Bradley, "The Folklinguistics of Women's Speech: An Empirical Examination," *Communication Monographs* 48 (1981): 73–90.

27. See discussions by Eakins and Eakins, *Sex Differences*, pp. 38–49; Bradley, "The Folklinguistics of Women's Speech," pp. 73–90.

28. B. R. Sandler, "Women Faculty at Work in the Classroom, or, Why It Still Hurts to Be a Woman in Labor." *Communication Education* 40 (1991): 6–15.

29. See discussions by Eakins and Eakins, *Sex Differences*, pp. 38–49; Bradley, "The Folklinguistics of Women's Speech," pp. 73–90.

30. R. B. Cialdini, *Influence: Science and Practice*, 4th ed. (New York: Harper-Collins, 2002).

31. Obama, "Elections," 2004.

32. See, for example, M. L. Houser, "Are We Violating Their Expectations? Instructor Communication Expectations of Traditional and Nontraditional Students." *Communication Quarterly* 53 (2005): 213–228; W. J. Potter and R. Emanuel, "Students' Preferences for Communication Styles and Their Relationship to Achievement." *Communication Education* 39 (1990): 234–249; G. Sorensen, "The Relationships among Teachers' Self-Disclosive Statements, Students' Perceptions, and Affective Learning." *Communication Education* 38 (1989): 259–276; J. Gorham, "The Relationship Between Verbal Teacher Immediacy Behaviors and Student Learning." *Communication Education* 37 (1988): 40–53; V. Downs, M. Javidi, and J. Nussbaum, "An Analysis of Teachers' Verbal Communication Within the College Classroom: Use of Humor, Self-Disclosure, and Narratives." *Communication Education* 37 (1988): 127–141; L. R. Wheeless, "Self-Disclosure and Interpersonal Solidarity: Measurement, Validation, and Relationships." *Human Communication Research* 3 (1976): 47–61.

33. L. K. Guerrero and T. A. Miller, "Associations Between Nonverbal Behaviors and Initial Impressions of Instructor Competence and Course Content in Videotaped Distance Education Courses." *Communication Education* 47 (1998): 30–42.

34. U.S. election feature on *The National* news show, Canadian Broadcast Corporation (CBC), October 29, 2004.

35. A. Mehrabian, "Attitudes Inferred from Non-immediacy of Verbal Communication." *Journal of Verbal Learning and Verbal Behavior* 6 (1967): 294–295.

36. Ray Bradbury, commencement speech, 2002.

37. Whitehead, Jr., "Factors of Source Credibility," pp. 59–63.

38. J. McCroskey, *An Introduction to Rhetorical Communication*, 7th ed. (Boston: Allyn and Bacon, 1997), pp. 91–101.

39. Interview with J. Baronet, Channel 10 Television, Lafayette, Louisiana, March 26, 1970.

40. Cited by M. Goldman, interview, Channel 3 television studio, Lafayette, Louisiana, March 24, 1970.

41. "News Updates," The Syracuse *Post Standard*, October 30, 2004. http://www.syracuse.com/news/updates/index.ssf?/mtlogs/syr_poststandard/archives/2004_10.html. Accessed on May 10, 2006.

42. W. C. Minnick, *The Art of Persuasion* (Boston: Houghton Mifflin Company, 1957).

43. See, for example, B. Reeves, J. Newhagen, E. Maibach, M. Basil, and K. Kurz, "Negative and Positive Television Messages: Effects of Message Type and Context on Attention and Memory." *American Behavioral Scientist* 34 (1991): 679–694. See also W. C. Minnick, *The Art of Persuasion* (Boston: Houghton Mifflin Company, 1957).

44. "The Third Man." Online at http://encyclopedia.thefreedictionary.com/The%20Third%20Man. Accessed August 31, 2004.

45. George W. Bush, excerpt from speech delivered from the Oval Office, Washington, DC, September 11, 2004.

46. See G. J. S. Wilde, "Effects of Mass Media Communications on Health and Safety Habits: An Overview of Issues and Evidence." *Addiction* 88 (1993): 983–996; T. E. Backer, E. M. Rogers, and P. Sopory, eds., *Designing Health Communication Campaigns: What Works* (Newbury Park, CA: Sage); and D. J. O'Keefe, *Persuasion: Theory and Research* (Newbury Park, CA: Sage).

47. F. J. Boster and P. Mongeau, "Fear-Arousing Persuasive Messages," in R. N. Bostrom and B. H. Westley, eds., *Communication Yearbook* 8 (Beverly Hills, CA: Sage, 1984), pp. 330–375. See also S. Sutton, "Fear-Arousing Communications: A Critical Examination of Theory and Research," in J. R. Eiser, ed., *Social Psychology and Behavioral Medicine* (New York: John Wiley, 1982), pp. 303–337.

48. See F. Cope and D. Richardson, "The Effects of Reassuring Recommendations in a Fear-Arousing Speech," *Speech Monographs* 39 (1972): 148–150; B. J. Fine, "Conclusion-Drawing, Communicator Credibility, and Anxiety as Factors in Opinion Change," *Journal of Abnormal and Social Psychology* 54 (1957): 369–374; H. Leventhal, J. C. Watts, and F. Pagano, "Effects of Fear and Instructions on How to Cope with Danger," *Journal of Personality and Social Psychology* 6 (1967): 313–321; and K. Witte, "Fear Control and Danger Control: A Test of the Extended Parallel Process Model." *Communication Monographs* 61 (1994): 113–134; R. E. Petty and J. T. Cacioppo, *Attitudes and Persuasion: Classic and Contemporary Approaches* (Dubuque, IA: William C. Brown, 1981); and J. B. Stiff, *Persuasive Communication* (New York: Guilford, 1994).

49. D. D. Johnston, *The Art and Science of Persuasion* (Madison, WI: WC Brown & Benchmark, 1994).

50. D. J. O'Keefe, *Persuasion: Theory and Research* (Newbury Park, CA: Sage Publications, 1990); G. J. S. Wilde, "Effects of Mass Media Communications on Health and Safety Habits: An Overview of Issues and Evidence." *Addiction* 88 (7): 983–996; E. B. Arkin, "Interview," in T. E. Backer, E. M. Rogers, and P. Sopory, eds., *Designing Health Communication Campaigns: What Works?* (Newbury Park, CA: Sage Publications, 1992), pp. 36–40.

51. Franklin D. Roosevelt, speech delivered on December 8, 1941, to the United States Congress, Washington, DC.

52. Franklin D. Roosevelt, address to the nation, Washington, DC, December 9, 1941.

53. Ronald Reagan, "A Time for Choosing," speech on behalf of Republican presidential candidate Barry Goldwater, Los Angeles, California, October 27, 1964.

CHAPTER 10

1. M. Rokeach, *The Nature of Human Values.* (New York: Free Press, 1973).

2. J. Dewey, *How We Think: A Restatement of the Relation of Reflective Thinking to the Educative Process* (New York: D.C. Heath, 1933).

3. A. H. Monroe, *Principles and Types of Speech* (Glenview, IL: Scott Foresman, 1945).

4. J. G. Barber, R. Bradshaw, and C. Walsh, "Reducing Alcohol Consumption Through Television Advertising." *Journal of Consulting and Clinical Psychology* 57 (1989): 613–618.

See also F. Cope and D. Richardson, "The Effects of Reassuring Recommendations in a Fear-Arousing Speech. "*Speech Monographs* 39 (1972):148–150; B. J. Fine, "Conclusion-Drawing, Communicator Credibility, and Anxiety as Factors in Opinion Change." *Journal of Abnormal and Social Psychology* 54 (1957): 369–374; H. Leventhal, J. C. Watts, and F. Pagano, "Effects of Fear and Instructions on How to Cope with Danger." *Journal of Personality and Social Psychology* 6 (1967): 313–321.

5. G. J. S. Wilde, "Effects of Mass Media Communications on Health and Safety Habits: An Overview of Issues and Evidence." *Addiction* 88 (7): 983–996.

6. S. Jackson and M. Allen, "Meta-Analysis of the Effectiveness of One-Sided and Two-Sided Argumentation." Paper presented at the annual meeting of the International Communication Association, Montreal, Canada, May 1987.

7. C. J. Hovland, I. L. Janis, and H. H. Kelley, *Communication and Persuasion* (New Haven, CT: Yale University Press, 1953).

8. W. J. McGuire, "The Effectiveness of Supportive and Refutational Defenses in Immunizing and Restoring Beliefs Against Persuasion." *Sociometry* 24 (1961): 184–197.

9. K. K. Reardon, *Persuasion in Practice* (Newbury Park, CA: Sage Publications, 1991).

10. E. P. Bettinghaus and M. J. Cody, *Persuasive Communication*, 5th ed. (Fort Worth, TX: Harcourt Brace College, 1994); J. C. Jahnke, "Serial Position Effects in Immediate Serial Recall." *Journal of Verbal Learning and Verbal Behavior* 2 (1963): 284–287.

11. Jackson and Allen, "Meta-Analysis." Also K. W. E. Anatol, "Fundamentals of Persuasive Speaking," in *Modules in Speech Communication* (Chicago: Science Research Associates, 1976), p. 19.

12. D. D. Johnston, *The Art and Science of Persuasion* (Madison, WI: William C. Brown/Benchmark, 1994), pp. 141–142.

13. H. Gilkinson, S. F. Paulson, and D. E. Sikkink, "Effects of Order and Authority in an Argumentative Speech." *Quarterly Journal of Speech* 40 (1954): 183–192; H. Sponberg, "A Study of the Relative Effectiveness of Climax and Anti-Climax Order in an Argumentative Speech." *Speech Monographs* 13 (1946): 35–44.

14. Bettinghaus and Cody, *Persuasive Communication*; Anatol, "Fundamentals of Persuasive Speaking," p. 19; R. S. Ross, *Understanding Persuasion*, 4th ed. (Englewood Cliffs, NJ: Prentice-Hall, 1994).

15. Anatol, "Fundamentals of Persuasive Speaking," p. 19.

16. Monroe, *Principles and Types of Speech*.

17. Sonia Genovesi, communication student, 2003.

18. E. Van Donkersgoed, "F for Environmental Stewardship." AG Net (October 12, 2001). http://131.104.232.9/agnet/2001/10-2001/agnet_october_16.htm. Accessed June 20, 2002.

19. Reported by Howard L. Nations. http://www.howardnations.com/themes/themes6.html. Accessed on May 5, 2006.

20. Excerpted from a speech by Leslie Revere, communication student, University of Ottawa, 2004.

21. S. E. Taylor and S. C. Thompson, "Stalking the Elusive 'Vividness' Effect." *Psychological Review* 89 (1982): 155–181.

22. T. R. Koballa, Jr., "Persuading Teachers to Re-examine the Innovative Elementary Science Programs of Yesterday: The Effect of Anecdotal Versus Data-Summary Communications." *Journal of Research in Science Teaching* 23 (1986): 437–449.

23. A. N. Miller, "An Exploration of Kenyan Public Speaking Patterns with Implications for the American Introductory Public Speaking Course." *Communication Education* 51 (2002), 168–182.

24. K. Jamieson, *Eloquence in an Electronic Age: The Transformation of Political Speechmaking* (New York: Oxford University Press, 1988). Also see T. S. Frobish, "Jamieson Meets Lucas: Eloquence and Pedagogical Model(s) in *The Art of Public Speaking*." *Communication Education* 49 (2000): 239–252; M. Javidi, V. C. Downs, and J. F. Nussbaum, "A Comparative Analysis of Teachers' Use of Dramatic Style Behaviors at Higher and Secondary Educational Levels." *Communication Education* 37 (1988): 278–288.

25. D. R. Roskos-Ewoldsen, H. J. Yu, and N. Rhodes, "Fear Appeal Messages Affect Accessibility of Attitudes Toward Threat and Adaptive Behaviors." *Communication*

Monographs 71 (2004): 49–69. Also F. J. Boster and P. Mongeau, "Fear-Arousing Persuasive Messages," in R. N. Bostrom and B. H. Westley, eds., *Communication Year-book* 8 (Newbury Park, CA: Sage, 1984), pp. 330–375.

26. See the following discussions of the relationship between esteem and persuasibility: J. Brockner and M. Elkind, "Self-Esteem and Reactance: Further Evidence of Attitudinal and Motivational Consequences." *Journal of Experimental Social Psychology* 21 (1990): 346–361; Bettinghaus and Cody, *Persuasive Communication*; H. Leventhal and S. I. Perloe, "A Relationship Between Self-Esteem and Persuasibility." *Journal of Abnormal and Social Psychology* 64 (1962): 385–388.

27. See the following discussions of the relationship between esteem and persuasibility: J. Brockner and M. Elkind, "Self-Esteem and Reactance: Further Evidence of Attitudinal and Motivational Consequences." *Journal of Experimental Social Psychology* 21 (1990), 346–361; E. P. Bettinghaus and M. J. Cody, *Persuasive Communication*, 5th ed. (Fort Worth, TX: Harcourt Brace College, 1994); and H. Leventhal and S. I. Perloe, "A Relationship Between Self-Esteem and Persuasibility." *Journal of Abnormal and Social Psychology* 64 (1962): 385–388.

28. Brockner and Elkind, "Self-Esteem and Reactance," pp. 346–361; Bettinghaus and Cody, *Persuasive Communication*; Leventhal and Perloe, "A Relationship," pp. 385–388.

29. Bettinghaus and Cody, *Persuasive Communication*.

30. Speech by William J. Kunstler, reported in *Indiana Daily Student*, October 8, 1970, p. 8.

31. Dennis Hastert, eulogy delivered at the state funeral of Ronald Reagan, Capital Rotunda, Washington, DC, AP wire story, *Baltimore Sun*, June 9, 2004. Online at http://www.baltimoresun.com/features/lifestyle/sns-ap-reagan-hastert-text,1,1889558.story?coll=bal-artslife-today. Accessed September 7, 2004.

32. Kennedy, inaugural address, 1961.

33. Ronald Reagan, address at the U.S.-French ceremony at Omaha Beach on the 40th anniversary of D-Day, June 6, 1984. Online at http://reagan.webteamone.com/speeches/omaha.cfm. Accessed October 17, 2004.

34. George W. Bush, eulogy to Ronald Reagan, delivered at the National Cathedral, Washington, DC, June 11, 2004. Online at http://www.whitehouse.gov/news/releases/2004/06/20040611-2.html. Accessed September 7, 2004.

35. Winston Churchill, speech delivered on June 4, 1940. Online at www.winstonchurchill.org/beaches.htm. Accessed October 10, 2001.

36. Andrew Gowing, communication student, 2003.

37. John F. Kennedy, farewell address to the people of Massachusetts, delivered to state legislature, January 9, 1961.

38. John F. Kennedy, inaugural address, 1961.

39. Nelson Mandela, speech at Rivonia trial, Pretoria Supreme Court, April 20, 1964. www.anc.org.za/ancdocs/history/rivonia.html. Accessed November 11, 2002.

40. George W. Bush, eulogy for Ronald Reagan, delivered at the National Cathedral, Washington, DC, June 11, 2004. Online at http://www.whitehouse.gov/news/releases/2004/06/20040611-2.html. Accessed September 7, 2004.

41. Barbara Jordan, speech delivered to the Democratic National Convention, New York, New York, July 12, 1976.

42. Winston Churchill, speech to the Canadian Parliament, December 30, 1941. Online at www.nebridge.org/varrieur/Other%20Events/churchill.htm. Accessed October 31, 2003.

43. Winston Churchill, "This Was Their Finest Hour," June 18, 1940. Online at http://mitglied.lycos.de/FrankGemkow/laku/gb/speeches/churchill-hour.htm. Accessed October 31, 2003.

44. Martin Luther King, "I've Been to the Mountaintop," speech delivered at Mason Temple in Memphis, Tennessee, April 3, 1968.

45. Bill Moyers, keynote address to the National Conference on Media Reform, Madison, Wisconsin, November 8, 2003. Published online at Common News Dream Center (November 12, 2003), http://www.commondreams.org/views03/1112-10.htm.

46. I. Mayers, "A Burning Topic: Tobacco and Death, *Canadian Respiratory Journal* 9 (2002). President's page. Online at http://www.pulsus.com/Respir/09_02/pree_ed.htm. Accessed February 14, 2003.

47. Martin Luther King, "I Have a Dream," speech delivered in Washington, DC, on the steps of the Lincoln Memorial, August 28, 1963.

48. Ronald Reagan, televised speech to the nation, January 28, 1986.

49. George W. Bush, speech to the nation, February 1, 2003.

CHAPTER 11

1. G. S. Jowett and Victoria O'Donnell, *Propaganda and Persuasion*, 2nd ed. (Newbury Park, CA: Sage, 1992), p. 54.

2. Jowett and O'Donnell, *Propaganda and Persuasion*, pp. 185–199.

3. J. Ellul, *Propaganda: The Formation of Men's Attitudes* (New York: Vintage, 1973).

4. H. Goering, interview with Gustave M. Gilbert, April 18, 1946. Reported in G. M. Gilbert, *The Nuremberg Diary* (New York: Da Capo Press, 1995).

5. *WordNet Dictionary*. Online at http://www.hyperdictionary.com/dictionary/demagogue. Accessed September 17, 2004.

6. *Webster's 1913 Dictionary*. Online at http://www.hyperdictionary.com/dictionary/demagogue. Accessed September 17, 2004.

7. Ellul, *Propaganda*.

8. K. Witte, "The Manipulative Nature of Health Communication Research: Ethical Issues and Guidelines." *American Behavioral Scientist* 38 (1994): 285.

9. Jowett and O'Donnell, *Propaganda and Persuasion*, p. 4.

10. W. L. Brembeck and W. S. Howell, *Persuasion: A Means of Social Control* (Englewood Cliffs, NJ: Prentice-Hall Inc., 1952).

11. S. L. Hayakawa, *Language in Thought and Action* (New York: Harcourt, Brace and Company, 1949).

12. Jowett and O'Donnell, *Propaganda and Persuasion*, p. 186.

13. Adolf Hitler, *Mein Kampf* (Volume I, Chapter 12). Trans. James Murphy (London: Hurst and Blockett LTD, 1939).

14. P. Knightley, *The Guardian*, October 4, 2001. Online at http://www.guardian.co.uk/Archive/Article/0,4273,4270014,00.html. Accessed September 20, 2004.

15. G. Orwell, "Politics and the English Language," *Horizon*, April 1946; also *George Orwell, Shooting an Elephant and Other Essays* (London: Secker and Warburg, 1950).

16. W. Lutz, *Doublespeak: From ROM Revenue Enhancement to Terminal Living: How Government, Business, Advertisers, and Others Use the Language to Deceive* (Harper Collins, 1990). Also W. D. Lutz, *Doublespeak Defined: Cut Through the Bull**** and Get to the Point* (New York: Harper Resource, 1999).

17. R. M. Weaver, "Ultimate Terms in Contemporary Rhetoric," in R. L. Johannessen, R. Strickland, and R. T. Eubanks, eds., *Language Is Sermonic: Richard M. Weaver on the Nature of Rhetoric* (Baton Rouge: Louisiana State University Press, 1970), pp. 87–112.

18. Hitler, *Mein Kampf*.

19. M. H. Prosser, "Introduction," *Sow the Wind, Reap the Whirlwind*, Vol. I (New York: William Morrow, 1970).

20. "Abu Ghraib General Blames Conspiracy," *Globe and Mail*, online edition (August 3, 2004): 1. Online at www.globeandmail.com. Accessed August 3, 2004.

21. K. Witte, "Putting the Fear Back into Fear Appeals: The Extended Parallel Process Model." *Communication Monographs* 59 (1992): 329–349.

22. Edwin Edwards, speech delivered to Optimist Club, Shreveport, Louisiana, April 10, 1970.

23. "Medbh Sings." Online at http://medbhsings.blogspot.com/2005/11/get-on-bandwagon-and-give-click.html. Accessed on April 25, 2006.

24. L. Taylor, "Confusing Statistics," July 22, 2004. Online at http://www.channel4.com/news/2004/07/week_4/22_crime_t.html. Accessed August 16, 2004.

CHAPTER 12

1. By *collectivist* cultures, I mean those that stress the group over the individual. A. N. Miller, "An Exploration of Kenyan Public Speaking Patterns with Implications for the American Introductory Public Speaking Course." *Communication Education* 51 (2002): 168–182.

2. Craig Senior, Toastmaster competition, Ottawa region, 2004.

3. M. Robesch, "The Spirit of Leonard Peltier at Evergreen State College," Washington Free Press (October/November 1993). Online at http://www.washingtonfreepress .org/06/Peltier.html. Accessed on May 6, 2006.

4. "Princeton University Confers 1,806 Degrees at 252nd Commencement." Office of Communications, Princeton press release, June 1, 1999. Online at http://www.princeton .edu/pr/news/99/q2/0601-stats.htm. Accessed February 13, 2005.

5. Leslie Tutty, speech commemorating the 11th anniversary of the Montreal massacre, Nickle Arts Museum, University of Calgary campus, Calgary, Alberta, December 6, 2000.

6. Edward M. Kennedy, eulogy delivered at St. Patrick's Cathedral, New York, June 8, 1968.

7. "Schwarzenegger Hits the Cruz Control." *The Insider* (January 9, 2005). Online at http://www.sacunion.com/pages/columns/articles/1633/. Accessed February 14, 2005.

8. "Schwarzenegger Hits the Cruz Control."

9. Robin Williams, "BrainyQuote." Online at http://www.brainyquote.com/quotes/ authors/r/robin_williams.html. Accessed June 18, 2005.

10. Margaret Smith, "Timeless Quotes." Online at http://www.timelessquotes.com/ author/Margaret_Smith.html. Accessed June 18, 2005.

11. Robin Williams, "BrainyQuote." Online at http://www.brainyquote.com/quotes/ authors/r/robin_williams.html. Accessed June 18, 2005.

12. Chris Rock, "DFR: Daily Fashion Report." April 1, 2003. Online at http://www .lookonline.com/2003_04_01_archive.html. Accessed June 18, 2005.

13. "Linda Ross, Reptile at Law." Canoe, CN News, December 16, 1999. Online at http://www.canoe.ca/CNEWSHeyMartha9912/16_two.html. Accessed February 11, 2005.

14. Carol Leifer, "Quote of the Day." Online at http://listserver.themacintoshguy.com/ pipermail/x-apps/2003-June.txt. Accessed June 18, 2005.

15. D. Russell, "Self-Deprecatory Humour and the Female Comic: Self-Destruction or Comedic Construction." *Third Space*, Vol. II (November 2002). Online at http:// www.thirdspace.ca/articles/druss.htm. Accessed June 21, 2005. Also Ron Jenkins, *Subversive Laughter: The Liberating Power of Comedy* (New York: The Free Press, 1994).

16. "The Battle of the N-Word." *The Observer* (January 20, 2002). Online at http:// education.guardian.co.uk/racism/comment/0,10795,636886,00.html. Accessed July 10, 2004.

17. R. Barreca, *They Used to Call Me Snow White . . . But I Drifted: Women's Strategic Use of Humor* (New York: Penguin Books, 1991). Also Torborg Lundell, "An Experimental Exploration of Why Men and Women Laugh." *Humor* 6 (1993): 301.

18. "Gender Differences in Comfort with Communication Situations Is Evident in Poll Results" (National Communication Association/Roper Starch Poll). *Spectra* (February 2000): 5.

19. B. W. Eakins and R. G. Eakins, *Sex Differences in Human Communication* (Boston: Houghton Mifflin Company, 1978), pp. 75–77. Also Mary Crawford, "Just Kidding: Gender and Conversational Humor," in R. Barreca, ed., *New Perspectives on Women and Comedy* (Philadelphia: Gordon and Breach, 1992), p. 24.

20. Barreca, *They Used to Call Me Snow White*.

CHAPTER 13

1. Little agreement exists in the management literature on the differentiation between goals and objectives. Some use goals to suggest a broader focus and objectives to suggest a more narrow focus; others use the terms in the opposite way. See P. G. Bergeron, *Modern Management in Canada: Concepts and Practices* (Scarborough, ON: Nelson Canada, 1989), p. 254.

2. J. E. Brooks-Harris and S. R. Stock-Ward, *Workshops: Designing and Facilitating Experiential Learning* (Thousand Oaks, CA: Sage Publications, 1999), pp. 55–56. See also J. W. Thatcher and P. N. Blanchard, *Effective Training* (Toronto: Pearson Prentice Hall), pp. 122–124.

3. L. Stoneall, "The Case for More Flexible Objectives." *Training and Development* (August 1992): 67–69.

4. See sources such as the following: J. Colquitt and J. Lepine, "Toward an Integrative Theory of Training Motivation: A Meta-analytic Path Analysis of 20 years of Research." *Journal of Applied Psychology* 85 (2000): 678–707; Thatcher and Blanchard, *Effective Training*, p. 126; J. Lewis, "Answers to Twenty Questions on Behavioral Objectives." *Educational Technology* (March 1981): 27–31.

5. P. N. Blanchard and J. W. Thacker, *Effective Training: Systems, Strategies, and Practices*, 2nd ed. (Upper Saddle River, NJ: Pearson Education, Inc., 2004), p. 193.

6. J. Lewis, "Answers to Twenty Questions on Behavioral Objectives," pp. 27–31.

7. See, for example, D. A. Kolb, *Experiential Learning: Experience as the Source of Learning and Development* (Englewood Cliffs, NJ: Prentice Hall, 1984).

8. A study completed by the U.S. Department of Health, Education, and Welfare is referenced in W. E. Arnold and L. McClure, *Communication, Training and Development*, 2nd ed. (Prospect Heights, IL: Waveland Press), p. 38.

9. *The Power of Listening* [motion picture] (Scarborough, ON: CRM McGraw-Hill, 1978).

10. D. A. Brunson and J. F. Vogt, "Empowering Our Students and Ourselves: A Liberal Democratic Approach to the Communication Classroom." *Communication Education* 45 (1996): 73–83.

11. S. S. Wulff and D. H. Wulff, "Of Course I'm Communicating; I Lecture Every Day: Enhancing Teaching and Learning in Introductory Statistics." *Communication Education* 53 (2004): 92–102; also P. Smagorinsky and P. K. Fly, "The Social Environment of the Classroom: A Vygotskian Perspective on Small Group Process." *Communication Education* 42 (1993): 157–171.

12. J. Middendorf and A. Kalish, "The Change-up in Lectures." Unpublished manuscript, Indiana University (1995), p. 6. Cited in P. H. Andrews, J. R. Andrews, and G. Williams, *Public Speaking: Connecting You and Your Audience*, 2nd ed. (Boston: Houghton Mifflin Company), p. 54.

13. R. Dunn and K. Dunn, *Teaching Secondary Students Through their Individual Learning Styles: Practical Approaches for Grades 7–12* (Boston: Allyn & Bacon, 1993).

14. M. L. Houser, "Are We Violating Their Expectations?" Instructor Communication Expectations of Traditional and Nontraditional Students." *Communication Quarterly* 53 (2005): 213–228; also M. D. Richardson and K. E. Lane, "Andragogical Concepts for Teachers of Adults." *Catalyst for Change* 22 (1993): 16–18.

15. M. L. Houser, "Are We Violating Their Expectations?" 213–228; also M. D. Richardson and K. E. Lane, "Andragogical Concepts for Teachers of Adults," pp. 16–18.

16. H. Gardner, *Frames of Mind: The Theory of Multiple Intelligences* (New York: Basic Books, 1983).

17. W. McKenzie, Multiple Intelligence Survey (1999). Online at http://surfaquarium .com/MI/inventory.htm. Accessed July 28, 2004.

18. Dunn and Dunn, *Teaching Secondary Students*.

19. Brooks-Harris and Stock-Ward, *Workshops*, pp. 30–31.

20. K. K. Dwyer, "Communication Apprehension and Learning Style Preference: Correlations and Implications for Teaching." *Communication Education* 47 (1998): 137–150.

21. J. A. Daly and C. A. Diesel, "Measures of Communication-Related Personality Variables." *Communication Education* 41 (1992): 405–414.

22. J. R. Kidd, *How Adults Learn* (New York: Association Press, 1955), p. 44.

23. C. R. Rogers, *On Becoming a Person: A Therapist's View of Psychotherapy* (New York: Houghton Mifflin, 1995). Cited by K. H. Dover, "Carl Rogers and Experiential Learning, http://adulted.about.com/cs/adultlearningthe/a/carl_rogers.htm. Accessed July 28, 2004.

24. Arnold & McClure, p. 21.

25. Brooks-Harris and Stock-Ward, *Workshops*, p. 29.

26. J. Vanden Hazel, Ontario Institute for Studies in Education, University of Toronto. At http://www.educationalconsulting.ca/icebreak.htm.

27. "Methodology: Energizers." Online at http://www.isodec.org.gh/workshop-cd/ workshops/methodology/energiser/Energisers.htm. Accessed March 2, 2003.

28. J. Neill, "Games and Activities with Balloons." Online at http://www.wilderdom .com/games/descriptions/gamesballoons.html. Accessed July 28, 2004.

29. Christina Kirkey, communication student, 2004.

30. This passage is a paraphrased version of "The Legend of the Dream Catcher." Online at http://www.y-indianguides.com/pfm_st_dreamcatcher.html. Accessed July 26, 2004.

31. This information was drawn from the following websites: http://lokrin.net/ nynees/superstitions.php and http://www.japan-guide.com/e/e2209.html. Accessed July 27, 2004.

32. "Survival: A Simulation Game." Online at http://scoutingweb.com/scoutingweb/ SubPages/SurvivalGame.htm. Accessed July 28, 2004.

33. B. S. Bloom, ed., *Taxonomy of Educational Objectives: Book 1, Cognitive Domain* (New York: Longman, 1956).

34. *The Ultimate WebCT Handbook: A Practical and Pedagogical Guide to WebCT*. Online at www.ultimatehandbooks.net/excerpts/presentations.html. Accessed October 2, 2004.

35. M. Burgoon, J. K. Heston, and J. McCroskey, "Communication Roles in Small Group Interaction," in S. D. Ferguson, *Organizational Communication*, 2nd ed. (New Brunswick, NJ: Transaction Publishers, 1990), pp. 386–390. Also K. Benne and P. Sheats, "Functional Roles of Group Members." *Journal of Social Issues* 4 (1948): 41–49.

36. J. L. Chesebro and J. C. McCroskey, "The Relationship of Teacher Clarity and Immediacy with Student State Receiver Apprehension, Affect, and Cognitive Learning." *Communication Education* 50 (2001): 59–68; B. S. Titsworth, "An Experiment Testing the Effects of Teacher Immediacy, Use of Organizational Lecture Cues, and Students' Notetaking on Cognitive Learning." *Communication Education* 50: 283–297; M. B. Wanzer and A. B. Frymier, "The Relationship Between Student Perceptions of Instructor Humor and Student's Reports of Learning." *Communication Education* 48 (1999): 48–62; L. J. Christensen and K. E. Menzel, "The Linear Relationship Between Student Reports of Immediacy Behaviors and Perceptions of State Motivation, and of Cognitive, Affective, and Behavioral Learning." *Communication Education* 47 (1998): 82–90; A. Moore, J. T. Masterson, D. M. Christophel, and K. A. Shea, "College Teacher Immediacy and Student Ratings of Instruction." *Communication Education* 45 (1996): 29–39; J. I. Rodriguez, T.G. Plax, and P. Kearney, "Clarifying the Relationship Between Teacher Nonverbal Immediacy and Student Cognitive Learning: Affective Learning as the Central Causal Mediator." *Communication Education* 45 (1996): 293–305; J. Comstock, E. Rowell, and J. W. Bowers, "Food for Thought: Teacher Nonverbal Immediacy, Student Learning, and Curvilinearity." *Communication Education* 44 (1995): 251–266; D. Christophel, "The Relationships among Teacher Immediacy Behaviors, Student Motivation, and Learning." *Communication Education* 39 (1990): 323–340; J. Gorham and D. Christophel, "The Relationship of Teachers' Use of Humor in the Classroom to Immediacy and Student Learning." *Communication Education* 39 (1990): 46–62; J. L. Allen and D. H. Shaw, "Teachers' Communication Behaviors and Supervisors' Evaluation of Instruction in Elementary and Secondary Classrooms." *Communication Education* 39 (1990): 308–322; J. Gorham and W. R. Zakahi, "A Comparison of Teacher and Student Perceptions of Immediacy and Learning: Monitoring Process and Product." *Communication Education* 39 (1990): 354–368; J. S. Gorham, "The Relationship Between Verbal Teacher Immediacy Behaviors and Student Learning." *Communication Education* 37 (1988): 40–53; D. H. Kelley and J. Gorham, "Effects of Immediacy on Recall of Information." *Communication Education* 37 (1988): 198–207; and V. P. Richmond, J. Gorham, and J. C. McCroskey, "The Relationship Between Selected Immediacy Behaviors and Cognitive Learning," in M. A. McLaughlin, ed., *Communication Yearbook* 10 (Newbury Park, CA: Sage, 1987), pp. 574–590; P. Andersen and J. Andersen, "Nonverbal Immediacy in Instruction," in L. Barker, ed., *Communication in the Classroom* (Englewood Cliffs, NJ: Prentice Hall, 1982), pp. 98–120.

37. P. L. Witt, L. R. Wheeless, and M. Allen, "A Meta-Analytical Review of the Relationship between Teacher Immediacy and Student Learning." *Communication Monographs* 71 (2004): 184–207.

38. Q. Zhang, "Immediacy, Humor, Power Distance, and Classroom Communication Apprehension in Chinese College Classrooms." *Communication Quarterly* 53 (2005): 87–

108; J. C. McCroskey, A. Sallinen, J. M. Fayer, and R. A. Barraclough, "Nonverbal Immediacy and Cognitive Learning: A Cross-Cultural Investigation." *Communication Education* 45 (1996): 200–211; J. C. McCroskey, A. Sallinen, J. M. Fayer, and R. A. Barraclough, "A Cross-Cultural and Multi-Behavioral Analysis of the Relationship Between Nonverbal Immediacy and Teacher Evaluation," *Communication Education* 44 (1995): 281–291; R. G. Powell and B. Harville, "The Effects of Teacher Immediacy and Clarity on Instructional Outcomes: An Intercultural Assessment." *Communication Education* 39 (1990): 369–379; J. A. Sanders and R. L. Wiseman, "The Effects of Verbal and Nonverbal Teacher Immediacy on Perceived Cognitive, Affective, and Behavioral Learning in the Multicultural Classroom." *Communication Education* 39 (1990): 341–353; P. Kearney, T. G. Plax, and N. J. Wendt-Wasco, "Teacher Immediacy for Affective Learning in Divergent College Classes." *Communication Quarterly* 33 (1985): 61–74.

39. See, for example, M. Z. Hackman and Kim B. Walker, "Instructional Communication in the Televised Classroom: The Effects of System Design and Teacher Immediacy on Student Learning and Satisfaction." *Communication Education* 39 (1990): 196–206.

CHAPTER 14

1. "Ghostwriters." From *Disinfopedia*, a project of the Center for Media and Democracy. Cited on www.disinfopedia.org/wiki.phtml?title=Ghostwriters. Accessed January 26, 2005.

2. L. J. Einhorn, "The Ghosts Unmasked: A Review of Literature on Speechwriting." *Communication Quarterly* 30 (1981): 41–47. Cited by Halford Ryan, *Speaker and Gavel*, Vol. 38 (2001): 1–15.

3. A. Wayman, "Even Presidents Use Ghost Writers." Online at http://freelancewrite.about.com/od/writingspecialties/a/ghost1.htm. Accessed January 21, 2005.

4. A. S. Felzenberg, "The Transition: A Guide for the President-elect." *Policy Review Online* 103 (October/November 2000) (Hoover Institution, Stanford University). Online at http://www.policyreview.org. Accessed January 22, 2005.

5. Felzenberg, "The Transition."

6. M. J. Gleason, "The Good Old Days," January/February 2000. Cited on www.bookmagazine.com/archive/issue8/gooddays.shtml. Accessed January 21, 2005.

7. Felzenberg, "The Transition."

8. M. Medhurst, "Importance and Role of Presidential Speech Writers." Online at www.tamu.edu/univrel/aggiedaily/news/stories/archive/083198-3.html. Accessed January 21, 2005.

9. "John Harvard's Journal." *Harvard Magazine.* Online at http://www.harvardmagazine.com/issues/so96/jhj.friends.html. Accessed January 22, 2005.

10. Felzenberg, "The Transition."

11. Felzenberg, "The Transition."

12. L. Sigelman, "Two Reagans? Genre Imperatives, Ghostwriters, and Presidential Personality Profiling." *Political Psychology*, 23 (December 2002): 839–851.

13. Tracy Jan, "Presidential Speechwriters Don Thinking Caps and Beepers," April 2, 2000. Cited online at www.asne.org. Accessed January 21, 2005.

14. Jan, "Presidential Speechwriters."

15. Medhurst, "Importance and Role of Presidential Speech Writers."

16. T. H. Neale, CRS Report for Congress, *Speechwriting in Perspective: A Brief Guide to Effective and Persuasive Communication* (Washington, DC: Congressional Research Service, The Library of Congress, 1998). Cited on http://countingcalifornia.cdlib.org/crs/ascii/98-170. Accessed January 21, 2005.

17. Neale, *Speechwriting in Perspective.*

18. Neale, *Speechwriting in Perspective.*

19. Neale, *Speechwriting in Perspective.*

20. This excerpt comes from a speech that I prepared on a contract basis for a government representative.

21. See S. E. Lucas, *The Art of Public Speaking*, 6th ed. (Boston: McGraw-Hill, 1998): 298.

22. F. J. O. Blachly, "Ghost Stories." Online at www.cosmos-club.org/journals/1999/blachly.html. Accessed January 21, 2005.

23. "John Harvard's Journal."

24. "D.C. Gator Writing Campaign Speeches." Online at http://www.jou.ufl.edu/pubs/communigator/Archives/S99/pages/alumni/kappalman.htm. Accessed January 18, 2005.

25. M. Koppel, S. Argamon, and A. R. Shimoni, "Automatically Categorizing Written Texts by Author Gender." *Literary and Linguistic Computing* 17: 401–412.

26. B. W. Eakins and R. G. Eakins, *Sex Differences in Human Communication* (Boston: Houghton Mifflin Company, 1978), pp. 75–77. Also M. Crawford, "Just Kidding: Gender and Conversational Humor," in R. Barreca, ed., *New Perspectives on Women and Comedy* (Philadelphia: Gordon and Breach, 1992), p. 24

27. Neale, *Speechwriting in Perspective.*

28. Neale, *Speechwriting in Perspective.*

29. T. Lundell, "An Experiential Exploration of Why Men and Women Laugh." *Humor* 6 (1993): 301.

30. Neale, *Speechwriting in Perspective.*

31. Jan, "Presidential Speechwriters."

32. J. Podhoretz, "The Breakfast Table: John Podhoretz and Michael Waldman" (August 14, 2000). Cited at http://slate.msn.com/id/2000191/entry/1005882. Accessed January 26, 2005.

33. Jan, "Presidential Speechwriters."

34. Jan, "Presidential Speechwriters."

35. Jan, "Presidential Speechwriters."

36. "D.C. Gator Writing Campaign Speeches."

37. Jan, "Presidential Speechwriters."

38. Jan, "Presidential Speechwriters."

39. "Presidential Genres," summarized from K. K. Campbell and K. H. Jamieson, *Deeds Done in Words: Presidential Rhetoric and the Genres of Governance* (Chicago: University of Chicago Press, 1990): 11. Cited online at http://www.janda.org/politxts/methods&links/genres.html. Accessed January 23, 2005.

40. J. Scalzi, "Whatever: The Stupidest Criticism of a Clinton, This Week" (June 12, 2003). Cited online at www.scalzi.com/whatever/002465.html. Accessed January 21, 2005.

41. P. J. Parsons, "Ethics: PR and Plagiarism." *PR Canada* (April 2003). Cited on www.prcanada.ca/ETHIX/PLAGT.HTM. Accessed January 25, 2004.

42. J. Deshaye, "The English Department's (Anti-) Plagiarism Road Show, Part II." Teaching and Learning Bridges, University of Saskatchewan, Vol. 2 (March 2004). Cited online at http://www.usask.ca/tlc/bridges_journal/v2n5_mar_04/v2n5_anti-plagiarism.html. Accessed January 23, 2005.

43. Parsons, "Ethics: PR and Plagiarism."

44. J. Gerstein, "Researcher Alleges Potential Plagiarism in 11 Passages of Kerry's Writings." *The New York Sun*, October 26, 2004. Cited online at http://daily.nysun.com. Accessed January 21, 2005.

45. Gerstein, "Researcher Alleges Potential Plagiarism in 11 Passages of Kerry's Writings."

46. B. Martin, "Plagiarism: A Misplaced Emphasis." *Journal of Information Ethics* 3 (1994): 36–47. Online at www.uow.edu.au/arts/sts/bmartin/pubs/94jie.html. Accessed January 21, 2005.

47. F. J. O. Blachly, "Ghost Stories."

CHAPTER 15

1. M. J. Medhurst, "Teaching Rhetorical Criticism to Undergraduates: Special Editor's Introduction." *Communication Education* 38 (1989): 175–190.

2. S. K. Foss, "Rhetorical Criticism as the Asking of Questions." *Communication Education* 38 (1989): 191–196.

3. An excellent (albeit sophisticated) discussion of the constituents of the rhetorical act appears in J. Andrews, *The Practice of Rhetorical Criticism* (New York: Macmillan Publishing Co., Inc., 1983).

4. Medhurst, "Teaching Rhetorical Criticism," pp. 175–190.

5. E. Stack, "Dressing Marcia: The Construction of Gender in the 1990s." Online at http://collection.nlc-bnc.ca/100/202/300/mediatribe/mtribe95/marcia.html.

6. For additional questions, see a classic article by L.F. Bitzer, "The Rhetorical Situation." *Philosophy and Rhetoric* 1 (1968): 1–14; also M. J. Medhurst, "Rhetorical Criticism: Forensic Communication in the Written Mode." *Communication Education* 38 (1989): 205–213.

7. See D. Henry and H. Sharp, Jr., "Thematic Approaches to Teaching Rhetorical Criticism." *Communication Education* 38 (1989): 197–204.

8. W. A. Linsley, classroom handout, University of Houston, 1968. Later published in W. A. Linsley, ed., *Speech Criticism: Methods and Materials* (Dubuque: William C. Brown, 1968).

ART CREDITS

INDEX